Exploring the New Exodus in John

Exploring the New Exodus in John
A Biblical Theological Investigation of John Chapters 5–10

Paul S. Coxon

FOREWORD BY
Stephen S. Smalley

RESOURCE *Publications* • Eugene, Oregon

EXPLORING THE NEW EXODUS IN JOHN
A Biblical Theological Investigation of John Chapters 5–10

Copyright © 2014 Paul S. Coxon. All rights reserved. Except for brief quotations in critical publications or reviews, no part of this book may be reproduced in any manner without prior written permission from the publisher. Write: Permissions. Wipf and Stock Publishers, 199 W. 8th Ave., Suite 3, Eugene, OR 97401.

Resource Publications
An Imprint of Wipf and Stock Publishers
199 W. 8th Ave., Suite 3
Eugene, OR 97401

www.wipfandstock.com

ISBN 13: 978-1-61097-952-8

Manufactured in the U.S.A. 03/06/2015

BWHEBB, BWHEBL, BWTRANSH [Hebrew]; BWGRKL, BWGRKN, and BWGRKI [Greek] PostScript® Type 1 and TrueType fonts Copyright ©1994-2013 BibleWorks, LLC. All rights reserved. These Biblical Greek and Hebrew fonts are used with permission and are from BibleWorks (www.bibleworks.com).

Bible Works ask for this notice to be displayed and the copyright preserved in any derived publications.

Unless otherwise indicated, all Scripture quotations are from The ESV® Bible (The Holy Bible, English Standard Version®) Copyright © 2001 by Crossway, a publishing ministry of Good News Publishers. Used by permission. All rights reserved.

Scripture quotations marked NKJV are taken from the New King James Version®. Copyright © 1982 by Thomas Nelson, Inc. Used by permission. All rights reserved.

For Sue

Whose worth is far above rubies (NKJV Prov 31:10)

Contents

Foreword by Stephen S. Smalley | ix
To the Reader | xi
Acknowledgements | xv
Abbreviations | xvii

PART I—Preliminary Considerations

Introduction: Why Has the New Exodus in GJohn been Largely Unexplored? | 3
1. Methodology: How Can We Explore the NE in GJohn? | 10
2. Historical Feasibility: Can We Find a Historical Background for GJohn in Keeping With a NE Interpretation? | 26
3. Ideological Feasibility: Can GJohn's Jewish OT Roots be Established? | 56
4. Theological/Christological Feasibility: Is GJohn Consistent in Its Theology? | 66
5. Literary Feasibility: Is GJohn a Literary Unity that Bears Witness to Jesus and the NE? | 70
6. Exodus/NE Scholarship on GJohn: What Have Others Said? | 73

PART II—Detailed Exegetical Examination of John 5–10

7. Anatomical Overview of John 5–10 | 85
8. Episode 1: The Sabbath Healing of a Lame Man, John 5 | 99
9. Episode 2: Jesus' Paschal NE Departure, John 6 | 148
   Excursus: The Future Salvation of Israel in the Plan and Purpose of God | 240
10. Episode 3: Jesus at the Feast of Tabernacles, John 7–8 | 244
11. Episode 4 Narrative: The Sabbath Healing of a Man-Born-Blind, John 9 | 269
12. Episode 4 Discourse: The Good Shepherd, John 10:1–21 | 281
13. Episode 5: Jesus Sanctified and Sent by the Father, John 10:22–42 | 332
14. Summary and Conclusions | 342

Bibliography | 349

Foreword

THIS BOOK INVESTIGATES THE Paschal-New Exodus motif in the Gospel of John as a leading interpretative key to its teaching, and in particular its Christology. By means of careful and detailed exegesis, notably of the central festal section, chapters 5-10, Dr Coxon reaches the conclusion that the Johannine Jesus inaugurates a new exodus, so that God's people may be led at last into the true and heavenly Temple. In it all, the author is sensitive to the rich intertextual echoes within the Fourth Gospel itself.

We have here an important monograph that fills a gap in the recent study of this theme in New Testament theology, and also provides helpful markers for further research in the field. Paul Coxon writes with clarity and confidence, and throws fresh light on the theological themes he treats, both in their Judaic and Johannine settings. While concentrating on John's Gospel, he also—and pleasingly—draws other parts of the Johannine literature, including Revelation, into his work.

I was glad to be involved with an early stage in the life of this book, when I examined it in the form of a doctoral thesis, presented to the University of Wales at Lampeter. I am delighted now to be invited to commend it, as I warmly do, to a much wider audience.

Dr Stephen S. Smalley
Dean Emeritus of Chester
January 2015

To the Reader

> The whole exodus of the people out of Egypt . . . was a type and image of the exodus of the Church which should take place from among the Gentiles; And for this cause He leads it out at last from this world into his own inheritance, which Moses the servant of God did not [bestow], but which Jesus the Son of God shall give for an inheritance.
>
> —IRENAEUS *HAER.* 4:29:4

> I, he says, am the Christ. Therefore, come, all families of men, you who have been befouled with sins, and receive forgiveness for your sins. I am your forgiveness, I am the passover of your salvation, I am the lamb which was sacrificed for you . . .
>
> —MELITO OF SARDIS, *PERI PASCHA*, 102–103

THE GREAT DELIVERANCE OF the Old Testament was the Exodus. At the Exodus, the Lord redeemed Israel from slavery through the blood of the paschal lamb. With a "strong hand" (Exod 13:9) he brought them out of Egypt, the "iron furnace" (Deut 4:2), and led them through the sea in a pillar of cloud by day and a pillar of fire by night. On eagles' wings he bore them to himself and, at Sinai, Israel became a nation under God (Exod 19:4–6). He gave them his Law and ordinances and entered into a covenant with them. He would be their God and they would be his people. From that time onwards the Lord would dwell with his people in a tent, leading them through the wilderness unto their promised inheritance. For forty years he fed them with bread from heaven and sustained them with water out of the rock. He also brought them into the Land that he had promised, defeating seven nations of Canaan (Deut 7:1) and dividing their Land for Israel's inheritance. There, if they would obey his voice, he would dwell in their midst forever.

So important was the Exodus to Israel that it became the type of a much greater deliverance to come—a cosmic New Exodus (NE) from sin and bondage that would eclipse the former deliverance (Isa 43:18–19). Thus, because of their sin and covenant unfaithfulness (as Moses had predicted) Israel would be scattered and exiled among the nations (Deut 28:58–64; 31:29). Nevertheless, when they remembered the Lord in their captivity and returned to him with all their heart he would restore them to their

Land, gathering them from the ends of the earth (Deut 30:1–4). In this NE, as elaborated in the prophets, the Lord himself would search for his "sheep" and seek them out from every place where they have been scattered (Ezek 34:12). The (divinely exalted) Servant of the Lord would redeem them and make them righteous, laying down his life as a vicarious (paschal) sacrifice for their sins (Isa 53:10–11). The Lord would tend his people like a flock, carrying the "lambs" in his bosom (Isa 40:11) and pasturing them upon the mountains as he leads them home (Isa 49:8–10). He would betroth them to himself forever—in righteousness and in justice (Hosea 2:19–20)—entering into a new covenant with them. He would forgive and cleanse their sin, bestow his Spirit upon them, and write his law upon their hearts (Jer 31:31–33 cf. Isa 59:20–21). The Gentiles would also be caught up in this redemption since the Lord would reveal his righteousness and his salvation before all the nations (Isa 51:4–5). Moreover, he would renew creation and bring his chosen people into a new (renewed) Jerusalem. He would abolish death and the curse (Isa 25:8) and dwell with them forever (Isa 65:17–25). So great would be the numbers of the redeemed that their land would be too small for them and they would spread abroad to fill the earth with God's glory (Isa 54:1–3).

For the writers of the NT, rooted as they were in OT Scripture, the typological significance of the Exodus was not lost and they interpreted the life and work of Jesus (as their Lord himself had done) in terms of the New Exodus promised by God. Thus Paul could speak of Christ as "our Passover" (1 Cor 5:7) and encourage and admonish believers from the example of Israel at the Exodus (1 Cor 10:1–11). Moreover, he proclaimed the good news of salvation to the Gentiles, calling them by faith in Christ to belong to the people of God (Eph 2:19–22 cf. Rom 9:24). Likewise, Peter spoke of redemption by the precious blood of Christ, as of a lamb without blemish or spot (1 Pet 1:18–19). He also addressed Gentile believers in terms previously reserved for Israel, as "a chosen race, a royal priesthood, a holy nation" (1 Pet 2:9 cf. Exod 19:6). Hebrews uses the example of Israel in the wilderness to admonish NT believers (Heb 3–4). It also proclaims Jesus as the mediator of the new covenant (Heb 8:8–13; 12:24) and the cross of Christ as the once for all time sacrifice that can take away our sins (Heb 10:11–14). Revelation is filled with allusions to the Exodus (e.g. Rev 5:9–10; 11:6) and its NE salvation culminates in the new Jerusalem, where God's people walk in the light of his presence and drink from the water of life (Rev 22:1–5).

From the earliest times, as Irenaeus and Melito testify, the Early Church Fathers also understood the typological significance of the Exodus and recognised its NE application in the NT. Only in recent scholarship, however, in the last sixty years, has the full extent of the NT use of the NE paradigm been investigated. This is particularly true for Paul and for the Synoptic Gospels. For the Gospel of John (GJohn), however, comparatively little work has been completed. The purpose of this book is to explore the NE in GJohn, specifically chapters 5–10. As such it is a revision of my Doctoral dissertation, submitted to the University of Wales in 2010.

To the Reader

The present work is divided into two parts. In Part I, I discuss the reasons why the NE in GJohn has been largely unexplored, how it can be explored (the methodology I employ), and why it is feasible that the NE motif is key to the interpretation of GJohn. For those particularly interested in the "Johannine puzzle," why GJohn differs from the Synoptic Gospels, I hope that this will offer an insight. In Part II, I give an anatomical overview of John 5–10, John's "Festival Cycle," which I divide into five episodes, each set against its OT festal background. For each episode I discuss its form, structure, and (where I deem it necessary) the integrity of the text. I then interpret the episode in the light of its festal background, the NE paradigm, and the NE allusions that it contains. For those who wish to come straight to the Gospel text, each episode is largely self contained and may be read as a unit. It is advised, however, that the anatomical overview (chapter 7) be read first to put the episodes into context.

This book is written from the perspective of one who holds unashamedly to the divine inspiration, inerrancy, and infallibility of Holy Scripture, as originally given. It is sent out to the glory of the Triune God who gave us his marvelous Word. It is hoped that it will stimulate further exploration of God's Word, particularly of the NE in John's Gospel, with a view to furthering our understanding of that Gospel. It is also hoped that interest will be stimulated generally in the way that the OT NE promises are fulfilled in Jesus throughout the NT.

Soli Deo Gloria

Acknowledgements

THIS BOOK IS A revision of my doctoral thesis presented to the University of Wales Lampeter in 2010. As such I would like to thank the many people who assisted both in the preparation of the original dissertation and also in its revision in book form. Firstly, thanks must go to my supervisors: Dr Tom Holland of WEST invited me to undertake this work. He also provided the initial stimulus and invaluable guidance throughout. Prof. D. P. Davies of Lampeter was also a constant source of help and encouragement. I am also grateful to the scholars, research staff, and librarians who aided me with advice and in obtaining books and papers. In particular I wish to thank Dr Elizabeth Magba and Dr David Instone-Brewer of Tyndale House, Prof. Gregory Beale (who I met at Tyndale), Kathy Miles of Lampeter, Dr Robert Letham and Marcus Hobson of WEST, and the many librarians of my local lending library in Crewe. Thanks are also due to my external and internal examiners, Dr Stephen Smalley and Dr Bill Campbell, for their careful scrutiny of my thesis. Dr Smalley and Dr Holland in particular encouraged me to publish my work and I am grateful for their friendship, advice, and support throughout. I am also grateful for Christian Amondson of Wipf and Stock for patiently guiding me through the publishing process, and for Calvin Jaffarian who typeset my book.

Last, but by no means least, I want to thank friends and family for their encouragement and support. In particular I wish to thank Dr Donald and Mrs Emma Kesson whose practical help and fellowship in the Gospel have meant so much to my wife and to me. Thanks also to all our many good friends at the Bethel Church and in the wider Christian family. Thanks to both sets of parents, Mr George and Mrs Alma Coxon, and Mr Alastair and Mrs June Legge, for their continual help and support. Thanks to my children, Josh, Daniel, Joel, Esther, and Micah, for their patience with Dad while he was "doing his PhD." Josh and Dan proof-read parts of my work prior to publication and my wife painstakingly read through the entire manuscript. Thanks are especially due to my wife Sue, to whom I dedicate this book: You have been a constant source of support, help, and encouragement, without which my work would never have been completed.

Abbreviations

AB	Anchor Bible
ABD	*Anchor Bible Dictionary*
ANE	Ancient Near East
ANET	*Ancient Near Eastern Texts Relating to the Old Testament*
ANF	Ante-Nicene Fathers
Apoc. Ab.	*Apocalypse of Abraham*
As. Mos.	*Assumption of Moses*
ASV	American Standard Version
b.	*Babylonian* (Talmud)
BD	Beloved Disciple
Bar	Baruch
2 Bar.	*2 Baruch*
4 Bar.	*4 Baruch*
Ber.	*Berakot*
BNTC	Black's New Testament Commentaries
BSC	Bible Student's Commentary
BST	The Bible Speaks Today
CBQ	*Catholic Biblical Quarterly*
CD	Damascus Document
CUP	Cambridge University Press
DSS	Dead Sea Scrolls
EP	Evangelical Press
EvQ	*Evangelical Quarterly*
ET	English Translation
GJohn	Gospel of John
Haer.	*Against Heresies*
HBT	Horizons in Biblical Theology
Hist. eccl.	*Ecclesiastical History*
HTFG	*Historical Tradition in the Fourth Gospel*

Abbreviations

ICC	International Critical Commentary
IFG	Interpretation of the Fourth Gospel

Ignatius

Ign. *Magn.*	Ignatius to the Magnesians
Ign. *Philad.*	Ignatius to the Philadelphians
Ign. *Rom.*	Ignatius to the Romans

ISBE	International Standard Bible Encyclopaedia
ITC	International Theological Commentary
IVP	Inter Varsity Press
JBap	John the Baptist
JBL	Journal of Biblical Literature
JECS	Journal of Early Christian Studies
JETS	Journal of the Evangelical Theological Society

Josephus

Ant.	Jewish Antiquities
Life.	The Life of Flavius Josephus
War	Jewish War

JPS	Jewish Publication Society
JSNT	Journal for the Study of the New Testament
JSNTSup	Journal for the Study of the New Testament: Supplement Series
JSOT	Journal for the Study of the Old Testament
JSOTSup	Journal for the Study of the Old Testament: Supplement Series
JTS	Journal of Theological Studies
Jub.	Jubilees

Justin

1 Apol.	First Apology
Dial.	Dialogue with Trypho

JVG	Jesus and the Victory of God
KJV	King James Version

Abbreviations

L.A.B.	*Liber Antiquitatum Biblicarum*
LXX	Septuagint
m.	*Mishnah*
Mek.	*Mekilta*
Midr.	*Midrash*
MT	Masoretic Text
NAC	New American Commentary
NC	New Covenant
NDBT	*New Dictionary of Biblical Theology*
NE	New Exodus
NI	New Israel
NICNT	New International Commentary on the New Testament
NICOT	New International Commentary on the Old Testament
NIGTC	New International Greek Testament Commentary
NKJV	New King James Version
NovT	*Novum Testamentum*
NovTSup	Supplements to Novum Testamentum
NT	New Testament
NTPG	*New Testament and the People of God*
NTS	*New Testament Studies*
OC	Old Covenant
OT	Old Testament
OTL	Old Testament Library
OUP	Oxford University Press
Pesiq. Rab.	*Pesiqta Rabbati*
Pesiq. Rab Kah.	*Pesiqta de Rab Kahana*
PFG	*Paul and the Faithfulness of God*

Philo

Cher.	*On the Cherubim*
Leg. All.	*Allegorical Interpretation*
Mos.	*On the Life of Moses*
Praem.	*Rewards and Punishments*
Spec.	*On the Special Laws*

Pss. Sol.	Psalms of Solomon
Pol. Phil.	Polycarp, *To the Philippians*
Rab.	Rabbah
RSG	*The Resurrection of the Son of God*
SBL	Society of Biblical Literature
SBLMS	Society of Biblical Literature Monograph Series
Sib. Or.	*Sibylline Oracles*
SJT	*Scottish Journal of Theology*
SNTSMS	Society for New Testament Studies Monograph Series
SPCK	Society for Promoting Christian Knowledge
Str-B	Strack and Billerbeck. *Kommentar zum Neuen Testament aus Talmud und Midrasch*
t.	Tosefta
T. Ab.	*Testament of Abraham*
T. Jud.	*Testament of Judah*
T. Levi	*Testament of Levi*
T. Mos.	*Testament of Moses*
TDNT	*Theological Dictionary of the New Testament*
Tg. Isa.	*Targum of Isaiah*
Tg. Neof.	*Targum Neofiti*
Tg. Onq.	*Targum Onqelos*
Tg. Ps.-J.	*Targum Pseudo-Jonathan*
TNTC	Tyndale New Testament Commentary
TOTC	Tyndale Old Testament Commentary
TynBul	*Tyndale Bulletin*
UBS	United Bible Societies
USC	University of South Carolina
VT	*Vetus Testamentum*
VTSup	Supplements to Vetus Testamentum
WBC	Word Biblical Commentary
WJK	Westminster John Knox Press
WTJ	*Westminster Theological Journal*
WUNT	Wissenschaftliche Untersuchungen zum Neuen Testament
y.	*yerushalmi* (Jerusalem Talmud)
YUP	Yale University Press
ZNW	*Zeitschrift für die neutestamentliche Wissenschaft*

PART I

PRELIMINARY CONSIDERATIONS

Introduction

Why Has the New Exodus in GJohn been Largely Unexplored?

IN THE 1950'S AND 60's scholarly interest was awakened concerning the use of the Exodus and NE motifs within the NT.[1] For the Gospel of John (GJohn[2]), several short papers were published, suggesting that the Exodus (the book or the event) was a key to its interpretation.[3] In the thirty years that followed, countless papers, monographs, and commentaries investigated OT citations, allusions, and typologies in GJohn, often noting NE motifs. But the idea that the (New) Exodus was an interpretative key to the Fourth Gospel was not taken further.

Since the 1990's there has been a renewed interest in the use of the NE paradigm within the NT, particularly in the Synoptic Gospels and Pauline epistles.[4] This movement has been headed up by Wright's scholarly exploration in *Christian Origins and the Question of God*,[5] and the enthusiastic reception these volumes have received.[6]

---

1. See, e.g., Sahlin, "Exodus," 81–95; Manek, "Luke," 8–23; Piper, "Promises," 3–22; Teeple, *Prophet*; Balentine, "Concept"; Williams, *Wilderness*; Daube, *Exodus*; Mauser, *Wilderness*; Nixon, *Exodus*. This interest was coincident with biblical-theological investigation of the NE motif in the OT prophetic literature, cf. Von Rad, *Theology*, 2:238–62; Fischer, "neuen Exodus," 111–30; Daniélou, *Sacramentum Futuri, 131ff.*; Zimmerli, *Ezekiel 1*; idem, *Ezekiel 2*. It was stimulated by investigations into the use of the OT within the NT, particularly in the form of apologetic testimonial material, cf. Lindars, *Apologetic*; Dodd, *According*; Bruce, *Old Testament*. It was also aided by the rehabilitation of typology, a discipline which had previously fallen out of favor, cf. Goppelt *Typos*; Ellis, *Paul's Use*, 126–35.

2. In what follows, GJohn refers to the Fourth Gospel, and John refers to its author.

3. Cf. Sahlin, *Typologie*; Enz, "Type," 208–15; McCasland, "Signs and Wonders," 149–52; Morgan, "Fulfilment," 155–65; Smith, "Exodus Typology," 329–42; Glasson, *Moses*; Balentine, "Concept," 349–411.

4. Cf. Garrett, "Exodus," 656–80; Marcus, *Way of the Lord*; Allison, *New Moses*; Schneck, *Isaiah*; Swartley, *Scripture Traditions*; Ravens, *Luke*; Watts, *Mark*; Davies, "Paul," 443–63; Pao, *Acts*; Holland, *Contours*; idem, *Romans*.

5. Wright, *NTPG*; idem, *JVG*; idem, *RSG*; idem, *PFG*. Wright's work takes the form of a historical investigation, in the vein of the third quest for the historical Jesus, and the quest for the historical Paul. On Paul, see Wright, *Climax*; idem, *Saint Paul*; idem, *Perspective*; idem, *Pauline Perspectives*. For a critical appraisal of Wright's "new perspective" on Paul's teaching on Justification, see Eveson, *Great Exchange*, 110–206. For a re-examination of E. P. Sander's teaching on "covenantal nomism" in idem, *Paul and Palestinian Judaism*, see Carson et al., *Justification and Variegated Nomism*, vol. 1–2.

6. See Newman, *Restoration*.

PART I—PRELIMINARY CONSIDERATIONS

According to Wright, the Jewish people of Jesus' day saw themselves in bondage and "exile," and looked for a fulfilment of the OT NE hope in their own days. Moreover, the Synoptic Gospels and Pauline Epistles reflect this Jewish NE hope.[7]

For the Fourth Gospel, however, comparatively little recent NE work has been completed. The main exception is the thesis of Brunson.[8] But although he sees the NE "everywhere" in GJohn, his focus is restricted to John's use of Ps 118. Other scholars have examined the NE motif in passing.[9] Besides this, several intertextual studies have explored Ezekiel's and Isaiah's relationship to GJohn, and Moses typology has been investigated,[10] but the idea of the NE as an *interpretative key* to GJohn has not been adequately exploited. Though surprising,[11] there may be several explanations:

1. Wright has not done for GJohn what he did for the Synoptics. Recognising that GJohn's uniqueness and complexity make it a vast field of study in its own right, he has not incorporated it in his groundbreaking historical work.[12] His agenda has also been dictated by the "Historical Jesus" debate:[13] Jesus Quest scholars, questioning GJohn's historical reliability,[14] have confined themselves largely to the Synoptics.[15]

2. For some scholars, GJohn has not escaped suspicion that its high Christology,

---

7. The tendency in Pauline studies has been to move away from a Hellenistic ethos and towards a Jewish one. For example, for Wright, Paul was a Shammaite Jew, who looked for the fulfilment of the NE. Wright's work has been stimulated by several factors, including recent scholarly attention given to historical study (especially Apocalyptic/Messianic) of the Dead Sea Scrolls and intertestamental and rabbinic literature, but above all, by the post-Bultmann sea-change that understands Paul and the Synoptic Jesus from a Jewish perspective. Cf. Daube, *Rabbinic Judaism*; Davies, *Paul*; Sanders, *Paul and Palestinian Judaism*; idem, *Jesus and Judaism*. Other NE scholars, who have taken a more literary, or biblical-theology approach, have been helped by the flourishing OT in NT movement (cf. Ellis, *Paul's Use*; Hanson, *Utterances*; Kaiser, *Uses*; Carson and Williamson, *It is Written*; Beale, *Right Doctrine*; Moyise, *Old Testament in the New testament*; idem, *Old Testament in the New*), the revival of Biblical Theology (Cf. Vos, *Biblical Theology*; Childs, *Biblical Theology*; Alexander and Rosner, *NDBT*; Beale, *Biblical Theology*), and the application of literary techniques to the NT (Particularly intertextuality, e.g., Hays, *Echoes*. See also Alter, *Biblical Narrative*, and the inner-biblical exegesis theories in Fishbane, *Biblical Interpretation*; idem, *Text and Texture*).

8. Brunson, *Psalm 118*.

9. For example, Motyer, *Your Father*, who notes that in GJohn Jesus leads a NE, and shows that this is applicable to the post A.D. 70 situation of the Jews. This insight, however, is tangential to his focus on John 8:31–59 and his main concern of absolving John from anti-Judaism. See also Beasley-Murray, *John*.

10. For example, see Boismard and Viviano, *Moses or Jesus*.

11. In as much as the earlier work has not been followed up.

12. See Wright, *JVG*, xvi. In his popular commentary, however, he gives clues as to the direction he might take in investigating the NE in GJohn. See Wright, *John 1–10*; idem, *John 11–21*.

13. He writes: "The debate to which I wish to contribute in this book has been conducted almost entirely in terms of the Synoptic tradition." See Wright, *JVG*, xvi; idem, "In Grateful Dialogue," 251.

14. Though Wright distances himself from this historical scepticism. See Wright, "In Grateful Dialogue," 251–52.

15. See Smith, *Four Dimensions*, 119, who cites Meir, *Marginal Jew*; Fredriksen, *Jesus of Nazareth*, as exceptions.

"dualism," and abstract language indicate that it is Hellenistic or Gnostic in its concepts. This has militated against the enthusiasm for enquiry into a Jewish NE ethos.[16] Many of these difficulties have been overcome,[17] but not all accept the solutions. Thus for the last 150 years, scholars have been preoccupied with the "Johannine puzzle"—the question of the Gospel's author, origins, and cultural milieu.[18] Westcott placed GJohn squarely in the Jewish world.[19] Hoskyns[20] set GJohn against a Christian background, as setting forth the theological significance of the Jesus of Synoptic and Synoptic-like tradition.[21] Dodd thought that GJohn reflected a wide background including Hellenism, Philo, and the Hermetic literature.[22] But the scholar, who above all set the agenda, was Bultmann. He believed that GJohn echoed Gnosticism; in particular the Johannine ascent and descent of the Son of Man was based on the Mandaean Gnostic Redeemer myth. Mandaean Gnosticism is discounted today, its sources clearly post-dating John.[23] Moreover, although John's Jewishness has been established,[24] the *type* of Jewishness it displays is in question. Thus Barrett thinks that John reflects a turn of the first century "eclectic" Judaism that was both "Jewish and anti-Jewish," and "Gnostic and anti-Gnostic."[25] Similarly Smith thinks that "the Mandaean affinities of John's

16. See Burge, *Interpreting John*, 19–20, who traces these ideas to the time of F. C. Baur and D. F. Strauss. Cf. Neill and Wright, *Interpretation*, 335ff.

17. In particular the DSS have done much to confirm that John's use of "dualism" and abstract language is more likely to be "Jewish" than "Hellenistic." See Hengel, *Judaism and Hellenism*, passim, where he minimises the difference between Palestinian and diaspora Judaism. Moreover, though J. A. T. Robinson's "New Look" at John has not commanded general support, an increasing number of scholars now accept the Jewishness of John, its foundation on historical traditions, and in some cases authorship by the apostle John.

18. Interest in the mystery of GJohn and its differences from the Synoptic Gospels goes back to the earliest writings of the Church, but preoccupation with this "puzzle" has considerably intensified during the last century.

19. See Westcott, *John*, 1:x–lii. The author was a Jew, a Jew of Palestine, an eyewitness, an apostle, the apostle John.

20. Hoskyns, *Fourth Gospel*.

21. See the comments of Smith, "Contribution," 275–94. He notes that Hoskyns was "amenable to the classical Christian understanding of the document [i.e. GJohn.]." Thus he stands in direct relation to both Clement of Alexandria, who referred to GJohn as a "spiritual Gospel" in relation to the other three, and Calvin, who characterised GJohn as the key to the proper understanding of the others. See Calvin, *John*, 1:6.

22. See Dodd, *IFG*. For an outline and critique of Dodd's position see Painter, *Quest*, 53–61. Cf. Bacon, *The Gospel of the Hellenists*; Scott, *Fourth Gospel*, cited by Robinson, *Priority*, 36; Brown, *Introduction to the New Testament*, 116ff.; Nash, *Greeks*, 226ff.

23. See Brown, *John I–XII*, lii–lvi; Dunn, *Christology*; idem, *Parting*, 14. Of Bultmann's thesis Dunn writes, "There is no real evidence of such a [Gnostic Redeemer] myth prior to Christianity." He also notes that the discovery of the Nag Hammadi texts has not altered this conclusion.

24. Cf. Brown, *John I–XII*, lix–lxiv; Barrett, *Judaism*; Robinson, "New Look," 338–50; idem, *Priority*, 36ff.

25. See Barrett, *Judaism*, 71–72. Cf. Painter, *Quest*, 61, who thinks that "Gnostic tendencies, present within some realms of sectarian Judaism, contributed to the development of distinctive Johannine

PART I—PRELIMINARY CONSIDERATIONS

Gospel and the best guess as to Mandaean origins combine to suggest . . . that the Johannine literature is related to sectarian, perhaps gnosticizing Judaism."[26]

The persistence of this Gnostic understanding has been underpinned by the scholarly consensus concerning the "Orthodox Johannophobia Theory"[27] of the way GJohn was received by the early Church—feared by the orthodox, but welcomed by Valentinian and other Gnostics. This consensus, which has developed over the last sixty years, owes much to J. N. Sanders,[28] who found no trace of GJohn in the Fathers, only cautious use of GJohn by the Apologists, but reception of the Gospel among the Gnostics of Alexandria.[29] He postulated that the Gospel was written in Alexandria for a group influenced by proto-Gnostic speculation, used the language of that speculation, and was consequently mistrusted by the Orthodox. This has led other scholars to postulate that John himself was proto-Gnostic[30] or that his community was on the margins of the Church. Brown postulated that the community split, a heterodox group taking the Gospel with them and that First John was written by an orthodox elder, explaining how GJohn is capable of orthodox interpretation.[31] Acceptance by the "Great Church," however, came only when Irenaeus used the Fourth Gospel against the Gnostics.[32]

3. The "aporias" and Christological tensions in GJohn cause many scholars to view it as being composed from various *conflicting* sources, carefully stitched together to give the appearance of a "seamless robe" (Strauss).[33] According to Bultmann there were at least three written sources: the *Offenbarungsreden*—a collection of revelational discourses, the *Semeia* (or miracle) source, and the Passion-Narrative source. To these must be added the contribution of the evangelist and the redactor. Moreover, each of these reflected a different Christology. The Christology of the *Offenbarungsreden* is that of the Gnostic redeemer myth, that of the *Semeia* source is the *theios anēr* (divine man), the evangelist's Christology is existential, and the Christology of the redactor is bound up with ecclesiastical concerns.[34] Bultmann was not the first to propose Johannine sources, but he set the standard

---

language and symbolism."

26. Smith, *Johannine Christianity*, 28. He cites the work of Odeberg, *Fourth Gospel*, who noted parallels between Jewish mystical sources and certain strata of Mandaean literature. See also, Scholem, *Jewish Gnosticism*; Painter, *Quest*, 35.

27. Coined by Hill, *Johannine Corpus*, 11.

28. Sanders, *Fourth Gospel*. Cf. Bauer, *Orthodoxy and Heresy*, which influenced Sanders.

29. Cf. Hill, *Johannine Corpus*, 15–16.

30. See Barrett, *John*, 66, who thinks John to have been one stage in the development towards Gnosticism.

31. Brown, *Community*, 107.

32. Ibid., 149–150.

33. Strauss's phrase is cited by Anderson, *Christology*, 252.

34. See Anderson, *Christology*, 6, 35.

that many have followed.[35]

The problem for a NE interpretation here is that, although NE typologies and motifs may appear in one source, they are likely to be absent or *contradicted* in the others. Thus both Martyn[36] and Fortna[37] detect a Moses typology in "the Semeia source," but Martyn thinks this has been "upgraded" to a Son of Man Christology by the evangelist.[38] This would not obviate NE studies in GJohn but might suggest that the NE is not *the* key to the Gospel.

4. Closely related to this is the idea that GJohn has "evolved" over a long period of time. Martyn speaks of three periods: during "the Early Period" Christian Jews—an "inner-synagogue messianic group"—preached Jesus as the Prophet-Messiah like Moses. One of their number collected these sermons and produced "a rudimentary, written Gospel."[39] In "the Middle Period," synagogue expulsion and martyrdom give birth to a separate community of Jewish Christians. Interpretation of their experience led to "new christological formulations," including the "Logos hymn" and above/below dualism.[40] In "the Late Period," the Johannine community formed its own theology and identity in relation to the parent synagogue and other Christian groups. During this time two editions of the "fully Johannine Gospel" were written.[41]

Brown speaks of five periods where:

a) The traditions of Jesus are collected, possibly from the Beloved Disciple.

b) Anti-Temple and Samaritan Christians join Christians with a "synoptic" heritage (reflected in John 1–4) and a "higher christology" is introduced.

c) Conflict with the world, the "Jews," and the Baptist's disciples produces the first edition of GJohn, reflecting this conflict.

d) Internal conflict divides the community, leading to a second edition of GJohn and the Johannine epistles.

e) The community splits into orthodox and Gnostic camps.[42]

---

35. See Fortna, *Signs*. Cf. Smith, *Johannine Christianity*, 31, who thinks GJohn's "principal components" include "originating eyewitness, miracle tradition, passion narrative, controversy with the synagogue, *incipient Gnosticism or quasi-Gnosticism*, and charismatic prophecy" (emphasis mine).

36. See Martyn, *History and Theology*, 101–23.

37. See Fortna, *Signs*, 100–1.

38. Martyn, *History and Theology*, 124–43.

39. Ibid., 150.

40. Ibid., 156.

41. Ibid., 157.

42. Brown, *Community*, passim. Cf. Burge, *Interpreting*, 73; Painter, *Quest*, 63.

PART I—PRELIMINARY CONSIDERATIONS

Anderson[43] and Painter[44] also think that GJohn "evolved" in relation to specific events. This diachronic emphasis and its fragmentation of the Gospel have important ramifications for NE studies. On this model, the Gospel is like an archaeological tell,[45] and the NE, if present in GJohn, is likely to be confined to particular strata, but is unlikely to provide *the* key to the final Gospel. Moreover, preoccupation with sources and community[46] has made the Gospel a window onto the early church,[47] to be exploited by social scientists, rather than a window onto Jesus and his ministry.[48]

5. The concept of a "Johannine School" is a further concomitant of sources and community. Dismissing the evidence of the early Church,[49] Brown speaks of a "school of writers who shared a theological position and style, to which the evangelist, the redactor, and the author of the Epistles all belonged."[50] Not only does this add extra complexity, but also it potentially allows a wider divergence in Johannine theological positions than Brown would allow.

6. In the absence of detailed historical evidence, sociological and sociolinguistic approaches have sought to apply the sociology of knowledge to illuminate the Johannine community, delineated by Martyn and others. Thus Meeks has used the approach of sociologists Berger and Luckmann to explore the role that the "ascent descent" language might have played in the Johannine community's "internalisation" under external hostility and alienation.[51] He has been criticized, however, for misapplying the theory, attempting a micro-sociological analysis of the community without the control of a macro-sociological analysis of the structure of society within which it operated.[52] The main problem here is that such approaches have tended to supplant historical research, or ignore what historical evidence we do have,[53] rather than augmenting it. Moreover, the focus has once again been diverted from interpretation of the Gospel to mirror reading of the

---

43. See Anderson, "Bread of Life," 42–43.

44. See the chapter on "Johannine Christianity," in Painter, *Quest*, esp. 61ff.

45. See Martyn, *History and Theology*, 145.

46. See Anderson, *Christology*, 30–31. "The historical interest of Johannine scholars has shifted from the search for the historical Jesus to the search for the historical Johannine community."

47. See Brown, *Community*, 69, where he says that the Gospel can be read "partly as an autobiography of the Johannine community."

48. See Robinson, *Priority*, 29–31.

49. See Brown, *Community*, 34, n. 46.

50. Ibid., 96.

51. Meeks, "Man from Heaven," 44–72. Cf. Neyrey, *Ideology*; Malina and Rohrbaugh, *John*; Rensberger, *Johannine Faith*. Rensberger has used the categories of the liberation theology of Jose Miranda to find John's description of an oppressed community seeking liberation from powerful authorities.

52. See Motyer, *Your Father*, 30–31.

53. Motyer, *Your Father*, 26, complains that even Rensberger's attempt to relate his theory to the wider political and social background is barely more than a page long.

Why Has the New Exodus in GJohn been Largely Unexplored?

community, assumed to be a small group marginalized from the wider Church.

7. The recent trend to approach the Gospel synchronically, from a literary perspective,[54] while bringing many important advances and serving to point up the thematic and literary unity of the Gospel, has only bracketed the historical-critical questions.[55] Moreover, though diverting attention from the Gospel as a window onto the early church, such studies tend to provide a mirror onto the reader rather than a window onto Jesus.[56]

None of these difficulties, though seemingly formidable, precludes a NE reading of GJohn. Indeed, much older scholarship has been challenged,[57] and much recent scholarship, though acknowledged and acclaimed, has been advanced in a very tentative manner.[58] Moreover, while progress has been made, the final universally acknowledged solution to the "Johannine puzzle" has not yet been found. Indeed, unless fresh external confirmatory evidence is unearthed,[59] a universally recognized solution may never be found. What is evident, however, is the need, in any plausible solution, for recognition of the Gospel's literary unity, satisfactory accommodation/accounting for the Johannine "aporias" and tensions, discernment of the Gospel's Weltanschauung (world-view), and its location in a plausible historical *Sitz im Leben* (situation in life). It is the contention of this book that the NE paradigm provides such a solution and, moreover, that the NE is a key, both to John's interpretation of Jesus' ministry and to many of the perceived difficulties of the Fourth Gospel. Before we can explore the NE motif in GJohn, however, we must establish a credible methodology.

---

54. See, for example, Culpepper, *Anatomy*.

55. But cf. Stibbe, *John as Storyteller*, 9ff.; Motyer, *Your Father*, passim.

56. So Culpepper, *Anatomy*, 4.

57. See, e.g., the criticisms levelled against Bultmann's source theories in Anderson, *Christology*, 70–89.

58. For example, Brown, *Community*, 7, admitted that he would be happy if 60 percent of his theory was correct. Painter, *Quest*, 2, admits the hypothetical nature of his reconstruction.

59. For example, the publication of P52 (1945) pushed back the Gospel's date and the discovery and translation of the Nag Hammadi library (1970s) has illuminated early Gnosticism. If we could discover Papias's missing work it could be a key to the Johannine question. See Hengel, *Question*, 16.

1

Methodology: How Can We Explore the NE in GJohn?

THE USE OF INTERTEXTUALITY

Introduction

THE PRIMARY METHODOLOGY WE will use to explore the NE in GJohn can be described simply as "intertextuality," but it is important to clarify what we mean. Intertextuality is an umbrella term that covers a multitude of meanings. Generally speaking, we can think of intertextuality as "the interrelationship between texts." From the standpoint of the literary critic there are many ways in which texts relate to one another. This is true, not only in terms of one text's citation or appropriation of other texts, but also in terms of such considerations as shared language, genre, the framing of texts, and the culture they reflect—even to the very act of reading texts.

From the perspective of biblical studies, there are also many different interrelationships between texts. For George Buchanan,[1] intertextuality covers such diverse fields as traditional source criticism, Jewish midrash, typology, and inner-biblical exegesis.[2] Though all of these approaches are broadly intertextual, and important for our consideration, we need to narrow down our definition, and the scope of intertextuality to be employed, and focus more narrowly upon the phenomenon.

Delimiting our approach

For our purposes, we will restrict the use of intertextuality to the examination of embedded "fragments" of Scripture texts within other Scripture texts.[3] These fragments are usually classified as quotations, allusions, and echoes. We will return to the distinction between these categories, and the way we identify them, at a later point. For

---

1. Buchanan, *Intertextuality*.
2. See, e.g., Fishbane, *Biblical Interpretation*, *passim*. Cf. Koptak, "Intertextuality," 332.
3. Clearly, there are other, extra-biblical, allusions within Scripture. In Acts 17:28, for example, Paul alludes to the Greek poet Aratus. Nevertheless, as will become clear, the OT is the one great background for the NT, upon which it rests, and to which it constantly alludes.

Methodology: How Can We Explore the NE in GJohn?

now, we will think of each of these fragments as an allusion to the OT. Moreover, in order to explore the NE in GJohn, we will consider fragments of the OT embedded within John's Gospel. The aim is to understand John's use of the OT NE paradigm by analysis of his OT quotations, allusions, and echoes. This is possible because of the phenomenon of biblical intertextual allusion.

Recognising the phenomenon

On a simple level, when one biblical text alludes to another biblical "source" text, it sets up a mutually interpretive relationship with that text, (implicitly or explicitly[4]) commenting, elucidating, explicating, or elaborating upon what was originally said.[5] This interpretation is not one-way, however, because the quotation, allusion, or echo, and the context in which it is set in the "source" text, informs, clarifies, and illuminates, the text that quotes it. The net result is a resonance between the two texts and their contexts that amplifies and elucidates their meaning.[6] Thus, to properly interpret a biblical text, we must take notice of the sources to which it alludes, and the context in which the allusions are set both in the source texts and in the text that makes the allusion.

A working definition

It follows that, from the perspective of inner-biblical allusions, intertextuality can be defined as "the mutually interpretive interrelationship between biblical texts."

An illustration of the phenomenon

Before we proceed further, we will look at an illustration. An example of this intertextual phenomenon is found in the opening words of GJohn, "In the beginning was the Word (Ἐν ἀρχῇ ἦν ὁ λόγος)." The phrase, "In the beginning," Ἐν ἀρχη, is an unmistakable allusion to Genesis 1:1, "In the beginning God created (בְּרֵאשִׁית בָּרָא אֱלֹהִים, LXX ἐν ἀρχῇ ἐποίησεν ὁ θεὸς)." If we examine the context of Genesis 1 and that of John 1, we find that there is a resonance between them. They both deal with God, creation,

---

4. A good example is the citation of Deut 25:4, "You shall not muzzle an ox when it is treading out the grain" in 1 Cor 9:8–10 and in 1 Tim 5:18. In the first instance, Paul *explicitly* says that God gave this directive in the Law, not because of his concern for oxen, but rather out of his concern that the ministers of his word should be provided for. In the second instance, Paul offers no explicit comments on Deut 25:4, but in the context in which the quotation is set he *implicitly* "says" that it applies to the remuneration of Gospel ministers. (I would also add that the context of Deut 25:4, the duty of God's people, whom he redeemed from Egyptian slavery, of dealing equitably and compassionately with one another and with strangers, informs the NT passages that make the quotation).

5. This accords with the principles of inner-biblical exegesis, whereby a later biblical author elaborates upon an earlier Scripture according to the unfolding of the progressive revelation of the mind of God.

6. See Hays, *Echoes*, 20.

PART I—PRELIMINARY CONSIDERATIONS

life, light, and darkness. The context of Genesis 1 deals with the creation of the world, *ex nihilo*, by God. In John 1, however, the creation of all things *ex nihilo* is attributed unequivocally to the Word (ὁ λόγος), a person who not only existed in the beginning "with God," but who mysteriously "was God," and is the source of "life." Thus John 1 elaborates upon Genesis 1, by insisting that the Word, later identified with Jesus, existed in the beginning, with God, and as God, and that he was the agent by which God created "all things." But Genesis 1 similarly informs John 1. Not only does the creation account detail the abundance, goodness, and glory of creation, and the wise and orderly way in which it was made by an all powerful creator, but it also describes the agency of creation in terms of the going forth of God's word, "God said (εἶπεν ὁ θεός) . . . and it was so."[7] Importantly, εἶπεν is indicative aorist active of λέγω, cognate of λόγος (Word). Moreover, this same "word of the LORD" (דְּבַר־יְהוָה), frequently personified throughout the OT, is God's agent, not only in creation, but also in providence, revelation, and salvation.[8] Importantly, in Isaiah 55:11–13, God's "preexistent" word, sent forth from God's mouth, will accomplish the forgiveness of sins and deliverance from bondage in a NE of salvation that will involve all creation. Thus this wider OT background also informs GJohn's use of "the Word," indicating that he (Jesus) is the one, promised long ago, sent forth from God to deliver his people in a NE.[9]

Several other echoes and allusions in the GJohn Prologue combine with this one to confirm and elucidate John's NE understanding of Jesus' mission. Thus Jesus' coming to his own people to deliver them (John 1:11) echoes Moses' coming to Israel to bring them out of Egypt (Exod 3:13). The light shining in the darkness, and the inability of the darkness to overcome it (John 1:5) is evocative, not only of creation (and fall[10]), but also of the struggle between light and darkness at the Exodus (Exod 10: 21– 23; 13:21; 14:19–20), and the shining of the light in the darkness at the NE (Isa 9:2; 42:6–7, 16; 60:1–3). The "crying out" of the forerunner echoes (John 1:15) and cites the NE "voice of one crying out in the wilderness, 'Make straight the way of the Lord'" (John 1:23 cf. Isa 40:3). The Word dwelling (in a tent) among us (John 1:14) alludes to God's dwelling in a tent among Israel, both at the Exodus (Exod 25:8–9; 29:44–45) and in the NE (Ezek 37:26–27; Zech 2:10). These allusions (and several others), together with their contexts, inform the meaning of the Prologue and enable us to build up a picture of the way John understood Jesus as the one who accomplishes the NE salvation.

The Prologue is particularly important for GJohn because, not only does it announce the great themes of the Fourth Gospel, but it also introduces Jesus' mission, and it is key to the plot of the Gospel. A NE interpretation of the Prologue is thus indicative of a NE interpretation of the entire Gospel.

---

7. Cf. Gen 1:3, 6, 9, 11, 14, 20, 24, 26.

8. Cf. e.g., Ps 33:6; Deut 8:3; 1 Sam 3:7, 21; 2 Sam 7:4; Isa 38:4; Jer 1:2; Ps 107:20; Isa 55:11.

9. Commenting on Isa 55:11, Oswalt, *Isaiah 40–66*, 446–47, notes its relationship to "the Word" of John 1:1, in the mind of John.

10. See Brown, *John I-XII*, 27.

Methodology: How Can We Explore the NE in GJohn?

For our purposes, in order to explore the NE in John 5–10, we must similarly take note of the allusions to the OT NE in these chapters, including the context in which they are originally set, and the context of their new setting in the Gospel, in order to investigate the way that John has used them to shape the meaning of what he says.

Accounting for the phenomenon

How do we account for this intertextual phenomenon? Scholars have done so in various ways.

1. First of all we can think of allusions to other texts as pointers to the context of those texts. C. H. Dodd said this many years ago. The reader must study the OT context and plot, to which he has been directed, in order to gain insight into its fulfilment in the NT events.[11] A. T. Hanson said something similar. Thus, when Jesus alludes to Psalm 82:6 in John 10:34, he is using the allusion as a pointer to the context of the whole psalm.[12] We have to read the whole psalm to understand the allusion. Bringing this up to date, we can think of the allusion as a hyperlink on an internet page—you click on the button and it redirects you to a new context.

2. A more elaborate explanation, one that has led the field in recent biblical intertextual studies, has come from Richard Hays. He explains biblical intertextuality in terms of a figure of speech, transumption or metalepsis. Transumption means to take from one place to another—and refers to the transportation of meaning from one context to another.

   Hollander, from whom Hays gets the idea of transumption (or metalepsis), advocates the application of this term to poetic or rhetorical diachronic allusion.[13] He notes that metalepsis comes from the Greek, μεταλαμβάνω, ("to partake in, succeed to, exchange, take in a new way . . . to explain").[14] He also notes that it has been described as early as the Roman rhetorician Quintilian, who lists it as a trope (figure of speech) that "effect(s) change of meaning," that provides a "transition from one trope to another."[15] Not only is this aesthetically pleasing, but also, in this "figure of linkage between figures," suppressed or unspoken correspondences are present, which the interpreter must recover to understand the allusion.[16]

---

11. Dodd, "Old Testament in the New," in Beale, *Right Doctrine from the Wrong Text*, 176; idem, *According*, 126–27.

12. Hanson, *Prophetic Gospel*, 148.

13. Hollander, *Figure of Echo*, 114.

14. See ibid., 133.

15. Ibid., 133. See his discussion in ibid., 133–49, where, in a survey of the historic use of the terms "matalepsis" and "transumption," Hollander shows the degree of confusion and bewilderment that has surrounded this figure of speech.

16. Ibid., 114–15.

PART I—PRELIMINARY CONSIDERATIONS

Building upon Hollander, and applying these ideas to biblical intertextuality, Hays helpfully provides us with a working definition:

> Metalepsis is a rhetorical and poetic device in which one text alludes to an earlier text in a way that evokes resonances of the earlier text *beyond those explicitly stated*. The result is that the interpretation of a metalepsis requires the reader to recover unstated or suppressed correspondences between the two texts.[17]

What Hays is saying is that, when the NT alludes to the OT, there are suppressed correspondences—unspoken whispers—that take place between the two contexts, which must be discovered to understand the allusion. This is similar to what Dodd says, but it transfers information in both directions, producing a resonance between the two contexts.

3. A third way of accounting for this mutual interpretation is given by Gregory Beale. He does so in terms of the principle that "Scripture interprets Scripture." What he says is that, when a NT text alludes to an OT Scripture, it *"unpacks the meaning"* of that OT Scripture. Similarly, the OT passage *"sheds light on"* the meaning of the NT passage.[18] The reason Beale uses these terms is because he wants to warn against the idea of the creation of new meanings that are incompatible with the original author's intentions—changing and distorting the original intended OT meaning. This is an important consideration that we need to bear in mind. NT allusion to the OT does not create meaning that isn't already there in the OT text, at least in embryonic form. Rather, it unfolds and develops what is *already present*, according to God's progressive revelation and in the light of Jesus Christ. Beale cites Geerhardus Vos's illustration of an early biblical "seed" idea (a text or a prophecy), being developed by later authors into roots, stems, and leaves, coming into full bloom in the NT. Though the different stages of development differ from one another and from the original thought, there is nevertheless an organic relationship that exists between them.[19]

The explanation adopted in this book combines the insights of these three approaches. Allusions to the OT act as pointers to the OT context and plot. More than that, however, they set up a resonance between the two contexts and result in unspoken whispers between them. Moreover, Scripture interprets Scripture, without distortion of the original OT author's intended meaning.

---

17. Hays, *Conversion*, 2 (emphasis original).

18. Beale, *Biblical Theology*, 3 (emphasis mine). He notes that this also applies when later OT texts allude to earlier OT texts.

19. Ibid., 4. He cites Vos, "Idea," 11–15.

ANSWERING OBJECTIONS

Answering objections of oversimplification

It may be objected that, in reality, the approach suggested above is an oversimplification. This is because, from the perspective of the literary theorist, the *entire language* that a text uses to communicate can be thought of as a system of signs and codes that derive their meaning from the culture and society from which they originate. For Julia Kristeva, since a text depends on prior codes, "every text is from the outset under the jurisdiction of other discourses which impose a universe on it."[20] Moreover, intertextuality becomes "the sum of knowledge that makes it possible for texts to have meaning."[21] For GJohn this might mean finding parallels in Philo, the Odes of Solomon, or Mandaean literature. Indeed, in our John 1:1 example above, scholars have found parallels to the "Word," (λόγος) in the Greek philosophical schools and in Philo that suggest to them that GJohn has been, at the very least, influenced by these backgrounds. I would argue, however, that, in view of GJohn's repeated allusions to Genesis and to the OT in the Prologue, the correct background for GJohn's "Word," is the OT.[22] Not only so, but also, in our search for GJohn's NE allusions, we must confine our attention largely to echoes of the OT alone. But can such an approach be justified?

For Paul, Hays has done just this, providing a "reading" by applying the insights of intertextuality largely to the citations and allusions in Paul to specific Scripture texts alone. Hays believes this "approach to reading Paul" is justified because Scripture is Paul's "privileged predecessor." Thus Paul "repeatedly situates his discourse within the symbolic field created by a single great textual precursor: Israel's Scripture."[23]

I argue similarly for the applicability of Hays's general approach to GJohn. Thus, John also repeatedly situates his discourse within the single great textual precursor of Israel's Scripture: though his explicit Scriptural quotations are relatively few,[24] his widely acknowledged allusions to Scripture are abundant.[25] Moreover, he repeatedly

---

20. Cited by Culler, *Pursuit of Signs*, 105.

21. Culler, *Pursuit of Signs*, 104.

22. Cf. Carson, *John*, 115.

23. Hays, *Echoes*, 15–16. He compares this to a citation from T. Green's comments on Renaissance poems: They "tend to reach out to a single privileged predecessor and bind themselves to that authenticating model with particularly intricate knots." Cf. Wright, *Perspective*, 150, "In all that He does [Paul] is engaged in implicit dialogue both with the Old Testament itself and with other first century readings of it."

24. According to the UBS Greek NT, 4th rev. edn., John has 14 quotations from the OT, compared with 54 in Matthew, 27 in Mark, 25 in Luke, and 60 in Romans. This may not accurately reflect a book's indebtedness to the OT, however, since Revelation, without any recognized OT citations, alludes to the OT many times (estimates ranging from 250 to over 1000). See Moyise, *Old Testament in the New*, 6.

25. Cf. Carson and Williamson, *It is Written*, *passim*; Hanson, *Utterances*, 115; Motyer, *Your Father*, 42; Brunson, *Psalm 118*, 149.

affirms that Jesus fulfils Scripture[26] and explicitly speaks of it as inviolable truth.[27] Furthermore, from a literary perspective, his abundant use of historical analepses (flashbacks) ties the narrative "to the central events of the larger biblical story . . . locating the story [of Jesus] squarely within the history and scriptural heritage of the Jewish people."[28] Nevertheless, if we seek to demonstrate John's *determinative* use of the NE paradigm, further justification is necessary. Thus granting John's privileged predecessor to be Scripture does not rule out (for some scholars) a non-Scriptural lens through which he viewed Scripture. Moreover, John's widespread use of universal symbols[29] (e.g., light and darkness) makes other, non-Scriptural, echoes possible.[30] Are we justified in confining our search for echoes and allusions largely to Scripture? Are we not just silencing other legitimate echoes? My justification is that we can *determine* what John meant.[31] Moreover, I will seek to show that John deliberately portrayed Jesus as fulfilling the OT NE hope, and that he intentionally echoed Scripture rather than Gnosticism or Hellenism, which were alien to his thinking. Furthermore, even where these other echoes are possible, they are better explained as OT echoes.

Answering Postmodern objections

Postmodern interpreters would disagree with the above. They say that once a text is cut free from its author, it takes on an independent identity (it has "semantic autonomy"[32]), and meaning depends upon a reader's (historically, culturally, and ideologically preconditioned)[33] interaction with the text. Thus there is never only one meaning, and a particular meaning only results if some interactions are privileged and others silenced.[34] Moreover, it would be equally legitimate to understand GJohn in the light of Gnosticism or Hellenism or the NE.

Hirsch disagrees: a text has just one correct meaning, that determined by the author,[35] and "Verbal meaning is whatever someone has willed to convey by a particular sequence of linguistic signs and which can be conveyed (shared) by means of

---

26. Cf. John 12:38; 13:18; 15:25; 17:12; 19:24, 28, 36.
27. Cf. John 10:35; 17:17.
28. Culpepper, *Anatomy*, 58.
29. See Smith, *Johannine Christianity*, 9.
30. And for some scholars irresistible, e.g., the suggestion of the Dionysius myth behind the miracle of the wine, or the Gnostic redeemer behind the descending and ascending Son of Man.
31. Cf. Dunn, "Let John be John," 312, who insists that the task of exegesis is to hear John on his own terms and in his own time, as its first readers heard him.
32. Cf. Hirsch, *Validity*, 1–2.
33. Cf. Vanhoozer, *Meaning*, 106–7, and his discussion of a reader's "horizon" and "preunderstanding."
34. Cf. Moyise, "Intertextuality," 18, 33–40; Cotterell and Turner, *Linguistics*, 53–56.
35. Hirsch, *Validity*, 1, speaks of "the sensible belief that a text means what its author meant."

those linguistic signs."[36] Thus our primary interpretative task is to discover that single meaning.

Cotterell and Turner discuss three objections to Hirsch, which he has also sought to answer[37]:

1. Authorial incompetence—the author may have generated meanings of which he is unaware, or he may not have understood what he has written, or accurately conveyed his own meaning.[38] There two issues here:

    a) The first two difficulties arise because of the author's poor understanding of his subject matter, or his inattentiveness to every aspect of his complex discourse.[39] Although such "incompetence" can be often be discerned by the competent interpreter, it does not invalidate the author's "verbal meaning."

    b) In the case of inaccuracies, we can usually *infer* what an author meant (his "verbal meaning") even when he makes mistakes.[40] Students are aware that textbooks frequently contain mistakes—and not only can these be detected, but also they can usually be resolved from the context of the text. This is possible because the author has given coherence to his text by the way he has organized his material.[41]

    It is interesting that John has been accused of authorial incompetence (e.g., due to old age) on account of his "aporias." Barrett, however, suggests that John knew exactly what he was saying,[42] and his tensions and seams are due to his dialectic thought.[43]

2. The "Intentional Fallacy,"—the author's intention is unavailable and thus irrelevant.[44] Hirsch retorted that we do not need to get inside the author's mind (or his *private* intentions) to understand his "verbal meaning."[45] Rather this is

---

36. Ibid., 31.
37. Cf. Cotterell and Turner, *Linguistics*, 58–71; Hirsch, *Validity*, 1–23.
38. See Hirsch, *Validity*, 19–23.
39. See ibid., 20–22.
40. See Cotterell and Turner, *Linguistics*, 58, 60.
41. Ibid., 61.

42. See Barrett, *Judaism*, 75. On the apparent contradiction between John 6:54, 63, Barrett writes, "I cannot believe that these apparently contradictory statements were left to stand side by side in the Gospel because John was too careless, or too stupid, to notice an actual incompatibility. He knew very well what he was doing . . ."

43. Cf. Robinson, *Priority*, 17. He cites Lindars, *Behind the Fourth Gospel*, 17, and Kümmel, *Introduction*, 210, who think Aporias are the product of "over subtle criticism" and an "inappropriate standard of logic." This judgement is most important and we will discuss it further in chapter 4, Theological/Christological Feasibility.

44. See Hirsch, *Validity*, 10–19.
45. See ibid., 14–19.

conveyed by the text.[46] Moreover, since the author gives his work coherence, we can "clear up the meaning of any ambiguous passage . . . by referring to what we *infer* to be the meaning of the work as a whole, as deduced from the relatively clear passages."[47] Furthermore, since texts (like speech) are written ("uttered") in specific contexts, once we establish the context no one can deny what the writing ("utterance") means.[48] On this model, it is essential to know both the context in which the author wrote and that in which the readers received the original text[49] as well as the way the text has been transmitted to us.[50] A plausible historical setting is thus indispensable.[51]

3. The problem of the intrusion of the world of the interpreter into the interpretation (and the hermeneutical circle). Hirsch insists that the authorial meaning of an ancient text (understood as a historical communication) remains unchanged—it is its significance that changes for successive generations.[52] Misunderstandings arise because later readers are limited by their own "horizon," the context in which they live, beyond which they cannot see. Moreover, this differs from the horizon of the author. The interpreter's task is to get back to the context of the original communication—to the author's "horizon"—in order to recover his original meaning.[53]

Cotterell and Turner emphasise the difficulty of this enterprise. Not only do we tend to read texts through the "spectacles" of our "own knowledge and experience" (our world), but also for ancient texts, we are separated from the original situation by a "gulf of time, language, culture, and presuppositions."[54] While accepting the Herculean nature of this task, I would also emphasize that, in the case of Scripture, we have Herculean shoulders to stand upon. Thus the labor of countless scholars, down through the centuries, has provided us with a world of archaeological, historical, textual, geographical, cultural, linguistic, and interpretative information; information that is accessible and readily available, reaching

---

46. See ibid., 16–17, cf. Cotterell and Turner, *Linguistics*, 61

47. Cotterell and Turner, *Linguistics*, 61 (emphasis original). This is in fact the principle of analogy, adopted and applied to the Bible at the Reformation. See *The Westminster Confession of Faith*, 1.9, "The infallible rule of interpretation of Scripture is Scripture itself; and therefore; when there is a question about the true and full sense of any Scripture, (which is not manifold but one) it must be searched and known by other places that speak more clearly."

48. Cf. Cotterell and Turner, *Linguistics*, 63.

49. Ibid., 64.

50. See Silva, *Exegetical Method*, 43.

51. Cf. Hays, *Echoes*, 28.

52. See Hirsch, *Validity*, 215–219.

53. See ibid., 222–23. Cf. Thiselton's comments on interpreting the parable of the Pharisee and the tax collector in *Two Horizons*, 10–17: "If a text is to be understood there must occur an engagement between two sets of horizons . . . those of the ancient text and those of the modern reader."

54. Cotterell and Turner, *Linguistics*, 69.

back to the world of the Bible. Not only so, but we can seek to read Scripture through biblical spectacles (Calvin), understanding and accepting Scripture's presuppositions and immersing our minds in its world. It follows that our interpretation need not be circular, because, as Grant Osborne asserts, we can spiral nearer "the text's intended meaning" as we "refine [our] hypotheses and allow the text to continue to challenge and correct . . . alternative interpretations,"[55] and this is the presupposition adopted here.

Presupposing "recoverable" authorial intent, therefore, and that GJohn's great textual precursor is Scripture, we can infer John's meaning, including his "take" on Scripture, both from the context of the internal coherence and semantic pattern of GJohn and from the clues from a plausible historical paradigm. In this, I take particular note of the Johannine corpus (including Revelation) and the wider NT, particularly Paul's epistles. I also make *cautious* use of intertestamental, DSS, and rabbinic literature where appropriate.[56] In doing so, while acknowledging that rabbinic literature post-dates the Gospel, I allow that *ideas* and *traditions* contained within these sources pre-date it and thus may possibly be reflected in GJohn as part of the wider historical background to the life and times of Jesus.[57] Furthermore, I will take note of particular webs of OT intertextual echoes and the biblical-theological development of important scriptural themes (as God's progressive revelation unfolded) both in the OT and by John. I will also take note of Johannine Paschal and NE typology and will seek, by careful exegesis of the Johannine text, to show how John has synthesized his NE themes to demonstrate their fulfilment in Jesus.

OTHER IMPORTANT CONSIDERATIONS

Having broadly stated my presuppositions and methodology, other important issues remain to be considered:

Do NT allusions to the OT respect the OT context?

A hotly debated issue in "OT in NT" studies is whether the NT authors show respect for the original context of their citations. Several scholars have suggested that they do not: Lindars believes that NT authors cited proof-texts, *ad hoc*, without respect for context.[58]

---

55. Cf. Osborne, *Spiral*, 6–15, 366–415; Cotterell and Turner, *Linguistics*, 72, 100–102.

56. Cf. Moyise, *Old Testament in the New*, 7. "In order to understand how the Old Testament functions in the New, we must immerse ourselves in the writings of the time." Cf. Smalley, *John*, 70–71.

57. See Glasson, *Moses*, 11. He notes that rabbinic names attached to their sayings enable us to be confident that "certain ideas were extant in the time when the New Testament was being written." Borgen, *Bread*, 13–14, shows that the "kernel" of *Exod. Rab.*, and *Mek. Exod.* manna traditions must go back to the time of Philo and the "beginning of the Christian era." Cf. ibid., 20; Neyrey, *John*, 3.

58. Lindars, "Place of the Old Testament," 137–45.

PART I—PRELIMINARY CONSIDERATIONS

Mead believes that citations are often detached from or violate their OT setting[59] and McCasland suggests that Matthew "twists the Scriptures" for his own purposes.[60] Moyise thinks that the strangeness of OT citations by NT authors is due to the fact that they "lived in a very different world to ours," and indeed, "it is fairly certain that it [their use of the OT in the New] did not appear 'arbitrary' or 'ad hoc' to them."[61] But this does not vindicate the NT authors by the standards of contemporary scholarship.[62] However, a credible explanation of the NT authors' use of the OT, one that indicates their respect for the OT context, has come from Dodd. Thus he believes that the independent quotation of different texts from particular passages[63] by several NT authors implies that these portions were particularly significant for the NT.[64] He points out that the original referent of the Isaianic Servant or the "Psalms of the Righteous Sufferer" was as disputed in antiquity as it is today.[65] But such passages, together with Daniel 7, Joel 3–4, Zechariah 9–14, and Isaiah 6:1–9:6, share the "same broad plot":

> The Son of man, who is the Servant of the Lord, who is the Man of God's right hand, who is the people of the saints of the Most High, who is the vine which God brought out of Egypt, who is the end of the whole human race, is first brought very low and then, by grace of God, exalted to glory.[66]

Dodd remarks that it is easy to see how the NT authors understood these passages as variations on the same basic plot, and referred them to Jesus. Importantly, as we have seen, he argues that they did not cite single verses or phrases for their own sake, but used them (*pace* Lindars) as "a pointer to a whole context." The reader is "invited to study the context as a whole, and to reflect upon the 'plot' there unfolded."[67] Thus he is helped to see the significance of the events of Jesus' life and death. Moreover, since all these passages reflect on the changing fortunes of Israel's history in the light of which they look forward to a coming day of the Lord, so "the Christ event" is seen as the fulfilment of Israel's history.[68]

---

59. Mead, "Dissenting Opinion," 153–63.
60. McCasland, "Twists," 146–52.
61. Moyise, *Old Testament in the New*, 5.
62. Not that contemporary scholarship always gets it right!
63. For example, Ps 69 or Isa 53.
64. Dodd, "Old Testament in the New," 171–72.
65. Ibid., 172.
66. Ibid., 174.
67. Ibid., 176. See above on the importance of context for intertextual allusions.
68. Cf. Sundberg's response to Dodd's view, and Marshall's counter response, in Beale, *Right Doctrine*, 182–216.

Are the NT authors faithful to the original OT meaning?

Related to the above is the question of the NT authors' faithfulness to the OT authors' intentions. Many scholars have accounted for the "strangeness" of the NT's interpretation of the OT in terms of contemporary hermeneutical practices.[69] Following Brooke, Marshall notes that the rabbinic *Middoth* were little different from the exegetical rules of Qumran, probably early and widespread, and may have influenced early Christians. However, the *Middoth* rules were very general and "many of the devices used at Qumran . . . do not function in the New Testament."[70]

A more important parallel is that, like Qumran, the NT authors saw themselves as the latter day referent of Scripture and thus as possessing the key to the OT.[71] Hays argues that Paul taught his (Corinthian) readers to adopt an "eschatological hermeneutic." Thus they were to place themselves, "a Gentiles congregation grafted into Israel," within the narrative world of Israel—which typified the Church—and to understanding themselves in terms of its eschatological fulfilment.[72] Furthermore, NT authors deliberately modified the *contemporary understanding* of the OT. Thus Wright speaks of Jesus' parables as "subversive stories," that challenged the world-view of his hearers.[73]

This does not explain, however, those occasions where the NT authors seem to deliberately misquote or misappropriate the OT. How do we explain, for example, Paul's citation of the OT in Rom 11:26–27, "The Deliverer will come from Zion, he will banish ungodliness from Jacob"; "and this will be my covenant with them when I take away their sins"? At first sight, Rom 11:26–27 seems to contain a misquotation of Isa 59:20–21a. In the Hebrew, Isaiah says that the Redeemer with come *to* Zion, but Paul says that the Deliverer will come *from* Zion. Isaiah says that he will come "to those in Jacob who turn from transgression," but Paul says that, "he will banish ungodliness from Jacob." Lenski resists any suggestion that Paul is quoting from a faulty memory and has accidentally got it wrong.[74] How then do we explain his apparent alteration of the OT text? Has Paul made an unjustifiable change to Israel's Scriptures to suit his own purposes?

To understand what is happening, we must begin with what Hays calls "a hermeneutic of trust," as opposed to a hermeneutic of suspicion and mistrust.[75] Thus, I argue that we must start from the premise that Paul cites the OT truthfully and accurately, and gives the correct sense and meaning of the OT authors that he quotes.

69. See Marshall's discussion of Stendahl, *School of St. Matthew*, in "Assessment of Recent Developments," 206ff.

70. Ibid., 209.

71. Ibid., 210.

72. See Hays, *Conversion*, 8–12.

73. Wright, *JVG*, 175.

74. Lenski, *Romans*, 729. Cf. Lloyd-Jones, *Romans 11*, 187, who makes a similar point.

75. See particularly Hays, *Conversion*, 190–97.

PART I—PRELIMINARY CONSIDERATIONS

This follows from the recognition that Paul writes as a prophet and an Apostle of Jesus Christ under the inspiration of the Holy Spirit. In Scripture's own terms this means that the words that Paul writes are "God breathed" (θεόπνευστος)[76] and that in the act of writing he was borne along by the Holy Spirit. Thus, although Paul actively engaged his own mind, faculties, personality, and gifts in writing, God so inspired, guided, and supervised his activity, taking him up and carrying him along as his instrument, that every word that Paul wrote was exactly what God intended that he should say[77]: what Paul said, God said.[78] The net result is that Paul's words (as originally given) possess divine authority and are infallible and inerrant.[79] Moreover, he stands in succession to the OT prophets who unfolded and developed God's progressive revelation according to the mind of God.[80]

From this position of trust, since we deny that Paul got it wrong, we are able to assert that one of two things has happened: either there has been an error in the transmission of the original OT or NT manuscripts, or Paul is conflating two or more texts and giving their general sense. In fact, in this case, most scholars opt for the latter explanation. Thus, as Martyn Lloyd-Jones writes, "What the Apostle has done is to take phrases out of a number of Old Testament statements, namely Isaiah 59:20, 21; Isaiah 27:9; Jeremiah 31:31–34 and Psalm 14:7, and to give their general sense."[81]

From a position of trust in the inspiration and inerrancy of Scripture, both of the OT and of the writings of Paul, Lloyd-Jones gives a brilliant exposition. Thus he notes that OT prophecies were capable of both an initial and an ultimate fulfilment. Moreover, for later fulfilments, the terms of the prophecies were often modified slightly to reflect the changed circumstances.[82] In Rom 11, writing as an inspired Apostle, Paul has prophesied that God will (again) restore national Israel to salvation, but he also wants to show that this was foreseen, in general terms, in the OT. Thus Paul conflates several OT verses, giving their general sense and applying them to this *second* restoration of the Jewish people from "captivity" (in which they have been broken off from their own "olive tree," Rom 11:17–24).[83]

Lloyd-Jones notes that Paul's reference to the Deliverer coming "from Zion," rather than the "to Zion" of Isa 59:20, has been taken from Ps 14:7, "Oh that the salvation of Israel were come out of Zion!"[84] (This psalm refers to the restoration of Israel, and so is very relevant to Paul's theme in Rom 11). He then proceeds to ask what Paul intends

---

76. 2 Timothy 3:16–17. Cf. Young, *Thy Word is Truth*, 21–23.
77. 2 Peter 1:21. Cf. Young, *Thy Word is Truth*, 23–26.
78. Cf. e.g., Heb 3:7 where what the psalmist wrote, Ps 95:7, the Holy Spirit says.
79. See Young, *Thy Word is Truth*, 112–82.
80. Cf. Hays, *Echoes*, 14.
81. Lloyd-Jones, *Romans 11*, 188.
82. Ibid., 188.
83. Ibid., 193–94.
84. KJV.

by using the words, "out of Zion"? This phrase does not signify Christ's first or second advent, as some commentators have thought. Rather, it is to be taken "in a spiritual sense," as in Gal 4, where there are two Jerusalems (Zions), earthly Jerusalem and spiritual Jerusalem—the Church—that has its headquarters in heaven.[85] In context, Paul is speaking of the Jews being restored to salvation (being grafted back into their own "olive tree") by Christ exercising his influence through spiritual Zion—the Church. Paul cites the LXX version of Isa 59:20b, "ἀποστρέψει ἀσεβείας ἀπὸ Ιακωβ"[86] (banish ungodliness from Jacob), in agreement with Isa 27:9, rather than the Hebrew, בְּיַעֲקֹב וּלְשָׁבֵי פֶשַׁע ("to those in Jacob who turn from transgression,"), to emphasise that this is something that God will do, "softening" Jewish hearts so that they will recognise their Messiah. "This is my covenant with them," comes from Isa 59:21a and signifies God's keeping his covenant promises to Israel (the nation as a whole), by the Redeemer (Jesus Christ). "When I shall take away their sins," comes directly from Isa 27:9. (Removal of Israel's sins in the context of the New Covenant is also alluded to in Jer 31:31–34).

If we reflect on this exposition, we see that Paul has accurately conveyed the sense of the OT prophecies. Thus the meaning of Isa 59:20, in context, is that the Redeemer (God/Christ) will come to Israel (Zion, referring to Jacob), to save them, in faithfulness to his covenant with them. This received an initial fulfilment at the first advent of the Lord Jesus Christ. Those who turned away from their sins (for example, the Shepherds, Zechariah and Elizabeth, the disciples, the women, and very many Jews from the day of Pentecost onwards) were indeed delivered from the power and penalty of sin. The nation as a whole, however, rejected their Messiah and (as we will see below in our exposition of John 10) went into a new "captivity." From that time onwards, the locus of "Zion" changed from Israel as a nation to the Church (comprising believing Jews and Gentiles). Nevertheless God's covenant promises to Jacob remained in force and, in Rom 11, Paul predicts a second fulfillment of Isa 59:20.

Since the referent of "Zion" has changed, however, Paul cannot quote the exact words of Isa 59:20, because "to Zion" now signifies "to the Church," rather than "to Israel," which is not what Isa 59:20 signified. Instead, in accordance with other OT prophecies, notably Ps 14:7, he notes that the salvation of Jacob will come from the Lord, "from (spiritual) Zion" ("the generation of the righteous"). Consideration of the other prophecies alluded to by Paul (Jer 31:31–34; Isa 27:9) shows that he has again given the correct sense of their original meaning.

It is argued that by interpreting the OT and NT Scripture from a position of trust, many of the perceived difficulties can thus be resolved. For those difficulties for which we cannot find an immediate answer, we will put our trust in Scripture, that

---

85. Lloyd-Jones, *Romans 11*, 190–91.

86. Cf. Cranfield, *Romans*, 577, who notes that Paul "agrees with the LXX version of Isa 59.20-21a exactly, except that ἐκ is substituted for the ἕνεκεν of the LXX, perhaps under the influence of Ps 14[LXX:13].7."

PART I—PRELIMINARY CONSIDERATIONS

Scripture has got it right and, like Abraham (Gen 15:1–6), believe where we cannot see the immediate solution.

How do we recognise quotations, allusions, and echoes?

Finally, we must have criteria for recognizing quotations, allusions, and echoes. Quotations consist of a series of words taken verbatim from the OT, (usually) identified by an accompanying formula such as, "as the Scripture has said," or "that the Scripture might be fulfilled."[87] Allusions lack an accompanying formula, are usually shorter, and are generally woven into the text. Echoes are the least distinct of all, and are often considered to be unintentional borrowings by biblical authors whose minds were immersed in Scripture.[88] In this work, following Hays, I make no systematic distinction between allusions and echoes.[89] Rather I will judge allusions and echoes as clear, probable, or possible. Moreover, I propose that the following tests, a modified version of some of the seven tests laid down by Hays,[90] listed in what I judge to be their order of importance, can be used to detect intertextual allusions and echoes in GJohn:

1. The main test proposed for the recognition of an echo or allusion to a particular source is the extent to which it makes its presence felt by the repetition of words, numbers, syntactical patterns, and ideas from that source. The greater extent to which this is demonstrable, the more probable an allusion or echo has occurred. It is *not necessarily* the number of words repeated, however, that identifies them, but often the impact that they make.[91] Thus mention of the date 1066, to anyone familiar with English history, immediately suggests the Battle of Hastings. Similarly the repetition of the words "Romeo, Romeo," "To be or not to be," or "My kingdom for a horse," would point to Shakespeare. Anyone familiar with his works would identify them with *Romeo and Juliet* (Act 2, Scene 2), *Hamlet* (Act 3, Scene 1), and *Richard III* (Act 5 Scene 4). These phrases "jump out" of the text, not only because of the profound influence Shakespeare has had upon the English language, but also because, out of all of his vast literary output, they are some of the most widely known and best loved words. This in turn is because of their literary artistry, uniqueness, and the prominent position they occupy

---

87. See the definition given in Menken, *Old Testament Quotations*, 11, "a clause (or series of clauses) from Israel's Scriptures that is (or are) rendered verbatim (or anyhow recognizably) in the NT and that is (or are) marked as such by an introducing or concluding formula . . ." Menken lists seventeen passages in GJohn that fit this definition: John 1:23; 2:17; 6:31, 45; 7:38, 42; 8:17; 10:34; 12:15, 34, 38, 40; 13:18; 15:25; 19:24, 36, 37. Cf. Moyise, *Old Testament in the New*, 5–6.

88. Moyise, *Old Testament in the New*, 6.

89. See Hays, *Echoes*, 29.

90. See Hays, *Echoes*, 29–32; idem, *Conversion*, 34–45.

91. Hays refers to the "volume" of an echo. Cf. Hays, *Echoes*, 30; idem, *Conversion*, 34–37; Moyise, *Old Testament in the New*, 6; Watts, *Mark*, 3.

within their respective plays, occurring at the commencement of a poignant speech or soliloquy, or at the climax of a battle. Similarly, because of its vast influence, many fragments of the King James Bible have become part and parcel of the English language. Phrases such as "a drop in a bucket" (Isa 40:15), "the twinkling of an eye" (1 Cor 15:52), and "the salt of the earth" (Matt 5:13), are immediately recognisable.

The fact that a literary fragment can be identified, however, does not mean that an author has intentionally alluded to its source. Biblical or Shakespearean phrases are often quoted without any knowledge of their origin, symbols are often universal, and numbers and semantic patterns can sometimes be coincidental.

2. Thematic connections (and resonance) between the alluding text and the source text tends to increase the likelihood that deliberate allusion has occurred.[92] Thus, if an author uses the number 1066 in the context of runs scored in county cricket, it is almost certain that he is not alluding to Hastings. Conversely, if this number appears in a text discussing English history, or mentioning Harold, William, and the Normans, it is almost certain that the year of the Norman Conquest is in mind. In our John 1 example, above, reference to God, creation, light, and darkness make it certain that John's "In the beginning" refers to Genesis 1:1. It is just possible, however, that an author may have used the words "In the beginning," in the context of the start of a holiday, or of a period employment, for example, without any intentional allusion to Genesis.[93]

3. Once a potential allusion or echo has been identified by the first two tests, historical feasibility makes an *intentional* allusion or echo probable. By historical feasibility, I mean not only that the author had access to the text from which the proposed allusion came, but also that he was likely to have alluded to it.[94] In the case of Johannine allusions, I have previously argued that not only did John have access to the OT Scriptures, but also the OT was his "privileged predecessor." Moreover, below, I provide a feasible historical model that shows that, not only was John likely to quote and allude to OT Scripture, but also that he has particular reasons to interpret Jesus' ministry in the light of the OT NE. Furthermore, I will show that, ideologically, John's world-view was Jewish rather than Hellenistic or Gnostic, which were alien to his thinking, and thus he would not have alluded to Hellenistic or Gnostic texts.

---

92. See "Thematic Coherence," in Hays, *Echoes*, 30; idem, *Conversion*, 38–41.

93. Cf. Dickens' *David Copperfield*, where the phrase "the beginning" is used of the main character's birth.

94. See Hays, *Echoes*, 29–31, who divides this test into "availability" and "historical plausibility."

2

Historical Feasibility: Can We Find a Historical Background for GJohn in Keeping With a NE Interpretation?

IN THE LIGHT OF the historical-critical and methodological difficulties discussed earlier, it is necessary to demonstrate the feasibility of my thesis by providing a plausible model. It is especially important to establish the historical context, which will affect the way GJohn was meant to be heard by its first readers. Wright's great contribution to the interpretation of the Synoptics is historical. By establishing the historical setting, he has made the NE a credible paradigm for these Gospels. If anything, this is even more important when we come to GJohn where:

> Only by uncovering the historical context of John can we hope to hear John as the first readers were intended to hear it, both the allusions and nuances as well as the explicit teaching.[1]

Here I consider general historical issues prior to a more detailed discussion of a specific *Sitz im Leben*.

AUTHORSHIP

I consider GJohn to be the product of a single great mind, rather than a school,[2] and that this person was the apostle John, as supported by external and internal evidence:

---

1. Dunn, "Let John be John," 310–11. He argues that we cannot understand GJohn by the way it was used by later heretical or orthodox groups, projecting back Gnostic ideas or Nicene orthodoxy. We must "let John be John" and seek to hear him on his own terms. While I agree in principle, I would insist that Nicene orthodoxy legitimately arises out of John's Gospel, whereas heretical interpretations cannot legitimately be defended by exegesis of GJohn. On GJohn's "trinitarian" theology cf. Letham, *The Holy Trinity*, 70–71.

2. Cf. Hengel, *Question*, ix.

External evidence

The main witness is Irenaeus who says that John the disciple of the Lord, who reclined on his breast, published the Gospel in Ephesus, remaining there until the time of Trajan.[3] He also wrote the letters and Apocalypse.[4] Though not specifically referred to as "the apostle," which title Irenaeus reserved for Paul, John is identified as one of the apostles.[5] Polycrates Bishop of Ephesus similarly speaks of John as the Beloved Disciple,[6] who reclined upon Jesus' breast, "witness and teacher,"[7] who sleeps in Ephesus.[8] Bernard believes that "witness" relates to the BD's testimony as the "final authority" behind GJohn[9] regarded as "Gospel [and] . . . rule of faith." Further support comes from the enigmatic evidence of the Muratorian Canon and the Anti-Marcionite Prologue.[10] Subsequent writers, including Tertullian, Clement of Alexandria, and Origen, agree with Irenaeus.[11] Even Gaius and the Alogoi, (witless ones), repudiating GJohn and Revelation as "unworthy" of the church, being forgeries by Cerinthus, testify to their early date and recognition by the Church.[12]

The modern take on this is that Irenaeus was "mistaken" and others followed him.[13] Irenaeus cannot easily be dismissed, however, because his testimony is based on established tradition, obtained orally during his youth from the elders in Asia Minor, especially Polycarp.[14] Writing to the Gnostic Florinus, he relates vivid memories of Polycarp, including the way he reported "his converse with John and with others

---

3. Irenaeus *Haer.* 3:1:1 (ca. A.D. 180) = Eusebius *Hist. eccl.* 5:8:4, cf. *Haer.* 2:22:5 = *Hist. eccl.* 3:23:3-4; *Haer.* 3:3:4 = *Hist. eccl.* 4:14:3-8; *Hist. eccl.* 5:20:4-8. See Guthrie, *Introduction*, 269. Trajan's reign began in A.D. 98.

4. For composition of the Gospel see Irenaeus *Haer.* 3:8:3; 3:11:1-9; 3:16:5; 3:22:2; 4:2:3; 4:6:1; 4:10:1; 5:18:2. On the letters of John see *Haer.* 3:16:5; 3:16:8. On the Apocalypse see *Haer.* 4:30:4; 5:26:1; 1:26:3; 4:17:6; 4:20:11; 4:21:3; 5:28:2; 5:34:2; 5:35:2. See Keener, *John*, 139.

5. Cf. Irenaeus *Haer.* 2:22:5; Eusebius *Hist. eccl.* 3:1:1; 3:23:1. See Hengel, *Question*, 4.

6. Hence BD.

7. Eusebius *Hist. eccl.* 3:31:2-3; 5:24:2-7, cf. John 13:25; Irenaeus *Haer.* 3:1:1. See Bernard, *John*, l.

8. He also speaks of John in terms of a High Priest, but I take this to be metaphorical. It is not impossible that John came from a priestly line, but I cannot accept that he was ever High Priest or that Polycrates came to this conclusion by exegesis of Acts 4:6. Cf. Hengel, *Question*, 3, n. 10; John 18:15; Bauckham, *Eyewitnesses*, 445-52; idem, *Testimony*, 41-50; Dodd, *HTFG*, 86-87; Morris, *John*, 752, n. 30; Borchert, *John 12-21*, 230, n. 40; Culpepper, *Son of Zebedee*, 6.

9. Bernard, *John*, li. Cf. John 21:24; 19:35; 3 John 12; Rev 1:2, 9. Bernard also thinks that "teacher" might refer specifically to the apostle John, as it does in the second century *Acts of John*. Cf. Bauckham, "Papias and Polycrates," 40.

10. Cf. Bruce, *Canon*, 158-69; 154-57; Smalley, *John*, 77.

11. In Eusebius *Hist. eccl.* 6:14:7, Clement says that "last of all, John [after the Synoptic Gospels] . . . composed a spiritual Gospel." Cf. Bernard, *John*, xlvi; Guthrie, *Introduction*, 271. Carson, *John*, 27-28.

12. Cf. Hengel, *Question*, 6; Carson, et al., *Introduction*, 141.

13. See Guthrie, *Introduction*, 270-71.

14. Cf. Eusebius *Hist. eccl.* 5:20:4-8; 3:23:1-4; 4:14; Irenaeus *Haer.* 3:3:4; 2:22:5.

PART I—PRELIMINARY CONSIDERATIONS

who had seen the Lord."[15] Thus there is a direct link from John through Polycarp to Irenaeus.[16] Moreover, as Hengel has shown, we can trace the use of GJohn as authoritative Scripture back to the first quarter of the second century, close to the time of its publication:[17]

1. It is unlikely that Tatian, Justin's pupil, would have used GJohn as the basis of his *Diatessaron*, ca. A.D. 170, if it were not already widely recognized *as having apostolic authority* [18] by the Church.[19]

2. In the Quartodeciman Controversy, Apollinaris of Hierapolis alludes to GJohn and Melito of Sardis uses GJohn in his *Peri Pascha*, A.D. 160–70.[20]

3. The *Epistula Apostolorum*, ca. A.D. 150, is heavily indebted to the Johannine corpus and attributes GJohn to the apostle John, one of the Twelve. [21]

4. GJohn influenced the secondary ending of Mark, (possibly dating from A.D. 110 to 130) and, "at a very early stage," the Western text of Matthew and Luke.[22]

5. Justin has many allusions to GJohn.[23] Though these are disputed,[24] some seem irrefutable, as the citation "Unless you are born again you will not enter into the kingdom of heaven."[25] Though he does not mention John as author of GJohn, his Christology shows dependence upon the Johannine Prologue.[26] He also speaks of a "certain . . . John, one of the apostles of Christ, who prophesied, by a Revelation that was made to him, that [believers] would dwell a thousand years in Jerusalem."[27]

---

15. Eusebius *Hist. eccl.* 5:20:5–6.

16. Cf. Lightfoot, *Ignatius*, 1:440-41; Barrett, *John*, 101; Bruce, *John*, 11; Carson, *John*, 26; Hengel, *Question*, 144, n. 30; Smalley, *John*, 75-76; Bauckham, *Eyewitnesses*, 456-57.

17. Following Hengel, *Question*, 7–23. Cf. Hill, *Johannine Corpus*, 40–42.

18. Matthew was identified as an apostle, and Mark and Luke derived their authority from apostolic association through Peter and Paul. Cf. Eusebius *Hist. eccl.* 3:39:15; Irenaeus *Haer.* 3:1:1; Muratorian Fragment. See Bruce, *Canon*, 161.

19. Cf. Hengel, *Question*, 4, 140, n. 14; Hill, *Johannine Corpus*, 40.

20. Cf. Hengel, *Question*, 4; Hill, *Johannine Corpus*, 40, 54, 295. As Hill points out, Melito clearly alludes to such "distinctive Johannine stories" as those of the man-born-blind, John 9, and Lazarus, John 11.

21. Hill, *Johannine Corpus*, 366–74; idem, "Epistula Apostolorum," 1–53; Bauckham, *Eyewitnesses*, 464–65.

22. Hengel, *Question*, 11. Cf. Mark 16:9–20; John 20. Cf. Hill, *Johannine Corpus*, 402–6.

23. Cf. Hengel, *Question*, 12-13; Hill, *Johannine Corpus*, 312–51.

24. See Haenchen, *John 1*, 13. Cf. Koester, *Introduction*, 2:184, 344 who thinks Justin "did not know the Gospel of John," but cited tradition older than GJohn, which John himself appropriated and modified. This speculative suggestion lacks supporting evidence and is not very credible.

25. Justin *1 Apol.* 61:4. Cf. John 3:3–4. See also Justin *Dial.* 88:7. Cf. Hengel, *Question*, 12–13. Hill, *Johannine Corpus*, 327–28.

26. Cf. Bernard, *John*, 1, lxxv; Hengel, *Question*, 13; Hill, *Johannine Corpus*, 316–25.

27. Justin *Dial.* 81. Cf. Rev 20:4–5.

6. Ignatius, martyred ca. A.D. 117, does not mention John, but has several clear allusions to GJohn and to Revelation, which indicate their authority.[28] Of particular interest is reference to "living water in me," desire for "the bread of God which is the flesh of Christ" rather than "corruptible food," and "for drink . . . his blood."[29] Other allusions include the Spirit knowing "whence it comes and whither it goes,"[30] the Lord doing nothing without the Father,[31] Jesus revealing himself more clearly by returning to the Father,[32] being hated by the world,[33] and "the door."[34]

7. In his surviving letter, Polycarp clearly alludes to 1 John, "whosoever does not confess that Jesus Christ is come in the flesh is antichrist . . . is of the devil," and possibly to GJohn.[35] Sparse allusion to GJohn and none to John are probably due to the letter's nature and destination.[36]

8. That Papias knew GJohn is clear from the Johannine order in which he lists the apostles.[37] That he was a hearer of John can be inferred from his famous statement,[38] which I take to refer to what the apostles said and what the apostle John as a living witness was still saying in Papias's youth.[39] It is also plausibly con-

---

28. See Hill, *Johannine Corpus*, 421–43.

29. Ign. *Rom.* 7:2–3. Cf. John 4:10; 7:38; Rev 21:6; 22:1, 17; John 6:27, 33, 53; Richardson, *Christian Fathers*, 105. Lightfoot, *Ignatius*, 2:224, 226, says that the whole of Ign. *Rom.* 7 is inspired by GJohn and "the indirect reference to the eucharistic elements is analogous to that which our Lord makes in John 6." Cf. Hill, *Johannine Corpus*, 432–33.

30. Ign. *Philad.* 7:1. Cf. John 3:8; Richardson, *Christian Fathers*, 109; Lightfoot, *Ignatius*, 2:266; Hill, *Johannine Corpus*, 437–38.

31. Ign. *Magn.* 7:1. Cf. John 5:19, 30; 8:28; Lightfoot, *Ignatius*, 2:121; Richardson, *Christian Fathers*, 96; Hill, *Johannine Corpus*, 434–35.

32. Ign. *Rom.* 3:3. Cf. John 7:33; 16:5; 13:3; 14:12, 28; 16:10, 16, 28; 8:28.

33. Ign. *Rom.* 3:3. Cf. John 7:7; 15:18-19; 17:14; 1 John 3:13; Lightfoot, *Ignatius*, 2:205.

34. Ign. *Philad.* 9:1-3. Cf. John 10:7, 9; Rev 3:8; Lightfoot, *Ignatius*, 2:275; Richardson, *Christian Fathers*, 110; Hill, *Johannine Corpus*, 438–39.

35. Pol. *Phil.* 7:1. Cf. 1 John 4:2-3; 2:22; 3:8; 2 John 7; John 8:44. Cf. also Pol. *Phil.* 10.1 and John 13:34; Pol. *Phil.* 7:2 and 1 John 2:7, 24; 3:11; 2 John 5, John 8:25, 16:4. Cf. Hill, *Johannine Corpus*, 418–19; Bernard, *John*, lxxii.

36. See Hill, *Johannine Corpus*, 417.

37. Cf. Eusebius *Hist. eccl.* 3:39:3-4; John 1:35-51; 21:2; Bauckham, "Papias and Polycrates," 51.

38. *Apud* Eusebius *Hist. eccl.* 3:39:4 "If anyone came who had kept company with the Elders, I would enquire about the words of the Elders: what Andrew or Peter said, or Philip, or Thomas, or James, or John, or Matthew, or any other of the Lord's disciples, and whatever Aristion and the Elder John, the Lord's disciples say."

39. Cf. Bruce, "Notes," 101; Smalley, *Thunder and Love*, 38; idem, *John*, 80–81. The theory that Papias refers to two Johns, apostle and Elder, tentatively muted by Eusebius, *Hist. eccl.* 3:39:5-7, is a red herring arising from Papius's ambiguous style, supported by two Ephesian memorials to John, and Dionitius's evaluation of Revelation as non-apostolic; apud Eusebius *Hist. eccl.* 7:25:7-27. On the two competing memorials to John see Schaff and Wace, *Fathers*, 1:171, n. 13. Interestingly, Eusebeus *Hist. eccl.* 3:18:1-5 upholds the tradition of the apostle John's banishment to Patmos under Domitian and his authorship of GJohn.

jectured that Papias is the written source for an exegetical harmonisation of Matt 13:3–8 with John 14:2, attributed to the "elders" and "disciples of the apostles."[40] Hill similarly argues that tradition concerning Matthew and GJohn, recorded in Eusebius, paraphrases a written account by Papias.[41]

9. The title "according to John" circulated with second century papyrus P66 and a little later with P72. It is likely that this title was affixed when the collection of the Gospels began to circulate together,[42] as early as A.D. 125. It may well be that the Gospels never circulated anonymously and thus the Gospel was always known by its title "according to John."[43]

This evidence points to the early acceptance of the Johannine corpus by the Church, towards the first quarter of the second century and its association with Asia Minor and with the apostle John bar Zebedee.[44] It suggests that he lived to a great age, continuing until Trajan, and that he was prevailed upon to write his "memoirs" of Jesus' ministry, in part to supply the Synoptic omissions.

Direct internal evidence

At face value, John 21:24, "This is the disciple who is bearing witness about these things, and who has written these things," directly identifies its author as the BD.[45] Modern scholarship has cast doubt on this:

1. "Has written" is interpreted as "caused to write."[46] This has been further weakened by the suggestion that the BD stood behind the testimony of the Gospel, but another "wrote" it.

2. The referent of "these things" has been interpreted to be either a source or chapter 21.

---

40. Cited by Irenaeus *Haer.* 5:36:1–3. Cf. Hengel, *Question*, 4–5; Hill, *Johannine Corpus*, 40; Bauckham, "Papias and Polycrates," 51.

41. Eusebius *Hist. eccl.* 3:24:5–13 alluding to John 3:24. Cf. 3:39:16; Hill, *Johannine Corpus*, 386ff., citing Lawlor, *Eusebiana*, 22. Could this be proved, it would be of great significance since it names the apostle John as the author of GJohn who having proclaimed the Gospel orally was finally prevailed upon to give an account of Jesus' ministry prior to JBap, to supply the omission by the Synoptics. But cf. Bauckham, *Eyewitnesses*, 433–37.

42. See Keener, *John*, 92.

43. Hengel, *Question*, 6–7, 74. Cf. idem, *Mark*, n. 6, 64–84, 162–83; Carson, *Introduction*, 138, 66; France, *Evangelist and Teacher*, 50–52.

44. See Hengel, *Question*, 134, "thirty or forty years after his death, church tradition identified him [John] with the son of Zebedee." In spite of this evidence, however, Hengel thinks that "the final redactor(s) [of GJohn]" deliberately superimposed "John the son of Zebedee" upon "John the Presbyter." Ibid., 129–30.

45. See Westcott, *John*, 1:lvii. "There can be no doubt as to the meaning of these words [of John 21:24]. The writing of the Gospel is distinctly assigned by them to 'the beloved disciple' (v. 21)."

46. See Bernard, *John*, 713, who cites the example of Pilate's "writing" the inscription on Jesus' cross.

3. Verses 24–25 are later editorial editions, which are mistaken or pseudepigraphical.

All these objections have been answered by Bauckham:

1. Though "Wrote" may include the use of an amanuensis, it always implies authorship.[47]
2. Since vv. 24–25 must be taken together, the referent of "wrote" has to be the entire Gospel.[48]
3. Chapter 21, including vv. 24–25, is not an editorial addition, but the work of the author, and integral to GJohn.[49]

Bauckham demonstrates the integrity of chapter 21 from its intricate design and function as an epilogue framed by parallel endings.[50] The Epilogue answers to the Prologue with mathematical symmetry;[51] the Epilogue foreseeing the Gospel's post-history in terms of the Church's mission, the Prologue sketching the Gospel's prehistory.[52] This means that John 21:24 was written by the author; "and we know . . ." cannot refer to corroborating witnesses or editors, exclusive of the BD, but must include him. Moreover, comparison with other Johannine usage indicates that it is not an associative or dissociative "we," but the "'we' of authoritative testimony," referring to John himself.[53] Thus not only does the BD claim to be a principle eyewitness of Jesus' ministry, death, and resurrection, but also that he is the author of GJohn.

Indirect internal evidence

Further clues to the identity of the author may be gleaned indirectly from the Gospel. The classic example of this approach is that of Westcott who presents evidence that the author is a Jew, of Palestine, an eyewitness, an apostle, the apostle John.[54] Although this argument has been challenged at every point it still has its defenders.[55]

---

47. Bauckham, *Eyewitnesses*, 360–61.
48. Ibid., 362.
49. Ibid., 364–68.
50. John 20:30–31 and 21:24–25.
51. See Bauckham, *Eyewitnesses*, 364, citing Menken, *Techniques*, 21. The Epilogue contains 496 words compared with the Prologue's 496 syllables; 496 is a triangular number with the same numerical value as *monogenēs*.
52. Ibid., 364.
53. Ibid., 371–83. Cf. 3 John 9–12; 1 John 1:1–5; 4:14; John 3:10–13; 1:14–16; John 12:38; Isa 53:1.
54. Westcott, *John*, 1:x–xlii.
55. Cf. Morris, *John*, 12–14; Keener, *John*, 89; Burge, *Interpreting*, 45; Köstenberger, *John*, 6–7.

PART I—PRELIMINARY CONSIDERATIONS

A Palestinian Jew.

The author's Jewishness[56] is reflected in his intimate detailed knowledge of Jewish history,[57] festivals,[58] theology,[59] and messianic expectations.[60] His literary style is Jewish[61] and his writings are rooted in OT Scripture.[62] His domicile in Palestine prior to A.D. 70 is evident from his precise political, cultural, religious, geographical and topographical knowledge.[63]

An Eyewitness

GJohn indicates the BD to be uniquely qualified as a perceptive witness to Jesus,[64] being intimate with Jesus,[65] present at key events,[66] evincing detailed knowledge,[67] and possessing spiritual insight.[68] Moreover, GJohn is full of incidental narrative detail that provides verisimilitude.[69] Although this feature was possible in a good storyteller,[70] it gives the impression of an eyewitness testimony and is characteristic of

---

56. The Jewishness of such concepts as the author's "dualism," the Logos, and the sending of Jesus will be examined below.

57. Cf. e.g., John 1:17; 2:20; 4:5, 12; 8:33, 40. See Westcott, *John*, 1:xxff.

58. Cf. John 6:25ff.; 7:2ff., 37; 8:12; 10:22ff.; 13:26; 18:28; 19:14, 41; 20:1. See Burge, *Interpreting*, 20. John understands "the theological symbolism behind the Jewish feasts (Passover, 6:25–59; Tabernacles, ch. 7; Dedication or *Hanukkah*, 10:22–39)." Westcott, *John*, 1:xxiv–xxv, notes John's familiarity with the Feast's various Temple settings.

59. John 4:24; 12:31, 48; 16:8–11; 19:11. See Bauckham, "Monotheism and Christology," 239–52.

60. Cf. John 1:20–21, 41, 49; 4:25; 6:14; 7:27, 31, 40, 41, 42, 52; 12:15–16, 34. See Bauckham, "Jewish Messianism," 207–38.

61. Westcott, *John*, 1:xii, mentions vocabulary, sentence structure, symmetry, numerical symbolism, and expression and arrangement of the author's thoughts as being "essentially Hebrew." Cf. Burge, *Interpreting*, 21.

62. OT citations are found in John 1:23; 2:17; 6:31, 45; 10:34; 12:14-15, 38, 40; 13:18; 15:25; 19:24, 28, 36, 37. To these we must add innumerable OT allusions. Westcott, *John*, 1:xiiff.; xxviff., argues that the OT is the source of the author's imagery, typology, and of his religious life. He affirms its "absolute authority" and notes that its details are fulfilled by Jesus. He notes that John was acquainted with the original Hebrew.

63. See Westcott, *John*, 1:xxi–xxv; I. Broer, "Knowledge of Palestine," 83–90; Smalley, *John*, 37–41.

64. So Bauckham, *Eyewitnesses*, 398–400. Cf. Dodd, *HTFG*, 244–45.

65. Bauckham, *Eyewitnesses*, 398–400. Cf. John 1:35–40; 13:23–26; 19:26–27.

66. Ibid., 398–400. Cf. John 1:35; 18:15–16; 19:31–37; 20:3–10.

67. Ibid., 398. He cites John 1:39; 13:26; 18:18; 19:33–35; 20:6–8.

68. Ibid., 399, citing 13:25–30; 20:8–9; 21:7.

69. Westcott, *John*, 1:xxxixff., provides evidence of the narrative being "marked by minute details of persons, and time, and number, and place and manner, which cannot but have come from a direct experience." For example, in ibid., xxii–xxiii, he references, in John 4, the heights of Gerizim, the cornfields, and the depth of the well as bearing the stamp of authenticity and the "vividness of an actual spectator."

70. So Lincoln, "Beloved Disciple as Eyewitness," 5.

good historiography.[71] Moreover, while corroborating Synoptic tradition, the Gospel possesses sufficient authority, such as possessed by eyewitness testimony, to relate its own special tradition.

The apostle John

Circumstantial evidence points to the identification of the BD with the apostle John.[72] His presence at the call of the first disciples,[73] at the Last Supper, empty tomb, and at Jesus' post resurrection appearance, coupled with his intimacy with Jesus, including knowledge of his inmost thoughts, are consistent with apostleship and indeed with his being one of the inner three.[74] His presence in John 21 means that he must have been either an unnamed disciple or one of the sons of Zebedee. That one of the initially unnamed disciples of John 1:35 turned out to be Andrew, who invited his own brother to Jesus, suggests that the other disciple did the same, and that he may well have been John, who also brought James to Jesus. The indications that he lived to a good old age[75] are consistent with the tradition. Above all, the BD is strongly associated with Peter, corresponding to the association of Peter and John in Synoptic Gospels and in Acts.[76]

Though I believe this evidence is strong, many think the identification impossible because of the perceived differences between GJohn and the Synoptics. Thus both Dodd and Barrett acknowledge the theoretical possibility that the apostle John authored GJohn, but reject it on the grounds of the Gospel's ideology and sophistication.[77] Others believe the GJohn rivalry between Peter and John to be evidence that John seeks to replace the Synoptics. GJohn does not contradict Synoptics tradition, however, but complements it.[78] Moreover, the GJohn rivalry is not polemical, as between rival traditions, but "friendly," portraying John as the ideal author in contrast to Peter's role as leader of the apostles.[79]

---

71. Bauckham, *Eyewitnesses*, 399. Cf. idem, "Historiographical Characteristics," 93–112.

72. See Hengel, *Question*, 128–30, who thinks GJohn takes the reader in this direction, but "wants the riddle to remain unsolved." Cf. Smalley, *John*, 82–84.

73. John 1:35ff. See Bauckham, *Eyewitnesses*, 127–29.

74. See Westcott, *John*, 1:xliv–xlvi.

75. John 21:22–23. This probably has a double meaning. Unlike Peter, John would himself remain (tarry) long after the other apostles; his Gospel witness would indeed remain until Jesus returns.

76. Cf. John 13:23–24; 18:15–16; 20:3–8; 21:7; 20–24; Mark 9:2; Acts 3:1. See Smalley, *John*, 83.

77. For Barrett, *John*, 132, n. 2, it is "a moral certainty" that John was not the author. Cf. Dodd, *HTFG*, 10ff. His main objection to apostolic authorship arises from the difficulty he finds in a Galilean fisherman becoming an accomplished theologian (cf. p. 16). I believe that to some extent both scholars misidentify Johannine concepts, as Hellenistic or Gnostic, and underestimate the level of achievement to which John was able to attain. History proves otherwise: Who would have thought of an English butcher's son becoming the Lord Chancellor, or a farmer becoming the Protector of England?

78. As evidenced by the narrative of John 6.

79. So Bauckham, *Eyewitnesses*, 128.

PART I—PRELIMINARY CONSIDERATIONS

Hengel and Bauckham argue that John cannot be an apostle because the Synoptics represent apostolic tradition, from which John's Gospel "radically differs."[80] In this, however, they overemphasize the (undeniable) differences between GJohn and the Synoptics. I believe that John must have been an apostle to have had his "different" Gospel so readily accepted by the Church.[81] While I accept that the Synoptics represent the primitive (Petrine) kerygma, as seen in Acts 10:36–43, I argue that GJohn is different, not because of a non-apostolic author, in possession of non-apostolic sources,[82] but because of the radically different "post apostolic" era in which he writes.[83] As the surviving apostle, he has returned to the totality of apostolic Jesus tradition, of which he is primary custodian, to retell the story, using previously unpublished material, so appropriate to the new situation in which the Church found itself.[84] The Synoptic Gospels selected their material to suit their primitive kerygmatic purpose.[85] Clearly this did not require the lengthy discourse material, Jesus' encounter with a Samaritan woman or his visits to Jerusalem at the feasts, which unnecessarily complicate the basic message. John has also been selective,[86] supplementing the Synoptic picture with much they had previously omitted, which has now found new relevance for the Church. He has nevertheless deliberately co-ordinated his material to the Synoptic account.[87] In so doing his different perspective has opened up a new dimension onto the ministry of Jesus.

RELATED ISSUES: TOWARDS A GENERAL SITZ IM LEBEN

Genre

What kind of book did John write? This has an important bearing upon historicity. Many scholars suggest that GJohn tells us more about John's community than it

---

80. Cf. Hengel, *Question*, 130; Bauckham, *Testimony*, 27-28, idem, *Eyewitnesses*, 179–80.
81. See Hill, *Johannine Corpus*, 468–69.
82. See Bauckham, *Testimony*, 28.
83. This anticipates my discussion of *Sitz im Leben* below.
84. See below.
85. See Green, *Luke*, 38.
86. John 20:30–31. Cf. Carson, *John*, 661; Bruce, *John*, 395.
87. See Bauckham, "John for Readers of Mark," 158–59. GJohn "rarely repeats and largely complements Mark's narrative in such a way that chronological dovetailing of the two narratives can easily be accomplished." He suggests that John has made reference to Mark, at crucial points in his narrative, to enable readers familiar with Mark to make sequential correlation. Cf. ibid., 154; Bruce, *John*, 93–94, 99, on John 3:24. The ancient church used John 3:24 as a "chronological datum for comparative study of John and the Synoptic Gospels." Cf. Eusebius *Hist. eccl.* 3:24:11–13. "John . . . relates what Christ did before the Baptist had been thrown into prison [John 3:24], but the three other evangelists narrate the events after the imprisonment of the Baptist. If this is understood, the Gospels no longer appear to disagree."

does about Jesus.[88] Guilding suggests that GJohn has a liturgical background, being a Christian commentary on OT lectionary readings.[89] Although it is plausible that some Jewish *haftarot* inform some of Jesus' Johannine discourses, especially the Passover of John 6,[90] Guilding's lectionary purpose for GJohn is not convincing.[91] A more fruitful approach is that of Burridge. By comparison with Graeco-Roman *Bioi*, he has demonstrated the similarities between the Gospels and the literary family of ancient lives.[92] GJohn is no exception: dominated by Jesus,[93] it shares such biographical features as a generic title, settings determined by Jesus' whereabouts, interest in his great deeds, respect for his person, and emphasis upon his last days.[94] Furthermore, Bauckham has shown that GJohn "conforms to good historiographical practice" in terms of topographical knowledge, chronological precision, eyewitness testimony, narrative asides, selectivity, and reporting of discourses and dialogues.[95]

This is not the whole story, however, because "the Gospels contain not just facts about Jesus, but facts about him which have been interpreted."[96] They are the good news of a life-imparting message of salvation, through Jesus, that must be proclaimed and believed.[97] This salvation has been accomplished not only by Jesus' life, but also particularly through his death and resurrection, by which he has led a NE from sin and death to righteousness and life in fulfilment of the OT prophecies.[98] These features suggest that (*pace* Burridge) they belong to "a literary type of their own."[99]

Among this unique literature GJohn has its own special place: "Not only historiography but also theology . . . [GJohn] incorporates history into metahistory."[100] GJohn supplements rather than replaces the Synoptic Gospels.[101] Like them he articulates Christian tradition in such a manner as to address it with new relevance to a given community, but for John's community, including the wider Church, radically altered circumstances have led to a new interpretative perspective on Jesus' life and works.[102]

---

88. See Martyn, *History and Theology*, passim.

89. Guilding, *Jewish Worship*.

90. See Brown, *John I–XII*, 278–80.

91. See Smalley, *John*, 173–74.

92. Burridge, *Gospels*, passim.

93. See ibid., 216, where analysis of verb subjects reveals that "over half the verbs are taken up with Jesus' words or deeds, performed by him or spoken by him (55.3 %)."

94. See ibid., 213–32. Cf. the helpful summary in Stibbe, *John's Gospel*, 57–59.

95. Bauckham, "Historiographical," 93–112.

96. Smalley, *John*, 205.

97. Mark 16:15–16; Matt 28:19–20; Luke 24:46–47; John 20:31. Cf. France, *Matthew*, 1114–15; Carson, *John*, 659–61.

98. Cf. Wright, *JVG*, passim, Watts, *Mark*, passim. On the NE in GJohn see exposition below.

99. Smalley, *John*, 205.

100. Bauckham, "Historiographical," 102.

101. See Guthrie, *Introduction*, 314.

102. Cf. Kysar, *Fourth Evangelist*, passim; Bauckham, "For Whom," 22ff. See below.

PART I—PRELIMINARY CONSIDERATIONS

A School or Community?

Did John found a school? Was he the head of a community? This is another important question. As Hengel points out, unlike the Platonic Academy or the Oxford Movement, we do not have independent references to a Johannine school, but "only to *one* John."[103] What we do have, however, is primary source evidence of a Johannine community in terms of the Johannine letters and Apocalypse:

The Johannine Letters

Many scholars would accept that the letters share a common author. Not only are they connected linguistically,[104] but also it is inconceivable that the last two would have circulated apart from the first. There is also clear evidence[105] that 1 John is connected to GJohn by:

1. Christology: Jesus is both the μονογενής Son of God sent into the world[106] and flesh and blood.[107] His word abides in believers.[108]

2. Monotheistic Theology.[109]

3. Soteriology: faith in Jesus, his atoning for the sins of the world, forgiveness and cleansing by his blood, being born of God, abiding, and walking in the light.[110]

4. Ethical "dualism": darkness and light, truth and lies.[111]

5. Advocacy and testimony.[112]

Such features convinced Brown that 1 John was an interpretation of GJohn, written by "the Elder" who sought to defend its Orthodoxy. Given the similarities of style, however, it is more likely that they share the same author,[113] John, who having

---

103. Hengel, *Question*, 24 (emphasis original). Cf. Bauckham, *Testimony*, 13–14.

104. Cf. Westcott, *Epistles of John*, lv; Kruse, *Letters of John*, 7–8. Both scholars note close linguistic resemblances between the first and second and second and third letters.

105. See Smalley, *Thunder and Love*, 19. It is "possible to establish a literary and theological linkage between the Gospel and Letters of John, to claim that those four documents emanate from the same circle if not necessarily from the same hand, and to argue that this community owed its inspiration in some way to the beloved disciple." He cites Houlden, *Johannine Epistles*, 37–38. Cf. Smalley, *1, 2, 3 John*, xx.

106. For example, 1 John 4:9 recalls John 3:16. See Smalley, *1, 2, 3 John*, 229.

107. Cf. ibid., 264–66; 1 John 5:6.

108. Cf. ibid., 75; 1 John 2:14; John 15:7.

109. Cf. 1 John 4:6–12; John 3:16. See Hengel, *Question*, 42.

110. Cf. Smalley, *1, 2, 3 John*, 24, 60–61, 122, 127–28.

111. Ibid., xxv.

112. 1 John 2:1; 5:7–9. Cf. Smalley, *1, 2, 3 John*, 34.

113. Cf. Bruce, *Epistles of John*, 30–31; Hengel, *Question*, 49, 177, n. 7; Howard, "Common Authorship," 12–25, reprinted in idem, *Fourth Gospel*, 282–95; Smalley, *Thunder and Love*, 57; idem, *1, 2, 3*

survived the apostolic era is referred to as *the* Elder as a mark of his age and authority. Given this identification, we can deduce that John had authoritative oversight over several churches, traditionally located in Asia Minor,[114] to which he ministered in person,[115] by letter, and by supporting itinerant missionaries.[116] They comprised many believers who were strong and discerning and some ("Fathers") capable of leadership.[117] They nevertheless needed reassurance of their Christian standing, having been troubled by defections, docetic heresy, and factious leaders.[118] Traditionally the heresy is connected with the teaching of Cerinthus, John's opponent at Ephesus:[119] that Christ came upon the man Jesus at his baptism and left him prior to his passion;[120] teaching strongly refuted in John's Gospel and letters. Importantly, 1 John is a catholic epistle showing no evidence of a dispute with the "mainstream Church" or polemic against other Christian communities.[121] Rather, the difficulties are internal to the churches.[122]

Revelation

Despite the "wide [generic, linguistic, ideological, and eschatological] gulf" often perceived to exist between the Apocalypse and the rest of the Johannine corpus, Stephen Smalley has established "striking resemblances"[123] to GJohn in terms of:

1. Jewish/Christian ethos.

2. Theology: Both share above below cosmologies, two worlds interacting, with intermediaries ascending and descending between them.

3. Christology: Jesus is God and man, the Word (and voice) of God, the lamb, and the Son of Man—who suffers, is vindicated, and who judges.[124]

John, xx.

114. See on external evidence above.

115. 3 John 10, 14; 2 John 12, where the "elect lady" is probably a local church.

116. 3 John 5–8. Cf. Smalley, *1, 2, 3 John*, 334–35.

117. 1 John 2:12–14. Cf. ibid., 67.

118. See, e.g., 1 John 2:19; 3 John 9. See ibid., 96.

119. Cf. Irenaeus *Haer.* 3:3:4; Eusebius *Hist. eccl.* 3:28:6; 4:14:6. See Hengel, *Question*, 54, 59, who thinks that this is plausible.

120. See Irenaeus *Haer.* 1:26:1.

121. Cf. Edwards, *John*, 102, "The idea of the Johannine 'community' at loggerheads with other Christians is a scholarly construct arising from a surfeit of sociological speculation"; Bauckham, *Testimony*, 13, n. 7.

122. Cf. e.g., 1 John 2:18–19, 22; 2 John 7–10; 3 John 10, 11.

123. Smalley, *Thunder and Love*, 58. Cf. Beasley-Murray, *Revelation*, 34. He speaks of "striking contacts" between Revelation and GJohn.

124. Smalley, *Thunder and Love*, 62. In Rev 1:13; 14:14, John "exactly recapitulates . . . the Son of man christology patterned in the Fourth Gospel," going back to the Danielic form, Dan 7:13.

PART I—PRELIMINARY CONSIDERATIONS

4. Eschatology: Realized/future tension,[125] God's wrath due to sin, connected to the cross, worked out in history, and disclosed at the Parousia.[126]

5. Testimony tradition: Clustering around themes, "such as the new Israel, and the suffering servant,"[127] evincing primitive interpretation.[128]

6. Language.[129]

7. Structural use of seven.[130]

To these we must add such common symbolism as water of eternal life, Jerusalem, and Jesus as the Temple.[131] In Revelation, a counterfeit church opposes God's people: "Jews" who rely on the power of Rome, similar to the situation in GJohn. Revelation's "trinitarian" theology (and its satanic counterfeit) compares with that of GJohn's. Most importantly, Revelation's Paschal NE redemption, involving new creation and Judgement upon the world,[132] is also key to GJohn.[133]

These resemblances suggest the same great theological mind stands behind GJohn and Revelation, and many scholars would argue that both come from the same school,[134] and some the same author.[135] As early as Dionysius, however, common authorship has been denied on the basis of the Revelation's "inaccurate and barbarous" Greek compared to GJohn's "flawless" Greek.[136] If the Seer's grammatical ignorance could be sustained this verdict might prove insurmountable.

There are, however, reasons to question it. Smalley notes that the Greek of GJohn and of Revelation have much in common: Both utilize "direct" Greek, "share some stylistic features, and turns of phrase,"[137] and neither is flawless or ungrammatical.[138] Ozanne cites words and phrases common to Revelation and the other Johannine writ-

---

125. Ibid., 62–63. GJohn is eschatologically realized but also future, (cf. John 5:28–29; 14:13). Revelation is eschatologically future, but also realized (cf. Rev 1:17–18; 3:20).

126. Ibid., 63. Cf. Rev 5:6–7; 6:16–17; John 3:35; 12:30–33; 1 John 3:14–16.

127. Smalley, *Thunder and Love*, 63. Cf. Dodd, *According, passim*; Lindars, *Apologetic, passim*.

128. See Smalley, *Thunder and Love*, 64.

129. See below.

130. GJohn is structured around seven signs, contains seven discourses, and seven "I am" sayings. Revelation has seven parallel sections, structured around the seven seals, trumpets and vials. Cf. Hendriksen, *More Than Conquerors, passim*; Smalley, *Thunder and Love*, 66.

131. See Walker, *Holy City*, 263–64.

132. See on the Paschal NE in Revelation in Part II, chapter 9, below.

133. As I seek to demonstrate below.

134. See Smalley, *Thunder and Love*, 60ff. Cf. Fiorenza, *Revelation*, 85–93.

135. See Keener, *John*, 126–39.

136. See Eusebius *Hist. eccl.* 7:25:24–27. Cf. Smalley, *Thunder and Love*, 65. Modern critics of the Greek employed by Revelation include Moule, *Birth of the New Testament*, 213; Selwyn, *Apocalypse*, 258.

137. Smalley, *Thunder and Love*, 72, n. 60. Cf. Rev 3:3 and John 7:6; Rev 12:11, John 15:13 and 1 John 3:16; Rev 14:12 and John 14:15; John 15:9–10 and 1 John 3:23–24; Rev 14:15 and John 4:35–38.

138. Smalley, *Thunder and Love*, 65.

Historical Feasibility

ings, "more or less restricted to this literary group."[139] Moreover, it has been argued that Revelation's abnormalities of grammar and vocabulary cannot be attributed to ignorance,[140] but are due to some other cause. Some suggest translation from Aramaic or Hebrew, or the seer's "thinking in Hebrew while writing in Greek." Others conceive of John's personal development over time.[141]

The most satisfactory solution, however, is the argument that John has adapted his style to his purpose: the Semitic element bringing his work in line with Jewish Greek Apocalypse.[142] Beale believes that the author's "grammatical irregularities" may have been a deliberate attempt to produce Semitic idioms in his Greek, demonstrating solidarity with OT Scripture.[143] Examining the Hebraisms of the Apocalypse, Ozanne shows that the author of Revelation modelled his grammar on OT Hebrew. He argues that this was to indicate that his Revelation was the final prophetic book.[144] There is thus "no longer . . . adequate reason for denying that the apostle John was the sole author of Gospel, Epistles, and Apocalypse."[145]

Revelation is thus able to shed further light upon the Johannine community. Its seven letters indicate John's authoritative oversight of the churches[146] and his intimate knowledge of the topography and history of their cities.[147] Starting from Ephesus, these represent the circuitous route he might take, visiting important localities from which his message might spread to the whole province.[148] Moreover, they are indicative of the circumstances faced by believers: Oppressed by Roman persecution, instigated by Domitian's imperial cult,[149] they were being betrayed to the authorities by "false

---

139. See Ozanne, "Language," 3–5. These include , ἀληθινός, νικᾷ, τηρεῖν τὸν λόγον, τηρεῖν τὰς ἐντολὰς, ὁδηγεῖν (of spiritual guidance), σκηνοῦν, ποιεῖν σημεῖον, μαρτυρία, and Ἑβραϊστί. Cf. Fiorenza, *Revelation*, 93, who cites "only . . . eight words in common that are found nowhere else in the NT."

140. Ozanne, "Language," 3, citing Beckwith, *Apocalypse*, 355. "The departures from correct grammatical usage are not due to ignorance; the writer shows a knowledge and command of Greek too accurate to make such a supposition tenable."

141. See Hengel, *Question*, 126–27, who thinks Revelation to have been written twenty or thirty years before the Gospel. Cf. Ramsay, *Seven Churches*, 82–92, who thinks John's style was affected by his "education" on Patmos.

142. See Smalley, *Thunder and Love*, 65.

143. See Beale, "Revelation," 332.

144. Ozanne, "Language," 4, citing Burney, *Aramaic Origin*, 15–16; Hort, *Apocalypse*, xxxviii.

145. Ozanne, "Language," 9.

146. See Ramsay, *Seven Churches*, 80, who speaks of John's "superintendence and oversight" of the churches.

147. Cf. Ramsay, *Seven Churches*, passim; Hemer, *Seven Churches*, passim.

148. Hemer, *Seven Churches*, 15.

149. Cf. Hemer, *Seven Churches*, 8–11; Caird, *Revelation*, 23.

Jews,"[150] described as belonged to "the Synagogue of Satan."[151] The pressure of pagan worship from without,[152] and the infiltration of antinomian teachers within, added to their troubles.[153] It is possible that the Nicolaitan heretics might be "the earliest representatives of the error of Cerinthus."[154]

History of the Community

I can now sketch a plausible history.[155] The apostle John moved to Ephesus, probably around A.D. 66–70, when the headquarters of the Church relocated from Jerusalem prior to its fall.[156] It is possible that he brought many Jewish Christians with him. These may have joined the mixed, Jewish-Gentile, churches, previously established during Paul's third missionary journey, or founded new churches. Being "zealous for the law"[157] they would in addition, or perhaps as an alternative, have sought fellowship with the Synagogue. The events of A.D. 70 brought an influx of unbelieving "Jews," which fueled existing resentment of Christians by the Synagogue.[158] John remained in Asia until the time of Trajan, becoming overseer of the Christian churches. Sometime during his stay in Ephesus he wrote GJohn, a new perspective on Jesus to suit the radically new conditions that applied not only to his followers, but also to the whole Church.[159] Since 1 John interprets and alludes to GJohn, the letters were written after the Gospel, particularly to combat heresy and division within John's community. Following a period of banishment to Patmos,[160] under Domitian, John later wrote Rev-

---

150. See Hemer, *Seven Churches*, 9, 67–70. "Probably . . . unbelieving Jews had become active in instigating persecution of the church or denouncing to the authorities those Jews who were also Christians."

151. Cf. Rev 2:9; 3:9; John 8:44; Lightfoot, *Ignatius*, 1:468-69, 3:482; Smalley, *Thunder and Love*, 125.

152. Rev 2:20, 24, alludes to the apostles' decree banning meat offered to idols, Acts 15:28–29. Hemer, *Seven Churches*, 117, notes that the trade guilds would have required their members to attend idolatrous feasts.

153. Cf. Smalley, *Thunder and Love*, 121–22; Hemer, *Seven Churches*, 91–92, 117–23.

154. So Irenaeus *Haer.* 1:26:3; 3:11:7. He also ascribes to them a Gnostic cosmology, but this might be an inference from 1 Tim 6:20. Cf. Hemer's comments, *Seven Churches*, 88.

155. For two slightly different version of events, cf. Martin Hengel's "provisional assessment" in idem, *Question*, 80–83, and Stephen Smalley's, "Conclusions" in Smalley, *Thunder and Love*, 67–69, 134-37.

156. Cf. Hemer, *Seven Churches*, 66, 232, n. 38; Lightfoot, *Ignatius*, 1:438, 440-41. Before Jerusalem's fall, "the principal leaders of the Church—the surviving apostles and other personal disciples of the Lord—sought a new home in proconsular Asia." It is possible that Lightfoot is correct in thinking that Philip and Andrew were alive at the time. If so, they could have encouraged John to write his Gospel as the Muratorian Cannon suggests.

157. Acts 21:20 speaks of Jerusalem's thousands of believing Jews, zealous for the law.

158. Acts 19:8–10. Cf. Lightfoot, *Ignatius*, 1:468-69; Hemer, *Seven Churches*, 66.

159. See Bauckham, "For Whom," 22ff.

160. See Caird, *Revelation*, 21–23. Tertullian correctly understands this as a lenient form of

elation at a time when the churches suffered intense persecution under the Romans, possibly aided by some local pagan and "Jewish" opponents.[161]

POINTS OF SENSITIVITY—TOWARDS A SPECIFIC SITZ IM LEBEN

Having suggested this general historical background, can we find a specific *Sitz im Leben* for the writing of GJohn? Scholars maintain that, GJohn shows "points of sensitivity" towards particular aspects of first century Judaism.[162] These can be exploited to reveal a possible *Sitz im Leben*.

Martyn's thesis.

In a highly influential monograph,[163] Martyn argues for a two level reading of GJohn where the "*einmalig* tradition about Jesus" has become a cipher for the history of the community.[164] In particular the ἀποσυνάγωγος expulsion of John 9:22 reflects the excommunication of Johannine Christians from the Synagogue and John 5 the martyrdom of their leaders.[165] The historical situation behind this was the formulation of the *Birkath ha-Minim*, a Synagogue prayer pronouncing a curse ("blessing") upon the heretics, that Martyn believes was used to exclude Christians.[166]

Martyn's work has been criticized from several angles: Though John doubtless wanted to apply his Gospel to the needs of his own community, the "two level drama" theory is not compatible with the Gospel's "biographical" *genre*.[167] Moreover, the model is contradicted elsewhere in the Gospel, as in John 11:1–41, where many of "the Jews" come to comfort the believing sisters.[168] It becomes especially far-fetched when it puts the words of a "Johannine" martyr-evangelist cum prophet into the mouth of Jesus. Reinhartz notes that GJohn "evinces a pattern of prophecy and fulfilment which in itself imputes historicity to the events and discourses [which it relates]."[169]

---

banishment, *religatio in insulam*, which could be imposed by the provincial governor.

161. Rev 2:9–10, 13; 3:9. On "Jewish" opposition, see Smalley, *Thunder and Love*, 89, 125. He emphasises that John speaks of "Judaism in its local, not its national expression." Cf. Hemer, *Seven Churches*, 29, 67, 86–87, *et passim*.

162. Cf. Dunn, "Let John be John," 309–39; Motyer, *Your Father*, 35.

163. Martyn, *History and Theology*. Cf. Smith, "Contribution," 280ff. He gives Martyn credit for "a sea change in Johannine studies."

164. Martyn, *History and Theology*, 129–30.

165. Ibid., 35–98. Cf. John 16:2, "they will put you out of the synagogue, the time will come when he who kills you will think he does God service."

166. Which Martyn, *History and Theology*, 56–66, thought to be reflected in John 9:22; 12:42; 16:2. Cf. Luke 6:22.

167. See Bauckham, *Testimony*, 13. On the GJohn's *genre*, see above.

168. John 11:19; 12:11. See Reinhartz, *Beloved Disciple*, 40–53.

169. Reinhartz, "Johannine Community," in Segovia, *'What is John?'* 2:132.

PART I—PRELIMINARY CONSIDERATIONS

Thus these events, including the ἀποσυνάγωγος passages, would have been regarded by John's earliest readers as historical stories of Jesus.[170] Motyer complains that Martyn's allegorization is unprecedented and unjustified, particularly when applied to Johannine narrative purporting to be history.[171]

Doubt has also been cast over the use of the *Birkath ha-Minim* as a means of excluding Christians from the Synagogue. Neusner has argued that the Yavneh academy under Yohanan ben Zakkai and Gamaliel II was not as influential as previously thought and that the pre A.D. 70 diversity within Judaism continued until the Bar Kokhba revolt, A.D. 132–35, and beyond.[172] It follows that the *Birkath ha-Minim* would not have been as universally important as Martyn thinks, and the rabbis of the Yavneh period would have lacked the power to enforce its use.[173] Some think that the *Birkath ha-Minim* may have not been particularly designed against Christians, though it possibly included them.[174] Boyarin argues that the earliest attestation of the curse in the Tosefta indicates that it was initially a "blessing" upon those who separated themselves from the community, and that the *minim* was appended later.[175] Moreover, he argues that it is foundational to the Babylonian Talmud's "Yavnean legend," which retrojected its own rabbinic orthodox patterns back to the first century Yavneh.[176] Thus "we cannot know" whether or not there was a first century curse against Christians or not.[177]

Despite these devastating criticisms, Martyn is correct, in my view, in one particular—in *pointing towards* a background of conflict that existed between Johannine Christians and the Synagogue.[178] Not, *pace* Martyn, conflict between the Church and a centralized Synagogue, able to wield the power of the *Birkath ha-Minim*, but conflict between John's Asia minor churches and the *local* synagogues.[179] Moreover, GJohn was primarily written to establish Jewish Christians in their faith.[180] Thus Reinhartz, who rejects Martin's thesis, acknowledges the relevance of the GJohn portrayal of the conflict between Jesus and "the Jews" to its readers.[181] Rejecting Martyn's model of

---

170. Ibid., 133.

171. Motyer, *Your Father*, 28–29. Cf. Martyn, *History and Theology*, 130ff.; Ashton, *Fourth Gospel*, 412–20. See Bauckham's criticisms in "For Whom," 19–22.

172. Neusner, "Destruction," 83–98. Cited by Motyer, *Your Father*, 75–76. Cf. Dunn, *Parting*, xxii.

173. Cf. Goodman, "Function," 505; Boyarin, *Border Lines*, 116.

174. See Motyer, *Your Father*, 93.

175. Boyarin, *Border Lines*, 69–70. Cf. t. Ber. 3:25.

176. Ibid., 70, 152. Cf. Goodman, *Rome and Jerusalem*, 448, who takes a similar position.

177. Boyarin, *Border Lines*, 71. Cf. Boyarin, "The Ioudaioi," 218–19.

178. In this respect he was not the first. Cf. Hoskyns, *Fourth Gospel*, 361–62, Bultmann, *John*, 239.

179. See Smalley, *Thunder and Love*, 89, 125.

180. Taking "believe," John 20:31, as present continuous rather than aorist. See Keener, *John*, 1215–16.

181. Reinhartz, "Johannine Community," 135. Cf. Barrett, *John*, 250, 137–38; Borchert, *John 1–11*, 311. "There is little doubt in my mind of the existence of double level thinking in John both theologically and historically, but I frankly have a little trouble with asserting that texts must represent *either* a

reading back community history into the days of Jesus, I affirm John's writing historical narrative, but selecting his material as being particularly applicable to his own community and also to the wider Church.

Martyn thinks that the controversy was over the high Christology of the community and its conflict with the "Jewish" understanding of monotheism. That this was of central importance seems undeniable, especially as John's stated purpose, John 20:30–31, is that his readers may believe that the Christ, the Son of God, is Jesus—where "Son of God" indicates deity.[182] But along with this there may have been another issue: who are the true people of God and what is the history of their salvation? For the "Jews" of GJohn, "Jewish" descent implies belonging to the redeemed community.[183] The great event that shaped Israel was the Exodus. She became a nation in covenant with God by this dramatic act of redemption from slavery. This event had been celebrated annually in the great feasts of Passover, Tabernacles, Firstfruits, and Pentecost. But in GJohn, Jesus' followers represent a new redeemed community, being taken out of "Judaism,"[184] and from wider humanity, by a New Moses.[185] It is not hard to see that this became a further flashpoint[186] between the Johannine community and the local synagogues—especially following the destruction of the Temple when resentment to Christians may have increased.

Writing at the time when the *Birkath ha-Minim* theory was in the ascendancy, Barrett has suggested that several liturgical attempts were made to expose and combat the Christians. One of the most interesting, that may have connections with GJohn, comes from the Passover Haggadah, *Maggid*, where the sole agency of the Lord in delivering Israel out of Egypt ("not by an angel, nor by a seraph, not by a messenger") receives particular emphasis:

> *I will in the same night go through Egypt*: I myself and not an angel (אני ולא מלאך).
> *And I will slay the firstborn in Egypt*, I myself and not a seraph (אני ולא סרף). *And I will manifest my judgement against all the gods of Egypt*: I myself and not the messenger (אני ולא השליח). *I, the Lord*: I am he and not another (ולא אחר אני הוא).[187]

Barrett thinks that the repeated emphasis upon the sole activity of God in the Exodus was aimed at combating Christian teaching concerning the deity of Jesus Christ.[188] He

---

Jesus period *or* a time of the early church."

182. See Barrett, *Judaism*, 17.

183. Cf. John 8:33ff.; Keener, *John*, 754; Carson, *John*, 349.

184. John 1:11–13. Cf. Keener, *John*, 402; Carson, *John*, 126.

185. Cf. Glasson, *Moses*, 10, 20–21, *et passim*; Allison, *New Moses*, 97–106.

186. Cf. Acts 13:44–51; 17:4–8, where Jewish jealousy over Paul's success led to persecution. See Robinson, *Priority*, 72–81. He specifically mentions the early persecution of the church in Acts 8 in the A.D. 30s, 40s, and 50s. Cf. Hengel, *Question*, 114; idem, *Between*, 1–29, 133–56.

187. Cited by Barrett, *Judaism*, 49, (his emphasis). Barrett believes this to be one of four liturgical alterations aimed against Christians within the Synagogue.

188. Ibid., 49. Cf. Gartner, *John 6*, 28–29. He believes that rabbinic texts were censored to remove

notes the importance of the expression השליח (the messenger) to GJohn, where Jesus is sent by his Father. Moreover, he notes the close relationship between אני הוא and the Johannine ἐγώ εἰμι. What Barrett does not point up, however, is the implication that Johannine believers understood that the pre-existent Jesus led the Exodus—or indeed that he was being presently hailed in GJohn as the leader of a NE. As we will see, John sees Jesus as the liberator from slavery to sin.[189] Moreover, in this context, Jesus is not only the messenger who delivers people, but also the absolute "I am."[190] Although this evidence may be relevant, however, we cannot be certain that it is as early as GJohn.[191]

Motyer's contribution.

Another important historical contribution has come from Stephen Motyer.[192] He is at the dialectically opposite extreme from Martyn, taking issue with him both as to his methodology and his conclusions.[193] Thus he has sought to defuse the anti-Semitic understanding of GJohn by proposing that it should be understood evangelistically, with the intention of winning Jewish people. Methodologically he has undertaken a three-stage investigation, seeking "points of sensitivity"[194] within the text that resonate with first century Jewish history, investigating that history, and returning to read the text against his historical findings.

Motyer finds a Johannine sensitivity to the Temple and its festivals to be particularly important, signalling the trauma resulting from destruction of the Temple and loss of its worship.[195] Thus "Destroy this Temple, and in three days I will raise it up," John 2:19, is programmatic, not for a two level reading of the Gospel,[196] but for GJohn's addressing the problem of the Temple's destruction and the loss of its worship (Feasts) and indicating their "replacement" by Jesus.[197] Other scholars have also found

---

the theophanic "I am" form because of Christian interpretation and that the Passover *Haggadah* being uncensored is the "only rabbinic text in which this form is encountered." He cites Daube, *Rabbinic Judaism*, 327–28, who argues that as a *liturgical* text it withstood this expurgation.

189. See below on John 8:31–59. Cf. Carson, *John*, 349–50; Lincoln, *John*, 270–71.

190. Cf. John 8:58; Barrett, *John*, 342.

191. See Goodman, *Rome and Jerusalem*, 250, who notes that the Passover Haggadah "existed roughly in its present form by the time of the Mishna in ca. 200 CE." Cf. Finkelstein, "Pre-Maccabean," 291–332.

192. Motyer, *Your Father*.

193. Ibid., 24ff.

194. Cf. Dunn, "Let John be John," 309–39.

195. Motyer, *Your Father*, 38.

196. *Pace* Ashton, *Understanding*, 414–16.

197. Motyer, *Your Father*, 39–42; 137ff. He notes that John 4:21 and 11:47–50, also carry poignant reminders of the trauma and its solution in a return from exile through Jesus. Cf. Duke, *Irony*, 87–89. On the trauma that this event caused to all Jews cf. Kerr, *Temple*, 34–49.

Jesus' "replacement" of the Temple to be a key Johannine theme, but they have not particularly connected it with the NE.[198]

Moving outside the text, Motyer finds that "rabbinic orthodoxy" fostered by the Yavneh academy under ben Zakkai and Gamaliel II did not become the dominant force within Judaism until after the Bar Kokhba revolt of A.D. 132–35, and that up to that time Jewish diversity continued.[199] Thus there were many diverse attempts to deal with the A.D. 70 trauma and comparisons were inevitably made with the destruction of the first Temple and the Babylonian exile that followed.[200] Importantly, some Jews understood the situation as that of "exile" and envisaged a return from "exile" either through divine intervention[201] or human activity.[202]

Re-reading the text against this background, Motyer approaches his target passage, John 8:31–59, through the context of John 5–12, and the "co-text" of John 7–8. His main concern is to show that its polemic does not vilify Jewish people *per se*, but was typical of the rhetoric of the day, reflecting the prophetic appeals of Hosea, and can be viewed as a "debate within [the] family."[203] In so doing, he suggests that GJohn addressed the post A.D. 70 crisis and appeals to Jewish people to believe in Jesus as the solution to their dilemma seen in terms of a New Temple and a NE. Importantly he finds Exodus and "exile" symbolism prominent in Jesus' signs and dialogue.[204] Following Trites, Motyer further suggests GJohn's employment of the lawsuit motif of Isaiah 40–55.[205]

Lincoln's contribution.

While several scholars have studied the lawsuit motif in GJohn,[206] Andrew Lincoln has produced a major literary, theological, and historical investigation. He understands

---

198. Cf. Walker, *Holy City*, 161ff.; Kerr, *Temple, passim*; Coloe, *God Dwells, passim*; Köstenberger, "Destruction," 69–108.

199. Motyer, *Your Father*, 75. In this he follows Neusner, "Destruction," 83–98, esp. 93. Cf. Boyarin, *Border Lines*, 152, 196, who speaks of the legend of Yavneh as a myth projected back into the first century.

200. See Motyer, *Your Father*, 79–87. Cf. 2 Macc 5:17–20; *Pss. Sol.* 2:1–3, 16; Jeremiah 7:13–15; Goodman, *Rome and Jerusalem*, 193.

201. For example, *4 Bar.* emphasised sixty-six years of "exile" after which God would step in.

202. See Motyer, *Your Father*, 98. Cf. *Apoc. Ab.* Motyer cites Mueller, "Apocalypse of Abraham," 348–49.

203. Motyer, *Your Father*, 212–13. He emphasises the diversity of this "family," at this (post A.D. 70) time.

204. Ibid., 136–40.

205. Motyer, *Your Father*, 145–46. See, e.g., Isa 41:2, 4; 41:26; 43, 9, 13; 44:7, 8. Cf. Trites, *Concept*, 78ff. Motyer also alludes to Gemser, "Rib," 120–37, Harvey, *Trial*, and Blank, *Krisis*.

206. See Lincoln, *Trial*. In addition to scholars mentioned in the footnote above (in connection with Motyer), Lincoln also cites Preiss, "Justification," 9–31, Boice, *Witness*, Beutler, *Martyria*, Pancaro, *Law*, Minear, *John*, and Maccini, *Testimony*, 32–62.

this motif to be central to the plot and a key to the Gospel's interpretation, with the trial running throughout the Gospel. In terms of Greimas's structuralism[207]:

> The Sender is . . . the Father . . . The Object is the trial constituted by Jesus' mission, with its witness issuing in the judgement of either life or death. The Receiver is the world (with Israel as its primary representative), which is put on trial . . . Jesus as the one who is sent [is] . . . the Subject . . .[208]

Importantly, John has reworked the OT lawsuits, such as the *rib* of Exodus 17:1–7 where Yahweh is put on trial by Israel, but particularly those of Isaiah 40–55 between Yahweh and Israel and between Yahweh and the Nations.[209] With the nations, Yahweh is involved in a cosmic lawsuit in which he shows himself to be the one true God over against pagan gods. This had been put in doubt by the Babylonian exile. But Yahweh establishes himself as "I am," the first and last, and the Lord of history, by *predicting* the advent of Cyrus and Babylon's downfall. Moreover, his word will not return to him void.[210] With Israel, Yahweh is guarantor of the covenant and also party to its actions.[211] Israel's complaint is that Yahweh has abandoned them. Accusing them of blindness and deafness, he retorts that he has not been blind or deaf to their cries or inactive in history. Rather, they have sold themselves into slavery and he has punished them for their sin by sending them into exile.[212] Moreover, he is able to redeem them, as evidenced by his sovereign power, already displayed at the Exodus.[213] Besides many Isaianic echoes,[214] GJohn's three direct quotations from Isaiah 40–55, placed strategically to form an *inclusio* with Jesus' ministry, point up the significance of this Scripture for the Gospel.[215]

The functions of the Johannine and Isaianic lawsuit are analogous. As the Babylonian exile had called into question Yahweh's sovereignty over history, so the controversy over Jesus' claims and Jesus' death by crucifixion called into question belief about God and his control over history. As Yahweh's ability to predict Cyrus demonstrated his Lordship in Isaiah, so Jesus' control over every situation and the reliability of his words demonstrated his trustworthiness before wavering believers. Moreover, the purpose of the lawsuits is the same: the salvation of the world.[216]

---

207. Cf. Greimas, *Sémantique structurale*.
208. Lincoln, *Trial*, 163.
209. Ibid., 51ff.; 38ff. Cf. Trites, *Witness*, 35–47.
210. Lincoln, *Trial*, 39–41, citing Isa 55:10–11.
211. Ibid., 41–43. Cf. Nielsen, *Prosecutor and Judge*, 25.
212. Lincoln, *Trial*, 41.
213. Ibid., 42.
214. See Ibid., 43, where Lincoln cites Hengel, "Old Testament," 31–32, "[John] prefers the bare terse clue, the use of metaphor or motif more than the full citation."
215. Ibid., 43. Cf. Isa 40:3 in John 1:23, Isa 53:1 in John 12:38, and Isa 54:13 in John 6:45.
216. Lincoln, *Trial*, 49–50.

In terms of historical setting, Lincoln follows the main tenets of Martyn's thesis: The Gospel's narrative and discourse are closely related to the experience of its author and readers. It is a witness to Jesus, but a witness that has been shaped by events relating to the community, resulting in a witness on two levels.[217] Moreover, the community has been put on trial by "the Jews," convicted and expelled by the synagogues. This threatened their "entire universe of shared perceptions, assumptions, beliefs, ideals, and hopes that had given meaning to their world within Judaism."[218]

Lincoln differs from Martyn, however, at several points.[219] Importantly he believes that the conflict with the synagogue was local rather than universal and preceded widespread influence of the rabbis over the synagogues and the use of the *Birkath ha-Minim*.[220] Consistent with Second Temple practice, the (locally) excommunicated Jewish Christians were under the ban: considered to be under the covenantal curses, exclusion served instead of the death penalty.[221] Exclusion divided families and brought betrayal and shame.[222]

It was for this reason, Lincoln argues, that John turned to the divine lawsuit. Only by this means could the sentence passed upon Jewish Christians by the synagogue be reversed, truth be established, and true (divine) honor recognized.[223] Moreover, Isaiah 40–55 was a particularly appropriate Scripture to appeal to, since it sought to overturn the shame and disgrace of Yahweh's people in exile and promised them assurances of Yahweh's glory.[224] Members of the Johannine community, in conflict with the local synagogue, would have likewise felt themselves to be in "exile," outside the majority group to which they had belonged. But the divine lawsuit would have given them an assurance of life and well-being and enabled them to make sense of their own history.[225]

Evaluation and synthesis

The situation of John's churches

The insights of these scholars are important. Martyn has identified probable tension between the Johannine community and the synagogues. Lincoln, building upon Martyn, has shown how John's use of the lawsuit motif might strengthen Johannine believers, but neither Lincoln nor Martyn have considered the impact of A.D. 70 upon

---

217. Ibid., 263–65. He thinks, however, that the Gospel transcends the experiences of the Johannine group and is addressed a wider audience.
218. Rensberger, *Johannine Faith*, 27. Cited in Lincoln, *Trial*, 278.
219. See Lincoln, *Trial*, 277.
220. Ibid., 274–277.
221. Lincoln, *Trial*, 279–81. He cites Horbury, "Extirpation," 13–38. Cf. Ezra 10:8; Neh 13:3.
222. Ibid., 285ff. Cf. Malina, *New Testament World*, *passim*; Neyrey, "'Despising,' 113–37.
223. Lincoln, *Trial*, 282; 298.
224. Ibid., 289.
225. Ibid., 327–28.

PART I—PRELIMINARY CONSIDERATIONS

the community. Motyer has provided an insight into the Johannine sensitivity to the destruction of the Temple, but his conclusions run counter to those of Martyn and Lincoln. Can we find a *via media* that recognizes their insights while harmonising their differences? This is possible if we abandon Motyer's conclusion that GJohn's purpose was primarily to evangelize the Jewish people[226] and affirm that GJohn was written primarily to strengthen the Johannine churches, devastated by the destruction of the Temple *and* in conflict with the synagogue. The links between Motyer and Lincoln are then the NE and lawsuit motifs.

Lincoln is surely correct that GJohn's lawsuit would vindicate the community in the synagogue ban and honor/shame context and (more importantly) reassure them of the verdict of eternal life, including forensic justification by faith[227] and bodily resurrection to life,[228] through Jesus' death and resurrection. He recognizes that the lawsuit is a vindication of God; "God's name, God's reputation, and God's truth, the reliability of the divine word, are at stake," including his saving purposes in Christ.[229]

I argue that, in addition to an understanding of their forensic justification, however, John's churches would have required instruction concerning God's NE purposes, including his purposes for the Temple, its sacrifices, and their fulfilment in Jesus. The Johannine believers had received a double blow: they had suffered the destruction of the Temple *and* expulsion from the local synagogues. The "Jews" may well have blamed them for the destruction of the Temple, their defection to Jesus the Christ, whom the "Jews" considered to be a blasphemer, John 10:33, bringing judgement. They not only needed legal vindication before God, but also, as those who felt "exiled"[230] by exclusion from the synagogue *and* loss of the Temple, they needed to *understand* the fulfilment of the NE hope in Jesus the Messiah, the Son of God.[231] Contrary to appearances, Jesus had called them out of "exile," laid down his life—the paschal sacrifice for their sin—raised up the new messianic Temple, and inaugurated the new heavens and earth.

Though he does not emphasize the NE, Lincoln recognizes the (NE) promises of salvation to be central to the Isaianic lawsuit, particularly that of Israel against Yahweh.[232] It is no coincidence that Isaiah 40–55, the Scripture most important for the lawsuit motif, is also the Scripture most important for the NE. Indeed, Israel brought

---

226. Though Motyer has made an able defense of GJohn against the charge of anti-Semitism, few will be persuaded that GJohn's *primary* purpose was to evangelise the Jews.

227. Lincoln, *Trial*, 218. He compares this with Paul's teaching on justification in Rom 3:25, 26; 5:18.

228. Ibid., 211.

229. Ibid., 188. Cf. the demonstration of the justice of God in justifying the ungodly, set forth in the cross, Rom 3:25–26.

230. See Motyer, *Your Father*, 137–40.

231. For example, that Jesus is the new Temple and the eschatological fulfilment of the symbolism of the feasts.

232. Lincoln, *Trial*, 207–8.

its lawsuit because they felt Yahweh to be unfaithful to the covenant as unable or unwilling to deliver them. The great demonstration of Yahweh's covenant faithfulness would be the fulfilment of his word, which would go forth to accomplish a NE, forgiving their sin, ransoming them from the grave, and inaugurating a new creation. In GJohn, Jesus, God's incarnate Word, accomplishes this by his sacrificial death upon the cross and his glorious resurrection from the dead.

The link between creation and covenant

It is important, at this point, to emphasize the inextricable relationship between creation and covenant.[233] Wright speaks of "problems" both within the OT covenant and within creation; each of these being invoked to deal with the difficulty of the other.[234] The problem within creation was the fall.[235] The covenant with Abraham and his seed was designed to remedy this, "to undo the sin of Adam," all nations being blessed in his seed.[236] Under the Deuteronomic covenant, return to paradise was envisaged in terms of the Land. The weakness of this covenant was Israel's inability to keep it.[237] In Isa 40–55 God is invoked, as creator, covenant Lord, and the one who delivered Israel at the Exodus, to fulfil his responsibilities: to "establish justice in the world and . . . vindicate his people."[238]

Wright finds these covenant-creation themes to be reflected in the Second Temple period [contemporary with John] in such diverse literature as the Wisdom of Solomon, Qumran literature, and apocalyptic writings such as 4 Ezra and 2 Baruch,

> Invoked as the reason why Israel's God, the creator, must eventually engage in a final showdown with the forces of evil, a dramatic event which will be like the Exodus in some respects and in other respects like a great court scene, a trial in which the powers of evil are judged, condemned and overthrown.[239]

---

233. See the discussion in Wright, *Perspective*, 21–39. I disagree profoundly with his denial of Reformed understandings of imputed righteousness, ibid., 25. In Romans 3, Paul speaks of the righteousness of God manifest now at this present time (in Christ), (imputed) unto all who believe (vv. 21–24) *as well as* the manifestation (demonstration) of the righteousness of God (the Father) in providing a means (the cross) whereby he can justify the ungodly (vv. 25–26).

234. Ibid., 24.

235. I would emphasize the perfection of creation, Gen 1:31, being spoiled by the invasion of sin that came through one man, Adam, Rom 5:12.

236. Ibid., 23. Cf. Gal 3:16, where Abraham's seed is Christ. It is important to point out the unconditional nature of the promise to Abraham compared to the conditional nature of blessings under the law, Gal 3:17–18.

237. I would emphasize the holiness and righteousness of God's law and covenant, its weakness being due to man's sinful nature, Rom 7:12–13; 8:3. Cf. ibid., 36.

238. Ibid., 24.

239. Ibid., 25, citing the importance of Daniel 7.

PART I—PRELIMINARY CONSIDERATIONS

Wright points up these themes in Paul, but they are just as prominent in GJohn. Thus in the prologue, the creator God comes to "his own" covenant people. Though they reject him, he gives power to become the sons of God, and thus members of the covenant, to everyone who receives him.[240] Moreover, Jesus' signs, as well as reflecting the Exodus, demonstrate the power of the creator God, who begins the work of re-creation. They culminate in the final showdown—the casting out of the Prince of this world—when Jesus is lifted up on the cross.[241]

The Problem of Sin

This is not the whole story, however, because the Lord could not just *create* a way out of the broken covenant, without dealing with sin.[242] God's law had been broken and the penalty of the law must be paid. The Lord would make a new covenant with Israel, gathering them to their own land, recreating them after his image, providing them with a new heart and a new spirit,[243] but to do so he had to deal with their sin. This would involve not only forgiveness and cleansing from defilement,[244] but also a means whereby satisfaction for sin, viewed as the breaking of God's law, could be made.[245] In addition, God's people required a righteousness and holiness, obtained by the perfect keeping of God's law from the heart. The logic of this is seen in the requirement of absolute obedience to the law as the condition by which the covenant promises would be obtained (Deut 28:1–14). Paul notes that it was by obedience, "one act of righteousness"—the culmination of a life of perfect obedience (Rom 5:18–19)—that Jesus gained righteousness, justification, and life on behalf of his people.

As Robertson argues, ultimately God himself was the guarantor of the covenant, as evidenced by his walking between Abraham's divided covenantal sacrificial pieces and thus invoking the covenant curse upon himself.[246] Thus God himself must bear the penalty for the sins of his people.

---

240. John 1:11. See Carson, *John*, 124–26. These themes also occur in "parallel" passages in Hebrews 1 and particularly in Colossians 1:15–20. See Wright, *Perspective*, 27.

241. See exposition below where the healing of the lame man makes him "completely whole." The healing of lame and blind signified a NE and new creation. Similarly, the multiplied loaves signalled eschatological fulfilment. See Carson, *John*, 442–43.

242. Cf. Jer 11:10; 31:31-34; Thompson, *Jeremiah*, 580–81.

243. See, e.g., Jer 31:31-34. See Thompson, *Jeremiah*, 579–81.

244. Cf. Ezek 36:25; Jer 31:34b. See Mackay, *Jeremiah*, 238–39.

245. Typically this was made by the Levitical sacrifices. As the letter to the Hebrews shows, however, the inefficacy of these sacrifices was seen in the fact that they could not purge the guilty conscience, but had to be continually offered, again and again. Rather, they were but pointers to the one great sacrifice of Christ, offered once for all time. Heb 10:1–12.

246. Gen 15. See Robertson, *Covenants*, 145–46. He understands that the Lord's presence passing between the divided sacrifice incurred upon God a "self-maledictory oath" whereby the covenant promise was guaranteed to Abraham who asked "How can I *know*? How can I be sure?" (emphasis original).

The Paschal Paradigm

When God redeemed his people from Egypt, he instituted the Passover. This provided the pattern for redemption from slavery and atonement for sin for the Israelites.[247] Tom Holland argues that the firstborn was the family representative whose vicarious death was to redeem the family and who in turn was redeemed by the death of the unblemished Paschal lamb.[248] That this did not deal definitively with Israel's sin problem is evident from her subsequent history. This understanding is reflected in the NT where Paul speaks of God "passing over"[249] former sins, but demonstrating his righteousness "at the present time" by setting forth Christ Jesus "as a propitiation [propitiatory sacrifice] by his blood."[250] Similarly, Hebrews teaches that while animal sacrifices could not take away sins, the "offering of the body of Jesus Christ once for all" has done so.[251] The reason is that "only the creator himself could redeem creation."[252] Moreover, only as God made flesh—a sinless righteous man and second (last) Adam—could God die on behalf of his people.

In the Isaianic NE the Servant "the righteous one" (Isa 53:11) takes the place of the Paschal lamb in that he suffers vicariously, bearing the people's sin,[253] and as the "arm of the Lord," inaugurates the global NE.[254] Enigmatically, he is described in terms not only of weakness, giving his "back to those who strike," and being led "like a lamb that is led to the slaughter," but also in terms appropriate only to God, "high and lifted up," and "exalted." As Oswalt points out, "High" and "lifted up" (רום and נשׂא) are used in combination four times in Isaiah and nowhere else in the OT. Commentating on Isa 52:13—53:12, he writes,

> In the other three places (6:1; 33:10; 57:15) they describe God. Whom do they describe here? The same point may be made concerning *exalted*. The section 2:6–22 speaks forcefully against every exaltation of the human; v. 17 says that God will humble the exaltation of man, so that only God will be lifted up.[255]

---

247. See Holland, *Contours*, 242. He argues that while the Passover became a memorial meal, "the sin of the nation was dealt with in the original Passover."

248. Ibid., 238.

249. An allusion to the Passover. Cf. Rom 3:25; Holland, *Contours*, 165.

250. Rom 3:25. See Cranfield, *Romans*, 214–218. He translates ἱλαστήριον as "a propitiatory sacrifice," and thinks that Isa 53:10 (אִם־תָּשִׂים אָשָׁם נַפְשׁוֹ) may have contributed to Paul's thought. Cf. Hodge, *Romans*, 92–93.

251. Heb 10:1–10. See Bruce, *Hebrews*, 238, 242–43.

252. See Holland, *Contours*, 265, 283.

253. Isa 53:4–6, 10–12. See Oswalt, *Isaiah 40–66*, 384–89.

254. Cf. Isa 42:4ff.; 49:5ff.; 52:9–12; 54:1ff. See discussion of the Passover Festival below.

255. Oswalt, *Isaiah 40–66*, 378 (emphasis original). He notes that Paul refers to this passage in Phil 2:5–11 when speaking of the exaltation of Christ following his voluntary sufferings on the cross.

PART I—PRELIMINARY CONSIDERATIONS

A similarly enigmatic suffering and atoning figure is found in a Paschal context in Zechariah.[256] Here, consequent upon the Lord's pouring out of "a spirit of grace and pleas for mercy," upon David's house, they shall "look on me, on him whom they have pierced." The piercing results in a "fountain opened . . . to cleanse them from sin and uncleanness." The identity of the pierced one is (once again) ambiguous. On the one hand it appears to be the Lord himself and on the other hand the Davidic King, firstborn and only son. Thus, the Shepherd-King/pierced one of Zechariah 12–14 and the Servant of Isa 53 are closely related.[257]

Significantly, anticipating more detailed exegesis,[258] all these motifs come together in GJohn. Thus John combines allusions to Jesus as the paschal sacrifice,[259] the arm of the Lord, the Suffering Servant,[260] the one lifted up,[261] and the pierced Lord himself.[262] Jesus is portrayed as the incarnate creator,[263] God's only begotten Son, John 3:16 (τὸν υἱὸν τὸν μονογενῆ), and thus firstborn, who lays down his life for his people.[264] The vicarious nature of his sacrifice is emphasized by his trial in which three times Pilate pronounces him innocent.[265] This verdict is reinforced by the repeated use of the trial motif throughout the Gospel, where Jesus is seen to be innocent and righteous, and in Jesus' challenge to the "Jews," "which one of you convicts me of sin" (John 8:46). Moreover, the new covenant gifts are bestowed precisely when Jesus dies on the cross. Thus the fountain for sin is opened in the blood and water (twin symbols for cleansing) that flow from his side (John 19:34) and the Spirit is bestowed when Jesus dies on the cross (John 7:39; 20:22). Furthermore, it is at this time that the Prince of the world is cast out, the standard is erected to signal the gathering of the nations, and the eschatological harvest initiated (John 12:31–32). Thus John portrays Jesus as the paschal sacrifice, God's firstborn and Servant, whose death satisfies the covenant curse and inaugurates the new covenant and NE—setting his people free from slavery to sin and Satan, and from the just demands of the law.

---

256. Zech 12:10–14. See Holland, *Contours*, 249–251, 268.

257. See France, *Jesus and the Old Testament*, 109–110. Cf. Provan, "Messiah," 83. "The suggestion of vicarious suffering in Zechariah 13:1 reminds us . . . of Isaiah 52:13–53:12."

258. See below on the exegesis of the relevant passages.

259. See, e.g., John 1:29, 36; 19:36. See Keener, *John*, 454.

260. John 1:29; 12:38. See Brown, *John I-XII*, 60–63.

261. John 3:14; 8:28; 12:32, 34. See Glasson, *Moses*, 35–36.

262. John 19:37 cf. Zech 12:10. See Bruce, *John*, 377–78.

263. Cf. John 1:3, 14; Keener, *John*, 408ff.

264. John 10:15, 17–18; 15:13. See Carson, *John*, 386.

265. John 18:38; 19:4, 6.

The Purpose of GJohn

If we apply this to the Johannine churches, John's purpose is to strengthen the faith of believers. Jewish believers, in particular, have seen the collapse of their world, not only in their expulsion from the local synagogues, but also in the destruction of the Temple with its worship. The evidence from Acts is that for many years Jewish Christians continued to esteem the Temple and observe the Feasts.[266] Such was the hold that these institutions had on Jewish Christians (and the pressure of their Jewish brethren on them to conform) that the letter to the Hebrews suggests that they may have been the reason for many being tempted to return to "Judaism" with its tangible Temple worship.[267] Moreover, the primitive Church, (both Jews and Gentiles) looked for a restoration of the Kingdom, the subjugation of the world to Christ, the Parousia, and the restoration of all things.[268] In the prophets, the Temple is at the center of the eschatological hope and the feasts share eschatological restoration connotations.[269] With the Temple gone, what now of this hope? Skarsaune argues that "from the very beginning the apostles valued the temple as the place from which the authoritative word of God was to go forth to all Israel and to the nations, according to Isaiah's prophecy (Is 2:3)."[270] With the Temple (the center of world mission) destroyed, what now will become of the Church's mission to Israel and to the world? The destruction of the Temple signalled a new "exile" for the Jewish people. What now of the NE hope for the salvation of Israel? Goodman argues that although the destruction of the Temple by Titus was "accidental" it was portrayed in the Flavian triumph, in A.D. 71, as a triumph over "Judaism" (and her God); the Temple furniture and sacred Torah scroll being carried

---

266. Acts 18:21; 21:20ff. See Dunn, *Parting*, xxi. He argues that "Christian leaders, as late as the fourth century, had to continually rebuke and warn their congregations against attending synagogues and observing Jewish feasts and customs." See The Quartodeciman controversy where churches of Asia dated Easter to 14th day of Nisan as the Christian Passover, no matter what day it fell on. See Bauckham, *Eyewitnesses*, 438–39.

267. While the destination and purpose of Hebrews is disputed many scholars think it was written to exhort Jewish believers, in danger of returning to "Judaism," to continue to trust in Christ. Cf. Bruce, *Hebrews*, 5; Guthrie, *Hebrews*, 31–38; Lane, *Hebrews 1–8*, lxi–lxii. Hughes, *Hebrews*, 11, thinks that a particular community of Jewish Christians was being pressured to abandon Christ and return to "Judaism": "Accommodation to judaistic beliefs and practices was the price that would purchase ease and acceptance." Attridge, *Hebrews*, 13, thinks that the factors causing Hebrew Christians to be disaffected "could well have involved Jewish or Judaizing pressure." He cites 7:11–19; 9:9–10; 13:9. Interestingly, the author uses the NE wilderness motif to urge them to press on to their promised Sabbath rest, Heb 3–4.

268. Acts 1:6–8; 2:33–6; 3:21. See Harvey, *Trial*, 9ff.; Evans, "Root Causes," 20–35. Evans argues that, "The fundamental sticking points for the many Jewish people were the simple facts that Jesus had been put to death and the *kingdom of God had failed to materialise*."

269. See, e.g., Isa 2:3; Zech 14; Ezek 40ff.; 45:21ff. Cf. Block, *Ezekiel 25–48*, 587–88, 667.

270. Skarsaune, *Shadow*, 157, 88, 148–9. Cf. Acts 1:6–8.

in procession as the spoils of the vanquished.[271] What now of the "triumph" of the Son of God over the nations?[272]

Wright speculates that Paul *expected* calamities such as the destruction of the Temple to come upon the "Jews" as an "interim judgement" for rejecting Messiah and, had he lived, would have interpreted the events of A.D. 70 as the "day of the Lord."[273] Be that as it may, ordinary Jewish (and Gentile) Christians may have been horrified and perplexed at the turn of events. Making comparison with the destruction of the first Temple many may well have understood this as a judgement upon themselves. Moreover, they may have asked many of the questions witnessed in contemporary Jewish literature: Who sinned? What of the NE? Will the Temple be restored? Is Satan responsible? Will our enemies be judged? Is God in control? Is there merit in our sufferings? To suffer, on top of this, expulsion from local synagogues would have been devastating. Moreover, it might have been tempting for them to doubt Jesus and to see themselves as morally responsible, as his followers, for the Temple's destruction.

Understood in this light John's strategy for strengthening his churches in their trials was:

1. To establish the Johannine believers in their faith in Jesus the Christ, the Son of God, John 20:31. Although recent events may have caused them to doubt, contrary to appearances, Jesus had fulfilled OT NE expectation of the coming of God, and of Messiah, to deliver his people and save the world.

2. To instruct them concerning the way that these NE purposes had been fulfilled. Jesus had already inaugurated the NE return of the Lord to his people, accomplished the Paschal sacrifice, brought cleansing, forgiveness, freedom from sin, given the gift of the Spirit, raised up the New Temple,[274] and established universal worship. Moreover, God's purpose of subduing the world to himself is not finished, but his new heavenly Temple is now the headquarters of world mission and the place to which all nations shall flow. Furthermore, he has lifted up a standard signalling the end of "exile," drawing *all people* unto himself. All this is just the prelude to future bodily resurrection, the Judgement of the world, and the glory of the Father's house.

3. To Justify them, by a cosmic lawsuit, acquitting them from the judgement of the synagogues, the destruction of the Temple, and the shame of the world. More importantly, to enable them to understand their forensic justification and righteousness before God, by faith in Christ, that had acquitted them from the Mosaic penalty for sin.

---

271. Goodman, *Rome and Jerusalem*, 452–53.
272. Ps 2:7–9. See Kidner, *Psalms 1–72*, 51.
273. See Wright, *Perspective*, 56. Cf. 1 Thess 2:16; 2 Thess 2:2; Matt 24;
274. Zech 6:15. See Walker, *Holy City*, 163–64.

4. To comfort and assure them, despite appearances to the contrary, concerning the depth of the Father's love for them, in that he offered his only Son for their salvation.[275]
5. To explain the destruction visited upon Jerusalem and the Temple as the consequence of sin.
6. To demonstrate that the judgement of their *true* enemies—Satan, his followers, and sin—has already begun and will culminate in a last day judgement.[276]
7. To enable them to endure the sufferings and shame of the present age, as they look forward to the hope of the resurrection and an inheritance in the world to come.

In this way John would enable believers to continue to trust Jesus, the Messiah and Son of God, under their present trials. Though they would have felt their situation to be that of "exile" from the Jewish people, John's proclamation of the NE in Jesus would have signalled the re-gathering of the "exiles," to God, to belong to his New Covenant people, and the start of their pilgrim journey to the Promised Land.[277] In fact, John understands their situation to be comparable to that of Israel in the wilderness: they had already been released from the penalty of the law and from sin's slavery by Jesus' paschal sacrifice and were en route to the Promised Land of the Father's house. Nevertheless, the way was hard and the time a period of testing.[278] Just as in Isaiah, Yahweh could be trusted because he had predicted the future, so Jesus was in complete control of every event. He had predicted not only the destruction of the Temple, but also his own death and resurrection, and the troubles that would come upon the Church. The Johannine believers needed to continue in Jesus' word and to continue to believe that the Christ, the Son of God is Jesus.[279] Moreover, they must understand their present sufferings, analogous to those of Jesus, as being glorious.

---

275. Cf. John 3:16; 15:13; 1 John 3:16.

276. John 12:31; 16:8, 11. Cf. Carson, *John*, 442–43; Lincoln, *Trial*, 219.

277. The "lifting up of Jesus" in GJohn, alludes to the standard raised in Isa 11:12 for the return of the exiles from the "four corners of the earth" in a second Exodus. Cf. Glasson, *Moses*, 56.

278. John 15:20; 16:1ff., 33; Heb 12:5–11; Deut 8:2–5. Cf. Glasson, *Moses*, 15–19.

279. John 20:31. See Keener, *John*, 1215–16.

3

Ideological Feasibility: Can GJohn's Jewish OT Roots be Established?

"Laying bare the presupposed *Weltanschauung* [is] . . . essential to any precise understanding of the evangelist's thought."[1]

"To us Jews, the Fourth Gospel is the most Jewish of the Four"—Israel Abrahams (1924).[2]

THE EVIDENCE THAT JOHN is Jewish rather than Hellenistic or proto-Gnostic is in two parts:

1. The external evidence of the reception by the early Church.
2. The internal evidence of its concepts and terminology:

EXTERNAL EVIDENCE.

The "Orthodox Johannophobia" consensus[3] suggests that the Church initially rejected GJohn because it was suspected of Gnostic tendencies. This theory has not gone unchallenged, however, and several scholars have put a different interpretation on the evidence from the Fathers and the recently published Nag Hammadi codices.[4] In particular, the reader is referred to the major recent study by Hill, which provides a significant rebuttal to the "three planks" of the Johannophobia paradigm:[5]

1. The silence of the earliest sources concerning GJohn.

---

1. Painter, *Quest*, 4. Painter envisages several changing situations, each with its own *Weltanschauung*. I argue for just one. I agree, however, that "laying bare" John's *Weltanschauung* (world-view) is essential.
2. Cited by Neill, *Interpretation*, 338. Cf. Burge, *Interpreting*, 20; Smalley, *John*, 65.
3. Outlined in the Introduction above. See Hill, *Johannine Corpus*, 13–55.
4. See, e.g., Braun, *Jean le Théologien*; Hengel, *Question*; Röhl, *Rezeption*.
5. Hill, *Johannine Corpus*, 62–65.

Ideological Feasibility: Can GJohn's Jewish OT Roots be Established?

2. Gnostic Johannophilia.

3. The suspicion of GJohn by pre-Nicene critics, particularly in Rome.

Hill finds that:

1. By disputing the necessity of a rigid formula quotation criterion, allusions to GJohn can be found in many early "orthodox" Patristic sources.[6]

2. Until Valentinians Ptolemy, Heracleon, and Theodotus, GJohn's use by heterodox or Gnostic groups was largely "critical or adversarial."[7]

3. There is no real evidence that the Great Church of the second century rejected GJohn. The Alogoi were either a cipher for Gaius or a grouping together of criticisms made against GJohn. Moreover, GJohn was probably well known in Syria, Asia Minor, Athens, and Rome, in the first part of the second century.[8]

INTERNAL EVIDENCE

Here I examine Johannine concepts that some scholars consider Hellenistic or Gnostic in origin. I argue that not only is this misconceived, Hellenistic and Gnostic ideas being alien to Johannine thought, but the concepts are fully explained by the OT NE paradigm:

"Hellenistic" concepts

The Johannine concept of the Word is sometimes seen as a reflection of the Greek *logos spermatikos*, reflected in Philo, synthesized with the Jewish concept of wisdom. But Greek thought, positing the eternity of matter, does not fit the Johannine Prologue that reflects the Genesis account of creation *ex nihilo*.[9] Neither does Heraclitus's[10] idea of *Logos*, nor the ideas of the Stoics who followed him.[11] Though Philo used the

---

6. Ibid., 67–71. See for example allusions to GJohn made by Ignatius, cited above.

7. Ibid., 466. He detects "underlying animosity" to GJohn in the *Acts of John*, *Apocryphon of James*, *Trimorphic Protennoia*, *Second Apocalypse of James*, and the *Gospel of Thomas*. Cf. Hengel, *Question*, 8–12; Dunn, "Let John be John," 312; Keener, *John*, 92.

8. Hill, *Johannine Corpus*, 468–69. He notes that artwork in the catacombs indicates early reception of GJohn at Rome. Cf. Glasson, *Moses*, 22–23, who also highlights this Johannine catacomb artwork.

9. Compare also Greek and Philonic ideas of the evil nature of the body, and the undesirability of bodily resurrection with GJohn's view of the resurrection.

10. See Morris, *John*, 115. The sixth century B.C. originator of the doctrine spoke of *Logos* as the eternal principle of order underlying the ever-changing universe, "sometimes as fire, sometimes as God, sometimes as Logos."

11. See Guthrie, *Theology*, 115. The Stoics conceived of ethereal fire, known as *logos spermatikos* (seminal reason), as the primordial source of all things. *Logoi spermatikoi* were forces responsible for the creative cycles of nature. Later Stoics embraced the highly pantheistic concept of the logos as a

term *Logos* in an attempt to synthesize Scripture and Greek thought,[12] there is little evidence that John showed familiarity with Greek thought,[13] nor did he attempt such a synthesis.

A more probable echo is the eternal,[14] creative (and predictive),[15] Word of the LORD (דְּבַר־יְהוָה). This fits the Genesis 1 context echoed in John 1.[16] Moreover, the personified Word is the eternal active agent of God, who proceeds from God (descends) and returns to God (ascends), to perform his works of creation, providence, judgement, and salvation.[17] This Word "came" to the Patriarchs and Prophets,[18] and goes forth from and returns to God to accomplish a second Exodus:

> As the rain and the snow come down from heaven and do not return there but water the earth, making it bring forth and sprout, giving seed to the sower and bread to the eater, so shall my word be that goes out from my mouth; it shall not return to me empty, but it shall accomplish that which I purpose, and shall succeed in the thing for which I sent it. For you shall go out in joy and be led forth in peace . . . Instead of the thorn shall come up the cypress; instead of the brier shall come up the myrtle; and it shall make a name for the LORD, an everlasting sign that shall not be cut off (Isaiah 55:10–13).

This passage has a particular importance for GJohn. In particular, Köstenberger posits "the evangelist's adaptation of Isaiah 55:9–11 for his basic christological framework."[19] Similarly, Dahms argues that Isaiah 55:11 "had a direct influence on" GJohn.[20] Thus the many references to Jesus having come from God (ἀπὸ θεοῦ ἐξῆλθεν) and going back to God (πρὸς τὸν θεὸν ὑπάγει)[21] allude to the motif of the Word going forth from God's mouth and not returning to him void without accomplishing his NE mission.[22]

---

world soul.

12. Philo used the *Logos* as a "philosophically respectable bridge between a transcendent God and this material universe," but he was inconsistent in his thinking. "Sometimes he speaks of the *Logos* as a 'second God,' sometimes as the one God in action." See Morris, *John*, 121.

13. See Morris, *John*, 117.

14. Isa 40:8. See Oswalt, *Isaiah 40–66*, 54.

15. See Lincoln, *Trial*, 46–47. See above.

16. As discussed earlier, in view of the Prologue's many allusions to the Genesis creation account, the Word, ὁ λόγος, alludes to God's creative word, Gen 1:3, 6, 9, 14, εἶπεν ὁ θεός, "God said," (εἶπεν, aorist indicative active, third person singular, from λέγω) which called the universe into existence.

17. Cf. Ps 33:6; 147:15, 18; Ps 107:20. See Kidner, *Psalms 1–72*, 136.

18. Cf. Gen 15:1; Jer 1:1; Ezek 1:3.

19. Köstenberger, *John*, 27. Cf. idem, *Encountering*, 53. Pao, *New Exodus*, 166, argues that Isa 55:11 lies behind the mission and activity of the word in Acts. He also links Isa 55:10–11 with Isa 45:22–24 and Deut 32:47.

20. Dahms, "Isaiah 55:11," 78–88.

21. See, e.g., John 7:28–29, 33; 8:14, 21–22, 42.

22. Dahms, "Isaiah 55:11," 80.

Ideological Feasibility: Can GJohn's Jewish OT Roots be Established?

Dahms further notes that συντελεσθῇ (end, complete, finish) of Isaiah 55:11 is echoed in Jesus completing (τελέω [cf. also τελειόω]) the Father's work.[23] It is significant that Genesis 2:2 (LXX) uses the same verb (τελέω) of God's finishing his works, καὶ συνετέλεσεν ὁ θεὸς ἐν τῇ ἡμέρᾳ τῇ ἕκτῃ τὰ ἔργα αὐτοῦ ἃ ἐποίησεν. It may well be that Isa 55:11 echoes this verse, and thus we have an instance of the New Exodus redemption being likened to a new creation.[24]

"Gnostic" concepts

Bultmann opines that Gnostic concepts were borrowed by the Church to make the Gospel understandable to the Hellenistic world.[25] For Bultmann, Gnostic terminology not only places its stamp on Jesus' GJohn discourses, but also it "runs through the whole Gospel and Epistles."[26] Moreover, John's ambiguous statements and concepts indicate "that he lives within the sphere of Gnostic-dualistic thinking."[27] Thus John presents Jesus' ministry in terms of a (demythologized) pre-Christian Gnostic redeemer myth: Primal man, from the world of light, is imprisoned in the evil physical world as sparks of light within certain pneumatic people. In order to re-gather these sparks, the highest god sends another light-Person to wake them and teach them passwords by which, at death, they may get past demonic watchmen and soar to the light world.[28]

Many scholars reject Bultmann's thesis, chiefly because there is no evidence of a pre-Christian Gnostic myth. Rather this is a retrojection[29] from the much later Mandaean documents.[30] Neither has the publication of the Nag Hammadi scrolls changed this fact.[31] Any borrowing that may have occurred is likely to have been done by the Gnostics—copying GJohn.[32] The syncretistic nature of Gnosticism makes this likely.[33]

---

23. Ibid., 80. Cf. John 19:28, 30; 4:34; 5:36; 17:4; 9:4.

24. Isaiah 55:10–13 suggests the removal of the creation's curse, by the replacement of thorn and brier with cypress and myrtle.

25. Bultmann, *Theology*, 1:164.

26. Ibid., 2:13.

27. Ibid., 2:14.

28. See Ibid., 1:166–67. Cf. Bultmann's summary cited in Neill, *Interpretation*, 180. See Yamauchi, *Pre-Christian Gnosticism*, 163.

29. See Meeks, "Man from Heaven," 45. Cf. Dunn, "Let John be John," 312.

30. See Nash, *Greeks*, 227. "There are absolutely no pre-Christian texts that support the existence of the Gnostic myth before the beginning of Christianity." Cf. Yamauchi, *Pre-Christian Gnosticism*, 164, "All the evidences cited . . . the Hermetica, the Hymn of the Pearl, the Mandaic literature—are of clearly post-Christian date." Cf. Colpe, "Gnostic Christology," 235. See, Dodd, *IFG*, 98, "There is no Gnostic document known to us . . . before the period of the New Testament." Cf. ibid., 130.

31. Cf. Nash, *Greeks*, 251ff.; Yamauchi, *Pre-Christian Gnosticism*, 187–249.

32. See Yamauchi, *Pre-Christian Gnosticism*, 166–67. He cites Grant, *Gnosticism*, 18; idem, *Historical Introduction*, 203; Cross, *Jung Codex*, 78. See also Dunn, *Christology*, 99.

33. See Dodd, *IFG*, 98. "Typical Gnostic systems all combine in various ways and proportions ideas derived from Christianity with ideas . . . draw[n] from Greek religion and philosophy, from

PART I—PRELIMINARY CONSIDERATIONS

Moreover, Gnosticism probably developed only as a parasite upon Christianity; even the pagan forms of Gnosticism only developed after Christianity.[34]

Even if Bultmann's pre-Christian Gnostic redeemer myth could be established, its basic postulates are totally alien to the Fourth Gospel.[35] Thus GJohn understands the physical world, including the human body, to be good, and the subject of the Father's redemption.[36] This is clear from Jesus' initial act of creation and his creative works performed in healing a cripple and a blind man, and in raising the bodies of Lazarus and of himself.[37] The circularity of Bultmann's argument is evidenced by his theory that John has *selectively* used Gnostic ideas: where Gnosticism cuts across such basic Christian teaching as Christ's humanity, John has resisted it as heresy.[38] Moreover, occurrences of future eschatological judgement and resurrection, that he cannot square with his model, Bultmann attributes to a later editor.[39] Most importantly, every instance of Johannine "Gnostic" thought is far more satisfactorily explained from the OT NE paradigm as the following examples illustrate:

1. The ascent and descent of the Son of Man and Jesus' travel between heaven and earth are of central importance to GJohn.[40] For Bultmann they reflect the Gnostic redeemer—as do Ephesians 4:8–10, Philippians 2:6–11, and 1 Timothy 3:16, which *parallel Johannine descent and ascent*.[41] Many scholars, however, would think these latter passages are better explained as alluding to the OT and few would accuse the Pastorals of Gnosticism. Ephesians 4:8 cites Ps 68:16. Probably composed for the occasion of the ascent of the ark to Jerusalem, Ps 68 charts "God's victorious march from Egypt [before his people], with its culmination at Jerusalem."[42] Interestingly, the Targums and midrash apply Psalm 68 to Moses' ascent of Mount Sinai, where he received the law.[43] Ephesians 4:8–10 applies Ps 68 to Jesus, who having descended to the lowest parts of the earth has redeemed his people in a NE and "ascended far above all the heavens."[44]

Jewish scriptures, probably from Iranian and other oriental traditions."

34. So Pétrement, "Colloque," 362, cited by Yamauchi, *Pre-Christian Gnosticism*, 20.

35. See Yamauchi, *Pre-Christian Gnosticism*, 34, who speaks of a "great gulf between both the concepts and the language used by John and the Gnostic texts as recovered in the Nag Hammadi library."

36. Cf. John 1:3; 3:16; 12:32.

37. For example, in John 7:23, Jesus refers to the John 5 healing in terms of his making "the whole man well." See Brodie, *John*, 249. Raising the dead is not alien to John, introduced by a questionable editor. Cf. Wright, *RSG*, 441ff.

38. Bultmann, *Theology*, 1:169, citing 1 John 2:22; 4:2, 15; 5:1, 5–8; 2 John 7:1; 1 John 5:6. Cf. ibid., 2:40–41.

39. Ibid., 2:39.

40. See Dunn, "Let John be John," 317.

41. Bultmann, *Theology*, 1:175–77.

42. Kidner, *Psalms 1–72*, 238. Cf. 2 Sam 6:12.

43. See Braude, *Midrash on Psalms*, 1:545, citing Exod 19:3.

44. Eph 4:10. See similar ideas in Ps 132:8, "Arise, O Lord, and go to your resting place, you and

Ideological Feasibility: Can GJohn's Jewish OT Roots be Established?

Importantly, in GJohn, Jesus' descent from and ascent to heaven employ similar Exodus and NE typology. Moses descended from the mount of God when sent to deliver Israel from Egypt and, having completed his mission and returned with the people, he ascended the mountain to meet with God and receive the law and heavenly design of the Tabernacle.[45] As Beale argues, Sinai was a mountain-Temple and a microcosm of heaven and earth.[46] Ultimately the mountain-Temple of God was to be Zion where God would ascend with his ark, into his rest among his people. In GJohn Jesus descends from God's presence (like Moses) to lead a NE and ascends back to God from Jerusalem to the new Temple of his Father's house.[47] Similar Temple imagery, used in connection with ascent and descent, is found in John 1:51 where Jesus is represented by Jacob's ladder, understood as the "house of God and . . . gate of heaven," Gen 28:17.

Philippians 2:6–11 echoes the Servant's voluntary humiliation and subsequent exaltation as the reward for his vicarious suffering.[48] But there is also an important allusion to Isa 45:22–24, "every knee shall bow."[49] Here, as in Isa 55:10–13, the *word* that has *gone forth from* [God's] *mouth* does not return (void), but will accomplish the cosmic subjection of creation to the Lord. As we have observed, the Isa 55:10–13 descent and ascent of God's Word, having accomplished the NE mission, is a paradigm for Jesus' mission.

In GJohn, Jesus comes into the world when as God's Word he becomes flesh and "tabernacles" among us.[50] As in Philippians, God becomes a man and offers perfect obedience to his Father, suffering death upon the cross. As a result of this, as his reward, he is glorified: lifted up, raised from the dead, and ascends to his Father.[51] Moreover, Jesus also speaks of his descent and ascent as that of the Son of Man, echoing Daniel 7, where a divine-human figure suffers and is exalted.[52] Thus GJohn interprets Jesus' descent and ascent in terms of the OT paradigm where the Son of man, God's Servant, suffers before his exaltation.[53]

2. Bultmann thinks Jesus' not acting of himself (ἀφ' ἑαυτοῦ) but doing what he sees the Father doing, John 5:19–22, echoes the Gnostic Redeemer. Though he admits

---

the ark of your might." Augustine applies this to Jesus' resurrection. See Hanson, *Prophetic*, 71–72. According to the Midrash on the Psalms it points to the messianic age.

45. See the comparison between Moses and Jesus in John 1:17–18.
46. Beale, *Temple*, 105.
47. Cf. John 13:3; 17:8, 13; 14:2. On the Mosaic Exodus typology see on John 6 below.
48. Isa 52:13–53:12. See Oswalt, *Isaiah 40–66*, 378.
49. Phil 2:10. See Silva, *Philippians*, 127–28.
50. John 1:14. See Bruce, *John*, 40–41.
51. John 12:23. Cf. Bruce, *John*, 264; Barrett, *John*, 258.
52. See below. See Brown and Moloney, *Introduction*, 10, where Moloney speaks of Brown's connection between the Son of Man and Ascent/descent as a determining feature.
53. See Dodd, "Old Testament in the New," 174, cited above.

PART I—PRELIMINARY CONSIDERATIONS

the similarity between this *modus operandi* and that of the prophets who spoke "not of themselves," Bultmann thinks that the differences are too great for Jesus' mission to be based on the prophetic model.[54] In particular, in the OT, the Prophet is never equal with God. Moreover, in GJohn, he says that Jesus speaks as the Gnostic "heavenly Revealer."[55] In fact, contra Bultmann, GJohn represents Jesus as a "prophet like Moses." God's sending Moses to deliver Israel at the Exodus is a type of his sending Jesus into the world to deliver the NE "sons of God."[56] But Jesus is much more than a prophet. The distinction is illustrated by the Synoptic parable of the Wicked Vinedressers where, having sent his servants to the tenants, he finally sends his Son.[57] Derrett argues that the slaves were unable legally to represent the owner because in order "to plead one's cause *through* an agent—one must actually transfer one's right to the 'representative'. Therefore the son had to be sent."[58] This concept is reflected in GJohn where, as God's Son, Jesus is appointed his heir—the Father giving all things into his hand. As Ashton notes,

> The phrase διδόναι ἐν τῇ χειρὶ (= ביד נתן), 'to give into the hand (of)' is a formal expression signifying the transmission of authority—authority in the first place over the owners (in this case the father's) property.[59]

He remarks that God's plenipotentiary powers, including the power to bestow life and authority to judge, were bestowed on Jesus from the very beginning of his mission.[60]

3. For Schnackenburg, the voice of the Son of God that calls from death to life, John 5:24–25, has its origin in the "'call' of the gnostic envoy" that awakens the pneumatics out of their sleep.[61] The opposite realms of life and death are "spatial," analogous to the Mandaean House of life and House of death.[62] He believes that this "must undoubtedly" be so, because there is not an analogous call in Jewish writings.[63]

---

54. Bultmann, *John*, 249–50. Cf. Dodd, *IFG*, 254ff.

55. Bultmann, *John*, 249.

56. Cf. Glasson, *Moses*, 80. "If one looks up the word 'sent' in a concordance he will find many cases where the word is used of Moses, and he will wonder if some of the involved and circuitous explanations of the Johannine 'sent one' have not missed a source which lies much closer at hand." Cf. Reim, *alttestamentalchen Hintergrund*, 130–32; Motyer, *Your Father*, 136.

57. Mark 12:1–11.

58. Derrett, "Wicked Vinedressers," 302–303, cited by Ashton, *Understanding*, 320 (emphasis original). Cf. Hengel, "Gleichnis," 28–28.

59. Ashton, *Understanding*, 321–22. See his citation of Bühner, *Gesandte*, 195–98, on the concept of "son of the house." Cf. John 3:35; 13:3; 10:18; 17:2.

60. Ashton, *Understanding*, 323—25. Cf. John 5:21–22.

61. Schnackenburg, *John*, 2:111. Cf. Odeberg, *Fourth Gospel*, 192.

62. Schnackenburg, *John*, 2:109.

63. Ibid., 111. Though he acknowledges a similarity with God's calling into being the works of creation (e.g., Isa 48:13) and calling into existence the things that do not exist (e.g., Rom 4:17).

Ideological Feasibility: Can GJohn's Jewish OT Roots be Established?

In fact, contra Schnackenburg, not only are these Gnostic ideas alien to GJohn,[64] but once again the correct analogy is found in the OT Exodus and NE paradigm as analysis of John 5:24 indicates. Thus "passed from death to life"[65] has deliberate dual forensic and spatial connotations: Forensically, it compares with Paul's doctrine of Justification by faith.[66] Spatially, it compares with the Colossian description of redemption from the domain (realm) of darkness and deliverance to the kingdom of God's beloved Son, to partake of the inheritance of the saints in light.[67] Importantly the Exodus and NE basis of the Colossian passage is "widely acknowledged."[68] The analogous NE context of John 5 is explored later.[69] For now, it is sufficient to note that Israel was delivered from the realm of death (Egypt) at the Exodus.

The call echoes God's call recorded in Hosea 11:1, "Out of Egypt I called my Son." That God continuously calls is clear from Psalm 95:7–8, "Today, if you hear his voice, do not harden your hearts." In the OT Israel was unable to obey (hear God's voice). Under the New Covenant God creates an obedient people by his powerful Word, raising the spiritually dead to new life.[70] Moreover, since there is an "explicit [OT] link of life with the land and death with exile," in the NE he calls his people from realm of death to that of life.[71]

4. Though Bultmann considers Johannine "dualism" to be Gnostic, many scholars have pointed out parallels between GJohn and the DSS. Moreover, "the Scrolls consistently offer better parallels than do any of the . . . Mandaean documents emphasized by Bultmann or the examples of Philo or the *Hermetica* offered by Dodd."[72] Price draws attention to the *Hodayoth's* and the Rule's affirmation of a supreme creator God, unlimited in power or glory, who created two spirits, in which men walk—the Prince of Light (Michael) and the Angel of Darkness (Belial). This "modified dualism" is far closer to the two impulses of rabbinic

---

64. See ibid., 110, where he acknowledges some of the differences between GJohn and Gnostic thought.

65. John 5:24 cf. 1 John 3:14, "passed (μεταβεβήκαμεν) out of death into life."

66. Cf. Rom 3:22–24; Barrett, *John*, 261; Carson, *John*, 256; Lincoln, *John*, 203–4; Smith, *John*, 136–37.

67. Col 1:12–13. Cf. Beasley-Murray, *John*, 76. "He has crossed over from the realm of death into the sphere of divine sovereignty, the characteristic of which is life for all who enter it (cf. Col 1:13)"; Carson, *John*, 256, who makes a comparison with Col 1:13; Barrett, *John*, 261, "The believer has already passed out of the world ruled by death and entered the realm of eternal life"; Westcott, *John*, 1:193. "Death and life are, as it were, two spheres of existence"; 1 John 3:14.

68. See Holland, *Contours*, 279. He cites Klijn, "Jewish Christianity," 119–31. Cf. Martin, "Reflections," 37–49; Wright, "Poetry and Theology," 444–60; Col 1:15–29.

69. See my analysis of John 5 below.

70. See, e.g., Col 2:13. See Wright, *Colossians and Philemon*, 109–10.

71. Wright, *RSG*, 92–93. He cites Deut 30:9–10; 28:1–14, 15–68; 29:14–28.

72. See Brown, "Dead Sea Scrolls," 7. Cf. Robinson, *Priority*, 40; Smalley, *John*, 33–36.

literature[73] and the "ethical dualism"/two sorts of men in John[74] than to Gnostic ideas. So too are Qumran's predestinarian and free will tensions,[75] light and darkness struggle,[76] and the concept of God revealing his own glory.[77] Moreover, GJohn's "two world dualism," once thought to be "proto-Gnostic," was "[probably] already a commonplace conceptual framework in Jewish apocalyptic and wisdom theology,"[78] and is significantly different from Gnostic models.[79]

I argue, however, that there is a much closer conceptual background in the OT;[80] in particular in the fall and in the Exodus and NE paradigm. Thus the Prologue's (ethical) light-darkness "dualism"[81] points back to the separation of light from darkness at creation. Here two opposing realms are encountered: the realm of obedience to God, associated with the garden and the tree of life, and the opposing realm of obedience (listening) to the Serpent, associated with lies, death, and "exile." The struggle between these realms, sons of God versus sons of the devil, alluded to in John 8,[82] is evident from Gen 3:15 onward, where (following the fall) mankind is divided into two seeds. Represented by Cain, the wicked seed replicate their father's murderous deeds, departing from God's presence, while Seth's righteous seed call upon the name of the Lord.[83]

The struggle continues in Egypt where the bondage and affliction of Abraham's seed in an alien land is represented as a "dreadful and great darkness."[84] At the Exodus, light and darkness take on ethical symbolism where they separate the two nations: Israel, God's "son," enjoys light while "Egypt," their sinister oppressor, is plunged into darkness.[85] The return of Abraham's seed to the land, coupled with obedience to the Lord, is understood in Deuteronomy as leading to blessing. Failure to listen, however, would bring (Babylonian) exile and death.[86] The great lesson of Israel's history is that neither natural descent nor possession

---

73. Price, "Light from Qumran," 13–15.

74. See, e.g., John 1:12–13; 3:18–21. See Leaney, "Johannine Paraclete," 53–55.

75. Price, "Light from Qumran," 16. Cf. 1QH 4:21–22; 15:15ff.; John 6:37; 10:26–27. Cf. Carson, *Divine Sovereignty*, 75–83, 181ff.

76. Price, "Light from Qumran," 18–19.

77. Ibid., 18. Cf. John 1:12–13, 18; 1 QH 1:21, 29ff.; 4:27ff.; 9:35ff.; 10:20–21.; 1 QS 11:17ff.

78. Ibid., 19.

79. Ibid., 20.

80. See Barrett, *John*, 34. Cf. Painter, *Quest*, 37–38.

81. Painter, *Quest*, 44, emphasises light and darkness as "the dominant symbols which give expression to the dualism of both Jn and Qumran."

82. See Leaney, "Johannine Paraclete," 55, citing John 8:33–44; 1 John 3:7–12.

83. Gen 4:8–16; 25–26. See Leupold, *Genesis*, 225–26.

84. Gen 15:12. See Wenham, *Genesis 1–15*, 331–32.

85. Exod 10:22–23. See Bush, *Exodus*, 128–29.

86. McConville, *Deuteronomy*, 408–10.

of the law could guarantee obedience or ensure the blessing[87] and, ultimately, disobedience led to exile in Babylon.

Because of the failure of Israel to keep the covenant, the prophets foresaw that return from Babylonian exile must involve not only atonement for sin (a new Passover lamb) but also cleansing and "rebirth" of the nation. This is provided for under the New Covenant, where God would effectively raise his people from their graves, washing them from defilement, forgiving their sin, bestowing his Spirit, and thereby writing his law upon their hearts.[88]

This perspective is evident in GJohn. Jesus comes into the world that he has created, but—as the realm now controlled by Satan and "enslaved" to sin—it opposes him. He comes to his own people, the seed of Abraham, but since natural descent and possession of the law are insufficient to secure their obedience, many reject him, siding with the world.[89] Those who do recognize and receive him, however, show that they are subjects of new birth by the Spirit, which, as Nicodemus should have recognized, is to be understood in terms of the NE promises.[90] To ensure the gift of the Spirit, however, Jesus must take away sin and obtain righteousness for his people as the atoning Passover lamb and obedient second (last) Adam and Son of God.[91] (It was on the basis of this once for all time sacrifice, that God previously passed over the sins of the OT sons of God, Rom 3:25). John's "dualism" is thus very similar to Paul's last Adam theology, Rom 5:12–19, where all men are headed up either in the first fallen Adam or in the last righteous Adam, Christ.

I conclude that not only are Gnostic concepts alien and inappropriate to GJohn, but the ideological interpretative key is rather the OT Paschal NE.

---

87. Ibid., 404.
88. Cf. Ezek 37:1–14; Jer 31:31–34. See Thompson, *Jeremiah*, 579–81.
89. See Carson, *John*, 124–26.
90. John 3: 5–8, 10. See Bruce, *John*, 84.
91. Cf. John 1:29, 36; 7:39; 19:30–34. On GJohn's Second Adam Christology see exposition in Part Two below.

4

Theological/Christological Feasibility: Is GJohn Consistent in Its Theology?

THE MORE THE GOSPEL reveals theological tensions and conflicting Christologies the harder it is to posit a single great mind and a unified theological paradigm for Jesus' ministry. For Anderson, the fact that both Arius and Athanasius were able to draw on GJohn in support of their teachings is evidence that such tensions exist.[1] Though many scholars agree with this verdict explanations differ widely:

Source critics have attributed theological tensions to conflicting emphases within John's sources. Haenchen believes that differences are due to different "hands" behind the Gospel.[2] On the archaeological tell model, tension arises due to representation of the conflicting theologies of the different eras of the Johannine school. Martyn believes that an early "low" Christological era, where Jesus was considered to be a prophet like Moses, was followed by a period of "high" Christology, where Jesus was understood to be the Son of Man.[3] Brown, considering the Gospel to be largely the work of the Evangelist, believes that John has produced a synthesis, placing the school's different theological insights side by side.[4]

All of these solutions are problematic. Source theories fail because of the uniform style of the Gospel,[5] making it impossible to separate out sources. Moreover, apportioning sources on the basis of perceived differences in theology is arbitrary[6] as is evident in the substantial disagreement among critics as to the extent and nature of the different

---

1. See Anderson, *Christology*, 1–2. My response is that while Arius was in serious error, Athanasius interpreted GJohn correctly.

2. Haenchen, *John 1*, 259. Cf. ibid., 94–95, where he speaks of "two theologically diverging evangelists."

3. See Martyn, *History and Theology*, 101–43, esp.125ff., 132–34. Cf. Neyrey, *Ideology*, 18ff.; idem, *John*, 106.

4. Brown, *Community*, 52–53.

5. See Schweizer, *Ego Eimi*; Poythress, "Asyndeton," 312–40.

6. This criticism is levied against Bultmann by Anderson, *Christology*, 10, who demonstrates that Bultmann's assumption of sources rests on *theological* rather than stylistic grounds. This is a weakness in Bultmann, because it rests on three layers of judgement: 1. Correct interpretation of the text. 2. Accurate assessment of incompatibility. 3. Superior reassignment.

sources.[7] Furthermore, outside GJohn, there is no textual evidence that sources, such as the "*Semeia* source," ever existed. Theories of redaction are limited by the relatively early date of GJohn. As Haenchen admits, since GJohn was "probably published as early as the end of the first century" there is no time for "a whole series of revisions."[8] Nor is there any textual evidence.[9] According to Bauckham, the Johannine School is a figment of scholarly imagination largely based on sociological speculation.[10]

A more satisfactory explanation is available in terms of John's dialectic thought. Barrett argues that John was engaging in dialectical Socratic dialogue.[11] Anderson attributes the GJohn dialectic, not to *Socratic* thought, but to a developmental psychological model for John's faith: he was at the "dialectic thought" stage of faith that holds apparently contradictory views in tension.[12] Though I have reservations,[13] there is merit in Anderson's approach: focusing on John 6, he has demonstrated that "tensions" highlighted by Bultmann cannot be explained by Bultmann's source and displacement solutions but are better understood as internal to the thinking of the evangelist.

My own position is that while John is perfectly consistent in his teaching, his perception and presentation of Jesus Christ, an inscrutable person, both God and man, cannot but involve tensions in the mind of his readers. The finite cannot fully comprehend the infinite. Guided by the Holy Spirit, John accurately reports that which he has witnessed of Jesus. Nevertheless, the nature of Jesus' person, how as God he became perfect man and died for men and women, will always remain a mystery (truth once hidden, but now revealed) that is unsearchable in its depths and beyond human comprehension in its fullness. The deity of Jesus Christ and his perfect humanity, two natures in one person, witnessed by John and recorded in his Gospel, must be received and held as true, according to the principle of Deut 29:29:

---

7. *Pace* Kysar, "Source Analysis," 134–52. Cf. Smith, "Sources," 336–51; Anderson, *Christology*, 49–52. Anderson points out that critical agreement largely depends upon the extent that scholars are dependent upon Bultmann.

8. Haenchen, *John I*, 257.

9. Ibid., 257. He thinks "an unpublished version of the Gospel was made usable successfully by a single editor." See Ashton, *Studying John*, 112–13, who observes that the concept of different editions of John is anachronistic and misleading. He suggests a better model is that of an author reworking or tinkering with his own work over a period of time. Cf. Hengel, *Question*, 49.

10. Cf. Bauckham, "For Whom," 19–26; Edwards, *John*, 102.

11. Cf. Barrett, "Dialectical Theology," 49–69; Hengel, *Question*, 199, n. 39; Lieu, *Second and Third Epistles of John*, 214–16. She thinks that the tensions in the Gospel are not indicative of layers of tradition or redaction, but are the result of the Evangelist's dialectical thought. See Painter, *Quest*, 62, 81, who, citing Barrett and Lieu, thinks that, *to some extent,* tensions might be explicable in terms of the Evangelist's dialectical thought.

12. Anderson, *Christology*, 142–66.

13. While I agree that GJohn represents the reflective thinking of the evangelist (on what he witnessed as an apostle), I disagree that GJohn reflects a historic dialogue between the evangelist and his community, *pace* Anderson, *Christology*, 1off., and Hengel, *Question*, 53.

PART I—PRELIMINARY CONSIDERATIONS

> The secret things belong to the LORD our God, but the things that are revealed belong to us and to our children forever, that we may do all the words of this law.

God has not told us everything, but he has told us all that we need to know and we must exercise a "hermeneutic of trust,"[14] treasuring and obeying that which he has revealed, and humbly accepting that there is truth that he has not been pleased to reveal, much of which is beyond our comprehension. Similar tensions between election and free will, realised and future eschatology, salvation that is already experienced—but not yet final, must likewise be held together in tension.

John reflects and engages with a similar "tension" already present in the OT in terms of its messianic and soteriological predictions. Taking John 20:30–31 seriously, John's purpose was to demonstrate that the Christ, the Son of God, is Jesus. Following Jesus' own example,[15] he interprets Jesus' ministry in the light of the whole gamut of OT Messianic expectation. Not only is this diverse and elaborated by inner-biblical exegesis and biblical-theological development,[16] but "dialectic thought" also runs through the OT and Jewish thought generally.[17] Thus Barrett is able to speak of the OT's Law versus love, cult versus worthless sacrifice, and Judaism's foresight versus free will, judgement by grace versus works.[18]

A further explanation of the GJohn Christological "tension" can be found in John's use of the NE paradigm. Thus Jesus is a prophet like Moses and the Exodus is a type of the redemption that Jesus brings. Much more, however, Jesus fulfils the NE and New Creation where the Lord himself returns to Jerusalem and delivers his people. The tensions in this NE model are evident. In Zechariah, the Davidic Messiah dies for the people, yet seemingly it is God himself who is pierced.[19] In leading the NE, the Servant takes on characteristics of Moses but also of David.[20] Yet signs were expected of the prophet like Moses, but none of the Davidic Christ. Though clearly a man, the Servant is also spoken of in terms reserved for God.[21] Similarly, Daniel's "one like the Son of Man" is seen to ride the clouds like the Lord.[22] Ezekiel's Shepherd is both the Lord himself and yet David.[23] Thus for John to portray Jesus as the Christ

---

14. This helpful phrase belongs to Richard Hays, *Conversion*, 192. See above.

15. Luke 24:27, 44–47. See Morris, *Luke*, 370.

16. Cf. Alexander, "Messianic Ideology," 19–39; Provan, "Messiah," 67–85.

17. See Barrett, *Judaism*, 75.

18. Ibid., 75, 91, n. 49. Cf. *m. P. Aboth* 3:16; Josephus *War* 2:162ff.; *Ant.* 13:172; Carson, *Divine Sovereignty, passim*.

19. Zech 12:10. See Baldwin, *Haggai, Zechariah and Malachi*, 190–91.

20. For example, in Isa 52:13—53:12 the Servant has both Mosaic characteristics leading the NE and Davidic characteristics, dividing the spoil with the strong.

21. See above.

22. Dan 7:13.

23. Ezek 37:24. See Block, *Ezekiel 25–48*, 301.

Theological/Christological Feasibility: Is GJohn Consistent in Its Theology?

and fulfilment or antitype of the NE hope, it is natural that his Christology will reflect the multifaceted and diverse OT statements of that hope.[24]

This also applies to Johannine eschatology. Many of the OT NE predictions have a here-and-now, this-world expectation. But others can only be posited of a New Creation regeneration of the universe. John expresses this hope in Jesus both as realized and future eschatology.

I conclude that, holding *apparently* inconsistent teaching in tension, the Evangelist is perfectly consistent in his theological, christological, and eschatological portrayal of Jesus and also in his employment of the NE paradigm.

---

24. Cf. Dodd, "Old Testament in the New," 180; Painter, *Quest*, 15–16; Stuhlmacher, "Spiritual Remembering," 57; Hengel, *Question*, 85.

5

Literary Feasibility: Is GJohn a Literary Unity that Bears Witness to Jesus and the NE?

LITERARY CRITICISM HAS DEMONSTRATED the "essential unity" of GJohn.[1] Literary "aporias" have been accounted for on the basis of Johannine "awkwardness,"[2] his episodic "slide show"[3] arrangement of material,[4] his misunderstanding motif and subtle irony,[5] or as the product of over-subtle or inappropriate criticism.[6] Motyer suggests that discontinuities in the narrative and dialogue, such as Jesus' "unexpected" replies and actions, are literary devices with a rhetorical purpose, "gripping" the reader and causing him to "pause and search for coherence."[7] Moreover, as Culpepper demonstrates and as the following examples indicate, all the literary features of GJohn have a particular purpose:

The Prologue introduces the plot which in turn unfolds Jesus' mission.[8] The signs and symbols point to the significance of Jesus.[9] Viewed against a background of Jewish feasts, institutions, and laws, they show how Jesus will fulfil and replace these.[10] The misunderstandings direct the reader as to the way in which the Gospel is to be understood, including its use of "metaphors, double-entendres, and plurisignations."[11]

---

1. See Culpepper, *Anatomy*, 4.

2. Thus Culpepper likens the evangelist to the eagle: magnificent in the air, but awkward on the land.

3. See Culpepper, *Anatomy*, 31.

4. See Keener, *John*, 634, who thinks John simply assumes major chronological and geographical gaps (e.g., 7:2; 10:22; 11:55). "After this" (μετὰ ταῦτα) is a common chronological transition device e.g., in LXX Gen 15:14; 23:19; Exod 5:1; Josephus *Life* 427; John 3:22; 5:14; 6:1; 7:1.

5. See Anderson, *Christology*, 82, 92–94. For a survey of Johannine irony See Duke, *Irony*; Culpepper, *Anatomy*, 165–80.

6. Cf. Robinson, *Priority*, 17; Lindars, *Behind the Fourth Gospel*, 17; Kümmel, *Introduction*, 210.

7. Motyer, *Your Father*, 117–18, 156. Cf. Burge, *John*, 171. On the sequence of chapters 5 and 6 he writes, "John's literary efforts are not haphazard. If anything, a careful study of this Gospel shows that sequence and image are never accidental, but quite sophisticated."

8. Culpepper, *Anatomy*, 87–88.

9. Ibid., 189.

10. Culpepper, *Anatomy*, 173. Cf. Burge, *Interpreting*, 77; Brunson, *Psalm 118*, 147ff.; Neyrey, *Ideology*, 11.

11. Culpepper, *Anatomy*, 165.

Is GJohn a Literary Unity that Bears Witness to Jesus and the NE?

The responses to Jesus, of various characters in the story, help the reader respond to Jesus, according to the purpose statement of 20:31.[12] Moreover, the use of historical analepses (flashbacks) and prolepses (flashforwards) serves to situate Jesus' ministry at the center of world history as the bridge between Israel and the Church[13]:

Pre-history, Creation, Great events of Israel's History, Jesus' Ministry, Church, Consummation.

Importantly, these literary features support my thesis:

1. The historical analepses and prolepses suggest that Jesus and the Church are the fulfilment (*telos*) of Israel's history just as the consummation is the fulfilment (*telos*) of prehistory/creation, including the fall.

    Prehistory, Creation (including the fall) ⟶ Consummation

    Israel's history ⟶ Jesus' ministry, the Church

2. The key to the great event of Israel's history, the Exodus, is prominent.[14] This points in the direction of Jesus and the Church fulfilling Exodus typology.

Exodus, great event of Israel's history ⟶ Jesus and the Church, the greater Exodus

3. Key symbols (such as light, darkness, hunger, thirst, bread, and water) have strong associations with the Exodus and NE.
4. The feasts function symbolically by pointing back to the Exodus and forward to the hope of a NE consummation.
5. The signs, reminiscent of Moses, are NE signs.
6. The Prologue introduces Jesus as the Word of God sent forth to lead a NE.[15]
7. The plot is dominated by the Passover.[16] Thus Jesus ministry is framed by three Passovers, at its beginning, mid point, and end. Moreover, as Culpepper and Stibbe both note, these are used to mark narrative time,[17] a year elapsing between the first and second Passovers and a year between the second and third. During the third Passover, time "slows down," twenty-four hours being covered

---

12. Ibid., 145–48.
13. Ibid., 57–58.
14. Allusions to the Exodus include John 1:17; 2:13; 3:14; 6:3, 4, 14, 31ff.; 7:2, 19, 22–23, 37–38, 40; 8:24, 32, 58.
15. See my brief analysis under "Methodology" above.
16. See Stibbe, *John's Gospel*, 37.
17. Culpepper, *Anatomy*, 72; Stibbe, *John's Gospel*, 36–38.

PART I—PRELIMINARY CONSIDERATIONS

by seven chapters.[18] Moreover, Jesus dies on the cross at the very same time that the paschal lambs are offered in the Temple.[19] Since Passover commemorates the Exodus the inference may be made that Jesus' death is the paschal sacrifice that initiates a *New* Exodus.

---

18. Stibbe, *John's Gospel*, 37.
19. Cf. Ibid., 38; John 19:14.

6

Exodus/NE Scholarship on GJohn: What Have Others Said?

H. SAHLIN[1]

SAHLIN PRESENTS A THOROUGHGOING typology of the Gospel of John based on people and events from Exodus through 1 Kings 8. Christ is progressively portrayed as a second Moses (John 1–9), a second Joshua (John 10–11), and a second Solomon (John 12–13, 17). Some of the more important typological events include: the call of Moses, the water turned to blood, salvation at the Red Sea, camping at Elim, the manna, Yahweh's appearance in the cloud, Israel's complaint, water from the rock, the golden calf, the appointment of Joshua, Joshua's deeds, Solomon's riding to Gihon to be appointed king, and Solomon's prayer of dedication. These find parallels in: the beginning of the Gospel, the wedding at Cana, Jesus' conversation with Nicodemus, the Samaritan woman, the feeding of the multitude, Jesus' walking on the sea, the "Jews'" rejection of Jesus, Jesus' offer of living water, the woman taken in adultery, Jesus the Good Shepherd, the raising of Lazarus, the anointing of Jesus, his riding into Jerusalem, the Last Supper, Jesus' high priestly prayer, and his passion.[2]

Evaluation

Sahlin's progressive Christology, based on consecutive OT books, is a little fanciful and strained. But although some of his types are ill founded, such as the comparison between the golden calf and the woman taken in adultery, he does highlight important OT echoes in GJohn. Thus Solomon's riding on a mule to Gihon *is* echoed in Jesus' riding to Jerusalem as a Davidic King.[3] Moreover, he may be right to highlight the concentration of Moses typology in the first half of the Gospel. If anything, the

---

1. Sahlin, *Typologie*. Cf. Smith, "Typology," 330.
2. Sahlin, *Typologie, passim*.
3. See Brunson, *Psalm 118*, 194.

PART I—PRELIMINARY CONSIDERATIONS

Gospel's typology becomes progressively Davidic as the story progresses. Above all he points up GJohn's rich background and roots in OT Scripture.

JACOB J. ENZ.[4]

In a short paper, Enz proposes that John has modelled his Gospel after the book of Exodus, which is its "literary type." Importantly, Jesus is the "New Moses," and both books use of a series of signs to lead to faith in Moses/Yahweh and Jesus respectively. Exodus has twelve signs, climaxing in the deliverance at the Sea, where the people "saw the great power [of the LORD] . . . and they believed in the LORD and in his servant Moses."[5] Moreover, Yahweh appears to Moses, that the people might "believe you [Moses] forever."[6] This compares with GJohn's seven signs, climaxing in the sight experience of the beloved disciple and the appearance to Thomas, followed by the Evangelist's purpose statement, "that you may believe."

Enz demonstrates how this literary typology is reflected in the structuring of the Gospel after Exodus:

1. They share similar beginnings. Both refer to the sending of a deliverer who is unrecognized by his people and is associated with the sign of the serpent given in the presence of Israel's rulers.[7] In both, the early signs are met with a response of faith.[8]

2. Their general sequence is built around a series of signs, climaxing in hardening of heart or belief.[9]

3. Their latter parts show common concern for the Lord's own, for the construction of the sanctuary, and for the law.[10] They also include prayers of intercession[11] and end with the completion of the work.[12]

Enz draws attention to several other parallels:

1. He compares God's dwelling among Israel with the "tabernacling" presence of Jesus.[13]

2. He compares the divine name with Jesus' use of the absolute "I am" and connects

---

4. Enz, "Type," 208–15.
5. Ibid., 209. Cf. Exod 14:31.
6. Ibid., 208. Cf. Exod 19:9; Exod 14:31.
7. Enz, "Type," 209. Cf. Exod 2:11–14; 4:4–5, 29; John 1:11; 3:14–15.
8. Ibid., 210. Cf. Exod.4:30; John 2:11.
9. Ibid., 210. Cf. Exod14:8; John 12:37–40; Exod 14:31; John 20:30–31.
10. Ibid., 210.
11. Ibid., 211. Cf. Exod 32–33; John 17.
12. Enz, "Type," 211. Cf. Exod 40:33b; John 19:30.
13. Ibid., 212. Cf. Exod 29:43–46; John 1:14.

GJohn's predicated "I am" with Exodus themes.[14]

3. He connects GJohn's "lamb" with that offered twice daily in the Tabernacle.[15]

Enz believes that this literary patterning of GJohn after Exodus is deliberate, serving to interpret Jesus in terms of Moses. He is surprised that the term "covenant" so prominent in Exodus is absent in John, but thinks "John surely assumes it."

Evaluation

Enz has many important insights, such as the positive evaluation of signs as leading to faith. Moreover, the general parallels he draws between Moses and Jesus, such as their being sent, initially rejected, and their intercession, are valid. This is because John's use of the Exodus paradigm is valid. It is unlikely, however, that the Evangelist attempted to model his Gospel *on the book* of Exodus. Moreover, this literary model understanding has led to some strained interpretations.

ROBERT H. SMITH.[16]

Smith believes Exodus typology to be important for the origins and structure of GJohn. Surveying three contributions,[17] however, he complains that there are too many competing hypotheses that cannot equally be correct, and proposes four basic criteria for their evaluation:

1. Typological analysis must be sensitive to various typological forms and functions. In particular single detail types[18] must be distinguished from extended types that occupy a structural role in the NT.[19]
2. Typology must respect form.
3. Extended typology must account for all the material in the units being compared.
4. The type must accord with the theology of the work using it.

On this basis he proposes his own extended typology between Moses' signs *in Egypt*, Exodus 1–12, and those of Jesus in GJohn. Since Johannine signs reflect the Mosaic background,[20] Smith attempts to correlate seven of Moses' signs with GJohn's

---

14. Enz, "Type," 213.
15. Ibid., 214.
16. Smith, "Typology," 329–42.
17. Those of Enz, "Type," 208–51; Sahlin, *Typologie*, and Hunt, *Johannine Problems*.
18. For example, Jesus = manna.
19. For example, Moses = Jesus.
20. Ibid., 334. Cf. Deut 4:34; Ps 78:43–51; Dan 4:2–3; 4 *Ezra* 7:26–27. He cites McCasland, "Signs and Wonders," 149–52; Braun, "Saint Jean," 165–84, esp. 179.

seven signs in the order in which they occur: Turning water to blood corresponding with water to wine; the death of the firstborn corresponding to the raising of Lazarus and the death and resurrection of Jesus.[21]

Smith also attempts to find some correlation between the narrative of Exodus 1–12 and that of GJohn. He notes that Johannine "Jews" play a "highly stylised" role, similar to Pharaoh and the Egyptians, while those who believe in Jesus parallel Israel. He notes a link between the Exodus "I am" sayings and signs and those of GJohn. He also suggests the correspondence of a "new period" of wilderness wandering following the death and resurrection of Jesus to that following the flight from Egypt.

Evaluation

Sensing the impossibility of finding an exact literary parallel between the book of Exodus and GJohn, Smith has proposed criteria that enable him to pattern GJohn after a large section of Exodus (i.e. Exod 2:23–12:51). But he has failed to see that John is dependent upon the paradigm of the Exodus event rather than the literary pattern of the book. Thus, his criterion that extended typology must account for all the material in the units being compared is misguided and does not take into account GJohn's reflection of the NE modification of the paradigm in other Scripture. Moreover, it forces him to ignore the clear parallels between Jesus' feeding miracle and the wilderness manna, in favor of a more obscure parallel with the locusts. Such forced literary parallels[22] are strained and wooden. Nevertheless, his insights into the revelatory function of the signs, heralding the eschatological event, and the parallels between "the Jews" and Pharaoh are important.

RICHARD MORGAN.[23]

Morgan challenges an alleged Greek background for GJohn, pointing up its OT foundations. As the Logos, Jesus is both the *dabar Yahweh*, active in creation and redemption, and the eternal wisdom of God.[24] He notes GJohn's Jewish feast "framework" that commemorates Israel's strategic history and points to a NE "deliverance yet to come." As Messiah, Jesus fulfils such festal imagery as the (sin bearing) Paschal lamb, water from the rock, and the pillar of fire. Furthermore, the Gospel's OT quotations occur at crucial moments in the Messiah's life (such as the Temple cleansing and especially at

---

21. He omits the "colourless" plague of frogs, gnats and flies, Exod 7:28–8:15; 8:16–19, 20–32, and inverts the order of the hail and locust to correspond to the feeding and stilling of the storm, Exod 9:13–35; 10:1–20; John 6:1–15, 16–18.

22. For example, the plague on the animals, Exod 9:1–7, finds its counterpart in the healing of the official's son, John 4:46–54.

23. Morgan, "Fulfilment," 155–65.

24. Ibid., 163. Cf. Ps 33:6; Gen 1; Prov 8:30. Morgan rejects the Greek origin for GJohn's Logos.

Exodus/NE Scholarship on GJohn: What Have Others Said?

the cross) and the Messiah manifests himself in situations when Israel's hope is most evident.[25]

Importantly, redemption in GJohn is presented as a "Second Exodus," begun with Israel at the Exodus and consummated in the NE by Jesus' life, death, and resurrection. This is indicated by the Baptist's citation of the voice in the wilderness, by Moses typology, and by the emphasis on Exodus imagery: light, water, the serpent, manna, and God's tabernacling presence.[26] Above all, Jesus' death is set forth within the framework of the Passover that averted divine judgement and brought release from slavery. Morgan finds Jesus to be presented as the *telos* of OT Scripture. He is the Messiah, "of whom Moses in the law and the prophets wrote;"[27] the *true* Israel, who accepts Israel's Servant vocation.

Evaluation

Morgan has provided a brief sketch that contains important ideas for interpreting GJohn. Above all, he has unveiled the Gospel's deep foundations in Israel's Scriptures at the heart of which is the Exodus/NE paradigm. He has correctly shown that GJohn does not use "proof-texts," but interprets the story of salvation as fulfilled in Christ.

T. F. GLASSON.[28]

For Glasson, the "main events of Israel's story," from the Exodus to the conquest of Canaan,[29] are reflected in Christian experience as set forth in the NT.[30] In particular, the Christian life is analogous to Israel's wilderness wandering and Christ is the new Moses. Moreover, this typology has been understood by the Church and is reflected in its art and literature through the centuries.[31]

Glasson traces these ideas to the NT's interpretation of the OT Messianic hope that developed from the Exodus.[32] He notes that, for Israel, the Exodus was not only the "outstanding deliverance of the past," but also a paradigm of future salvation.[33] Thus, the Jews of Jesus' day expected a second deliverance analogous to that from Egypt and a second deliverer, Messiah, comparable to the first, Moses.[34] Importantly

---

25. For example, at the Feasts and in the Temple. See ibid., 157.
26. Ibid., *passim*.
27. Ibid., 165.
28. Glasson, *Moses*.
29. Ibid., 9.
30. See, e.g., Heb 4; 13:20; 1 Cor 5:7–8; 10; 1 Pet 1:18–19. See ibid., 9ff.
31. Ibid., 22–23.
32. He cites Klausner, *Messianic Idea*, 18. Cf. Fischer, "Problem," 111–30.
33. Glasson, *Moses*, 15.
34. Ibid., 20–21. He cites *Eccl. Rab.* 1:9, "As the first redeemer was, so shall the latter redeemer be

this "new Exodus," "second Moses," approach is a key to GJohn.[35] An OT and Judaic background is also a more probable source for GJohn's distinctive teaching than "circuitous" explanations (such as Gnosticism[36]).

Rather than expounding particular sections of GJohn, Glasson's method is to trace Exodus themes through the Gospel. Thus he provides detailed studies of such motifs as the Serpent, the gifts of water, bread, light, the Shepherd, and the Lamb of God. He notes how GJohn reflects particular rabbinic and Jewish interpretations[37] and how these were, in turn, later interpreted by the early Church. He also shows how GJohn has applied each theme to set forth Jesus as the reality foreshadowed by Moses and the Exodus. Thus, for example, Jesus is contrasted not only with Moses, but also with the Torah, thought of in terms of bread, water, and light. While the latter cannot impart life, Jesus is the "true"[38] life-giving reality behind these symbols. Finally, he compares the use of the same "wilderness terms" in GJohn and Revelation. He argues that in the Gospel they are used to support the evangelist's realized eschatological emphasis, but in the Apocalypse they support the Seer's emphasis upon future fulfilment. For Glasson, this makes it "difficult to believe" [sic] in common authorship of the two books, although common themes and vocabulary testify to their "common background."

Evaluation

Glasson's monograph provides thorough scholarship and balanced judgements and his work is an invaluable source on the NE in GJohn. He also demonstrates GJohn's roots in the OT and Judaism, suggesting that these are more likely his sources than Gnosticism. Though he does not provide a NE framework for interpreting GJohn, he has provided much important material and a sound exegetical example. His comparison of the eschatology of GJohn and Revelation, however, is too brief to be conclusive and thus gives little support to an argument in favor of their different authorship.

G. L. BALENTINE[39]

Balentine's wide-ranging study is divided into two parts. In the first, he investigates the background of the NE in the OT, Judaism, and the early Church. In the second he explores its use in the Gospels.

. . ." He also refers to the messianic pretenders mentioned by Josephus.

35. Ibid., 10.
36. Implied. Cf. ibid., 80.
37. Ibid., 11.
38. Ibid., 90.
39. Balentine, "Concept."

Exodus/NE Scholarship on GJohn: What Have Others Said?

In Part 1, Balentine emphasizes the importance of the Exodus to Israel as central to her history and cult, reflected in her credo, hymns, and feasts.[40] These in turn make Creation and Exodus the basis of Yahweh's kingship.[41] Moreover, with national apostasy, foreign oppression, and failure of the monarchy, Exodus became the prototype of the messianic hope and national rebirth.[42] Balentine traces the development of this hope from Elijah's desert experience, through Hosea, Isaiah, Jeremiah, and Ezekiel.[43]

This NE hope is further modified within Judaism: In the Apocrypha, reference is made to a future eschatological Prophet-Messiah, signs and wonders, and a NE,[44] and in the Pseudepigrapha a diverse NE hope is expressed.[45] The Qumran community modelled its life upon Israel after the Exodus, retreating to the wilderness in expectation of the messianic age after a period of forty years.[46] Josephus indicates a "widespread" NE (and new Moses) messianic hope.[47] In rabbinic Judaism also, the Exodus was regarded as a "prototype" for "messianic redemption."[48] This NE deliverance would coincide either with Passover or Tabernacles and last from forty to four hundred years.[49]

Balentine finds extensive use of the NE paradigm in the early Church in Acts 1–15, 1 Corinthians, Hebrews, 1 Peter, and Revelation. He finds a primitive Prophet like Moses typology, but thinks that this was replaced with an understanding of Jesus as "far superior to Moses."[50] He also highlights the motifs of the wilderness, "exile," pilgrimage, Passover, plagues, redemption, wilderness provision, and restoration.[51] In particular, he finds a baptismal typology based on the deliverance at the Sea, redemption from sin by the blood of the new Passover lamb, and Christian experience understood as wilderness wandering with the goal of a New Jerusalem.[52]

In Part 2, Balentine finds that Mark has structured his Gospel around the NE with Jesus as the new Moses and his disciples the new Israel whom he feeds in the

---

40. Ibid., 8–25. See, e.g., Deut 26:5b–9; Ps 66,77; Exod15:1–18, 19–21; Deut 32:1–43.

41. Balentine, "Concept," 12, 15. He cites Pedersen, *Israel*, 3:728, Cf. Bentzen, *King and Messiah*, 59; Mowinckel, *Psalms*, 2:228ff.

42. Balentine, "Concept," 26. Cf. Jeremias, "Μωυσῆς," 857ff.; Str-B 1.68ff., 85ff.

43. Balentine, "Concept," 36ff. Cf. Isa 10:24–27; 11:11, 13–16; Davies, *Torah*, 6–8.

44. Balentine, "Concept," 73–77. Cf. 1 Macc 4:46; Ecclus 36:3, 6, 11; 48:10–11; 2 Macc 2:4–8, 18.

45. Ibid., 81–83. Cf. 1 Enoch 1:4; 2 Esdras 13; 14; 2 *Bar.*; Ecclus 36:3; *Sib. Or.* 5:256–59.

46. Ibid., 89.

47. Ibid., 93. He notes the Mosaic characteristics of the messianic pretenders in *Ant.* 20:5.1; 20:8.6, 10; *War.* 2:13.4. Cf. Jeremias, "Μωυσῆς," 862.

48. Ibid., 98–105. Cf. *Ruth Rab.* 5:6; *Eccl. Rab.* 1:9; Meyer, "Μάννα," 462–66; Str-B 2.481; *Exod. Rab.* 2:4; *Song Rab.* 1:8; Str-B 1.86.

49. Balentine, "Concept," 105. Cf. *b. Sanhedrin* 99a., 669.

50. Balentine, "Concept," 118. Cf. Acts 7; Teeple, *Eschatological Prophet*, 94.

51. Ibid., 114–83. See, e.g., 1 Cor 5:6–8; 10:1–13; Heb 3:1–4:11; 11:1–13:14; Rev 2:17.

52. Ibid., 155–67. Cf. 1 Pet 1:13–19; 3:19–22; Rev 1:5b–6; 5:9–10; Selwyn, *First Peter*, 144, 146.

wilderness and rescues at the sea.⁵³ As the "eschatological Passover," Jesus initiates the final deliverance and, as the "new Joshua," completes the NE by his conquest of death. Matthew and Luke have not only understood Mark's interpretation, but also have heightened it with their own additions⁵⁴

For GJohn, Balentine finds that while the Gospel adopts the NE paradigm, it has not followed the Synoptics. Thus John has not used the wilderness or journey motifs, but has structured his Gospel around three Passovers. Within these he incorporates materials from other Jewish festivals.⁵⁵ Jesus is seen to accomplish the NE deliverance by his tabernacling presence and as the Paschal lamb who lays down his life for the sins of the world.⁵⁶ John has also incorporated the NE into his Christology: "Such leading Christological concepts as the Lamb of God, the greater than Moses, the 'I am,' and the Tabernacling Presence . . . have come directly out of the Exodus tradition."⁵⁷ The major difference between GJohn and the Synoptics, however, is eschatological. Thus in GJohn, there is no concept of a NE journey to a goal [*sic*] with the danger of falling by the wayside. Rather, the NE goal of passage from death to life is realized in the present.

Evaluation

Balentine has succeeded in producing a valuable overview of the development of the NE hope within the OT and Judaism and has demonstrated its importance to the NT generally and to the Gospels in particular. While he has provided important insights into the NE in GJohn, however, the vast scope of his work has meant that he has been unable to treat this Gospel in sufficient detail.⁵⁸ His paschal framework and christological NE emphases are important, but, as I will seek to show, GJohn *does* utilize the NE journey motif and employs a future, as well as a realized NE eschatological goal.

A. C. BRUNSON⁵⁹

Brunson's work is a major investigation of the presence and function of Psalm 118 in GJohn. His method is to combine "intertextuality" with study of the mediation of Scripture through Intertestamental and rabbinic literature. His procedure is to analyze the Psalm's use in its Jewish setting, and within the Synoptics, prior to investigation within GJohn.

---

53. Balentine, "Concept," 267.
54. Ibid., 271–307; 310–43. Cf. Luke 9:51–18:14.
55. Ibid., 394–409.
56. Ibid., 377–87.
57. Ibid., 410.
58. Just 61 of his 436 pages are devoted to GJohn.
59. Brunson, *Psalm 118*.

Exodus/NE Scholarship on GJohn: What Have Others Said?

Though Psalm 118's *Sitz im Leben* is elusive, Brunson connects its earliest usage with the Autumn Festival. In particular he thinks it was probably used in celebration of the kingship of Yahweh and his vice-regent David, where the king re-enacted his humiliation and subsequent exaltation by the Lord.[60] He notes the connection of the Psalm not only with Tabernacles, but also, as part of the (Egyptian) *Hallel*, with Dedication and Passover. These feasts, and the *Hallel*,[61] all came to have eschatological and messianic significance for Second Temple Jews, who increasingly viewed themselves as in continuing "exile" and longed for deliverance consummate with the return of Yahweh.[62]

Having surveyed the use of Psalm 118 in the Synoptics and made broad comparisons with GJohn,[63] Brunson sketches the general context of GJohn's use of the Psalm, including his use of OT quotations and the NE motif. He finds that John employs extensive complex allusions to Scripture, his "fundamental background,"[64] especially to "eschatological" passages that send the reader to search the OT context. OT symbolism is also important, especially that connected with the Feasts. The latter form an interpretative framework for the Gospel. Moreover, GJohn's "replacement" of Jewish institutions by Jesus[65] "provides a pattern" that is of fundamental importance to GJohn.[66]

Citing Wright, Brunson argues that many Second Temple Jews saw themselves as living in a state of "exile," awaiting the inauguration of the eschatological era.[67] He understands their NE hope to comprise return from "exile," defeat of their enemies, and the return of Yahweh.[68] In GJohn, the return of Yahweh is achieved not *merely* representatively (as for Wright) by Jesus as God's agent, but ontologically, by his mediating God's presence.[69]

Brunson's major allusions to Psalm 118 are found in the entrance narrative, the "coming one," Abraham's rejoicing to see Jesus' day, and "the door." In Jesus' Jerusalem entrance, the quotation of Ps 118:25–6, supported by contextual thematic parallels, becomes a pointer to the whole psalm, viewed as a Tabernacles processional enthronement of Yahweh's vice-regent and signalling the Lord's eschatological return to Zion. Moreover, Jesus "deflects comparison to . . . the Davidic Messiah, Moses, [and] the eschatological prophet."[70] Rather, the "coming one," "king," palm branches, and donkey, in the context of Ps 118, Zech 9:9, and Zech14, identify him with Yah-

---

60. Ibid., 44–45.
61. Ibid., 75, 82–83.
62. Ibid., 63–64.
63. See ibid., 133.
64. Ibid., 149. Cf. Hanson, "John's use of Scripture," 365; Chilton, *Templum Amicitiae*, 335.
65. Brunson, *Psalm 118*, 147ff.
66. Ibid., 153.
67. Ibid., 153.
68. Ibid., 154. He cites Wright, *JVG*, 201.
69. Ibid., 179.
70. Ibid., 281.

PART I—PRELIMINARY CONSIDERATIONS

weh, returning to inaugurate the NE. Similarly an allusion to Ps 118:24 (modified by Jubilees 16:20–31) in Abraham's rejoicing of John 8:56 points to Jesus' actualising the day of Yahweh's kingship and eschatological rule. Moreover, an echo of the "door," of Ps 118:19–20, in John 10:7–10 establishes Jesus as the Temple "door" and sole means of access to Yahweh.

Evaluation

Brunson's erudite work is an important contribution to Johannine NE studies—particularly in his understanding of Johannine allusions as contextual pointers and his identification of Jesus as the messianic vice regent of Yahweh, who fulfils the coming of Yahweh to Zion. His arguments are always very thorough, if at times a little convoluted. His focus on Ps 118, however, has meant that other important NE issues have been marginalized, particularly GJohn's Isaianic NE background. Moreover, in recognising Jesus' superiority to Moses and David, he has minimized the New Moses and messianic typology. Furthermore, as he admits, he has demonstrated the *probability* of a NE interpretation as the complex summation of individual symbols that could *possibly* be interpreted differently. The problem here is his bracketing of the historical issues concerning the Gospel's origin—without which the defining context of John's message is missing. In particular he makes no attempt to consider the situation of the original post A.D. 70 readers, or how John has sought to relate his Gospel to them.

CONCLUSION

In the first part of my work I have shown the scholarly interest in the Exodus paradigm in GJohn and the hiatus in that work commencing in the 1970s. I have suggested that this hiatus was caused by a combination of interpretative strategies that have taken Johannine studies in different directions, some of which have been perceived as inimical to NE studies. I have demonstrated, however, some of the weaknesses of some of these new approaches. Moreover, taking on board what are in my opinion the best of their insights, I have sketched feasible historical, ideological, theological, and literary alternatives conducive to the furtherance of NE studies in GJohn. Having surveyed and analyzed existing NE scholarship on GJohn, I turn in the second part of my work to my own approach, seeking to provide new insights that will further Johannine NE scholarship.

PART II

DETAILED EXEGETICAL EXAMINATION OF JOHN 5–10

7

Anatomical Overview of John 5–10

MY THESIS IS THAT the Paschal NE paradigm is key to the interpretation of GJohn. In this second part of my work I seek to demonstrate this, focusing attention upon chapters 5–10, which I seek to explore as individual episodes. Before doing so, I commence with an anatomical overview that will yield a roadmap of the chapters:

BEGINNING AND END OF THE SECTION

Many would agree that John 5 commences a new section, a turning point in Jesus' ministry, marked by an increasing hostility towards him by the authorities.[1] Their intention of destroying him, first suggested in John 2:19, now becomes clear, building to a concerted plan in John 11:48–57. It is significant that this hostility goes hand in hand with the "Festival Cycle,"[2] where attention is focussed on "the Jews,"[3] Moses,[4] the law,[5] the Synagogue, Jerusalem, the Temple, and its festivals. All of these, the Jewish people and their institutions, are particularly, for the promised Messiah and only Son, Jesus' "own." Thus the programmatic statement of John 1:11–12, "he came to his own, and his own people did not received him," is particularly applicable to this section.[6] Since this "coming" to his people is a NE motif, this section is central to the NE paradigm.

There is less agreement as to the Festival Cycle's conclusion. My own assessment is that this comes at John 10:42.[7] Though some would include chapters 11–12 in this

---

1. John 5:18. Painter, *Quest*, 22, notes that John 5 signals a change to conflict and rejection of Jesus. Cf. Lincoln, *John*, 190; Carson, *John*, 240; Brown, *John I-XII*, 213.

2. John 5–10. Cf. Brown, *John I-XII*, CXLI, CXLIV, 201–4; idem, *Community*, 49; Burge, *Interpreting*, 78, Fig. 4; Borchert, *John 1–11*, 224.

3. For an analysis of the referent of the Johannine "Jews," see below.

4. Moses receives nine mentions in John 5–10 compared with three in John 1–4.

5. See Brooke, "Christ and the Law," 102–12. He notes allusions to each of 10 commandments in John 7–10. Moreover, five commandments feature in 8:40–49. Cf. Pancaro, *Law*, passim.

6. See Meeks, "Galilee and Judea," 165. "The journeys to Jerusalem in John symbolize the coming of the redeemer to 'his own.'" Cf. Ashton, *Understanding*, 301.

7. See Painter, *Quest*, 28, who suggests that John 5 and 10 form a literary *inclusio*, with 11–12 acting as a secondary conclusion to Jesus' public ministry.

PART II—DETAILED EXEGETICAL EXAMINATION OF JOHN 5-10

section, they are in fact transitional, showing how Jesus' penultimate sign leads inevitably to his death and summarising "Jewish" unbelief at the close of the public ministry. Thus Stibbe sees John 5–10 as the "development towards the central point" of the plot (attained in 11–12), where the "Jewish" hierarchy, the "enemy of God," comes to the fore and conflict emerges between the "Jews" and Jesus.[8]

ANALYSIS OF ITS STRUCTURE

John portrays Jesus' ministry as a series of episodes.[9] In John 5–10 these are chapters 5; 6; 7–8; 9–10:21, and 10:22–39. John 10:40–42 is an epilogue that brings the entire Festival Cycle to a close.[10] Each episode follows a similar pattern: Set against a particular Jewish feast, somewhere in the background is either the Jerusalem Temple or a synagogue. Coming to the Jewish people,[11] Jesus finds a testing situation, often tragic, that reflects festal imagery and represents the situation of Jewish crisis that confronts him. To these people in crisis Jesus ministers by performing signs, revealing himself to be the Messiah and antitype of the Temple[12] and its feasts.[13] Though some believe, many of the "the Jews" (especially the "Jewish" authorities), feeling threatened, reject and oppose Jesus. Dialogue and discourse result, in which "the Jews" bring their lawsuit against Jesus and he brings God's lawsuit against them. While the "Jewish" authorities become increasingly hostile, determining to kill Jesus, and the crowds increasingly desert him, a minority gather around him as his followers. Jesus leads these outside the Jerusalem Temple and synagogue to belong to a new worshipping community that worship him in the Spirit and in truth.

WHO ARE "THE JEWS" IN GJOHN?

This question has perplexed readers of the Fourth Gospel, particularly in the light of GJohn's frequent "negative" depictions of "the Jews." Motyer writes,

> "The Jews" appear frequently [in GJohn] . . . notably as those who first "persecute" Jesus and plot to kill him (5:6–18), who call him demon-possessed

---

8. Stibbe, *John's Gospel*, 35–36. Cf. Moloney, *Signs and Shadows*, ix.

9. See Brown, *John I–XII*, cxlii. Dodd, *IFG*, 290, divides John 2–12 into seven episodes. Cf. Culpepper, *Anatomy*, 72; Brunson, *Psalm 118*, 146.

10. See Moloney, *Signs and Shadows*, 151.

11. John 6 is an exception in that Jesus travels away from Jerusalem and the crowds follow him.

12. Cf. Kerr, *Temple, passim*; Coloe, *God Dwells, passim*; Walker, *Holy City*, 161ff.; Köstenberger, "Temple," 97ff.

13. See Burge, *Interpreting*, 20, who notes that Jesus' discourses "presuppose knowledge of the theological symbolism behind the Jewish festivals (Passover, 6:25–59; Tabernacles, chap. 7; Dedication or Hanukkah, 10:22–39)."

(8:48) and throw his followers out of the synagogue (9:22), and who finally cry for his crucifixion (19:12).[14]

In the wake of the holocaust, this has proved to be a source of acute embarrassment and many scholars have sought to defend GJohn against accusations of "anti-Semitism" or, more accurately, "anti-Judaism."[15] Motyer for example, insists that GJohn's argument with "the Jews" is an argument "within family," one group complaining against another, paralleled by the language of the OT prophetic literature, and not to be identified with the later vile hatred of the Jewish people.[16] More importantly, by limiting the referent of the term "the Jews," many scholars insist that GJohn can be understood to speak about a particular historical group of Jesus' day, and not of the Jewish people as a whole. Furthermore, if we lived at that time we would understand the referent of the Johannine "Jews."[17]

Some would not accept this defense. Jewish scholar Adele Reinhartz speaks of her initial encounters with GJohn, in which "each Johannine usage of the term *Jew* felt like a slap in the face."[18] Moreover, although time has inured her to this effect, she argues that GJohn speaks negatively about the historical Jewish people and that "anti-Jewish elements are inherent in [GJohn]."[19] Importantly, she rejects attempts to limit the referent of the Johannine "Jews" to a particular group. Thus, she argues that the numerous uses of the word "Jew" in a variety of contexts tends to blur contextual distinctions and to generalize the referent to the Jewish nation as a whole.[20]

Against this argument, other scholars would urge that, "the Jews" cannot refer to the Jewish people in general, but only to some subset. As Boyarin insists, this is demonstrated in John 3:25, where JBap's[21] disciples are differentiated from a "Jew."[22] While many would agree with this position, the difficulty has been in trying to determine the subset of ancient Israel to which "the Jews" refers. Various attempts have been made to render "the Jews" as "the Judeans,"[23] or "the Jewish authorities,"[24] or the "powerful [Temple centered] party."[25] While each of these has its supporters, however, none of

14. Motyer, "Salvation of Israel," 93.

15. On the question of definition, see Dunn, "Embarrassment," 41.

16. Motyer, "Salvation of Israel," 93–94. Cf. Dunn, "Embarrassment," 52. "John's language is more the language of *intra-* Jewish polemic than of *anti-*Jewish polemic" (emphasis original). Cf. Ashton, *Understanding*, 140, 159.

17. So Motyer, "Salvation of Israel," 96–97.

18. Reinhartz, "'Jews' and Jews," 213 (emphasis original).

19. Ibid., 214.

20. Reinhartz, "John," 114. Cf. Kysar, *Voyages*, 149. "The impression the reader gains of the Jews . . . is blurred with ambiguity."

21. JBap here and elsewhere is an abbreviation for John the Baptist.

22. Boyarin, "Prehistory," 221.

23. See Lowe, "ΙΟΥΔΑΙΟΙ," 101–30.

24. See Von Wahlde, "Johannine 'Jews,'" 33–60. Cf. Bruce, *John*, 46.

25. Ashton, *Understanding*, 155. Cf. Boyarin, "Prehistory" 221.

them are without problems. "Judeans" makes good sense in John 11:7–9, but not in John 6:41 where "the Jews" appear to be Galileans.[26] The "Jewish authorities" makes sense of many of the Johannine references, but there are references to "the Jews" (for example, John 11:19) that do not denote the rulers.[27]

The "powerful [Temple centered] party," proposed by Ashton, is difficult to evaluate because of the tenuous nature of some of his arguments.[28] Importantly, he thinks that there is evidence of the term "Jews" being used to denote a particular religious party within the Jewish nation, that emerged at the end of the Babylonian captivity.[29] Moreover, Josephus hints at this in his discussion of the origin of the word Ἰουδαῖοι (the Jews), which derives from the tribe of Judah and dates from the return from Babylon. Thus the term applied to the group who returned from exile, who rebuilt the Temple, and were opposed by "the people of the land" (עַם־הָאָרֶץ, Ezra 4:4), who had remained behind at the exile.[30] The returnees regarded the latter as polluted and excluded them from the rebuilding work.[31] The situation is portrayed in the books of Ezra and Nehemiah which represents the "official position" of the "powerful party"; Ezra himself becoming one of their leading representatives.[32] The Temple remained a source of contention until its destruction and beyond. Although its importance was never questioned, its administraters were often perceived as being corrupt and its rites were questioned by various sectarian groups.[33]

In Jesus' day, the Temple was controlled by a coalition of chief priests and Pharisees, heirs of the powerful Temple centered group that originated with Ezra. These, Ashton suggests, were the Johannine "Jews."[34] As such they stood for a rigid Temple-centered "orthodoxy" against "the people of the land" and a large number of widely divergent "heterodox" sects.[35] That they were a minority is evidenced by the small numbers of their adherents, as listed by Josephus, compared to the wider population.[36]

Ashton further suggests that after the catastrophe of A.D. 70, the chief priests, having lost their power base, "regrouped," together with the Pharisees, seeking to

26. Cf. Motyer, "Salvation of Israel," 94; Boyarin, "Prehistory," 237; Carson, *John*, 292.

27. Cf. Motyer, "Salvation of Israel," 94; Bruce, *John*, 243.

28. As he himself admits. See Ashton, *Understanding*, 159.

29. Ashton, *Understanding*, 153.

30. Ibid., 153–54, citing Josephus *Ant.* 11:84, 22; Ezra 4:12, 17–22; Neh 2:17ff.; 3:35.

31. Ibid., 154. Ashton notes that Josephus refers to "the people of the land" as Samaritans. Cf. Josephus *Ant.* 11:19–30, 84–88.

32. Ibid., 154–55.

33. Ibid., 155, citing 1 Enoch 89:73; *T. Mos.* 5:1–6; CD 4:16–18; 5:6–7; *Pss. Sol.* 1:8; 2:2.

34. Ibid., 158.

35. Ibid., 151. Ashton acknowledges that his use of the terms "orthodoxy" and "heterodox" are anachronistic and uses them "loosely." Cf. Boyarin, "Prehistory," 216.

36. Ashton, *Understanding*, 156. He suggests that together they numbered some 10,000, compared with the "several hundred thousand" of the country's inhabitants. Cf. Josephus *Ant.* 17:42; 18:20, who, for example, tells us that there were some 6,000 Pharisees.

preserve their power and traditions.[37] This suggestion has been questioned by Boyarin, who argues that the early emergence of such a powerful controlling group is a myth, propagated by the redactors of the Babylonian Talmud.[38]

Boyarin's own proposal[39] is that "the Jews" refers to a "purity-oriented community" based in Jerusalem and its environs.[40] Like Ashton, he arrives at this conclusion by going back to Israel's history after the return from Babylonian exile and to the books of Ezra and Nehemiah.[41] He argues that those Judeans who returned from exile expanded the traditional endogamy principle, which precludes intermarriage with ethnic foreigners, to apply also to non-Judean Israelites. This resulted in a three-tier system consisting of an "inner group," an "in group," and a non-Israelite "out group."[42]

The "inner group," who controlled the Jerusalem Temple-State and identified themselves as the "holy seed" were known as "the Jews," a name that they had received in Babylon and which from the beginning was a "geo-religious term."[43] The "in group," "the people of the land," were regarded as Israelite "non-Jews." Their ranks were swelled as the Hasmoneans expanded the state of Judea and ruled the entirety of Palestinian hinterland, from Upper Galilee to the Negev, and the people who dwelled within its boundaries were included within Israel. Thus a mixed multitude of Edomites, Samaritans, and Galileans of remote Israelite descent became Israelite "non-Jews."[44] Although accepted as belonging to Israel, they were regarded with disdain by "the Jews," who they in turn resented. It is this tension, Boyarin argues, that lies behind the conflict between the Johannine Jesus and "the Jews." Thus he suggests that for GJohn, Jesus and his disciples belonged to the Israelite "non-Jews," at variance with "the Jews."[45]

This last point of Boyarin cannot be correct. In Christian tradition, Jesus' Jewish ancestry and descent from David is central to his messianic claims.[46] Moreover, this is no less true for GJohn. Not only is GJohn aware of Jesus' Davidic ancestry, necessary for the Messiah,[47] but he positively identifies Jesus as a "Jew."[48] Moreover, "in giving him [Jesus] the title 'King of the Jews' the Gospel is appealing to one of the best

---

37. Ibid., 157.
38. See Boyarin, *Border Lines*, 151–201, *et passim*.
39. Cf. Boyarin, "Prehistory," 223, n. 24, where he compares his position to that of Ashton.
40. Ibid., 235.
41. Ibid., 223.
42. Ibid., 225.
43. Ibid., 227, citing Ezra 4:12, 23.
44. Ibid., 227.
45. Ibid., 235.
46. See, e.g., Matt 1:1–17; Luke 3:23–28. Cf. France, *Matthew*, 25–35; Green, *Luke*, 188–90.
47. Cf. Bruce, *John*, 183–84; Carson, *John*, 329–30; John 7:42.
48. Cf. Kysar, *Voyages*, 152; Ashton, *Understanding*, 131; Carson, *John*, 218; John 4:9.

attested stories in the whole tradition."[49] Furthermore, John's inside knowledge and understanding of "the Jews" suggests that he also is a Jew.[50]

The distinction, however, between "the Jews" and "the people of the land" seems valid. Carson notes that, although "the people of the land" could refer to Israel or to the common people as opposed to the rulers, it ultimately signified the racially mixed people of Judea and Samaria as opposed to the "pureblood Jews" that returned from the exile.[51] Nevertheless, this in itself, "pureblood Jews" distinguished from "the mixed population," does not sufficiently narrow down the identity of the Johannine "Jews," which in most of its occurrences is used of a small section of the people.[52] Commenting on John 7:49, however, Carson notes that for the rabbis, "the people of the land" refers to "impious" people, "ignorant" of the Mosaic law and the oral tradition.[53] His citation of the school of Rabbi Meir is particularly appropriate, "If anyone has learned the Scripture and the Mishna but has not served as a student of the Learned he is one of the people of the land."[54] Thus use of the label, "the people of the land," seems to have been extended to a far wider group than just racially mixed people, and would have included all but the religious elite who had studied under the rabbis.

Although the rabbinical writings post-date GJohn, these attitudes fit the John 7:49 context where, at the feast of Tabernacles, the "Jewish leaders" (chief priests and Pharisees) insist that "this crowd [mob] that does not know the law is accursed." Clearly, the crowd was neither impious nor ignorant of the Scripture, and many of them would also have been "pureblood Jews." Rather, the attitude of the "Jewish leaders" smacks of an elitism that says, "We are the true Jews, who can not only trace our Jewish ancestry,[55] but who also have been schooled in the Law, and are the spiritual leaders of the people." Thus it seems likely that they referred to themselves as "*the Jews*,"[56] to the exclusion of others, and that John refers to them thus in his Gospel.

This is not the whole story, however, because "Jew" was also used in other senses in John's day, both of the Jewish nation, including the diaspora, and with geographical connotations, denoting the Judeans.[57] Moreover, a careful reading of GJohn shows that John uses the term in these other ways. In each case, the context is the key to his meaning.[58]

---

49. Ashton, *Understanding*, 134.

50. Cf. Westcott, *John*, 1:x–xx; Morris, *John*, 12–14; Keener, *John*, 89; Burge, *Interpreting*, 45.

51. Carson, *John*, 331. Cf. Ezek. 22:29; Jer 1:18; Ezra. 10:2, 11.

52. See, e.g., John 2:20; 3:25; 5:10, 15–18; 6:41–42; 7:1, 11, 13, 15; 9:18, 22; 10:24. Cf. Keener, *John*, 732.

53. Ibid., 331.

54. Ibid., 332, citing Str-B 2.468.

55. As could Paul, Rom 11:1; Phil 3:5.

56. Cf. Rom 2:17, "you call yourself a Jew."

57. See Ashton, *Understanding*, 153.

58. Cf. Carson, *John*, 141–42; Bruce, *John*, 46.

Who then are "the Jews" in GJohn? I suggest that Ashton's thesis is basically correct. The *primary* referent is to a powerful religious group, consisting largely of the chief priests and Pharisees, whose power base was in Jerusalem, who exercised control over the Temple and religious authority over the people. They were a small elite subset of the descendants of the returnees from the exile who primarily lived in Judea. GJohn distinguishes between these "Jews" and the ordinary Jewish people.[59] In general, it is the "Jews" who are the bitter enemies of Jesus. Their intractable argument with him is not because he is not a Jew, but because *being a man* he claims to be divine. The ordinary Jews are often sympathetic to Jesus or divided in their opinions about him. Even among the "Jewish" leaders, however, there are some who believe,[60] and thus, for GJohn, "Jewish" is not synonymous with unbelief. Moreover, that "salvation is of the Jews," John 4:22, indicates clearly that GJohn is not anti-Semitic, but understands the salvation of the world to have come through the Jewish people. Accordingly, throughout this book, inverted commas are used to distinguish "Jews," John's special usage, from the Jewish people generally, both then and now.

COMPARISON WITH THE EXODUS

How do chapters 5–10 relate to the Exodus? All the characteristic features of these chapters point back to the Exodus. The feasts mark the various stages in the history of salvation by which the Lord delivered his people from bondage and brought them to the Promised Land.[61] Moses and the law are reminders of God's bringing the people into covenant relationship with himself. Jerusalem and the Temple point back to a typical consummation of that process where God takes up a permanent dwelling among his people.[62]

Ironically, however, GJohn suggests that in the present situation Israel is again in bondage. This was indicated from the outset when, at his first visit to the Temple, Jesus found his Father's house occupied by merchants.[63] For GJohn, the "Jewish" custodians of the Temple, under their Roman overlords,[64] are morally responsible for the destruction of the Second Temple (as Pharaoh "destroyed" Egypt) by bringing judgement upon it.[65] Since the Temple is the place of God's royal throne from where the law is

---

59. Cf. Carson, *John*, 141–42; Brown, *John I–XII*, 428; Motyer, "Salvation of Israel," 97.
60. John 12:42.
61. See Yee, *Jewish Feasts, passim*.
62. Cf. Kidner, *Psalms 1–72*, 238.
63. Cf. Brown, *John I–XII*, 121; Evans, "Continuing Exile," 97; Keener, *John*, 524–25; Zech 14:21; Mal 3:1.
64. See Keener, *John*, 525.
65. Cf. Exod. 10:7; John 2:19; 11:48. Cf. Brown, *John I–XII*, 122; Barrett, *John*, 199; Kerr, *Temple*, 81, 88; Keener, *John*, 524–25; Motyer, *Your Father*, 39–42, citing Josephus *War* 5:412; *Apoc. Ab.* 25:1–6; *2 Bar.* 10:18; *4 Bar.* 1:1, 8; 4:7–8; *t. Menahot.* 13:22.

PART II—DETAILED EXEGETICAL EXAMINATION OF JOHN 5-10

to go out to all the earth, the focal point of the cosmos,[66] Jerusalem and the world are "in bondage." In this, the "Jewish" authorities are analogous to Pharaoh, who resisted God's deliverance of Israel by Moses.[67] Pharaoh did this by force, but the "Jews" do so by fear,[68] by their legalistic interpretation of the Torah, at variance with that of Jesus, and by bringing their lawsuits against Jesus.[69] Moreover, they show their own allegiance to Satan by manifesting his works, seeking to destroy Jesus.[70] Jesus' repeated coming to the Jewish people and his confrontation with the "Jewish" authorities and their supporters is analogous to that of Moses, who bearing God's name ("I am") and performing signs, demanded of Pharaoh, "Let my people go."[71] Jesus' final sign, his being lifted up in death, analogous to the paschal death of the firstborn, secures his people's redemption.[72]

JESUS LEADS A NE

The crisis confronting Jesus is not an Egyptian bondage, however, but must be understood in the light of the eschatological promises made in connection with the return from Babylonian exile. In exile the Israelites saw themselves as "dried up," with their hope lost,[73] but in the prophets God had promised to return to Zion and to bring Israel back to her land.[74] This NE would deal with the problems that had caused the exile: sin and idolatry would be atoned for and cleansed, a new covenant would be inaugurated, and the people would be transformed to love God wholeheartedly.[75] Moreover, a new eschatological Temple would be built, God would dwell with his people, his law would go forth to the Gentiles, creation would be renewed, and paradise restored.[76]

The Babylonian exile ended when, after conquering Babylon in 539 B.C., Cyrus proclaimed that the Jews could return to their own land.[77] About 50,000 Jews availed

---

66. Ezek 43:7. Cf. Wright, *NTPG*, 416; Walker, *Holy City*, 164; Goodman, *Rome and Jerusalem*, 177-78.

67. See Morgan, "Fulfilment," 158.

68. See Keener, *John*, 711; John 7:13. See my exposition of John 5 and 9, below, where the lame man and the parents of the blind man fear "the Jews."

69. See e.g., my exposition of John 5, below, where the "Jewish" interpretation of Sabbath rest conflicts with that of Jesus and consequently they bring a lawsuit against him.

70. John 8:44. Cf. Keener, *John*, 758; Barrett, *John*, 349; Brown, *John I–XII*, 357-58.

71. Reim, *Hintergrund*, 119-29, 132-40, finds twenty two references to the eschatological prophet in the Fourth Gospel and underlines the Moses background to the signs, finding several detailed points of correspondence. Cf. Smith, "Typology," 340.

72. Cf. Morgan, "Fulfilment," 158-59; Holland, *Contours*, 238ff.

73. Ezek 37:11. See Block, *Ezekiel 25–48*, 379-80.

74. See, e.g., Isa 40:3-11. See Oswalt, *Isaiah 40-66*, 51-55.

75. See, e.g., Jer 31:31-37. See Thompson, *Jeremiah*, 580 -81.

76. See, e.g., Ezek 40-47; Isa 2:1-3; 11:1-9. Cf. Oswalt, *Isaiah 1–39*, 117, 283-84; Brown, *John I–XII*, 122.

77. Ezra 1:1-4. Cf. Reicke, *New Testament Era*, 5; Pfeiffer, *Between the Testaments*, 19.

themselves of this opportunity.[78] Though the returnees encountered many difficulties, they eventually rebuilt the Temple and the city walls of Jerusalem. Moreover, although for many years they were controlled by successive Persian and Greek monarchs, a heroic struggle under the Maccabees against the oppressive Seleucid king, Antiochus IV "Epiphanes," led gradually to political independence in 142 B.C.[79] Under the Hasmoneans the frontiers of the small kingdom were extended to make it comparable to the territory ruled by David and Solomon.[80] Moreover, the inhabitants of the territories incorporated into the Hasmonean kingdom were assimilated into Israel.[81] Independence came to an end in 63 B.C. when Hyrcanus II welcomed the Romans into the land and "Judea... became once more a small temple land under foreign domination."[82] Even so, under the Romans, the Jewish people enjoyed a certain amount of freedom to worship God after their Mosaic traditions.[83] Under Herod the Great, the Temple was beautified and extended to rival the magnificence of Solomon's Temple.[84]

All this, however, fell far short of the prophetic vision.[85] Although the Babylonian exile had ended, Wright proposes that many of the Jewish people in the late Second Temple period considered themselves to be in "exile," under the dominion of foreigners. Moreover, "the glorious message of the prophets remained unfulfilled," notably the Lord's promised return to Zion.[86]

This proposal, adopted by several scholars,[87] has been challenged by others. In particular, Casey argues that Israel cannot be regarded as being "in exile" in Jesus' day because many Jews lived in Jerusalem, others came from all over Israel and the diaspora to the major feasts, and in the Temple the offering of the Tamid sacrifice twice a day was symbolic of God's presence with Israel. "We would need stunningly strong arguments to convince us that these Jews really believed they were in exile when they were in Israel."[88] Similarly, arguing from the advantages enjoyed by the Jews of Jesus' day, Goodman writes,

---

78. Ezra 2:64–65. Cf. Pfeiffer, *Between the Testaments*, 19.

79. Cf. Bruce, *New Testament History*, 5; Reicke, *New Testament Era*, 62; Pfeiffer, *Between the Testaments*, 94; 1 Macc 13:41–42.

80. Pfeiffer, *Between the Testaments*, 99; Cf. Reicke, *New Testament Era*, 69.

81. Cf. Pfeiffer, *Between the Testaments*, 100; Reicke, *New Testament Era*, 66.

82. Reicke, *New Testament Era*, 83. Cf. Bruce, *New Testament History*, 13; Josephus *Ant.* 14:74.

83. See Goodman, *Rome and Jerusalem*, 392–93.

84. Ibid., 194.

85. So Wright, *NTPG*, 268–72, 299–301; idem, *JVG*, 126–27, 203–4.

86. Wright, *NTPG*, 269.

87. See, e.g., Brunson, *Psalm 118*, 153ff.; Evans, "Continuing Exile," 77.

88. Casey, "Where Wright is Wrong," 99.

> The notion that the Jews in the late Second Temple period saw themselves as sinners permanently punished by God and in need of salvation from the sufferings of exile and Roman domination is a myth.[89]

This assertion has to be balanced against others, however, such as Goodman's statement that "the brutal reality of the Roman empire was that the power of the emperor could reach almost every corner of . . . [the Mediterranean] world."[90] Moreover, in the same context, he cites the passionate speech of Agrippa II before his fellow Jews on the eve of the rebellion in A.D. 66,

> Passing to your present passion for liberty, I say that it comes too late. The time is past when you should have striven never to lose it . . . when you should have strained every nerve to keep out the Romans.[91]

Considerable support for Wright's position has come from Evans. He argues that the "Action Prophets," Theudas and "the Egyptian," described by Josephus, may have considered themselves as Mosaic successors who sought to liberate the land, which was possessed by foreigners. Thus many Jews regarded themselves as being in a state of bondage and even "exile."[92] He also finds the "idea of exile"[93] and "exilic imagery"[94] in several Second Temple texts. Importantly, he finds support for a continuing "exile" in the Hebrew Scriptures. Thus Ezra describes the returnees as "slaves" and "bondmen" in the land.[95] Moreover, "exile" and redemption theology is also found in the Gospels. The appointment of Twelve apostles, for example, symbolizes the restoration of Israel's twelve tribes,[96] and the request for a sign (Mark 8:11–13) indicates an awareness that signs would precede the eschaton.[97] Moreover, Jesus warns Israel's rulers of a further future "exile" and of the destruction of the Temple.[98]

The position adopted in this thesis is that the exile describes a specific geographical and historical experience for Israel that came to an end with the return from Babylon. Nevertheless, Wright is certainly correct in pointing out that many of the prophecies, associated with return from exile, were not fulfilled at that time; in particular the glorious eschatological return of God to Israel, to gather the diaspora, and

---

89. Goodman, *Rome and Jerusalem*, 194.

90. Ibid., 68.

91. Ibid., 68. Cf. Josephus *War* 2:355–64, 370, 378.

92. Evans, "Continuing Exile," 78–82. Cf. Balentine, "Concept," 93; Josephus *Ant.* 20:97; 20:167; *War* 2:258–263. Cf. Bauckham's analysis in his "Jewish Messianism," 216–17.

93. Ibid., 82–83, He cites Sirach 36:10, 14–16; Tobit 13:3, 16–18; Bar 2:7–10; 2 Macc 2:5, 7, 18.

94. Ibid., 83–87, citing such texts as CD 6:4–5; *1 Enoch* 89:73–75; *T. Mos.* 4:8–9; *2 Bar.* 68:5–7; Josephus *War* 5:375–419.

95. Ibid., 83–87. Cf. Ezra 9:8–9; Neh 9:36.

96. Evans, "Continuing Exile," 92. Cf. Sanders, *Jesus and Judaism*, 98; Wright, *JVG*, 430–31.

97. Evans, "Continuing Exile," 93. Cf. Deut 13:1–3; 18:21–22; Isa 7:10–14; Jer 44:29.

98. Ibid., 98 –97. He cites Luke 13:34–35; 19:41–44; Matt 23:37–38.

the exaltation of Israel above the nations.[99] In Jesus' day these cherished hopes were expressed in the celebrations of the Jewish feasts, particularly Tabernacles.[100] Moreover, although many Second Temple Jews would not have considered themselves to be in "exile," some at least did consider their experience to be analogous to that of bondage and "exile." Importantly this is reflected not only in the Synoptic Gospels, but also in GJohn. Thus "the Jews" of John 8 consider that they have never been in bondage to anyone, but Jesus warns them that they are in bondage to sin and thus liable to be cast out of God's house.[101] In John 6:14-15, the crowd, having seen the sign that Jesus performed, seek to make him their political deliverer.[102] In John 5 and 10, Jesus' healings of the lame and the blind are NE signs, pointing to eschatological deliverance.[103] It was to this situation of bondage that Jesus came, to fulfil God's promised return to his people and to deliver them from "exile" (exile from God) in a NE. Accordingly, throughout this thesis inverted commas are used to distinguish this analogical use of "exile" from the Babylonian exile.

WHY DOES JESUS VISIT THE TEMPLE?

Although the Temple was God's royal seat, and the center of Messiah's worldwide kingdom, in Jesus' first visit, John 2:13-22, he signals that it is under God's judgement and will soon be destroyed.[104] Jesus will nevertheless raise up the Temple of his body in its stead.[105] Why then did Jesus repeatedly return to the Temple? Jesus was fulfilling the promise of Yahweh's return to Zion to lead a NE[106] and the Temple was the central sanctuary, the place where God's people (sheep) gathered. He would call the people to believe on him as the NE fulfilment of the symbolism of the Temple and its feasts, which delineated God's eschatological timetable of salvation. He could not do this at a distance, however, but must identify with the Temple and its feasts as the one who fulfils their symbolism.[107] Moreover, it is against the background of the feasts that Jesus performs his signs. These are creative acts that signal the coming of God among his people to lead them out of bondage that they might follow him in a NE that leads to a new creation.[108]

---

99. Cf. Wright, *NTPG*, 269, 271, 30; idem, *JVG*, 126, 205-6; Oswalt, *Isaiah 40-66*; 52.

100. Cf. Moloney, *Signs and Shadows*, 67; Yee, *Jewish Feasts*, 75-77. See below on John 7-8.

101. See Moloney, *Signs and Shadows*, 105.

102. See Keener, *John*, 670-71.

103. Cf. Carson, *John*, 243; Motyer, *Your Father*, 137-39. See my exposition below on John 5 and 9.

104. See Goodman, *Rome and Jerusalem*, 445. Cf. Motyer, *Your Father*, 39-42; Josephus *War* 5:412; *Apoc. Ab.* 25:1-6; *2 Bar.* 10:18.

105. Cf. Brown, *John I-XII*, 122; Walker, *Holy City*, 165-66, 170; Ezek 40-46; John 2:19-21.

106. See, e.g., Isa 40:1-11; 59:20; Mal 3:1. See Brunson, *Psalm 118*, 175-76.

107. Cf. Brown, *John I-XII*, lxx; Walker, *Holy City*, 167.

108. See my exposition of John 5 below.

PART II—DETAILED EXEGETICAL EXAMINATION OF JOHN 5–10

In chapters 5–10, however, Jesus progressively withdraws from the Temple, John 10:22–39 being his last visit recorded in GJohn. Why does he withdraw? In Ezekiel's day, failure of the people to obey God led to the progressive withdrawal of the glory of the Lord from the Temple signifying that its destruction was at hand.[109] Similarly, Jesus withdraws, because of the progressive failure of the people to hear him, signifying that the Second Temple will no longer be the locus of God's presence, but will soon be destroyed.[110] Jesus has now fully manifested God's presence among the people in the Tabernacle of his body.[111] Moreover, as the Mosaic Tabernacle led Israel to the Promised Land, and as the Lord promised to lead the Babylonian exiles back to Zion, Isa 52:12, so Jesus leads his followers out of the old Temple.

WHERE DOES JESUS LEAD HIS PEOPLE?

Balentine understands Jesus' deliverance of his people in terms of realized eschatology. Brunson maintains that Israel's re-gathering is spiritual.[112] Certainly realized eschatology is prominent in GJohn. Jesus translates his people from being under the dominion of the law of sin and death into the domain of eternal life. He leads them out of bondage to sin unto the freedom of the sons of God.[113] Alongside this, however, and in perfect harmony with it, is a future eschatology. The present enjoyment of eternal life is only the beginning. The ultimate destination to which Jesus leads his people is his Father's house, John 14:2, to which Jesus goes before to prepare a dwelling place for them. As Walker notes, most commentators (correctly) understand this as a reference to heaven, but as indicated in John 2, Jesus' Father's house *also* refers to the new Temple of Jesus' body. Ultimately it also incorporates believers who become consecrated dwelling places for God's Spirit.[114]

That this is not a mere spiritual release and re-gathering (*pace* Brunson and Balentine) is evident from Jesus' physical resurrection and ascension, his promised return, his resurrection of the dead, and Judgement of the world on the last day, all integral to GJohn. These concepts are compatible with Revelation where the redeemed are brought into the Father's house, the New Jerusalem, which descends to earth from God on the last day. Here the Johannine symbolism (water, manna, light) of eternal life is fulfilled and the new Temple is the Lord God and the Lamb, dwelling among God's people, effectively making the whole of the new creation God's Temple.

---

109. Ezek 10:1–22. See Block, *Ezekiel 1–24*, 317–27.
110. Cf. Davies, *Gospel and the Land*, 295; Kerr, *Temple*, 248; Carson, *John*, 127–28.
111. John 1:14, 18.
112. Brunson, *Psalm 118*, 178.
113. See Smith, *Theology*, 81–82. Cf. John 1:12; 8:32.
114. John 17:17–19; 20:22. Cf. Walker, *Holy City*, 171.

HOW DOES JESUS ACCOMPLISH THE NE?

He initiates it by his vicarious paschal death whereby he inaugurates the new covenant, makes atonement for his people, provides cleansing for their sins, ransoms them from the domain of death, bestows the Holy Spirit, and casts out Satan.[115] His lifting up on the cross becomes the symbol for the worldwide gathering of the nations.[116] His resurrection from the dead becomes the basis of the new creation.[117] His sanctifying and sending out his disciples with his word becomes the means by which people are powerfully called to new life and the NE through the Gospel.[118] Those who believe are set free from bondage to sin, and restored from "exile," to belong to his people.[119] Not only do they enjoy present communion with the Father, but also their ultimate heavenly destination is the Father's house.[120]

A STRUCTURAL REPRESENTATION:

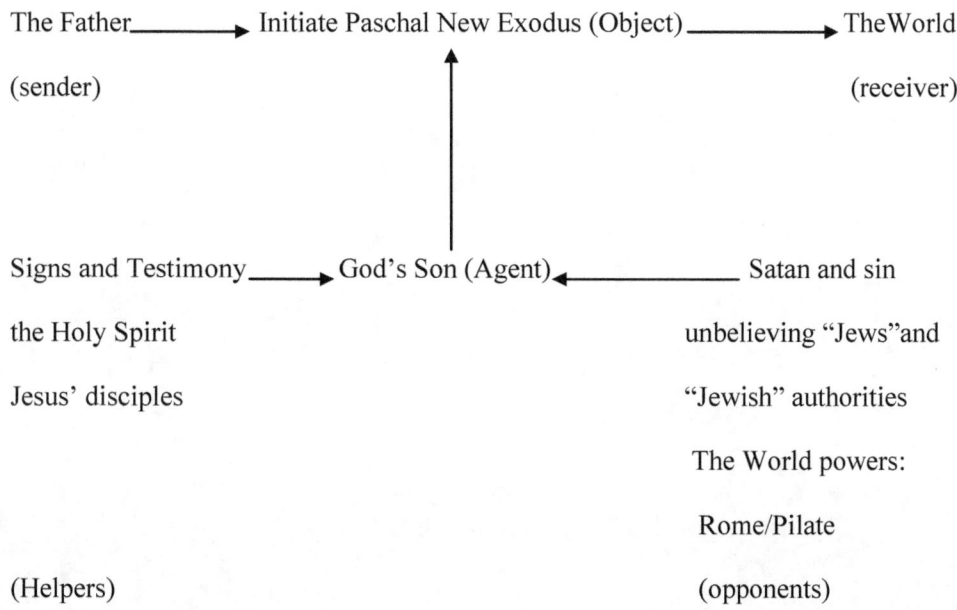

---

115. See below. Cf. John 5:21–22; 10:11ff.; 19:34–37; Carson, *John*, 253–54, 622ff.; Keener, *John*, 818ff.; Bruce, *John*, 227-28, 337-38; Morgan, "Fulfilment," 158–59.

116. John 12:32. See Bruce, *John*, 267-68.

117. See below where this is symbolically represented in the healing of the lame man and the resurrection of Lazarus, John 5; 11.

118. John 20:21–23. See Bruce, *John*, 391–92. See below on interpretation of John 5.

119. See Morgan, "Fulfilment," 158–59.

120. Cf. Bruce, *John*, 297; Glasson, *Moses*, 9–19.

PART II—DETAILED EXEGETICAL EXAMINATION OF JOHN 5-10

CONCLUSION

I have sketched my understanding of chapters 5–10 and their place in the GJohn Paschal NE paradigm. I will proceed to analyze these chapters in the light of this paradigm, dividing them according to the episodes that they contain. For each episode I will explore the OT festal background, so important to its narrative and discourse. This will be followed by a detailed intertextual exegesis in the light of the Paschal NE paradigm.

8

Episode 1
The Sabbath Healing of a Lame Man, John 5

BOUNDED BY THE *INCLUSIO*, "after this,"[1] this chapter is the first episode of the Festival Cycle where Jesus goes up to Jerusalem during a "feast of the Jews." Though many commentators have sought to identify the unnamed feast of John 5:1,[2] the episode focuses on the Sabbath[3] and, as Borchert recognizes, the Sabbath has taken on the festal motif.[4] Moreover, like the other Feasts, the Sabbath points forward to Jesus and he "replaces" and fulfils it.[5] The OT/Jewish background to the Sabbath is thus crucial to understanding this episode.

THE SABBATH FESTAL BACKGROUND

The OT memorial Sabbath

The Sabbath "day of rest"[6] has a dual *raison d'être*, pointing back both to God's creation rest and to the Exodus where the Lord redeemed Israel from slavery.[7] Accordingly, Israel was to rest and to give rest to servants on the Sabbath. This emphasis on compassionate rest is also found in the Sabbath year where the fruits of the land were left

---

1. Cf. John 5:1; 6:1.

2. Bernard, *John*, 226, argues for Tabernacles. Westcott, *John*, 1:204–77; Guilding, *Jewish Worship*, 69–72, advocate *Rosh ha-Shanah* (the Feast of Trumpets, Lev 23:23–25). Bowman, *Fourth Gospel*, argues for the Feast of Purim. Schnackenburg, *John*, 2:92, favors Pentecost, but both he and Carson, *John*, 241, think that the feast is not named because it is unrelated to the material in John 5. Cf. Barrett, *John*, 250–51; Brown, *John I-XII*, 206.

3. Cf. Brown, *John I-XII*, 216; Lee, *Narratives*, 111–12.

4. See Borchert, *John 1–11*, 228, 230. In Exod 34:21; Lev 23:1–3, the Sabbath is listed among the feasts as a "festival" in its own right. Cf. Keener, *John*, 634–36; Brown, *John I-XII*, 206; Burge, *John*, 171.

5. Cf. Neyrey, *Ideology*, 11; idem, "Jacob Traditions," 419–37; Keener, *John*, 643; Pancaro, *Law*, 499–500; Schnackenburg, *John*, 2:101, 461, n. 29, 30; Cullmann, "Sabbath und Sonntag," 129.

6. See Lohse, "σάββατον," 3, n. 6. "שָׁבַּת always means 'day of rest' in the OT."

7. Craigie, *Deuteronomy*, 157. Cf. Gen 2:2–3; Exod 20:8–11; 23:12; Deut 5:15.

for the poor and release was made from slavery and debt.[8] Compassionate release is also reflected in the Jubilee where, after seven Sabbath years, the fiftieth year was a general release of land and of slaves.[9]

Wright argues that Jesus was celebrating the Sabbath as redemption from slavery when he loosed the daughter of Abraham whom Satan had bound for eighteen years on the Sabbath.[10] More than that, however, he was also initiating the eschatological Sabbath: "[Jesus] was claiming that Israel's great coming sabbath day *was already breaking in* in his own ministry."[11] Similarly, Ringe argues that in Luke, the Jubilee imagery of Isaiah 61:1 is programmatic for Jesus' ministry.[12]

A Future eschatological Sabbath

The roots of the eschatological Sabbath lie not only in the Sabbath memorial but also in the OT idea of future rest within the Promised Land.[13] The bridge between the two ideas occurs in Deuteronomy.[14] First, its Decalogue gives an additional reason for Sabbath observance (compared to that of Exodus 20); namely Israel's release from bondage.[15] This effectively co-joins God's creative rest with his people's rest from slavery.[16] Then it promises future rest, which will only be fulfilled in the Promised Land, in connection both with rest from enemies and *God's resting place* among his people.[17] God would bless the land with paradisal fruitfulness on condition that Israel would faithfully *obey the voice* of the Lord.[18]

Von Rad denies that Deuteronomic "rest" has eschatological connotations,[19] but McConville disagrees: Israel is promised the land and rest on condition of covenant faithfulness, but two key passages make it clear that she is *unable* ultimately to *remain* faithful:

1. Deuteronomy 1:26–46 relates the debacle of Num 13–14, anticipating Israel's

---

8. See Ringe, *Biblical Jubilee*, 18. She refers to Exod 21:2–6; 23:10–11.
9. Cf. ibid., 16–17; Lev 25:8–55.
10. Luke 13:10–17. See Wright, *JVG*, 394.
11. Wright, *JVG*, 395, (emphasis original).
12. Ringe, *Biblical Jubilee*, 66. Cf. Luke 4:18–19.
13. See e.g., Attridge, *Hebrews*, 126.
14. See Von Rad, "Rest," 95.
15. Deut 5:15 cf. Exod 20:11.
16. See Weinfeld, *Deuteronomy 1–11*, 302.
17. Cf. Deut 12:9–18; cf. Lev 26:11–12; Ps 132:8, 14; 2 Chr 6:41. See Num 10:33 where, in the wilderness, the Ark of the Covenant, symbolic of God's presence, went before the people to search out a *resting place* for them.
18. Deut 28:1–14 cf. Lev 26:3–13. See McConville, *Deuteronomy*, 404–5.
19. Von Rad, "Rest," 95. He says that there is no eschatological rest "of the kind known to the prophets."

The Sabbath Healing of a Lame Man, John 5

tendency "to *trust their own perception*" and to distrust God.[20]

2. Deuteronomy 9–10 recalls the apostasy at Sinai, emphasising that Israel is a "stubborn" people.[21]

Deuteronomy itself provides the solution to this dilemma by prophesying the Lord's intervention: Although covenant faithfulness will result in blessing in the land, Israel will disobey God's voice and ultimately be sent into (Babylonian) exile. Nevertheless, Israel's repentance in exile will result in their restoration and return to the land. Crucially the Lord will circumcise their hearts that they may obey his voice and live.[22]

The "Deuteronomic pattern" is reflected in Israel's subsequent history. God gave rest from enemies, within the land, to obedient Joshua, the (early) Judges, David, and Solomon[23] and, in connection with that rest, set up his sanctuary among them.[24] But these periods of rest were followed by disobedience and curse.[25] Even at the dedication of the Temple, where God was petitioned to arise into his resting-place,[26] Solomon's prayer hinted that rest would not be permanent, but exile would follow Israel's disobedience.[27] Among prolonged times of social unrest, idolatry, and bloodshed that followed, only two short periods of rest were granted—to Asa and Jehoshaphat.[28]

It was possibly during this late Kings period[29] that Psalm 95 was written, expressing longing for rest.[30] Set in a context of worship, possibly as part of the Tabernacles liturgy,[31] like Deuteronomy, its "Today" re-actualizes[32] the Sinai covenant appearance of Yahweh before the worshippers.[33] This "epiphany" places them (and us) as sheep in the presence of their God, the Promised Land before them, enabling them to hear his

---

20. McConville, *Grace in the End*, 133, (emphasis mine). Interestingly this theme of not judging by appearances is important in GJohn. See e.g., John 7:24; 8:15. Cf. Isa 11:3.

21. McConville, *Grace in the End*, 134. Cf. Deut 9:7–21. Merrill, *Deuteronomy*, 191, notes that Israel's propensity to rebel is a point that is repeatedly made in Deut 4–11.

22. Deut 30:1–6. Cf. McConville, *Grace in the End*, 135–37. Merrill, *Deuteronomy*, 387–89; Ridderbos, *Deuteronomy*, 268–69; Craigie, *Deuteronomy*, 363–64.

23. Cf. Josh 14:15; 21:44; Judg 3:11, 30; 5:31; 2 Sam 7:1; 1 Kgs 8:56.

24. Cf. Deut 12:10–18; Josh 18:1; 2 Sam 7:1–29; 1 Kgs 8:1–11, 56; Baldwin, *1 and 2 Samuel*, 212–13.

25. See e.g., Judg 2:7–19.

26. See 2 Chr 6:41; Ps 132:8. Cf. Von Rad, "Rest," 96, 98, who thinks that the idea of *God's rest among the people* is a new "eschatological" development, arising from Ps 132, where David sought a permanent place for the Lord among Israel; Ps 132:14, "This is my resting place forever." I have argued that this eschatological note was already present in Deuteronomy.

27. 1 Kgs 8:46–50; 2 Chr 6:36–39. See Wiseman, *1 and 2 Kings*, 122.

28. See 2 Chr 15:15; 20:30, where Asa and Jehoshaphat wholeheartedly sought God and he rewarded them with rest. Cf. Deut 30:2–3.

29. See discussion in Kraus, *Psalms 60–150*, 246.

30. Cf. Kraus, *Psalms 60–150*, 246; Von Rad, "Rest," 99.

31. Cf. Mowinckel, *Psalms*, 1:121–22; Weiser, *Psalms*, 625; Kidner, *Psalms 73–150*, 343.

32. See Childs, *Introduction*, 216.

33. See Weiser, *Psalms*, 626.

voice and re-make for themselves the fateful decision to harden their hearts and die in the wilderness or to obey and follow into the promised rest. Like Deuteronomy it emphasizes *hearing God's voice* (obedience) as the condition for obtaining rest. Moreover, like Deuteronomy it highlights the failure of Israel, here at Massah and Meribah, but obliquely also in the debacle of Num 13–14, where God swore "they shall not enter my rest."[34]

Further revelation came through the prophets. Despairing that Israel would ever be faithful to the covenant,[35] they progressively elaborated the hope, first outlined in Deuteronomy,[36] of a NE from bondage unto a new creation and return to paradise, bringing in the eschatological Sabbath.[37] This would be accompanied by cleansing from the sin and defilement that had made the exile inevitable, together with the New Covenant gifts of the Spirit, forgiveness of sin, and the law written upon the heart.[38] Thus in a NE and new creation context, Isaiah says of the messianic deliverer, "his resting place shall be glorious."[39] In a similar context all people would worship before God "from Sabbath to Sabbath,"[40] and the Lord's own resting-place would be among his people.[41] In Isaiah 61, in return from exile context, God's eschatological reign is predicted in terms of Jubilee imagery. Thus God's Servant the Davidic Messiah announces,

> The LORD has anointed me to bring good news to the poor; he has sent me to bind up the brokenhearted, to proclaim liberty to the captives, and the opening of the prison to those who are bound; to proclaim the year of the LORD's favor."[42]

Significantly, the phrase translated "opening of the prison" is ambiguous, being used elsewhere of "opening of the eyes,"[43] a concept important to GJohn.

Daniel bases his *apocalyptic* eschatological Sabbath on the Levitical Sabbath theology.[44] Thus, although the Babylonian captivity would last for "seventy years," Dan

---

34. Ps 95:11 Cf. Num 14:22–23; Kraus, *Psalms 60–150*, 248; Kidner, *Psalms 73–150*, 346.

35. See, e.g., Isa 3:8–9; 5:5–7; Jer 17:1; Hos 6:4; 11:7–8. Cf. Oswalt, *Isaiah 1–39*, 154; McComiskey, "Hosea," 91.

36. See Deut 30:3–6.

37. See, e.g., Isa 11; 65:17–25; 66:22–23; Jer 31:1–14; Hos 14; Amos 9:13ff.; Joel 3:18ff.; Hag 2:7–9; Zech 2:4–5. Cf. Oswalt, *Isaiah 40–66*, 656, 691–92; Thompson, *Jeremiah*, 569–70.

38. Cf. Isa 44:3–5; Jer 31:31–34; Ezek 36:24–26; Zech 3:4; 12:10–11; 13:1; Oswalt, *Isaiah 40–66*, 166; Thompson, *Jeremiah*, 579–81; Block, *Ezekiel 25–48*, 353–57.

39. Isa 11:10. See Kaiser, *Isaiah 1–12*, 263, n. 5. He thinks this resting place to be the royal palace and Temple or "the whole city of Jerusalem."

40. Isa 66:23. See Calvin, *Isaiah*, 438, who translates "depuis un Sabbat jusques à son autre Sabbat." Cf. Zech 14:16–21.

41. See, e.g., Zech 2:10–12; Hag 2:7; Joel 3:21; Ezek 37:27–28; 43:7; Jer 3:16–17; Lev 26:11–12.

42. Isa 61:1–2. Cf. Ringe, *Biblical Jubilee*, 30.

43. Ibid., 30. Cf. Isa 61:1; 42:7.

44. Dan 9:24. Cf. Collins, *Daniel*, 352–53. Montgomery, *Daniel*, 373; Baldwin, *Daniel*, 168, 170; Fishbane, *Biblical Interpretation*, 482–84; Grelot, "Soixante-dix," 178–81.

9:2, the eschatological consummation, involving forgiveness of sin, the bringing in of "everlasting righteousness," and anointing the "most holy" would only occur after seventy Sabbaths of years, equivalent to 490 years or ten Jubilees.[45] By implication from the Jubilee concept, the completion of the 490th year would usher in the Sabbath year of release. Moreover, the end-time context points to an eschatological Sabbath,[46] and the seventy weeks have "overtones ... of apocalyptic determinism" and "periodization of history" that often conclude with a perpetual Sabbath.[47]

Developments within Judaism and Christianity

We find various developments of the eschatological Sabbath in the Pseudepigrapha, rabbinic literature, and within primitive Christianity:

In the Pseudepigrapha

In the *Life of Adam and Eve*, "the seventh day is a sign of the resurrection, the rest of the coming age, and on the seventh day the Lord rested from all his works."[48] In 2 Baruch the writer urges his readers to: "Prepare ourselves that we may ... *rest* with our Fathers and not be punished with those who hate us. For the youth of this world is passed away, and the power of creation is already exhausted, and the coming of the times is very near and has passed by."[49] Moreover, the world is sometimes conceived of as lasting for seven successive periods that culminate in a new creation and a millennial Sabbath.[50] This Sabbatical division of time probably reflects the OT "seven weeks of years" that led to the Jubilee release (Lev 25:8–13) and Daniel's seventy Sabbath-year periods, to be completed before eschatological redemption is accomplished,[51] as well as the seventh creation day of Genesis 2.

---

45. Cf. Dan 9:24; Lev 25:8; Collins, *Daniel*, 352; Baldwin, *Daniel*, 168; Calvin, *Daniel*, 196–97; Lev 26:18; 2 Chr 36:21.

46. Dan 9:24, "Seventy weeks are decreed about your people and your holy city, to finish the transgression, to put an end to sin, and to atone for iniquity, to bring in everlasting righteousness, to seal both vision and prophet, and to anoint a most holy place." See Baldwin, *Daniel*, 161–62., 168–69. "We are being told about the final triumph of God's kingdom and the end of human history." Cf. Dan 3:25; 7:9–10, 13–14.; 22, 26–27. 12:1–4, 13. For a survey of the different interpretations of the "seventy weeks" see Baldwin, *Daniel*, 172–78.

47. See Collins, *Daniel*, 352–53. He cites 1 Enoch 10:11–12; 4Q180, 181; *T. Levi* 16:1; 1 Enoch 93; 91:11–19; 89:59.

48. *Life of Adam and Eve* 51:1, 2, in Charlesworth, *Pseudepigrapha*, 2:294. This is dated 100 B.C. to A.D. 200 (probably towards A.D. 100) by M. D. Johnson in ibid., 2:252.

49. 2 *Bar.* 85:9–10, in Charlesworth, *Pseudepigrapha*, 1:651 (emphasis mine). The author writes in the wake of the destruction of the second Temple and in expectation of coming Judgement. The (eschatological) "rest" of which he speaks contrasts with the judgement of the wicked.

50. Cf. 2 Enoch 33:1–2; *T. Ab.* 19:7; 7:16. See Lohse, "σάββατον," 19–20.

51. Dan 9:2, 24–27; Jer 25:11–12. See above.

PART II—DETAILED EXEGETICAL EXAMINATION OF JOHN 5-10

In Rabbinic Judaism

For the rabbis, "The day of rest which the Patriarchs celebrated grants a foretaste already of eternal glory, which will be an unending Sabbath."[52] Moreover,

> The future world . . . is characterized by the kind of holiness possessed by the Sabbath of this world . . . the Sabbath possesses a holiness like that of the future world. And thus it says: 'A Psalm; a song of the Sabbath day.' (Ps 92:1), referring to a world in which there is a Sabbath all the time."[53]

Furthermore, "If Israel kept the Sabbath properly, even for one day, the son of David would come."[54] Significantly, this idea is also connected with Ps 95.[55]

In the NT

The most elaborate NT exposition of an eschatological Sabbath comes in Hebrews 3:7—4:13, as a reflection upon Ps 95:7–11 and Gen 2:2. Here Canaan is a "type" of rest in Christ, participation in God's finished work of creation and redemption.[56] Ultimately this refers to the heavenly city prepared for those who endure.[57] In a realized/future eschatology, believers *already* hold the title deeds,[58] but must labor to enter *future* rest.[59] Importantly, Hebrews refers to Israel's testing God and his oath that they would not enter Canaan but would die in the wilderness.[60] Accordingly, they traveled through the wilderness for thirty-eight years, from Kadesh Barnea to Zered, "until the entire generation . . . perished."[61]

---

52. Lohse, "σάββατον," 8. He cites Str-B 4.839–40.; *b. Ber.* 57b.

53. *Mek. Shabbat* 1:38ff., Lauterbach, 2:495. Cf. *m. Tamid* 7.4, in Danby, 589, where Ps 92 was reportedly sung by the Levites on the Sabbath in the Temple and the title is interpreted as "a Psalm, a song for the time that is to come, for the day that shall be all Sabbath and rest in the life everlasting." Cf. *Jub.* 2:30.

54. *Exod. Rab.* 25:12, in Freedman, 3:315. Cf. Lohse, "σάββατον," 8; *b. Shab.*, 118b.

55. See Ps 95 in Braude, *Midrash on Psalms*, 2:137, "If the children of Israel kept but one Sabbath as it ought to be kept, they would be redeemed forthwith, for it is said *The day—if ye would but hearken to His voice*, the day of which it is written *Observe the Sabbath day, to keep it holy* (Deut 5:12)" (emphasis original).

56. See Kidner, *Psalms 73–150*, 346. He cites Gen 49:15; Ps 132:14; 1 Kgs 8:56.

57. See Bruce, *Hebrews*, 110.

58. Heb 3:14. See Guthrie, *Hebrews*, 108. "Confidence (*hypostasis*) . . . appears in the present context to be connected with the assurance that an owner of property may have because he possesses the title deeds." Attridge, *Hebrews*, 128, speaks of "the same tension between . . . 'realized' and future' eschatology that characterises much early Christian literature."

59. Bruce, *Hebrews*, 109, n. 30, notes the "remarkable parallel" with Heb 4:10 in Rev 14:13, where the dead in the Lord rest from their labors and their works follow them. Cf. Isa 57:1–2.

60. Cf. Heb 3:11; Num 14:20ff.

61. Deut 2:14. See Bruce, *Hebrews*, 98.

Interestingly, Bruce thinks that the forty years of Ps 95:10 may have held special eschatological significance for the writer to the Hebrews as a "probationary period" between Jesus' "exodus" and the destruction of the Temple.[62] If so, the generation contemporary with Jesus of those who rejected him might be understood to parallel their "fathers" who tested God in the wilderness and died in their sin.

The Eschatological Sabbath in John 5

Theories

Two alternatives have been suggested, both centered around John 5:17.

1. Bruce argues that Jesus' defense in John 5:17 presupposes the view found both in Philo and also in Hebrews, that God's creation Sabbath rest has not ceased but is still ongoing.[63] Jesus enables people to enter *that* rest. Carson agrees, proposing that Jesus' work and rest are one with the Father's.[64]

2. Cullmann takes the position that many of the Church Fathers adopted,[65] that God *did not rest* after creation but only after Jesus' death and resurrection.[66] Jesus worked during his ministry, but by his death he completed the work of redemption thereby inaugurating the eschatological Sabbath.[67] This is indicated by Jesus' words, "my Father is working *until now*, and I am working."[68] Pancaro tentatively agrees,

> The *heos arti* [until now] points to a time when Jesus (and the Father) will no longer 'work,' at least not in the same manner in which Jesus (in unity with the Father) 'works' during his earthly ministry.[69]

Pancaro further notes that in Jesus' defense of John 7:21–24, "Moses has prepared the way for a correct understanding of Jesus' Sabbath work by prescribing circumcision." The point here is that Sabbath day circumcision (which makes a

---

62. Bruce, *Hebrews*, 99. He speaks of a "belief that God's dealings with Israel, which began with a probationary period of forty years, would be rounded off at the end-time by a probationary period of like duration." He cites CD 20:14–15 (echoing Deut 2:14–16); 4QpPs. 37, fragment A, 1.6ff. He notes that *b. Sanhedrin* 99a speaks of the days of the Messiah as lasting forty years.

63. Bruce, *John*, 127. Cf. Heb 4:3–10.

64. Carson, *John*, 248–49.

65. See Brown, *John I–XII*, 217.

66. John 9:4; Heb 4:9–10. Cf. Cullmann, "Sabbath und Sonntag," 127–31; Keener, *John*, 649.

67. John 5:36 cf. 19:30; 4:34; 5:36; 17:4; 9:4. See above on the echo of Isa 55:11 in 19:28, 30. Cf. Dahms, "Isaiah 55:11," 80.

68. John 5:17 (emphasis added).

69. Pancaro, *Law*, 159–60.

man ceremonially whole) foreshadows Jesus' Sabbath work, which makes a man entirely whole and thus gives rise to God's eschatological Sabbath.[70]

Evaluation

The fact that Jesus' statement that the Father works on the Sabbath, John 5:17, was not challenged seems to reflect Jewish understanding of a perpetual creation Sabbath. That the Father continued to work during his Sabbath was explained in various ways: For Philo, God's work was effortless and thus did not violate his rest.[71] For the rabbis, though God had ceased from his work of creation, the Sabbath did not bring his *moral/providential* activity to an end—the exercise of his twin powers[72] to judge and impart life.[73] Alternatively it was argued that technically he did not work.[74]

As Cullmann suggests, however, along with inferences of God's creation rest there are clear indications in Jesus' temporal note, "until now," ἕως ἄρτι, of another rest.[75] Barrett thinks this phrase connotes "up to the present" and does not imply an immanent or future cessation of work.[76] Bultmann thinks it primarily refers to constancy—my Father and I constantly work, but he also correctly allows the connotation of the cessation of Jesus' work.[77] This accords with the recurring idea of the cessation or completion of Jesus' work found in GJohn.[78]

---

70. Ibid., 508.

71. "It is the property of God to be creating," *Leg. All.* 1:3:5, in Yonge, *Philo*, 25. This does not violate his rest, however, for "God is . . . free from fatigue . . . and that, which has no participation in weakness, even though it moves everything, cannot possibly cease to enjoy rest for ever." *Cher*, 90, in Yonge, *Philo.*, 89. Cf. Haenchen, *John I*, 248.

72. Cf. Dodd, *IFG*, 320ff.; Neyrey, *John*, 108; Philo *Mos.* 2:99.

73. *Gen. Rab.* 11:10, in Freedman, 1:86, says God "rested from the work of [creating] His world, but not from the work of the wicked and the work of the righteous, for He works with the former and with the latter." Cf. Schnackenburg, *John*, 2:101; Brown, *John I-XII*, 217; Barrett, *John*, 213.

74. Since the whole world is "the courtyard of God" and since he fills heaven and earth he neither carries out of his own courtyard nor for a distance greater than his height and so he does not break the Sabbath. Cf. *Exod. Rab.* 30:9; Str-B 2.461–62; Bruce, *John*, 127; Barrett, *John*, 256. Carson, *John*, 247; Dodd, *IFG*, 320.

75. John 5:17. See Cullmann, "Sabbat und Sonntag," 127–31. He Takes this to be the Christian Lord's Day which "replaces" the Jewish Sabbath. He also relates it to Jesus' resurrection and the new creation.

76. Barrett, *John*, 255–56. Cf. Haenchen, *John I*, 248, who translates "up to the present moment," i.e. without a Sabbath break.

77. Bultmann, *John*, 245.

78. Cf. John 5:36; 4:34; 9:4; 17:4; 19:28–30. In the last reference the context is that of Jesus' death as fulfilment of the Scriptures.

Proposal

The nature of the eschatological Sabbath rest in GJohn

Rather than deny God's creation rest, with Cullmann, or posit an unbroken rest, with Bruce, it is better to posit two rests, or perhaps better a *resumption* of God's creation rest that has been broken. Thus both OT and NT assume a "fall" following creation, that necessitated a further work of God, that of redemption.[79] The OT paradigm for this new rest is redemption from slavery in Egypt (and Babylonian exile) followed by Deuteronomic rest in the Promised Land, elaborated by the Prophets as a new creation rest. In GJohn this is accomplished by the Father sending his Son, his powerful and creative Word, to ransom fallen mankind from the power of Satan, sin, and death, in a NE, and to re-create them as his people (illustrated by the healing).[80] This results in a return to paradise and restoration of the rest and fellowship that was lost in the beginning—God making his resting place in and among his people whom he has redeemed.[81] This work of redemption is accomplished at the cross where Jesus cries out, "It is finished," and yields up his life to God on behalf of his people.[82] They are able to enter His rest here and now.[83] Nevertheless, the full enjoyment of that rest awaits the consummation and the redemption of the body, when Jesus returns to raise the dead and to judge the world.[84]

Hearing God's voice: the way of entering His rest

The way of entering God's rest both in Deuteronomy and in GJohn is by *hearing God's Word* or *voice*. In Deuteronomy, "hearing God's voice" is reminiscent of Israel's Sinai *encounter* with God when they heard his voice from heaven and he called them to obedience. They were unable to hear (obey) God because they could not bear to listen.[85] Moreover, the debacle at Kadesh-barnea demonstrated their inability to believe or obey.[86] "Hearing God's word" is used similarly, except that *word* frequently connotes the written word, the means by which Israel *continues to hear God's voice*.[87] The Word was also mediated by God's prophets. Thus Moses spoke God's word to the people and

---

79. In GJohn this is implicit in 8:44. See Bruce, *John*, 201.
80. See below.
81. Cf. e.g., John 1:14; 6:56; 14:3; 15:4; 17:3.
82. John 19:30.
83. John 5:24–25.
84. Cf. John 5:28–29; 6:40
85. Cf. Deut 5:22–32; 18:16.
86. Cf. Deut 1:19–26, 32–43; 9:23–24. See McConville, *Grace in the End*, 134–35.
87. Thus they are exhorted to hear God's *voice* and then told that this is equivalent to keeping his commandments "written in this Book of the Law." Cf. Deut 30:2, 8, 10; 13:4, 18; 15:5; 26:17; 27:10; 28:1–2, 15, 45. This is not too hard for them because the *word* is "very near" to them, Deut 30:14 cf. Rom 10:8.

PART II—DETAILED EXEGETICAL EXAMINATION OF JOHN 5–10

promised that God would raise up a prophet like himself. Crucially, life would depend upon hearing his word.[88] For this, however, it would be necessary for God to write his word upon their hearts.[89]

In GJohn, "hearing God's voice" is again reminiscent of Sinai,[90] but now life and rest depend on hearing (obeying and believing)[91] Jesus' voice in a personal encounter with him. This is particularly emphasized in John 5 and John 9–10 where the dead hear Jesus' voice and live, and his sheep hear his voice and follow.[92] Significantly these passages contain parallel signs; each performed on the Sabbath.

"Hearing Jesus' *word*" functions similarly, but frequently connotes the word handed down from the Father to Jesus and then to the disciples, who wrote and preached it.[93] In this, Jesus functions as the "Prophet like Moses" who mediates the Father's word. More importantly, Jesus is the Word made flesh, the complete revelation of God embodied in human form.[94] Moreover, to a greater degree than in Deuteronomy, GJohn emphasises the *power* of Jesus' word: creating, cleansing, revivifying, drawing, and judging.[95] This suggests:

1. The contrast between the giving of the law by Moses and the grace and truth that came through Christ.[96]

2. Fulfilment of the Deuteronomic eschatological hope through the circumcision of the heart by Jesus' word.

3. The fulfilment of the Isaianic NE by Jesus the Word of God.[97]

Response to the Word made flesh

I propose that John 5 and John 9–10 echo the Sinai theophany and Deuteronomic ideal of Psalm 95.[98] In these chapters, the Jewish people (and we ourselves) appear before one who is our creator, life-giver, and judge,[99] to whom we owe divine honor.[100]

---

88. Deut 18:15–19.
89. Cf. Deut 30:2, 6, 10, 14; Jer 31:33; Ezek 36:26.
90. Cf. John 5:37; 12:28; Deut 4:12, 36. See Hübner, *Vetus Testamentum*, 154.
91. See Barrett, *John*, 261.
92. Cf. John 5:25, 28, 37; 10:3, 4, 5, 16, 27. John 11:43 is also similar.
93. See, e.g., John 5:38; 8:31, 37, 51, 55; 12:49; 17:14; 2:22. Cf. Cullmann, *Christology*, 260.
94. John 1:14; 14:9. Cf. Cullmann, *Christology*, 260.
95. See, e.g., John 5:24; 12:48; 15:3; 17:17. See Barrett, *John*, 261. But cf. Deut 8:3.
96. John 1:17. See Bruce, *John*, 43–44.
97. Isa 55:10–15.
98. That this Psalm was associated with the Sabbath is significant. See Bruce, *Hebrews*, 97–98.
99. Cf. John 5:21–22; 9:39; 10:28, 36.
100. Ps 95:6 cf. John 5:23.

Moreover, he is the Good Shepherd,[101] who calls his sheep to obey and believe his voice.[102] While his *true* sheep do this,[103] however, many unbelieving "Jews" are *unable* to bear Jesus' word.[104] Though they see his works· they have not known God's ways.[105] Thus they harden their hearts and rebel, questioning his claim and putting him to the test.[106] Consequently, they fail to enter life and rest.[107] Furthermore, as I will seek to show, the lame man and blind man act as alternative paradigms for response to Jesus, by which John teaches us, his readers, how we must respond.

Conclusion

I have argued that in John 5 Jesus fulfils the Sabbath rest by bringing life and redemption to all those who hear (obey) and believe in him. This is understood in terms of the fulfilment of the Deuteronomic rest promised to the Israelites and its elaboration as their eschatological NE hope.

INTEGRITY, FORM, AND STRUCTURE OF JOHN 5

Integrity

Though most scholars consider vv. 3b–4 to be a gloss,[108] many would also consider this chapter to be the product of radical redaction attributed to:

1. Different sources.
2. Different "hands."
3. Use of Synoptic material.[109]
4. Different Phases of the Johannine community.

None of these theories, however, can be substantiated. As previously indicated, source and redaction theories are impossible to substantiate because of the uniformity of

---

101. Cf. Ps 95:7. In John 5, the shepherd motif is implicit in Jesus seeking out the man. This becomes clear in the parallel healing in John 9, with its explication in the Shepherd discourse of John 10. See Keener, *John*, 636.

102. Cf. Ps 95:7; John 5:25, 28; 10:3–4, 16, 27.

103. John 9:38.

104. They *cannot* hear, because they do not love God, or seek his glory, nor are they Jesus' sheep or of the truth. Moreover, Jesus' word is "hard" to bear, cf. John 5:42, 44; 10:26; 8:43–44; 18:37; 6:44, 60.

105. Cf. Ps 95:9–10; John 5:37–38, 44.

106. Cf. Ps 95:8–10; John 5:16, 18, 40, 42; 10:33.

107. Ps 95:11 refers to God's oath of Num 14:28–35. Interestingly the Israelites wandered for thirty-eight years following this, the same period that the lame man had been invalid, John 5:5.

108. Used to explain verse 7. The best witnesses (P66, P75, B, C, D) omit vv. 3b–4. Cf. Brown, *John I–XII*, 207; Lincoln, *John*, 191; Beasley-Murray, *John*, 70; Carson, *John*, 242; Haenchen, *John I*, 257.

109. Haenchen, *John I*, 256, n. 67.

PART II—DETAILED EXEGETICAL EXAMINATION OF JOHN 5-10

the Johannine style and the lack of time for, or independent textual evidence of, different versions of GJohn.[110] The suggestion that John used Mark 2:1–12 must be discounted.[111] This is made on the basis of similarities between the infirmity of the one healed, the connection of sin with his illness, and the words of Jesus, "Ἔγειρε ἆρον τὸν κράβαττόν σου" ("Rise, take up your bed").[112] Scholars ancient and modern, however, have remarked on the much greater differences between the two healings,[113] indicating that John 5 contains a unique tradition from Jesus' ministry. Likewise the idea that the story first circulated without the Sabbath motif[114] is implausible because pointless: "One almost needs the Sabbath motif to give this story significance."[115] Above all the narrative bears the marks of eyewitness testimony and authentic tradition.[116] Not only are the incidental details vivid, but also their accuracy has been archaeologically confirmed. Moreover, the Evangelist had no doubts concerning its authenticity,[117] plausibly because he was an eyewitness.[118]

Various attempts have been made to find different John 5 strata that corroborate the Johannine school model. Brown moves in this direction.[119] He cites Sundberg's contrast between the Son who could do nothing of himself, John 5:19, 30, and the extension of the Father's "autonomous self existence" to the Son, John 5:26.[120] Brown believes that this is evidence of the Evangelist's synthetic approach, juxtaposing old insights against new.[121] For Martyn, John 5 is important to his thesis, representing the community's "middle" period,[122] where following persecution, the Mosaic Prophet/Christ was increasingly transformed into the Son of Man and stranger from heaven.[123]

---

110. See above on Christological Feasibility.

111. This idea is still repeated today, e.g., by McHugh, "In Him was Life," 135–36.

112. Cf. NKJV John 5:8; Mark 2:11.

113. See Chrysostom, *Homilies*, 128–29, who pointed out the differences in persons, replies, seasons and time, place, manner of cure, and charges of the Jews. See Brown, *John I–XII*, 208–10, who considers the healing of the lame man of John 5 and that of Mark 2:1–12 to be "quite diverse" in setting, local details and emphasis. Cf. Schnackenburg, *John*, 2:96.

114. Cf. Fortna, *Signs*, 52–54; Neyrey, *Ideology*, 10. They believe that vv. 9c–16 is a Johannine addition, the mention of the Sabbath in 9c being appended post script to change the focus from a healing sign to a controversy. But cf. Bultmann, *John*, 238.

115. Brown, *John I–XII*, 209–10. Contra Haenchen, he argues that the Sabbath motif is original to the story. Cf. Barrett, *John*, 249, 254.

116. Cf. Dodd, *HTFG*, 174–80; Barrett, *John*, 249, 254; Brown, *John I–XII*, 209.

117. See Haenchen, *John I*, 258.

118. See on authorship above. See Bauckham, *Eyewitnesses, passim*.

119. Cf. Brown, *Community, passim*; Brown and Moloney, *Introduction*, 250–51.

120. Brown, *Community*, 53.

121. Ibid., 52.

122. See Martyn, *History and Theology*, 72–76, 154–57.

123. Ibid., 125, 130–34.

The Sabbath Healing of a Lame Man, John 5

Neyrey believes that a redactor has added the charge of Sabbath breaking and Jesus' defence (John 5:10–16, 30–47) to a traditional healing (John 5:2–9).[124] Later redaction has turned this into a defence against the charge of blasphemy, based on Jesus' exercise of the "two powers" of creation and judgement (John 5:17–29).[125] The result is *two* forensic processes and *two* defenses representing two different strata of the Gospel.[126] The first, emanating from a period when the synagogue sought to separate from Jesus' disciples, represents a "low" Christology that views Jesus as a "a reforming prophet."[127] The second, coming from a time when the Johannine community had been excommunicated by the synagogue, represents a high Christology that understands Jesus as being equal with God.[128]

In reply, I note that Jesus' healing of the lame man, like his healing of the blind man, are NE signs that would only be fulfilled at the coming of God to his people.[129] They bear witness to Jesus that he is the Son of God.[130] His "breaking" of the Sabbath is akin to that in the Synoptics where "the Son of Man is Lord even of the Sabbath."[131] This is definitely *not* low Christology (*pace* Neyrey) and certainly does not support Martyn's theory of Christological development.[132] Furthermore, Neyrey's two judicial processes artificially carve up one trial into two fragments: one containing a defense without witnesses, the other having witnesses without a defense. The tension, observed by Brown, between Jesus' dependence and self-existence, though impossible to comprehend, is easy to explain in terms of Jesus' incarnation, mission, agency, and exaltation.

Finally, John's realized-future eschatological tension, thought to be redactional,[133] is in fact analogous to that of Jesus and of Paul. In the Synoptics, Jesus proclaims the kingdom to be both present and future.[134] Paul teaches present justification followed by future resurrection, judgement, and glorification.[135] Thus there is no great difficulty in ascribing both realized and future eschatology to John.[136] Moreover,

---

124. Neyrey, *Ideology*, 10–15.

125. Ibid., 18–29, 36.

126. Ibid., 15–18.

127. Ibid., 15.

128. Ibid., 21.

129. Cf. Isa 35:4–6; Ps 146:8.

130. Cf. John 5:36; 10:25.

131. Matt 12:8 NKJV. Cf. Mark 2:28; Luke 6:5.

132. Cf. Martyn, *History and Theology*, 72–73, 152.

133. Cf. Bultmann, *John*, 261; Haenchen, *John I*, 253; Schnackenburg, *John*, 2:114. But cf. the criticism of Bultmann in Kysar, *Voyages*, 22–23.

134. See Brown, *John I–XII*, cxix, who notes that both realized and final eschatology were "already present in Jesus' thought."

135. See Ibid., cxx.

136. Cf. de Jonge, "Eschatology and Ethics," 176; Painter, *Quest*, 227, 229; Brodie, *John*, 249; Kysar, *John*, 84; Carson, *John*, 258; Smalley, *John*, 265–69.

PART II—DETAILED EXEGETICAL EXAMINATION OF JOHN 5-10

> There is no reason whatever for regarding vv. 28f. as a supplement to the original Johannine discourse unless it is held incredible that John should have thought of resurrection and judgement under both present and future aspects. The combination of the two, however, is one of John's principal theological affirmations.[137]

Affirmation of present justification and future hope is just what the Johannine community and the wider Church needed to hear, especially in their current situation of crisis.[138]

Form and structure

This chapter divides into two: 1. A narrative story detailing Jesus' healing of a lame man and its aftermath. 2. Discourse where Jesus defends his actions against "Jewish" accusations. John has framed the narrative using a series of scenes in a similar fashion to that of the blind man of John 9.[139] Verses 9c–16 are transitional, introducing the reader to the preliminary steps of a forensic process typical in John 7–10.[140] A principal question is whether or not vv. 16–18, containing the accusations, belong with the narrative[141] or with Jesus' defense.[142] A good case can be made either way: on the one hand they seem *preliminary* to the discourse proper, but on the other hand they also belong to the "trial." I include them with the latter. In effect v. 16 contains the first charge brought against Jesus and v. 17 is his first defense. This leads to a second accusation, v. 18, and a second defense, vv. 19–47. Moreover, the two defenses are parallel, the first being a summary statement and the second an elaboration of that statement. A further issue concerns the division of the discourse, whether v. 30 should be taken with vv. 19–30 as an *inclusio* or as the commencement of a new subsection vv. 31–40.[143] I opt for the former, since v. 30 concludes the judgement theme.

---

137. Barrett, *John*, 263, 67–70.
138. See Brown, *John I-XII*, cxx. Cf. Painter, *Quest*, 233.
139. See Windisch, "John's Narrative Style," 25–64. Cf. Fortna, *Signs*, 52–53; Lincoln, *John*, 192, 198–99; Martyn, *History and Theology*, 37, 73.
140. See Neyrey, *Ideology*, 10–11.
141. So Barrett, *John*, 255–57. Cf. Lincoln, *John*, 196–200.
142. So Brown, *John I-XII*, 212ff.; Carson, *John*, 246ff.; Brodie, *John*, 241ff.
143. See discussion in Brodie, *John*, 241ff.

NE INTERPRETATION OF JOHN 5:1–15 NARRATIVE: JESUS HEALS A LAME MAN ON THE SABBATH

The background of Jewish crisis, vv. 1–3

A multitude of sick people

Brodie emphasizes the crisis that confronted Jesus at Bethesda, referring to it as "a scene of swarming suffering."[144] Gathered around the pool,[145] sheltering beneath "five roofed colonnades," lay "a multitude of invalids—blind, lame, and paralyzed," John 5:2–3. The position of the pool and the importance of its water made it a notable landmark and blot upon Jerusalem's landscape. Its association with sheep is suggestive of the multitude as a pathetic flock of sheep,[146] and these were Jewish sheep.[147] Moreover, the description of the invalids as ξηρῶν ("withered" or "dried up") is particularly poignant. The crowds were adjacent to the water, yet in desperate need of water. Moreover, Jesus who could give living water was present, but nobody moved or asked Jesus for help.[148]

Echoes of Israel in exile

The imagery, made more vivid by John's use of the present historic tense ("Now there is in Jerusalem . . ."), may deliberately echo Israel encamped by water in the wilderness or in Babylonian exile by the River Chebar.[149] It is possible that the bitter undrinkable waters of Marah may be in mind since these were made sweet and there the Lord, "your healer," promised to put "none of these diseases" on Israel if they will *listen to his voice*.[150] The sequence in Exodus 15–17, healing, bread, and water from the rock, might then lie behind John 5–7.[151] The motif of "exile" is also present: on account of their being "unwhole," the invalids were excluded from the Temple worship.[152]

---

144. Brodie, *John*, 235.

145. See Smalley, *John*, 38. "Until excavation began in 1878 on the Bethesda site . . . no knowledge of this pool existed outside the Fourth Gospel." In 1931, however, "Two tank-like pools," surrounded on four sides by colonnades, were discovered near St. Anne's Church, north-east of the Temple. Initially, these were thought to be the Bethesda pool itself, but fresh discoveries have pointed in the direction of "shallower pools adjacent to the tanks." Cf. Jeremias, *Rediscovery of Bethesda*; Mare, *Archaeology*, 166–68; Brown, *John I–XII*, 207; Schnackenburg, *John*, 2:94; Keener, *John*, 636ff.

146. Brodie, *John*, 236. Cf. Hoskyns, *Fourth Gospel*, 264.

147. Brodie, *John*, 236. "The flavor of the text is heavily Jewish."

148. Cf. Ibid., 236.

149. Ezek 3:15. See Manning, *Echoes of a Prophet*, 161, who, compares the "crowds of the sick around the pool" to "the dead" of Ezekiel 37.

150. Exod 15:22–26.

151. See Brown and Moloney, *Introduction*, 44.

152. So Neyrey, *John*, 101–2. The pool and the Temple "correspond to the persons in them; at the pool are people who are unwhole and thus unclean, but in the Temple, all persons must be whole and

PART II—DETAILED EXEGETICAL EXAMINATION OF JOHN 5-10

The failure of the invalids' hope

The invalids had been drawn to the waters by popular belief in their healing powers,[153] so close to the Sheep Gate,[154] through which sacrificial animals were brought into the Temple; the place-name, Bethesda, signifying "House of Mercy," "House of springs," or "House of outpourings."[155] Not only had the invalids suffered, but also many had apparently waited for a long time by the pool, hoping in vain to be healed; one man in particular having had his infirmity for thirty-eight years, John 5:5. The use of the adjective ξηρῶν ("dried up"), John 5:3, may deliberately echo the feeling of hopelessness expressed by the exiles in Ezek 37:11, "Our bones are dried up [LXX ξηρά], and our hope is lost." If so, the Ezek 37 passage points to the only solution: the Son of Man prophesying, first to the bones and then to the wind (Spirit), to raise the dead from their graves to new life, enabling them to return to the land in a NE. Significantly, this resonates with the John 5 healing. In John 5:25–27, Jesus is able to raise the dead and impart life "because he is the Son of Man." Moreover, like the Son of Man in Ezek 37, Jesus does those things that the Father shows him, John 5:19–20.

The blind and lame

While "withered"[156] sums up the hopelessness of the "exiled" invalids, "blind" and "lame" also have a particular NE significance. They are frequently joined as conditions associated with outcasts, unacceptable sacrifices, and excluded priests.[157] The blind and lame were David's enemies.[158] Blindness, mentioned in the context of oppression and Egyptian plagues, boils, and itch, is a Deuteronomic consequence of failure to hear

---

clean."

153. V. 7. Probably built as a water supply, the pool may at one stage have been used to wash sacrificial lambs on their way to the Temple or (according to Origen) used as a place into which their viscera were thrown, and thus thought to possess healing powers. Much later it became a pagan healing sanctuary, suggesting its prior association with healing. Cf. Lincoln, *John*, 193; Haenchen, *John 1*, 244, citing Origen, *Commentary on John*, fragment 61; Smalley, *John*, 38; Brown, *John I-XII*, 207; Keener, *John*, 638.

154. The word "gate" (supplied in the light of Neh 3:1) is missing from the original. See Lincoln, *John*, 190, n. 2; 193. Cf. Brown, *John I-XII*, 206 and Schnackenburg, *John*, 2:94 who prefers "sheep pool," though Brown affirms the association with the area north-east of the Temple where sheep were brought into Jerusalem for sacrifice. Carson, *John*, 241, thinks that in the light of Neh 3:1, 32; 12:39, "near the sheep gate" seems best. Barrett, *John*, 251, suggests that no ancient writer supplies πύλη with προβατικῇ, but Origen, *Commentary on John*, fragment 61, does in fact speak of the sheep gate. Cf. Haenchen *John I*, 244.

155. The name is uncertain, but cf. Barrett, *John*, 251–53 who tentatively prefers Bethesda on the evidence of the Copper Scroll 3Q15. C Schnackenburg, *John*, 2:94; Bruce, *John*, 122.

156. Cf. John 5:3; 15:6.

157. Cf. Mic 4:6; Deut 15:21; Mal 1:8, 13; Lev 21:18. See Malina, *New Testament World*, 187, where the lame and blind belong to those "barred from the Temple and sacrifice because of some sort of permanent impediment or lack of wholeness."

158. 2 Sam 5:6, 8.

the Lord's voice.[159] Moreover, lameness and blindness describe Israel at the time of the exile. Metaphors for their spiritual condition,[160] they evinced God's judgement;[161] though God will yet make the blind to see and understand, Isa 29:18. Isaiah 59:10 is particularly important, clearly alluding to Deut 28:29. In Isaianic context, God is able to save, but Judah feels helpless and is in despair of salvation. Because of this spiritual paralysis, however, God's own arm steps in to bring salvation and judgement. It is significant that in John 5 and 9, Jesus, God's 'arm,' administers life and judgement to the lame and spiritually blind.

The blind and lame were also candidates for mercy.[162] One of God's properties is that he heals the blind and sets the prisoners free.[163] Moreover, the lame and blind are specifically mentioned as subjects of the NE; their healing being a specific sign of its dawn.[164] The Servant himself, a light and covenant to the nations, will open their eyes and free them from their dark dungeons.[165] Importantly, God's work of saving the lame and blind in a NE is specifically presented as evidence in his lawsuit against the nations, blind Israel becoming the chief witnesses[166] to the Lord's claim that "I am."[167] In John 5:36, Jesus' works, including healing the lame, are used as evidence in his lawsuit with "the Jews" that he is "equal with God": commissioned as the Father's representative and possessor of divine prerogatives.

"Waiting for the moving of the water"

Though not original to GJohn, this phrase summarizes the hope of healing reflected in the lame man's words of John 5:7, "I have no one to put me into the pool when the water is stirred up." The multitudes were "blind, lame, and paralyzed," waiting for a divine intervention, God "troubling the water," that would restore them. There may well be an echo of the NE hope here.

> Given the possible exodus allusion in the "thirty eight years" (5:5), the "troubling of the waters" (John 5:7) might suggest an allusion to the exodus; the

---

159. Deut 28:15, 27–29 cf. Exod 10:21–23. Cf. Craigie, *Deuteronomy*, 338f; Oswalt, *Isaiah 40–66*, 521.

160. Cf. Isa 29:9–12; 42:18–19; 6:10; John 9:40–41; 12:40. See Rom 9–11, "blindness in part happened to Israel."

161. Cf. Oswalt, *Isaiah 1–39*, 189; Isa 6:9–10; 59:10; Zeph 1:17; Lam 4:14.

162. Job 29:15.

163. Ps 146:8 cf. Isa 29:18.

164. Cf. Isa 35:5–6; 42:16 Jer 31:8; Zeph 3:19; Mic 4:6; Isa 2:1–5; Matt 15:30–31; 21:14. See Matt 11:5; Luke 7:22, where they are specific evidence of the dawn of the messianic era.

165. Isa 42:6–7.

166. Isa 43:8–13. See Childs, *Isaiah*, 334ff.

167. Ibid., 335, citing Isa 41:4; 43:10, 13; 46:4; 48:12. Cf. Exod 3:14; Deut 32:39.

same language appears in Ps 77:16 (76:17 LXX), which depicts the time when God led his people "like a flock" by Moses and Aaron.[168]

The same term, ταράσσω ("trouble," "stir up"), appears as a possible Exodus allusion in Hab 3:15 and in Isa 51:14–15. The latter promises that "the captive exile will soon be loosed" on the basis of Yahweh's activity of troubling the sea. Other more general applications of ταράσσω suggest God's doing battle with the waters, which represent his enemies.[169]

The lame man as a representative, vv. 5–7

Out of the invalid multitude, Jesus focuses on one man who had been ill for thirty-eight years, who represents their plight and that of Israel at the time of Jesus.[170] Thirty-eight years is of symbolic importance, being the time that Israel spent in the wilderness following the debacle at Kadesh.[171] Moreover, though controversial, this symbolism has significant support.[172]

The allusion to thirty-eight years

From the earliest times scholars have debated whether or not an allusion is intended. Cyril of Alexandria thought so and saw the man as symbolic of the Jewish people who will find grace in the end.[173] Many others have followed his lead, though some have understood the symbol as indicative of Jewish failure.[174] Other scholars have allowed the possibility,[175] while many have dismissed it outright.[176] I argue that it is an intentional allusion:

168. Keener, *John*, 638.

169. Cf. Ps 46:3; Isa 17:12.

170. On the representative nature of Johannine characters cf. Culpepper, *Anatomy*, 145; Koester, *Symbolism*, 37; Brown, *Community*, 72; Neyrey, *John*, 6, 104–5.

171. Cf. Brodie, *John*, 238–39, 249, 252; Schnackenburg, *John*, 2:95.

172. See e.g., Brodie, *John*, 239.

173. See Cyril of Alexandria, *John*, 236. Cf. citation in Schnackenburg, *John*, 2:95.

174. See Schnackenburg, *John*, 2:95, "Since the patristic period . . . it has been common to point a symbolic allusion contained in this figure to the number of years which the Israelites spent in the desert between Kadeshbarnea and the brook Zered (Deut 2:14)." He cites Cyril of Alexandria; Apollinaris of Laodicea, fr. 19; Strathmann, *Johannes*, 103ff. Cf. Haenchen, *John I*, 255. He cites Holtzmann's comments on his predecessors who interpreted the healing allegorically. He also quotes Hirsch who sees the thirty-eight years as an allusion to Deut 2:14. Cf. Hengstenberg, *John, ad. loc.*; Barclay, *John*, 1:210; Smith, *John*, 131; Köstenberger, *John*, 179; Hengel, "Johannesevangelium," 293–334; Borchert, *John 1–11*, 232; Temple, *Readings*, 107–8; Brodie, *John*, 238ff.

175. Cf. Sloyan, *John*, 79; Lange, *Commentary*, 9:183.

176. Scholars who deny any allusion or think it improbable include Barrett, *John*, 253, Brown, *John I–XII*, 207, Carson, *John*, 242, Bernard, *John*, 229, and Burge, *John*, 180–81. Those who are undecided or doubtful include Westcott, *John*, 1:183; Hoskyns, *Fourth Gospel*, 265; Morris, *John*, 302, n. 17.

The Sabbath Healing of a Lame Man, John 5

1. Numbers have significance for John elsewhere.[177] For a community steeped in the OT, thirty-eight years would bring to mind the period from Kadesh to the border of Moab.[178]

2. The very fact that so many scholars have felt the need to affirm or deny the allusion suggests its persistence and undeniable "volume."

3. One of the reasons for rejecting the allusion is distaste for allegorical interpretation.[179] Clearly *arbitrary* and *uncontrolled* allegory is not appropriate, but an author's clues concerning the symbolic nature of his allusions should be followed. Moreover, the highly symbolic nature of GJohn is widely recognized.[180] This symbolism does not negate the reality of the man's thirty-eight year illness or that of his healing by Jesus.

4. Some have argued that if an allusion to the wilderness period was intended, forty rather than thirty-eight years would have been more symbolic, but thirty-eight specifically pinpoints the period from God's sentence upon the wilderness generation until the time that they had all died in the wilderness.

5. Carson rejects the allusion on the basis that there are no contextual indicators to support it.[181] This would be a strong argument, but in fact, I suggest that the opposite is the case: The allusion indicates the failure to enter Sabbath rest, crucial to the passage.[182] Moreover, like the wilderness generation, the man had failed to enter rest because of his sin.

Given the allusion, I propose that the man represents those Jewish people, "in the wilderness" and "exile," in Jesus' day, who fail through their own sin and unbelief to enter into rest. The rabbis speculated regarding the wilderness generation, whether or not they would finally share in the world to come.[183] If this speculation is in mind, the man becomes an important test case. More importantly, as one outwardly transformed by his encounter with Christ, but inwardly unchanged and ultimately defecting to "the Jews," he is a warning to the Johannine community (and to ourselves) of the failure to hear (obey) Jesus' voice.[184]

---

177. See Borchert, *John 1–11*, 254–56, who notes that for John numbers can be theologically significant. Cf. Jones, *Water*, 126–27.

178. Deut 2:14–18. See Watts, *Mark*, 30, 32–33, who refers to the effect of the mention of "four score and seven years" on American students in recalling Lincoln's Gettysburg address.

179. See Burge, *John*, 180–81, who speaks of allegorisation of John 5 by Augustine, Tertullian, and Chrysostom as "unnecessary and likely inappropriate."

180. See Dodd, *IFG*, 133–43; "The discourses appended to various narratives show that they are to be understood symbolically." Cf. Culpepper, *Anatomy*, 180–202; Koester, *Symbolism, passim*; Jones, *Water*, 20–26, 127; Lee, *Narratives, passim*.

181. Carson, *John*, 242.

182. Cf. Jones, *Water*, 127–28.

183. Cf. Balentine, "Concept," 102; *b. Sanhedrin* 110b; *Exod. Rab.* 2:4.

184. Cf. Jones, *Water*, 135.

PART II—DETAILED EXEGETICAL EXAMINATION OF JOHN 5-10

I further suggest that for John the thirty-eight years represent the time from Jesus' death and resurrection to the A.D. 70 destruction of the Temple, as a "probationary period." During this time, although many of the Jewish people responded to Jesus' word (preached by the apostles, e.g., in Acts 2:41) and entered into his rest, unbelieving "Jews" and their followers rejected Jesus, failed to enter rest, and wandered "in the wilderness" until they were ultimately doomed to disaster in the overthrow of Jerusalem.[185]

Reluctant to be healed, vv. 6, 7

That Jesus "saw him . . . and knew that he had already been there a long time," might reflect the Lord's looking upon the afflictions of his people, coming down to deliver them, prior to the Exodus.[186]

From the outset, the man's reactions are not promising. Jesus' question, "Do you want to be healed?" seems strange since ostensibly that was the reason for his lying by the pool.[187] It may imply the man's deep-seated disbelief, or unwillingness. The question meets with an excuse, "I have no one to put me into the pool," that effectively blames God for his condition. This attitude is confirmed when, accused by the Pharisees, he blames God's Son for instructing him to carry his mat on the Sabbath.[188]

Jesus' NE sign: He heals the lame Man on the Sabbath, vv. 8-9

There are significant features of the sign: Jesus healing the lame, instantly by his word, using the command "arise" (ἔγειρε), on the Sabbath, that make it a paradigm of resurrection and new creation and therefore a pointer to the NE and eschatological Sabbath.

A New Creation

The power of Jesus' word recalls the creation of the cosmos.[189] Thus Brodie speaks of the healing as "Creatorlike" and notes that it is followed by mention of the Sabbath.[190] Wright affirms that "Israel's God was . . . launching a *new creation*." Moreover, "[Jesus' signs might] correspond in some way to the 'days' of the old creation."[191] Keener points to Jesus finishing the Father's works as an allusion to and parallel with the Father

---

185. See comments of Bruce, *Hebrews*, 99, cited above.
186. Exod 3:7-9.
187. So Lincoln, *John*, 194.
188. John 5:7, 15 cf. Gen 3:12-13.
189. Gen 1:3, 6, 9. Cf. 2 Cor 4:6; Heb 11:3.
190. Brodie, *John*, 237. Cf. Painter, *Quest*, 223, who compares the healing to Creation.
191. Wright, *John 1-10*, 59 (emphasis original). Cf. Brodie, *John*, 245.

finishing creation prior to his seventh day rest.[192] He further thinks that the reference to the healing as "making" (ποιέω) the "man" (ἄνθρωπον) well, alludes to Gen 1:26 (LXX), "Let us make man (ποιήσωμεν ἄνθρωπον) . . ."[193] The five-fold repetition of the term ὑγιής, 'well' or 'whole,' is also significant, suggesting the lame man's complete restoration or re-creation by Jesus.[194]

A Resurrection

In the ancient world, paralysis or lameness was associated with death.[195] This is reinforced by the mention of thirty-eight years, linking the man with those sentenced to die in the wilderness. This fact and the command "arise" (ἔγειρε), followed by the immediate restoration to wholeness, point to the resurrection to life. This is in fact a reversal of the Adamic curse of death and dissolution of the body and a restoration to Edenic blessing. Moreover, the "resurrection" effected in the cripple becomes the pattern for Jesus' eschatological raising of both the spiritually dead by his voice and of the physically dead by his voice at the "last day."[196]

A New Exodus

The healing of the lame, never performed in the OT, was itself a NE sign.[197] In Isa 35:6, God himself will come and heal the lame, making a way for them in the wilderness, which will be transformed by the gift of living (rivers, springs, pools of) water. Moreover, the Lord's redeemed and sanctified people will return to Zion with everlasting Joy.[198] Similarly in Jeremiah God himself will bring the lame back to Jerusalem, gathering them as part of a great company from the farthest parts of the earth, leading them by rivers of water.[199] In Micah, God himself will assemble the lame, make them a remnant and strong nation, and reign over them forever.[200] In Zephaniah, God himself will save the lame, gathering them from every land, changing their shame into praise, restoring their fortunes, and turning back their captivity.[201]

---

192. See Keener, *John*, 649. Cf. John 5:20, 36; Gen 2:2–3.

193. See Ibid., 649. See John 5:15; 7:23.

194. John 5:6, 9, 11, 14, 15. See Lincoln, *John*, 199–200. Cf. John 7:23.

195. See Lincoln, *John*, 199–200.

196. John 5:25, 28. See Haenchen, *John I*, 256, who acknowledges that ἔγειρε points "to the resurrection of the (spiritually) dead." Cf. Keener, *John*, 649; Lincoln, *John*, 199–200.

197. In Isa 35:6 healing of the lame signifies the messianic era (as does giving of sight to the blind). Neither sign was performed by the OT prophets. Cf. Keener, *John*, 325.

198. Isa 35:6 cf. vv. 1–10. See Carson, *John*, 243.

199. Jer 31:8–9.

200. Mic 4:6–7.

201. Zeph 3:19–20.

PART II—DETAILED EXEGETICAL EXAMINATION OF JOHN 5-10

These images find resonance in John 5. Here Jesus, equal with God, doing the works of God shown to him by his Father, has come and healed the lame, outcast man, associated with death and the wilderness, representative of many Jews. Moreover, Jesus has provided living water as opposed to the mocking water of the pool,[202] offering the way of life and redemption, and a return to worship in the New Jerusalem and new Temple that he represents.

A further NE motif occurs in the concept of Jesus' re-creation, "finishing" (τελειώσω),[203] the Father's works. We have already observed Dahm's suggestion that this echoes the accomplishment (συντελεσθῇ) of God's creative NE work of Isa 55:10–13.[204] This itself echoes συντελέω, Gen 2:2 (LXX), describing the NE of salvation as a new creation by God's Word.[205]

An Eschatological Sabbath

The use of the imperfect tense in John 5:16, "the Jews were persecuting Jesus, because he was doing these things on the Sabbath," points to Jesus' continual Sabbath activity.[206] It may be that Jesus was deliberately choosing the Sabbath as his day to heal.[207] Wright suggests that Jesus was operating on a different timescale from "the Jews."[208] They were observing the rest of the old creation (still under the curse), while Jesus was ushering in the rest of the new redeemed creation.[209] Moreover, in John 7:22–23, Sabbath circumcision under the law of Moses, making a man ceremonially acceptable, merely points to and foreshadows the much greater work of making the man completely whole through Christ.[210] The idea that this involved resurrection, which comes on the "last day,"[211] evokes the eschatological Sabbath.

---

202. See Jones, *Water*, 136.

203. John 19:28, 30 cf. 4:34; 5:36; 17:4; 9:4

204. See Part I, above. See Dahms, "Isaiah 55:11," 78–88.

205. "My word . . . shall accomplish that which I purpose, and shall succeed in the thing for which I sent it . . . For you shall go out in joy and be led forth in peace; the mountains and the hills before you shall break forth into singing, and all the trees of the field shall clap their hands." Isa 55:11–12 cf. Isa 65:17–18.

206. Cf. Bultmann, *John*, 243; Haenchen, *John I*, 248; Carson, *John*, 247.

207. See Beasley-Murray, *John*, 74.

208. Wright, *John 1–10*, 59.

209. Following Cullmann, Pancaro argues that the finishing of Jesus' works would bring the Sabbath rest at his glorification. Pancaro, *Law*, 159–60. Cf. Lincoln, *John*, 197.

210. John 7:21–24. See Pancaro, *Law*, 508.

211. Cf. John 6:39, 40, 44, 54; 11:24; 12:48. See Bruce, *John*, 154–55.

"Jewish" opposition, vv. 10–13

"The Jews" confront the man

Like Moses' signs, Jesus' miracles manifested God's glory[212] and authenticated his mission.[213] Their self-authenticating nature should have convinced "the Jews" that he was from God and enabled them to believe. Although they "saw his works," however, they did not "know his ways."[214] Instead of glorifying God at the healing, they immediately find fault with the very thing that demonstrated it, the man's carrying his bed,[215] accusing him of breaking the Sabbath. They did so on the basis of the very law that testifies to Jesus, but interpreted by their own tradition. To carry out a bed constitutes one of the Mishnah's thirty-nine classes of work that violates the Sabbath.[216] Though they interpret the law's letter,[217] they do not observe its spirit regarding the man's Sabbath release from bondage,[218] but rather they interrogate him.

Opposition to the Exodus/NE

This reflects Pharaoh's opposition to Moses, God's Exodus agent. From the time that Moses first sought to effect Israel's release from bondage and at every step thereafter, notably in connection with his signs, Pharaoh opposed him. He did so on the basis that he *did not know the Lord* and he expected Israel to work as his slaves.[219] Opposition to Moses also came from within Israel, from both its leaders and its people, even though they had seen God's works.[220] This opposition, which came to all God's prophets, including Moses, and Christ as the 'Prophet like Moses,' is summed up in Stephen's speech (Acts 7:51–53).

Similar opposition was made to the announcement of God's NE at the time of the exile. The Lord had promised to bring his exiles home, defeating Babylon through

---

212. Cf. John 1:14; 2:11; 11:4, 40; Exod 9:16; Deut 5:24.

213. Cf. John 5:36; 10:25; 10:37–38; 14:11; 15:24; Exod 4:1–9; 7:17; 8:10, 22; 9:14, 29.

214. Ps 95:9, 10 cf. John 5:37–38; 15:24. "If I had not done among them the works that no one else did, they would not be guilty of sin, but now they have seen and hated both me and my Father."

215. Cf. Carson, *John*, 244; Barrett, *John*, 254.

216. That is, "taking out aught from one domain into another," *m. Shabbath* 7:2, in Danby, 106. In *m. Shabbath* 10:5, taking out of a man on a couch is permissible if the man is carried out alive but forbidden if he is dead. Cf. Lincoln, *John*, 195; Schnackenburg, *John*, 2:97; Str-B 2.454–61; *Jub.* 2:29–30.

217. The unlawfulness of carrying burdens on the Sabbath is enshrined in the OT. Cf. Jer 17:21–22; Num 15:32–36; Neh 13:16.

218. Deut 5:14–15. Jesus gives several instances of compassionate release in the Synoptics, e.g., Matt 12:2–8, 11–12. Lohse, "σάββατον," 5, notes that there was no objection to the desecration of the Sabbath when Jehoiada overthrew Athaliah on the Sabbath day. Cf. 2 Kgs 11:5, 7, 9.

219. Exod 5:2.

220. See, e.g., Num 16:1–3; Exod 17:7; Ps 95:8–10.

Cyrus.[221] But they objected to God's plan to use a Persian king to rescue them, their persistent "blindness and deafness," a consequence of their idolatry,[222] leading them to oppose God. This disobedience brought the postponement of the NE glory;[223] a new obedient Suffering Servant must bring about its fulfilment.[224] This person, who is both God's Servant and the representative of his people, will himself become the subject of disbelief, reproach, rejection, and a violent death.[225] Importantly, John applies this prophecy to Jesus as God's Servant in whom the crowds do not believe, "even though he had done so many signs before them," John 12:37–38. Moreover, their disbelief is attributed to the Lord's judicial blinding of their eyes and hardening of their hearts, reminiscent of the hardening of Pharaoh.[226]

Opposition to the community

Mirror reading of the "Jewish" authorities' treatment of the lame man, and later the blind man, might suggest "Jewish" opposition to the Johannine churches.[227] In particular, the methods employed by the "Jews" of Jesus' day, targeting those who had witnessed Jesus' miracles and been influenced by him, but had not yet made a formal commitment to him, may also have been employed by the local synagogues against those on the fringes of the Johannine community.[228] Thus it is possible that they would interrogate such people with a view, not only to deter them from Christian discipleship, reclaiming them for the "Jewish" fold, but also to gain information that they could use against the Christian churches.[229] Thus, although I reject Martyn's "two level" approach, it is likely that this episode was relevant to the localized opposition that John's readers faced.[230]

The motif of testing

Protracted suffering had tested the lame man's devotion to God. The allusion to the thirty-eight years of wilderness wandering reinforces this idea, as does lameness and

---

221. Cf. Isa 44:28; 45:1.

222. Cf. Ps 115:4–8; Isa 40–48. See Watts, "Consolation," 44–45.

223. So Watts, "Consolation," 31.

224. Isa 49–55. See Watts, "Consolation," 54–55.

225. Isa 52:13–53:12. Cf. John 12:37–38.

226. John 12:39–40. Cf. Isa 6:9–10; Exod 4:21; 9:12; 10:1, 20, 27; 11:10; 14:8; Cole, *Exodus*, 71–72; Oswalt, *Isaiah 1–39*, 189; Barrett, *John*, 431–32.

227. Cf. Barrett, *John*, 250, 137–38; Bultmann, *John*, 239, 247; Martyn, *History and Theology*, 72–76; Hoskyns, *Fourth Gospel*, 361–62; Carson, *John*, 240.

228. Cf. Bultmann, *John*, 239.

229. Ibid., 239.

230. See above. Cf. Rev 2:9–10; 3:9; Smalley, *Thunder and Love*, 89, 125–26; Hemer, *Seven Churches*, 29, 67, 86–87.

blindness, which echo Israel's spiritual condition during the exile. Jesus' healing sign and the subsequent reaction of the "Jewish" authorities, however, proved to be the moment of crisis for the man and those he represented. He must listen to Jesus' voice and enter God's rest, "today,"[231] facing the wrath of authorities, or he must be reconciled with the "Jewish" authorities and remain forever "exiled" from God. The seriousness of the charge of Sabbath violation would have affected his perception of the situation. Jesus had offered him life, but in the light of the hostility of the authorities, faith and obedience to Jesus may have been *perceived* as an impossible option.[232]

This may be compared with Israel's wilderness testing, commencing immediately after deliverance from bondage. When hemmed in by the sea, with Pharaoh's soldiers pursuing them, "they did not have a steadfast hold of the vision of faith . . . [but] focused very much on the immediate danger confronting them."[233] The choice before Israel was between their *perceptions*, the impossibility of escape at the sea and of living in the desert without bread or water, and faith and obedience to the word of God who promised life (cf. Deut 8:1–3). The ultimate test occurred at Kadesh, however, where God sent leaders from every tribe to spy out the Promised Land, the spies brought a bad report, and the people sought to return to Egypt. This was because they *perceived* themselves to be "like grasshoppers" before the powerful inhabitants of the land and did not believe that God could enable them to conquer it.[234] Because of this, God swore that they would not see the Land, but would wander for a further thirty-eight years in the wilderness, until that generation perished.[235] Similar testing also occurred at the time of the Babylonian captivity and at the return from exile where it *seemed* to Israel that God was not in control of history and that the gods of the nations were his equals. This perception resulted in God's lawsuit against the nations where his chief witness was blind and deaf Israel.[236]

Deflecting the blame

The answer the man gives to the "Jewish" authorities immediately indicates where his loyalty lies. Remarkably, although he has seen Jesus' works he does not *know* him and, like Israel by the Sea and in the wilderness, he is quick to point the finger at the one who has delivered him.

---

231. Carson, *John*, 246, thinks that "the syntax of *Stop sinning* is chosen to stress urgency. The *something worse* must be final judgement (cf. v. 29)" (emphasis original).

232. Cf. Barrett, *John*, 250; Carson, *John*, 244–45.

233. Mackay, *Exodus*, 252. Cf. Exod 14:9ff.; Deut 8:2ff. See Craigie, *Deuteronomy*, 185.

234. Num 13:32–14:4.

235. Num 14:28–35. Cf. Deut 2:14.

236. See above.

PART II—DETAILED EXEGETICAL EXAMINATION OF JOHN 5–10

Warning: Jesus seeks out and warns the man, v. 14

Jesus finds the man in the Temple. Ostensibly, return to the Temple is a sign of return from "exile," but here it indicates a return to the "Jewish" fold. John's readers would understand that the destruction of the Second Temple has been signalled from the outset of Jesus' ministry. They will be only too aware that this was fulfilled in A.D. 70. They will also be aware that Jesus' reference to raising it up in three days indicates the "replacement" of the Temple as the locus of God's glory by Jesus' body, John 2:19–21.[237] Thus they will understand that the man has made the mistake of choosing the wrong worshipping community and worshipping at the wrong Temple.[238] The warning "sin no more, that nothing worse may happen to you," John 5:14, reinforces this. Not only was the man's infirmity the result of his sin,[239] but also his present conduct and prospective betrayal are viewed as sinful.[240] Moreover, these actions will bring eternal consequences, the worse thing being Gehenna.[241] The warning is not malicious; Jesus' shepherd-like action in seeking the man out indicates real concern.

Defection: He reports to "the Jews," v. 15

Jesus' healing of the lame man, making him completely whole, has been taken as hope for the Jewish people, but this hope is now largely dashed. Despite all that Jesus has done for the man he remains unmoved,[242] betraying Jesus to his persecutors.[243] As a representative of *some* of his people, those who reject Jesus, he personifies their disbelief and foreshadows their fate, choosing to wander in the wilderness until finally destroyed with the Second Temple.[244] This is not the whole story.

---

237. John 2:19–22. On the Johannine replacement pattern cf. Neyrey, *Ideology*, 11; Brunson, *Psalm 118*, 147ff.

238. See Lightfoot, *John's Gospel*, 138. "He who was formerly infirm is found 'in the Temple' [5:14], and appears at the first opportunity to link himself with the Jews [5:15] rather than with his Benefactor." Cf. John 9:38 where the blind man worships Jesus.

239. Cf. Mark 2:10–12; Lincoln, *John*, 195; Carson, *John*, 245–46.

240. Bruce, *John*, 124, notes that unlike the paralytic of Capernaum, Mark 2:1–12, he did not receive assurance of his sins forgiven. Martyn, *History and Theology*, 5, thinks the man is being warned against the specific sin of being an informant.

241. Cf. Beasley-Murray, *John*, 74; Hoskyns, *Fourth Gospel*, 253; Barrett, *John*, 255; Lincoln, *John*, 200; Schnackenburg, *John*, 2:98, 461; Str-B 1.495.

242. Cf. Jones, *Water*, 122.

243. The idea that he is naïve (Brown, *John I–XII*, 209) or "dull" (Carson, *John*, 246) is untenable. The man was aware of the "Jews'" attitude to his carrying his mat on the Sabbath and understood that they were seeking the identity of the person who had told him to do so. Cf. Lincoln, *John*, 196; Borchert, *John 1–11*, 235.

244. Cf. Matt 11:20–24; Luke 10:13–15.

The parallels with John 9

In the light of striking parallels and contrasts between John 5:1–15 and John 9,[245] we cannot deal with these passages in isolation but need to consider them together.[246] As we have seen, the blind man and the lame man are frequently understood as paradigms for potential converts to the Johannine community.[247] The lame man who sides with the "Jewish" authorities is usually thought of as a foil for the blind man, who believes and obeys Jesus.[248] While this is surely correct, it is not the whole story, for they may also be understood as models for *different groups of Jewish people* in "exile"[249] offering alternate responses to restoration from "exile" through Jesus.

Motyer has argued that the John 9 healing of the blind man represents Jesus' mission to Israel to restore her from exile. Moreover, it is a theodicy addressing the A.D. 70 crisis. Just as the blind man was absolved from guilt by Jesus and worshipped him outside the synagogue, so also those whom he represents are absolved from blame for the destruction of the Temple (which occurred in the wider purposes of God) and are called to worship Jesus outside the synagogue.[250]

I would argue that the blind man represents only a part of Israel—those who have been restored from "exile" by hearing the voice of the Good Shepherd, the true believers of the Johannine churches (and of the Church generally). By parallel reasoning I argue that the lame man represents a similar but different scenario. He stands for those of Israel who continue in "exile" due to their sin and unbelief.[251] Like the blind man he is called out of "exile" by Jesus, through a new creation and NE sign. Unlike the blind man, however, he turns his back on Jesus and sides with the hostile "Jewish" authorities in order that he may participate in the "Jewish" synagogue and Temple worship.

One theodicy with two outcomes

The lame man and the blind man represent two possible outcomes for Jewish people confronted by the claims of Jesus in the probationary period before the A.D. 70 calamity. Either they side with the "Jewish" authorities and remain "exiled" from Jesus, or they are "exiled" from (unbelieving) "Jews" and restored to true worship in Jesus. They are thus two sides of the same theodicy. Many of "the Jews" who tragically perished in A.D. 70 did so because of their own sin and hardness of heart. Those who worshipped

---

245. See below on John 9.

246. Rensberger, *Johannine Faith*, 37–49, also links Nicodemus and the blind man as those who make "choices of faith and community."

247. Cf. Bultmann, *John*, 239; Barrett, *John*, 250, 137–38; Carson, *John*, 240.

248. See Martyn, *History and Theology*, 74–75.

249. See above on the lame and the blind.

250. See Motyer, *Your Father*, 137–38.

251. Cf. Bruce, *John*, 208, who thinks that John 5:14 implies that the cripple was blameworthy.

outside the Temple were willing subjects of Jesus' mercy. Furthermore, it is in the crucible of testing that their loyalty is revealed.

Two examples with one lesson

More than just a theodicy, however, these two examples teach all of us who read GJohn an important lesson: how to respond to Jesus. We must not emulate the lame man, who responded in unbelief, betraying Jesus in order to save his own skin. Rather we must be like the blind man, who believed in Jesus, venturing all upon him, to gain eternal life.

Conclusion

In this narrative, the vast crowds of invalids surrounding the pool typify Israel in exile. Jesus the Son of Man has been sent by the Father to raise them from (spiritual and ultimately physical) death to life, to initiate the eschatological Sabbath rest, and to restore them in a NE. One man in particular represents the response of a particular section of the Jewish people during the probationary period following Jesus' death. Although he is the subject of Jesus' sign and a witness of Jesus' power to raise the dead, when tested by "Jewish" persecution he fails to obey Jesus' voice and rejects Jesus in favor of a legalistic Second Temple worship. Consequently he (and those he represents) fails to enter rest, perishing together with the Temple some thirty-eight years later. This passage is thus the first part of a two-part theodicy regarding the destruction of the Temple. More than a theodicy, however, together with John 9, it teaches us how Jesus fulfils the eschatological Sabbath and NE resurrection promises. It also shows us the wrong and the right way to respond to Jesus.

NE INTERPRETATION OF JOHN 5 DISCOURSE: JESUS ON TRIAL VV. 16–47

The Dialogue takes the form of a trial or lawsuit against Jesus.[252] As in the case of Israel's lawsuit against Moses this effectively becomes a lawsuit against God.[253] Two charges are made and two defenses given. In the latter defense, Jesus is revealed to be the eschatological Judge who turns the tables on his accusers, who become the accused.

---

252. See Lincoln, *John*, 202, who points to the frequency of key forensic terms in the dialogue. Cf. Beasley-Murray, *John*, 77–78.

253. Cf. Exod 15:24ff.; 16:2, 7–8; 17:3–7.

Accusation: He breaks the Sabbath, v. 16

The attack on the lame man was an attack on Jesus, and, when the man deflected responsibility, "the Jews" put Jesus on trial[254] on the charge of breaking the Sabbath.[255] That they later sought "all the more to kill him," v. 18, suggests that from the outset of the trial they wanted to kill Jesus for Sabbath violation.[256]

Jesus' Defense: He acts as his Father's Son, v. 17

The vv. 17, 19 use of ἀπεκρίνατο ("answered"), aorist middle deponent, has "legal overtones," suggesting Jesus' legal defense.[257] Jesus' first response, his Father works until now and he works, is his defense in essence. It suggests that Jesus copies his Father who is re-creating and redeeming his creation, whose work will be completed, culminating in an eschatological Sabbath. Since "the Jews" understood that God worked on the Sabbath, this effectively answered the Sabbath charge, but it raised the new issue of Jesus' claim to equality with God.

Accusation: He *makes* himself equal to God, v. 18

It was not considered wrong for a Jew to refer to God as "Father." What "the Jews" objected to was Jesus' reference to God as *his special* Father[258] and to his suggestion that *he* may do what God does. In their eyes this was tantamount to *making himself equal to God*. In certain circumstances it was not considered wrong for men to be spoken of as God. "The Jews" gloried in Moses' being made like God to Pharaoh, Exod 7:1, but to make oneself equal to God, as Pharaoh and the king of Babylon had done (Isa 14:13–14), was "a revolt of the creature against his creator"[259] that called down judgement upon oneself.[260] Bruce, notes that desire to be like God drove Adam from paradise and the devil from heaven.[261]

Making oneself equal to God was to seek independence from God, as a rebellious son grasps at equality with his father.[262] Ironically it was Israel who had been

---

254. See Lincoln, *John*, 197. Cf. Harvey, *Trial*, 51.

255. Carson, *John*, 247, thinks that the imperfect in v. 16, "was doing these things on the Sabbath," suggests several occasions.

256. Sabbath violation could be punishable by death in the Torah, Exod 31:14, 15; Num 15:32–36. Cf. Carson, *John*, 249; Keener, *John*, 644; *y*. Megillah 1:6, 2; Sanders, *Jewish Law*, 18–19.

257. See Carson, *John*, 247.

258. See Schnackenburg, *John*, 2:102.

259. Ibid., 2:102.

260. Cf. Exod 7:1; Ps 86:2; Beasley-Murray, *John*, 75. Carson, *John*, 249, Dodd, *IFG*, 320–28; Barrett, *John*, 256; Philo *Leg. All.* 1:49; 2 Thess 2:4; Phil 2:6; Dodd, *IFG*, 32; Str-B 2.462–64.

261. Bruce, *John*, 127.

262. Odeberg, *Fourth Gospel*, 203, notes that a son who rejected his father's authority was described

rebellious sons, in the wilderness, and before the Babylonian exile, and "the Jews" who were now rebelling, taking the place of Pharaoh in resisting the redemptive NE work of both God the Father and of Jesus.

Jesus' defense: Equality with God does not imply his independence from God, vv. 19–23

Jesus does not deny his equality with God, but only that he is a rebellious son.[263] He is not acting independently of God nor did he *make himself* equal to God. Contrary to "the Jews," Jesus' equality with God means *dependence* upon his Father. "The Son can do nothing of his own accord, but only what he sees the Father doing," v. 19. Following Dodd, many understand Jesus' words as a parable of a son apprenticed to a Father.[264] It is more probable, however, that there is an OT echo here: the idea of God "showing" Jesus all things may echo God showing Moses the signs[265] or the pattern for the Tabernacle.[266] Similarly, David was shown the pattern of the Temple.[267] In Ezekiel 37, the Son of Man is shown how to raise Israel from their graves. It is also possible that there is a hint of "Second Adam" Christology here. According to Luke 3:8, Adam was God's son. Moreover, God created him in his own image and showed him all his works, making him vice-regent over all creation.[268]

While these ideas may lie in the background, however, they cannot begin to describe the equality with God that Jesus claims the Father has bestowed upon him. The Father so loves the Son that he shows him *all things that he himself is doing*, committing the twin powers of life and judgement into his hands, with the intention "that all may honor the Son, just as they honor the Father," v. 23. I suggest that this showing and bestowing indicate the commissioning of the Son to act not only (as Moses) as the Father's agent,[269] but also, as the Son in the Parable of the Vinedressers, as his legal representative to whom he *transferred his own rights*.[270] Consequently, the Son

---

as "one who equated himself with his father." Cf. Str-B 2.465.

263. See Deut 21:18–21. Cf. Keener, *John*, 648; McGrath, "Rebellious Son," 470–73; Brown, *John I–XII*, 218; Beasley-Murray, *John*, 75; Carson, *John*, 240.

264. Cf. Dodd, "Hidden Parable," 30–40; Brown, *John I–XII*, 218; Haenchen, *John I*, 250, who affirm use of a parable. But cf. Carson, *John*, 250; Beasley-Murray, *John*, 75, who think that this is unlikely.

265. Exod 4:2ff.

266. Cf. Exod 25:9, 40; 26:30; Num 8:4.

267. 1 Chr 28:11–12, 18–19.

268. Cf. Gen 1:26–30; Ps 8:6–9.

269. Meeks, *Prophet-King*, 301–5, suspects that the idea of Moses as God's envoy lies behind the Johannine formula. Cf. Schnackenburg, *John*, 2:108; Str-B 3.2; Rengstorf, "ἀποστέλλω," 1:407ff.; Blank, *Krisis*, 70; Haenchen, "Der Vater," 208–216.

270. See Derrett, "Wicked Vinedressers," 302-303. cited by Ashton, *Understanding*, 320. Cf. Rengstorf, "ἀποστέλλω," 404.

is to receive the same honor as the Father, "that all may honor the Son, just as they honor the Father."[271] Many of the ideas are similar to those of Paul, particularly the theology of Phil 2:5–11.[272]

In the verses that follow, Jesus proceeds to explain why the Father has bestowed all things into his hand, making the Son his representative. He is God's agent who executes eschatological resurrection and judgement. That this is understood in terms of the NE and eschatological Sabbath will become clear from the OT allusions, many of which refer to Israel's end-time Sabbath and NE hope. It is also a work of cosmic dimensions;[273] Jesus' obedience to the Father reverses death and the curse—brought into the world through Adam's independence from God. Moreover, it proceeds in two stages:[274] Jesus judges and grants eschatological life in the present. In the future his work will culminate in the Final Resurrection and Judgement.[275]

Jesus inaugurates a Paschal NE and eschatological Sabbath, vv. 24–25

Jesus speaks here of a realized eschatological blessing that he bestows on those who obey him. Here and now, "Whoever hears my word and believes him who sent me has eternal life. He does not come into judgement, but has passed from death to life," v. 24. "Passed from death to life," is practically identical to the realized eschatology of 1 John 3:14.[276] As we have seen it involves both forensic justification[277] and spatial translation,[278] a NE from one realm to another analogous to Col 1:12–13.[279]

Comparisons with the Colossian passage are worthy of further investigation. Thus both passages:

1. Contrast the opposing realms of death and darkness with life and light.[280] In Colossians 1:13 the realm of darkness is a hostile dominion,[281] whilst "light" characterizes the "inheritance" and the kingdom of God's Son.[282] In GJohn, death and

---

271. John 5:23. Cf. "they will reverence my Son," Matt 21:37; Mark 12:6; Luke 20:13.

272. Cf. Barrett, *John*, 258; Carson, *John*, 250–51; Bruce, *John*, 130; Isa 45:22–23. Cf. the exaltation of the Servant in Isa 52:13–53:12. See Knight, *Servant Theology*, 43.

273. Cf. John 5:28, "all who are in the tombs shall hear his voice," speaking of a general resurrection.

274. Cf. Barrett, *John*, 261.

275. Cf. vv. 24–25; 28–29; 12:48. See Barrett, *John*, 260–61.

276. In 1 John 3:14, believers have "passed (μεταβεβήκαμεν) out of death into life."

277. Cf. Barrett, *John*, 260–61; Carson, *John*, 256.

278. Barrett, *John*, 260–61, compares the use of μεταβέβηκεν in 5:24 to Jesus' departure μεταβῇ from this world to the Father in John 13:1.

279. See discussion in Part I, Ideological Feasibility, above. Cf. Carson, *John*, 256; Beasley-Murray, *John*, 76, who cite Col 1:13.

280. In GJohn both death and darkness, and life and light, are used synonymously. For light and life synonyms cf. John 1:4; 8:12. For darkness and death parallels cf. John 3:17–19; 12:35 13:27, 30–31.

281. Cf. Col 1:21.

282. See Dunn, *Colossians and Philemon*, 76.

PART II—DETAILED EXEGETICAL EXAMINATION OF JOHN 5–10

darkness are characteristic of Satan and his followers—in opposition to life and light which are characteristic of Jesus and his followers.[283]

2. Speak of a translation or crossing over from one realm to the other.

3. Relate the translation to the believing reception of the Word. In Colossians, the translation occurred when the gospel came and the Colossians heard and believed it.[284] In John 5:24–25, the spiritually dead hear the Word of Jesus, the voice of the Son of God, and live.

4. Are eschatological.[285]

5. Employ a realized eschatology.[286]

6. Imply a two-stage eschatology. In the Col 1:13 context, Wright speaks of Paul's conception of a "two-stage" process, whereby the kingdom is established, "which begins with Christ's resurrection and exaltation and continues until all enemies are subdued. Then there comes the final kingdom of God, the restoration of all things."[287] This two stage restoration is also present in Col 3:4, Rom 8:19–25, and 1 John 3:2, in terms of the regeneration of creation that occurs at the revelation of the sons of God at Jesus' Parousia. Two stages are also implicit in the parallel sections of John 5:24–25 and 5:28–29.

Importantly, as Holland has emphasized, the Colossian passage echoes Israel's New Exodus and her Exodus redemption from the power and realm of Pharaoh.[288] Invoking the Exodus imagery, Colossians 2:12–14 portrays:

> The time when Israel's God showed himself to be God of the whole world by defeating both the Egyptians and the mighty waters of the sea. The New Exodus was the act of New Creation, bringing the chosen race to a new birth out of chaos and slavery.[289]

---

283. Cf. John 3:19–21, 21; 8:12; 9:5; 12:36; 12:46.

284. Col 1:5, 6 cf. 1 Thess 1:5–6, where the gospel came to the Thessalonians, and 1 Thess 2:12–13, where God calls them into his kingdom by the gospel which is in truth "the word of God." Cf. "the Gospel of God," Rom 1:1.

285. Dunn, *Colossians*, 77. "Particularly notable is the way the [Col. 1:12 'inheritance'] language could be transferred to the eschatological hope of share in the resurrection and/or life beyond death in the eternal life of heaven (Dan 12:13 . . .)."

286. Cf. Dunn, *Colossians*, 77; Barrett, *John*, 261; Carson, *John*, 256.

287. Wright, *Colossians and Philemon*, 62.

288. See Holland, *Contours*, 279. He cites Klijn, "Jewish Christianity," 119–31; Martin, "New Testament Hymns," 37–49; Wright, "Poetry and Theology," 444–60.

289. Holland, *Contours*, 280, citing Wright, "Poetry and Theology," 452–54. Cf. 2 Cor 5:17.

Moreover, in the context of the Colossian hymn, Jesus' death is the Paschal sacrifice that initiates the NE.[290] Similarly in GJohn, at Jesus' paschal death the world is judged, its ruler is cast out, and Jesus draws all people unto himself,[291] initiating the NE.

The related idea of present possession of "eternal life" has similar implications. That this echoes "eternal life" (ζωὴν αἰώνιον) in Daniel 12 seems clear, not only from the verbal agreement, but also from the evident John 5:29 allusion to the "resurrection to eternal life" in Dan 12:2.[292] In context, this latter text connects eternal life to Promised Land, since Daniel himself is given hope of participation in the "resurrection to eternal life" in terms of arising to his inheritance (lot) at the end of the days.[293] Collins believes this to be reflected in Col 1:12, "the lot of the saints in light."[294] If so, this strengthens the conceptual parallel previously observed between John 5:24 and Col 1:12–13,[295] since both then imply the possession of an inheritance in connection with a realized eschatological NE.

The concept of eternal life in connection with the land may also be present elsewhere in the OT. Many scholars would deny this. Since the Hebrew, לְחַיֵּי עוֹלָם, ("everlasting life") occurs only in Dan 12:2, they think eternal life (and bodily resurrection) to be a Danielic innovation, introduced in connection with the Maccabees. Other scholars, however, argue that, in view of the beliefs of the Egyptians and others, it is inconceivable that Israel had no hope of eternal life.[296] Thus Dahood finds עַד־הָעוֹלָם חַיִּים, ("life forevermore") Ps 133:3, to reflect the concept of eternal life. Moreover, on the basis of Ugaritic parallels, he believes that there are many expressions of hope for immortality and resurrection in the Psalms.[297] This accords with NT interpretation of such OT episodes as Abraham receiving Isaac "from the dead," and Joseph giving instruction concerning his bones as expressing hope of life after death.[298]

I argue that while several texts such as Ps 16:11; 133:3; Dan 12:2, explicitly express such a hope, the main eschatological focus is upon eternal life in connection with the land. Joseph's hope lay in the burial of his bones within the land. Isaac's "resurrection" was bound together with promises of land. Abraham's body as good as dead was given

---

290. See Holland, *Contours*, 280, who notes that the Paschal context of the Colossian Hymn is the major determining factor, in interpreting the material.

291. John 12:31–33.

292. Cf. John 5:24; Dan 12:2 LXX. This is the only occurrence of ζωὴν αἰώνιον in the OT. On the allusion to Dan 12:13 in John 5:28 see below.

293. Dan 12:13.

294. See Collins, *Daniel*, 402. Cf. Baldwin, *Daniel*, 210.

295. See above.

296. Cf. Smick, "Ugaritic," 115; Baldwin, *Daniel*, 204–5, n. 2.

297. For example, in Ps 17:15, he translates "when I awake," as, "at the resurrection," linking it with Isa 26:19 and Dan 12:2. Cf. Dahood, *Psalms 1–50*, 106; Kidner *Psalms 1–72*, 90.

298. Cf. Heb 11:17–19, 22; Gen 22; 50:25.

PART II—DETAILED EXEGETICAL EXAMINATION OF JOHN 5-10

life in connection with the promise.[299] Thus, though not always patent, the hope of eternal life was always latent in connection with the Promised Land.

"An hour is coming, and is now here, when the dead will hear the voice of the Son of God and those who hear will live," John 5:25, is a parallel statement to John 5:24 expressed in terms of a realized eschatological resurrection. Remarkably similar to the Pauline spiritual resurrection,[300] this echoes the Ezekiel 37 resurrection at the word of the Son of Man[301] and is itself echoed in the resurrection of Lazarus, as a symbolic narrative for spiritual resurrection from the dead.

In terms of the hearing Jesus' voice (word) that brings life, I have already suggested that this echoes the hearing God's voice (obeying him) of the OT.[302] This is explicitly connected with the land and life: In paradise Adam was to obey God's voice, dwell in the garden, and have access to the tree of life. Failure to do so meant expulsion and death.[303] Because Abraham believed and obeyed the voice of God, he inherited the land.[304] Failure to hear the voice of God resulted in the unbelieving generation dying in the wilderness.[305] Deuteronomy connects hearing God's voice with return to the land and failure to hear with (Babylonian) exile and death.[306] In Isaiah, the direct connection is made: "Incline your ear, and come to me [Yahweh]; hear, that your soul may live," in the context of God making an everlasting Davidic covenant with Israel and sending forth his word, which will accomplish a NE.[307] Wright believes that,

> This explicit link of life with the land and death with exile, coupled with the promise of restoration the other side of exile, is one of the forgotten roots of the fully developed [resurrection] hope of ancient Israel.[308]

How and why he acts: The twin powers have been bestowed upon Jesus the Son of Man, vv. 26–27

Though Jesus has not *made himself* equal to God, the Father has bestowed divine prerogatives upon him—to have life in himself and to execute judgement. Possession of "life in himself," John 5:26, is the explanation of Jesus' ability to carry out his mission

---

299. Rom 4:17 cf. Heb 11:9–12.

300. Cf. Rom 6:4; Eph 2:5,6; Col 2:12; 3:1.

301. See Carson, *John*, 256.

302. See Part I, above.

303. Gen 3:6, 17.

304. Cf. Gen 12:1–4; 15:6; 17:23; 18:19; 22:1–18, esp. v. 18, "because you have obeyed my voice." Cf. Heb 11:8–19.

305. Ps 95:7–11.

306. Cf. Deut 13:4; 27:10; 28:62; 30:2, 8, 20.

307. Isa 55:3–13.

308. Wright, *RSG*, 93.

The Sabbath Healing of a Lame Man, John 5

of raising the dead, both in the present and future.[309] It means that he is not dependent upon anyone for his own life and no one can take it from him, John 10:18. Moreover, he can bestow life on others, whoever he will, including the dead.

That the Son of God eternally possesses this divine attribute is clear from the Prologue, where "in the beginning," the eternal Word possessed life in himself.[310] This raises the question of how and when the Father has "granted the Son ... to have life in himself"? It is possible to relate John 5:26 to the doctrine of the "eternal generation of the Son."[311] This is the (Nicene) teaching that the Son is eternally begotten of the Father: The Father eternally generates the personal subsistence (but not the essence) of the Son, of necessity, but also willingly, communicating to him the whole of the divine essence, in a manner that is wholly spiritual, eternal, and divine.[312] In this way the Son is (in the words of the Nicene Creed) "God of God, light of light, very God of very God, begotten not made, being of one substance with the Father."[313]

In the context of the passage, however, Jesus is speaking of himself, in terms of his messianic mission, as the one who has been sent by the Father, to do the Father's will (John 5:30). Thus it is possible (likely) that John 5:26 relates to the incarnation and refers to the Father's authorization of the Son, as the Messiah, to exercise the divine prerogative "to have life in himself."[314] At the incarnation the eternal Word took upon himself human nature and came to do the Father's will. "He became what he was not, without ceasing to be what he was." As the Word made flesh, however, the Son of God voluntarily "restricted himself to human limitations"[315] (Phil 2:6–11) in order to redeem fallen mankind in accordance with the Father's will. Nevertheless, as the Messiah and the Father's emissary, God the Father has granted (authorized the exercise of) "life in himself" upon Jesus the Son of Man in order that he might fulfil his messianic mandate, including raising the dead and imparting eternal life to his people (John 10:27–28). This is why he has received "authority to lay ... down [his life] and ... authority to take it up again" from the Father (John 10:18). Moreover, functionally, this makes him equivalent to Paul's "last Adam [who] became a life-giving spirit."[316]

Authority to execute judgement, John 5:27, explains why Jesus can forensically justify believers (John 5:24) and condemn unbelief (John 3:19). Moreover, Jesus' verdict

---

309. Cf. vv. 24–25 and 28–29.

310. John 1:4. Cf. Bruce, *John*, 33; Carson, *John*, 118.

311. Cf. Carson, *John*, 257; Bruce, *John*, 132.

312. See Berkhof, *Systematic Theology*, 93–94.

313. Traditional text. For an excellent summary of Athanasius's defense of the Nicene teaching on the relationship between the Father and the Son see Letham, *The Holy Trinity*, 133–38.

314. Cf. Reymond, *Systematic Theology*, 326; Hodge, *Systematic Theology*, 1:470–71. Hodge writes, "What this passage [John 5:26] teaches ... concerns the constitution of Christ's person as He appeared on earth, and not the nature of the relation of the Father and Son in the Godhead."

315. Letham, *The Holy Trinity*, 37–38.

316. 1 Cor 15:45, "'The first man Adam became a living being'; the last Adam became a life-giving spirit." Cf. Hodge, *I&II Corinthians*, 350.

will be confirmed on the last day (John 12:48) when he will call the dead to his judgement (John 5:28–30). Importantly, the reason for this gift of authority to judge is also stated. Surprisingly it is not because he is the Son of God, as might be expected, but "because he is the Son of Man." To understand this we must investigate the OT allusions.

Allusion to Daniel 7:13

Many scholars acknowledge Jesus' anarthrous use of "Son of Man," John 5:27, to be an explicit allusion to Dan 7:13.[317] Barrett suggests that John "may even be returning to the wording of Daniel 7:13, (ὡς) υἱὸς ἀνθρώπου."[318] In support of this he notes the correspondence of John 5:27, ἐξουσίαν ἔδωκεν αὐτῷ ("he has given him authority"), with Dan 7:14, ἐδόθη αὐτῷ ἐξουσία ("authority was given to him").[319] Further confirmation is provided by the context of final judgement. In Daniel, the Ancient of Days is seated upon his chariot throne, thousand times ten thousand stand before him, the court is set in judgement, and the books are opened; in GJohn, Jesus is the eschatological judge.[320]

To some, however, John 5:27 seems to be a development *beyond* Daniel 7.[321] Schnackenburg thinks that in Jewish thought "judgement is reserved for God himself in almost all texts" and the Messiah does not carry out judgement, but "remains very much in the background."[322] I argue that the differences should not be exaggerated:

1. Already from "thrones," Daniel 7:9, it might be inferred that others were associated with God in judgement.[323]

2. Daniel's Son of Man shares divine glory.[324]

3. The OT *does* suggest that the Messiah as the Son of God has authority to Judge.[325] Indeed, he is God's vice-regent who judges on God's behalf. The "thrones for Judgement" belong to David, the "root of David" *judges* the poor and slays the wicked, the Servant brings מִשְׁפָּט (judgement) to the nations, and the nations are given into the power of the Son of God.[326] This is analogous to the ancient idea

---

317. Cf. Beasley-Murray, *John*, 77; Carson, *John*, 257, 259; Brown, *John I–XII*, 220; Lincoln, *John*, 204.

318. Barrett, *John*, 262.

319. So also Martyn, *History and Theology*, 132; Manning, *Echoes*, 164.

320. Cf. Dan 7:9–10; Rev 20:12; John 5:22, 27.

321. See Beasley-Murray, *John*, 77.

322. Schnackenburg, *John*, 2:107, n. 52. He cites Str-B 4.1104ff.

323. Cf. Matt 19:28; 1 Cor 6:2; Rev 4:4; 20:4; Dan 7:22 LXX. See Collins, *Daniel*, 301.

324. He rides on the clouds, comes near to the Ancient of Days, and receives glory and an everlasting kingdom so that all nations should serve him. Cf. "that all may honor the Son, just as they honor the Father," John 5:23; Dan 7:14. See Morris, *John*, 320.

325. *Pace* Schnackenburg, *John*, 2:107.

326. Cf. Ps 122:5; Isa 11:3–4, (echoed in John 7:24); Isa 42:1, 4; Ps 2:8–12. Cf. also Zech 3:7, where

The Sabbath Healing of a Lame Man, John 5

that the shepherd-king is the son of the god, ruling on his behalf.[327] That the Son of Man receives a kingdom suggests that he is given authority to judge.

4. In John 5 the Father has not relinquished his office of Judge to the Son. Rather, Jesus acts as the Father's agent, judging on his behalf, according to his word and will.[328]

Importantly, for GJohn, the Son of Man is "the Son in his role as eschatological redeemer," who suffers for his people.[329] This reflects the pattern in Daniel, where the Son of Man represents the people of God, suffers, and receives the kingdom on their behalf.[330] Baldwin suggests that the term "Son of man" may indicate the (messianic) King, as in Ps 80:15–17.[331] Bauckham notes that in the late Second Temple period, the Son of Man of Daniel 7 was thought to represent the Davidic Messiah.[332]

Scholars have also noted similarities with the Servant of the Lord, Isa 52:13–53:12, and the Shepherd figure of Zech 9–14.[333] Hengel notes possible links with the Servant's exaltation, the reward of his suffering, Isa 52:13b, and the exaltation of the Lord, Isa 6:1. This is the reverse of the "high-as-heavens presumption of the king of Babylon" who was cast down to hell. The kings who "shut their mouths," Isa 52:15, may correspond to judgement in Dan 7:10–14.[334] Barrett also notes parallels between John 5 and Philippians 2:5–11.[335] This fits the pattern recognized by Dodd of the Messiah being brought low and lifted up.[336]

Importantly, in the wider context of Daniel, the Son of Man inaugurates the kingdom of God, in parallel with the end-time and return from exile motifs that usher in the Jubilee-based eschatological Sabbath.

> Seventy weeks are decreed about your people and your holy city, to finish the transgression, to put an end to sin, and to atone for iniquity, to bring in everlasting righteousness, to seal both vision and prophet, and to anoint a most holy place.[337]

Joshua the messianic priest-king is given authority to judge God's house.

327. See discussion in ch. 12 below on sacral kingship.

328. John 5:30. See Bultmann, *John*, 256.

329. Beasley-Murray, *John*, 80. Cf. John 10:15, 17–18; 11:50–52; Barrett, *John*, 262; Smalley, "Son of Man Sayings," 292; idem, *John*, 241–42.

330. Dan 7:18, 21, 27. See Baldwin, *Daniel*, 150–51. Cf. Smalley, *Thunder and Love*, 62.

331. Baldwin, *Daniel*, 151.

332. Bauckham, "Jewish Messianism," 237, citing 2 *Bar.* 39–40; 4 *Ezra* 13; *Sib. Or.* 5:414–27.

333. Cf. Baldwin, *Daniel*, 150–51; Dodd, *IFG*, 245, n. 1; Smalley, *John*, 137–38.

334. Hengel, "Effective History," 97–98.

335. Barrett, *John*, 258. Cf. Carson, *John*, 255; Lincoln, *John*, 203; Bruce, *John*, 130.

336. See Dodd, "Old Testament in the New," 174–75.

337. Dan 9:24. See Baldwin, *Daniel*, 168, where she interprets Dan 9:24 as the "final triumph of God's kingdom and the end of human history." Cf. Ibid., 161.

PART II—DETAILED EXEGETICAL EXAMINATION OF JOHN 5–10

Although not directly alluded to in John 5, these ideas may belong to unstated points of resonance[338] between Daniel and GJohn; their prophetic themes being understood as fulfilled through Jesus.[339] Of particular importance might be the anointing of the Temple, fulfilled in the descent of the Spirit upon Jesus (John 1:33), the cutting off of the Messiah with nothing, and the destruction of the city and Sanctuary in a flood, which John would have understood in terms of the events of A.D. 70.[340]

An Allusion to Psalm 8:4–6

A further possible allusion is to Psalm 8:4–6, where the Lord has made the Son of Man a little lower than the angels, but crowned him with glory and honor and set all things under his feet. Hebrews 2:6–9 applies Psalm 8 to "him who for a little while was made lower than the angels, namely Jesus, crowned with glory and honor because of the suffering of death, so that by the grace of God he might taste death for everyone." Bruce notes that Hebrews "applies these words . . . to Christ as the last Adam, the head of the new creation and ruler of the world to come." Moreover, he thinks that Hebrews identifies the Son of Man in Psalm 8 with the "one like a son of man" in Dan 7:13.[341] Bruce adds that "Only one who is capable of undoing the effects of Adam's fall and thus ushering in a new world-order" could "take the place of Adam."[342] This is exactly what Jesus claims for himself here. Interestingly, this is what Ezekiel, as Son of Man, does (typically) in calling Israel to rise from their graves in exile and in judging Israel, Judah, and Jerusalem.[343] Importantly, as in Philippians 2, Isaiah 53, and Daniel 7, it is because of his voluntary sufferings that God exalts Jesus to the highest place and (as part of his messianic mandate) gives him authority to judge.

Summary

Jesus' words of John 5:26–27, together with his allusions to Daniel 7 and Psalm 8, indicate that the Father has bestowed divine prerogatives (authority to have life in himself and to judge) upon Jesus, the Son of Man and Messiah, in order that he might fulfil his messianic mission. This mission involves representing his people (as the new man, last Adam, King, and Messiah), laying down his life for them in order to atone for their sin,

---

338. See Hays, *Echoes*, 20.

339. For example, as the Lamb of God, Jesus "takes away the sin of the world," John 1:29, making atonement for sin by his death upon the cross. His body is the Temple, John 2:19–21. He is anointed by the Spirit, John 1:32. The bringing in of "everlasting righteousness" might be understood in terms of the forensic "passing from death to life," John 5:24, and the righteousness of Christ, John 16:10. The sealing of the prophecy may be understood in terms of the fulfilment of Scripture, John 19:28.

340. Cf. The Synoptic interpretation of Daniel 11:31 in Matt 24:15; Mark 13:14; Luke 21:20.

341. Bruce, *Hebrews*, 72–73.

342. Ibid., 73.

343. Cf. Ezek 37:1–14; 20:4; 22:2; 23:36.

The Sabbath Healing of a Lame Man, John 5

rising from the dead, being exalted to glory, inheriting the kingdom on their behalf, and raising them from death to spiritual life. As we shall see, it culminates in his raising and judging the dead in the general resurrection and judgement of the last day.

His work culminates in future eschatological resurrection and judgement, vv. 28–30

"The Jews" are not to marvel at Jesus' words for

> An hour is coming when all who are in the tombs will hear his voice and come out, those who have done good to the resurrection of life, and those who have done evil to the resurrection of judgement, John 5:28–29.

This parallels the resurrection of John 5:24–25, but the absence of "and now is" and the reference to "all who are in the tombs" points to a future general resurrection of the body, followed by the last judgement.[344] That this is understood as a NE and eschatological Sabbath is evident from the OT allusions.

An allusion to Daniel 12:2

"And many of those who sleep (καθευδόντων) in the dust of the earth shall awake (ἀναστήσονται), some to everlasting life (ζωὴν αἰώνιον), and some to shame and everlasting contempt." Several scholars have noted this allusion.[345] Verbal parallels are evident in John's use of "everlasting life," ζωὴν αἰώνιον,[346] and "resurrection," ἀνάστασιν,[347] but the conceptual parallels are much stronger: There is "virtually unanimous agreement," in view of the mention of "everlasting life," that Daniel 12:2 refers to the resurrection of people who have died.[348] "Sleep," שֵׁנַת, and "awake," יָקִיצוּ are used in the OT of death and resurrection.[349] Moreover, Daniel envisages bodily resurrection. This may be inferred from the reference to the "dust of the earth," אַדְמַת־עָפָר, which echoes the הָאֲדָמָה and עָפָר of Gen 3:19, used of Adam's bodily dissolution.[350] Daniel 12:2 also alludes to Isa 26:19, "Your dead shall live; their bodies (נְבֵלָתִי) shall rise. You who dwell in the dust (עָפָר), awake and sing for joy!" which Daniel clearly understood as speaking of bodily resurrection.[351] Furthermore, Daniel envisages a *general* resur-

---

344. See Bruce, *John*, 133. Cf. John 6:40, 54; 11:24–26.
345. Cf. Barrett, *John*, 263; Smith, *John*, 138; Lincoln, *John*, 205; Brown, *John I–XII*, 220; Manning, *Echoes*, 163; Baldwin, *Daniel*, 204; Matt 24:46.
346. John 5:24 cf. LXX Dan 12:2. Cf. the Hebrew, לְחַיֵּי עוֹלָם.
347. John 5:29 cf. LXX Dan 12:13.
348. Collins, *Daniel*, 391–92.
349. Cf. Jer 51:39, 57; Job 14:12. See ibid., 392.
350. Cf. Baldwin, *Daniel*, 205.
351. Cf. Collins, *Daniel*, 392; Fishbane, *Biblical Interpretation*, 493. "To reinforce the hope of . . . resurrection, a strategic exegetical reference is made in Dan 12:2 to Isa 26:19 and its promise of

rection (at the end of the world) of the just to eternal life and of the unjust to eternal shame. This has been disputed on the basis of the word "many" (רַבִּים), in conjunction with the preposition מִן, which might give the sense, "a large part of (the dead)."[352] As Baldwin insists, however, the OT Hebrew רַבִּים "many" tends to mean "all" with an emphasis upon the numbers involved.[353]

In John 5:28–29 we also have a general resurrection at the end of the world, "all who are in the tombs" signifying all the dead. At Jesus' voice, both good and evil will come forth to eternal life and judgement respectively. The difference here is that in John 5:24–29 a spiritual resurrection or condemnation *precedes* the general physical resurrection to life or judgement. Moreover, the general resurrection at the end of the age confirms the verdict bestowed in the present by Jesus upon a person's reaction to his Word. Those who obey Jesus' voice and trust in him will participate in the final resurrection to eternal life (vv. 24, 29), but those who reject Jesus now will arise to judgement and condemnation on the last day.

Daniel's idea of an inheritance is also reflected in the translation from the realm of death to the realm of life.[354] It is also clear that, like Daniel, GJohn understands death as sleep from which one may "awake."[355] Moreover, GJohn envisages the resurrection at "the last day," τῇ ἐσχάτῃ ἡμέρᾳ, similar to Daniel's "end of the days," הַיָּמִין לְקֵץ (MT), συντέλειαν ἡμερῶν (LXX).[356] Daniel's understanding of these end-time events as a return from exile, ushering in an eschatological Sabbath, is reflected in the Johannine narrative.

An allusion to Isaiah 26:19

Verbal parallels with Isa 26:19, which Dan 12:2 echoes, are also evident in John 5:28–29. In Isaiah, the MT has יִחְיוּ מֵתֶיךָ נְבֵלָתִי יְקוּמוּן, "Your dead shall live; their bodies shall rise." The LXX has, ἀναστήσονται οἱ νεκροί καὶ ἐγερθήσονται οἱ ἐν τοῖς μνημείοις, "the dead shall rise, and they that are in the tombs shall be raised." The identical phrase οἱ ἐν τοῖς μνημείοις, is found in John 5:28. Moreover, ἀναστήσονται and ἐγερθήσονται, LXX Isa 26:19, are echoed in the Johannine cognates ἀνάστασιν and Ἔγειρε, John 5:29, 8. It is also possible that there is an allusion to this in the "symbolic narrative" of the raising of Lazarus who was ἐν τῷ μνημείῳ.[357] Significantly, in Isaiah the dead corpses are *called* to awake, which pattern is reflected both in John 5:28–29, and the Lazarus narrative.

---

resurrection." Cf. Hengel, "Effective History," 90–91, citing Baily, "Intertextual," 305–8.

352. See Collins, *Daniel*, 392.

353. Baldwin, *Daniel*, 204. Cf. Deut 7:1; Isa 2:2, 3; 52:14, 15; 53:11, 12; Jeremias, "πολλοί," 536–45.

354. Dan 12:13 cf. John 5:24. See above esp. the similarity to Col 1:12–13.

355. John 11:11, 13.

356. Cf. John 6:39, 40, 44, 54; 11:24; 12:48; Dan 12:13.

357. John 11:17. See Manning, *Echoes*, 165.

The Sabbath Healing of a Lame Man, John 5

The Isaianic background is important. Looking forward to God's final judgement[358] and "eschatological salvation,"[359] Isaiah complains that the nation has been ruled by foreign overlords and has labored like a woman undergoing birth pangs, only to bring forth wind.[360] Thus he confesses the community's inability to save itself together with an acknowledgement that in the past it was the Lord who delivered and blessed his people Israel, "an understanding . . . formed in Israel by the event of salvation at the Red Sea."[361] Importantly not only will Yahweh raise Israel's dead, but he will also enlarge the borders of her land and make smooth the way of his redeemed people to enter Jerusalem in a NE.[362] The allusion in John 5:28–29 points to a future fulfilment of this hope through Jesus.

An allusion to Ezekiel 37

A further important parallel connected with the above,[363] echoed in John 5:25–29,[364] is Ezekiel 37:1–14. Here the valley of dry bones to which Ezekiel prophesies represents the exiles, their bones standing for the "whole person" dried up (ξηρός) and without hope because of the exile.[365] Their restoration is interpreted as a national resurrection and return to the land in a NE.[366] This occurs in two stages: The bodies of the Israelites are raised, prior to the gift of the life bestowing Spirit, Ezek 37:7–10. (Is it possible that Ezekiel envisages a physical restoration of national Israel *prior to* their spiritual quickening by God? A return to the land *prior to* spiritual awakening?) The eschatological nature of this passage is seen from the context, it being the second of a series of three related oracles: Ezek 36:16–38, the "new heart"; Ezek 37:1–14, the "dry bones"; Ezek 37:15–28, the "two sticks." These passages are connected by the themes of the salvation of God's people through a NE return to the land, the gift of the Spirit, cleansing, and covenant renewal. Moreover, the first passage speaks of Deuteronomic circumcision of the heart and return to paradise, while the last speaks of the appointment of the Davidic messianic shepherd over the people.[367] Eschatological rest is implied by the Deuteronomic notion of the perpetual abode of God's sanctuary in Israel's midst (Ezek 37:26–27).

---

358. See Kaiser, *Isaiah 13–39*, 214.

359. Ibid., 210, on Isa 26:1–6.

360. Isa 26:17–18. Cf. Isa 42:14, where God will cry as a woman in labor as he leads the blind in a NE; John 16:21–22, where Jesus uses the illustration of a woman in labor of his passion, but promises that it will not be in vain.

361. Kaiser, *Isaiah 13–39*, 212, on Isa 26:12–15. Cf. Ex. 14:4

362. Isa 26:1–6, 7, 15. See Kaiser, *Isaiah 13–39*, 207.

363. Ibid., 217. Cf. Isa 26:19; Ps 88:11; Ezek 37:4ff.

364. Cf. Hübner, *Vetus Testamentum*, 152; Brown, *John XIII–XXI*, 220.

365. Allen, *Ezekiel 20–48*, 186. See above.

366. See Ibid., 186–87.

367. Cf. Ezek 36:25–27, 29–30, 34–35; Deut 30:6, 8; Ezek 37:24.

PART II—DETAILED EXEGETICAL EXAMINATION OF JOHN 5–10

John has several verbal parallels with Ezek 37 that encapsulate the key points of Ezekiel's vision and confirm the allusion to this passage.

> Both passages describe the dead (νεκρός) hearing (ἀκούω) from God through the prophet, coming alive (ζάω), and leaving their tombs (μνημεῖον/μνῆμα). The prophet who mediates the revivification is called 'son of man' in Ezek. 37.3, 9, 11, and both 'Son of Man' and 'Son of God' in Jn. 5.25, 28.[368]

Moreover, Ezekiel's actions foreshadow those of Jesus.[369] Both Ezekiel and Jesus call forth the dead unto life by their word.[370] Ezekiel is given power to raise the dead, shown exactly how to use it by God, and exercises his power in complete submission to God. This compares with Jesus' relationship to the Father, where he does only those things that the Father shows him, healing, raising the dead, and judging, in submission to the Father.[371]

Importantly, as we have previously remarked, the bestowal of life in Ezekiel is a two-stage process; the resurrection of the body is followed by the bestowal of the Spirit and life. This echoes Gen 2:7 where God first formed man's body from dust of the ground and then in-breathed life into it.[372] In John 5 the same two stages are employed, but, in accordance with its realized eschatology, the process is modified: The spiritual life bestowed on those who hear Jesus' voice in this life precedes the last-day resurrection of the body by Jesus' voice.[373] Arguably, Ezekiel's order is retained in John 11:25, 26, which speaks of resurrection of the body prior to speaking of spiritual bestowal of eternal life. Moreover, the resurrection of Lazarus's dead body occurs prior to the gift of the Spirit, John 20:22.

Significantly, John 20:22 echoes both Ezek 37:9 and Gen 2:7,[374] evident from the use of the rare verb ἐμφυσάω (breath into/on), which occurs only six times in the LXX and only here (John 20:22) in the NT.[375] In Gen 2:7, God's in-breathing the "breath of life" into the man's nostrils is a creative act that imparts life to man as a creature made in God's image. Thus in both John and Ezekiel it also suggests a new-creation in God's

---

368. Manning, *Echoes*, 161.
369. Cf. Ibid., 163.
370. Cf. Ezek 37:4–7, 9–10, 12; John 5:25, 28.
371. Cf. John 5:19–22, 26–27, 30; Manning, *Echoes*, 163–64.
372. See Allen, *Ezekiel 20–48*, 185.
373. See Bruce, *John*, 131.
374. See Keener, *John*, 1204. There may also be an echo of Isa 42:5, where the creator gives people breath/spirit. Knight, *Servant Theology*, 48, understands this soteriologically as a re-creation. Cf. Thompson, "Breath of Life," 71; Ridderbos, *John*, 634; Schnackenburg, *John*, 3:325.
375. See Manning, *Echoes*, 166.

image.[376] Moreover, in the Johannine context it is connected with the consecration of the apostles as temples of the Spirit and their commissioning as agents of Jesus' word.[377]

The correspondence between John 5 and Ezekiel 37 suggests that Jesus is in the process of fulfilling the long awaited NE promises that had only partially been fulfilled at the time of the return from Babylon. The ultimate fulfilment will occur at the second advent of Jesus, when he returns to raise the dead and judge the world. Nevertheless, prior to that great end-time event, Ezekiel 37, alluded to in John 5, continues to hold out the hope of the national salvation of Israel (and of the world), through their hearing of the voice of Christ (through the preaching of the gospel) and his gift to them of the Spirit.

Conclusion

These allusions suggest that John envisages a last day return from "exile" in terms of a general resurrection, final judgement, and new creation, that ushers in a Deuteronomic Sabbath rest, brought about by the powerful voice of the Son of Man, last Adam, and Son of God. The concept of a new creation links to the theology of Rom 8:18–25 where creation, "groaning . . . in the pains of childbirth," will be renewed at time of the manifestation of the children of God and the redemption of their bodies.

He calls his witnesses and begins to turn the tables, vv. 31–40

Jesus' calling his witnesses is

> Reminiscent of trial scenes in the OT, when witnesses are summoned by Yahweh to testify on behalf of the gods of the nations in the face of the manifest truth of the only God, whose witnesses his people are (see esp. Isa 43:8–13; 44:6–11).[378]

The context of these Isaianic trials is Israel in Babylonian exile. As Yahweh's servant, they are responsible for testifying to the heathen nations that the Lord is God.[379] Since they have both heard and seen God's great acts, especially at the time of the Exodus, they are particularly qualified to bear witness.[380] Having seen God's acts and heard his word, however, Israel is blind and deaf, not having perceived or understood God.[381]

---

376. Cf. Keener, *John*, 1204; Manning, *Echoes*, 166–68; Ross, *Creation and Blessing*, 122–23; Wenham, *Genesis 1–15*, 60–61; Haenchen, *John 2*, 211.

377. Cf. John 20:21–22; Keener, *John*, 1204–5.

378. Beasley-Murray, *John*, 77–78.

379. See Knight, *Servant Theology*, 53.

380. Cf. Westermann, *Isaiah 40–66*, 121; Knight, *Servant Theology*, 65.

381. See Knight, *Servant Theology*, 54.

The Lord, therefore, summons the nations and Israel to trial to decide who is God, the gods of the nations or Yahweh. He calls on the gods to prove their existence by predicting the future, just as he had directed history at the Exodus and now predicts a "new thing," Isa 43:19, the NE of salvation where he will bring his people home from exile. The gods cannot speak because they do not exist.[382] In the final analysis, therefore, it is only God's creative, powerful, self-authenticating word that counts. Nevertheless, he also calls blind and deaf Israel to be his witnesses;[383] he will yet make the blind to see and the deaf to hear.[384] This is not for his sake, but for theirs, that they may "know and believe me and understand that I am he."[385]

Similarly in John 5, Israel is in "exile,"[386] blind and deaf towards God, and the issue is the identity of Jesus as God. The "Jews" have seen Jesus' NE works and should have been his witnesses, but they have not perceived or understood his equality with God. They have never heard God's voice or seen his form, proof of their blindness and deafness.[387] Jesus will enable the blind to see and the deaf to hear in order that they may know, understand, and believe in him (the "I am").[388] But in the final analysis it is Jesus' own witness that counts.

> God reveals himself in Jesus and testifies to himself in the works which Jesus performs. All other testimony pales besides this divine testimony.[389]

This principle will arise again in John 8:13–18 where Jesus' self-testimony is valid because the Father is with him and speaks through him.[390] The situation is different here, however, since Jesus is *formally* on trial and in condescension to Jewish law he calls another witness.[391]

Jesus' other witness, vv. 31–32

Following the principle of Deut 19:15, Jesus' self-witness is not valid in a court, but must be corroborated by other testimony.[392] This testimony is that of the Father, but

---

382. Isa 41:26, 29. Cf. Oswalt, *Isaiah 40–66*, 105–6.
383. See Schnackenburg, *John*, 2:121.
384. Cf. Westermann, *Isaiah 40–66*, 122.
385. Isa 43:10b, (אֲנִי הוּא, MT; ἐγώ εἰμι, LXX). See Childs, *Isaiah*, 335. Cf. Isa 29:18.
386. See my discussion above.
387. John 5:37. See Carson, *John*, 262–63.
388. Cf. John 9:35–38; 8:25. See Carson, *John*, 376–77.
389. Schnackenburg, *John*, 2:121. He cites Blank, *Krisis*, 199–20, 212–13.
390. Cf. John 8:16, 28; 12:49; Beasley-Murray, *John*, 78; Schnackenburg, *John*, 2:120.
391. See Schnackenburg, *John*, 2:120.
392. See *m. kethuboth* 2:9, where no man can bear witness on his own behalf.

The Sabbath Healing of a Lame Man, John 5

since "the Jews" do not know the voice and form of the "other" Witness, he will adduce three ways in which the Father bears a witness that they can understand.[393]

Jesus does not receive man's witness, vv. 33–35

Jesus alludes first to JBap's witness because the "Jewish" authorities had sent to him and because his testimony still stands.[394] He does not "receive" this human witness because it does not compare to God's self-authenticating testimony, but he introduces it in compliance with human legal convention and in order that "the Jews" may be saved, for JBap did indeed testify "to the truth."[395]

Brown thinks the description of JBap as a "burning and shining lamp" may echo Sirach's description of the word of Elijah as "a flame like a torch."[396] More importantly, the "lampstands" of Rev 11:4 are described in terms of the ministry of Elijah.[397] Thus, it is possible that Jesus is reflecting on JBap in terms of Elijah.[398] Neugebauer traces Jesus' designation of JBap as a lamp to Ps 132:17, "I have prepared a lamp for my anointed."[399] This psalm resonates with the John 5 context, commemorating David's re-installation of the Ark of God in the Tabernacle and thus his rest among his people. The rabbis connect Ps 132:14, "this is my resting place forever," with the Deuteronomic rest.[400] Moreover, Augustine alluded to Ps 132:8, "Arise, O LORD, and go to your resting place," as speaking of Jesus' resurrection.[401] The rejoicing[402] in the lamp may echo the saints shouting for joy at the tabernacling of the Ark among them.[403] David's enemies being put to shame, v. 18, is ominous for Jesus' enemies. If the echo of Ps 132 is intentional it may suggest that JBap was the Elijah-like forerunner of Jesus, the Davidic Messiah and the Lord who has now come to dwell among his people, to introduce the eschatological Sabbath, and to reign over them forever.

---

393. Beasley-Murray, *John*, 78.

394. Indicated by the perfect tense μεμαρτύρηκεν.

395. John 10:41. See Lincoln, *John*, 206.

396. Cf. Sir 48:1; Brown, *John I–XII*, 224.

397. Rev 11:3–12. Cf. 1 Kgs 17:1; 2 Kgs 1:10.

398. Cf. Brown, *John I–XII*.

399. Ps 132:17 LXX ἡτοίμασα λύχνον τῷ χριστῷ μου. Cf. Neugebauer, "Miszelle," 130; Beasley-Murray, *John*, 78; Barrett, *John*, 265; Ecclus 48:1; Hanson, *Prophetic*, 71–72.

400. Deut 12:9, "For you have not as yet come to the rest and to the inheritance that the LORD your God is giving you," is connected with Ps 132:14, "[Zion] . . . is my resting place forever," in Braude, *Midrash on Psalms*, 2:318.

401. Ps 132:8; Augustine, cited by Hanson, *Prophetic*, 71–72.

402. ἀγαλλιαθῆναι, rejoiced greatly, is used in John 8:56 of Abraham who rejoiced to see the day of Christ.

403. Ps 132:9, 16.

Barrett thinks "the Jews'" willingness to rejoice in JBap *for a while* suggests that they "preferred" him to the Messiah,[404] but the contrast between this short time and the lasting power of his testimony (μεμαρτύρηκεν) may indicate that the "Jewish" authorities ultimately rejected JBap's witness.[405] They have not been willing to listen to a messenger sent from God.

The Father bears witness, vv. 36–40

Here it becomes clear that Jesus' "other witness" is that of the Father. It is possible to take these verses as speaking of three distinct ways in which the Father testifies to Jesus: through the works, by direct testimony, and through the Scriptures. Alternatively, "the Father has born witness" may be epexegetical,[406] leaving the Works and the Scriptures as the (two) *modi operandi* of the Father's witness. Schnackenburg thinks this latter possibility makes sense of "His voice you have never heard,"[407] but it may be preferable to interpret this as referring to "the Jews'" deafness and blindness rather than as an inference that the Father has not spoken directly, which is disproved in John 12:28. This means that the Father has testified to Jesus in three ways.

THE TESTIMONY OF THE WORKS, V. 36

The Father has given Jesus the works to accomplish. Bultmann thinks that this refers to the "whole activity of Jesus as Revealer,"[408] but it is better to apply the latter to Jesus' *work* and to understand *works* (here) of Jesus' individual redemptive healing signs that point up the significance of his mission.[409] In this way, the works parallel the signs that God gave to Moses to accomplish before Israel and Pharaoh as proof that God had spoken to him.[410] These signs brought judgement on Egypt,[411] but signified salvation for Israel. Moreover, they culminated in Israel's redemption in the death of the firstborn. Similarly, Jesus' works spell judgement for unbelieving "Jews," hardening their hearts, but salvation for believers, culminating in redemption attained through Jesus' paschal death. The difference here is that Jesus' works are NE signs and, rather than being destructive, have "overtones of renewing creation"[412] and Isaianic NE of

---

404. Barrett, *John*, 265.
405. See Schnackenburg, *John*, 2:122.
406. v. 37. See Schnackenburg, *John*, 2:124.
407. See ibid., *John*, 2:122.
408. Bultmann, *John*, 265.
409. Cf. John 7:21; 9:4ff.; Brown, *John I–XII*, 224, Schnackenburg, *John*, 2:123; Lindars, *John*, 229.
410. Exod 4:1ff. See Schnackenburg, *John*, 2:123. Jesus always appeals to his works to prove his divine mission, John 10:25, 32, 37–38; 14:10–11; 15:25.
411. Exod 12:12.
412. Schnackenburg, *John*, 2:123.

The Father's Direct Testimony, vv. 37–38

The Father himself has given direct witness to Jesus.[414] This witness has been interpreted as an inward testimony,[415] but it is better thought of as an outward manifestation. This is clear from the allusion to Sinai here and in John 12:28.[416] Brown thinks the idea may be that at Sinai God gave witness to Jesus in the sense that he gave the Mosaic law that testifies to Jesus.[417] It may be, however, that John is referring to the voice at Jesus' baptism, which he does not mention, but knows his hearers are aware of.[418] If so, the Father's testimony to his Son, the incarnate word, is possibly being implicitly compared to his testimony to the law. "His voice you have never heard, his form you have never seen, and you do not have his word abiding in you," refers not to the fact that God has not spoken, but to "Jewish" deafness, blindness, and disobedience—similar to that of the Exodus generation and of the Babylonian exiles.[419] This was manifest in their disbelief in the one the Father sent.[420]

The Testimony of Scripture, vv. 39–40

The indicative, "You search the Scriptures," is to be preferred to the imperative. This corresponds to *darash*, bible study and exposition, the principal activity of rabbinic Judaism.[421] It was on the basis of this study that the rabbis expected to have eternal life.[422] Jesus insists, however, that Scripture study is not an end in itself, but all Scripture testifies to him. Their culpable blindness is evident. "You refuse to come to me

---

413. τελειώσω. Cf. ibid., 123; idem, *John*, I. 515ff.

414. μεμαρτύρηκεν (perfect tense). The witness the Father has born continues to stand.

415. Cf. Barrett, *John*, 266–67, who thinks this is the witness of 1 John 5:9–10, the Father's voice to believers. Cf. Brown, *John I-XII*, 225, 227; 1 John 2:14.

416. See Lincoln, *John*, 206–7. Cf. Brown, *John I-XII*, 225, 227; *Mek. Bahodesh* 3:37ff.

417. Brown, *John I-XII*, 225; Exod 19:9, 11.

418. See John 7:28, where he assumes the readers' knowledge of the details of Jesus' birth. See Bruce, *John*, 136.

419. Isa 48:8, "You have never heard, you have never known, from of old your ear has not been opened. For I knew that you would surely deal treacherously, and that from before birth you were called a rebel." See Carson, *John*, 262.

420. John 5:38. See Lincoln, *John*, 207.

421. Barrett, *John*, 267. Bruce, *John*, 136–37, notes that ἐραυνᾶτε (search) indicates keen scrutiny.

422. Barrett, *John*, 267. Cf. *m. P. Aboth* 2:7, in Danby, 448, "If a man has gained . . . for himself words of the Law he has gained for himself life in the world to come"; *m. P. Aboth* 6:7, in Danby, 460, "Great is the law, for it gives life to them that practice it both in this world and in the world to come." Cf. Borgen, *Bread*, 136; *m. P. Aboth* 3:14; ibid., 130, where Torah is bread that nourishes the soul. But cf. Rom 7:10; 10:4; Gal 3:21.

that you may have life," indicates their deliberate wilful rejection of Jesus, comparable to Israel of old when they rejected God and brought judgement upon themselves.[423]

Jesus' lawsuit against "the Jews," vv. 41–47

Jesus has already indicted the "Jews" for refusing not only the testimony of the forerunner, JBap, but more seriously that of God himself. He now proceeds to try their hearts in a polemic that is "only surpassed in 8:37–58."[424]

"The Jews" reject Jesus because of their pride, vv. 41–44

Jesus does "not receive glory from people," v. 41, because he is orientated towards the glory of God. Isaiah had said that the Lord's glory would be revealed in his return with his people to Zion.[425] Jesus has come in his Father's name to reveal this glory.[426] The "Jewish" leaders are morally guilty because they do not love God[427] and are idolaters in not seeking the glory of the "only God."[428] Rather they are orientated towards seeking "glory from one another." Consequently, because their hearts are evil they *cannot* believe, but reject God's plenipotentiary, preferring another coming in his own name and glory. This reflects their inability to perceive God and their judging by outward appearances rather than by true judgement.[429]

It has been suggested that "another [who] comes in his own name," v. 43, may refer to the devil.[430] Bruce points to one "outstanding fulfilment," when Bar Kokhba was hailed by Akiba as the messianic "star out of Jacob."[431] Josephus details several similar pretenders.[432] Schnackenburg notes that "in your own name" was the rebuke given by Jeremiah to the false prophets.[433] Most commentators agree, however, that the reference is probably general, akin to the "thieves and robbers" who have climbed

---

423. Cf. Ps 95:8–11; Isa 1:2–3.

424. Schnackenburg, *John*, 2:126.

425. Isa 40:5.

426. Cf. John 2:11; 7:18; 8:50; 11:4, 40; 17:22.

427. "Love of God," ἀγάπην τοῦ θεοῦ, is objective genitive here signifying love for God. See Bruce, *John*, 137.

428. Cf. Schnackenburg, *John*, 2:128; Brodie, *John*, 254–55.

429. Cf. John 7:24. See Bruce, *John*, 137. Cf. Isa 53:2 where the Servant, "had no form or majesty that we should look at him, and no beauty that we should desire him."

430. So Bultmann, *John*, 270.

431. Num 24:17 See Bruce, *John*, 138.

432. Cf. Josephus *Ant.* 20:97–99, 160–172; *War* 2:258–265. See Barnett, "Jewish Sign Prophets," 679–97.

433. Schnackenburg, *John*, 2:127. Cf. Jer 14:14–15; 23:25; 29:9; Deut 18:20.

The Sabbath Healing of a Lame Man, John 5

into the sheepfold[434] and so might include not only these specific examples, but also the "Jewish" leaders.

Moses is their chief prosecutor, vv. 45–47

"The Jews" have set their hope on Moses, their advocate (paraclete) at the Exodus, whom they hoped would plead their cause before God both now and in the Last Judgement.[435] Jesus, however, cites him as their accuser since they do not believe him. This is evident because Moses wrote about Jesus, v. 46, whom they reject. It is possible that Jesus refers here to the whole of the Torah of Moses. If a particular Scripture is intended it is probably Deut 18:15, referring to the "prophet like Moses."[436] Either way, Moses' testimony to Jesus will be illustrated in the next episode in John 6. Thus, while "the Jews" looked to Moses, he himself looked to Jesus as the advocate to come. Moreover, since they do not believe Moses, they cannot possibly believe Jesus.

Conclusion

In the John 5 discourse, Jesus is on trial accused of breaking the Sabbath and *making* himself equal to God. His defense is that he is not a rebellious son, but the Father has bestowed upon him the twin powers, life in himself and authority to judge, in order to do the Father's work. As Son of Man and last Adam, he is inaugurating a NE return from "exile," new creation, and Sabbath rest by his paschal sacrifice. This takes place in two stages. Here and now the spiritually dead are called to new life by Jesus' word. In the last day Jesus will raise the dead by his powerful voice and judge the world. The Father witnesses to Jesus by the works, directly by his voice, and through Scripture. The "Jews" have not received God's testimony, but prefer the honor that comes from one another. Though they think that the Scriptures bestow eternal life, they testify to Jesus. Though they look to Moses, he spoke of Jesus and will become their chief prosecutor.

---

434. Cf. Barrett, *John*, 269; John 10:8.

435. See *As. Mos.*, 11:17; 12:6, where Moses intercedes "every hour, day and night" and has been appointed by the Lord to pray for Israel's sins and to "make intercession for them." Cf. *Exod. Rab.* 18:3, where Moses is said to have successfully interceded for Pharaoh's daughter.

436. Alluded to in John 1:21; 6:14; 7:40, 52, and possibly 4:19.

9

Episode 2
Jesus' Paschal NE Departure, John 6

THIS SECOND FESTIVAL CYCLE episode is again bounded by the *inclusio*, "after this."[1] In this chapter, however, it is the Passover that dominates, being the "proper background for [Jesus'] acts and works."[2] Recalling the OT deliverance and eschatological hope, it contextualizes Jesus' signs, informs his teaching, and explains the expectation and actions of the crowd.

PASCHAL FESTAL BACKGROUND

The OT Passover commemorates the Exodus from Egypt.[3] As such it is closely associated with the dedication of the firstborn and *Massot* (the festival of unleavened bread) which in turn are connected to the offering of the wave sheaf of the barley harvest.[4]

The first OT Passover

This protected Israel's firstborn from the tenth and final Plague God brought on Egypt and initiated the Exodus. The plagues had the purpose of making God's name and sovereignty known in all the earth[5] and delivering Israel through Judgement on Egypt and her gods[6] including the "divine" firstborn of the Pharaoh-god.[7] In nine plagues, Yahweh had overthrown the Egyptian gods' "authority" over nature (water, frogs, lice, flies, plague, boils, hail, locusts, and darkness) by his word. The tenth pre-eminently

---

1. John 6:1; 7:1.
2. Hoskyns, *Fourth Gospel*, 289.
3. Woudstra, *Joshua*, 102, n. 22. "Whatever earlier meaning the festival may have had, its present biblical meaning is the only legitimate one for the interpreter." Cf. Gispen, *Exodus*, 115.
4. Cf. Exod 13:1–16; Lev 23:5–12.
5. Exod 9:14–16.
6. Exod 12:12; 18:11.
7. "The son of Ra from his body." Cf. Holland, *Contours*, 241; Yahuda, *Accuracy*, 85–86.

demonstrated his sovereignty: God himself went out into the midst of Egypt[8] to avenge his own firstborn Israel, redeem them from slavery, and bring them forth as a nation to himself.[9]

The nature of the deliverance that Passover afforded Israel is intimated etymologically, though the meaning is not clear. Non-Hebrew roots of *Pesach*, such as to appease or placate, are tenuous.[10] That *Pesach* means "to defend or protect" has been urged on the basis of Isa 31:5.[11] This would indicate the Lord's protecting the house from the destroying angel. Alternately, the usual understanding of "pass-over" suggests the Lord's mercifully passing by and sparing the houses sealed with blood.

Clarification is obtained from the ritual. The Passover was a "sacrifice" to the Lord (Exod 12:27; Deut 16:2) partaking of many of the features of the priestly consecration—where the Ram of Consecration was an animal of the flock, without blemish, its blood was sprinkled, and its flesh eaten with unleavened bread.[12] What remained was to be burned with fire and the priests were not to go out of the Tabernacle door until their consecration was completed lest they die. Hyssop was also associated with their cleansing.[13] These priestly parallels suggests that the Passover both purified and consecrated those who ate it and atoned for their sin:

> The sacrifice of the animal atones for the sin of the people, the blood smeared on the doorposts purifies those within, and the eating of the sacrificial meat consecrates those who consume it. By participating in the Passover ritual the people sanctify themselves as a nation holy to God (cf. 19:6).[14]

The blood was "a sign" of Israel's relationship to God that he would look upon and spare/pass-over them when he visited Egypt with the plague. Moreover, the concept of propitiation of God's wrath by blood sacrifice is implied. To avert God's holy wrath against their own sins, the Israelites had to shelter within their blood-marked houses,[15] just as Aaron and his sons must fulfil their atoning consecration ritual, remaining within the Tabernacle to avert wrath.[16] (In fact the Passover is a model for Paul's teaching on propitiation in Rom 3:25 where God "passed over former sins").

Holland has demonstrated the significance of the part played by the firstborn:[17] that firstborn signified status rather than birth order is clear from the Ishmael, Isaac,

---

8. Exod 11:4–8. See Gispen, *Exodus*, 112–14.
9. Exod 4:22–23.
10. See Wilson, "Passover," 676.
11. Cf. Exod 12:23; Glasson, "Passover," 79–84; Woudstra, *Joshua*, 102, n. 22.
12. Cf. Exod 28; Lev 8.
13. Cf. Exod 12:22; Lev 14:4, 49, 52; Num 19:18–19; Ps 51:7.
14. Alexander, *Paradise*, 173 cf. Exod 29; Lev 8. Cf. Morris, *Apostolic*, 131, n. 1, "Lv. 17:11 connects atonement with 'the blood' . . . and not with any particular sacrifice."
15. Exod 12:12–13, 27.
16. Cf. Lev 8:33–35; Exod 12:22–23.
17. Holland, *Contours*, 237–91.

Jacob, and Esau narratives.[18] This status conferred not only family succession, but also a double portion of the inheritance.[19] It thus bestowed the power and obligation to act as the family's redeemer. This is why God's wrath was born by the firstborn at Passover.[20] For the Israelites, however, the firstborn was himself redeemed by a sacrificial lamb[21] and became consecrated to the Lord. In fact the Levites were later substituted for the firstborn and given to the priests to do the service of the sanctuary.[22]

How did the Passover precipitate the Exodus? It brought God's final judgement upon Egypt, such that Pharaoh was forced to acknowledge the power of the Lord, and unable to resist his demand to let the people go.[23] But it also released the people from Egypt, seen as the realm of death that had a hold on them because of their sin. The lamb without blemish was sacrificed to God as the price of their redemption from sin and death, and its blood on the doorposts and lintel of their houses propitiated the wrath of God because of their sin (anticipating the sacrifice of Messiah, Rom 3:21–26). Once sin had been dealt with it was "impossible" that they should be held any longer in slavery.[24] Thus the Paschal victim redeemed the people, at the cost of its life.

Subsequent memorial Passovers

The importance of the Passover is such that directions for its perpetual observation are intertwined with its historical inauguration. It was to be celebrated on the fourteenth of Nisan in family groups, the Father recounting the Exodus deliverance, elements of the meal acting as an *aide-mémoire*: the unleavened bread testimony to hasty departure and bitter herbs a reminder of bondage. Each generation was to consider themselves as partakers of the original redemption.[25] Only the circumcised were to partake,[26] signifying the covenantal nature of the Passover meal.

Memorial Passovers were kept in the wilderness during the second year of the Exodus[27] and on entrance to the Promised Land, when the manna ceased, being replaced by the fruit of the land.[28] In First Temple Judaism, however, Passover became

---

18. Cf. Gen 22:1, Deut 21:16. See Holland, *Contours*, 239.

19. Cf. Gen 43:33; Exod 13:2; Deut 21:17. See Sarna, *Exploring Exodus*, 93–94.

20. See Holland, *Contours*, 238ff.

21. Cf. the substitution of a ram for Abraham's firstborn Isaac, Gen 22.

22. Num 8:18–19. Holland, *Contours*, 246, suggests that their presence around the Tabernacle provided atonement for Israel (Num 1:53).

23. Exod 12:30–33.

24. Cf. Acts 2:24.

25. Exod 12:24–27.

26. Exod 12:48.

27. Num 9:1ff.

28. Josh 5:10–12.

one of three great pilgrim feasts celebrated only at Jerusalem.[29] The lambs, selected by the family, were sacrificed by the priests in the Temple to the singing of the *Hallel* (Pss 113–18); the blood being poured out at the base of the altar. Furthermore, the Davidic king played an increasingly important role in Passover,[30] being the Lord's firstborn, representative, and priest after the order of Melchizedek.[31]

When the First Temple was destroyed, paschal sacrifice could not be observed, but the festival was not forgotten. It was celebrated, by the returnees from exile, on completion of the Second Temple.[32]

The Future Eschatological Passover

The Egyptian Exodus was so foundational to Israel that it became an OT model for future NE deliverance from captivity.[33] On a cursory reading the Passover itself is not prominent within the NE model. I argue, however, than on closer inspection the Passover plays a key role in the NE hope.

Ezekiel's Passover

The Passover plays an important part in the sacrifices of Ezekiel's eschatological Temple where it has merged with the Day of Atonement.

> The eschatological Passover will propitiate for the sins of the people. Indeed Ezekiel anticipates what the Son of David himself will do, for he brought atonement right into the centre of the Passover celebration (Ezek. 45:21ff.).[34]

Howard avers that the link between these two feasts was "widely understood in Second Temple Judaism."[35] The evidence suggests that the death of the paschal lambs (substituted for the firstborn) provided atonement for Israel's sins.[36]

---

29. Deut 16:5–7.
30. Cf. 2 Kgs 23:21ff.; 2 Chr 30:1ff.; 35:1ff.; Ezek 45:21ff.
31. Cf. Ps 89:27; Ps 110:4.
32. Ezra 6:19.
33. Cf. Isa 40–55; Jer 30ff.; Ezek 36ff.
34. Holland, *Contours*, 161, 251–53. Cf. Fairbairn, *Ezekiel*, 485; Zimmerli, *Ezekiel 2*, 484ff.; Cooke, *Ezekiel*, 504.
35. Cf. Howard, "Passover and Eucharist," 329–37, esp. 331–32; idem, "Christ our Passover," 97–108.
36. See Holland, *Contours*, 253.

PART II—DETAILED EXEGETICAL EXAMINATION OF JOHN 5–10

Isaiah's Servant

Although not explicitly Paschal, I argue that the Servant functions in the NE in an analogous way to the Paschal victim and firstborn redeemer in the Exodus. That is, he represents his people,[37] providing cleansing, propitiation, and vicarious atonement for their sins,[38] making them righteous (Isa 53:11), effecting their redemption from bondage and exile according to God's plan. The Servant Songs provide evidence of this.

That the Servant is to be instrumental in NE redemption is evident from the promises made to him. In particular he will be given "as a covenant for the people, a light for the nations" (Isa 42:6 cf. 49:8). He will deliver the captives, "bring[ing] out the prisoners from the dungeon" (Isa 42:7). He will also lead a NE, guiding his people "by springs of waters," pasturing them upon "upon all bare heights" (Isa 49:9–10), and causing them to "apportion the desolate heritages" (Isa 49:8).

That the Servant effects the release of his people as a paschal sacrifice is evident from the strategic positioning of the fourth Servant Song (Isa 52:13—53:12). This describes the Servant's vicarious sufferings immediately following the call to depart from Babylon. This NE is compared and contrasted with the Exodus from Egypt on the night of the Passover. As at the Exodus, the Lord would go before his people and be their "rear guard" (Exod 13:21; 14:9). Unlike that night, however, when the Passover was eaten in haste and the people fled from Egypt, departure from Babylon would neither be "in haste" nor "in flight."[39] Immediately this comparison has been made attention is drawn to the Servant's vicarious sufferings, "Behold my Servant," suggesting that he is the paschal victim that accomplishes his people's deliverance.

More importantly, as Oswalt points out, the Servant's vicarious sufferings (of Isa 52:13—53:12) initiate the transformation of Israel's fortunes (in Isa 54 onwards). Thus, prior to the Servant's intervention, Israel is in captivity, like a divorced wife, bereaved of her children, enslaved because of her sin, and whose plight seems hopeless.[40] Isaiah has to plead with her to convince her that God is willing and able to save her. After the Servant's sacrificial death, however, everything has changed.[41] Israel is married to the Lord, she has been restored to the Land, her children have been restored to her, she "will spread abroad to the right and to the left," and her descendants "will

---

37. He sums up Israel in himself. See France, *Jesus and the Old Testament*, 111, n. 102, who speaks of "corporate personality." This concept is widely understood in the OT where the King, High Priest, Son of Man, and "Branch" are individuals who represent Israel.

38. Isa 53:10. See Oswalt, *Isaiah 40–66*, 400–1, who speaks of him offering "'a full and sufficient sacrifice' [for sins] . . . satisfying all the unpaid debts of their behavior." Cf. Spieckermann, "Conception and Prehistory," 8. "God's will or 'pleasure' in afflicting the Servant is . . . the wiping out of guilt (אשם) through the Servant's suffering." Cf. Westermann, *Isaiah 40–66*, 268. Ridderbos, *Isaiah*, 484, speaks of "substitutionary satisfaction."

39. Isa 52:11–12. "you shall not go out in haste" alludes to the hasty Exodus departure. Cf. Exod 12:11, 33; Deut 16:3; Oswalt, *Isaiah 40–66*, 372, n. 49; Westermann, *Isaiah 40–66*, 253.

40. Cf. Isa 49:21; 50:1; Jer 3:8ff.; Hos 2:2ff.

41. See Oswalt, *Isaiah 40–66*, 413.

possess the nations and will people the desolate cities" (Isa 54:3). Moreover, the Lord has established his lovingkindness and his everlasting covenant of peace with her (Isa 54:7–10) signifying the turning away of his wrath.[42] This "shift is unaccountable" unless the Servant's work in the Isa 52:13–53:12 song is understood as instrumental in the Isa 54 salvation.[43]

Further confirmation of the paschal nature of the Servant's sacrificial death is found in the paschal typology which he fulfils. His being taken away "by oppression" to be "cut off out of the land of the living" might recall the paschal lamb that was taken from the sheep or goats on the tenth day and kept until the fourteenth day when it was killed by the "whole assembly of the congregation of Israel" (Isa 53:8 cf. Exod 12:3–6). That he is lamb-like and sinless answers to the unblemished nature of the paschal victim.[44] The making his soul a sin offering (אָשָׁם) corresponds to its atoning function,[45] as does "because he poured out his soul unto death," which "could also be translated, 'because he poured out his blood . . . [נֶפֶשׁ] to death.'"[46] His "sprinkling" many nations may suggest covenant confirmation.[47] The public nature of his sacrifice, lifted up, seen by kings and nations, corresponds to the public nature of Passover.[48] Moreover, his firstborn status is inferred from his Davidic-messianic[49] character: a root (שֹׁרֶשׁ),[50] dealing wisely,[51] lifted up before the nations,[52] exalted,[53] connected with the Davidic covenant,[54] and status as an intercessor for others.[55]

The Suffering Servant passage[56] is particularly important because it is unprecedented in the OT: Nowhere else is vicarious *human* sacrificial sin-bearing explicitly

---

42. Isa 54:7–10. Cf. Gen 9:8–17; Num 25:12; Block, *Ezekiel 25–48*, 302. Cf. Isa 48:18–19 where Israel's peace (שָׁלוֹם) has been forfeited by her disobedience.

43. Oswalt, *Isaiah 40–66*, 413.

44. Exod 12:5. See Young, *Isaiah 40–66*, 351, who thinks that "lamb" might reflect "upon the sacrificial lamb of Exodus 12:3." Cf. Oswalt, *Isaiah 40–66*, 391–92.

45. See above.

46. So Westermann, *Isaiah 40–66*, 268. Cf. Lev 17:11, "the life of the flesh is in the blood (נֶפֶשׁ)."

47. Cf. Exod 24:6–8. The translation "sprinkle" is defended by Young, "Interpretation of *yzh*," 125–32; idem, *Isaiah 40–46*, 338; Bruce, *Old Testament Themes*, 86. n. 6.

48. Exod 12:6. Cf. Holland, *Contours*, 165–66.

49. Schultz, "King," 141–65, reveals numerous links between the messianic King and Servant texts of Isaiah suggesting that the two figures are integrally related.

50. Isa 53:2 cf. Isa 11:1, 10. Young, *Isaiah 40–66*, 342, thinks an echo of Isa 11:1 "quite likely."

51. See Oswalt, *Isaiah 40–66*, 378, n. 78.

52. Cf. Isa 49:22; 52:13, 15; 11:10, 12. The verb ὑψόω LXX 52:13 is used of Jesus' being lifted up in John 3:14. Cf. Oswalt, *Isaiah 40–66*, 310.

53. Cf. Isa 52:13; Ps 89:27.

54. Isa 55:3.

55. Isa 53:12. See Westermann, *Isaiah 40–66*, 269. "With his life, his suffering and death, he took their place and underwent their punishment in their stead." See ibid., 268, This is "a once for all expiatory act."

56. Isa 52:13–53:12.

sanctioned.⁵⁷ Thus, whereas the paschal lamb was substituted for the firstborn, the Servant is himself the sin-bearing 'lamb'. Other important features include:

1. His divine exaltation: "High and lifted up, and . . . (very) exalted," (וְנִשָּׂא וְגָבַהּ מְאֹד יָרוּם) Isa 52:13, are used of the Lord in distinction from men.⁵⁸

2. The voluntary nature of his sacrifice, pouring out his life like a drink offering.⁵⁹

3. The once for all nature of his sacrifice.⁶⁰

4. The intimation of his resurrection.⁶¹

5. The Servant's provision of salvation for the nations according to the plan of God.⁶²

6. The cosmic nature of the NE his death initiates, fulfilling the promises to Abraham and to David.⁶³

These unique characteristics of the Servant Songs cannot be predicated of any ordinary individual of Isaiah's day, or of any other time, or of the nation of Israel, but are prophetic of the Messiah. As the NT recognizes, they have their fulfilment in Jesus Christ.⁶⁴

Zechariah's Pierced one

Zechariah 12 associates Jerusalem's eschatological redemption and the New-Covenant blessings of the Spirit and cleansing with one enigmatically described as God, "me," and man, "him."⁶⁵ Put to death by his own Davidic house, he is lamented as "firstborn" in separate family groups.⁶⁶ All these features: redemption, cleansing, grieving over the firstborn,⁶⁷ family group participation, faith in the firstborn's death ("look on

---

57. See Spieckermann, "Vicarious Suffering," 1–15.

58. Cf. Isa 6:1; 33:10; 57:15; 2:17. Oswalt, *Isaiah 40–66*, 378 infers that "This is the messiah or no one." Moreover, Phil 2:5–11 "almost certainly" reflects on Isa 52:13–53:12.

59. See Michel, "σπένδομαι," 533, "poured out his life unto death . . . denotes the substitutionary sacrifice which is offered with the voluntary surrender of life." Cf. Westermann, *Isaiah 40–66*, 268. "The first part [of v. 12b] could . . . be translated, 'because he poured out his blood . . . to death.' This suggests a sacrifice . . . corresponding to the sacrificial term . . . [אָשָׁם] (guilt offering) in v. 10."

60. Cf. Spieckermann, "Vicarious Suffering," 3; Westermann, *Isaiah 40–66*, 268.

61. Isa 53:10. Cf. Young, *Isaiah 40–66*, 355f.; Oswalt, *Isaiah 40–66*, 402f.; Westermann, *Isaiah 40–66*, 266ff. It is "only the other side of his death that his deliverance and ours is realised."

62. See Spieckermann, "Vicarious Suffering," 14. "The nations will . . . themselves participate in the wiping out of guilt effected by the Servant."

63. Cf. the promises of Isa 54:3; Gen 15:5; 17:4–8; 22:17–18; Ps 72; 89:1–37.

64. Cf. e.g., Matt 8:17; 12:18–21; John 12:38.

65. Zech 12:10.

66. Cf. Rev 1:7 where it is Jesus, described in terms of the cloud riding Son of Man, Dan 7, who has been pierced, provides cleansing, and is mourned by all earth's tribes.

67. Zech 12:10. See Holland, *Contours*, 250. "The loss of the firstborn could not but recall the Passover."

me") are paschal. Significantly, the Davidic (messianic) Prince was regarded both as a priest and as God's firstborn.[68] Moreover, allusion to the death of Josiah at Megiddo confirms this Davidic connection, suggesting that here the messianic prince is put to death by the people and on their behalf. Interestingly, Josiah is firmly linked to Passover, celebrating a Passover that had not been seen since the Judges.

A further point of interest is the connection with the Servant. Lamarche has proposed that four passages of Zechariah 9–14 present four aspects of a single messianic conception, the "Shepherd King." Concentrating on Messiah's coming, rejection, and death, the concept has been built up through reflection on the figure of the Servant of Yahweh. Though verbal echoes are not impressive, the conceptual parallels are very strong and the "same prophetic current, foretelling a humble and suffering Messiah" runs through the two writings.[69]

This connection is supported by Rudolph who identifies the pierced one[70] with the messianic shepherd of Zech 11:4ff.; 13:7, claiming the influence of Isa 53 where the verbs חלל (pierced) and דכא (crushed) in Isa 53:5 are synonymous with דקר (pierced) in Zech 12:10.[71] Hengel finds further Isaianic Servant connections:

1. Victory over the peoples of the world.[72]
2. The collective lament of the community that followed the victim's death.[73]
3. Sin and guilt being overcome.[74]

Traces of Isaiah 53 in Daniel

Fishbane posits an exegetical relationship between the wise (מַשְׂכִּלִים) of Daniel 12:3, who "turn many (הָרַבִּים) to righteousness (צדק)," and Isaiah's righteous (צַדִּיק) Servant who "will prosper (יַשְׂכִּיל)" and "vindicate (יַצְדִּיק) . . . the many (לָרַבִּים)."[75] Moreover, he believes that Dan 11–12 portrays them as "heir to the mantle" of the Suffering Servant in terms of their suffering and resurrection,[76] their resurrection hope being reinforced in Dan 12:2 by a "strategic" allusion to Isa 26:19, juxtaposed with an allusion to Isa 66:24 that signals the doom of the wicked.

68. Cf. Ps 110:4; Ps 89:27.

69. Cf. Zech 9:9–10; 11:4–17; 12:10–13:1; 13:7–9; Lamarche, *Zecharie IX–XIV*, 145–47; Bruce, *Old Testament Themes*, 101ff.; Lindars, *John*, 110ff.; France, *Jesus and the Old Testament*, 103ff.

70. Zech 12:10.

71. Rudolph, *Haggai*, 223–24, cited by Hengel, "Effective History," 88.

72. Zech 12:9–13:1, reflecting Isa 52:13–15.

73. Zech 12:10 cf. Isa 53:1–9.

74. Zech 13:1 cf. Isa 53:10–12. See Hengel, "Effective History," 89.

75. Cf. Dan 12:3; Isa 52:13; 53:11; Fishbane, *Biblical Interpretation*, 493; Hengel, "Effective History," 90–98; Collins, *Daniel*, 385, 393.

76. Fishbane, *Biblical Interpretation*, 493.

PART II—DETAILED EXEGETICAL EXAMINATION OF JOHN 5-10

I would argue, however, that the wise are not identical to their suffering head and messianic King, but are identified with him, just as the "saints of the most high" (Dan 7:18-27) are identified with the Son of Man (Dan 7:13-14). Moreover, while the Servant "make(s) many to be accounted righteous," the wise "turn many to righteousness" by their instruction and witness.[77] Furthermore, the Dan 12:2 resurrection is the General Resurrection of the righteous and the wicked at the end of the age. The resurrection and glorification of the Servant (Isa 53:10-12) is distinct from this, being his vindication and the reward for his vicarious sufferings that effect the redemption (and resurrection) of his people. This is the same relationship that the NT recognizes as existing between Jesus (the Son of Man, Servant, Messiah, and Son of God) and his people. He suffers vicariously for their salvation and is glorified on their behalf. They suffer with him and share in his glory.[78] Thus attempts to find the Servant's vicarious atonement for "the many" in the death of the "wise" are not convincing.[79]

A more fruitful parallel in this respect is Dan 9:24 where seventy weeks are determined for Jerusalem "to finish the transgression (פֶּשַׁע), to put an end to sin, and to atone for iniquity (עָוֹן), to bring in everlasting righteousness (צֶדֶק), to seal both vision and prophet, and to anoint a most holy" (place/person). This compares with the work of the Servant who was "wounded for our transgressions (פֶּשַׁע), crushed for our iniquities (עָוֹן,)," "his soul makes an offering for sin," and he will "make many to be accounted righteous (צדק)."[80] Similarities have also been noted between Dan 9:26, "an anointed one shall be cut off (כָּרַת)," and Isa 53:8, "he was cut off out of the land of the living."[81] Baldwin notes that the verb כָּרַת is used of cutting a covenant, by means of a sacrificial victim (as in Gen 15:10, 18). She further considers this anointed one important to the accomplishment of the purposes of Dan 9:24.[82] Daniel 9:27, "he will make a firm covenant with many," may *possibly* reflect the "*He* and the *many*" contrast of Isa 52:13-53:12.[83] Importantly, these Danielic events which interpret Jeremiah,[84] like the Servant's suffering, are associated with the end of exile and the restoration of God's people and Jerusalem. It is therefore likely that the accomplishments of the Servant

---

77. Dan 11:33-35. See Collins, *Daniel*, 386, "The death of the martyrs is not vicarious. They are the ones who are purified." Cf. Dan 12:3, ibid., 393; Baldwin, *Daniel*, 205-206.

78. Cf. Rom 8:11, 17; Matt 10:38; 16:24; John 16:2-3; 1 Cor 15:22-23.

79. *Pace* Hengel, "Effective History," 91-92, 98.

80. Isa 53:5, 10, 11.

81. Cf. Young, *Daniel*, 206-7; Olyott, *Dare to Stand Alone*, 124. Collins, *Daniel*, 356, with many scholars, interprets this as *vaticinium ex eventu* of the murder of the High Priest Onias III, ca. 170 B.C., recorded in 2 Macc 4:23-28. As Young, *Daniel*, 24, points out, however, this interpretation stems from an unwillingness to accept the integrity of supernatural prophecy. Moreover, it is not without its own difficulties. For the traditional messianic interpretation, accepted here, cf. Young, *Daniel*, 204-7; Keil, *Daniel*, 354-55; Wallace, *Daniel*, 169-70; Baldwin, *Daniel*, 171.

82. Baldwin, *Daniel*, 171.

83. Young, *Daniel*, 213, "particularly 53:11."

84. Dan 9:2 cf. Jer 25:11, 29:10-14.

are reflected upon in Dan 9:24, 26, and possible that the latter reflects a vicariously suffering Messiah[85] and paschal NE victim.

Daniel's expectation of such a messianic individual is supported by "one like a son of man," Dan 7:13.[86] Moreover, parallels with the Servant have been suggested including the concept of judgement, the establishment the messianic kingdom,[87] and the divine exaltation of the two figures: the Son of Man riding on the clouds, brought near to the ancient of days, and the Servant, "high and lifted up, and . . . exalted."[88] Furthermore, the Servant and the Son of Man both have relationships to larger groups, "the saints" or "the many," which they represent in a capacity that can be likened to a firstborn-redeemer.[89]

Developments within Judaism

1. The Paschal victim's blood, linked with the blood of circumcision,[90] was viewed as atoning. For example, God says "Fix . . . this month for Me and for you, because I will see therein the blood of the Passover and will make atonement for you."[91] The analogy is used of a king whose sons offer gifts in order to commute capital offenses.[92] In Midrash on Exod 12:6, the blood of the Paschal victim is considered as atoning covenant blood.[93] Elsewhere, however, the atoning efficacy of Passover and circumcision lies in meritorious works: Thus when God saw Israel in her bloods[94] and "bare of any religious deeds," He assigned two "duties" for them, Passover and circumcision, "which they should perform so as to be worthy of redemption."[95] Moreover, the blood on the lintel and doorposts reflects the merit of Abraham's circumcision and the merit of Isaac and Jacob by which Israel was protected.[96] The bloods are also linked with the covenant by way of Zech 9:11.

---

85. See Young, *Daniel*, 200, 220.
86. Cf. Young, *Daniel*, 154–56; Baldwin, *Daniel*, 150–51; Beasley-Murray, "Daniel 7," 44–58.
87. Cf. Hengel, "Effective History," 98.
88. Cf. Dan 7:13; Isa 52:13. See Kellermann, "Danielbuch," 50–75, esp. 59ff.
89. On the idea of the representative nature of the Son of Man cf. Baldwin, *Daniel*, 151.
90. See *Tg. Ps.-J.* Exod 12.
91. *Exod. Rab.* 15:12, in Freedman, 3:174.
92. Ibid., 3:176, God says to Israel: "I am now occupied in judging souls, and I will tell you how I will have pity on you, through the blood of the Passover and the blood of circumcision, and I will forgive you."
93. Cf. Midrash on Exodus 12 cited by Howard, "Passover and Eucharist," 329–37, esp. 332; Holland, *Contours*, 162. See Morris, *Apostolic*, 132, n. 1–4, 131, n. 1., who believes all sacrifices were atoning on the basis of shedding of blood (cf. Lev 8:33–35; Exod 12:22f.). He cites Josephus *Ant.* 2:312.
94. Cf. Ezek 16:6 (where דם is plural).
95. *Mek. Pisha* on Exod 12:6, Lauterbach, 1:24. Cf. *Pesiq. Rab Kah.* 7, 4; *Tg. Ps.-J.* Exod 22.
96. Cf. *Exod. Rab.* 17:3.

A further explanation, discussed by Holland, relates to a rabbinic *Aqedah* tradition in which Isaac, "firstborn of the covenant people," is viewed as sacrificed to make atonement on behalf of his people.[97] Vermes suggests that all expiatory sacrifices offered on the Mountain of the Lord's House were thought to obtain their efficacy from the sacrifice of Isaac.[98] This was particularly true of the Passover: when God saw the paschal blood, "He beheld the blood of the sacrifice of Isaac, as it is said: 'God will Himself see the lamb,' etc. (Gen 22:8)."[99] It is possible that a Jewish Aqedah doctrine developed in conjunction with or in response to Christian teaching on the significance and efficacy of Christ's death.[100]

2. Passover became linked with messianic expectation and "overlaid with eschatological ideas."[101] Because of its immense importance and connection with significant events as the entrance into Canaan and the dedication of the Temple[102] there was a tendency to associate it with other important events[103] and traditions such as Sarah's baking of Gen 18, unleavened bread, manna, heavenly food, Torah, and life.[104] Since manna initially fell on the 15th day of the second month,[105] associated with Passover, and ceased on Passover eve,[106] "the expectation grew that the Messiah would come on Passover, and that the manna would begin to fall again on Passover."[107] Moreover, in the messianic age the manna would be restored: "the treasury of manna will come down again from on high, and they will eat of it in those years because these are they who will have arrived at the consummation of time."[108] Passover became the night when the Messiah would redeem Israel.[109]

---

97. Holland, *Contours*, 254ff.

98. Cf. Gen 22:14; Holland, *Contours*, 256, citing Vermes, "Redemption," 193–227.

99. *Mek. Pisha* on Exod 12:13, Lauterbach, 1:40. Cf. Exod 12:13, 23; Gen 22:14; *Mek. Pisha* on Exod 12:23; *Exod. Rab.* 15:12; Josephus *Ant.*; Pseudo Philo, *L.A.B.*, and 4 Macc, the latter linking Isaac's "martyr" death to Isa 53:7. See Holland, *Contours*, 254ff.

100. See Holland, *Contours*, 262.

101. Cf. Howard, "Passover and Eucharist," 329–37; Yee, *Jewish Feasts*, 57.

102. Cf. Josh 5:1–11; Ezra 6:15–20; Ezek 45:21.

103. See *Poem of the Four Nights*, in *Tg. Neof.* Exod 12:42.

104. *Gen. Rab.* 48:12. Cf. Gartner, *John 6*, 19; Yee, *Jewish Feasts*, 56.

105. Cf. Exod 16:1ff.; Num 9:11; *Mek. Exod.* 16:1.

106. Josh 5:10–12.

107. Gartner, *John 6*, 19. Cf. Brown, *John I-XII*, 265.

108. *2 Bar.* 29:8, in Charlesworth, *Pseudepigrapha*, 1:631. Cf. *T. Levi* 18:11; *Mek. Exod.* 12:42; *Eccl. Rab.* 1:9, 28. Barrett, *John*, 288, notes that though most of these references are late, the *2 Bar.* reference is "roughly contemporary with John." Dodd, *IFG*, 335, cites a fragment from the Sibylline Oracles, which "may be pre-Christian": "Those who fear God will inherit true eternal life . . . feasting from the sweet bread from the starry heaven." Cf. Howard, "Passover and Eucharist," 334.

109. Cf. Howard, "Passover and Eucharist," 329–37; *Exod. Rab.* 15:1; 18:11, 12; *Mek. Exod.* 12:42. The second redeemer would be "as the first redeemed," giving manna (*Eccl. Rab.* on 1:9). Cf. Brown, *John I-XII*, 265.

3. The Passover Haggadah Developed.

Not finalized until at least the second century A.D., it is likely that much of the Passover Haggadah precedes the time of Jesus, being based upon the instruction of Exod 12,[110] ultimately adapted for a lamb-less Passover.[111] The singing of the *Hallel* (Pss 113–18) in the *Seder* is ancient.[112] Of particular interest are:

   a) The Call to the hungry: "Whoever is hungry, let him come and eat," echoing Isa 55:1–2[113]

   b) The emphasis on the Lord's kingship, particularly the declaration "We have no King but you."[114]

   c) The spilling of the Cup into a broken dish to the words "blood, and fire, and pillars of smoke," symbolising God's wrath poured out in judgements upon the wicked; the remaining wine becoming the "cup of joy." This is not too dissimilar to the idea of Jesus' blood poured out in judgement, but bringing life to his people.[115]

   d) Prayers that the Lord would look upon Messiah Son of David and rebuild Jerusalem, linked with future expectation "This year here; next year Jerusalem. This year slaves; next year free people." At the conclusion of the *Seder* the door is left open for Elijah, precursor of Messiah.

   e) The apologetic affirmation, "I and not an angel . . ."[116]

   f) The association of all the events of the Exodus with Passover. "Two of the great 'benefits' or historic remembrances . . . rehearsed are the control of the sea and the feeding of manna . . . the celebration of Passover focuses not merely on the lamb but on the entire Exodus rescue experience."[117]

   g) The singing of the *Hallel*, culminating in the messianic Psalm 118, important to John.

---

110. Cf. Deut 26:5–8.

111. Cf. Gartner, *John 6*, 49–50; Finkelstein, "Passover Haggadah," 291–332.

112. Jeremias, *Eucharistic Words*, 57ff.; 45.

113. The same verse is echoed in John 4:13–15; 6:35; 7:37.

114. In *Hallel Nirtzah*. Cf. Isa 43:15 "I am the LORD, your Holy One . . . Your King." Note John's emphasis on Jesus' kingship and his rejection by the "Jews," "We have no king but Caesar," John 19:15.

115. Especially given the OT association of wine with blood, e.g., Isa 63:1–4. See below.

116. See above.

117. Borchert, *John 1–11*, 249. Cf. Ps 78:13–30 where "water control and food supply were very significant to the psalmist."

PART II—DETAILED EXEGETICAL EXAMINATION OF JOHN 5-10

Developments within the NT

Paul

Holland has shown that Passover is basic to the interpretation of Paul's theology; redemption, propitiation, and the passing over of sins all share a paschal, Exodus, and return from exile background where Jesus is the firstborn redeemer of the cosmos from the curse of sin.[118] In particular, the crucial Rom 3:21–26 passage interprets Christ's death in terms of the first Passover.[119]

I argue that in Rom 3:21–26 Paul uses the paschal paradigm to teach the forensic justification of sinners by God, the judge of all men, by grace through faith. This is accomplished through God's righteousness manifested in two ways:

1. God's righteousness has been manifested in terms of the righteousness of Christ, who was born under the law and fulfilled the law on behalf of his people (Gal 4:4–5). In this he became the second (and last) Adam (Rom 5:19; 1 Cor 15:22, 45), "holy, innocent, unstained, separated from sinners" (Heb 7:26), the federal head and redeemer of his people (believers). Jesus' righteousness was foreshadowed by the paschal lamb without blemish (Exod 12:5), and foretold in terms of God's righteous Servant who makes many to be accounted righteous (Isa 53:11). Just as our sins were laid upon Jesus (Isa 53:5–6), reckoned to his account, and he bore the punishment that we deserve, even so Christ's righteousness is imputed (reckoned) to all who believe (Rom 3:22; 4:22–24), and we are accepted as righteous in God's sight,[120] declared justified—the moment we believe. It is through this great exchange, our sins for Jesus' righteousness, that God justifies the ungodly.

2. God the Father's righteousness was demonstrated. This was necessary because "in his divine forbearance he had passed over former sins," an allusion to the Passover.[121] How could a righteous God have executed judgement on Egypt and yet spared his own people who committed the same sins, for example murder (Exod 2:12) and idolatry (Exod 32:4), as the Egyptians had? How could God have justified the ungodly (Rom 4:5), something he had clearly done in the case of Abraham and David (Rom 4:3, 6–8)? To do so would apparently mean the flouting of his own holy law, the violation of his own holy character and righteous wrath against sin, and the tolerance of injustice, something he himself had strictly forbidden.[122] Paul explains the moral and legal basis of justification, how God can be just (righteous) and the justifier of the ungodly, in terms of three key words, *redemption*, *propitiation*, and *demonstration*, that explain what took place

---

118. Cf. Holland, *Contours, passim*; idem, *Romans*, 91–94.
119. Holland, *Romans*, 96–101.
120. See Williamson, *The Shorter Catechism*, 1:130–34, answer to question 33.
121. Rom 3:25. Cf. Holland, *Romans*, 100.
122. Cf. Exod 23:7; Deut 25:1; Isa 5:23 where God expressly forbids the justification of the ungodly.

at Jesus' cross.[123] Believers are justified "freely by His grace through the *redemption* that is in Christ Jesus, whom God set forth *as a propitiation* by His blood, through faith, to *demonstrate* His righteousness . . ."[124]

Redemption is the purchase of a release by payment of a ransom. The great biblical model for redemption, to which Paul alludes, is the Passover. At the Passover, Israel was redeemed from slavery at the cost of the unblemished lamb, whose blood was shed on their behalf. At the cross believers are redeemed from the penalty of the law, that holds us as its prisoners, by Christ whose blood was the ransom price that was paid to satisfy the demands of the law and set us free.

Propitiation is the placating of wrath by means of a sacrifice. As we have seen, the blood of the paschal lamb turned away the holy wrath of God who passed through Egypt in judgement. At the cross, God set forth his own Son as the sacrifice whose blood was shed to placate his own righteous wrath and indignation against our sins.[125] This public setting forth of Christ's wrath-satisfying blood is foreshadowed by the setting forth of the wrath averting paschal blood on the doorposts and lintel of the houses.[126]

Paul further explains that the public nature of Calvary was a *demonstration* of God's righteousness, made necessary by his "passing over" former sins, because God in his forbearance had left his people's sins unpunished. No animal sacrifice could atone for sins. The blood of the paschal lambs was only a type and shadow that pointed forward to the one sacrifice of Christ that alone could atone for sin (Heb 10:4–10). It was at the cross, upon his own Son, that God publicly meted out the punishment that all his people's sins (past, present, and future) deserve. Thus God demonstrated both his mercy in forgiving believers and his justice in punishing their sins.

Finally, faith in Christ's blood (Rom 3:25) also alludes to the Passover. Just as the Israelites exercised faith by sheltering inside the bloodstained houses, so believers put their trust in the blood that Jesus shed upon the upright and crosspiece of his cross. Those who, like Pharaoh and the Egyptians, do not shelter under the blood must answer for their sins at the final judgement (Rom 2:5–16).

Paul's use of the paschal paradigm is also evident in other epistles.[127] Significantly this usage conceptually unites such christological titles as the Second Adam, Son of God, Davidic King, and Servant.[128]

---

123. See Stott, *Romans*, 113.

124. Rom 3:24–25, NKJV (emphasis added).

125. Rom 3:25. On Christ's death as a propitiation see Stott, *Romans*, 113–116.

126. See Holland, *Romans*, 99.

127. Cf. 1 Cor 5:7; 10:16; 2 Cor 5:17, 21; Eph 1:7; 5:25–27; Gal 1:3–4; 4:3ff.; Col 1. See Holland, *Contours*, 173–74; idem, *Romans*, 93–94.

128. See Holland, *Contours*, 283–85.

PART II—DETAILED EXEGETICAL EXAMINATION OF JOHN 5-10

The Synoptic Gospels

Conscious of the Passover season at which Jesus died, the Synoptic Gospels present him as the messianic King who offers his life as a paschal sacrifice for the redemption of his people. Importantly, Jesus himself signifies the paschal roots of his sacrifice by transforming a Passover Meal into the Eucharist.[129] Moreover, he conflates paschal themes with those of the Suffering Servant; for example Jesus' New Covenant (NC) blood is "poured out for many."[130] Such conflation is also present in the heavenly voice where Jesus is designated God's Son (firstborn) and Servant, Matt 3:17.

That Jesus understood his ministry in terms of the vicarious sufferings of Isaiah's Servant,[131] has been challenged by Barrett, and Hooker, but upheld by France.[132] The crux of the matter is whether or not allusions to Isa 53 are sufficient to establish intentional reference to the context and the mindset of the Servant's sufferings and mission. Though Hooker denies this, careful examination of such texts as Mark 10:45; 14:24 and Luke 22:37 show the cumulative effects of the allusions. Their "almost incidental" occurrence points to a deep-seated conviction on Jesus' part that he had come "to fulfil the task of the *ebed Yahweh*."[133] Stuhlmacher describes Mark 10:45 as "an authentic word of Jesus," which "interprets Jesus' mission and sufferings from the perspective of Isaiah 43:3–4 and 53:11–12." It indicates that Jesus,

> Understood himself as the 'man' or Son of Man whom God had sent to save Israel and whose life he had designated as a 'ransom' . . . to redeem the existence of 'the many' (Israel: cf. Isa 53:11–12) from the final judgement.[134]

First Peter

Peter bases his inaugurated and futuristic soteriology and eschatology on a paschal NE model. Believers have *already* been redeemed and purified by Christ's sprinkled blood as "of a lamb without blemish."[135] As such they have been begotten of God to become a kingdom of priests and a holy people.[136] At present, however, they are un-

---

129. Cf. Howard, "Passover and Eucharist," 329–30; Jeremias, *Eucharistic Words*, *passim*.

130. Mark 14:24 cf. Isa 53:12.

131. See Jeremias, "παῖς θεοῦ," 712–17.

132. Cf. Barrett, "Background of Mark 10:45," 1–18; Hooker, *Servant*, esp. 156–58; France, *Jesus and the Old Testament*, 110–32.

133. France, *Jesus and the Old Testament*, 121; idem, "Servant of the Lord," 28. Cf. Stott, *The Cross*, 31; Cullmann, *Christology*, 65; Lindars, *Apologetic*, 77–79; Zimmerli and Jeremias, *Servant of God*.

134. Stuhlmacher, "Isaiah 53," 151.

135. 1 Pet 1:18–19. See Davids, *First Epistle of Peter*, 71. "Here the imagery is of the Passover lamb." Moreover, the OT background of redemption is the "great redemption of slaves that God accomplished in the Exodus."

136. See Grudem, *1 Peter*, 111, who notes that 1 Pet 2:9–10. alludes to the Exodus, Exod 19:6, and to "redemption from captivity in Babylon," Isa 43:14, 21.

dergoing testing, awaiting entrance into their heavenly inheritance.[137] Importantly, Peter merges Paschal and Suffering Servant imagery in describing Jesus' sin-bearing death, meek endurance, healing stripes, and suffering leading to glory.[138]

GJohn

GJohn indicates the paschal nature of Jesus' ministry by three Passovers at its commencement, mid point, and end. These mark narrative time[139] and relate the feast to Jesus' death.[140] The final Passover, covered in John 11–19, overshadows Jesus' final week, culminating in his death at the same time that the paschal lambs were sacrificed in the Temple. Moreover, the word "Passover" occurs ten times while "the feast" is used of the Passover on another nine occasions,[141] and the idea of Christ as the paschal lamb pervades the whole Gospel.[142] Howard maintains that John is "concerned with presenting Jesus as the perfect Paschal victim, the complete antitype of the old order."[143] John's Christology confirms this paschal interpretation:

1. Jesus' denotation as God's "only begotten Son," makes him the firstborn, heir, and redeemer of the cosmos.[144] He functions similarly to Israel's firstborn in Egypt, but uniquely he himself is not redeemed and his death initiates the NE from bondage unto the liberty of the New Creation.[145] Moreover, he is continually compared to Moses, leader of the Exodus from Egyptian bondage: not just as the reality that answers to the type, but more as the Son who compares to a servant.[146] Thus Jesus redeems the world from slavery to sin and death and grants his followers the prerogative of becoming God's sons.

2. As God's Word, Jesus is the powerful agent of NE redemption and re-creation promised by Yahweh in Isa 55:10–13, which Moses and the Exodus foreshadowed. As the Word, he came from God and does not return empty, but accomplishes God's will—completing (συντελεσθῇ) it by his *death* and resurrection,[147] effecting NE redemption and re-creation, and returning to the Father.[148] Isaiah 55:10–13

---

137. 1 Pet 1:4–7. Grudem, *1 Peter*, 56, makes comparison with Canaan.
138. See Grudem, *1 Peter*, 129. "All four verses [1 Pet. 2:22–25] . . . are dependent on Isaiah 53."
139. See Stibbe, *John's Gospel*, 36–38.
140. Cf. John 2:13, 19–23; 3:14–16; 6:51–58, 71; 11:54–57; 12:1, 20; 13:1–2, 29; 18:28, 39; 19:14.
141. See Howard, "Passover and Eucharist," 331.
142. Cf. Lightfoot, *John's Gospel*, 96–97; Keener, *John*, 454.
143. Howard, "Passover and Eucharist," 330.
144. Cf. John 1:14, 18; 3:16–18; 5:19–30; 1:12; 1 John 3:2; 4:9; Rom 8:29–30, 32.
145. John 12:31–33 cf. 1 John 3:2 Rom 8:19–23; Rev 21:1–2, 5.
146. Cf. John 1:17; 3:14; 5:45f.; 6:32; 7:19, 22f.; 9:29; Heb 3:1–6.
147. Cf. John 19:30, Τετέλεσται; Isa 55:11 συντελέω.
148. Cf. John 13:3; 14:12, 28; 16:10, 17, 28; 20:17.

is particularly important for GJohn, not least for John 6, since it relates to midrash on the manna, God sending rain *down* to cause bread to grow,[149] and the NE from bondage. Moreover, it belongs to Guilding's Passover *haftarah*,[150] which contains an invitation to the hungry,[151] on which Jesus' discourse is based, and God's promise to teach Israel's children.[152]

3. Many scholars understand Jesus' designation as the "Lamb of God,"[153] in Johannine context, as undoubtedly paschal. Some object that Passover is "not usually associated with removal of sin," but as we have seen above, this does not apply to the initial and eschatological Passovers. The first Passover undoubtedly provided a type for Christ's death as the redemption of his people and the propitiation of God's wrath because of their sins. Holland also points up the sin offerings of Ezekiel's atoning eschatological Passover[154] as providing a correct background.[155]

This is not the whole story, however, since other possible referents are particularly suggestive, particularly the lamb led to the slaughter, Isa 53:7, and the lamb that God provides, Gen 22:8.[156] This leads Morris to conclude that the allusion is to "all that is foreshadowed in the sacrifices."[157] A more probable suggestion is that the evangelist, who "constantly interweaves Old Testament themes,"[158] has conflated the Paschal lamb, the primary referent, with an allusion to the Suffering Servant, of Isa 53:7.[159]

Rather than seeing this as the merging of *unrelated* motifs, however, I propose that John has followed Jesus[160] by identifying certain key passages,[161] *already related in the OT*, as indicating Messiah's paschal self-offering, and brought them together as types of Jesus' one great messianic paschal sacrifice. Evidence of this synthesis appears below.

---

149. See Odeberg, *Fourth Gospel*, 241. Rain and food are synonymous in rabbinic thought.

150. Isa 54:9 to 55:5.

151. Echoed in John 4:10–14; 7:37–38. See Oswalt, *Isaiah 40–66*, 435.

152. Isa 55:1–2; 54:13 cf. John 6:35; John 6:45.

153. John 1:29, 36.

154. Ezek 45:22ff.

155. Holland, *Contours*, 251–52. Cf. Howard, "Passover and Eucharist," 332; Num 28:22; Exod 24:8; Zech 9:11; Jub 49:3, 11, 15.

156. Cf. Morris, *Apostolic*, 133, 139–40; Taylor, *Jesus and his Sacrifice*, 228; Vermes, "Redemption and Genesis 22," 225.

157. Morris, *Apostolic*, 143.

158. Hooker, *Servant*, 104.

159. Cf. Barrett, "Lamb of God," 210–18; idem, "Old Testament," 155–56; Stauffer, *Theology*, 132; Howard, "Passover and Eucharist," 332; Brown, *John I–XII*, 60–63; Schnackenburg, *John*, 1:298–300; Hooker, *Servant*, 104; Koester, *Word of Life*, 113; idem, *Symbolism*, 221.

160. Cf. Luke 24:25–27, 44–47.

161. Isa 52:13–53:12; Gen 22; Zech 12:10ff.

4. John identifies Jesus as the *paschal* Suffering Servant in his "lifting up" sayings,[162] in his Isa 53:1 quotation,[163] and possibly in his burial.[164] Hooker disputes this arguing that:

   a) John's conception of "lifting up" differs from that of Isaiah. Thus while in GJohn, Jesus and the Father are glorified at the crucifixion, for Isaiah, the Servant is glorified only at his restoration and the Father only at Israel's regathering.[165]

   b) Rather than referring to Jesus' death as that of the Suffering Servant, John 12:38 is used as evidence of "Jewish" obduracy.[166]

Both these objections have been refuted:[167]

   a) Ironically, Hooker's summary of the Servant's being "lifted up" (ὑψωθήσεται, Isa 52:13 LXX) describes GJohn's depiction of Jesus' descent and ascent where, in being lifted up at his crucifixion, he is "restored to the Father."[168] Moreover, in John 10:14–16 where the sheep are gathered in conjunction with Jesus' death, the Father is glorified by the re-gathering of the true Israel.[169] Importantly, the idea that both the Father and Son are to be glorified is Johannine (John 13:31–32). Thus Hooker's contrasts between Isaiah's and John's understanding actually underlines their "theological affinity."[170]

   b) Though the citations of Isa 53:1 and 6:10 in John 12:38–41 *do* refer to "Jewish" obduracy, they also act as pointers to Isa 52:13–53:12 and 6:1–10 respectively, which relate to each other in terms of the rabbinic rule of *gezerah shawah* ("textual correspondence"). Thus they present parallels not only in speaking of obduracy, but also on other themes, especially the theme of exaltation/glorification.[171] It was because these themes are important to his Christology that John linked these texts. Moreover, in view of this linkage, Evans tentatively suggests that "he spoke of him," John 12:41, may even refer to Isaiah's speaking of Jesus in terms of the Servant Songs[172] as well as (I

---

162. Cf. John 3:14; 8:28; 12:32; Isa 52:13. Koester, *Symbolism*, 221, notes that *hypsoun*, used of the Servant in Isa 52:13, is used of Jesus in John 3:14.

163. John 12:38.

164. John 19:38–42 cf. Isa 53:9.

165. Hooker, *Servant*, 106.

166. Ibid., 106. Cf. Schnackenburg, *John*, 2:413–14.

167. See Evans, "Obduracy," 221–34.

168. Ibid., 230.

169. See also on John 6 below, where the gathered fragments represent Israel's regathering, accomplished by Jesus' death.

170. Evans, "Obduracy," 230.

171. Ibid., 231.

172. Ibid., 232.

would add) in terms of his encounter with the exalted Lord in the Temple. Since John 12:1–43 is paschal, I suggest that John viewed the Servant's sufferings as a paschal sacrifice in which the Lord died for his people.

Importantly, as the Servant, firstborn, and paschal lamb, it is Jesus' *death* that *perfects* redemption and re-creation[173] and initiates the NE. As the Servant, Jesus' death is rewarded by a harvest that includes the gathering of the Gentiles.[174]

5. Both the Passover victim and the *Aqedah* are reflected in John 3:16.[175] This Passover and *Aqedah* link is also made in Jewish and rabbinic thought.[176]

6. John's Son of Man Christology relates NE Redemption to the Danielic Sabbatical periodization of history and hope of eschatological resurrection.[177] I argue that John understands the Son of Man as the descending and ascending Lord who becomes "flesh," suffers, and rises higher than the heavens.[178] He also views him as the Second Adam who redeems humanity by his vicarious obedience and suffering,[179] and is consequently exalted, as their representative, becoming eschatological King and Judge.[180] God's judgement on the world and the casting out of its prince, simultaneous with Jesus' death, echo not only the Passover-night Judgement on Egypt, but also the judgement of the nations associated with the Son of God, Servant, and Son of Man.[181]

7. Since the king is God's firstborn redeemer, who offers himself for the people,[182] the prominence given to Jesus' kingship[183] relates to his role as Davidic Messiah[184] and paschal victim. Thus Jesus is the Shepherd who lays down his life for the sheep. I suggest that John views the Son of Man and Servant as the Davidic King.

8. In John 19:31–37, the piercing of Jesus' side, with the resultant flow of blood and water is seen by John as the fulfilment of several scriptural types. The quotation in John 19:36 shows that Jesus' legs were not broken in order to fulfil the paschal lamb typology.[185] John may *also* have in mind God's preservation of the

---

173. Cf. John 19:30 Τετέλεσται; Isa 55:11 συντελέω.
174. John 12:20–24.
175. Cf. 1 John 4:9; Gen 22.
176. See above.
177. See above on John 5.
178. Cf. John 1:51; 3:13; 6:62.
179. Cf. John 3:14; 6:27, 53; 8:28
180. Cf. John 5:27; Dan 7:13ff.
181. Cf. John 12:31–33; Ps 2:8–9; Isa 52:15; Dan 7:9ff.
182. See below on Sacral Kingship, Episode 4 Discourse, John 10:1–21.
183. Cf. John 1:49; 12:13–15; 18:33–39; 19:12–15, 19–22.
184. Cf. John 1:17, 41; 3:28; 7:26–27, 31, 41–42; 9:22; 10:24; 11:27; 17:3; 20:31.
185. Exod 12:46; Num 9:12. Cf. Carson, *John*, 627; Barrett, *John*, 558; Köstenberger, *John*, 553.

righteous man, Ps 34:19–20,[186] and by extension the preservation of his "righteous Servant."[187] That Jesus was pierced primarily fulfils Zech 12:10, but John may *also* have had in mind Zech 13:7,[188] Ps 22:16, and Isa 53:10.[189] Similarly, both blood and water are symbols of purification and probably indicate the fountain opened for sin and uncleanness, Zech 13:1, but they may *also* indicate the paschal blood, which was not to congeal.[190]

9. Other paschal imagery includes Jesus' washing of the disciples' feet, John 13:1–11, providing purification in preparation for his Passover in contrast to those who sought Levitical purification for the "Jewish" Passover.[191] The mention of hyssop at Jesus crucifixion is also paschal imagery.[192]

First John

Though not overtly paschal, GJohn's Paschal NE themes are echoed in this letter. The world lies under the power of the devil,[193] but God sent his only begotten Son, thus firstborn, heir, and Redeemer of the world, to save and deliver the world.[194] He provided propitiation for sins[195] and cleansing through his shed blood.[196] By vicariously laying down his life,[197] the sinless one takes away the sins of others.[198] "So in the letter, as in the Gospel, we come across the use of Isa 52:13–53:12."[199] Those who believe become God's sons,[200] passing from death to life, and from the realm of darkness unto light.[201] Consequently they are hated by the world,[202] but hope in future transformation at Christ's coming.[203]

---

186. Cf. Lindars, *John*, 590; Hengel, *Question*, 189, n. 68.
187. Isa 53:11 NKJV. Cf. Carson, *John*, 627.
188. Ibid., 627.
189. So Köstenberger, *John*, 554.
190. So Sloyan, *John*, 213–14.
191. John 11:54–57. Cf. Lightfoot, *John's Gospel*, 234, 352–53; 1 John 3:3; Hengel, *Question*, 66.
192. Cf. John 19:29; Exod 12:22.
193. Cf. 1 John 5:19; John 12:31; Smalley, *1, 2, 3 John*, 291.
194. Cf. 1 John 4:9; John 3:16; Smalley, *1, 2, 3 John*, 229.
195. 1 John 2:2; 4:10. Cf. Stott, *Epistles of John*, 81–84.
196. Cf. 1 John 1:7, 9; 5:6, 8; John 19:34, 37; Stott, *Epistles of John*, 75, 179.
197. Cf. 1 John 3:14, 16; John 10:15–18; Hengel, *Question*, 67; idem, *Atonement*, passim.
198. Cf. 1 John 3:5; John 1:29; Hengel, *Question*, 66.
199. Hengel, *Question*, 67.
200. Cf. 1 John 3:1–2, 9–10; 5:2, 18–19; John 1:12; Cf. Smalley, *1, 2, 3 John*, 134.
201. 1 John 3:14 cf. John 5:24; ibid., 178–79; Stott, *Epistles of John*, 141.
202. 1 John 3:13 cf. John 15:18; 17:14; Stott, *Epistles of John*, 141.
203. 1 John 3:2 cf. John 14:2–3; ibid., 118–20.

PART II—DETAILED EXEGETICAL EXAMINATION OF JOHN 5-10

Revelation

Revelation's cultic language,[204] Christology, and soteriology are paschal. John has conflated Davidic, Son of Man, and Servant themes with the Paschal lamb, suggesting that the latter interprets their soteriological function: In Rev 1:5–7, Jesus is described in terms of the Son of Man, pierced one, and paschal redeemer, "the firstborn of the dead," who has "freed us from our sins by his blood." Similarly, in Rev 5:5–14 the Root of David is the slain Lamb who has redeemed his people by his blood from every nation, making them kings and priests to God and consequently receives universal dominion and worship. In Rev 7:9–17 the redeemed are arrayed in festal garments, hold palm-branches, and sing Psalm 118 (Imagery associated both with Jesus' Passover and Tabernacles). They have washed their robes in the Lamb's blood and neither hunger nor thirst because the Lamb shepherds them to fountains of living water. Moreover, they are before God's throne and serve him day and night in his Temple.

Not only are these themes remarkably similar to those of GJohn, but in fact the whole concept of salvation through judgement is the same as that of GJohn: John divides his Revelation into seven parallel sections that commence with Christ's first coming and sacrificial death. This not only initiates a NE salvation for the redeemed, but also the outpouring of plagues upon the earth that culminate in final judgement.[205] The final outcome is the unveiling of the New Jerusalem, the ultimate home of Jesus' servants, where the Lord God and the Lamb are the Temple.

Conclusion

We have seen the way that the Passover, which was of foundational importance to Israel, was developed to become a basis of the eschatological messianic hope in the OT and in the Jewish literature. In the NT Jesus' death is interpreted as a paschal sacrifice, not least in the Johannine corpus where it sums up all other messianic expectation.

INTEGRITY, FORM, AND STRUCTURE OF JOHN 6

Integrity

This chapter's sudden geographical dislocation, points of contact with the Synoptics,[206] "eucharistic" symbolism, theological tensions,[207] and disputed unity have made it the subject of innumerable source, redaction, dislocation, midrashic, and Synoptic

---

204. Cf. Holland, *Contours*, 163.
205. Cf. Rev 15:1–4; 19:11–21.
206. See Barrett, "Dialectical Theology," 51.
207. See Ibid., 63, where Barrett discusses such theological tensions as seeing/believing; working/working; coming and coming; free will/predestination; faith/works; ecclesiastical sacraments/no sacraments.

dependent[208] composition theories. It is thus central to Johannine investigation and crucial to the integrity and interpretation of the Gospel.[209]

The integrity of John 6 has been defended on the basis of stylistic unity[210] and John's "dialectic" thought.[211] "Aporias" have been accounted for on the basis of Johannine misunderstanding motif or subtle irony,[212] or as the product of over-subtle or inappropriate criticism.[213] Its unitive character has been demonstrated by Borgen's midrashic composition theory,[214] which has received strong support.[215] Nevertheless many issues are still debated including:

1. GJohn's use of Mark. The crux of the problem of GJohn's relation to the Synoptics lies in its wide divergences on the one hand compared with its lower level of verbal agreements on the other.[216] Scholars emphasising the similarities insist that John used Mark.[217] Those emphasising the differences insist that he used an independent source.[218] My own position is that although John (and his readers) knew Mark, as an apostle and eyewitness[219] he possessed the authority to write an independent account, alluding to or supplementing Mark[220] or going his own way as it suited his purpose.

2. The nature and origin of the discourse. Following Borgen, many scholars accept

---

208. See Smith, *John Among the Gospels*, passim.

209. See Anderson, *Sitz im Leben*, 1. "In no other place does the same confluence of historical, literary, and theological debates come to the fore as they relate to the Gospel of John." Cf. Culpepper, *Critical Readings*, vii, who refers to John 6 as the "focus in recent scholarship of theories regarding the composition history of the Gospel, the history of the Johannine Community, the relationship between sign and discourse material . . . the tension between free will and determinism . . . the role of the Eucharist in John . . ." Cf. Barrett, "Dialectic Theology," 54.

210. Cf. Schweizer, *Ego Eimi*; Ruckstuhl, *Einheit*; Poythress, "Asyndeton," 312–40.

211. Cf. Barrett, "Dialectical Theology," passim; Anderson, *Christology*, passim.

212. See Anderson, *Christology*, 82, 92–94.

213. Cf. Robinson, *Priority*, 17, citing Lindars, *Behind the Fourth Gospel*, 17, and Kümmel, *Introduction*, 210.

214. Borgen, *Bread*, passim.

215. Cf. Barrett, *John*, 284; Lindars, *Behind the Fourth Gospel*, 74–75; idem, *John*, 251–52, 234; Carson, *John*, 287; Keener, *John*, 675; Brown, *John I-XII*, 277–78.

216. See Smith, *John Among the Gospels*, passim.

217. Bernard, *John*, xcvii–xcviii, thinks John scrutinised and corrected the Marcan narratives. Cf. Hoskyns, *Fourth Gospel*, 76–77, The Marcan "Feeding of the Five Thousand [is John's] . . . primary source." Cf. De Solages, *Jean et les synoptiques*, (Leiden: Brill, 1979), 98–99 (cited by Smith, *John Among the Gospels*, 173–74) who notes the exact correspondence of numbers in Mark and John. Cf. Barrett, *John*, 43, 45, 271.

218. Cf. Bultmann, *John*, 210; Dodd, *HTFG*, 196ff.; Brown, *John I-XII*, 244; Haenchen, *John I*, 274; Lindars, *John*, 236ff.

219. See above on authorship. Cf. De Solages, *Jean et les synoptiques*, 170–266; Hengel, *Question*, 194, n. 8; idem, *Four Gospels*, 105–6. See also Bauckham, *Eyewitnesses*, 358ff.; idem, "John for Readers of Mark," 147–71.

220. See Carson, *John*, 267, 269, 272.

that the discourse is a unified synchronic composition. Many consider it to be the Evangelist's creation,[221] composed under the influence of the Spirit,[222] to combat Docetism or to reflect the history of his community.[223] Brown believes that it is based on tradition,[224] although he thinks that vv. 51–58 is a "eucharistic interpolation," recast from material taken from the Last Supper.[225] My position is that, as inspired and inerrant Scripture, it accurately represents Jesus' original discourse:[226]

The Passover and Synagogue setting and schema are "authentic"[227] and the discourse is suited to Passover synagogue readings.[228] The *yelammedenu* homiletical technique, involving dialogue and questioning and answering, could easily have given rise to the form of the discourse in the context of the synagogue.[229] Moreover, scholars have recognized that it contains much traditional material.[230] Neither is it anachronistically "eucharistic," but, at home in its Galilean setting, it is paschal and proto-eucharistic, helping prepare the disciples for the inauguration of the Eucharist just before Jesus' death. Interestingly, the Synoptic Last Supper discourses give no indication of demur on the part of the disciples at "drinking Jesus' blood," which is hardly credible if they had not been previously prepared.

3. The supposed dislocation of John 6 from an "original" position following John 4 to its present location suggested on the basis of the awkwardness of its geographical transitions.[231] There is no textual evidence for a different sequence[232] and, since John 6 is a discrete episode in Jesus' ministry, no need for a precise geographical transition. Moreover, relocation only improves geographical transitions at the

---

221. See Dodd, *HTFG*, 220.

222. So Haenchen, *John I*, 289–90. Cf. Stuhlmacher, "Spiritual Remembering," 55ff.

223. Cf. Martyn, *History and Theology*, 122, n. 188; Anderson, *Christology*, 54, n. 5; idem, "Sitz im Leben" 15–16; Painter, *Quest*, 272.

224. Brown, *John I–XII*, 275, 286.

225. Brown, *John I–XII*, 284–87.

226. Carson, *John*, 280, considers the discourse to be an authentic witness to Jesus' "creative" OT exegesis. Cf. Anderson, "*Sitz im Leben*," 15, who thinks that John 6 may represent "a stylised transmission of *an actual debate that may have occurred during the ministry of Jesus*" (emphasis mine).

227. Cf. Gartner, *John 6*, 38ff.; Brown, *John I–XII*, 278.

228. According to Guilding, *Jewish Worship*, 61, n. 61, the Passover synagogue readings are Gen 6:9ff.; Exod 15:1ff. or 22ff. and Num 11; the *haftarah* corresponding to Gen 6:9ff., is Isa 54:9–55:5. Cf. Brown, *John I–XII*, 279–80. He refers to a three-year cycle for the synagogue readings for the 6 weeks around Passover: Year 1, Gen 1–7; Year 2, Exod 11–16; Year 3, Num 6–15, and several of the corresponding *haftarot*: Isa 51:6ff.; 54–55; 63. Cf. Gartner, *John 6*, 14–15. He mentions Exod 12:1–21; 13:1, 17; 22:24; 34.1; Lev 22:26; Num 9:1; Deut 15:19; 2 Sam 22; Isa 10:32; Josh 5:9ff.; 2 Kgs 23. He cites *b. Meg* 31a; Str-B 4.154ff.; Finch, *Synagogue Lectionary*.

229. So Lincoln, *John*, 224–25.

230. See Brown, *John I–XII*, 275, 263.

231. Cf. Bultmann, *John*, 209–10; Bernard, *John*, xvii–xix, 171; Schnackenburg, *John*, 2:5–9.

232. Cf. Barrett, *John*, 24; Carson, *John*, 267; Lincoln, *John*, 210.

expense of thematic links and theological sequence.[233] John 5–7 may deliberately recall the Exodus 15–17 sequence: healing by the waters of Marah (John 5); manna from heaven (John 6); water from the rock (John 7).[234] More importantly, John 6 is a profound illustration of the principles of John 5, particularly the John 5:46 allusion to Jesus as the "prophet like Moses."[235] Moreover, the John 5 allusion to Israel in the wilderness, represented by the invalid as good as dead for thirty-eight years, re-appears in John 6 where the multitudes emulate their fathers who rebelled, turned back, and died in the wilderness.

I propose that there is a further reason, however, for the John 6 sharp geographical break. In the Festival Cycle, Jesus is always located in Jerusalem or Judea. In John 6, however, he *goes away* to the other side of Galilee, at Passover. I believe that this is a paradigm for his ultimate Passover departure from "the Jews" of which he repeatedly warns them.[236] As such it symbolizes the whole of Jesus' ministry as a paschal NE. The geographical break draws attention to this, as does the fact that John 6 is the central Passover of GJohn's three Passovers and as such it occurs at the mid point of Jesus' ministry. John is effectively showing us that Jesus' paschal sacrifice, by which he bestows eternal life on his people and leads them in a NE, is at the heart of all that Jesus came to do and to teach.

Form and Structure

The chapter divides into three sections: narrative, explanatory discourse, and epilogue. The narrative, takes the form of a great "drama,"[237] similar to the OT dramatic narratives, where Jesus leads a paschal NE and performs NE signs. This subdivides into four "scenes": vv. 1–4 introduce the episode with Jesus' NE departure, vv. 5–15 detail the feeding and its aftermath, vv. 16–21 narrate Jesus' rescue of his disciples on the sea, and vv. 22–24 depict the crowds' pursuit of Jesus on the following day.

The crowds' question on finding Jesus, v. 25, introduces his synagogue discourse. This takes the form of a dialogue in which Jesus brings a lawsuit against the crowds to which they raise objections. Verses 26–27 are Jesus' "text,"[238] by which he reproves and exhorts them to labor for the true life giving bread that he alone gives. The crowds "trump"[239] this, v. 31, by quoting from the OT, "He gave them bread from heaven to

---

233. Cf. Barrett, *John*, 24; idem, "Dialectical Theology," 51; Lincoln, *John*, 210; Haenchen, *John I*, 270–71; Brown, *John I–XII*, 235–36; Carson, *John*, 267; Smith, *Composition and Order*, 128–30.

234. See the similar sequence in Neh 9:13–20: the Sabbath, law, manna, water, Israel's rebellion, land and light. Cf. Brown, *John I–XII*, 236; Odeberg, *Fourth Gospel*, 238ff.

235. Deut 18:18. Cf. Lindars, *John*, 208–9; Lincoln, *John*, 210, 225.

236. Cf. John 7:33–36; 8:21–24; 14:28; 16:7.

237. Brodie, *John*, 258–59.

238. See Lincoln, *John*, 224.

239. Cf. Anderson, *Christology*, 58–59; Malina, *Palestinian*.

eat," speaking of Moses and manna. Jesus expounds this text, subordinate to his own, as a witness to himself and against them, showing that they have not understood it. In a series of further exchanges, he explains that he is the true bread from heaven given by the Father, vv. 32–51, and they must eat his flesh and drink his blood to gain life, vv. 52–58. Verse 59 concludes by locating the discourse in the Capernaum synagogue.

The epilogue, vv. 60–71, reveals the aftermath of the discourse with respect to two groups: the larger group of disciples desert Jesus, but the inner core of the Twelve, with the exception of Judas, remain loyal.

NE INTERPRETATION OF THE JOHN 6 NARRATIVE: JESUS' PASCHAL NE SIGNS

Scene 1: Jesus leads a Paschal NE, vv. 1–4

This episode commences with Jesus signalling a Paschal NE by departing across the sea, followed by multitudes, ascending a mountain, and sitting down with his disciples, all at Passover. That these actions comprised a sign-act is clear from a comparison with popular "Action Prophets,"[240] described by Josephus,[241] and from GJohn's NE echoes.

Prophetic Praxis

The "Action Prophets" led their followers into a desert place, promising to show signs of deliverance, thereby signalling the advent of a NE or new conquest whereby God would intervene to overthrow the Romans.[242] Though the prophetic "pretenders" mentioned by Josephus post-dated Jesus, it is possible that others were earlier[243] and that Theudas and Judas of Galilee, Acts 5:36–37, were such.[244] The Essenes and JBap certainly understood the significance of the wilderness as the OT place to which God would return to launch a NE.[245] Jesus likewise could not but be aware of the

---

240. Cf. Horsley and Hanson, *Bandits, Prophets and Messiahs*,135; Horsley, "Popular Messianic Movements," 484; Beasley-Murray, *John*, 88.

241. See Josephus *Ant.* 20:97–99, 167–72, 188; *War* 2:258–60, 261–63; 6:283–87; 7:437–50; *Life* 424–25. Cf. Acts 5:36; 21:38.

242. See Bauckham's analysis in his "Jewish Messianism," 216–17.

243. Josephus provides scant information prior to Theudas, A.D. 45–46. Cf. Bauckham, "Jewish Messianism," 221; Wright, *JVG*, 344–45.

244. See Bock, *Acts*, 250, who postulates two Theudases: "Given the popularity of the name and the turmoil of the period leading to the census." Cf. Bruce, *Acts*, 147; Witherington, *Acts*, 238–39.

245. Cf. Isa 35:6; 40:3, 18–19; 43:19; Jer 3:2; Hos 2:14; Ezek 20:10–38; Mark 1:3–4. Cf. Marcus, *Way of the Lord*, 22–24; Bauckham, "Jewish Messianism," 219, 221; Mauser, *Wilderness*, 104-5, 135.

Jesus' Paschal NE Departure, John 6

significance of his actions,[246] heightened by paschal messianic expectation.[247] Moreover, the crowd recognize him as the prophet like Moses.[248] The fact that Jesus rejected their attempt to make him king does not invalidate this, but qualifies it. He had not come to inaugurate a "this worldly" kingdom by force of arms, but a heavenly one inaugurated by his death.

Jesus' prophetic praxis is highlighted by OT allusions. "Nothing in John's Gospel is there by accident"[249] and each of Jesus' actions has allusive NE significance:

Departure across the sea, vv. 1–2

In the Synoptics parallels, the reasons given for Jesus' withdrawal into a "desert place" are the need for rest following the mission of the Twelve[250] and Jesus' hearing of the death of JBap.[251] In the Johannine context, however, the emphasis falls upon Jesus' departure from "the Jews."[252] "Departure" is a motif for Jesus' "exodus" from the world and return to the Father, by death, where "the Jews" would seek to find him, but will not be able.[253] John 6 becomes a paradigm for his paschal death and departure—Going away, leading a Paschal NE to the Father, drawing all people unto himself,[254] feeding them upon the mountains with the bread of life—confirmed by OT allusion:

1. "Went away," (ἀπῆλθεν) may reflect Israel's going out (and away) from Egypt: "Go out from (Heb יְצֵא Go out/forth from; LXX ἐξέλθατε) among my people, both you and the people of Israel; and go (Heb הָלַךְ go; walk; depart; go away LXX βαδίζετε walk/go), serve the LORD, as you have said";[255] They "went out (Heb יְצֵא; LXX ἐξῆλθεν) from the land of Egypt."[256] The same idea is present in Isa 52:11–12, "Depart, depart, go out from (Heb יְצֵא; LXX ἐξέλθατε) there . . . go out (Heb יְצֵא; LXX ἐξέλθατε) from the midst of her." Although this provides little by way of verbal parallels, with the combined mention of sea crossing, multitudes, mountain, and Passover, the *idea* of an Exodus begins to crystallize.[257]

---

246. See Wright, *JVG*, 344–45, who believes Jesus' sitting on the Mount of Olives, Mark 13:3 and par., was an intentional symbolic allusion to Zech 14:4–5. Cf. ibid., n. 10.

247. See above. Cf. Bauckham, "Jewish Messianism," 220; Beasley-Murray, *John*, 88.

248. Deut 18:18.

249. Wright, *John 1–10*, 71.

250. Cf. Mark 6:7ff., 31–32; Luke 9:10.

251. Matt 14:13.

252. Following on from chapter 5 and preceding John 7:1, "he would not go about in Judea . . ."

253. Cf. John 7:33–36; 8:21–23; 13:33; 14:28; 16:5–7.

254. John 6:2 cf. 12:32.

255. Exod 12:31.

256. Exod 12:41.

257. See Borchert, *John 1–11*, 249, who speaks of the sea crossing, crowd, and mountain region in terms of a "picture perfect setting" for considering how Jesus could be related to the Exodus.

If legitimate, these echoes suggest that the Jerusalem from which Jesus departs[258] is equivalent to Egypt and Babylon. This accords with Johannine thought where Judea is equated with "the world,"[259] the "Jewish" authorities proclaim their allegiance to Caesar,[260] and Satan is the "ruler of this world."[261] Similar ideas are found in Revelation where Jerusalem is equated with Sodom and Egypt,[262] and God's people are warned to depart from Babylon, identified with Rome,[263] lest they share her plagues. Jesus' departure may also suggest the purpose of the Exodus, to "serve the Lord," on the Mountain of God, indicated in John 6:3 by the Mountain location.[264]

2. "The other side of the sea," v. 1, suggests the Exodus crossing of the sea.[265] "The other side of the Sea of Galilee," πέραν τῆς θαλάσσης τῆς Γαλιλαίας, might also have connotations of darkness, bondage, and Gentiles, as expressed in Isaiah's "way of the sea (LXX θαλάσσης), the land beyond (LXX πέραν) the Jordan, in Galilee (LXX Γαλιλαία) of the nations,"[266] The context speaks of the people passing through the land, *hungry*, and *speaking against their king* and their God.[267] In this chapter, the crowds hunger and speak against their King (and God). If there is an intentional echo, it might also connote the breaking of that yolk of bondage by the universal reign of the Son of David.[268] Jesus launched his ministry in Galilee in fulfilment of Isa 9:1–2, as a springboard to the nations.[269] Reference to "Tiberias" after Caesar is not redundant, but it evokes the Roman empire, perhaps as a reminder that the whole world, including the Jewish people, was "in bondage" under Rome.[270]

---

258. Cf. John 7:1; 4:3.

259. John 7:3–4.

260. John 19:15, "We have no king but Caesar." Cf. Isa 43:15, "I am the LORD, your Holy One . . . your King." Cf. the affirmation made to God in *Hallel Nirtzah*, Passover *Haggadah*, "We have no king but you."

261. John 12:31.

262. Rev 11:8.

263. Rev 18:4 cf. Rev 17:5, 9. See Bauckham, *Climax of Prophecy*, 207–8: "If the great city has some of the characteristics of Jerusalem, it also has those of Babylon. John's purpose here is to merge . . . the two cities." Cf. Beasley-Murray, *Revelation*, 177, 187; John "sees in the great city an image of the world"; Walker, *Holy City*, 254.

264. Exod 3:12; 12:31.

265. This sea imagery is utilised in NE context in Rev 15:2–3 where the redeemed stand on the sea of glass and sing the song of Moses and of the lamb.

266. Isa 9:1ff.

267. Isa 8:21.

268. Isa 9:6–7.

269. Matt 4:12–16. So Robertson, *Understanding*, 33, 35–36, 116. He notes that the traffic of three continents made their exchanges by way of Galilee.

270. See Brodie, *John*, 261.

3. That, "a large crowd was following him," v. 2, suggests the language of discipleship,[271] as does their "coming" to Jesus, v. 5, used in GJohn to depict faith.[272] The imperfect tense, ἠκολούθει, (was following) implies that "people are continually coming to [Jesus]."[273] Suggestive of the multitudes that departed from Egypt,[274] or the multitudes that gather to Zion at the NE,[275] this foreshadows the drawing of all people to Jesus.[276] Here, however, the crowd's motivation, "Because they saw the signs that he was doing (ἐθεώρουν τὰ σημεῖα ἃ ἐποίει) on the sick" is ominous. It echoes "many believed in his name when they saw the signs that he was doing (θεωροῦντες αὐτοῦ τὰ σημεῖα ἃ ἐποίει)," John 2:23, which indicated only a "signs faith" to which Jesus "did not entrust himself," John 2:24.[277] Significantly, this also took place at Passover and involved many Galileans.[278] There may also be an echo of Israel's seeing the signs and wonders that the Lord did in Egypt,[279] despite which they provoked God's wrath.[280] The sick (ἀσθενούντων), suggests their need, being under the Deuteronomic maledictions and thus in "exile."[281]

Ascending and Sitting upon the Mountain, v. 3

Ascent of the mountain has symbolic significance. Mountains were "regarded as a crucial symbolic place of divine encounter."[282] Several commentators note an allusion to Moses tradition,[283] the use of the definite article[284] possibly suggesting a "Christian Sinai."[285] Sinai was "*the* mountain of God" from which Moses was sent to deliver Israel and to which he was to return as the initial destination of the Exodus.[286] Thus Jesus' departure, signs, being followed by a multitude, and ascending *the* mountain echo the

---

271. Keener, *John*, 665.

272. See, e.g., John 1:35–39; 4:30; 5:40. Cf. Brown, *John I–XII*, 79, 233; Brodie, *John*, 261; Barrett, *John*, 274.

273. Cf. Bultmann, *John*, 211; Brodie, *John*, 258–59.

274. Exod 12:37–38.

275. Isa 49:18.

276. John 12:32.

277. Cf. John 6:2, 14, 26, 30; Keener, *John*, 665.

278. John 2:23; 4:45.

279. Cf. Deut 7:19; Exod 14:31; John 4:48.

280. Cf. Ps 78:11, 40, 56, 58, Heb 3:9.

281. See above on John 5:3.

282. Borchert, *John 1–11*, 251.

283. Cf. Brown, *John I–XII*, 232; Keener, *John*, 664, Lincoln, *John*, 211; Barrett, *John*, 273; Matt 5:1; 15:29.

284. τὸ ὄρος in John 6:3, 15.

285. Brown, *John I–XII*, 232.

286. Exod 3:1, 12.

PART II—DETAILED EXEGETICAL EXAMINATION OF JOHN 5–10

Exodus. Sinai was a mountain-Temple,[287] the place where Israel received the Torah, entered into covenant with the Lord, and were consecrated to him as "a kingdom of priests and a holy nation" (Exod 19:6). These echoes are present in the Synoptics where Jesus gave his law, met with God, revealed his glory, and appointed the Twelve upon the mountain.[288] For GJohn, Jesus' sitting down may indicate teaching and reference to his disciples the reconstitution of Israel, especially since four of John's five references to "The Twelve," occur in this chapter.[289]

While these Exodus echoes seem probable it is likely that NE allusions are also intended. In Ezek 20:33–44, having been gathered from the peoples and purged in the wilderness, Israel would serve the Lord on his holy mountain and he would accept their firstfruits and offerings. As in Isa 2, *the* eschatological (Temple) mountain of the Lord's House is not Sinai but Zion, to which the nations shall flow and from which the law (תּוֹרָה) and the word of the Lord (דְּבַר־יְהוָה) shall go forth (יֵצֵא).[290] This is the same "mountain of the Lord," where Abraham offered up Isaac resulting in the ratification of the promise of the covenant people.[291] The contrast between the two mountains, Zion and Sinai, taken up by Paul,[292] is similar to the Johannine contrast between Christ and Moses, and New Israel and "the Jews."[293] For Jesus, the NE goal is the new Zion, his heavenly Father's House (John 14:2).

In spite of the definite article, however, Carson thinks it likely that τὸ ὄρος is being used generically to signify "mountainous country."[294] Though I would place the emphasis on *the* mountain, it is not impossible that generic mountain country echoes are present, especially in the light of the feeding on the mountain and the gathering of the leftover fragments. France confirms that this double meaning is likely.[295] This would widen the allusions to reflect the NE upon the Mountains:

In Ezekiel, the mountains of Israel will yield fruit to God's returning people, Israel, who will inhabit them.[296] Moreover, there, God will make the *scattered* children of Israel and Judah one nation under one shepherd-King, his servant David.[297] He will

---

287. See Beale, *Temple*, 105.

288. Cf. Matt 5:1; 8:1; 14:23; 28:16–17; 17:1–2; Mark 6:46; 9:9; 3:13; 9:2; Luke 9:28–36; 6:12–13. Davies and Allison, *Matthew*, 1:427, speak of a "developed Exodus typology," reflected in every part of Matt 1–5. Cf. Lane, *Mark*, 133, "The Twelve represent in a new form the people of the twelve tribes, Israel."

289. Cf. John 6:13, 67, 70, 71; 20:24; Evans, "Continuing Exile," 92; Sanders, *Jesus and Judaism*, 98.

290. Cf. Isa 55:11, where the word of the Lord goes forth from his mouth.

291. Gen 22:14, 17–18.

292. Cf. Gal 4:25–27; Heb 12:18–24.

293. John 1:11–13, 17.

294. Cf. Carson, *John*, 268; Nolland, *Matthew*, 192–93.

295. See France, *Matthew*, 157.

296. Ezek 36:1–15, esp. v. 8.

297. Ezek 37:22, 24, alluded to in John 10:16.

cleanse them and sanctify them before the nations, make a covenant of peace with them, and tabernacle among them. He will be their God and they will be his people.[298]

Similarly in Isaiah the mountains and hills sing before the redeemed who have been led forth from captivity, by the instrumentality of the Servant, according to the word of God.[299] Of particular importance is the NE return of the Lord and his Servant with God's people to Zion, where the Lord announces:

> They shall feed along the ways; on all bare heights shall be their pasture; they shall not hunger or thirst, neither scorching wind nor sun shall strike them, for he who has pity on them will lead them, and by springs of water will guide them. And I will make all my mountains a road, and my highways shall be raised up (Isa 49:9–11).

As we shall see, several of these themes are echoed in John 6, particularly Jesus' having the multitudes recline upon the mountain grass, feeding them, and satisfying their hunger and thirst. Moreover, this feeding prefigures Jesus' own NC sacrifice. Like the Servant, Jesus represents (New) Israel, offers himself as their paschal sacrifice, is lifted up and glorified, raises up Israel's tribes, and calls the Gentiles.[300]

At Passover, v. 4

"Now the Passover, the feast of the Jews, was at hand," is transitional. As part of the introductory verses, 1–4, it heightens Jesus' initial sign-act, emphasising its *paschal* NE nature, signifying that this theme will dominate this chapter,[301] setting it in the "context of the paschal lamb."[302] Connected logically with "then" (οὖν) of v. 5, it also introduces the vision of the multitudes and the subsequent feeding narrative as paschal. Together with the deliverance across the sea, vv. 16–21, the latter reflects Moses' two outstanding miracles, both associated with Passover: the crossing of the Red Sea (Exod 14) and the feeding of Israel in the wilderness with manna (Ex 16:35). These form the background to Jesus' deeds in Galilee.[303]

The "feast of the Jews," v. 4, like the mention of Tiberias, is not redundant but evokes the "Jewish" people. Together these details indicate the worldwide scope of the NE initiated by Jesus,[304] as do the sea crossings, the mountain, and the great crowds that continually follow Jesus.[305]

---

298. Ezek 37:19–28.
299. Cf. Isa 49:13; 55:12.
300. Cf. Isa 49:3, 6; John 15; Isa 53:12; John 10:15–18; Isa 42:6; 49:6; John 11:50–53; 12:19–24, 32.
301. Wright, *John 1–10*, 72. See above.
302. Keener, *John*, 665.
303. See Burge, *John*, 192.
304. Brodie, *John*, 260–261.
305. Ibid., 259.

PART II—DETAILED EXEGETICAL EXAMINATION OF JOHN 5-10

Scene 2: Jesus' miraculous provision of food, vv. 5–13

Jesus' NE vision of the approaching multitudes, v. 5

For John, "coming," evokes discipleship.[306] Jesus' lifting up his eyes can denote his prayerful attitude,[307] but here it signifies his vision of messianic harvest.[308] This is confirmed by NE echoes:

Isa 49:18

Here, God bids Zion to behold her returning sons: "Lift up your eyes around and see (LXX ἆρον ... τοὺς ὀφθαλμούς σου καὶ ἰδὲ); they all gather, they come to you (LXX ἤλθοσαν πρὸς σέ)." In John 6:5 Jesus does this, "Lifting up his eyes (ἐπάρας ... τοὺς ὀφθαλμοὺς), then, and seeing (καὶ θεασάμενος) that a large crowd was coming toward him (ἔρχεται πρὸς αὐτὸν) ..." Not only are there verbal similarities, but as we have already seen the context is similar. In Isa 49 the Servant leads and feeds the redeemed on the mountains and they neither hunger nor thirst. Moreover, God lifts up his standard to the nations who bring Zion's sons and builders from afar.

Isa 60:4

"Lift up your eyes all around, and see," (LXX ἆρον κύκλῳ τοὺς ὀφθαλμούς σου καὶ ἰδὲ). Here, Zion is glorified with kings and nations coming to her light and her sons being brought from afar. GJohn echoes this note of high expectation, in contrast to Mark's account where Jesus viewed the crowds with compassion as "sheep without a shepherd [king]."[309] As John will show, however, large crowds of followers will be whittled down to a nucleus of true disciples. The multitudes are nevertheless symbolic of the harvest that would *ultimately* be reaped by the Church, regarded as the true Israel.[310]

The Resultant Crisis, vv. 5–9

The crowds that followed Jesus result in a crisis, insufficient bread in a deserted place. In the Synoptic accounts the necessity of providing food arises at the end of the day in connection with the hunger of the multitudes.[311] In GJohn, however, it seems logically

---

306. V. 5 cf. ibid., 261; Brown, *John I–XII*, 79, 233; Barrett, *John*, 274.

307. Cf. John 11:41; 17:1.

308. In John 4:35, Jesus had instructed his disciples to *lift up their eyes* to witness the messianic harvest where the ploughman overtakes the reaper, Amos 9:13–14. Cf. Barrett, *John*, 241–42, 274; Keener, *John*, 665.

309. Mark 6:34 cf. Num 27:17; 1 Kgs 22:17; 2 Chr 18:16; Zech 10:2.

310. Cf. Rev 7:4–9.

311. Cf. Matt 14:15; Mark 6:35–36; Luke 9:12.

connected with the multitudes coming to Jesus *at Passover*, vv. 4–5. Gartner suggests that the background to John 6 is Jesus' celebration of a lamb-less Passover;[312] traces of the Passover Haggadah being found in the "four" questions of the crowd.[313] Though I consider these parallels overdrawn, the crowds' questions not exactly corresponding to Gartner's four categories, I suggest that GJohn portrays Jesus as hosting a feast that foreshadows the great paschal feast provided by his cross. In the discourse the bread is connected with manna and, to contemporary Jewish minds, this is also connected with the unleavened bread and Passover lamb.[314] In Jesus' mind, however, the bread is especially connected with his "flesh," that he will give for the life of the world, John 6:51–56. Hoskyns affirms that:

> The movement from miracle to discourse, from Moses to Jesus (*vv.* 32–35 cf. i. 17), and, above all, from *bread* to *flesh*, is almost unintelligible unless the reference in *v.* 4 to the Passover picks up i. 29, 36, anticipates xix. 36 (Exod. xii. 46; Num. xi. 12), and governs the whole narrative.[315]

Thus, at that time when Jewish families were preparing to eat the Passover, the crisis involved Jesus' obligation to provide food as a Passover host. Moreover, it echoes similar crises faced by Israel in the past:

The post Exodus crisis

"Where (Πόθεν) are we to buy bread, so that these people may eat?" v. 5, echoes Moses' question, "Where (LXX πόθεν) am I to get meat to give to all this people?"[316] To Moses, the possibility of satisfying the multitude in the wilderness seems absurd: "Shall flocks and herds be slaughtered for them, and be enough for them? Or shall all the fish of the sea be gathered together for them, and be enough for them?" Moses was told that he would see whether or not God's *word* would come true (Num 11:22). Though quantitatively less difficult,[317] the disciples' challenge seems equally impossible.[318]

---

312. Gartner, *John 6*, 38–42; 47–48. Cf. Josephus *Ant.* 14:214; *Mek. Exod.* 12:8.
313. Gartner, *John 6*, 25–29.
314. See above.
315. Hoskyns, *Fourth Gospel*, 281 (emphasis original).
316. Num 11:13. Cf. Brown, *John I-XII*, 233; Burge, *John*, 193; Köstenberger, *John*, 201. Cf. Matt 15:33, "Where are we to get enough bread in such a desolate place to feed so great a crowd?"
317. Cf. the Gospel's 5000 men as opposed to Moses' 600,000 footmen fed with flesh for a month, Num 11:21.
318. Vv. 7–9, "Two hundred denarii would not buy enough bread . . ." and "What are they for so many?"

PART II—DETAILED EXEGETICAL EXAMINATION OF JOHN 5–10

Brown notes several parallels between John 6 and Numbers 11[319]: grumbling (γογγύζω);[320] the manna;[321] flesh to eat";[322] and reference to fish (ὄψος) of the sea being gathered together (συνάγω).[323] These echoes, particularly Israel's lust for flesh and their murmuring, are ominous for the situation here.

THE NE CRISIS

A similar crisis is implicit in Isa 55 with regard to the returning exiles who need to "buy bread." God anticipates and averts this by his abundant provision freely available. In contrast to the Exodus, however, emphasis is placed upon spiritual rather than physical bread.[324] Invitation is made to buy milk and wine without money rather than to work for that which is not bread. But they must repent and believe God's word, receiving the life that he offers "through the sacrifice of the Servant."[325] Thus God offers his sure (unconditional and eternal) covenant with David, linked with his messianic Servant, in contrast to the conditional Mosaic Sinai covenant that Israel had broken.[326]

Isaiah 55:5 is God's word to his Davidic messianic Servant[327]: "You shall call a nation that you do not know, and a nation that did not know you shall run to you, because of the Lord your God, and of the Holy One of Israel, for he has glorified you." This situation is guaranteed by God's powerful *word*,[328] as effective as life-giving rain. As rain *descends* (Heb. ירד, LXX καταβῇ) from heaven and produces seed and bread before returning thither, so God's *word* will come from heaven and will not return to him without accomplishing his NE purposes.[329]

This passage is clearly alluded to in John 6.[330] Moreover, the spiritual versus physical contrast between Isa 55 and Num 11 stands behind and is reflected throughout the discourse. The crowd desires the physical bread of the Exodus that led to death, but Jesus freely offers true life-giving bread available through his sacrificial death.

---

319. See Brown, *John I–XII*, 233.

320. Num 11:1 cf. John 6:41, 43.

321. Num 11:7–9 cf. John 6:31.

322. Num 11:13 cf. John 6:51ff.

323. Num 11:22 cf. fish (ὀψάρια) and "gather up" (συνάγω) in John 6:9, 12.

324. See Oswalt, *Isaiah 40–66*, 435.

325. Ibid., 437 cf. Isa 55:6, 7.

326. Ibid., 437–39 cf. Jer 31:31; Fishbane, *Biblical Interpretation*, 495.

327. See Oswalt, *Isaiah 40–66*, 440.

328. This compares with the efficacy of God's word in Num 11:23, "Is the LORD's hand shortened? Now you shall see whether *my word* will come true for you or not" (emphasis mine).

329. Summarised in Isa 55:12–13, "For you shall go out with joy . . ."

330. Cf. esp. Isa 55:1, being echoed in John 6:27, Jesus' discourse text, and Isa 55:10, "come down from heaven," echoed in John 6:38.

The crisis in Elisha's day

John 6 also echoes the miraculous feedings of 2 Kgs 4:38–44.[331] "Barley loaves," echoes the ἄρτους κριθίνους firstfruits.[332] Andrew's disbelief, "what are these among so many?" echoes that of Elisha's servant, "How can I set this before a hundred men?"[333] That they eat and have leftover bread echoes "They shall eat and have some left ... according to the word of the Lord."[334]

Given John's NE paradigm, the reason for these allusions is not immediately obvious, but several explanations are possible. In meeting God at Sinai and standing against idolatry Elijah resembled Moses. As Elijah's successor, Elisha was not only a "Prophet like Moses," but also stood in the Mosaic prophetic succession from which the ultimate "Prophet like Moses" (Jesus) would come.[335]

The provision of bread is also significant: in Elisha's day the Northern Kingdom was apostate and the famine was a Deuteronomic curse upon covenant unfaithfulness. This is akin to the situation in John 6, where the religious hierarchy is corrupt and Israel is under Roman occupation. Bread of the firstfruits, first offered when Israel entered the Promised Land,[336] and linked to Unleavened Bread and Passover,[337] was the prerogative of the priests.[338] That it was given to the sons of the prophets indicates that they represented the legitimate worship of God as opposed to Jeroboam's illegitimate "state church."[339] Likewise in GJohn, Jesus is the true "bread of God," and those who trust in him belong to the true Israel, "priests and kings," who belong to his Temple. Importantly, like the other passages, the miraculous provision of bread was "according to the word of the Lord."[340]

Its use as a test

In all the above passages, God tested his people that they might learn to *depend upon his word*. Here Jesus explicitly set the crisis before his disciples as a test. "He said this to test (πειράζων) him," echoes the Lord's testing (ἐκπειράζω) Israel: He led them through the wilderness, allowed them to hunger, and fed them with manna that they might know that "man does not live by bread alone, but man lives by every *word* that

---

331. Cf. Brown, *John 1–XII*, 233; Carson, *John*, 269; Dodd, *HTFG*, 206–7.
332. In John 6:9, John uniquely mentions that the loaves were of barley. Cf. 2 Kgs 4:42.
333. John 6:9 cf. 2 Kgs 4:43.
334. John 6:12–13 cf. 2 Kgs 4:43–44.
335. Deut 18. See Keil and Delitzsch, *Pentateuch*, 3:395–96.
336. Cf. Lev 23:10; Deut 26:1–11.
337. Cf. Exod 23:15–16; 34:25–26.
338. Cf. Num 18:12; Deut 18:3. See McConville, *Deuteronomy*, 298
339. See Keil, *Kings*, 316.
340. 2 Kgs 4:44 cf. Num 11:23; Isa 55:11. See Oswalt, *Isaiah 40–66*, 446.

comes from the mouth of the Lord."³⁴¹ Unlike Moses and Elisha,³⁴² however, Jesus knew what he would do, suggesting his divine plan and initiative: Jesus is God's powerful Word and agent, in whom the disciples, as founder members of the NI, must learn to trust.

Jesus hosts a paschal messianic banquet, vv. 10-11

While in Mark, the seating of the multitudes by ranks may suggest an eschatological army,³⁴³ absence of militaristic overtones in GJohn and the use of ἀναπεσεῖν (sit at table) suggests a messianic banquet. People reclined at feasts and this, together with the abundant grass, points to the Passover.³⁴⁴ Moreover, the picture of Jesus making the people recline on the mountain's green grass recalls Ps 23:1, "He makes me to lie down in pastures of grass (Heb בִּנְאוֹת דֶּשֶׁא יַרְבִּיצֵנִי; cf. LXX εἰς τόπον χλόης, "in a place of green grass"),³⁴⁵ where the referent is David's Lord. A further possible echo is the Servant pasturing the people on all desolate heights.³⁴⁶ The ideas may reflect the background of Ps 78:19 where Israel tested God saying, "Can God spread a table in the wilderness?"

For Barrett, Jesus' words and actions, in both Mark 6:41 and John 6:11, "recall the Last Supper."³⁴⁷ Dodd avers that John's use of εὐχαριστήσας (having given thanks) instead of Mark's εὐλόγησεν (blessed) is sacramental language.³⁴⁸ In fact, both εὐχαριστεῖν and εὐλογεῖν are used in connection with ancient Jewish thanksgivings for food and wine: "Blessed are thou, O Lord our God, King of the universe, who bringest forth bread from the earth ... Blessed are thou ... who createst the fruit of the vine."³⁴⁹ Moreover, John omits to mention such "eucharistic" details as Jesus' breaking the bread, or the role of the disciples in the distribution. It follows that there is nothing in Jesus' acts or words here that is specifically "eucharistic," or out of place in a Jewish meal at the season of Passover.³⁵⁰

---

341. Deut 8:2-3 (emphasis mine), echoed in Isa 55:11. Cf. John 6:6.

342. Cf. Keil, *Kings*, 316. "Elisha did not produce the miraculous increase of food, but merely predicted it."

343. Mark 6:40, 34 cf. Exod 18:21; Ezek 37:10; Keener, *John*, 667; France, *Mark*, 267.

344. John 6:10. So Edersheim *Temple*, 234.

345. See Brodie, *John*, 261.

346. Isa 49:9.

347. Barrett, *John*, 276, cf. Mark 14:22; 1 Cor 11:23.

348. See Lincoln, *John*, 23.

349. Used, for example, in the Passover *Haggadah*. Cf. Barrett, *John*, 276; Carson, *John*, 270.

350. Barrett, *John*, 276.

The satisfying of the multitude, "As much as they wanted," "And when they had eaten their fill,"³⁵¹ again suggests the lavish provision of a messianic banquet.³⁵² "As much as they wanted" may recall, "Each of them gathered as much [manna] as he could eat."³⁵³ Satisfied (ἐνεπλήσθησαν) appears only here in GJohn. Both it and the Synoptic equivalent (ἐχορτάσθησαν)³⁵⁴ are used in LXX to translate the Hebrew שׂבע, although Brown suggests that ἐχορτάσθησαν is more redolent of the divine promises of abundance in the OT.³⁵⁵ These OT references suggest satisfaction in the context of God's presence, inheriting the land, and obeying God's voice, having been delivered from Egypt and from testing. The term is also used, however, of the satisfaction of enemies, of the earth, and of the Psalmist with God's likeness.³⁵⁶ In John 6:26 ἐχορτάσθητε is used "pejoratively,"³⁵⁷ of physical rather than spiritual satisfaction. This contrast also appears in John 6:27, where "food that perishes," is contrasted with "food that endures."

Dodd suggests that John may have preferred ἐνεπλήσθησαν, as reflecting Jer 31:14 "I will feast the soul of the priests with abundance, and my people shall be *satisfied* with my goodness, declares the LORD."³⁵⁸ The background here is the restoration of Israel, the NE, and the NC.ABottomdd points out the importance of Jer 31 for the NT and its "affinity of language," with GJohn.³⁵⁹ If John intends these associations here, however, it is on the basis of the word *in context* rather than on the word alone, since ἐμπίπλημι is used some 36 times in the LXX of satisfaction in widely differing contexts.

What these references might suggest is that true satisfaction comes from God,³⁶⁰ rather than from hostility, vengeance,³⁶¹ persecution,³⁶² material prosperity,³⁶³ sin,

---

351. Vv. 11–12.

352. Cf. Witherington, *John's Wisdom*, 149. The crowd does not receive "sacramental-sized portions."

353. Exod 16:18. The word "gather" appears in John 6:12.

354. "To be satisfied, filled," Mark 6:42.

355. Cf. Brown, *John I–XII*, 247; LXX Ps 37:19; Ps 81:16; Ps 132:15.

356. Cf. Ps 59:15; Ps 104:13; Ps 17:15.

357. So Brown, *John I–XII*, 234.

358. (emphasis mine). Cf. Dodd, *According*, 85; Barrett, *John*, 276.

359. Dodd, *According*, 44–46; 85–86. Cf. New Covenant knowledge, Jer 31:34; John 4:42; 1 John 2:12–14; The gathering (συναγαγεῖν) of God's scattered people; Jer 31:10; John 11:52; God's feeding them (βόσκων) as his flock Jer 31:10; John 10:9; 21:17; The feeding of the hungry and their hungering no more Jer 31:12 LXX (οὐ πεινάσουσιν); John 6:35 (οὐ μὴ πεινάσῃ).

360. Cf. Ps 22:26; 63:5; 65:4; 90:14; 91:16; 105:40ff.; 145:16; Prov 12:10–14; 18:20; 20:13; Isa 58:10–11; Deut 14:29; Ruth 2:14, 18; Isa 66:11; Jer 31:14; 50:19; Joel 2:19, 26.

361. Exod 15:9.

362. Job 19:22.

363. Cf. Ps 17:14–15; Eccl 1:8; 4:8; 5:10; 6:2–3; Hab 2:5.

unfaithfulness, idolatry,[364] or mere physical bread and water.[365] Importantly, want of satisfaction due to lack of bread is a Levitical curse, imposed for covenant breaking.[366]

The gathering of the fragments so that nothing is lost, vv. 12–13

The leftover bread echoes 2 Kgs 4:44, "they ate and had some left." Here, however, the abundance of fragments not only underlines the miraculous,[367] but also makes it a "messianic sign"[368] of eschatological blessing[369] and messianic banquet.[370] In Amos 9:13 the context of this blessing is Israel's restoration from captivity to the Promised Land. Brown also alludes to Isa 49:9ff., where the Lord promises, "They shall feed along the ways; on all bare heights shall be their pasture; they shall not hunger or thirst . . ." The context is the *Servant* leading the people forth from captivity towards the Promised Land.

The command to "gather up the leftover fragments," unique to John, is also significant. Several scholars note allusions to this gathering in the "eucharistic" prayer of Didache 9:4:

> As this broken bread (κλάσμα) was scattered (διεσκορπισμένον) upon the mountains, but was gathered up and became one (συναχθὲν ἐγένετο ἕν), so let the Church be gathered up from the four corners of the earth into your kingdom.[371]

In addition to the John 6:12 gathering of the fragments echo, Brown also notes John's mountain location and the attempt to make Jesus *king*. There is also an acknowledged echo of John 11:52, where John interprets Caiaphas's words as a prophecy that "Jesus would die for the nation, and not for the nation only, but also to gather into one (συναγάγῃ εἰς ἕν) the children of God who are scattered abroad."[372]

The inference often made is that the Didache viewed John 6 as eucharistic. Even *if* this were so, it does not follow that John himself viewed the feeding as a eucharist or

---

364. Cf. Prov 6:30–31; Isa 44:16; Ezek 7:19; 16:28, 29; 27:33–34.
365. Cf. Prov 30:16; Isa 9:20; Amos 4:8; Mic 6:14.
366. Lev 26:26.
367. Cf. Bultmann, *John*, 213, Haenchen, *John 1*, 272.
368. Cf. Brown, *John I–XII*, 247; Dodd, *HTFG*, 207. For Dodd, the command to gather up the pieces has made the large surplus "an *additional* 'sign'"; the pieces that are collected "symbolize the bread which 'abides' and is not 'lost'" (emphasis original).
369. Joel 2:19–26; 3:18; Amos 9:13. See Keener, *John*, 668.
370. Cf. Lightfoot, *John's Gospel*, 156; Witherington, *John's Wisdom*, 152; Beasley-Murray, *John*, 88, citing Isa 25:6–9.
371. Cf. Brown, *John I–XII*, 248, citing Moule, "Note on Didache IX. 4," 240–43.
372. Cf. Brown, *John I–XII*, 248; Haenchen, *John I*, 275; Moule, "Note on Didache IX. 4," 240–43; Robinson, "Problem of the Didache," 347–48.

based his account anachronistically upon the Eucharist.[373] Importantly, however, what Didache 9:4 *does* do is to draw attention to is the parallel between John 6:12–13 and John 11:50–53. Examination of the two passages confirms this parallel.

1. The verbs Συναγάγετε (gather up) and ἀπόληται (be lost/perish) in John 6:12 are used elsewhere in GJohn of the *gathering* and the *perishing* of people.[374] Thus the gathering of the fragments that nothing may be lost symbolizes the gathering of believers that they might not perish.[375] Comparing v. 12 with v. 39, which speaks of Jesus not losing (μὴ ἀπολέσω) any that the Father has given him, Lindars thinks that John has applied the tradition symbolically to "Christian mission."[376]

2. In John 11:50–52, these same verbs are both used of the *gathering* of Israel into one, and the necessity of Jesus' death that the nation might not *perish*.

3. In John 11:50–52, emphasis is placed upon Jesus dying for the *nation* (mentioned three times) and for the children of God scattered abroad—implying the inclusion of the Gentiles, and their gathering into one.[377] Barrett thinks this might be alluded to metaphorically in John 6:12–13.[378]

I argue that the gathering of the children of God into one nation is symbolized by the collection of twelve baskets; twelve being the number of the apostles, who represent the regeneration of Israel's twelve tribes.[379] I suggest that in effect John 6:12–13 is an enacted parable that *interprets* Caiaphas's prophecy of the gathered (New) Israel effected by Jesus' death.

The objection that the bread represents Jesus *rather than* his people does not hold[380] since for John, as for Paul, those who partake of Christ are one with him.[381] Brown notes the link between the Church as "one body" and the "one bread," 1 Cor 10:17. Moreover, he affirms that it is "scarcely incidental," that the John 11:52 gathering of Jew and Gentile into one echoes the John 6:13 gathering of the fragments.[382]

---

373. *Pace* Brown, *John I–XII*, 248; Schweitzer, *Mysticism*, 362–66. Rather, I have argued (above) that the feeding in John 6 is the precursor to the Eucharist in the same way that OT baptism into Moses and spiritual food and drink prefigure the NT sacraments of baptism and the Lord's table, 1 Cor 10.

374. For "gather" cf. 11:47, 52; for "perish" cf. e.g., 3:16; 6:39; 10:28; 11:50.

375. Cf. Barrett, *John*, 276.

376. Lindars, *John*, 243 cf. 11:52; 17:12; 18:9; Lincoln, *John*, 213.

377. Cf. John 1:11:12; 10:16; Barrett, *John*, 407; Brown, *John I–XII*, 442–43; Carson, *John*, 422; Keener, *John*, 857.

378. Barrett, *John*, 407.

379. Cf. Evans, "Continuing Exile," 92; Sanders, *Jesus and Judaism*, 98; Carson, *John*, 271; Kruse, *John*, 163; Hoskyns, *Fourth Gospel*, 290; Bruce, *John*, 145, 167, n. 3.

380. *Pace* Keener, *John*, 669.

381. Cf. John 6:56 –57; 15; 14:20; 15:1–9; 17:21, 23, 26; 1 Cor 10:16–18.

382. Brown, *John I–XII*, 443.

PART II—DETAILED EXEGETICAL EXAMINATION OF JOHN 5-10

The ramifications of these parallels are important: It is widely recognized that John 11:50-52 echoes the NE *gathering* and restoration of Israel.[383] It is not surprising therefore that John 6:12-13 also echoes the same passages, of which the following are particularly important for the John 6 context:

Ezek 20:33-44

With a mighty hand the Lord will be King over Israel. He will bring them out from the peoples and *gather* (קבץ) them from the countries where they are scattered, bringing them into the wilderness. There he will enter into judgement with them face to face, as he entered into judgement with their fathers in the land of Egypt. He will make them pass under the rod and bring them into the bond of the covenant, purging out the rebels and transgressors, who will not enter the Promised Land. Then they will know that he is the Lord. In his holy mountain, they will serve him and he will accept them, being sanctified among them, and they will loathe their former sinful ways.

This OT passage is programmatic for John 6 where Jesus is the messianic King, performs mighty signs, and gathers the people in the wilderness. Face to face, God with men, he enters into judgement with them, as their fathers were judged in the wilderness,[384] purging out the rebels by a "whittling down" process,[385] of tests, trials, and "hard sayings" concerning his death. The multitudes are reduced to the Twelve, representative of NI, members of the NC, among whom he is sanctified,[386] and by whom he is recognized as the Lord.[387]

Jer 31:8-11

The Lord will gather (Heb קבץ; LXX συνάγω)[388] the remnant of Israel from the end of the earth, among them "the blind and the lame,"[389] "a great company." He will keep them as a shepherd does his flock[390] and satisfy them with his goodness.[391] The NC context of this chapter (Jer 31:31-34) where God (Israel's husband) teaches his people, writing his law upon their hearts, is alluded to in John 6:45.

---

383. The following echoes have been suggested: Isa 11:12; 43:5-6; 49:5-6; Jer 23:2-3; 31:8-11; Ezek 11:17; 20:34; 34:12-13; 37:21-22; Mic 2:12; Ps 106:47; 107:3;as well as *Pss. Sol.* 8:34; *4 Ezra* 13.47; Philo *Praem*. 163-72. Cf. Barrett, *John*, 407; Brown, *John I–XII*, 443; Borchert, *John 1–11*, 367; Lincoln, *John*, 330.

384. Ezek 20:36, 35 cf. John 6:31, 49, 58.

385. See Witherington, *John's Wisdom*, 149.

386. John 6:69.

387. Ezek 20:42, 44 cf. John 6:20, 35, 41, 48, 51, 69; 8:28.

388. Jer 31:8, 10.

389. Jer 31:8 cf. John 5; 9.

390. Jer 31:10 cf. John 10.

391. See above.

Isa 11:12

The Lord will "raise a signal for the nations and will assemble (LXX συνάξει) the banished of Israel (LXX τοὺς ἀπολομένους Ισραηλ, "the lost/perishing ones of Israel"), and gather (Heb קִבֵּץ; LXX συνάξει) the dispersed of Judah from the four corners of the earth." John 6:12, Συναγάγετε and ἀπόληται, echo this. It is also possible that "leftover fragments," echoes "the remnant that remains of [the Lord's] people (עַמּוֹ אֲשֶׁר יִשָּׁאֵר אֶת־שְׁאָר)," Isa 11:11.

In support of the allusion is the importance of Isa 11 for GJohn. The context is the emergence of a branch from the root of Jesse who will set up his messianic kingdom. GJohn echoes several of the Isa 11 messianic characteristics, applying them to Jesus, including: The Spirit resting on messiah,[392] "He shall not judge by what his eyes see, or decide disputes by what his ears hear,"[393] and the "Root of Jesse."[394] Of particular interest to GJohn is the Isa 11:10, 12, *lifting up* of the "root of Jesse," as a standard or *sign* (נֵס) for the nations (Gentiles) to which he *gathers* the remnant of his people in a NE.[395] The same idea is present in Isa 49:22 where the Lord will lift up his hand to the nations and set up a standard to the people in connection with the Servant whose purpose is to *gather* Israel.[396]

John combines these ideas[397] with the Servant's exaltation[398] to signify Jesus' glorification or lifting up in death as the means by which people might *not perish*,[399] the "Jews" will know him,[400] and all peoples will be drawn (and so gathered) to him.[401] Associated with this lifting up is the Johannine emphasis on looking to and believing in Jesus, found in John 6:40.[402]

---

392. Isa 11:2, echoed in John 1:33.

393. Isa 11:3 alluded to in John 7:24.

394. Isa 11:10 in Rev 5:5 cf. Rom 15:12; Dodd, *According*, 83.

395. Cf. Glasson, *Moses*, 35–39; Isa 5:26; 13:2; 18:3; 62:10.

396. Isa 49:5. Cf. The Servant's pasturing the people on the mountains; Isa 49:9, 10, they shall not hunger and thirst, is echoed in John 6:35, where the one who comes and believes never *hungers or thirsts*.

397. Cf. John 3:14; 8:28; 12:32, 34.

398. Isa 52:13.

399. Cf. John 3:14 cf. 6:12, 39–40, 47, 50.

400. John 8:28.

401. John 12:32.

402. Cf. John 1:14, 29, 36, 39, 46, 50; 6:40; 12:21; 14:9, 19; 16:16; 17:24; 19:35; Glasson, *Moses*, 34–35.

PART II—DETAILED EXEGETICAL EXAMINATION OF JOHN 5-10

Isa 54:7

In exile Israel (like an unfaithful wife) had been deserted by God and bereaved of her children. As a result of the vicarious "paschal" sacrifice of the Servant,[403] however, she has been redeemed from exile and everything has changed. The Lord is once again her husband, he has established his everlasting mercy and covenant of peace with her, and she has been restored to the land. Her children will return in such numbers that the land can no longer contain them, but they will spread out to "possess the nations and . . . people the desolate cities" (Isa 54:3). Thus the Lord will *gather* (Heb קָבַץ) Israel (to himself) with great mercies, Isa 54:7. Moreover, she will be protected from her enemies, established in peace and righteousness, and all her children "shall be taught by the LORD" (Isa 54:13). Not only does Isa 54:13 correspond to the NC context of Jer 31:31–34, alluded to in John 6, but also it is cited by Jesus in John 6:45.

Isa 43:5–6

The Lord has redeemed Israel and will *gather* (Heb קָבַץ) her offspring from the east, west, north, and south,[404] guiding and protecting them as they pass through the waters. The nations are also gathered together before the Lord for judgement and God brings his lawsuit against them. The gods of the nations cannot predict the future (because they do not exist), but (blind and deaf) Israel are God's witnesses that he is the Lord, the "I am" (Heb אֲנִי הוּא; LXX ἐγώ εἰμι). Israel's witness bearing is for her own sake that she might "know and believe me and understand that I am he" (Isa 43:10). The Lord, who delivered Israel at the Exodus, and who directs the future, will yet deliver his people in a NE (Isa 43:16–17).

Importantly, there are several allusions to this passage in GJohn. "I have called you by name, you are mine" (Isa 43:1) is echoed in "he calls his own sheep by name" (John 10:3). "Fear not . . . when you pass through the waters I will be with you" (Isa 43:1, 2), "the LORD, who makes a way in the sea, a path in the mighty waters" (Isa 43:16), and "I am" (Isa 43:10) are all echoed in the John 6:19–21 theophany where Jesus walks upon he water and delivers his disciples. "I am" is used by Jesus as a self-designation throughout the Gospel. The Lord's lawsuit against the nations is echoed in Jesus' lawsuits against the "Jews."[405] "There is none who can deliver from my hand" (Isa 43:13) is alluded to by Jesus in John 10:29.

---

403. See above.
404. Isa 43:5–6.
405. See e.g., above on John 5:31–40.

Ps 107:2, 3

The Lord has *gathered* his redeemed people from east, west, north, and south, rescuing them from hunger and thirst in the desert, from affliction and bondage, from folly and disease, and from peril on the sea. [406]

Exod 16:16–31

The gathering of the manna, a further possible echo,[407] does not contradict the above ideas, but complements them. This is because Jesus will be contrasted with the manna in the discourse as he is with Moses, Jesus ushering in an altogether superior redemption. Manna is the bread that perishes, which the fathers ate; He is the bread that endures to eternal life.[408]

Reaction: Attempt to make Jesus King, vv. 14–15

Having witnessed the sign, as Israel saw the Lord's great work,[409] the crowds comprehend something of its significance: Jesus is the Prophet like Moses of Deut 18:18. On a deeper level, however, they have not understood. Ironically, "who is to come into the world (ὁ ἐρχόμενος εἰς τὸν κόσμον)," echoes John 1:9, "The true light ... was coming into the world (ἐρχόμενον εἰς τὸν κόσμον)," indicating Jesus' divine origin, reflected in his ability to read their hearts.[410] To their carnal understanding[411] they can only interpret the fulfilment as the coming of a political deliverer who will liberate them from the Romans. Thus they do not fear him or listen to his word,[412] but seek to force him to do their will, making him a figurehead for rebellion.

To Jesus, this is the antithesis of all that he stands for: He is a King, but not according to their worldly standards.[413] At Jesus' trial Pilate will repeatedly refer to him as King,[414] but will three times pronounce him innocent of sedition.[415] Jesus' hasty withdrawal from the crowds signals not only his fear of being misrepresented, but also his rejection of and judgement upon the crowds. Symbolically, return to the

---

406. On the importance of this psalm for John 6, see below.
407. Cf. Brown, *John I–XII*, 234; Lindars, *John*, 243; Lincoln, *John*, 213.
408. John 6:48–51.
409. Exod 14:31.
410. Cf. John 6:15; 1:48; 2:24; 5:42; 6:36, 64.
411. Cf. John 3:6; 6:63; 8:15.
412. Cf. Exod 14:31; Deut 18:19.
413. Cf. John 18:36–37; 1:49.
414. Cf. John 18:37, 39; 19:14–15, 19.
415. Cf. John 18:38; 19:4, 6.

mountain⁴¹⁶ may represent Jesus' return to heaven, the ultimate NE destination, when "the Jews" will seek him and not find him.

There has been much debate as to whether "Prophet like Moses" was a recognized messianic title, especially when linked to an attempt to make Jesus king. Though hope of the Mosaic Prophet is not generally reflected in first century literature, it would likely have been considered a messianic designation among the common people at the pilgrim feasts.[417] Meeks demonstrates that Moses was viewed as the ideal king, particularly among the Samaritans.[418] Bauckham argues that to be made king over the people is consistent with being a prophet like Moses,[419] thus John has not assimilated the figures of Mosaic prophet and Christ.[420] While John clearly recognizes the distinction,[421] however, I argue that:

1. It would be easy for the people to link the two figures from the Scriptures.

2. John himself links such figures as Mosaic Prophet with Christ as different facets of the one person in whom all are fulfilled.

3. Such linkage is already made in Scripture by "inner-biblical exegesis." For example, the Servant exhibits both Mosaic and Davidic characteristics.

4. Linkage is also made in some later rabbinic writings.[422]

Scene 3: Jesus delivers his true disciples through the waters, vv. 16–21

Scholars have argued that because these verses are "not directly expounded" in the discourse, John included them to get the disciples to the other side of the Lake, or because they are inseparable from the tradition. In fact, they are integral to the paschal NE theme of the chapter.[423] Much that John narrates is not "expounded." Rather its allusive character indicates a deeper significance to what has transpired, which draws the reader into the story in search of ever-deeper meaning. Here it will be seen that allusions are made to the sea crossing of the Exodus and to the NE deliverance from the nations through the waters.[424]

---

416. Forming an *inclusio* with v. 3. See Keener, *John*, 664.
417. Bauckham, "Jewish Messianism," 220–21.
418. Meeks, *Prophet-King, passim*.
419. Bauckham, "Jewish Messianism," 223.
420. Ibid., 222.
421. Cf. John 7:41, cited by Bauckham, "Jewish Messianism," 222.
422. See, e.g., *Eccl. Rab.* 1:9, in Freedman, 8:33, "As the first redeemer was, so shall the latter Redeemer be," which compares Moses who rode on a donkey, Exod 4:20, to the messianic king of Zech 9:9, who comes lowly and riding on a donkey.
423. *Pace* Bultmann, *John*, 218; Barrett, *John*, 279. Cf. Carson, *John*, 273–74. Richardson, *Miracle Stories*, 117–18, believes that they are expounded in chs 13–17.
424. See below. Cf. Brown, *John I–XII*, 255; Beasley-Murray, *John*, 89; Jones, *Water*, 136–37;

Jesus' Paschal NE Departure, John 6

Importantly, the sea crossing is closely linked with the gift of manna and the Passover both in Scripture and also in Jewish exegesis:

1. In Ps 78 and Neh 9.[425] Both of these texts are alluded to in John 6:31.
2. Indirectly in Ps 107, alluded to in John 6:16–21.[426]
3. Through the Passover synagogue readings: directly[427] and indirectly—through the themes of faith and disbelief,[428] death and resurrection.[429] Interestingly the theme of death and resurrection is found in all John's Passover sections.[430]
4. Through Paul's linking of the manna and sea crossing as OT sacraments that prefigure the New (1 Cor 10:1–5).
5. In the Passover Haggadah.[431]

Guilding argues that Jesus' walking on the sea symbolizes his death and resurrection, analogous to the overthrow of Pharaoh (symbolic of death and Satan) in the Red Sea.[432] Though these ideas have found little acceptance,[433] several considerations might make them possible:

1. Jesus' withdrawal to a mountain may be symbolic of his return to God. Such withdrawals progressively occur[434] until they become final at his death.
2. "Jesus had not yet come to them," v. 17, is enigmatic. Why should they expect this on the sea?[435] In fact the pattern illustrates Jesus' saying, "a little while, and you will see me no longer; and again a little while, and you will see me" (John 16:16–22), spoken of his death and resurrection.
3. Finding an analogy with Jesus' sudden appearance, Keener thinks that there is an

---

Guilding, *Jewish Worship*, 66–67. As with the miraculous multiplication of the food, above, Greek parallels are not relevant. See Keener, *John*, 672–73.

425. See, e.g., Neh 9:11, 15; Ps 78:13, 24. See Brown, *John I-XII*, 255.

426. See below.

427. Cf. Exod 14:15–16:27; Num 11; Isa 51:6–16; 54:9–55:5; 63:11; Guilding, *Jewish Worship*, 61–63.

428. See Guilding, *Jewish Worship*, 64–65, 62. In Exod 14:31, Israel saw great work of Lord and believed. Cf. *Exod. Rab.* 15:1 and *haftarah* Isa 26:1ff., "Keep in perfect peace whose mind stayed on you." Confidence in God's *provision* is a traditional theme of Nisan synagogue readings (Guilding, *Jewish Worship*, 65). Cf. *Sifre* on Num 11:6; *Mek. Exod.* 14:31; *Exod. Rab.* 15:1. The theme of unbelief is also present.

429. Cf. the Nissan synagogue readings Gen 2:4ff.; Exod 15:22, and their *haftarah*, Isa 51:6–16; 63:11, possibly connected to Isa 26:19 by Isa 51:14.

430. See, e.g., John 2:19; 6:39; 12:24–33.

431. See Brown, *John I-XII*, 255.

432. Exod 15. See Guilding, *Jewish Worship*, 58–59.

433. Cf. Barrett, *John*, 279; Schnackenburg, *John*, 2:29–30.

434. Cf. 5:13; 7:1; 8:59; 9:12; 12:36.

435. See Brown, *John I-XII*, 251.

allusion forward to John 20 where the risen Lord appears to disciples.[436]

4. A similar analogy may be drawn with Jesus' John 21 appearance. In both passages the disciples go down to the Tiberias sea shore, apparently on their own initiative, and embark in a boat by night. They see Jesus but fail to recognize him until he manifests himself to them by a sign.

More probably the sea crossing represents the disciples' NE deliverance through death alluded to in the Passover synagogue readings. At the Exodus God delivered his people through death at the Passover, in the deliverance through the sea, and by the provision of bread in the wilderness.[437] In the Isaianic NE the Lord preserves his people as they pass through the waters (Isa 43:1–2). Similarly, in Ps 107, God delivers the redeemed from the hand of the enemy and the shadow of death in a NE; The disciples' sudden arrival at their destination, John 6:21, just one of several echoes of this psalm,[438] likewise symbolizes deliverance by Jesus *through* death to safety.[439] Just as their participation in the bread will point to participation in Jesus (and his paschal sacrificial death) as their life giving spiritual food,[440] so their deliverance here is symbolic of baptism into Jesus' death and resurrection. Moreover, these experiences prefigured life through Jesus' death and resurrection, as the Eucharist and Christian baptism look back upon it. This is plausible because Paul makes the same association between the Exodus Sea crossing and manna and their NT sacramental counterparts in 1 Cor 10.

With these ideas in mind, the functionality of John 6:16–21 becomes apparent. The incident contrasts and separates out (after the Ezekiel 20 model) the true disciples from the unbelieving "Jews" and the crowd. The former are "baptized" into Jesus, delivered by him, and come through trial by wilderness and water to recognize his divine identity.[441] The latter seek only a political deliverer and follow Jesus for bread that perishes. They have no true faith that stands the test, but turn back because of inability to hear Jesus' word. This division becomes progressively clear in the discourse section and also in the reactions of the different groups to Jesus' words.

Trial by water—An ominous departure, vv. 16–17

Everything about the departure is ominous. Evening is not the usual time to embark on a journey, let alone one by sea. But this departure had been occasioned by the actions of a potentially violent crowd from whom Jesus had withdrawn and from whom

---

436. Keener, *John*, 674–75. Cf. John 20:19, 26.
437. See, e.g., Exod 14:11–12; 16:3; 17:3.
438. Cf. Ps 107:30; Barrett, *John*, 281; Carson, *John*, 276; Lightfoot, *John's Gospel*, 157.
439. See Lightfoot, *John's Gospel*, 157, "We seem to have here [in 6:20–21] the teaching of 14:5–6; 15:4–5, in another form."
440. John 6:51–58. See below.
441. Cf. 6:5–6; Heb 3:8–11; 1 Pet 1:7; 4:12.

Jesus' Paschal NE Departure, John 6

the disciples had effectively escaped under cover of darkness. That the disciples went "down" on to the sea suggests not only topography, but also travel away from Jesus into imminent danger and testing.[442] Situated in a depression surrounded by hills, the Sea of Galilee was notorious for its sudden perilous storms[443] and it was now late and dark. For GJohn, darkness, common to all the Passover sections,[444] is synonymous with evil, ignorance, danger, and death.[445] Here it is reminiscent of the darkness that descended at the Red Sea.[446] According to Mark, Jesus had instructed the disciples to go before him, but as yet, "Jesus had not yet come to them," (John 6:17).[447] Jesus' later absence would be compared to the sorrow occasioned by birth pangs.[448]

Survival threatened, vv. 18–19

The rough sea, occasioned by the strong winds, appears adversarial and even sinister, halting the disciples' progress and threatening their survival.[449] In the OT God is always in ultimate control of the winds and the sea, but occasionally he allows the powers of heaven to test his people.[450] Added to this is the terrifying sight of an unidentified figure,[451] walking on the waters and approaching. The disciples in the boat are effectively the Church in embryo,[452] whom the adversary[453] is seeking to destroy. God will not allow this to happen, but will use it to test the disciples.

ALLUSION TO PS 107 (LXX PS 106)[454]

This psalm celebrates the Lord's gathering of Israel from the nations, from the east, west, north, and south—redeeming them from exile, from "the enemy," and from

---

442. Cf. Ps 107:23; Jones, *Water*, 139.

443. See Bruce, *John*, 148, citing Smith, *Historical Geography*, 441–42.

444. See Guilding, *Jewish Worship*, 59–60. Cf. John 3:2, 19; 12:35–36; 13:30.

445. Cf. John 1:5; 3:19; 8:12; 12:35, 45; 1 John 1:5–6; 2:8–11; Isa 5:10; 8:22; 9:2; 42:7, 16; 60:2; Jones, *Water*, 139; Heil, *Jesus Walking on the Sea*, 146.

446. Exod 14:20. Cf. Ellis, *Genius*, 110; Jones, *Water*, 136; Guilding, *Jewish Worship*, 66–67.

447. Cf. Exod 32:1, where Moses delayed to come down from mount, and 1 Sam 13:11, where Samuel did not come within the appointed days. Both delays had disastrous consequences. Cf. Jones, *Water*, 139.

448. John 16:6–7, 19–22.

449. Cf. Matt 14:24. Keener, *John*, 674, notes that modern boats remain on land during storms on Galilee; *pace* Lincoln, *John*, 217.

450. Cf. Job 26:13; 28:25-26; 1:16, 19; Dan 7:2-3.

451. Cf. Matt 14:26; Mark 6:49.

452. For a recent reiteration of this ancient idea cf. Brodie, *John*, 265.

453. Cf. Ps 107:2.

454. Cf. Barrett, *John*, 281; Brown, *John I-XII*, 255; Carson, *John*, 276; Lightfoot, *John's Gospel*, 157; Kidner, *Psalms 73–150*, 386.

PART II—DETAILED EXEGETICAL EXAMINATION OF JOHN 5–10

"the shadow of death." It depicts four contrasting predicaments and divine interventions: the Lord delivering people from wilderness wanderings, prison, sickness, and storm. Not only are all these concepts utilized by John,[455] but also the first and last are reflected here. Verbal parallels include "gathered (LXX συνήγαγεν)";[456] "wilderness (LXX ἐρήμῳ)";[457] "hungry and thirsty (LXX πεινῶντες καὶ διψῶντες)";[458] and "satisfies (LXX ἐχόρτασεν; Heb שָׂבֵעַ) . . . and . . . fills (LXX ἐνέπλησεν)."[459] Ps 107:23, "Some went down to the sea in ships (LXX Ps 106:23 οἱ καταβαίνοντες εἰς τὴν θάλασσαν ἐν πλοίοις)" compares with John 6:16, "His disciples went down to the sea, [and] got into a boat (κατέβησαν οἱ μαθηταὶ αὐτοῦ ἐπὶ τὴν θάλασσαν καὶ ἐμβάντες εἰς πλοῖον)." There are also many parallel ideas:

1. "They saw (LXX εἴδοσαν) the deeds of the LORD (LXX τὰ ἔργα κυρίου), his wondrous works in the deep," is descriptive of the disciples who saw Jesus walking upon the waters and experienced his miraculous deliverance.[460] The "works of God" (τὰ ἔργα τοῦ θεοῦ), are what Jesus performs.[461]

2. "The stormy wind, which lifted up the waves of the sea."[462]

3. "At their wits' end," signifying the limits of their *seamanship*, and their cry to the Lord, who stilled the storm and made them glad, are reflected in the Synoptics.[463]

4. "He brought them to their desired haven."[464]

5. "He sent out his word and healed them (LXX ἀπέστειλεν τὸν λόγον αὐτοῦ καὶ ἰάσατο αὐτούς), and delivered them from their destruction."[465]

Although the Psalm suggests suffering because of sin, this is not apparent for the seafarers.[466] Rather they have encountered powerful forces, superior to their abilities, at the "hand of the enemy (LXX χειρὸς ἐχθροῦ; Heb מִיַּד־צָר)," Ps 107:2. The Lord has rescued and redeemed them from this and brought them to the "Promised Land."

---

455. Cf. also the restoration of those sick through sin, vv. 17–22, with John 5; 9, and the deliverance of the prisoners, vv. 10–16, with John 8.

456. Ps 107:3 cf. John 6:12–13.

457. Ps 107:4 NKJV cf. John 6:31.

458. Ps 107:5 cf. John 6:35.

459. Ps 107:9 cf. John 6:12.

460. Ps 107:24 cf. John 6:19.

461. Cf. John 9:3–4; 10:32; 17:4; 4:33; 7:21. In John 6:28, the crowds think that God requires the works of God from them.

462. Ps 107:25 cf. John 6:18.

463. Cf. Ps 107:27, 28–30; Mark 6:48–51; Matt 14:26–33; Kidner, *Psalms 73–150*, 386.

464. Ps 107:30, suggestive of John 6:21, "Immediately the boat was at the land to which they were going." Cf. Beale and Carson, *New Testament Use*, 444.

465. Ps 107:20 cf. John 5:8–11.

466. Ps 107:23–30 cf. Ps 107:11, 17.

Likewise in John 6, the disciples are unable to accomplish their own deliverance because the enemy is too powerful, but the Lord delivers them through the waters.

Possible allusion to Isa 42:10

"You who go down to the sea" (LXX οἱ καταβαίνοντες εἰς τὴν θάλασσαν καὶ πλέοντες αὐτήν. Literally: "those that go down to the sea and sail upon it"). The context is a call for the world to praise the Lord in the light of his announcement of the Servant who will manifest God's grace and glory, and bring his justice and salvation to the whole world.[467]

Delivered by Jesus, vv. 19–21

Jesus miraculously rescues the disciples by walking to them upon the water, being received by them into their boat, and immediately transporting them to their destination. Jesus' appearance to the disciples is a theophany,[468] a manifestation of his divine glory. This is indicated by his use of the divine name, "I am," his walking on the sea, the fear his presence evokes in the disciples, and his words of reassurance, "do not be afraid." In the OT "theophanies evoke fear," to which the Lord responds with, "fear not," usually linked with a self-revelation formula.[469] Likewise here, the disciples are afraid, not only because of the storm, but also because of Jesus' supernatural appearance,[470] and he responds by disclosing his divine identity, and dispelling their fears Εγώ εἰμι μὴ φοβεῖσθε (literally, "I am; fear not"), John 6:20. All the elements of Jesus' appearance, the walking upon the sea, the "I am," and the "fear not," echo OT theophanies, many of which are associated with the Exodus or the NE:

Job 9:8

Here God walks on "the waves of the sea," and "passes by" unperceived.[471] The context is God's omniscience, omnipotence, and holy otherness, that makes it impossible for men to justify themselves before God. Job also mentions the allies of Rahab, emblematic of Egypt, being bowed before the Lord.

---

467. See Oswalt, *Isaiah 40–66*, 123.

468. Cf. Lincoln, *John*, 218 –19; Keener, *John*, 673; Grigsby, "Reworking," 296; Ellis, *Genius*, 110 –11; Appold, *Oneness Motif*, 82; Smith, *John*, 150.

469. See Lincoln, *John*, 218–19, citing Gen 15:1; 26:24; 46:3; Judg 6:23. Cf. Exod 14:13, where Israel was afraid at Red Sea, and Moses said "fear not." Cf. Beale and Carson, *New Testament Use*, 444: "Do not be afraid," was God's message in the OT. Cf. Gen 26:24; Deut 1:21, 29; 20:1, 3; Josh 1:9.

470. Cf. Matt 14:26; Mark 6:49, where they think they have seen an apparition.

471. Cf. John 6:19; Job 9:11; 38:16; Beale and Carson, *New Testament Use*, 444; Beasley-Murray, *John*, 89; Keener, *John*, 678; Lincoln, *John*, 218.

PART II—DETAILED EXEGETICAL EXAMINATION OF JOHN 5-10

Ps 77:19

Referring to the Exodus, the psalmist writes, "[God's] way was through the sea, . . . [his] path through the great waters; yet . . . [his] footprints were unseen."[472] The waters saw him and fled and he led his people by the hand of Moses and Aaron.

Isa 43

As we have seen (above), the Lord's walking upon the waters at the Exodus becomes a paradigm for a NE where he will redeem his people from the east, west, north, and south. Thus he will be with his people when they "pass through the waters," (v. 2). Promising to do "a new thing," God bids them to "fear not," (v. 1), declaring himself, "I am," (v. 10), Israel's Lord, Holy One, Creator, and King "who makes a way in the sea, a path in the mighty waters," (v. 16).

Isa 51:9-15

Here, Isaiah calls on the "arm of the LORD" to awake, and fulfil his word that "the ransomed of the LORD shall return and come to Zion . . ." He reminds God, "Was it not you who cut Rahab in pieces . . . Was it not you who dried up the sea . . . who made the depths of the sea a way for the redeemed to pass over? The Lord replies, v. 12, "I, I am he (Heb אָנֹכִי אָנֹכִי הוּא, LXX ἐγώ εἰμι ἐγώ εἰμι ὁ . . .) who comforts you; who are you that you are afraid . . . He who is bowed down shall speedily be released; he shall not die . . . neither shall his bread be lacking. I am the LORD your God, who stirs up the sea."

Ps 8

It is just possible that there is also an echo of Ps 8, where the Son of Man has dominion over the works of God's hand, having "put all things under his feet . . . whatever passes along the paths of the seas," (vv. 6, 8). "Crowned . . . with glory and honor," he exercises divine prerogatives, walking upon the sea (cf. the Son of Man riding upon the clouds, Dan 7:13–14). As such Jesus is a second-Adam and head of a redeemed humanity.[473]

---

472. Ps 77:19, 15. Cf. Beasley-Murray, *John*, 89–90; Brown, *John I–XII*, 255; Lincoln, *John*, 218; Keener, *John*, 673; Witherington, *John's Wisdom*, 153.

473. See Kidner, *Psalms 1–72*, 68. Cf. Heb 2:8; 1 Cor 15:27–28.

Jesus' use of "I am," v. 20

This use of the absolute "I am" prepares the way for the (first) predicated "I am" saying, "I am the bread of life."[474] While some scholars accept this, others deny that anything more than "it is I" is intended.[475] Barrett argues that similar usage in Mark 6:48–51, John's "source," has no overtones of an epiphany. In response I argue that:

1. The context determines the meaning of the ἐγώ εἰμι.[476]

2. Mark does indeed indicate Jesus' appearance to be an epiphany. Not only does he share John's echoes, but he also speaks of a theophanic "passing by" (v. 48), echoing the manifestation of the Lord at Sinai before Moses and at Horeb before Elijah.[477] Mark 6:48–49, "walking on the sea. He meant to pass by . . ." may also echo Job 9:8, 11, where God walks on the sea and passes by unperceived.

3. GJohn's Ἐγώ εἰμι μὴ φοβεῖσθε (John 6:20, literally "I am, do not be afraid") and Mark's Θαρσεῖτε, ἐγώ εἰμι· μὴ φοβεῖσθε (Mark 6:50, literally "take courage, I am, do not be afraid") rest ultimately on Exod 3:14[478] and unmistakably echo "the formula of [God's] self-revelation."[479] GJohn echoes several OT passages that contain "I am," or "fear not," or both.[480] Two of these coincide with passages echoed by Jesus' walking on the water,[481] suggesting that God, walking upon the water, has become manifest in Jesus[482] and has come to deliver his people in a NE.[483] The boat's arrival immediately at land (John 6:21) compares with God bringing his people through the sea.[484]

These ideas are further strengthened by consideration of the importance of "I am" to the Passover. Bruce thinks that "I am He" (Heb אֲנִי־הוּא, LXX ἐγώ εἰμι), repeatedly used in Isa 40-55, was probably the origin of the divine name, "I and He" (אֲנִי וְהוּא), used

---

474. John 6:35. Cf. Lincoln, *John*, 217.

475. Cf. Brown, *John I–XII*, 1, 252; Carson, *John*, 275; Haenchen, *John I*, 280.

476. Clearly for the man-born-blind, the ἐγώ εἰμι of John 9:9 can only be the colloquial "I am he." In John 8:24, 28, 58, however, most would recognize that the context demands an absolute use of "I am," identifying Jesus with God, Isa 41:4. Cf. Bruce, *John*, 193, 195; Barrett, *John*, 341–42.

477. Cf. Mark 6:48; Exod 33:19, 22; 1 Kgs 19:11; Lane, *Mark*, 236; Schneider, "ἔρχομαι," 681–82; Denis, "Jesus' Walking on the Waters," 284–97; Lincoln, *John*, 220; Keener, *John*, 673.

478. See Beale and Carson, *New Testament Use*, 444.

479. See Lane, *Mark*, 237. He cites Ps 115:9ff.; 118:5–6; Isa 41:4ff., 13ff.; 43:1ff.; 44:2ff.; 51:9ff. Moreover, "the emphatic overtone [in Mark] . . . is confirmed . . . in verse 51f." See ibid., 237, citing *Baba Bathra* 73a; *b. megillah* 3a; 1 Enoch 60:16; Wisd. 17:3–4, 15, Str-B 1.691.

480. Cf. Exod 3:14; Isa 40:9; 41:4, 10, 13–14; 43:1–2; 44:2–8; 45:5–6, 18, 21–22; 46:4; 48:12; 51:9–12; 54:4. Cf. Lincoln, *John*, 219; Beasley-Murray, *John*, 89–90.

481. Cf. Isa 43; 51:9–15, above.

482. Cf. Lincoln, *John*, 219.

483. See Beasley Murray, *John*, 89. Cf. Witherington, *John's Wisdom*, 153.

484. John 6:21. Cf. Ellis, *Genius*, 111; Keener, *John*, 674.

at Tabernacles and Passover in the processional singing of Ps. 118:25.[485] "I am" is especially emphasized in the Passover Haggadah in the context of the Exodus deliverance.

Scene 4: The Left-Behind Crowd's Quest for Jesus, vv. 22–24

These verses reveal the division that has opened up between the crowd and Jesus: The next day indicates that time has moved on, but the people have not. Separated physically, they "remained on the other side of the sea" (John 6:22). They are also incapable of thinking on a spiritual level, but use natural ("carnal") reasoning concerning Jesus' baffling departure.[486] This illustrates the situation that Jesus says will obtain following his death, "You will seek me and you will not find me. Where I am you cannot come." Of this, "the Jews" speak more than they know: "Does he intend to go to the Dispersion among the Greeks and teach the Greeks?" (John 7:34–36). Here they set about seeking Jesus, not because they believe in him, but for what they can get from him.[487]

Conclusion

We have seen that John 6:1–24 is a symbolic narrative in which, against the Passover background, Jesus signals the paschal NE. First, he performs a prophetic sign-act: departing from Judea, crossing the sea, followed by multitudes, he ascends the mountain. Reflecting the Exodus, this becomes a paradigm for Jesus' paschal departure to his Father's house, by way of the cross, by which he initiates the NE.

This leads to a crisis, typical of the Exodus and NE: the need to provide the multitudes with bread, not merely physical bread, but a paschal messianic banquet and God's NC mercies. Jesus is this paschal bread, God's Servant, and Word from heaven, who feeds the multitudes by virtue of his paschal sacrifice. In this Word his disciples must learn to trust. The gathering of the fragments that none perish, represents the NE gathering of "exiles" from all the world and the reconstitution of twelve tribes in one NI. The crowds, however, failing to understand or to perceive Jesus' true identity, seek to make him a political king and source of perishable bread.

The disciples' deliverance through the sea is a further NE sign. Jesus' absence, perhaps symbolic of his death, leads to imminent danger and death by which they are "baptized" into Jesus. He manifests his divine glory to them, revealing himself to be the embodiment of the covenant God, the "I am," who delivers his people through the waters in a NE. This separates them from the left-behind crowds, who search in vain for Jesus, in hope of physical bread.

---

485. Bruce, *John*, 193, 206, n. 5. Cf. Keener, *John*, 673, n. 104; Harner, *"I Am,"* 18, 61.
486. Cf. 1 Cor 2:14; 3:1–4.
487. Cf. John 6:14–15, 26, 36.

NE INTERPRETATION OF THE JOHN 6 DISCOURSE ON THE BREAD OF LIFE, VV. 25–59

This discourse takes place in the Capernaum Synagogue, where the crowds catch up with Jesus (v. 59). It follows the *yelammedenu* homiletical pattern involving a series of exchanges where the crowds question Jesus as rabbi and he answers them with his teaching.[488]

Throughout the discourse several previously announced Johannine themes, particularly those of John 3 and 5, are reintroduced. These include the cooperation between the Father and the Son in the work of salvation, the contrast between perishing and eternal life, life as a gift, looking unto/believing in Jesus, the ascending and descending Son of Man, and the last day resurrection to life. In John 3, these themes interpreted the typology of the serpent uplifted in the wilderness. Here in John 6, they interpret the typology of the bread given in the wilderness. As Joseph said of Pharaoh's dreams, they "are one." John understood both the uplifted serpent and the gift of manna as different types of the same event: Jesus' life-giving death. Importantly, as we will see, *looking* to the serpent and *feeding* on the bread are equivalent. They both signify participation in the salvation that Jesus brings through faith in his life giving death.

First exchange, vv. 25–27

The crowds' enquiry, v. 25

The crowds commence with their curiosity concerning Jesus' disappearance from them and reappearance in the Capernaum synagogue, v. 25, "Rabbi, when did you come here?"

Jesus warns the crowds: their motivation for seeking him is wrong, vv. 26–27

"Jesus answered them, 'Truly, truly, I say to you, you are seeking me, not because you saw signs, but because you ate your fill of the loaves. Do not labor for the food that perishes, but for the food that endures to eternal life, which the Son of Man will give to you. For on him God the Father has set his seal.'"

As in John 3:2–3, Jesus does not answer them directly, satisfying their idle curiosity, but changes the subject to confront their condition, addressing their deepest spiritual need. Jesus' answer is the "text" on which the discourse is based. It sums up the whole discourse as God's lawsuit against them:

1. They are seeking him for the wrong reason. "You are seeking me . . . because you ate your fill of the loaves," v. 26. Their reason for seeking Jesus is because their

---

488. See Lincoln, *John*, 224–25.

PART II—DETAILED EXEGETICAL EXAMINATION OF JOHN 5-10

stomachs were filled. Their vain desire is for a this-world political deliverer, not a savior from sin who will bestow eternal life upon them.

2. They must exert themselves for the right reasons. "Labor . . . for the food that endures to eternal life, which the Son of Man will give to you," v. 27. They must stop seeking Jesus for a supply of perishable food (food that causes people to perish) and begin to seek him for food that endures (food that bestows eternal life). As Son of Man, Jesus is authorized by the Father to "give" them this food in contrast to their "labor" (persistent efforts) to obtain food that only temporarily sustains life. This is analogous to John 4:10–14, where Jesus offers "living water" in contrast to that which involves constant effort to draw and only temporarily alleviates thirst.

3. They are spiritually blind. "You are seeking me, not because you saw signs," v. 26, probably alludes to the miraculous feeding, but may also include Jesus' sign-act, his "disappearance," or the "signs that he was doing on the sick."[489] The "formal contradiction" with v. 2, "a large crowd was following him, because they saw the signs that he was doing," is explicable by the difference between sight and perception: though they saw what Jesus did, they did not perceive its significance. This principle, illustrated in John 9:39, is explicit in John 12:40 (citing Isa 6:10), "He has blinded their eyes and hardened their heart, lest they see with their eyes, and understand with their heart." Like idolaters they have eyes, but "cannot see."[490] As in God's lawsuit with the nations, his witnesses (Israel) are blind (Isa 43:8–10).

4. They must recognize Jesus' divine authority. "For on him God the Father has set his seal," v. 27, recalling John 3:33,[491] is the reason that people should come to Jesus. The seal is the mark of authority designating irrevocable approval of a person or decree. Jesus, the Son of Man, has been uniquely approved as God's Son and Servant, marked out as the only Savior. This took place when Jesus was anointed with the Holy Spirit at his baptism.[492] As we have seen, God also continually bears a threefold witness to Jesus: by the works, directly, and through Scripture.[493] This divine witness is self-authenticating and so, if they fail to heed it, they have no excuse.

Several OT passages stand behind, and are possibly deliberately echoed in, Jesus' words:

---

489. John 6:2 cf. Matt 14:14.
490. Cf. Ps 115:5; Ps 135:16; Isa 44:18; 32:3.
491. See Lincoln, *John*, 226.
492. John 1:32–33 cf. Matt 3:16–17; Mark 1:10–11; Luke 3:22.
493. John 5:36–39.

Jesus' Paschal NE Departure, John 6

AN ECHO OF GEN 3:17–19

"Cursed is the ground because of you (LXX ἐπικατάρατος ἡ γῆ ἐν τοῖς ἔργοις σου; cursed is the ground in your *labors*). In pain (Heb עִצָּבוֹן, toil) you shall eat of it all the days of your life ... By the sweat of your face you shall eat bread, till you return to the ground ..." In this passage God pronounces the curse because of Adam's sin. It highlights the futility of his labors (under the curse) to produce bread that will ultimately sustain his life. Thus it will be to him bread that causes him to perish, in contrast to God's gift of the tree of life that was freely available prior to the fall.[494]

AN ECHO OF ISA 55:2

"Why do you spend money for that which is not bread (לֶחֶם), and your *labor* (יְגִיעֲכֶם toil [husbandry] or its result) for that which does not satisfy?"[495] This predicts a NE crisis when the returnees, though in need of food, will have far greater need of covenant mercy.[496] God, whose thoughts are higher than theirs, freely offers the sure (eternal) covenant mercies of David,[497] whom he has appointed as a witness to and leader of the peoples. The fatness (Hebrew דֶּשֶׁן),[498] in which those who respond will delight, can be understood as luxury, abundance, fertility, or as "fat ashes" of a sacrificial victim. God's NE purposes of grace will be accomplished by his powerful word, going forth and returning to him like the rain from heaven.

This Isaianic contrast between spiritual and physical bread governs the whole John 6 discourse. Jesus is the true life-giving bread, God's Word, and Servant, come down to execute God's will by offering himself as a paschal victim. All who believe in him receive eternal life. Those seeking only temporary satisfaction, like the wilderness fathers, will perish.

AN ECHO OF EXOD 16:15–21

"Food ... which the Son of Man will give you," John 6:27, might echo "It is the bread that the LORD has given you to eat" (Exod 16:15). Moreover, "food that perishes"

---

494. Gen 2:4ff., which may have been a Passover synagogue reading (So Guilding, *Jewish Worship*, 61).

495. See Lincoln, *John*, 226. This passage is directly alluded to in John 6:45 (cf. Isa 54:13) and comes from the *haftarah*, Isa 54:9–55:5, corresponding to a possible Paschal synagogue reading, Gen 6:9ff.

496. See above where this crisis is echoed in vv. 5–9.

497. See Fishbane, *Biblical Interpretation*, 495, who believes that Isa 55:1–5 is a nationalisation of the promises made to David in Ps 89.

498. Isa 55:2.

PART II—DETAILED EXEGETICAL EXAMINATION OF JOHN 5–10

might echo the manna that constantly had to be gathered and that bred worms (indicative of death) when left (Exod 16:20).[499]

An echo of Num 11:32–34

The concept of laboring for food that causes people to perish might echo Israel's rising all day and all night and all the next day, to gather quail. "While the meat was yet between their teeth . . . the anger of the LORD was kindled against the people, and the LORD struck down the people with a very great plague . . . there they buried the people that had the craving," Num 11:33–34. This is recalled in Ps 78:18–31, alluded to in John 6:31.

An echo of Num 21:5–9

This may also be reflected in food that causes people to perish: When the people spoke against Moses, "There is no food (bread) and no water, and we loath this worthless food," Num 21:25, the Lord sent fiery serpents, which bit them and many *died*. When Moses prayed, the Lord instructed him to lift up a bronze serpent and all who looked to it were healed.

Second exchange vv. 28–29

They ask for clarification, v. 28

"Then they said to him, 'What must we do, to be doing the works of God?'" Jesus has spoken concerning their labor and his gift. That they have picked up on the former together with the repetition of "works" suggests their "legal mentality."[500] They think they can earn God's favor. In fact, only Jesus can procure God's favor for them. As Barrett notes, "doing the works of God" (John 6:28; ἐργαζώμεθα τὰ ἔργα τοῦ θεοῦ) echoes "perform the work of the Lord," (Num 8:11 NKJV; LXX ἐργάζεσθαι τὰ ἔργα κυρίου), which the Levites (offered to God instead of the firstborn) were to do that they might eat the bread of God. In fact,

> Jesus, the true Holy One of God and true firstborn has worked the works of God, "offered his flesh for the life of the world."[501]

The Levites served in the Tent of Meeting, but Jesus, God's "only Son" and firstborn, "tabernacled among us."[502] Having been consecrated by the Father and sent into the

---

499. Cf. Lincoln, *John*, 224.
500. Haenchen, *John I*, 290.
501. Barrett, *John*, 61. Cf. Haenchen, *John I*, 290.
502. John 1:14 cf. Num 8:22.

world, Jesus works God's works among us.[503] The Levites made atonement for the children of Israel typically,[504] but Jesus, God's firstborn and paschal redeemer, makes atonement for his people in reality.

Jesus corrects them: God's work is to believe in Him, v. 29

"Jesus answered them, 'This is the work of God, that you believe in him whom he has sent.'" Jesus does not deny that they can eat the (Levitical) consecrated bread of God (as priests in his new Temple), but only that they can do God's works.[505] There is only one "work" that they can do: believe in him whom God has sent. He will *give* them the bread of life. This is very close to Paul's doctrine of justification by faith.[506]

Third exchange, vv. 30–33

They ask for a sign, v. 30

"What sign do you do, that we may see and believe you? What work do you perform?" This indicates that the people understand something of Jesus' claim to be God's emissary and as such they expect him to perform a validating sign.[507] In particular they have in mind the restoration of manna, associated with Passover and Messiah.[508] Bultmann thinks that this is an aporia, because they have already witnessed such signs. As Anderson points out, however, the motivation for their request is another free lunch.[509] In fact, they still have not stopped striving for a this-world political deliverer.

AN OMINOUS ECHO

John 6:30, "Sign . . . see and believe," echoing "Israel saw the great work which the LORD had done . . . and they believed in the LORD," (NKJV Exod 14:31), might suggest the validity of their request for a sign. The context is the Exodus deliverance through the sea. Jesus has just performed such a deliverance for the Twelve and clearly they do believe. A more applicable and ominous echo, however, is of John 4:48, "unless you see signs and wonders you will not believe," spoken by Jesus to the Galileans. This indicated that the majority of Jesus' Galilean followers had only a "signs faith."

---

503. John 10:36–37 cf. John 9:3–4; 4:34; 17:4; 5:20, 36; 10:25, 32, 37–38; 14:10–12; 15:24.

504. Cf. Holland, *Contours*, 246.

505. See above on v. 9, where the barley bread echoes the priestly bread of the firstfruits that the sons of the prophets were given to eat.

506. Cf. Rom 3:21–24, 28; Barrett, *John*, 287; Carson, *John*, 285.

507. Cf. Exod 4:8; Bauckham, "Jewish Messianism," 217ff.

508. See above. Cf. *Eccl. Rab.* 1:9, in Freedman, 8:33, "As the former redeemer caused manna to descend . . . (Ex. XVI, 4), so will the latter Redeemer cause manna to descend . . . (Ps. LXXII, 16)."

509. Cf. Anderson, *Christology*, 92, 97.

PART II—DETAILED EXEGETICAL EXAMINATION OF JOHN 5–10

These Galileans whom he now addresses are no different. They have witnessed Jesus' signs, but have not reposed their trust in him.

They cite a scriptural precedent: Our fathers ate manna, v. 31

They point out that "Our fathers ate the manna in the wilderness," John 6:31, suggesting that Jesus should likewise continually provide them with bread. They fail to realise that by identifying themselves with their fathers they are testifying to their own disobedience and unbelief.

"Our fathers" (οἱ πατέρες ἡμῶν) occurs in 1 Cor 10:1–5:

> Our fathers were all under the cloud, and all passed through the sea, and all were baptized into Moses in the cloud and in the sea, and all ate the same spiritual food, and all drank the same spiritual drink [Christ] . . . Nevertheless, with most of them God was not pleased, for they were overthrown in the wilderness.

In 1 Cor 10:6–11, this passage warns of the dangers of emulating the sinful acts of the wilderness generation (such as idolatry, testing Christ, and grumbling). The many parallels with John 6 suggest a fearful outcome for the crowds.[510]

Another foreboding parallel passage is the account concerning "your fathers," Heb 3:8–19, who tested God and saw his works, but could not enter rest because of their disobedient and unbelieving hearts.

They back up their request with an OT quotation, v. 31

Oblivious to the danger that they are acting just like their rebellious fathers, the crowds play their "trump" card—a scripture quotation,[511] introduced by a citation formula, "as it is written, 'He gave them bread from heaven to eat,'" (John 6:31). In John 6 context, this suggests that *Moses* gave the manna[512] and thus, if Jesus is to be the Prophet like Moses, he must at least do the works that Moses did. In their eyes this means *continually* supplying them with bread.

---

510. Cf. Barrett, *John*, 288.

511. See Anderson, *Christology*, 58–59.

512. Cf. Beasley-Murray, *John*, 91; Menken, *Old Testament Quotations*, 54–55. Menken believes that "in such Moses-centred piety there was a tendency towards deification of Moses," based on Exod 7:1. Cf. ibid., 57–61; Meeks, *Prophet-King*, 100–131.

The Source of the Quotation

Scholars disagree as to the source of the quotation.[513] Ps 78:24 is closest,[514] but there is no exact match and we either have a free quotation or a conflation of two or more texts. Evidence for the latter practice is found in Qumran exegesis, Philo, the NT, and in the rabbinic homiletical rule, *gezerah shawah* ("textual correspondence").[515] Menken thinks ἐκ τοῦ ("from") LXX Exod 16:4, has been added to Ps 78:24b (LXX Ps 77:24), ἄρτον οὐρανοῦ ἔδωκεν αὐτοῖς ("gave them the bread of heaven"), to accommodate John's "from heaven" Christology.[516] Similarly, φαγεῖν ("to eat"), important to John 6, has been appended from Ps 78:24a. Echoes of the following passages, however, make it possible that Exod 16:4; Neh 9:15; Pss 78:24; 105:40, have all been combined, or at least stand behind the quotation:[517]

An Echo of Exod 16:4, 15

"The LORD said to Moses, 'Behold, I am about to rain bread from heaven for you.'" "When the people of Israel saw it, they said to one another, 'What is it?' For they did not know what it was. And Moses said to them, 'It is the bread that the LORD has given you to eat (φαγεῖν).'"[518] Resonance with John 6 is found in Israel's murmuring,[519] gathering the manna,[520] and the bread that perished.[521]

An Echo of Neh 9:15

"You gave them bread from heaven for their hunger." Nehemiah 9:6–15 emphasizes God's *covenant mercy* (Heb הַבְּרִית וְהַחֶסֶד)[522] to Israel in performing signs and wonders (Heb אֹתֹת וּמֹפְתִים) against Egypt, parting the sea, providing the cloud and fire, appearing on Sinai, making known the law and Sabbath by Moses, and providing manna and water from the rock. By contrast, Israel forgot God's wonders, rebelled, and appointed

---

513. Suggestions include Exod 16:4, 15; Ps 78:24; 105:40; Neh 9:15.

514. See Menken, *Old Testament Quotations*, 49ff.

515. See Menken, *Old Testament Quotations*, 52, citing Brooke, *Exegesis at Qumran*, 166, 294, 297–98, 306–8, 319. Cf. Luke 4:18–19; Mark 1:2.

516. Cf. John 6:38, 41–42, 50–51, 58; 3:13, 31; 8:32, 42, 47.

517. Cf. Barrett, *John*, 289; Beasley-Murray, *John*, 91; Carson, *John*, 286.

518. See Barrett, *John*, 289. This passage may well have been the synagogue reading when Jesus taught, John 6:59.

519. Exod 16:2, 7–9, 12 (LXX γογγυσμός), against Moses Aaron and the Lord, echoed in John 6:41, 43, 61.

520. Exod 16:16–17 cf. John 6:12–13.

521. Exod 16:20 cf. John 6:12.

522. Neh 9:8, 32, 38.

PART II—DETAILED EXEGETICAL EXAMINATION OF JOHN 5–10

a leader to take them back to Egypt (Neh 9:17).[523] God did not forsake them in the wilderness, however, but gave his good Spirit to instruct them,[524] preserving them for forty years until their children inherited the land. Even then they rebelled and ultimately their repeated rebellion and covenant unfaithfulness led to the Babylonian Captivity.

This passage finds resonance with John 6 in the theophany, sea crossing, satisfaction of hunger and thirst,[525] Spirit teaching, and rebellion against God's word.[526] Whereas Nehemiah places Spirit instruction alongside the gift of manna, John 6 contrasts physical bread with living bread and Spirit-led teaching. John's readers, pointed to this passage, would reflect upon Jesus' gracious forbearance towards the crowds and their culpable rejection of him, turning back to "captivity."[527]

An echo of Ps 78:24 (LXX Ps 77:24)

"He rained down on them manna to eat (Heb לֶאֱכֹל; LXX φαγεῖν) and gave them the grain of heaven (Heb וּדְגַן־שָׁמַיִם נָתַן לָמוֹ; LXX ἄρτον οὐρανοῦ ἔδωκεν αὐτοῖς)." There is resonance between John 6 and the whole of this Psalm, which deals with the rebellion of the Exodus fathers.[528] They had seen the Lord's wonderful works in Egypt yet tested him, rebelled, broke his covenant (Ps 78:10, 37), and turned back.[529] They witnessed the parting of the sea, the pillar of cloud and fire, and water from the rock (Ps 78:13–16). God redeemed them from the foe, displaying his signs and wonders[530] in Egypt, sending his plagues—including the death of the firstborn. He led them to his mountain and brought them into the Promised Land (Ps 78:54–55). Despite this they did not believe, but tested God, desiring food that they craved and asking whether God was able to provide this (Ps 78:19). God was angry and slew them.[531] Ultimately their apostasy resulted in captivity (Ps 78:61).

In John 6, the disbelieving crowds, having failed to perceive the meaning of Jesus' NE signs (v. 26), and desiring the perishable bread that their fathers craved, tempt him to produce it by a further sign (vv. 30–31). Ultimately, they turn back (John 6:66). By following the pointer to this psalm (John 6:31), John's readers would be able to understand that the reason many disciples defected was because they were never true

---

523. Cf. Num 14:4.

524. Neh 9:20, Heb וְרוּחֲךָ הַטּוֹבָה נָתַתָּ לְהַשְׂכִּילָם cf. Neh 9:30; John 6:63, τὰ ῥήματα ἃ ἐγὼ λελάληκα ὑμῖν πνεῦμά ἐστιν καὶ ζωή ἐστιν. See below.

525. Neh 9:20 cf. John 6:35.

526. John 6:60, 66 cf. Neh 9:29–30.

527. Neh 9:17 cf. John 6:66; 1 John 2:19.

528. LXX Ps 77:5, τοῖς πατράσιν ἡμῶν cf. John 6:31 οἱ πατέρες ἡμῶν.

529. Ps 78:9, 57. cf. John 6:66.

530. LXX Ps 77:43, τὰ σημεῖα αὐτοῦ καὶ τὰ τέρατα αὐτοῦ cf. the σημεῖα καὶ τέρατα of John 4:48.

531. Ps 78:21, 31, 33–34 cf. John 6:49.

believers, but followed Jesus on their own terms, according to the flesh.[532] They might also understand that the overthrow of Jerusalem, following God's long forbearance (Ps 78:38), was the ultimate judgement on their rebellion and rejection of Jesus. This amounted to covenant unfaithfulness, rejecting God's Word and agent.[533] Believers would be encouraged that God has chosen Jesus, the Davidic King, to shepherd/feed (Heb רָעָה; LXX ποιμαίνειν) the true Israel.[534] Moreover, they would recall that all who believe in Jesus have been given the right to become covenant children of God (John 1:12–13).

An echo of Ps 105:40 (LXX Ps 104:40)

"He . . . and gave them bread from heaven (Heb וְלֶחֶם שָׁמַיִם יַשְׂבִּיעֵם; LXX καὶ ἄρτον οὐρανοῦ ἐνέπλησεν αὐτούς)." Recited to give thanks in connection with the David's procession with the ark to Jerusalem, this Psalm rehearses the history of God's marvelous works, signs, and the judgements of his mouth (Heb מִשְׁפְּטֵי־פִיו) which he performed in faithfulness to his covenant, "the *word* that he commanded."[535] Importantly, it was by the agency of this *word* (Heb דָּבָר; LXX λόγος) that deliverance came for his chosen people. Thus he *promised* Canaan by *oath* [536]and *rebuked* kings for Israel's sake. He *called* for a famine (v. 16) sending Joseph ahead of Israel into Egypt. Joseph was tested by God's *word*, being brought low "until the time that his (God's) *word* came to pass,"[537] when he was exalted as Lord over Egypt. Having multiplied the people and turned the Egyptians against them, God sent Moses and Aaron, who established the *words of* (Heb דִּבְרֵי) his signs and wonders among them in Egypt. The last of these, the death of the firstborn, resulted in their deliverance (Ps 105:36–37). Furthermore, God gave the pillar of cloud and fire, manna, quails, water from the rock, and ultimately the Promised Land in remembrance of his promise (Heb דָּבָר; *word*) to Abraham (Ps 105:42, 44).

Jewish interpreters understand that "the word that he [God] commanded, for a thousand generations," is the Torah.[538] John's readers, however, directed to the background of this Psalm, would understand Jesus to be God's Word and agent of creation and redemption (John 1:1–18). They could compare the instrumentality of Moses and Jesus in providing bread: while God told Moses what to do, Jesus "himself knew what he would do."[539] It is possible that they would also make a comparison between Joseph, who, being brought low and then exalted, provided Israel with bread in Egypt, and

---

532. See below on John 6:63.
533. Ps 78:10, 37, cf. John 1:11.
534. Ps 78:70–71. cf. John 6:35, 37–40.
535. Ps 105:8 (emphasis mine) cf. 1 Chr 16:12–15.
536. Ps 105:9, 11.
537. NKJV Ps 105:19 (emphasis mine).
538. Ps 105:8 cf. Braude, *Midrash on Psalms*, 2:181.
539. Cf. John 1:17; 6:6.

PART II—DETAILED EXEGETICAL EXAMINATION OF JOHN 5-10

Jesus who suffered and was glorified that he might provide the bread of life for the world.[540]

Jesus corrects them: My Father gives you the true bread, v. 32

"Truly, truly, I say to you, it was not Moses who gave you the bread from heaven, but my Father gives you the true bread from heaven." Comparison shows that Jesus' answer presents a parallel to his teaching in vv. 26–27,[541] where "the bread" that "Moses ... gave" is equivalent to "food that perishes," and "the true bread from heaven," which "my Father gives you," is equivalent to "food that endures to eternal life, which the Son of Man will give you." Thus v. 32 restates v. 27, the "text" for Jesus' discourse, in different but equivalent terms, progressing his argument.[542] This restatement uncovers the crowd's motivation for a repetition of the Mosaic gift of manna as satisfaction of physical hunger, rather than as a *sign* pointing to something far higher. It is this attitude, as well as their understanding and exegesis of the OT, which Jesus corrects:

1. Not Moses, but my Father. John does not deny Moses' importance, but points to the Father in conjunction with the Son of Man as Israel's true benefactors.
2. Not gave, but gives. Moses, God's instrument, gave the manna, but only as a shadow or type of the present reality, eternal life, *now being given* and available, having descended from the Father.
3. Not bread, but the *true* bread. This is the crux of the matter. Physical bread causes people to perish, but "true bread" bestows eternal life.

Jesus' explanation: he is the bread come down from heaven, v. 33

"For the bread of God is he who comes down from heaven and gives life to the world." In the Greek, ὁ καταβαίνων ἐκ τοῦ οὐρανοῦ is ambiguous, meaning "that which," or "he who," "comes down from heaven." John's readers will recall other parts of the Gospel where Jesus speaks of himself coming from heaven to give eternal life.[543] Particularly important is the echo of John 3:13, "he who descended from heaven, the Son of Man (ἐκ τοῦ οὐρανοῦ καταβάς, ὁ υἱὸς τοῦ ἀνθρώπου)." "Gives life to the world (ζωὴν διδοὺς τῷ κόσμῳ)," echoes John 3:16, "God so loved the world (τὸν κόσμον,) that he gave (ἔδωκεν) ... eternal life (ζωὴν αἰώνιον)."

---

540. Cf. the testing of Philip, John 6:6, and that of Jospeh.
541. Note the "truly, truly," vv. 26, 32.
542. Thus John 6:31 is not, *pace* Borgen, *Bread*, the text on which the discourse is based.
543. Cf. John 1:4; 3:15–16; 4:14; 5:21; 10:10; 17:2.

An echo of Isa 55:10–13

Isaiah 55:10–13, is another important echo: "As the rain and the snow *come down from heaven* and do not return there but water the earth . . . giving . . . bread . . . so shall my word be that goes out from my mouth . . . For you will go out in joy . . ." Not only is this part of a Passover *haftarah* from which Jesus quotes,[544] but it also compares God's word to rain from heaven that produces bread. The context is the promised NE. The parallel suggests that Jesus, God's Word from heaven, has come down to give (the bread of) life to the world, leading to a NE from death and the curse.

Fourth exchange, vv. 34–40

The peoples' request for bread, v. 34

"Sir, give us this bread always," v. 34, echoes John 4:15, "Sir, give me this water, so that I will not be thirsty or have to come here to draw water," indicating that, like the woman at the well, they are still thinking on a purely materialistic and temporal level. They want a Moses-like prophet who will continually feed them. Conversely, in speaking of alleviation of hunger and thirst, Jesus is speaking on a spiritual and eternal level. Thus Jesus proceeds to disclose his person, mission, and "Galilean" unbelief

His self disclosure, "I am the Bread of Life," v. 35

This is the first of a series of "I am" (ἐγώ εἰμι) sayings with an explicit predicate. These sayings simultaneously critique Judaism's rituals as becoming obsolete and point to Jesus as their fulfilment and the true object of desire. Jesus reveals himself to be the Lord, the one who bears God's covenant name, "I am," and God's presence before the world. Moreover, this divine name, associated with the Exodus (Exod 3:14) and repeatedly used in Isa 40–55 in the context of the NE, is the guarantee of God's all-sufficient provision (bread, light, water, way, door, shepherd) for the NE.[545] Here the people crave repetition of the Mosaic gift, but Jesus is the reality to which it points: "I am the bread of life; whoever comes to me shall not hunger, and whoever believes in me shall never thirst," v. 35. Between this "I am the bread of life" saying and its (*inclusio*) restatement in vv. 48–51 is enclosed an exposition of this metaphor, punctuated only by Jewish grumbling, vv. 41–43.

---

544. Cf. Isa 54:13; John 6:45.
545. Cf. Isa 41:4, 10, 13–14; 43:1–2; 5, 10–11, 25; 44:2–8; 45:5–6, 18, 21–22; 46:4; 48:12; 51:9–12.

PART II—DETAILED EXEGETICAL EXAMINATION OF JOHN 5–10

Jesus' satisfaction of hunger and thirst: intertextual echoes

Hunger and thirst evoke a web of intertextual echoes, running through salvation history, but particularly associated with the Exodus and NE. The cause of hunger and thirst is associated with man's disobedience to God's word and covenant, and their alleviation with messianic redemption and the inauguration of the New Covenant:

HUNGER AND THIRST FOLLOWING THE FALL

In Genesis, God abundantly provided for the first man and woman in the Garden of Eden, granting them access to "every tree that is pleasant to the sight and good for food," including the tree of life (Gen 2:9). Moreover, "a river flowed out of Eden to water the garden" (Gen 2:10). At that time, mankind (in Adam, our federal head, Rom 5:12) was in a covenant relationship with God, under probation, bound to obey his word (Gen 2:16–17). Had Adam remained faithful to God's command, the implication is that in him all mankind would have been established in righteousness and life, and would never have known hunger, thirst, or death.[546] Having believed the satanic lie, however, and disbelieved and disobeyed God's word, man was "exiled" from paradise and from the tree of life; cast out to till the ground for his food, by the sweat of his face, under the curse and sentence of death (Gen 3:17–19). Nevertheless, God promised salvation through the (messianic) seed of the woman (Gen 3:15), who would defeat the satanic serpent and thus undo his work. God later revealed that it would be through Abraham that the promised seed (Messiah) would come—through whom the curse would be removed and the nations would be blessed (Gen 22:17–18 cf. Gal 3:13–14, 16).

HUNGER AND THIRST FOLLOWING THE EXODUS

At the Exodus, God entered into a covenant relationship with Israel, Abraham's descendants, delivering them from Egyptian bondage in order to bring them to "a land flowing with milk and honey" (Exod 3:8), represented as a return to Paradise. As they journeyed to that land, through the wilderness, the Lord provided bread from heaven and water from the rock (Neh 9:15). But he also allowed them to hunger and to thirst to test their hearts and to train them to rely upon his life-giving word rather than upon physical bread (Deut 8:2–3). In the Promised Land, obedience to God's covenant would lead to an abundance of bread and water, paradise restored, but disobedience

---

546. Cf. Berkhof, *Systematic Theology*, 213–14; Reymond, *Systematic Theology*, 404–5; Williamson, *The Shorter Catechism*, 1:45–69, questions, 12–19.

would lead to covenant curse: hunger, thirst,[547] famine, drought,[548] and exile.[549] Although Israel was God's son (Exod 4:22) and servant (Isa 44:1), through whom deliverance would come to the world, she consistently failed to keep God's covenant and was ultimately sent into exile.

Hunger and thirst at the exile

Having been exiled to Babylon, for covenant unfaithfulness, Israel would serve her enemies "in hunger and thirst" (Deut 28:48). Unable to keep God's covenant, Israel's case seemed hopeless. Nevertheless, God promised a new unconditional and eternal covenant, associated with the Davidic Messiah, that would remove the curse forever.[550] Moreover, God's word would go forth like the rain, to deliver his people from exile, that they might enjoy abundant provision in the Land (Isa 55:1–3, 10–13). The days of Messiah would bring a messianic banquet: abundant supply of the finest of wheat, milk, and wine, in association with the return to the land.[551] In particular, given "as a covenant to the people" (Isa 49:8 cf. 55:3), the (messianic) Servant would redeem God's people and atone for their sin (Isa 53:11–12). He would lead them from bondage in a global NE, abundantly providing for them along the way: "They shall feed along the ways; on all bare heights shall be their pasture; *they shall not hunger or thirst* (LXX οὐ πεινάσουσιν οὐδὲ διψήσουσιν),[552] neither scorching wind nor sun shall strike them" (Isa 49:9–10).

Hunger and thirst experienced by Jesus

The Synoptic Gospels record Jesus' hunger in the wilderness.[553] This is part of his recapitulation and fulfillment of Israel's calling: He is called, as God's Son, out of Egypt (Matt 2:15), baptised through the waters (as Israel was baptized in the cloud and in the

---

547. Deut 28:48 cf. 28:3–5, 8,11–12.

548. Cf. Isa 8:21; 9:19–20; 44:12; 65:13; Hos 2:3.

549. Cf. Deut 27–28; 28:48; Jer 15:14; Ps 107:5 (see echoes above). In Deut 28:48, hunger and thirst constitute a curse ("a sign and a wonder," v. 46) for covenant unfaithfulness; failure to hear and obey God's voice and keep his commandments. Israel's enemies are presented as a swooping eagle (v. 49). Moreover, they would put "an iron yolk" on Israel's neck until she was destroyed. This resonates with the situation presented in John 6, where Israel is under the tyranny of Rome, and hunger and thirst, together with desire for a political deliverer, are important themes.

550. Cf. Jer 31:31–34; Isa 55:1–3; Ezek 37:11–14, 24–28. See Block, *Ezekiel 25–48*, 380.

551. Cf. Amos 9:11–15; Joel 3:17–18; Isa 49:8–10; Jer 31:10–14. See Dodd, *According*, 44–46; 85–86. Cf. LXX Jer 31:12 (οὐ πεινάσουσιν ἔτι); John 6:35 (οὐ μὴ πεινάσῃ).

552. (Emphasis mine). Cf. John 6:35, "Whoever comes to me shall not hunger (οὐ μὴ πεινάσῃ), and whoever believes in me shall never thirst (οὐ μὴ διψήσει πώποτε)."

553. Cf. Matt 4:2; Luke 4:2.

sea, 1 Cor 10:1–2), anointed as Messiah by the Spirit (Matt 3:16), designated God's Son and Servant by the voice from heaven,[554] and then tested in the wilderness (Matt 4:1).

Jesus refutes the tempter, citing "Man shall not live by bread alone, but by every word that comes from the mouth of God" (Matt 4:4 cf. Deut 8:3). He also cites "You shall not put the Lord your God to the test" (Matt 4:7 cf. Deut 6:16), alluding to Israel's testing God at Massah—where Israel thirsted for water, grumbled, and God provided water from the rock that Moses struck.[555] Jesus' final quotation, "You shall worship the Lord your God and him only shall you serve" (Matt 4:10 cf. Deut 6:13),[556] carries a reminder of Israel's idolatry, from the time of the golden calf onwards (Exod 32:4). Thus, at the very points at which Israel (and Adam) had failed, distrusting God, tempting him, and being unfaithful to him, Jesus was obedient unto death. As the federal head and representative of all who believe, he "fulfill(ed) all righteousness," (Matt 3:15) on their behalf.

The Gospel of John records Jesus' words, "I thirst," from the cross (John 19:28), noting that Jesus spoke them "to fulfill the Scripture." The Scripture to which Jesus alluded is Ps 69:21, "They also gave me gall for my food, And for my thirst they gave me vinegar to drink."[557] This messianic Psalm foreshadows Jesus' sufferings, when he bore the curse, being hung upon the tree (Gal 3:13).

The import of Jesus' hunger and thirst is twofold. Jesus fulfilled Israel's commission as a Second Adam, being tested like Adam and Israel. But unlike them he obeyed God, "fulfilling all righteousness," and obtaining everlasting life on behalf of his people. Jesus also bore the curse, as the federal head and representative of his people. The Second Adam and "seed of the woman," he bruised Satan's head, being bruised himself in his heel.

Conclusion

Together, these passages lead to the principle previously demonstrated:[558] that God's word and covenant are the ultimate source of life to which bread and water are subservient as mere secondary agents and symbols.[559] They indicate that Jesus has not only borne the curse of the broken covenant on behalf of his people, but has also fulfilled its demands of their behalf, that he might bestow righteousness and life upon them.

---

554. Matt 3:17. Cf. Mark 1:11; Luke 3:22. This voice conflates Ps 2:7, "You are my Son," with Isa 42:1, "Behold my servant, whom I uphold, my chosen, in whom my soul delights." Isa 42:1 also speaks of God putting his Spirit upon his Servant.

555. Cf. 1 Cor 10:4, where the rock is a type of Christ.

556. See France, *Matthew*, 135.

557. NKJV. See also Matt 27:34, where Jesus is offered vinegar mixed with gall to drink.

558. We have already observed this principle in the provision of bread *according to God's word* at the crises of the Exodus, NE, and in the days of Elisha.

559. Cf. Amos 8:11; Isa 55:1–3, 10–11.

In John 6:35, that those who believe in Jesus will never hunger or thirst, likewise suggests that he is the one who removes the curse (by providing atonement for sin) and ratifies the New Covenant, "fulfilling all righteousness" on behalf of his people. Moreover, his self designation, "I am the bread of life," confirms his identity as the covenant Lord, who has life in himself, the Servant who redeems and feeds his people, the Davidic Messiah who provides the messianic banquet,[560] and the Word of God sent forth into the world (as the rain that produces bread) to lead a NE.

The life that Jesus bestows begins here and now, but it is consummated in the heavenly New Jerusalem, the Promised Land to which Jesus leads his people. There:

> They shall *hunger no more, neither thirst any more*; the sun shall not strike them, nor any scorching heat: For the Lamb in the midst of the throne will be their shepherd, and he will guide them to springs of living water (Rev 7:16–17).[561]

These verses refer to an innumerable multitude from every nation who have washed their robes in the blood of the (paschal) lamb. They stand before God holding palm branches[562] and serve him day and night in his Temple where he will tabernacle (σκηνώσει)[563] among them.

From these findings the symbolic nature of Jesus as the bread of life is clear. Moreover, this runs counter to a sapiential understanding of "bread" urged by scholars who cite Prov 9:5 and Ecclus 24:21, where eating and drinking of wisdom cause hunger and thirst for more.[564] Furthermore, it also runs counter to some Jewish interpretations that identify bread with Torah.[565]

"Galilean" unbelief disclosed, v. 36

Some think, in view of their "positive" response, "Sir, give us this bread always," v. 34, that Jesus' charge of unbelief, brought against the Galileans, "You have seen me and yet do not believe," is unwarranted. It is justified, however, by their materialistic outlook (demonstrated above) and by Jesus' knowledge of their hearts (John 6:61, 64). Moreover, it accords with Galilean sign faith (John 4:48) and the "temporary faith" to which Jesus would not commit himself (John 2:23). It also reflects Israel's

---

560. See Ps 72:16, that speaks of the abundant prosperity in the days of the Messiah. In John 6, this is evident in the lavish provision of bread for the multitude. Cf. also the abundant gift of wine in John 2:6–11, and the harvest of John 4:35–36, where the sower overtakes the reaper.

561. (Emphasis mine), alluding to Isa 49:10. Cf. John 1:29, 36; 4:10–11; 7:38; 10:11, 14.

562. Rev 7:9 "clothed in white [festal] robes, with palm branches in their hands, and crying out . . . 'salvation belongs to our God . . .'" Cf. John 12:13, where, at Passover, "they took branches of palm trees and went out to meet him [Jesus], crying out, 'Hosanna! [save now!] . . .'" Cf. Ps 118:25.

563. Cf. John 1:12, where the Word tabernacled (ἐσκήνωσεν) among us.

564. Cf. Carson, *John*, 289.

565. Cf. e.g., Ecclus 24:23; Str-B 2.483–84; Odeberg, *Fourth Gospel*, 243.

experience: Though, at the sea, they "*saw* the great power that the LORD used against the Egyptians . . . *and they believed* in the LORD,"[566] their faith proved temporary. In the wilderness they "saw [God's] work," but hardened their hearts.[567] At the close of Jesus' public ministry, GJohn will summarize the multitude's unbelief, seeing but not believing, as fulfilment of Isaianic prophecy given in connection with the Suffering Servant and the prophet's vision of the Lord (Jesus).[568]

Jesus' mission disclosed, vv. 37–40

Jesus' mission is to impart eternal life to "everyone who looks on" (believes in) him, v. 40. Though, in the face of unbelief, Jesus' mission is seemingly put in question, he has unshakeable confidence in God's saving purposes: "All that the Father gives me (Πᾶν ὃ δίδωσίν μοι ὁ πατὴρ) will come to me, and whoever comes to me I will never cast out," v. 37.[569]

THE FATHER HAS GIVEN A PEOPLE TO JESUS

"All that the Father gives me," echoes Abraham's request "O Lord God, What will you give me (LXX τί μοι δώσεις) for I continue childless . . . Behold, you have given me no offspring" (Gen 15:2–3). In response, the Lord promised Abraham that his seed would be as innumerable as the stars (Gen 15:5). Moreover, God covenanted with Abraham that he would be "the father of a multitude of nations" (Gen 17:4). Significantly, the promise was ratified when Abraham offered up Isaac, because he had obeyed God's voice.[570] Called into question by Israel's apostasy,[571] the promise was reiterated in connection with the Davidic covenant,[572] and in connection with the suffering of the Servant.[573] In all of these promises it is intimated that the Gentiles will belong to God's people.

These echoes suggest that the promise is fulfilled through Christ, the seed of Abraham and David, along Pauline lines.[574] They also suggest that Jesus' people have

---

566. Exod 14:31 (emphasis mine).

567. Ps 95:8ff. Israel's unbelief in the face of God's mighty works is emphasised in the Passover synagogue readings (see above). Cf. also Deut 1:32.

568. John 12:39–41 cf. Isa 53:1; 6:10. See the idea of seeing but not perceiving in Barrett, "Dialectical Theology," 49–69.

569. Cf. Carson, *John*, 290.

570. Gen 22:16–18. Cf. Heb 11:19 where Abraham figuratively received Isaac back from the dead.

571. Cf. Isa 1:9; 6:9–13; 10:22.

572. Isa 55:3–5. Cf. 2 Sam 7:8–16; Ps 89:3–4, 20–29, 33–37; 105:6–11. In Ps 22:27, 30–31, the seed are the reward of the Righteous Sufferer. Cf. Kidner, *Psalms 1–72*, 109.

573. Isa 53:10–11; 54:1–14.

574. Christ is the seed of Abraham and David. Cf. Gal 3:16–19, 29; Rom 1:3; 4:13ff.; 9:6–16; Heb 11:17–19.

been given to him (from eternity), by his Father (in the covenant of redemption[575]), in connection with his sufferings as the messianic Righteous Sufferer, Servant, and Son of God. Since Abraham (and his seed) was effectively to fulfil the commission given to Adam,[576] Jesus becomes the new man and Second Adam.[577] The antithesis between those who disbelieve and those given to Jesus by the Father was announced in the Prologue.[578]

THEY WILL COME TO HIM AND HE WILL NOT CAST THEM OUT

The fact that the Father has given a people to Jesus ensures that they will come to him. He in turn will surely keep them.[579] The logic is similar to that of Rom 8:29–39. As above, "coming," echoes the return to Zion of her sons.[580]

"Cast out," echoes several important passages: In Gen 21:10, Abraham was told to "Cast out this slave woman with her son," that Ishmael might not be heir with Isaac. Paul draws an analogy between these two sons and their mothers. Hagar represents Mount Sinai and its covenant, equivalent to "the present Jerusalem," and Sarah represents the NC and "Jerusalem above." Hagar's children represent those "in slavery," under the law, and Sarah's children are NC believers, "children of promise," free in Christ. Significantly, Paul identifies the latter with the seed of Isa 54:1 (promised in connection with the Servant's suffering).[581]

At the Babylonian exile, those who sinned against God were *cast out* of their inheritance.[582] Ironically, some of the more powerful among the returnees *cast out* their brethren who trembled at God's word.[583] Similarly in GJohn, the man-born-blind and healed by Jesus (paradigmatic of believers) is cast out by the "Jewish" authorities,[584] but not by Jesus. In fact, Jesus is the true vine and true Israel, and those who do not abide in him (thus demonstrating that they are not genuine believers) will be "cast out" (ἐβλήθη ἔξω) by the Father and will wither (John 15:6).

---

575. See Berkhof, *Systematic Theology*, 265–71.
576. Cf. Gen 1:28; 28:14. See Beale, *Temple*, 94–96; 113–17.
577. Cf. Rom 5:12–19; 1 Cor 15:45.
578. John 6:36–37 cf. John 1:11–13.
579. Cf. Carson, *John*, 290.
580. Isa 49:12, 18. Cf. above on v. 5.
581. Cf. Gal 4:27; Isa 53:10.
582. Cf. Jer 7:15; 52:3; Mackay, *Jeremiah*, 587.
583. Isa 66:5. Cf. Oswalt, *Isaiah 40–66*, 670.
584. John 9:34. See below.

PART II—DETAILED EXEGETICAL EXAMINATION OF JOHN 5-10

Further explanation: Jesus has come down to do the Father's will, vv. 38–40

The reason Jesus will not cast out those who come to him is because he has come down to do (not his own will, but) the will of his Father who sent him. This involves Jesus keeping all those that the Father has given him (identified as all who look on the Son and believe in him) and raising them up on the last day.

"Come down (καταβέβηκα) from heaven," v. 38, is indicative perfect active. Once again Jesus speaks of a specific time past when he "descended from heaven" (John 3:13). Because John portrays Jesus as fully human, this hints not only at Jesus' pre-existence (cf. John 8:58), but also at his incarnation: a point in time when he became a man (cf. John 1:14). The crowds could not accept this teaching (John 6:41). The reader, however, familiar with the Synoptics, will understand this to refer to the virgin conception and birth (Luke 1:35; Matt 1:18). Καταβέβηκα ἀπὸ τοῦ οὐρανοῦ ("I have come down from heaven") echoes Isa 55:10, καταβῇ ... ἐκ τοῦ οὐρανοῦ, spoken of the rain and snow to which God's powerful Word is likened. His word will not return to him void but will accomplish his will (LXX συντελεσθῇ ὅσα ἠθέλησα), Isa 55:11, just as Jesus, God's Word, came down from heaven to do the will of the one who sent him (ποιῶ ... τὸ θέλημα τοῦ πέμψαντός με).[585] Jesus completed (τετέλεσται) this will, by his lifting up in death, when he returned to the Father.[586]

Other agents of God's will[587] (and of the NE) are Cyrus and the Suffering Servant: In Isa 44:28, The Lord says of Cyrus "'He is my shepherd, and he shall fulfill all my purpose'; saying of Jerusalem, 'She shall be built,' and of the Temple, 'Your foundation shall be laid.'" In GJohn Jesus builds God's Temple. Of the Servant, Isaiah writes, "When his soul makes an offering for sin ... the *will of the LORD* shall prosper in his hand."[588] In GJohn Jesus offers his life as a redemptive paschal sacrifice in fulfilment of God's will.

A further possible echo is "Sacrifice and offering you have not desired ... Behold, I have come; in the scroll of the book it is written of me: I desire to do your will O my God; your law is within my heart" (Ps 40:7–8). In Heb 10:5–12 this is interpreted Christologically: God does not require ineffectual animal sacrifices, but Jesus came (became a man) in order to do God's will by offering "for all time a single sacrifice for sins." This accords with the Johannine concept of Jesus' sin-bearing paschal death.[589] Jesus' preferring God's will to his own, foreshadows Gethsemane (familiar to readers of Mark), "Father ... Remove this cup from me. Yet not what I will, but what you will" (Mark 14:36).

---

585. Cf. John 4:34 where Jesus says of his food, ποιήσω τὸ θέλημα τοῦ πέμψαντός με καὶ τελειώσω αὐτοῦ τὸ ἔργον. Cf. John 5: 17, 19–22; 9:4; 10:32; 17:4; 19:30, "It is finished."

586. John 19:30 cf. John 4:34; 17:4.

587. Cf. also Acts 13:22, where David is a man after God's heart who will do all God's will.

588. Isa 53:10 (emphasis mine) cf. 50:4–5.

589. Cf. John 1:29; 10:11, 15; 17:4ff.; 19:30.

From these allusions we can deduce that Jesus performs the Father's will by suffering death for the sins of his people in order to bring about their redemption. This accords with what follows, John 6:39. God's will is that Jesus should lose nothing of all that he has given him (ἵνα πᾶν ὃ δέδωκέν μοι μὴ ἀπολέσω ἐξ αὐτου). This echoes the gathering of leftover fragments, "that nothing may be lost," (ἵνα μή τι ἀπόληται), John 6:12. Rather than have them perish (John 3:16), God has given his Son that by his death he may bestow upon them eternal life. That Jesus will "raise it [them] up (ἀναστήσω αὐτὸν ἐγώ) on the last day," John 6:39, echoes John 2:20 (ἐγερεῖς αὐτόν), where Jesus speaks of the resurrection of his body from the dead. Here, as in John 5:29, the reference is to the Danielic resurrection of believers to eternal life on the last day.[590] This signifies the reversal of death and the curse, that came through Adam's sin.

God's will is further elaborated in v. 40: that everyone who looks on (believes in) the Son, shall have eternal life. "Looking" is implicit in the parallel concept in John 3:14–16, where Jesus is lifted up as the serpent in the wilderness to which those bitten by serpents *looked* and lived.[591] In Isaiah, the "Root of Jesse" will be lifted up as an ensign to which the nations and the outcasts of the diaspora will gather.[592] A further possible echo is, "when they look on me, on him whom they have pierced" (Zech 12:10). This is likely, because in John 19:37 John cites, "They will look on him whom they have pierced." As noted previously, the setting is the paschal mourning for a firstborn, associated with cleansing of sin. Looking may also allude back to John 1:29, "*Behold* the Lamb of God who takes away the sin of the world."[593]

The repetition of I will "raise him up" (ἀναστήσω αὐτὸν ἐγώ)[594] makes Jesus' word emphatic. There can be no doubt that Jesus will raise the bodies of his people to eternal life on the last day.

Fifth exchange, vv. 41–51

"The Jews" grumble about Jesus, vv. 41–42

Up to this point, Jesus has been disputing with the crowds. Here the focus falls upon "the Jews" among the synagogue congregation. That "the Jews grumbled about him, because he said, 'I am the bread that came down from heaven,'" is explained by their perception of him: "Is not this Jesus, the son of Joseph, whose father and mother we know?" They "knew" everything that there was to know about his humble origins; οὗτός (this fellow) is a mark of their contempt. This is a case of Johannine irony,[595]

---

590. Cf. Dan 12:2, 13; Isa 26:19; John 11:24; 12:48.
591. Num 21:8–9. Cf. Glasson, *Moses*, 34ff.
592. Isa 11:10, 12 cf. 49:22, where the ensign is raised in the context of the work of the Servant.
593. My emphasis.
594. John 6:39, 40, 44, 54 cf. Dan 12:2, 13; Isa 26:19; John 11:24; 12:48.
595. See Duke, *Irony*, 65. Their blindness is revealed "again and again."

however, for they knew neither Jesus nor his Father.⁵⁹⁶ The locus of the irony is the incarnation, the Word becoming flesh (John 1:14). John's readers, familiar with the tradition, would know how this took place through the virgin conception and birth.⁵⁹⁷

The grumbling echoes the (Mark 6:3) response of Galileans at Nazareth, giving credibility to John's account: "'Is not this the carpenter, the son of Mary and brother of James and Joseph and Judas and Simon? And are not his sisters here with us?' And they took offense at him." There are also echoes of Israel's grumbling in the wilderness:

The grumbling of Israel in the wilderness

At Marah Israel grumbled because of the bitter waters and God made them sweet (Exod 15:24–25). In the Wilderness of Sin they remembered the Egyptian fleshpots and grumbled that God had brought them into the desert to kill them with hunger (Exod 16:1–15). Nevertheless, the Lord rained "bread from heaven" upon them (Exod 16:4). At Rephidim they murmured that God would slay them with thirst and he brought water from the rock, a Pauline type (τύπος) of Christ.⁵⁹⁸ At Taberah they murmured and were smitten by fire. Moreover, they despised the manna and lusted for meat (Num 11:1–6). At Kadesh they murmured that they could not conquer Canaan: God had brought them to the Land to die by the sword and it would be better to return to Egypt.⁵⁹⁹ Because of this grumbling and their unbelief, God swore that they would never enter the Land and, turning back, they wandered in the wilderness for thirty-eight years until that generation had died. On the way from Hor, they complained "there is no food and no water, and we loathe this worthless food" (Num 21:5). This gave rise to the fiery serpents and Moses' lifting up of the bronze serpent. In all these incidents, the people murmured because they did not perceive or believe God's covenant love (חֶסֶד), or ability to provide, and they lusted for flesh, loathing and despising his gift of manna as "this worthless bread" (NKJV Num 21:5).

Its recapitulation in John 6

"The Jews" in John 6 make the same mistake as their forefathers. Jesus is leading a NE and God has assured his people that in the NE he will provide food and water, even on barren heights, and a way in wilderness.⁶⁰⁰ Jesus has disclosed his divine identity to the people using the designation, "I am the bread of life," combining God's covenant name, "I am," with the promised supply of the bread of life. He has interpreted this life in terms of eternal life and last day resurrection obtained through faith in him-

---

596. Cf. John 8:19, 55; 15:21; 16:3; 17:25.
597. Cf. Barrett, *John*, 164, 330; Carson, *John*, 292, 329–30.
598. Exod 17:3, 6 cf. 1 Cor 10:4, 6.
599. Num 14:2–3. Cf. Deut 1:27ff.
600. Cf. Isa 41:18; 49:9.

self. Although the people have seen his signs, however, they have not perceived his divine origin, and do not believe in him. Ominously, as Israel despised the manna, they despise Jesus, because of appearances (their perception of his humble origins), and grumble at his claims. Like the wilderness generation, many will ultimately turn back from following him.

Jesus rebukes them: You must be drawn by the Father, vv. 43–44

"Jewish" murmuring is fruitless. Salvation is a divine initiative: No one can come to Jesus except the Father draw him (ἑλκύσῃ αὐτόν). In John 12:32 it is Christ who, by being lifted up from the earth, draws all people to himself. This is not a contradiction, because the Father and Son are jointly active in salvation.[601] The Father's drawing echoes God's drawing Israel to himself:[602]

An echo of Jer 31:3

"The LORD appeared to him *from afar* (Heb מֵרָחוֹק LXX πόρρωθεν), *saying*, 'I have loved you with an everlasting love; Therefore I have drawn you (Heb מְשַׁכְתִּיךְ LXX εἵλκυσά σε) with lovingkindness (Heb חֶסֶד covenant love, faithfulness).'"[603] This echo is not obvious since the verb מָשַׁךְ (draw) can also be translated, *draw out, prolong*, or *continue*.[604] This would make good sense in context, especially if מֵרָחוֹק (from afar) is translated "from of old." If this is so, Jer 31:3 becomes, "From of old the Lord appeared to him, *saying*, 'I have loved you with an everlasting love, therefore I have prolonged unfailing faithfulness to you.'"[605] This would mean that Jer 31:3 has nothing to do with God drawing Israel to himself, and thus John 6:44 is not a valid echo. There are good reasons, however, both for accepting the LXX translations "from afar," and "drawn," in Jer 31:3, and also for confirming the likelihood of a Johannine echo:

1. In speaking of a NE, Jer 31 alludes to God's deliverance of Israel from Egypt, his care of them in the wilderness, and the Sinai theophany.[606] Thus, Jer 31:2, "The people who survived the sword found grace in the wilderness," looks back (alludes) to the Exodus. It is therefore possible that "The LORD appeared to him

---

601. John 5:17, 20. Thus the Father lifts up the Son. Cf. Phil 2; Isa 52:13; 11:12; 49:22; 59:19. The Father teaches and the Son is God's Word; the Son draws and so does the Father. Both Father and Son work, raise the dead, and judge.

602. See Barrett, *John*, 295.

603. My emphasis and translation. See Thompson, *Jeremiah*, 566–67. חֶסֶד occurs 245 times in the OT, mostly in a covenant or treaty context.

604. As in Ps 36:10.

605. Cf. Thompson, *Jeremiah*, 565–67; Keown et al., *Jeremiah 26–52*, 106–8; Holladay, *Jeremiah 2*, 182.

606. Jer 31:2, 3 cf. Thompson, *Jeremiah*, 566.

PART II—DETAILED EXEGETICAL EXAMINATION OF JOHN 5-10

from afar, *saying*, 'I have loved you with an everlasting love; Therefore I have drawn you with lovingkindness,'" is the correct translation of Jer 31:3, and that this reflects Exod 19:4, "I bore you on eagles' wings and brought you to myself." Here, having delivered the people from Egypt, God "drew" them to himself at the mount of God, and entered into a covenant relationship with them, that they might be his special people. In the NE God similarly brings his children "from afar."[607] Jeremiah 30:10 speaks of this and uses the same term, "from afar" (מֵרָחוֹק), as Jer 31:3.

2. Elsewhere the verb מָשַׁךְ means "to draw."[608] Moreover, "the thought [in Jer 31:3] is akin to Hos 11:4"[609] (which speaks of God drawing Ephraim to himself). Mackay thinks God's drawing the people to himself is possibly pictured as a farmer drawing his recalcitrant animal to a place of safety.

3. Jeremiah 31 reflects Hosea 11 elsewhere, particularly Yahweh's compassion towards his people, personified as his son.[610] Hosea 2:18–25 also anticipates Jer 31:31–34, Jeremiah's NC passage.[611] (On the basis of the above, therefore, I would argue that Jer 31:3 alludes to God appearing to his people from afar and drawing them to himself at Sinai, at the time of the Exodus. Thus it is possible that John 6:44, where God draws people to Jesus, echoes this. Further considerations make this echo not only possible, but also probable).

4. John 6:37-40, 44-45, and Jer 30-31 share the same subject matter: "Yahweh's [gracious] plan of salvation."[612]

5. In Jer 30–31, as in John 6, this takes the form a NE and NC, "echoing the theology of salvation in Isaiah 40–55."[613]

6. In both Jer 30–31 and John 6, the emphasis is on God taking the initiative in salvation. The concept of God's drawing his people to himself fits in with this.

7. GJohn frequently alludes to Jer 31,[614] thus a deliberate allusion to Jer 31:3 seems likely.

---

607. Cf. Isa 43:6; 49:1, 12. NB Jeremiah's reflection of Isaiah's NE themes. See Thompson, *Jeremiah*, 566.

608. Cf. Gen 37:28; Jer 38:13; Hos 11:4.

609. Cf. Thompson, *Jeremiah*, 567; Mackay, *Jeremiah*, 209. See below.

610. Cf. Jer 31:9, 20; Hos 11:1-4, 8-9; Holladay, *Jeremiah 2*, 201; Thompson, *Jeremiah*, 567, 570, 575.

611. Cf. Ezek 36:26; Isa 42:6, 9; 43:19.

612. McConville, *Judgement and Promise*, 95.

613. Cf. Jer 30:10-11; 31:2-14, 31-34; McConville, *Judgement and Promise*, 96. See esp. on John 6:45 for Johannine New Covenant allusions.

614. See on John 6:45 below. See Dodd, *According*, 44-46, 85-86. Jer 31 refers to: God as "Father," 31:9, and Israel as his people, 31:1; the wilderness, 31:2; gathered from farthest parts of the earth . . . the blind and the lame, 31:8, 10; rivers of water, 31:9; God as Israel's shepherd and Israel as his flock, 31:10.

Jesus' Paschal NE Departure, John 6

The immediate context of Jer 31:3 is the certainty of God's latter day redemption and restoration of scattered Israel to their land. Just as God delivered Israel at the Exodus, so he will certainly judge the wicked (Jer 30:23) and deliver Israel in a NE, drawing them with lovingkindness to himself.

At the time when Jeremiah wrote this prophecy, God's people had broken his covenant and judgement and exile seemed to be the only possibilities. Nevertheless, following the exile, God would gather his people from the farthest parts of the earth, the blind and lame, shepherding them by rivers of water (Jer 31:8–10). He would cause them to rejoice, multiplying their grain, oil, and wine, and abundantly satisfying them with his goodness (Jer 31:12–14). He would also heal them, build and plant them in the land (Jer 31:28), restore the Davidic Messiah to them (Jer 30:9), and establish His NC with them (Jer 31:31–34 cf. Jer 30:22). God's discipline of Israel (like "an untrained calf"),[615] his drawing and instructing them, writing his law upon their hearts, would guarantee the success of this divine plan of salvation.

This context resonates with that of John 6, with its NE deliverance, gathering of the remnant, and messianic banquet. Crucially, as in Jeremiah, the unbelief and disobedience of the people suggest that coming judgement is inevitable. Nevertheless, as in Jeremiah, God's irresistible drawing and effectual teaching of those given by the Father to the Son will ensure the success of the divine plan of salvation.

AN ECHO OF HOS 11:4

"I drew them [אֶמְשְׁכֵם] with cords of a man, with bands of love," KJV. Although there is no verbal agreement with the LXX, there is a verbal parallel between John's ἕλκω and the Hebrew מָשַׁךְ, both of which mean to draw or drag.[616] Still more important is the conceptual parallelism: in both Hosea and GJohn the background is Israel's wilderness rebellion and the turning away of God's people from himself.[617] In both cases it is the Father who draws the people to himself (Hosea), or to Jesus (GJohn), and the Father who calls or teaches them to walk (Hosea, תִרְגַּלְתִּי), or teaches them to come (GJohn). "Cords of a man," and "bands of love," "describe the lovingly . . . humane . . . treatment with which God taught and guided his people";[618] "young people who can easily go astray . . . [guiding them] . . . through the wilderness into the arable land."[619]

The Hosea context is "a legal trial"[620] (similar to the lawsuit of John 6), where Yahweh complains against Israel as a Father against his stubborn son.[621] The *consequences*

---

615. Jer 31:18 cf. Hosea 4:16.
616. See above.
617. Cf. Hos 11:2, 5, 7; John 6:49, 66.
618. Hubbard, *Hosea*, 189.
619. Wolff, *Hosea*, 199–200.
620. Hubbard, *Hosea*, 185.
621. Cf. Deut 21:18–21; Isa 1:2ff.; Amos 4:6ff.; Isa 9:7ff.; Ezek 16; 20; Wolff, *Hosea*, 199–200.

of Israel's rebellion are captivity and the sword, Hos 11:5–7.[622] The Lord's compassion is such, however, that he cannot altogether abandon his firstborn son, but promises salvation to follow judgement, when he will roar for Israel to come home from Egypt and Assyria.[623]

The echo indicates that God's drawing people to Jesus parallels his drawing of Israel to himself having delivered them from Egypt. The locus of God's revelation is now Jesus. Consequently, the people are being tested[624] by the way they treat Jesus. Those who reject him rebel against God. Judgement is visited upon them, not maliciously, but as a direct consequence of their continual impenitence and obstinacy. Nevertheless, God's compassion to his Old Covenant (OC) people is such that he cannot completely give them up, but has reserved mercy following judgement. The A.D. 70 destruction of Jerusalem is thus in some measure explained to John's readers as a fearful judgement[625] upon obstinate sons,[626] similar to that visited upon the Northern Kingdom of Israel. Mercy remains, however, by way of a NE led by Jesus.

The Son's raising up the dead is mentioned for the third time not only for emphasis, but also as the future eschatological fulfilment of mercy promised by God in the prophets in terms of Israel's resurrection.[627]

He offers further explanation: believers are taught by God, v. 45

Jesus further explains the Father's drawing in terms of *instruction*,[628] citing the OT: "It is written in the Prophets, 'And they will all be taught by God.' Everyone who has heard and learned from the Father comes to me." The introductory formula, used only here, is vague. It may refer to just one quotation from the second division of the OT canon, "the Prophets," in which case Isa 54:13 is favorite.[629] It is also possible, however, that the vagueness is deliberate with several passages from different prophets in view, all dealing with God's eschatological teaching and all supportive of the main Isa 54 reference. Thus Jer 31:33–34 or Ezek 36:26–27 may also be in mind.[630]

---

622. See Wolff, *Hosea*, 194.
623. Hos 11:10–11. Cf. Exod 4:22–23, where Israel is God's firstborn.
624. As in Ezek 20:33–38.
625. Cf. Matt 23:37; Luke 13:34.
626. Deut 21:18.
627. Cf. Hos 6:2 and the allusion to this in John 10. Cf. Jer 30; 31; Ezek 36; 37; Isa 26:19.
628. Cf. Menken, *Old Testament Quotations*, 68.
629. See ibid., 67–71.
630. Other suggested allusions include Jer 24:7; Joel 2:27; and Hab 2:14.

An echo of Isa 54:13

This is a widely accepted allusion. Not only does Isa 54:13 belong to a possible paschal *haftarah*, but the John 6:45 verbal resemblance is sufficiently strong to make the latter an accurate paraphrase of the former.[631] Thus John 6:45, "And they will all be taught by God (Καὶ ἔσονται πάντες διδακτοὶ θεοῦ)," paraphrases Isa 54:13 "and all your children shall be taught by the LORD (LXX καὶ πάντας τοὺς υἱούς σου διδακτοὺς θεοῦ, Heb וְכָל־בָּנַיִךְ לִמּוּדֵי יְהוָה)." Importantly this reference defines the subjects of the divine teaching, GJohn's "they," as "your children." These are the vast numbers of Jews and Gentiles, redeemed by the vicarious paschal sufferings of the Servant, restored from captivity to Zion from the ends of the earth.[632] Their being taught by the Lord *ensures* their enjoyment of abundant peace, since, being established in righteousness, they will stand in the judgement (confuting every tongue that rises against them) and the Lord will deliver them from all their enemies (Isa 54:13–17).

That this is a NC blessing is clear from the context. Under the OC, the Lord had taught and guided Israel through his commandments, written on tablets of stone and taught by fathers to children.[633] Nevertheless, Israel had disobeyed with dire consequences: Her peace (שָׁלוֹם) had been removed and her children destroyed or exiled.[634] Because of her sin, Yahweh had "divorced" Israel-Judah and put her away; she was "barren" and her hope of restoration had gone.[635] In Isa 54, however, this situation has completely changed. The Lord has restored Zion's children in such numbers that they will spread abroad and possess the nations, fulfilling the promise made to Abraham.[636] Her former shame and disgrace will be forgotten because the Lord is her husband and redeemer (Isa 54:5). Moreover, the NC of peace, involving the putting away of wrath, will "not be removed."[637]

The manner in which this restoration takes place is particularly important. The Lord himself will deliver Zion's children, contending with their captors whom he will cause to eat their own flesh and to "be drunk with their own blood, as with wine" (Isa 49:24–26). He will also lift up his hand and set up (lift up, Heb רוּם, the same verb that is applied to the exaltation of the Servant, Isa 52:13) a standard or ensign (Heb נֵס) to the nations who, together with their kings and queens, will carry Zion's children home, Isa 49:22–23. This reflects Isa 11:10–12, where the Lord will extend his hand to recover the exiles, setting up the Davidic Messiah as an ensign (Heb נֵס), and assembling Israel's outcasts from the ends of the earth. This implies that the Servant is

---

631. See Barrett, *John*, 296. Cf. Menken, *Old Testament Quotations*, 71ff.
632. Cf. Isa 54; 52:13–53:12 See above on the Suffering Servant.
633. Cf. Isa 48:17–18; Jer 31:32, 34; Deut 6:7; Ps 78:5–7.
634. Isa 48:18–19, 22.
635. Cf. Isa 49:21; 50:1; 54:6–8; Jer 3:8; Hos 2:2ff.
636. Cf. Isa 54:3; Gen 22:17–18.
637. Cf. Isa 54:8–10; 55; Jer 31:31ff.; Ps 89:34–37.

PART II—DETAILED EXEGETICAL EXAMINATION OF JOHN 5–10

the Davidic Messiah, and his exaltation (by virtue of his death) is the signal (to which the nations look) that initiates a global NE.

The ramifications for John 6 are important. It is by his lifting up (glorification) in death, by the Father, that Jesus draws all men to himself (John 12:23, 32–33). Moreover, it is by looking to the uplifted Son that men are saved (John 6:40 cf. John 3:14–16). Furthermore, Jesus' death is that of the Servant who, as a paschal sacrifice, atones for human sin, placates God's anger, ratifies the NC of peace, and redeems God's people. The Father draws and teaches men to come to his uplifted Son. Those who come follow Jesus in a NE from sin and the curse to eternal life and last day resurrection. They constitute the New Israel.

Echoes of Jer 31:33–34 and Ezek 36:26–27[638]

Although there are few verbal parallels, connections between Jer 30–31, Ezek 36, and Isa 54 are widely recognized and the conceptual parallels are clear. In each case the Lord teaches his people, with whom he enters into a NC, redeeming them from exile in a NE. Moreover, the divine teaching under the NC differs from that under the Old, in that it is guaranteed success.

Jeremiah 31:31 predicts the coming of a NC, superior to the OC. Under the OC God delivered his people from bondage, instructed them, "took them by their arms,"[639] and became their "husband." But he gave his covenant law externally, to be taught by one generation to the next, and Israel ultimately failed to keep it.[640] Under the NC, however, the Lord would teach them by internalising the law, writing it upon their hearts (Jer 31:33).[641] Moreover, God would "forgive their iniquity . . ." (Jer 31:34) and guarantee the NC forever.

In Ezekiel 36:26–27 the solution is similar. The mountains of Israel have been bereaved of their children because of Israel's infidelity to Yahweh. God, however, will bring the exiles home, cleanse them, give them a new heart, and put a new Spirit within them, *causing* them to obey his statutes and rules. The covenant will be renewed, the curse removed, and Edenic blessing restored.[642] Ezekiel 37 illustrates this return as a resurrection from the dead.[643]

---

638. Cf. Barrett, *John*, 296; Carson, *John*, 293.

639. Cf. Hos 11:1–4.

640. See Jer 31:34, alluding to Ps 78:5–8.

641. Cf. Rom 7:6, where service "under the old written code" is contrasted with "the new life of the Spirit."

642. Ezek 36:28, 29–30, 35.

643. Cf. Isa 49:20.

Jesus qualifies this divine teaching: God reveals himself through Jesus, v. 46

They must not expect a mystical encounter with God the Father that will lead them to Jesus.[644] "Not that anyone has seen the Father except he who is from God; he has seen the Father," alludes back to John 1:18, where Jesus is the exegete and mediator of God.[645] Thus, to be taught by God and drawn to Jesus, people must listen to Jesus. Though apparently "circular," the point is that the process is not initiated by humans, but by God the Father, working and speaking through Jesus.[646]

He continues to correct them: the contrast between manna and Jesus, vv. 47–51

In v. 32, Jesus began to correct their erroneous exegesis and serious misunderstanding of the OT gift of heavenly bread: "Truly, truly, I say to you, it was not Moses who gave you the bread from heaven, but my Father gives you the true bread from heaven." Here, "Truly, truly," links back to and continues that solemn correction, but now from the perspective of those who receive the respective gifts of manna and of the "true bread from heaven." Four contrasts are presented:

1. Present believing and eating (vv. 47, 50) with past eating (v. 49). As in John 6:35, believing is parallel to eating the bread of life, confirming the metaphorical nature of the latter. This is contrasted with the consumption of manna in the wilderness, suggesting that as a physical act it did not necessitate faith.

2. Believers (v. 47) with Your fathers (v. 49). The people wished to emulate their fathers, who were led by Moses and supported all their lives with manna, but the contrast suggests that the latter were not believers and neither are they.

3. Jesus the bread of life (v. 48) with the manna (v. 49). The repetition of "I am the bread of life"/"living bread"[647] and "that came (comes) down from heaven" is emphatic. There can be no doubt that Jesus, not manna, is the life giving heavenly bread. The use of the present tense, "comes down," v. 50, suggests that manna was a predictive type of the reality now available.

4. Eternal life (v. 47) with death (v. 49). The fact that the fathers ate manna profited them only a little. It sustained their lives for a short period, but it was unable to stave off death, in contrast to the bread of life that imparts eternal life (v. 50–51).

---

644. Cf. Barrett, *John*, 296.

645. John 1:18 suggests that OT theophanies were pre-incarnate appearances of Jesus. So Hanson, *Prophetic*, 21ff., Cf. John 12:41.

646. Cf. Barrett, *John*, 296.

647. ὁ ἄρτος ὁ ζῶν cf. John 4:10–11; 7:38, τὸ ὕδωρ τὸ ζῶν; John 6:57, ὁ ζῶν πατήρ, the living Father.

PART II—DETAILED EXEGETICAL EXAMINATION OF JOHN 5-10

Allusion to Num 14:22-29

"Your fathers ate the manna in the wilderness, and they died," v. 49, alludes to the incident at Kadesh and its repercussions:

> None of the men who have seen my glory and my signs that I did in Egypt and in the wilderness, and yet have put me to the test these ten times and have not obeyed my voice, shall see the land that I swore to give to their fathers. And none of those who despised me shall see it . . . Your dead bodies shall fall in this wilderness . . . who have grumbled against me.[648]

Thirty-eight years elapsed from Kadesh to the entrance to the Land, during which "the entire generation . . . perished."[649] Rabbinic speculation has questioned whether the rebellious wilderness generation would ultimately be resurrected to enter heaven,[650] but Jesus' contrast between their death and eternal life answers that question negatively. Believers, however, will "not die," but will receive present eternal life and future bodily resurrection. Nevertheless, "the Jews" prove themselves the heirs of their fathers; having seen Jesus' glory and signs they have disbelieved, grumbled, and put him to the test.

The Hook, v. 51

Jesus' words end with a "hook": "And the bread that I will give for the life of the world is my flesh," that leads inexorably to one final exchange. Commentators who think this verse eucharistic struggle with John's use of "flesh" (σάρξ) rather than "body" (σῶμά).[651] In fact, "flesh" echoes "The LORD gives you . . . (בָּשָׂר, flesh) to eat," Exod 16:8, spoken to those who grumbled in the wilderness. It also echoes the flesh (בָּשָׂר) of the Paschal victim or the peace offering eaten by those who participated in the sacrifice.[652]

Sacrificial connotations are confirmed by "for the life of the world" (ὑπὲρ τῆς τοῦ κόσμου ζωῆς). Comparison with John's use of "for" (ὑπὲρ) elsewhere shows "conclusively" that the giving of Jesus' flesh in death is intended and suggests a vicarious sacrificial meaning.[653] This voluntary, vicarious sacrifice is provided by the Father, who gives his Son, and by Jesus who lays down his life for the life of the world (John 3:16 cf. John 10:18). The concept is that of the Servant, who voluntarily suffers vicariously, for the redemption of "the many," according to the plan of God.

The John 6 paschal background (John 6:4) suggests that (as the Suffering Servant) Jesus becomes the paschal sacrifice on behalf of the world; specifically all who believe

---

648. Num 14:22-23, 29 cf. Num 14:32-35; 32:13; Deut 1:35.
649. Deut 2:14. Cf. the man lame for thirty-eight years in John 5:5ff., above.
650. Cf. Balentine, "Concept," 102; b. Sanhedrin, 110b; Exod. Rab. 2:4.
651. Cf. Barrett, John, 297-98; Carson, John, 295.
652. Cf. Exod 12:8, 46; Lev 7:15; 8:31.
653. Cf. John 10:11, 15; 11:50-52; 15:13; 18:14; Barrett, John, 298; Carson, John, 295.

Jesus' Paschal NE Departure, John 6

(John 6:47). Eating the flesh of the paschal victim indicated personal participation in the redemption procured by its sacrifice. Eating Jesus' flesh thus signifies believing participation in Jesus and of the benefits of his sacrifice, including redemption from sin and death. That this concept offended Jewish sensibilities is evident from Targumic exegesis of the Suffering Servant, revealing their inability to accept that the Messiah should suffer.[654]

Sixth exchange, vv. 52–58

"The Jews" object: How can he give us his flesh to eat? v. 52

The verb "disputed" (ἐμάχοντο) indicates strong contention or fighting over Jesus' words. μάχεσθαι is often used to translate the Hebrew term ריב (strive/contend), reflecting the Exodus narrative where Israel not only grumbled against the Lord and Moses, but also strove with them.[655] The anger of "the Jews" against Jesus turns to fighting among themselves. Division is characteristic of the effect Jesus has on his enemies.[656] Though they disagreed, however, none could rise above a wooden interpretation or disbelief. Their reply is crassly literal and derisory: "How can this man (οὗτος) give us his flesh to eat?"

Jesus issues his final correction, vv. 53–55

Although "the Jews" do not address their difficulties to Jesus, he responds to their question, using the solemn asseveration, "Truly, truly, I say to you," that he has previously used to correct them.[657] Not only can he give them his flesh to eat, but unless they "eat the flesh of the Son of Man and drink his blood," they have no life in them, v. 53. This teaching is driven home in vv. 54–55, "Whoever feeds on my flesh and drinks my blood has eternal life . . . For my flesh is true food, and my blood is true drink." Thus, as so often in the discourses, in similar fashion to the Synoptic passion predictions,[658] rather than removing difficulties, Jesus' words are becoming progressively explicit and progressively offensive to "the Jews," culminating in their inability to hear him.

---

654. Cf. France, *Jesus and the Old Testament*, 111, n. 102; Zimmerli and Jeremias, *Servant*, 37–79; Tg. Ps.-J. Isa 53.

655. Cf. Exod 17:2, 7; Num 20:3, 13; 27:14; 26:9; Beasley-Murray, *John*, 94; Schnackenburg, *John*, 2:60.

656. See, e.g., John 7:34, 43; 9:16.

657. See above on vv. 32, 47.

658. Cf. Matt 10:34–39; 16:24–26; Mark 34–38; 10:21; Luke 9:23–26.

PART II—DETAILED EXEGETICAL EXAMINATION OF JOHN 5–10

The stumbling block: eating Jesus' flesh and drinking his blood

If eating human flesh was repulsive, consuming ("eating") blood was explicitly prohibited by the law:[659] God would set his face against the person who did so and would cut him off from his people.[660] This was because blood represented the life of a person or animal[661] and blood poured out before the altar or sprinkled upon it was the means of making atonement for sin (Lev 17:11). Since mankind bears God's image, human blood was especially sacrosanct and God would require a person's blood at the hand of that man or beast that spilled it (Gen 9:4–6). The acceptance of Jesus' words was thus the ultimate test of their obedience and faith. The disciple must "believe to understand."

Eating and drinking as metaphors for faith in Jesus

For true disciples this is possible. Eating and drinking Jesus' flesh and blood are not to be taken literally, but are metaphors for believing in and looking to Jesus' sacrificial death[662] (which the repetition of "my flesh" and "my blood" emphasize). This is evident from the close parallel between verses 54 and 40, where eating and drinking Jesus' flesh and blood (v. 54) is equivalent to looking on and believing in him:

> v. 54 ὁ τρώγων μου τὴν σάρκα καὶ πίνων μου τὸ αἷμα ἔχει ζωὴν αἰώνιον, κἀγὼ ἀναστήσω αὐτὸν τῇ ἐσχάτῃ ἡμέρᾳ.

> v. 40 πᾶς ὁ θεωρῶν τὸν υἱὸν καὶ πιστεύων εἰς αὐτὸν ἔχῃ ζωὴν αἰώνιον, καὶ ἀναστήσω αὐτὸν ἐγὼ [ἐν] τῇ ἐσχάτῃ ἡμέρᾳ.[663]

Importantly, the OT supports a metaphorical use of *drinking* as applied to blood: In all the scriptures banning human consumption of blood (cited above) the verb "eat" (Heb אָכַל; LXX ἐσθίω) is used. Reference to humans *drinking* blood is only used metaphorically. A unique instance of this is David's refusal to benefit by drinking water at the expense of the lives of his men, pouring it out as their "blood" in an offering to the Lord.[664] Applying such a metaphorical use to the drinking of Jesus' blood suggests partaking of the benefits he has obtained at the expense of the shedding of that blood.[665]

---

659. Cf. Gen 9:4; Lev 3:17; 7:26–27; 17:10–11, 12; 19:26; Deut 12:16, 23; 15:23.

660. Cf. Lev 7:27; 17:10–14.

661. Cf. Gen 9:4; Lev 17:11, 14; Deut 12:23.

662. We have seen (above) that John 6 is connected with the uplifted Serpent, John 3, and with the uplifted standard of Isa 11, connected with David, and of Isa 49:22, connected with the Servant.

663. Cf. Bruce, *John*, 159; Lincoln, *John*, 233. See Carson, *John*, 297, who cites Augustine, "Believe, and you have eaten." We have already noticed the parallel in v. 35 (see above).

664. Cf. 2 Sam 23:16–17; 1 Chr 11:19.

665. See Ryken et al., *Dictionary of Biblical Imagery*, 219, who note that "Drinking is employed figuratively in a variety of ways in Scripture to indicate *partaking* in or even experiencing something" (emphasis mine). Cf. Job 6:4; Ps 80:5; Prov 7:18; Song 5:1; Deut 11:11.

Eating and Drinking as Metaphors for Judgement

Another group of references relates "drinking of blood" to the judgement of nations or individuals—either in terms of others drinking their blood or their drinking their own blood. In Deut 32:41–42, God's sword will "eat flesh" (תֹּאכַל בָּשָׂר) and he will make his arrows drunk with blood (Heb אַשְׁכִּיר ... מִדָּם; LXX μεθύσω ... ἀφ' αἵματος) in eschatological judgement. Thus he will avenge the blood of his children and take vengeance upon his adversaries. Such judgement fell upon Egypt, at the hand of Babylon,[666] and will be yet be visited upon Gog and Magog in the last days.[667] Coming against the people of God in "battle," they will be given as a sacrificial feast to the birds and beasts that will eat their flesh and drink their blood until drunk (Heb דָּם לְשִׁכָּרוֹן שְׁתִיתֶם; LXX πίεσθε αἷμα εἰς μέθην). Elsewhere, Israel's vengeance on her enemies is portrayed as *her* drinking their blood.[668]

At the Exodus God judged Egypt, *giving them* blood to drink, turning the Nile into blood, so taking vengeance upon the shedding of Israel's blood.[669] Similarly, at the NE, he would make her captors eat *their own flesh* (Heb הַאֲכַלְתִּי ... אֶת־בְּשָׂרָם LXX φάγονται ... τὰς σάρκας αὐτῶν) and become drunk (Heb שָׁכַר LXX μεθύσω) with *their own blood* as with wine (Isa 49:26). At the Babylonian captivity, Israel had drunk of the cup of God's wrath and become drunk as with wine. Nevertheless, God would take the "cup of his wrath" out of her hand and give it to her enemies to drink.[670] In the Isaianic context, removal of God's wrath from Israel in his "covenant of peace" is due to the Servant's vicarious atoning sacrifice by which he bears their sin,[671] pouring out his blood (נֶפֶשׁ) unto death.[672]

Applied to Jesus, this concept of drinking his blood suggests God's fearful judgement poured out upon him, and thus removed from his people, and their participation in the benefits of his atonement for their sin[673] In the Synoptics, Jesus is portrayed in Gethsemane as preparing to drink the cup of God's wrath as he faces the approaching cross and the pouring out of God's wrath upon him.[674]

---

666. Jer 46:10–13.
667. Ezek 39:19 cf. Rev 20:8–9.
668. Cf. Num 23:24; Zech 9:15.
669. Cf. Exod 7:17–21; 1:15, 22.
670. Isa 51:17–23 cf. Jer 25:15ff.; Rev 14:10; 16:9; 19:18.
671. Isa 53:10–12. Cf. Oswalt, *Isaiah 40–66*, 373–410, esp. 402.
672. See Westermann, *Isaiah 40–66*, 268, who notes the possibility of this translation, suggesting "a sacrifice of expiation," corresponding to the use of אָשָׁם in Isa 53:10. Calvin, *Isaiah*, 125, relates this term to Christ's "expiation and satisfaction for sin," and the pacifying of God's wrath, by Christ's death.
673. In Rev 14:10; 16:19, those who do not participate by faith in Jesus must drink this cup themselves.
674. Cf. Mark 14:36; Matt 26:39; Luke 22:42.

PART II—DETAILED EXEGETICAL EXAMINATION OF JOHN 5–10

JUDGEMENT UPON JESUS HAS BROUGHT LIFE AND JOY FOR BELIEVERS

Interestingly, in the Passover Haggadah, in connection with the retelling of the Exodus (*Maggid*), wine is spilt from the (second) cup into a chipped dish, to symbolize God's wrath and judgements poured out upon the accursed ("principle of evil"). The wine that remains becomes the "cup of joy" for participants of the Passover. An imprecation is also uttered following the pouring of the fourth cup, associated with the kingdom, "Pour out your wrath upon the nations that do not acknowledge you . . ." Jesus would not drink from this cup again until the final heavenly fulfillment of the kingdom.[675]

If these imprecatory practices were contemporary with Jesus they might hold significance for the (third) "cup of blessing,"[676] which became the "communion of the blood of Christ,"[677] symbolising judgement poured out upon Jesus, but life and joy for his followers, through the ratification of the NC of peace. For GJohn, Jesus' transformation of water into wine at the marriage feast is the antithesis of the Mosaic transformation of water into blood and symbolizes the eschatological banquet and marriage supper of the Lamb.[678]

THE BREAD THAT SYMBOLISED THE PASSOVER LAMB

A further tentative suggestion, mooted by Gartner, is that a lamb-less Passover *Seder*, perhaps similar to the Passover Haggadah, originated during the captivity and was practised in Palestinian synagogues antedating the time of Jesus.[679] If so, it is possible that unleavened bread (*matzot*) broken and initially *hidden* became the "Afikoman," that "symbolised the Paschal lamb," eaten prior to the third cup of wine. This would facilitate the representation of the paschal victim by the bread in the feeding of the multitude. It is interesting that this "hidden Messiah" motif is applied to Jesus from John 7 onwards.

The Eschatological Son of Man, vv 53–55

Jesus has spoken of giving his flesh as a future event,[680] but he also links it to eschatological events by speaking of himself as the Son of Man (v. 53) who bestows eternal life and last day resurrection (v. 54). In our study of John 5 we saw that last day resurrection to eternal life and an inheritance are connected in Daniel and Psalm

---

675. Cf. Mark 14:25; Matt 26:29; Daube, *Rabbinic Judaism*, 330–31; France, *Matthew*, 995.

676. Cf. *b. Berakoth*, 51a; Daube, *Rabbinic Judaism*, 330–31.

677. 1 Cor 10:16 KJV.

678. Rev 19:7–9.

679. See Gartner, *John 6*, 47–48. He resolves tensions between the Synoptic and Johannine dating of the Last Supper by assuming that the Last Supper was such a lamb-less Passover. Cf. Josephus *Ant.* 14:214; *Mek. Exod.* 12:8.

680. John 6:51, where δώσω is future indicative.

Jesus' Paschal NE Departure, John 6

8 to a messianic Son of Man and Second Adam, to the tree of life, and to a NE from the curse and bondage. This heavenly Son of Man receives glory, universal dominion, and an eternal kingdom on behalf of his people (Dan 7:14, 18). In John 3, these connections are present in terms of the kingdom of God and the heavenly Son of Man, descended from heaven and exalted (lifted up) through suffering. We have also noted possible links between the Danielic Son of Man and the Suffering Servant who suffer (vicariously) as the representative of their people and who (as such) are highly exalted.

Eating Jesus' flesh and drinking Jesus' blood thus become participation in him as the head of a redeemed humanity who gives himself for his people as a paschal sacrifice that removes the curse and prepares the way for last day resurrection to eternal life and paradise restored. Jesus' flesh is "true food." His blood is "true drink," v.55.

The means and fruits of abiding, vv. 56-57

"Whoever feeds on my flesh and drinks my blood abides in me, and I in him. As the living Father sent me, and I live because of the Father, so whoever feeds on me, he also will live because of me."

PARTICIPATION AND ABIDING IN JESUS IS BY FAITH

The reason Jesus bestows eternal life and bodily resurrection upon those who feed upon (trust in) his sacrificial death is because faith in him is the means of participating in and abiding (μένω) in him.[681] Life is in the Son.[682] Outside of him, and his life-giving sacrifice, death is the only possibility.[683] These ideas are very similar to the Pauline concept of the communion of the blood and body of Christ (1 Cor 10:16–17). Here, (believing) participation in the cup of blessing (the third cup of the Jewish Passover feast) symbolises participation in the (life giving) blood of Christ and (believing) participation in the breaking of bread symbolises participation in the (life giving) body of Christ. Moreover, the many participants in the one bread are one body, because all share fellowship in the one, Christ.

UNION WITH THE SECOND ADAM

This in turn is in harmony with Paul's teaching on the Second Adam, "As in Adam all die, even so in Christ all shall be made alive" (1 Cor 15:22). All people, participating in Adam by natural birth, have participated in his sin, and thus die, because all sinned when Adam (their federal head) sinned. Similarly, all those who by faith participate

---

681. V. 56, "Whoever feeds on my flesh and drinks my blood abides in me, and I in him."
682. Cf. John 1:4; 1 John 5:11–13.
683. Cf. John 3:18; 5:24; 8:51–52.

PART II—DETAILED EXEGETICAL EXAMINATION OF JOHN 5-10

in Christ, participate in the free gift of righteousness and life that Christ obtained for his people. He obtained this by his righteousness and obedience unto death when he fulfilled the demands of the law and atoned for their sin upon the cross (Rom 5:12–21). These concepts accord with the OT representative principle of the Suffering Servant and the Son of Man where the people are summed up in one, who suffers and triumphs on their behalf.

The relationship between Father, Son, and Holy Spirit

Abiding (μένω) is very important for John, who speaks of the relationship between Father, Son, and Holy Spirit in terms of abiding.[684] At Jesus' baptism, the Spirit descended upon him and remained (μένω) upon him (John 1:33). The Father himself dwells (μένω) in Jesus (John 14:10) and, by keeping his Father's commandments, Jesus abides (μένω) in his Father's love (John 15:10). John understands this communion of Father, Son, and Holy Spirit, to be that between three infinite and eternal persons. From eternity past, the Son, as God, was with the Father and shared his glory (John 1:1–4; 17:5). The Spirit also (though less is explicitly said in GJohn about his relationship to the other divine persons) clearly (eternally) shares their deity, being sovereign in his operations (John 3:8; 16:8) and equal in his person.[685]

Communion with God

By faith in Jesus and obedience to his word, believers are called, in a measure, to share in this divine fellowship (v. 56 cf. 1 John 1:3). Thus, Jesus' words abide in them (John 15:7) and by keeping his commandments they abide (μένω) in his love (John 15:10). Moreover, all three persons of the Godhead dwell within them: They abide (μένω) in Jesus and he in them (John 6:56). The Holy Spirit abides (μένω) with them and dwells in them (John 14:16–17). The Father and the Son will come to them and make their home (μονή) with them because they love Jesus and keep his word (John 14:23).

The mutual indwelling of Jesus and the believer

The mutual indwelling between Jesus and believers is the source of their life. As Jesus lives because of the Father who sent him, v. 57, so also, those who feed on him will have life through him. Nevertheless, Jesus' relationship with his Father differs from that between believers and Jesus. From eternity, as the Son of God, Jesus has enjoyed "life in himself" (John 1:4). Moreover, from the perspective of his messianic mission, in which he voluntarily humbled himself that he might do the will of the Father who

---

684. Cf. Barrett, *John*, 299; Carson, *John*, 298; Bruce, *John*, 160.

685. Cf. John 14:16; 16:12–15. The Holy Spirit is "another paraclete," of the same kind, as Jesus. See Letham, *The Holy Trinity*, 58–59.

sent him, he has been given to exercise "life in himself."[686] By contrast, believers derive their life from Jesus as they continue to trust in him and obey him, but they are never independent of him, nor do they have life in themselves. Moreover, the life-bestowing union that they enjoy with the Son of God (although conceived in eternity, when they were given by the Father to the Son[687]) has only been effected in time, when they were "born again" of God's Spirit and baptized into (grafted into) Christ.

Abiding in the Vine and the Olive Tree

In John 15, this relationship between believers and Jesus is further elaborated in terms of the image of the vine: Jesus is the "true vine," His Father is the "vinedresser," and Jesus' disciples are the branches. The branches are of two sorts: those that abide in the vine receive their life from the vine and bear fruit, proving that they are genuine disciples (John 15:8). Those that do not abide in Jesus cannot bear fruit (John 15:4), but are cast out and wither, proving that they never truly belonged to Jesus. Importantly, in the OT the vine is both Israel and (in Ps 80:17) its messianic representative, the Son of Man.[688] Thus Jesus, the Son of Man, is the true Israel, who fulfils her destiny, reversing the fall, heading up and giving life to a people that bring forth fruit to God.[689] All who abide in him belong to "the Israel of God" (Gal 6:16).

Paul uses similar (Olive tree) imagery in Rom 11:16–24, where the tree is Israel, the natural branches are the natural descendants, and branches cut from a wild olive and grafted in are believing Gentiles, grafted into Israel. Although many of the natural descendants have been "cut off" because of unbelief, God is able to graft them back into the tree provided that they do not continue in unbelief.

From the perspective of these images, it can again be seen that Christ is the Second Adam. Thus Israel was chosen by God to undo Adam's sin and fulfil Adam's commission, filling the world with a people who would bring God's blessing to all the nations (Gen 22:17–18 cf. Gen 1:28). Throughout the OT, Israel failed to do this. Nevertheless, Christ, the seed of Abraham, the root and offspring of David (Rev 22:16), has atoned for sin, conquered death, and brought life and immortality through the gospel (2 Tim 1:10) to all the nations of the world (Matt 24:14).

The Children of Promise

Interestingly, in Gal 4:26–28, Paul understands believers in Christ to be the fulfilment of Isa 54:1–4, the "children of promise," the spiritual descendants of Abraham, as opposed to those in bondage under the law (Gal 4:25). This promised seed are the vast

---

686. See above on John 5:26.
687. See above on John 6:39.
688. Cf. Kidner *Psalms 73–150*, 292; Baldwin, *Daniel*, 151.
689. Cf. Isa 5:1–7, where the whole purpose of Israel, God's vine, was to bear fruit unto God.

PART II—DETAILED EXEGETICAL EXAMINATION OF JOHN 5–10

multitudes of God's people, redeemed, restored from "exile," and "taught by the Lord" (Isa 54:13 cf. John 6:45), who will spread abroad to possess the nations and thus fill the world with God's glory. As we have seen above, these children (of Isa 54:1–4) are the very people who are redeemed by the vicarious sufferings of the Suffering Servant of Isa 52:13–53:12.

The nature of the NE

Jesus is thus both the Suffering Servant and the Second Adam and the NE is the exodus from death and "exile" (from God) in Adam unto life and union with God in Jesus. Participation in the NE involves both participation in the benefits of Jesus' vicarious death, as the Suffering Servant, and being transplanted from Adam into Christ. In John 5:24, this transition has been depicted as crossing over from the realm of death into the realm of life.[690]

Believers become part of God's Temple

Importantly for GJohn, abiding also has Temple connotations. "John's frequent use of the idea of 'abiding/dwelling' (μονή, μένω) should be understood against the background of the Temple."[691] Jesus is the new Temple because the Father dwells in him and he in the Father. Believers become part of this new Temple by abiding in Jesus and by the Holy Spirit dwelling in them.[692] Admission to this Temple is by way of trust in Jesus' paschal sacrifice that cleanses and atones for sin. The Temple continues to grow as believers, described elsewhere as living stones (1 Pet 2:5 cf. Eph 2:19–22), are added. Ultimately, at Christ's second advent, the Temple will be complete and will reach its NE fulfilment in the New Jerusalem that descends from God (Rev 21:1–3). This eternal Temple will fill the world with God's glory.

Jesus concludes his teaching, vv. 58–59

Jesus concludes the discourse by restating his rebuttal of the unbelieving "Jews":[693] "This is the bread that came down from heaven, not as the fathers ate and died. Whoever feeds on this bread will live forever." "He will live forever," ζήσει εἰς τὸν αἰῶνα, is only used here and in v. 51 in the NT. It echoes Gen 3:22 where man was forbidden access to the tree of life lest he "eat, and live forever" (φάγῃ καὶ ζήσεται εἰς τὸν αἰῶνα). In Revelation, those who have washed their robes have the right to eat of the tree of

---

690. See above on John 5:25.
691. Walker, *Holy City*, 171–72.
692. Ibid., 172.
693. Linking back to v. 31.

life.[694] The implication is the reversal of the fall and the restoration of Paradise through Jesus the Second Adam.

THE AFTERMATH, VV. 60–71

The episode does not end with the discourse and its rejection by the crowds and "the Jews," but culminates with the reaction of two groups of disciples. First, bracketed by "many of his disciples," πολλοὶ ἐκ τῶν μαθητῶν αὐτοῦ, vv. 60–66 focuses on the majority who react by abandoning Jesus. Following their departure, the spotlight falls, vv. 67–71, on the Twelve as the remaining nucleus, representative of the New Israel (true Church). The chapter seems to be heading towards a climax with Peter's positive representative confession. Alarmingly, however, all is not well. Jesus points out that even within this inner group there exists a traitor who will ultimately betray him.

This whittling down of the great numbers of Jesus' followers reflects the apostasy and unbelief that followed both the Exodus and return from captivity under Cyrus.[695] It is paradigmatic of the NE sifting of Israel[696] and her stumbling at the Gospel. "Though your people Israel be as the sand of the sea, only a remnant of them will return."[697] This does not mean that Jesus' mission is a failure, however, since all those whom God has given to Jesus will come to him. None of these true disciples will be lost. Moreover, the door has been opened to the Gentiles who will come to Jesus in vast numbers.[698] This will commence when Jesus is lifted up on the cross as "an ensign for the nations."[699]

Mass defection vv. 60–66

These verses provide an external description of the actions of disciples who turn back from following Jesus and Jesus' own penetrating critique of their inner motives.

Externally

Like the wilderness generation and "the Jews" who oppose Jesus, many disciples murmur at Jesus' words, finding them difficult or harsh. The v. 62 reference to the ascent of the Son of Man (the counterpart to the descent) suggests that not only are they offended at Jesus' heavenly origin, but they will be more offended by the manner of his

---

694. Cf. Rev 22:14 cf. Rev 4:9, 10; 15:7, where God is said to "live forever and ever." Cf. Deut 32:40; Dan 4:34; 12:7.

695. Cf. e.g., Exod 32:4–8; Num 14:1–24; Malachi 1:6–10; 2:1–17.

696. See Ezek 20:33–44.

697. Isa 10:22 cf. Rom 9:27ff.

698. Cf. John 1:11–13; 12:20–32; Isa 2:1–4; 49:22; 54:3; Acts 28:28.

699. Isa 11:12, KJV.

PART II—DETAILED EXEGETICAL EXAMINATION OF JOHN 5-10

ascent, being lifted up on the cross.[700] They reach the point where they turn away and walk no more with Jesus. This signals a complete and final rejection. "Turned back" echoes the situation at Kadesh where the disbelieving people turned back to Egypt, to die in the wilderness.[701]

Jesus' critique

In addressing the apostates Jesus points out the reasons for their failure.

1. They have been caused to stumble (σκανδαλίζει) by his words, v. 61. This echoes Isa 8:14, "a stone of stumbling and a rock of offense." Both Paul and Peter use σκάνδαλον, citing this verse, Paul conflating it with Isa 28:16.[702] In context it refers to the Lord who would be a sanctuary for the Isaianic remnant, but a stumbling block to Israel and Jerusalem. In the Synoptics Jesus speaks of himself as the messianic Temple cornerstone, rejected by the builders, on which those who fall would be broken.[703]

2. Greater offenses will follow. "What if you were to see the Son of Man ascending . . ." v. 62, is a reference to the Jesus' glorification and return to God by way of the cross, echoing the Suffering Servant and suffering Son of Man. If these disciples have been offended by talk of his heavenly origin and consumption of his flesh, how much more so when they see his crucifixion?

3. Their understanding is according to the flesh (fallen human nature), not the Spirit (John 6:63).[704] John frequently uses the same words with different meanings, depending upon the context,[705] and "flesh" refers here, not to Jesus' flesh, which is "true food,"[706] but to their carnal reasoning which "is of no avail." In contrast to their carnality, Jesus' words are "spirit and life."[707] The linking of the Spirit to instruction is found in the context of the Exodus where God gave his "good Spirit to instruct them and did not withhold . . . [his] manna from their mouth and gave them water for their thirst."[708] God's life giving NC gift of the Spirit is

---

700. Cf. Beasley-Murray, *John*, 96.

701. Num 14:4, 43. Cf. Ps 78, where the Fathers, who saw the Lord's wonderful works (Heb נִפְלְאוֹתָיו) in Egypt, nevertheless tested him, rebelled, broke his covenant (vv. 10, 37), and turned back (Ps 78:9, 57, Heb. הָפְכוּ; LXX ἀπέστρεψαν cf. John 6:66 (ἀπῆλθον εἰς τὰ ὀπίσω).

702. Cf. Rom 9:33; 1 Pet 2:8; Gal 5:11; Mark 6:3; Matt 15:37.

703. Ps 118:22 cf. Matt 21:42–44; Luke 20:17–18.

704. Cf. John 8:15; 1:13; 3:6, where flesh and Spirit are contrasted.

705. Cf. Cotterell and Turner, *Linguistics*, 176, who cite several meanings of "world" in GJohn.

706. John 6:55 cf. 1 John 5:8 where the Spirit bears witness along with the water and the blood: Thus Jesus' "flesh" *does* profit.

707. Cf. 1 Cor 2:14–15, where Paul contrasts the "natural person," who cannot accept the Spirit's teaching, with the "spiritual person," who possesses spiritual discernment.

708. Neh 9:20, Heb וְרוּחֲךָ הַטּוֹבָה נָתַתָּ לְהַשְׂכִּילָם cf. v. 30; John 6:63, τὰ ῥήματα ἃ ἐγὼ λελάληκα ὑμῖν

also linked to his instruction of Zion's children in perpetuity, in the context of the NE.[709]

In Jesus' reference to himself as speaking words that are "spirit and life" there is a hint of Ezekiel's raising Israel's dead bones by his word and the Spirit.[710] The reason these followers are offended is because they have not been regenerated by the Spirit (cf. John 3:3–6). Paul has a similar understanding, not only of Jesus as the last Adam, made a "life giving Spirit," but also of those who cannot understand, being "natural" rather than "spiritual."[711]

4. They do not believe. Jesus knows all people and from the beginning some (many) of them "did not believe," v. 64. This is because they have not been given to Jesus by the Father, v. 65.

The New Israel, vv. 67–71

In v. 13, John alluded to Twelve baskets used to gather up the fragments, representative of the gathering together of the scattered people of God as the NI. Here "the Twelve" are mentioned three times in the space of five verses,[712] focusing upon the small nucleus of disciples who will become the founder members of this NI. Their labors will result in an eschatological worldwide ingathering.[713]

Jesus' question to the Twelve, "Do you want to go away as well?" addresses the question of the future of the Church, threatened by mass defection. It is not asked because Jesus does not know the outcome,[714] but to elicit Peter's answer.[715] This rises to great heights as a confession of faith, indicating the willingness of the Twelve to cleave to Jesus, despite the difficulties felt by others. It affirms:

1. The uniqueness of Jesus: There is no other leader or teacher to whom they might go to provide what they are seeking. From the context this includes Moses, in whom "the Jews" placed their hopes.[716]

2. The centrality of faith in Jesus' word: Jesus uniquely has the "words of eternal life," v. 68. This alludes to v. 54, whosoever eats "has eternal life," and v. 63, "The words that I have spoken are . . . spirit and life." It indicates that Peter has grasped that faith in Jesus' word is central to the hope of eternal life, rather than literal

---

πνεῦμά ἐστιν καὶ ζωή ἐστιν.

709. Cf. Isa 59:21; 30:20–21; 44:3; Ezek 36:27; 37:14; 39:29.
710. Ezek 37:1–14 cf. John 5:25.
711. Cf. 1 Cor 15:45; 2:13–15.
712. Vv. 67, 70, 71. Outside this chapter, the Twelve are only mentioned in 20:24.
713. Cf. John 4:35–38; 21:11; Amos 9:13; Barrett, *John*, 242–43; Bauckham, "153 Fish," 281.
714. Cf. 6:64, 70–71; 2:24–25.
715. Cf. Matt 16:13ff.; Mark 8:27ff.
716. Cf. 5:45; 9:28.

consumption of Jesus' flesh. This supports the metaphorical interpretation: to eat is to believe.

3. The content of the disciples' faith: They had come to believe and know (perfect tense) that Jesus is "the Holy one of God" (ὁ ἅγιος τοῦ θεοῦ). This is possibly a messianic title, though it is not found outside the NT. In the context of the Gospel, it signifies that "Jesus shares the Father's holiness" and has been set apart by the Father in order to be sent into the world,[717] John 10:36, referring to Jesus as the new Temple. Interestingly, in Dan 9:24, a "most holy" (place or person, possibly a reference to the Temple or to Christ) will be anointed.[718]

In OT Scripture, the Lord is *Israel's* Holy One (Heb קְדוֹשׁ יִשְׂרָאֵל ; LXX ὁ ἅγιος τοῦ Ισραηλ).[719] Men are occasionally referred to as *God's* holy ones. The Aaronic High Priest is referred to as holy (Heb הַקָּדוֹשׁ LXX ἅγιος).[720] The Davidic King is also God's holy one, but the adjective employed is ὅσιος rather than ἅγιος:[721] God will not allow his "holy one (τὸν ὅσιόν σου) to see corruption";[722] cited in Acts by Peter as predictive of Jesus' resurrection.[723] Another connection with Peter and the Capernaum synagogue is the demonic identification of Jesus as "ὁ ἅγιος τοῦ θεοῦ."[724] It is quite conceivable that this incident had been etched on Peter's memory and that he had repeated the identification.

Jesus' unsettling retort, vv. 70–71

Jesus answers, "Did I not choose you, the Twelve? And yet one of you is a devil." It may be memory of the demonic confession that prompts Jesus to speak in this way. The warning is that an orthodox confession on its own does not guarantee election; "the demons believe—and shudder!" Judas belonged to the Twelve and yet he would betray Jesus. Parallels drawn with Peter's Caesarea Philippi confession suggest that Peter is shown here in favorable light. There is no polemic between Johannine and Petrine believers as some have suggested.

---

717. Lincoln, *John*, 239. Cf. John 17:11.

718. See on John 10:36 in Episode 5 below. Cf. Baldwin, *Daniel*, 169.

719. Cf. Isa 10:20; 40:25; 41:14; 43:14–15; 45:11; 60:14; Jer 51:5; Ezek 39:7; Hos 11:9.

720. Cf. Num 16:3, 5, 7; Deut 33:8, where he is referred to as לְאִישׁ חֲסִידֶךָ, LXX τῷ ἀνδρὶ τῷ ὁσίῳ.

721. Interestingly, ὁ ὅσιος is used of God, in Rev 16:5, indicating that the two words share enough semantic content to be interchanged.

722. Ps 16:10 cf. Ps 89:19 (τοῖς ὁσίοις σου).

723. Acts 2:27–32. Cf. Acts 13:35, where the same scripture is cited by Paul.

724. Mark 1:24 cf. Luke 4:34.

CONCLUSION

When the crowds catch up with Jesus he brings a lawsuit against them whereby he warns them not to work for bread, under the curse, that causes to perish, but for bread that he the Son of Man gives that leads to eternal life. They interpret Jesus' words of legal works that enable them to eat the sanctified bread, but Jesus directs them to faith in himself. In hope of physical bread, they ask him to repeat the sign of the manna, but Jesus corrects them: the Mosaic gift was just a shadow of the one who comes down from heaven to give eternal life to the world. Using the covenant name, "I am," Jesus discloses himself to be the true bread and Word of God come down from heaven to lead a NE from hunger and thirst under the curse.

Though many do not believe, the Father has given Jesus a people, as the Last Adam. They will come to him and he will not cast them out or lose them, but on the last day he will raise them up to eternal life in a new heaven and earth. The crowds show that they are truly the descendants of their wilderness fathers by murmuring and despising Jesus, the bread of God. Like their fathers, the physical bread they crave will only lead to their death. The Father, however, will teach Jesus' people, drawing them out of bondage to Jesus, lifted up as a NE signal of salvation. Jesus bestows eternal life on them as God's Suffering Servant by giving his flesh as a paschal sacrifice, vicariously bearing the wrath of God for them, and initiating a NE from sin to salvation. They partake of this sacrifice by faith, abiding in him, deriving life from Jesus, the Second Adam, becoming part of God's new Temple, and awaiting the last day resurrection to eternal life.

For many of Jesus' disciples his words cause offense and they turn back. Greater offenses are ahead when Jesus will die on the cross. These disciples turn back because they do not have true faith in Jesus, lack spiritual illumination, and stumble at his words. The Twelve, however, the basis of the NI, have come to know and believe that Jesus is God's holy one, the messianic King, and the locus of his divine presence. Even among them, however, there is a traitor.

Jesus' discourse explains why "the Jews," having rejected their Messiah, were left to "wander in the wilderness" for some thirty-eight years before the destruction of the Second Temple. It explains why Israel as a nation largely rejected Jesus as their Messiah. They sought salvation by works by which they thought to commend themselves to God and stumbled at the teaching of Jesus' vicarious death upon the cross and the necessity of faith in him for salvation. It also explains defections from the Johannine community—they were offended (as Docetics?)[725] by Jesus' cross; without true faith and spiritual illumination.

---

725. Cf. 1 John 2:19; Hengel, *Question*, 52; Smalley, *Thunder and Love*, 58.

PART II — DETAILED EXEGETICAL EXAMINATION OF JOHN 5-10

EXCURSUS: THE FUTURE SALVATION OF ISRAEL IN THE PLAN AND PURPOSE OF GOD

In John 6 we have seen that not only did "the Jews" largely reject Jesus' words, but also the majority of Jesus' disciples (Israelites by birth or assimilation) stumbled because of Jesus and turned back from following him. Moreover, we have remarked that their turning from Jesus is paradigmatic of the stumbling of Israel at the Gospel. This is confirmed by the John 12 quotations from Isaiah that sum up the obduracy of Israel at the conclusion of Jesus' ministry: "'Lord, who has believed our report? And to whom has the arm of the LORD been revealed?' Therefore they could not believe, because Isaiah said again: 'He has blinded their eyes and hardened their hearts, Lest they should see with *their* eyes, Lest they should understand with *their* heart and turn, So that I should heal them.'"[726]

This raises the question of Israel's future salvation in the plan and purpose of God. A little consideration will underline the enormous difficulty that their rejection of Jesus presents: Israel are the OT people of God to whom the NE promises of salvation were made and through whom and to whom the Messiah came (cf. Rom 9:4–5). Yet Israel, for the most part, have rejected the gospel. Have God's gracious purposes for his ancient covenant people come to nothing? Is God unable or unwilling to save them? Has he reneged on his covenant (Jer 31:35–37)? Has the Gospel lost its power to save the Jew (Rom 1:16)? While John does not give a specific detailed solution to this problem, he does provide teaching that helps us to formulate an answer to it.

Israel's salvation depends upon faith in Jesus

GJohn makes it clear that the only way of salvation from sin and from its penalty is through the redemption accomplished by the atoning paschal sacrifice of Jesus. Jesus' words, John 6:53, are categorical, "unless you eat of the flesh of the Son of Man and drink his blood, you have no life in you." John 14:6 is equally categorical, "I am the way, and the truth, and the life. No one comes to the Father except through me." In John 15, Jesus makes it clear that he is the true vine, the true Israel, and that abiding in him is essential to eternal life. We have also noted parallels between this illustration and that of the olive tree of Romans 9, where natural branches are broken off because of unbelief. It follows that any teaching that affirms that Israel will be saved in some other way than that in which the Church is saved is erroneous (cf. Acts 15:11). Partaking in Christ by faith is the only way of salvation for Jew and Gentile alike.

---

726. John 12:38–40 NKJV cf. Isa 53:1; 6:10.

Israel's rejection of the Gospel has happened in the sovereign purposes of God

Jesus' ultimate explanation for his rejection by his people lies in election. No one can come to Jesus unless it be given him from the Father (John 6:65). In Romans, Paul argues similarly that salvation depends upon the sovereign choice of God. "So then it depends not on human will or exertion, but on God, who has mercy," Rom 9:16. Moreover, Scripture has foreseen Israel's rejection of the Gospel in the sovereign purposes of God.[727] As Paul explains, Israel has stumbled in order that the door of salvation might be opened to the Gentiles, that the blessing of Abraham might come to all the world.[728] GJohn makes several allusions to the coming of salvation to the Gentiles.[729]

Israel's rejection of the Gospel is only partial

It is important to emphasise that GJohn does not envisage a total rejection of the Gospel by Israel. Indeed the first disciples of Jesus were Israelites. In particular, the Twelve, the founders under Jesus of the NI, were not only Israelites themselves, but also represent the reconstitution of the Twelve tribes. Moreover, as I have argued, many of the members of John's churches were Jewish believers. Paul was also able to affirm that God has not cast away his people, but, as in the days of Elijah, "so too at the present time there is a remnant, chosen by grace" (Rom 11:5).

Israel's rejection of the Gospel is not final

It is important to recognise that, along with John's allusions to Scriptures that predict Israel's fall, he also makes many other allusions to Scriptures that suggest that national Israel will afterwards be restored.[730] Indeed, all the NE promises, made in the first place to God's OT people, come into this category. Though they enjoy their fulfilment through the Christian Church, it seems inconceivable that they do not include the regathering of Israel (into the Church/NI). Prophecies such as Isaiah 54, alluded to above, are interpreted by Paul as the gathering of Christian believers, the "children of promise" (Gal 4:27–28). While this includes multitudes of Gentile believers, gathered from all the world, it seems inconceivable that it excludes the future gathering of the Jewish people in great numbers. Likewise, while John 6 points to Israel's larges-cale defection, the enacted parable of the gathered fragments indicates a subsequent worldwide ingathering of people into the body of Christ, that must surely include the coming of Jews to Jesus.

---

727. Cf. Rom 9:27–29, citing Isa 10:22–23; 1:9.
728. Cf. Rom 9:24–26; 11:11, 19–20.
729. Cf. John 7:35; 10:16; 11:52; 12:20–21.
730. Cited throughout this work.

PART II—DETAILED EXEGETICAL EXAMINATION OF JOHN 5-10

The clearest teaching on Israel's future salvation, however, comes in Romans 11. While this chapter is controversial, and it is beyond the scope of this work to give a detailed exegesis, there are certain indications that it points to a future gathering of Israel to Jesus Christ through the gospel:

1. Israel's fall has brought salvation to the Gentiles, which in turn is intended to provoke them to jealousy, v. 11.

2. Their "full inclusion"/"acceptance" will bring great blessing to the world/"life from the dead," vv. 12, 15.

3. God's consecration of the patriarchs (the "dough offered as firstfruits"/the "root") extends to their descendants ("the whole lump"/the "branches"), v. 16.

4. God is able to graft the broken branches back into "their own olive tree," vv. 23–24.

5. As "natural branches," their future inclusion into "their own olive tree" is "much more" consonant with the "Israelitish nature of the covenant,"[731] than the inclusion of the Gentiles, v. 24.

6. Concerning election, they are beloved for the sake of the patriarchs ("fathers"), v. 28.

7. God's gifts and calling (of Israel, cf. Rom 9:4–5) are "irrevocable," v. 29.

All Israel will be saved

While these points drawn from Rom 11 indicate God's purpose of salvation for Israel, in Rom 11:25–27 Paul specifically predicts the salvation of "all Israel." There are, however, difficulties of interpretation of this passage and Paul's meaning and is hotly disputed. In particular:

1. Does Paul refer to the salvation of national Israel or of the Church (Calvin)?

2. Does "the fullness of the Gentiles come in" refer to the completion of the full number of the elect Gentiles, at the end of the world, or does it refer to a great latter day work of God by which a great multitude of Gentiles will be saved, filling up their number?

3. Should v. 26 be translated, "And in this way all Israel shall be saved . . ." referring to the mode of Israel's salvation, or as "and so all Israel will be saved . . ." referring to the time of their national turning to Christ (in great numbers), following a revival of God's work among the nations.

4. How are we to understand Paul's OT citation in vv. 26–27?[732]

---

731. Murray, *Romans*, II, 90.

732. We have discussed the interpretation of these verses above, as an example of the NT citation of the Old, under Methodology.

My own understanding of Rom 11:25–27 is that Paul is referring to the end time salvation of the nation of Israel when, following a mighty work of God among the nations, they will be provoked to jealousy and brought into the Kingdom of Christ in great numbers. This fits well with Paul's triumphant exaltation in the wisdom and glory of God whose purpose is to "have mercy on all" (Rom 11:32–36).

10

Episode 3
Jesus at the Feast of Tabernacles, John 7–8

IN THIS EPISODE, INTRODUCED by "after this," Jesus goes up to Jerusalem at the Feast of Tabernacles, which feast forms the background not only for chapters 7–8, but also for 9:1—10:21.[1]

THE TABERNACLES FESTAL BACKGROUND

I argue that from the outset Tabernacles contained the seeds of eschatological fulfilment of Yahweh's covenant promises and ultimately came to anticipate the eschatological Day of the Lord and the fulfilment of the NE hope. To appreciate this I trace its development from Mosaic times.

Tabernacles and the Mosaic Exodus

Tabernacles is a Mosaic institution[2] given to Israel that she might reflect on Yahweh's covenant love at such a time *when the covenant promises are fulfilled.* Thus the Lord's redeemed people were to celebrate it in the Promised Land, at a central sanctuary chosen by the Lord,[3] as the ultimate of three great pilgrim feasts. Since it was envisaged that God would deliver his redeemed people from their enemies, all the males would be able to attend without fear of the land being invaded.[4] Moreover, it marked a time of great joy, at the turn of the year,[5] when Israel had gathered in their threshing floor,

---

1. See Kerr, *Temple*, 228. "The whole of John 7:1–10:21 can be placed under a Tabernacles rubric."

2. Though modern critical scholarship has questioned Mosaic authorship of the Pentateuch, both the NT and Jesus recognize it. Cf. e.g., Matt 8:4; 19:7–8; 22:24; John 1:17, 45; 5:46; 7:19. For a contemporary defense of the Mosaic authorship and contents of Deuteronomy see Thompson, *Deuteronomy*, 47–68; Kline, *Treaty*.

3. Cf. Deut 16:15; 31:11. See Thompson, *Deuteronomy*, 41, who speaks of the central sanctuary as the Mosaic ideal.

4. Exod 34:24.

5. Tabernacles was celebrated for eight days from 15th to 22nd Tishri. Cf. Lev 23:23–36, 39; Num

and the final harvest of olives and grapes had been reaped.[6] At such a time they could look back over all the way that Yahweh had led them through the wilderness, providing light and water;[7] the construction of leafy booths aiding a festive re-enactment of the wilderness journey. Every seventh year, the year of release, Tabernacles became the occasion for covenant renewal and the reading of the law before all Israel.[8]

Tabernacles and the Davidic Sacral Kingship

Under David, Israel's enemies were subdued, Zion became God's chosen sanctuary, the king became God's priest and son,[9] and the Abrahamic promises were subsumed under the Davidic covenant.[10] First Kings represents typical fulfilment of these promises under Solomon when God had given peace, Judah and Israel were as numerous as the sand, Solomon ruled from the Euphrates to Egypt, and every man sat under his vine and fig tree.[11] The crowning act of fulfilment, however, was the Tabernacles dedication of the Temple:[12] Here, as sacral king, Solomon presided over the installation of the Ark, symbolic of Yahweh's enthronement,[13] sealed by his Shekinah Glory filling the Temple.[14] Solomon's priestly Deuteronomic prayer, however, was tacit admission that this typical fulfilment of the covenant blessing embodied in Tabernacles could and would soon be lost.[15]

Tabernacles and the NE

When Israel broke covenant, bringing divine displeasure and ultimately exile, Tabernacles began to take on a new importance—prospective of eschatological NE judgement and salvation foretold in the prophets. When the exiles returned, Tabernacles was the first feast to be celebrated in conjunction with the rebuilding of the altar and

---

29:12–38.

6. Cf. Exod 34:22; Lev 23:39–43.

7. Lev 23:40–43.

8. Cf. Deut 31:10–13; Neh 8:14 – 18. See Thompson, *Deuteronomy*, 290–92.

9. Cf. 2 Sam 7:12–14; Ps 2:6–7; 110:4. On sacral kingship see below on John 10.

10. Cf. e.g., Ps 72:8, 11, 17; Ps 89:3–4; 27–29.

11. Cf. 1 Kgs 4:20–25; 8:24; Deut 8:8; Mic 4:4; Zech 3:10; Gen 22:17; De Vries, *1 Kings*, 72 –73; Davis, *1 Kings*, 59–61.

12. Cf. 1 Kgs 8:15–20; 2 Chr 6:4–11; 7:8–10.

13. Mowinckel, *Psalms*, 1:136, connects this enthronement with the Babylonian New Year Akitu festival, but this is unwarranted and unnecessary, since the Lord's enthronement, dwelling among his people, is the logical climax of the covenant. See the analysis of Mowinckel's view in Brunson, *Psalm 118*, 28–29. Cf. Kraus, *Worship in Israel*, 8ff., 16ff.; Rubenstein, *Sukkot*, 20ff.

14. Cf. 1 Kgs 8:1–11; 2 Chr 5:2–14.

15. 1 Kgs 8:22–53; 2 Chr 6:12–42.

PART II—DETAILED EXEGETICAL EXAMINATION OF JOHN 5–10

the restoration of the cult, "recall[ing] the dedication of Solomon's temple."[16] It was later celebrated in conjunction with the public reading of the law under Ezra.[17] This return from exile failed to live up to prophetic expectations, however, since Israel still failed to be true to the covenant and were still "slaves" within their own land.[18] Thus the feast and its prophetic elaboration continued to be the focus of future expectation. The following passages represent this hope:

Isa 12:3

This is inseparably connected with the Tabernacles' water-pouring ceremony to which it either alludes, as an existing ritual, or for which it is the source.[19] In context it represents the paradisal conditions ushered in by the reign of the fruitful Davidic Branch, initiating Israel's NE gathering from among the nations and the dwelling of God among his people.[20] Several points are important:

1. The messianic "branch"[21] sprouts from the truncated root of Jesse.
2. The Spirit of the Lord will rest upon him.
3. He will judge the world, not by appearance, but will decide justly for the poor and smite the wicked.
4. He is lifted up as an ensign to the nations.
5. The Lord will come as a divine warrior and smite the Egyptian Sea.[22]
6. A united Israel will spoil the nations.
7. They will celebrate Tabernacles, drawing water from the wells of salvation, and sing the song of Moses.[23]

---

16. Cf. Ezra 3:1–4; Rubenstein, *Sukkot*, 33.
17. Neh 8–9.
18. Ezra 9:9; Neh 9:36. Cf. Wright, *NTPG*, 269.
19. So Edersheim, *Temple*, 279–80.
20. See Isa 11:1–12:6.
21. See Kaiser, *Messiah in the Old Testament*, 157, who thinks that the "Branch" terminology probably comes from 2 Sam 23:5, where God will bring David's salvation to fruition (cause it to sprout, branch out, Heb צמח). Cf. Oswalt, *Isaiah 1–39*, 279; Jer 23:5; 33:15; Zech 3:8; 6:12.
22. For the Divine Warrior motif in connection with the Exodus see Longman and Reid, *God is a Warrior*, 83–88.
23. Isa 12:4 quotes Ps 105:1. This psalm celebrates God's judgements upon Egypt, the Exodus journey, and the possession of the Promised Land. Isa 12:5 reflects Exod 15:1, the Song of Moses at the Red Sea, and (perhaps) Ps 98:1, which is "a new song," celebrating the victory of the Divine Warrior. Cf. Rev 5:9.

Isa 4:2–6

Following the fearful judgements of the Day of the Lord, by which he will cleanse Zion's survivors, the (messianic) "branch"[24] of the Lord will be glorious, the fruit of the land excellent, and the Lord will create the cloud and fire over Zion and her assemblies (associated with Tabernacles) and a booth for shade.[25] If "the fruit of the land" alludes to Num 13:26,[26] it would refer to the "first ripe grapes,"[27] and the branch might be understood as the "true vine," and messianic representative of Israel (who have failed to bear good fruit, Isa 5:4).[28] It is significant that in Isa 63:1–6 winepress imagery is used to depict messianic eschatological judgement, and that this is alluded to within the Johannine corpus.[29]

Isa 30:19–29

Supernatural light imagery associated with eschatological Tabernacles is employed: the light of the sun will be sevenfold, rain will be given for the seed, water will flow on the mountains, and Israel's divine Teacher will no longer hide himself.[30] The Lord will sift the nations and Israel will sing as in the Feast (Tabernacles).[31] This day will only come, however, after Israel's affliction, her abandonment of idolatry, and after "the day of the great slaughter."[32]

Isa 35:1–10.

Rivers will flow in the desert and the dry ground will become a pool, for God will come to save and recompense his people, opening the eyes of the blind, creating a highway for his redeemed who will return to Zion with everlasting joy.

---

24. Cf. Oswalt, *Isaiah 1–39*, 146–47.
25. See Moloney, *Signs and Shadows*, 69. Cf. Bar 5:8–9; Song Rab. 1:7, 3.
26. So Kaiser, *Messiah in the Old Testament*, 157. Cf. Deut 1:25.
27. Num 13:20.
28. This makes sense, juxtaposed as it is against Isaiah's vineyard parable, where Israel is a vine bearing wild grapes and ripe for judgement. Moreover, it tells exactly the same story as Ps 80, where Israel, God's vine under judgement, hopes in the messianic branch, the Son of Man. Cf. Kidner, *Psalms 73–150*, 291, who compares Ps 80:8–13 with Isa 5:1–7 and Jesus' saying, "I am the true vine," John 15:1. See also Ezek 15; Baldwin, *Daniel*, 150–51.
29. Cf. Rev 14:18–20; 19:11–16.
30. Cf. Oswalt, *Isaiah 1–39*, 560; Kaiser, *Messiah in the Old Testament*, 172; Joel 2:23.
31. See Moloney, *Signs and Shadows*, 66.
32. Isa 30:20, 22, 25. Cf. Kaiser, *Messiah in the Old Testament*, 172.

PART II—DETAILED EXEGETICAL EXAMINATION OF JOHN 5–10

Isa 60:1–20.

Jerusalem will be glorified, the glory of the Lord having risen upon her. Her exiled sons will return, all nations will serve her, the branch of the Lord's planting will possess the land, and the Lord will be Israel's everlasting light.[33]

Joel.

Tabernacles imagery is repeatedly employed to announce the coming Day of the Lord. A locust-like army will descend upon Israel, devastating the grain, oil, and wine harvests, bringing drought and darkness.[34] God's people must repent, with mourning and fasting rather than feasting, imploring him to turn away his anger.[35] He will then restore an abundant harvest, giving the former as well as the latter rain,[36] prayed for at Tabernacles, and Israel will know that "I am the LORD."[37] Afterwards he will pour out his Spirit upon all flesh, showing wonders, delivering the remnant in Zion.[38] Moreover, God will bring the nations into Judgement, thrusting in the sickle and treading the winepress, because "their evil is great."[39] For Judah and Jerusalem, the mountains will drip sweet wine, streambeds will flow with water, and a fountain shall come forth from the house of the Lord.[40] The Lord will cleanse his people and dwell among them.[41]

Importantly, Dillard notes that the phrase "the early rain for your vindication" (Heb הַמּוֹרֶה לִצְדָקָה), Joel 2:23, is ambiguous, since מוֹרֶה can signify either "(early) rain" or "teacher."[42] Though the context favors "rain," several scholars maintain an individual messianic teacher interpretation.[43] Teaching and rain are associated in Isa 30:19–26,[44] a passage that (as we have already indicated) is linked to Tabernacles. Moreover, Isa 55:10–11 likens the word that proceeds from God's mouth to the rain that waters the earth. We have already noted the association of the teaching of the law with Tabernacles (and its prayers for rain). Thus the rain/teacher ambiguity may well be deliberate,

---

33. Cf. Rev 22:5.

34. Cf. Joel 1:5, 7, 9–12, 17–19, 20; 3:15.

35. Cf. Joel 1:7, 13–14; 2:12–17.

36. Joel 2:18–26. Cf. Dillard, "Joel," 290.

37. Joel 2:27.

38. Joel 2:28–32.

39. Joel 3:12–13. Cf. Rev 14:15, where the sickle is used to reap because "the harvest of the earth is fully ripe" (for judgement). In Rev 14:19, the grape harvest of the earth is gathered and thrown into the "winepress of the wrath of God."

40. Joel 3:18 cf. Ezek 47:1ff.

41. Cf. Dodd, "Old Testament in the New," 174.

42. Dillard, "Joel," 289.

43. See summary in Allen, "Joel," 92–93. Cf. Dillard, "Joel," 289, who notes that a personal interpretation of the phrase is found in the targums, Vulgate, and Symmachus.

44. The same association is made by the rabbis. Cf. Wolff, *Joel and Amos*, 55; Dillard, "Joel," 289.

indicating not only the bestowal (life-giving) rain, but also the (life-giving) teaching of God's word.[45]

Interestingly, when the Spirit is outpoured all God's people will "teach."[46] Moreover, the command to instruct children's children concerning the judgement echoes that concerning the Egyptian signs and deliverance.[47] Allen notes that following their deliverance they were to praise God as in the return from exile.[48]

Ezekiel 47

Important Tabernacles symbolism is used, particularly the life-giving healing waters that issue from the altar of the eschatological Temple. In John 7:37–38, living waters proceed from Jesus, and in Rev 22:1, in the New Jerusalem, "the river of the water of life . . . [flows] from the throne of God and of the Lamb." The exceeding many fish taken by fishermen who spread their nets, Ezek 47:9–10, may be reflected in John 21, symbolic of the Church.[49]

Zechariah 14

An eschatological final battle is depicted where the nations fight against Jerusalem and Yahweh the divine warrior intervenes to save his people, punishing their enemies whom they will plunder.[50] The Lord will be universal King, re-creating an eschatological Jerusalem that towers above the flattened land; daylight will be continuous and waters will issue from Jerusalem to the seas. The survivors of the nations acknowledge God's sovereignty by annual worship at the Feast of Tabernacles. For those who fail to do so, rain will be withheld.

As Lightfoot points out, in NT times, Zechariah 14 would become a Tabernacles "lesson," forming the basis of popular belief concerning the coming day of the Lord and the messianic age.[51]

---

45. Cf. Dillard, "Joel," 289, who also cites Amos 8:11.

46. Joel 2:28. Cf. Numbers 11:17, 25, 29, where Moses wished that "all the LORD's people were prophets."

47. Joel 1:3 cf. Exod 10:1–2.

48. Allen, "Joel," 91–92.

49. See Bauckham, "153 Fish," 278ff.

50. Cf. Rubenstein, *Sukkot*, 45; Lightfoot, *John's Gospel*, 182. See Rev 20:7–10, where a similar final onslaught against Jerusalem ushers in the Judgement and final state.

51. Lightfoot, *John's Gospel*, 182.

PART II—DETAILED EXEGETICAL EXAMINATION OF JOHN 5-10

Conclusion

Several themes are common to eschatological Tabernacles fulfilment: Jerusalem will be surrounded, but delivered by God who will judge the world. The Lord will reign from Jerusalem and the messianic branch or teacher will be restored, resulting in paradisal blessing, perpetual supernatural light, and living waters that will issue from the Temple.

Developments within Judaism

Jubilees extrapolates the festivals back to patriarchal times. Thus Abraham celebrates Tabernacles, in the seventh month, for seven days, building "booths for himself and for his servants," "rejoicing with all his heart."[52] 1-2 Maccabees relate Tabernacles to *Hanukkah*.[53]

Tabernacles celebration in NT times

Referred to as "The Feast,"[54] Tabernacles was the most popular of the three pilgrim feasts (*hagim*), "a most holy and most eminent feast."[55] The Mishnah details Second Temple celebration:[56] On the first day of Tabernacles the Israelites constructed booths from branches of "splendid" leafy trees, on rooftops and in the Temple courts, in which they dwelt for seven days.[57] Throughout the feast they carried *lulabs*, willow and myrtle twigs tied with palm, in their right hands, marking the different stages of their Exodus journeys and perhaps a sign of victory.[58] In their left hands they held an *ethrog*, a piece of citrus fruit, symbolising the in-gathered harvest of the Promised Land.[59] Willow branches were also arranged around the altar, forming a leafy canopy for it.[60] A specified (diminishing) number of sacrifices were to be offered on each of the seven

---

52. Cf. Jubilees 16:21, 25, in Charlesworth, *Pseudepigrapha*, 2:89; Lev 23:40; Rubenstein, *Sukkot*, 51-52.

53. See below on John 10:22-42.

54. Cf. 1 Kgs 8:2, 65; 2 Chr 7:8; Neh 8:14; Isa 30:29; Ezek 45:23, 25. In Lev 23:39 and in Judg 21:19 it is referred to as "the Feast of the LORD." Cf. Jubilees 16:27.

55. Josephus *Ant.* 8:100-1, in Whiston, 219.

56. See tractate *m. Sukkah*. Although second century A.D., it is thought that this accurately reflects the practice when the Temple was standing. Cf. the collection of other relevant material in Str-B 2.774-812.

57. *m. Sukkah* 2:9, in Danby, 175.

58. Cf. Rev 7:9-10.

59. *m. Sukkah* 3:4-8. Cf. Edersheim, *Temple*, 274-75; Morris, *John*, 419-20.

60. *m. Sukkah* 4:5. Cf. Morris, *John*, 420; Edersheim, *Temple*, 278.

days.⁶¹ The feast was characterized by exuberant joy, reciting of specific Psalms, flute playing, and dancing.

Early in its development, water and light ceremonies had come to be associated with the daily ritual: On the seven days of the Feast a golden flagon filled with water drawn from the pool of Siloam was carried in procession led by the High Priest up to the Temple to the singing of Isa 12:3, "With joy you will draw water from the wells of salvation." When the procession reached the Water Gate, a trumpet was sounded three times. Through this gate eschatological waters of life would one day flow from the Temple.⁶² The priests then carried the pitcher in procession around the altar while the temple choir sang the *Hallel*⁶³ and the pilgrims looked on. On the seventh day, the altar was encompassed seven times, apparently symbolic of the march around the walls of Jericho.⁶⁴ When the choir reached Psalm 118:1, "O give thanks to the LORD," and again at v. 25, "Save us, we pray, O LORD! O LORD, we pray, give us success!" all the males shook their *lulabs* and shouted "Hosanna."⁶⁵ The water, together with the wine drink offering, was then offered to God, about the time of the morning sacrifice. Both were poured into their respective silver bowels, from which proceeded pipes, conveying the offering to the base of the altar.⁶⁶ Rabbinic tradition linked the water with expectation of a messianic Moses-like teacher who repeats the gift of the "well" of the Torah that followed the Israelites.⁶⁷

On the first night of the feast, and some think for each night, four enormous lamps, each with four bowls, were lit in the women's court. So brilliant was the light that every court in Jerusalem was said to be illuminated by it.⁶⁸ Men of Piety and good works danced through the night, torches in hand, singing hymns and songs of praise before the people. "Countless levites," with "instruments of music," stood on the fifteen steps (corresponding to the fifteen Songs of Ascent) that led from Israel's court to the court of women, playing and singing hymns.⁶⁹ At cockcrow, two priests proceeded

---

61. Cf. Num 29:12–13; *m. Sukkah* 5:6.

62. Rabbi Eliezer ben Jacob identified it as the south gate of Ezek 47:1–5, from which living waters would flow. Cf. *t. Sukkah* 3:2–10; *Gen. Rab.* 28:18; *Shekalim* 6:3; *Middot* 2:6. Cf. living waters of Zech 14:8.

63. Pss 113–18. *m. Sukkah* 4:9. See Edersheim, *Temple*, 280. His order of events places the encompassing of the altar after the pouring of water.

64. *m. Sukkah* 4:5.

65. *m. Sukkah* 3:9, in Danby, 177.

66. *m. Sukkah* 4:9. Cf. Lightfoot, *John's Gospel*, 182; Carson, *John*, 321–22; Jeremias, "λίθος," 277–78.

67. Cf. Num 21:18; *Tg. Onq.* Num 21:18; *t. Sukkah* 3:10–12; Pseudo Philo *L.A.B.* 10:7; 11:15; 28:7–8; *Eccl. Rab.* 1:8. Cf. Moloney, *Signs and Shadows*, 68.

68. *m. Sukkah* 5:2–3. This light, associated with that of Zechariah 14:6–8, was probably also linked with the pillar of fire in the wilderness, Exod.13:21, and its expected return at the end of time. Cf. Isa 4:5; Bar 5:8–9; *Song Rab.* 1:7, 3. Molney, *Signs and Shadows*, 69.

69. *m. Sukkah* 5:4, in Danby, 180.

down the steps, blowing trumpets, and advancing towards the Beautiful Gate, opening to the east. Turning their backs and facing west, towards the Holy Place, they said:

> Our fathers when they were in this place turned *with their backs towards the Temple of the Lord and their faces towards the east, and they worshipped the sun towards the east*; but as for us, our eyes are turned toward the Lord.[70]

On the eighth day the booth dwelling and ceremonies ceased and the day was dedicated to prayer for superabundant rain as a sign of Yahweh's continuing blessing.[71]

Tabernacles in the NT

Although Tabernacles motifs are possibly found in the Transfiguration,[72] explicit Sukkot references only occur in John 7–8. Rubenstein draws attention to other Johannine allusions. In John 12:12–15, the crowds wave palm branches and cry "Hosanna" ("Save, I pray"), associated with Tabernacles.[73] In Rev 7:9–17, the redeemed wear festal robes, carry palm branches, cry "Salvation belongs to our God,"[74] worship around God's throne, and God shelters (σκηνώσει) them with his presence.[75] Springs of living water, to which the Lamb leads them, relate to the water ceremony.[76]

Rubenstein asks if the lack of reference to Sukkot, compared to Passover and Pentecost, is due to disinterest? My explanation is that, unlike the other Pilgrim feasts, Tabernacles is understood as awaiting ultimate fulfilment. The Transfiguration is just a glimpse of the glory yet to be revealed. In GJohn, however, written after A.D. 70, the feast and Temple had disappeared without apparent fulfilment. GJohn solves this dilemma by showing that Jesus identified with the feast as something he was starting to fulfil, by leading a NE, and would ultimately accomplish, on the last day, but "not yet." In John 12:12–15, however, the crowds' use of Tabernacles symbolism at the Triumphal Entry signalled their desire for eschatological consummation, along the lines of Tabernacles.

In Revelation, written still later,[77] John uses abundant Tabernacles imagery to show how the feast will yet be fulfilled, including the nations' surrounding of the

---

70. *m. Sukkah* 5:4, in Danby, 180 (emphasis original); Cf. Edersheim, *Temple*, 284.

71. Cf. Moloney, *Signs and Shadows*, 67; Yee, *Jewish Feasts*, 74–77.

72. These include the booths, Jesus' shining face, and the overshadowing cloud. Cf. Mark 9:2–8; Matt 17:1–8; Luke 9:28–36. See Rubenstein, *Sukkot*, 84, n. 133, for the literature.

73. Cf. Ps 118:25, shouted at Tabernacles. See Rubenstein, *Sukkot*, 85–86.

74. Cf. "Save us" in Ps 118:25.

75. Cf. Rev 7:15; Isa 4:5; Rubenstein, *Sukkot*, 91–92.

76. Cf. Rev 7:17; Rubenstein, *Sukkot*, 92.

77. ca. A.D. 95. Cf. Caird, *Revelation*, 5–6; Hemer, *Seven Churches*, 2–5.

saints,⁷⁸ the final judgement,⁷⁹ and the ultimate state of the redeemed that follows Jesus' paschal sufferings and the NE. Here, in the New Jerusalem, God tabernacles with his people, the Lord God and the Lamb are the new Temple, a river of living water proceeds from God's throne, and the glory of God and of the Lamb provide unceasing light to which the nations come.⁸⁰

FORM AND STRUCTURE OF JOHN 7–8

Bounded by "the Jews'" desire to kill Jesus and the secrecy motif,[81] John 7–8 comprises a third Festival Cycle episode, focusing on Jesus' Tabernacles visit to Jerusalem. Unlike the previous two, the lack of "after this," at John 9:1, indicates that it concludes with Jesus' continuous residence in Judea for a period corresponding to the last six months of his ministry.[82] The adultery pericope is a late addition that interrupts the narrative.[83] Omitting this, the episode divides into four main sections: going up to the feast, at the middle of the feast, on the last day of the feast, and leaving the feast.

Within these sections the structure is chaotic.[84] Brodie believes it is deliberately obscure.[85] John reveals the turmoil of the occasion: Jesus' delay, failing to appear, and then appearing in the middle of the feast, has confounded the people.

NE INTERPRETATION OF JOHN 7–8

Going up to the feast, John 7:1–13

Will Jesus go up? vv. 1–10

The introduction to this episode is dominated by the question, "Will Jesus go up (ἀναβαίνω) to the feast"? "Go up" has a double meaning, being a motif for Jesus' ascent (as Son of Man) to the Father by way of the cross.[86] Similarly, Jesus' brothers' challenge to him, "Leave (μεταβαίνω, cross over) here and go to Judea," v. 3, echoes Jesus' departure from this world to the Father.[87] These allusions to Jesus' death are confirmed by the context: the "Jewish" authorities are seeking to kill him, v. 1, but his time is not yet.

---

78. Rev 20:8–10 cf. Zech 14.
79. Rev 14:15–20 cf. Joel 3:12–13.
80. Cf. Rev 21:3; 22:1–2; 21:6; 21:23–24; 22:5; 21:24, 26.
81. John 7:1, 4, 10, 8:59.
82. Cf. Mark 10:1ff.
83. Cf. Barrett, *John*, 589–92; Brown, *John I–XII*, 335–36; Carson, *John*, 333–34.
84. See Beasley-Murray, *John*, 104.
85. Brodie, *John*, 304.
86. Cf. John 3:13; 6:62; 20:18; Dan 7:13–14; Brown, *John I–XII*, 308; Brodie, *John*, 312; Carson, *John*, 309.
87. Cf. John 13:1, where "his hour had come to depart (μεταβαίνω) out of this world to the Father."

PART II—DETAILED EXEGETICAL EXAMINATION OF JOHN 5-10

Jesus must fulfil God's eschatological timetable in due time and in due order; Passover must precede Pentecost, with Tabernacles being the ultimate fulfilment. The hour of Jesus' departure (μεταβαίνω) will not come until his final Passover.

"Go up" (ἀναβαίνω) also echoes the enthronement of Yahweh, symbolized by the ascent of the ark into the sanctuary, associated with Tabernacles, "completing the Exodus."[88] This echo points to the powerful messianic manifestation by which Jesus will ultimately fulfil Tabernacles symbolism, including the bringing in of eschatological deliverance and the judgement of the nations. Jesus' disbelieving brothers challenge him to accomplish this in a worldly manner. They want his disciples to see his works and for him to "show [himself] . . . to the world."[89] Jesus knows, however, that the world hates him and seeks to kill him and he does not want to make a "triumphal entry" *at this feast*, which will lead prematurely to his death. Ironically, Jesus' brothers have equated Jerusalem and "the Jews" with the world, in hostile opposition to Jesus.[90] Moreover, "Show yourself to the world," is what will take place at Jerusalem when Jesus is lifted up.[91] As Brown points out, the brothers' words parallel the satanic temptation of Jesus to throw himself from the Temple to be spectacularly rescued.[92]

There is also a parallel with John 2:3, where Jesus' mother suggests that he should miraculously provide wine for the wedding *publicly*, symbolic of the messianic banquet, and thus of Jesus' broken body and blood. In response, Jesus objects that such thinking is totally out of accord with his own[93] and that his hour has not yet come. Nevertheless he provides wine *secretly*, manifesting his glory to his disciples, but not to the world.[94] Similarly here, Jesus does eventually go up to the feast, but *secretly*, as the hidden Messiah, at a time when the risk of a triumphal entry, precipitating his death, has passed.

Where is Jesus? vv. 11-13

These thoughts are now advanced from the perspective of the worshippers at the feast. "The Jews" are looking for Jesus to put him to death. Moreover, the multitudes, like Jesus' brothers, are in suspense, waiting for Jesus to make his move and manifest himself as the messianic deliverer who destroys their enemies. Murmuring (γογγυσμός) indicates their disbelief and discontent, directed against Jesus, reflecting that of Israel

---

88. Cf. Ps 47:5; Ps 68:18, 24; Kidner, *Psalms 1-72*, 177-78, 242; Davis, *1 Kings*, 61, n. 5.
89. John 7:4. See Schnackenburg, *John*, 2:140.
90. See Brown, *John I-XII*, 306-7.
91. Cf. John 2:14-15; 12:32; Bruce, *John*, 171.
92. Cf. Brown, *John I-XII*, 308.
93. Τί ἐμοὶ καὶ σοί can be translated "what have I to do with you?" as in 2 Sam 16:10. The suggestion is that Jesus' mother thinks that this is her son's opportunity to show himself to the world.
94. John 2:9-11.

against God, both in the wilderness and in relation to the delay of the NE.[95] Throughout this episode Jesus is put on trial by public opinion, just as Israel had put God on trial. Here the verdict is divided. At best he is "a good man," indicating the crowd's failure to perceive his divine glory. At worst, "he is leading the people astray," an allusion to the Deuteronomic false prophet. In fact, as in the Exodus and Isaianic lawsuits, they are themselves on trial, since they will be judged by the verdict they pass on God's envoy before whom they cannot remain neutral.[96]

At the middle of the feast, John 7:14–36

When the feast was half over, Jesus "went up" into the Temple and began to teach. Previously, however, he had acted in secret, (ἐν κρυπτῷ), so why does he now act in public (παρρησίᾳ)?[97] At this juncture, he has averted the expectation that he will immediately fulfil a messianic intervention associated with the feast. Nevertheless, he must identify with it as the one who begins to fulfil its NE agenda, in terms of the Lord's return to Zion, and as the one who will ultimately fulfil it in the New Jerusalem. Thus from now on he progressively reveals his identity, but as this revelation is progressively rejected, he gradually withdraws.

The messianic teacher, vv. 14–24

Jesus' "going up" to the Temple and teaching is a symbolic action. As previously mentioned "going up" echoes the ascent of the ark into the Temple, associated with the enthronement of the Lord at Tabernacles. Here, however, Jesus has not gone up in triumph, but in judgement, the suddenness of his appearance echoing Yahweh's sudden coming to his Temple where he sits as a refiner, purifying the sons of Levi, and coming near to judgement (Mal 3:1–5). This appearance will later be matched by Jesus' sudden withdrawal at the end of the feast, signalling Yahweh's judgement on the Second Temple.

Jesus' teaching is also significant since it identifies him as Israel's divine teacher who would no longer be hidden, but would be restored at Tabernacles:[98] he does not seek his own glory, nor speak from himself, but from the Father who sent him. The people are amazed at his knowledge of the Mosaic law (γράμματα)[99] since he has not

95. See above on the murmuring in John 6. See Watts, "Consolation," 31–59.

96. Cf. Deut 13:1–5; 18:19–20; Meeks, *Prophet-King*, 36. Similarly Pilate's trial of Jesus will become his own hour of crisis and trial when he unjustly condemns an innocent man. Likewise "the Jews" will stand self-condemned, delivering their king to death and swearing allegiance to another: "We have no king but Caesar."

97. Cf. vv. 10, 26.

98. See above on Joel 2:23 and Isa 30:20, where the Teacher is restored at Tabernacles.

99. See Bruce, *John*, 175. Jesus' knowledge of letters (grammata) refers to the writings of Moses. Cf. John 5:47.

PART II—DETAILED EXEGETICAL EXAMINATION OF JOHN 5-10

been educated at the rabbinical schools. Recognition of the divine origin of his teaching, however, depends on the attitude of their hearts and their desire "to do God's will," v. 17. These words allude to Psalm 40:8, "I desire to do your will, O my God; your law is within my heart."[100] Hebrews recognizes this psalm as messianic, speaking of Jesus who comes to offer his body as a sacrifice for sins.[101] Here, "I have preached righteousness in the great congregation . . . I have not concealed thy lovingkindness and thy truth," is also echoed,[102] as is "those . . . who seek to snatch away my life,"[103] in the "Jewish" authorities who "seek to kill me." Jesus is thus the messianic teacher who declares God's truth to his people though surrounded by those who seek to destroy him.

Because the discussion of the law, vv. 19–24, alludes to the healing of the lame man of John 5, some think that these verses have been displaced.[104] This is not necessary, however, since exposition of the law is part of Tabernacles. Moreover, Jesus looks back on that healing as the time when "the Jews" decided to kill him. Furthermore, the contrast between Jesus' making the man completely whole, and Moses, making people ceremonially whole, fits the present context. This recapitulation of Jesus' teaching is typical of GJohn.

In v. 24, "Do not judge by appearances, but judge with right judgement," Jesus alludes to Isa 11:3–4, "He shall not judge by what his eyes see, or decide disputes by what his ears hear, but with righteousness he shall judge the poor, and decide with equity for the meek of the earth."[105] As we have seen this refers to the Davidic Messiah who will judge the earth and remove the curse. Lifted up as an ensign to the nations he initiates a NE that ultimately results in the Tabernacles imagery of water drawn from the wells of salvation. Israel's great failure throughout their wilderness wanderings, at Kadesh, and at the return from exile, was to judge God by appearances. "The Jews" were making the same mistake here as their reactions to Jesus would show.

Reactions, vv. 25–32

The Jerusalemites sarcastically demonstrate their superior knowledge. Knowing of the plot to kill Jesus, they are amazed that he can speak openly without reproof. Surely the authorities cannot think that he is the Christ? They, however, are convinced that he is not, because, unlike Jesus, the Christ's origins are unknown.[106] The irony is that

---

100. So Hanson, *Prophetic*, 96–97.

101. Heb 10:5–10 cf. Psalm 40:6–8.

102. Ps 40:9–10, KJV. "Righteousness" and "truth," are echoed in John 7:18, ἀληθής ἐστιν καὶ ἀδικία ἐν αὐτῷ οὐκ ἔστιν.

103. Ps 40:14 cf. John 7:19, "why do you seek to kill me." Cf. Hanson, *Prophetic*, 97.

104. Cf. Bultmann, *John*, 247ff.; Schnackenburg, *John*, 2:90ff., 130–36.

105. Cf. Bernard, *John*, 265; Brown, *John I-XII*, 313; Barrett, *John*, 321; Hanson, *Prophetic*, 97; Lincoln, *Trial*, 197.

106. Cf. *1 Enoch* 46:2–3; *4 Ezra* 7:28; 13:32.

although they have a superficial knowledge of Jesus, as he points out, they have no idea as to his divine origins.[107] Such exchanges would help guide the churches in their debates with the synagogues[108] and the attempt to arrest Jesus would warn them of the hostility they would engender. The crowds' belief in Jesus as the Christ because of his miracles[109] echoes Israel's temporary faith at the Exodus.

Jesus warns of his departure, vv. 33–36

Far from delivering Jerusalem from the Romans, Jesus warns that he is departing (by his death and resurrection) to the one who sent him.[110] This echoes Jesus' NE departure of John 6, which has become a paradigm for his initiation of the NE. Like the Isa 55 *word of God* he will not return to God without accomplishing God's purpose. For "the Jews," however, this means that they have but a little while to seek him before their opportunity of finding and following him will be forever lost.[111] Ominously, "a little while" echoes OT passages anticipating the eschatological judgement of God.[112] Jesus later says the same words to his disciples (John 16:16–20). In their case, however, they would experience pain, as in childbirth, at his death, but would see him again following his resurrection and would rejoice. Significantly, birth-pain not only illustrates God's judgement, but also precedes eschatological salvation and resurrection.[113]

Reference to Jesus' going to the diaspora and teaching the Greeks, v. 35, is ironic. In the NE the Davidic Servant will indeed enlighten the Gentiles and gather the dispersed people of God.[114] As in John 6, the indications are that many of Jesus' own people will stumble because of him, but this will be the opportunity for the Gospel to go to the Gentiles and to be preached in all the world.

On the last day of the feast, John 7:37—8:20

The day is probably the eighth (Sabbath) day.[115] Now, when the water and light ceremonies have ended (permanently for John's readers) and the worshippers pray for

---

107. Vv. 28–29.
108. Cf. Justin *Dial.* 8:4; Beasley-Murray, *John*, 104; Lincoln, *John*, 251.
109. Cf. Meeks, *Prophet-King*, 162–64; Carson, *John*, 319; Beasley-Murray, *John*, 112. The merging of the prophet like Moses with Messiah as the "second Redeemer" led to an expectation that Messiah would perform miracles (greater than those of Moses) at the NE.
110. John 7:33. See Brown, *John I–XII*, 318.
111. John 7:34–35, echoing Isa 55:6. Cf. Hanson, *Prophetic*, 98–99; John 13:33.
112. Cf. Isa 10:25; 29:17; Jer 51:33; Hos 1:4. See Beasley-Murray, *John*, 285–86.
113. Cf. Isa 21:3ff.; Jer 13:21ff.; 22:23ff.; Mic 4:9–10; Isa 66:7–14; Isa 26:16–21; Hos 13:13–14.
114. Cf. Isa 42:1, 6; 49:6; 60:3; 62:2; 55:5.
115. Cf. Josephus *Ant.* 3:245; Bruce, *John*, 181; Carson, *John*, 321; Lincoln, *John*, 254.

PART II—DETAILED EXEGETICAL EXAMINATION OF JOHN 5–10

superabundant rain, symbolic of the Messianic teacher[116] (and his gift of the Spirit), Jesus reveals himself to be the reality to which the ceremonies pointed.

"Last day . . . the great" has eschatological connotations,[117] echoing Joel 2:28–31, where the Lord will pour out his Spirit upon all flesh and perform signs and wonders, before the coming of the "great and awesome day of the LORD." Upon Mount Zion and in Jerusalem there shall be deliverance for the remnant that escape, and "everyone who calls on the name of the LORD shall be saved." In Acts 2:16–21, Peter refers to this prophecy as being fulfilled in the outpouring of the Holy Spirit at Pentecost, by the crucified and risen Lord Jesus, prior to the coming of the "great and magnificent day [of the LORD]."

Jesus is the source of living waters, vv. 37–39

Bruce believes that,

> There are good reasons for revising the traditional punctuation of Jesus' invitation, so that it runs:
> If anyone is thirsty, let him come to me;
> And let him drink who believes in me.[118]

This allows a Christological referent for the scripture citation, "Out of his (Jesus') heart will flow rivers of living water." Jesus, not the believer, is the source of living water, equated here to the gift of the Spirit.[119] Moreover, this corresponds to the water and blood that flow from Jesus' side at his crucifixion, which is his glorification.[120] In John 19:34–37 the piercing that produced this flow fulfils Zech 12:10, where God pours out his Spirit on the house of David, opening a fountain for sin and uncleanness (Zech 13:1). Jesus' blood and water also fulfil the symbolic Tabernacles wine and water, poured out beside the altar by the priest, flowing from the Temple to the foot of mount Zion, becoming the river that waters and heals the land.[121]

JESUS SATISFIES THE BELIEVER'S THIRST

"If anyone thirsts," recalls John 6:35, "whoever believes in me will never thirst," and John 4:14, "whoever drinks of the water that I give him will never be thirsty forever."

---

116. See above on Joel 2:23 and Isa 30:19–26.
117. Cf. Joel 2:11, 31; Zeph 1:14; Mal 4:5; Isa 30:25; Jer 30:7; Num 24:14; Dan 12:13.
118. Bruce, *John*, 181. He thinks that this reflects the rhythm and rhyme of the original Aramaic. Cf. Beasley-Murray, *John*, 115.
119. Cf. John 1:33; 4:10–14; 15:26; 16:7; 20:22; Lincoln, *John*, 255.
120. John 19:34. Cf. Lincoln, *John*, 255; idem, *Trial*, 189; Dodd, *IFG*, 349, n. 2; Brown, *John I–XII*, 323; Carson, *John*, 324.
121. Cf. *m. Sukkah* 4:9–10; Ezek 47:1–12.

Jesus' reference to this water becoming a spring or well of water bubbling up to eternal life calls to mind Isa 12:3, "with joy you will draw water from the wells of salvation," a Scripture that is linked to Tabernacles. Satisfaction of thirst also alludes to the Isa 51:1 invitation to the thirsty, and to the Servant's satisfaction of thirst.[122] Thirst in the wilderness, satisfied by water from the rock, is also in the background.[123] "Let him come to me," indicates that Jesus is the sole fulfillment of all the aforementioned types of salvation. As in John 6:53, drinking is a metaphor for believing. Participation in the salvation that Jesus brings is by faith in him.

The OT citation

The source of the Scripture citation "Out of his heart will flow rivers of living water" is disputed, but several scriptural allusions are probable—especially the water that flowed from the smitten rock in the wilderness and the water that will flow from Jerusalem and its Temple in the eschatological Tabernacles.[124] Jesus is thus the source of living waters on the NE journey. He is also its fulfilment at the journey's end, in the New Jerusalem on the Last Day, when he gives to the thirsty "from the spring of the water of life" (Rev 21:6), and the "river of water of life" flows "from the throne of God and of the Lamb" (Rev 22:1).

The GJohn scheme of salvation

The chronological note, "as yet the Spirit had not been given, because Jesus was not yet glorified," v. 39, is important. It is in his paschal death and resurrection (and ascension to the Father, John 20:17) that Jesus is glorified (John 12:23). The gift of the Spirit follows this glorification. If we accept that John understands the ultimate fulfilment of Tabernacles to be that of Rev 22:1–5,[125] his chronological scheme is as follows:

Jesus' paschal death and resurrection initiates the NE redemption from bondage, opening a fountain for sin and uncleanness, and ensuring the gift of the Spirit. This gift is first bestowed in the upper room, when the disciples are commissioned to preach the gospel (John 20:21–23). Following the shedding forth of the Spirit at Pentecost (alluded to in John 16:7–11), the gospel will be preached in all the world to both Jews and Gentiles. The message of an uplifted Savior will be the ensign that signals the NE from sin and death to life and salvation and that draws people from all nations unto Jesus. Those who believe not only receive forgiveness of sins and eternal life, now in this present time, but are also called to journey to the Father's house, the heavenly New Jerusalem (John 14:1–6). The Tabernacles consummation of salvation

---

122. Isaiah 55:1; 49:10.
123. Cf. Exod 17:3; Neh 9:15, 20, where the gift of water is paralleled with the gift of the Spirit.
124. Cf. Exod.17:3–6; 1 Cor 10:4; Zech 14:8; Isa 33:21; Joel 3:18; Ezek 47:9; Bruce, *John*, 182.
125. See above.

PART II—DETAILED EXEGETICAL EXAMINATION OF JOHN 5–10

is realized in the Kingdom of God on the Last Day when Jesus will return to judge the world, raise the dead, and bring in the eschatological new heaven and earth (John 5:28–29). Jesus' redeemed people will then experience full enjoyment of eternal life and be able to look back with joyful celebration on the way that God has fulfilled his promised salvation.

Reactions, vv. 40–52

Once again Jesus' words divide the multitude. Many, in view of his promise of living water, believe that he is the Mosaic Prophet,[126] some think he is the Christ, but the Pharisees, who have attempted to arrest Jesus, think that he is the False Prophet who leads men astray (John 7:47). The objection that the prophet-Christ does not come from Galilee, but is David's seed from Bethlehem, is ironic.[127] It points up the "Jewish" authorities' ignorance of Jesus' origins, enabling John's readers to see through the curse that the authorities consider imposed on simple believers, John 7:49. Nicodemus's question, John 7:51, "Does our law judge a man without first giving him a hearing and learning what he does?" points up their utter unreasonableness, judging a man before hearing him. It indicates, however, that even among the Pharisees, and the ruling council, there was one who was prepared to listen to and perhaps believe in Jesus (cf. John 19:39).

Jesus is the light of the world, John 8:12–20

JESUS' DIVINE PROVISION FOR THE JOURNEY

Jesus' claim, "I am the light of the world," John 8:12, is the second "I am" (ἐγώ εἰμι) saying with a predicate.[128] It reveals Jesus to be the Lord, alluding not only to the divine revelation of Exod 3:14, but also to God's use of this name in Isa 40–55, in the context of the NE. The predicates of these "I am" sayings echo God's Exodus provision for Israel.[129] They also point to his divine all sufficient provision for the NE in terms of Jesus, the Son of God and messianic Suffering Servant. Jesus is the bread of life, the door of the sheep, the good shepherd, the resurrection and the life, the way, and the truth, and the life, the true vine, and (in this case) the light of the world.[130] In him, and in him alone, is everything that men and women need in this world and in the world to come.

---

126. Cf. John 7:40; 6:14; Deut 18:15; Exod 17:6; Num 20:11.
127. John 7:41–42. Cf. Bruce, *John*, 183–84; 2 Sam 7:12–16; Isa 9:7; 55:3; Mic 5:2.
128. For the first of these sayings, see above on John 6:35.
129. Cf. Enz, "Type," 213.
130. Cf. John 6:35; 10:7, 11; 11:25; 14:6; 15:1; 8:12.

Light at the Exodus and NE

Light is the means by which God separates his people (the children of light[131]) from their enemies (who are in darkness[132]) and by which he leads and guides them. At the Exodus, God gave light in the dwellings of the Israelites, while the Egyptians had "pitch darkness in all the land of Egypt three days" (Exod 10:22–23). When God led Israel out of Egypt, he went before them in a pillar of cloud and in a pillar of fire, to lead them and to give them light for their journey (Exod 13:21–22). He also went behind them to separate and protect them from the Egyptians, becoming a cloud of darkness to their enemies, but giving light to Israel (Exod 14:19–20). Similarly, in the NE, the Lord promises that he will go before and behind his people to guide and to protect them (Isa 52:12 cf. Isa 58:8).

The symbolism of light and darkness

As we have seen, in Scripture, not least in GJohn, light is symbolic of the realm of God, righteousness, life, understanding, knowledge, and truth, while darkness represents the realm of Satan, sin, death, blindness, ignorance, and falsehood.[133] Moreover, there is a struggle going on between the kingdom of light and the kingdom of darkness. "The light shines in the darkness, and the darkness has not overcome it," John 1:5. The fact that GJohn introduces this conflict in the context of creation, and "the beginning," John 1:1–4, points to its entrance into the world at the fall (Gen 3:1–7) when Satan sought to wrest mankind's allegiance from God to himself. God's first response was to pronounce judgement upon the serpent and to announce the coming Savior of men and women, the seed of the woman (Gen 3:14–15). According to their allegiance, mankind would be divided into two "seeds" at enmity with each other. The seed of the serpent would include all those, born by natural descent from Adam, who continue to follow (and take after) the satanic serpent. The seed of the woman is Christ, miraculously conceived and born of a virgin by the power of God.[134] Included in him are all those whom he represents, who are "born again" by the Holy Spirit (John 3:3–8). The Gen 3:15 conflict would result in the Christ inflicting a mortal wound upon the serpent ("he shall bruise your head") while the Christ himself would also suffer ("you shall bruise his heel"). This was fulfilled at the cross, of which Jesus says, "Now is the judgment of this world; now will the ruler of this world be cast out" (John 12:31).

---

131. Cf. Eph 5:8; 1 Thess 5:5;
132. Cf. John 3:19; 2 Cor 6:14; 1 John 2:11.
133. See above on Ideological Feasibility. Cf. John 3:20–21; 12:35–36; 46; Col 1:13; 1 John 1:5, 7.
134. Cf. Wenham, *Genesis 1–15*, 80–81; Isa 7:14; Matt 1:23; Luke 1:35.

PART II—DETAILED EXEGETICAL EXAMINATION OF JOHN 5-10

Light for the Gentiles

That Jesus is "the light of the world," indicates not only his divine person (in Johannine theology, "God is light, and in him is no darkness at all," 1 John 1:5), but also his office and work as God's messianic Servant, and Savior of the world, who will bruise the serpent's head (Gen 3:15) and set the captives free (Isa 61:1). In the NE, the Servant will be the light to the Gentiles, opening their prisons and calling them out of darkness, guiding and pasturing them, and leading them by springs of water, back to the Promised Land (Isa 49:6–10 cf. Acts 26:17–18). Thus it was always God's plan that the nations should be included among the people of God (Isa 2:2–4). The task of giving light to the Gentiles had belonged to Israel, in whom all the nations of the world would be blessed (Gen 28:14). When Israel failed to accomplish this, however, God revealed his Servant, the embodiment of Israel, who would fulfil his purpose in making atonement for sin and accomplishing worldwide redemption.[135]

Jesus' offer of light

Jesus' offer of redemption, "Whoever follows me will not walk in darkness, but will have the light of life," v. 12, is made to all the people of the world, without exception, on the condition that they follow him. The journey upon which he leads them is a NE from darkness to light. As we have seen, translation from the realm of darkness to the realm of light occurs the moment a person believes in Jesus.[136] For those who truly believe, this initial act of faith results in a lifelong commitment to Jesus, following him on a journey to the New Jerusalem and his Father's house (John 14:2). "The Jews" who were opposed to Jesus and who "were seeking to kill him" (John 7:1), were resisting his mission to deliver their fellow countrymen from darkness and bondage. In this they fulfilled a similar role (in the NE) to that of Pharaoh (at the Exodus), when he withstood Moses and God and would not let Israel go free. Moreover, they were walking in moral and spiritual darkness. Ominously, Jesus would soon depart from them and from their Temple.

Jesus is the Fulfillment of the Tabernacles light

"I am the light of the world," has especial significance for Tabernacles. We have already noticed that the Isaianic "I am he" (ἐγώ εἰμι) was probably the origin of the divine name, "I and He" (אֲנִי וְהוּא), used in the processional singing of Ps. 118:25 at Tabernacles.[137] Moreover, Jesus' provision of light, together with his provision of water, fulfils the symbolism of the illumination of the Temple courts and of the water

---

135. Cf. Isa 42:1–4; 49:1–6; 50:4–9; 52:13–53:12; 61:1–11.
136. See above on John 5:24–25.
137. See above on John 6:19–21. Cf. Isa 41:4; 43:10, 25; 46:4; 48:12; 51:12; 52:6; *m. Sukkah* 4:5.

ceremony respectively. These ceremonies not only look back to the Exodus, but also point froward to the NE journey and to the eschatological consummation that Tabernacles represents. Within the Johannine corpus, the New Jerusalem, the destiny of the redeemed, is illuminated by the glory of God; "the city has no need of sun or moon to shine on it, for the glory of God gives it light, and its lamp is the Lamb. By its light will the nations walk." (Rev 21:23–24). Thus, in his declaration, "I am the light of the world," Jesus reveals himself to be Israel's Lord, who not only saves and delivers his people in a NE from darkness, sin, and death, leading and providing for them in their NE journey, but who also is their reward at their journey's end. The bitter irony of this situation is that Jesus is the fulfillment of Tabernacles, Israel's Lord, to whom and for whose coming the worshippers prayed, but, although he freely offers himself to them, they fail to recognize his true identity and ultimately reject him.

They Judge by appearances

The Pharisees' objection that Jesus' self-witness is invalid harks back to John 5:31 and Jesus' trial and defense. Here, again on trial,[138] he defends his testimony as the self-authenticating[139] Word, come from and returning to God. Moreover, his Father bears witness.[140] Once again they are judging by appearance. "Where is your Father?" reveals their contempt and ignorance.

Leaving the feast, John 8:21–59

Jesus again announces his departure, vv. 21–30

He warns that they will die in their sins

Again Jesus tells "the Jews" that he is going away and they cannot follow him. Rather, he thrice warns them that they will die in their sins. This echoes the generation that, having judged by appearances, sinned at Kadesh, and died (in their sins and rebellion) in the wilderness. The ironic "will he kill himself?" v. 22, is contemptuous, indicating that they belong to a different realm than Jesus: They are from below, of this (dark) world, whereas he is from above, the realm of light and life. He has been sent into the world to speak the Father's message of deliverance from the realm of death, but unless they recognise Jesus' divine identity, they will die in their sins.

---

138. See Lincoln, *Trial*, 82–96, esp. 84.
139. See ibid., 85.
140. John 5:37.

PART II—DETAILED EXEGETICAL EXAMINATION OF JOHN 5-10

They must perceive and believe that "I am"

Jesus tells "the Jews" that it is absolutely imperative that they "believe that I am," v. 24. At the Exodus, God announced himself as "I am," the self-existent, all-powerful one, who is able to deliver Israel—who were meant to trust him through the wilderness that he might lead them into the Promised Land. Their perceptions, however, that God had brought them out of Egypt to die (Num 14:3; 20:4), led to further disbelief, rebellion at Kadesh (Num 14:4), and death in the wilderness (Num 14:29)—where they wandered for a further thirty-eight years. Likewise, in the Isaianic lawsuits, Israel's perception of Babylon's power and of God's apparent inability to deliver them led to disbelief in his sovereignty. Thus Yahweh calls Israel, as his witnesses, to "know and believe me and understand that I am he," Isa 43:10. He is Israel's only God and Savior who makes a way in the sea for his people, destroying their enemies (as at the Exodus). He will do a new thing, making a way in the wilderness and rivers in the desert for his people (Isa 43:19). Πιστεύσητε . . . ὅτι ἐγώ εἰμι, LXX Isa 43:10 ("believe . . . that I am"), are the exact words that Jesus uses here.[141] "Who are you?" indicates that they do not understand what he is saying. Only when they have lifted up the Son of Man (in death), as the Servant is lifted up (John 8:28 cf. Isa 52:13), will they recognize his divine glory.

This section concludes with a surprising act of faith on the part of "the Jews," v. 30, "As he was saying these things, many believed in him." John's readers will recollect, however, that previously such "faith" has proved spurious.[142]

Jesus addresses those who believe in him, vv. 31-59

The truth will set you free

Jesus does not accept mere "temporary faith," but looks for disciples who will abide (μένω) in his Word, v. 31. Such will know the truth and the truth will set them free, v. 32. Release from slavery, of which Jesus speaks, is associated with the Exodus and the return from exile. The ultimate realisation of Israel's emancipation from slavery was to be celebrated at Tabernacles, where, enjoying the freedom of the Promised Land, every seventh year, the Israelites were to release their slaves.[143] Such releases are only a paradigm, however, of a more important release from bondage, release from the slavery of sin and death. Moreover, "the truth," of which Jesus speaks, v. 32, stands in opposition to the satanic lie, "You will not surely die," that first brought man into bondage.[144]

---

141. Cf. Lincoln, *Trial*, 88.
142. See John 2:23-25. Cf. Carson, *John*, 345.
143. See on Tabernacles above.
144. Gen 3:4, referred to in John 8:44.

Jesus at the Feast of Tabernacles, John 7-8

CHILDREN OF ABRAHAM?

The "Jews'" protestation that as Abraham's seed they have "never been enslaved," v. 33, is ironic, recalling their slavery in Egypt and Babylon, and their present bondage under Rome. Jesus solemnly reminds them that "everyone who commits sin is a slave to sin," v. 34. Moreover, alluding to Ishmael who was 'cast out' as a slave by Abraham, and thus did not remain in Abraham's house,[145] Jesus reminds them that their physical descent from Abraham does not guarantee permanent membership of the family of Abraham or of God. Only Jesus, the Son, has authority to set slaves free.[146] Furthermore, by rejecting the truth and seeking to kill Jesus,[147] these unbelieving "Jews" (as they prove to be) demonstrate their true parentage; they belong to the devil, the father of lies and of murder.[148] If they were children of Abraham and of God they would love Jesus and hear (understand and obey) his word because he has come from God, v. 42, is manifestly sinless,[149] and speaks the truth from God, v. 46. Though "the Jews" counter by slandering Jesus,[150] suggesting that he is demon possessed, God seeks to honor his Son and will judge them.

THE SLAVE WILL NOT ABIDE IN THE HOUSE

What does it mean to abide in the house forever? "The house," τῇ οἰκίᾳ, echoes the Father's house or Temple.[151] Moreover, there are definite links between this passage and John 14:2-3 where Jesus returns to the Father's house.[152] Τῇ οἰκίᾳ also refers to the family, incorporating not only Jesus, but also his disciples. They are his children, τέκνα,[153] widening the communion between Father and Son to include those the Father has given to Jesus. In John 10, Jesus will be seen to be the royal priest who has charge over God's house and who builds the house. The concept of Jesus "replacing" the Temple is similar to Rev 21:22 where the Lord God Almighty and the Lamb are the Temple. The concept of believers being included in the Temple becomes clear in the "upper room," where, "John presents the whole episode . . . (chs. 13–17) as a

---

145. John 8:35 cf. Gen 21:10–14; Barrett, *John*, 346; Hanson, *Prophetic*, 124–25.

146. John 8:36 cf. John 1:12.

147. Anticipating v. 59.

148. v. 44, alluding to the devil's part in the fall, Gen 3. Cf. Carson, *John*, 353.

149. He is the Second Adam, who by obedience to God's will bestows righteousness and life upon his people. Cf. Rom 5:17–19.

150. References to not being "born of sexual immorality," John 8:41, may imply "like you," indicating that the "Jews" were familiar with Jesus' conception prior to Mary and Joseph being married. This and the John 7:42 reference to messiah's birth in Bethlehem imply Johannine familiarity with the virgin birth.

151. See Walker, *Holy City*, 171.

152. See Kerr, *Temple*, 298–99.

153. Cf. John 1:12; 1 John 2:1; 3:18.

PART II—DETAILED EXEGETICAL EXAMINATION OF JOHN 5–10

'Temple experience'" and the disciples are "encouraged to see themselves as places in which God will 'dwell' by his Spirit (14:17, 20, 23)."[154] This is similar to the Pauline and Petrine view of believers as living stones built upon Jesus, the chief cornerstone.[155]

JESUS DISCLOSES HIS DIVINE GLORY

Jesus' solemn asseveration that whoever keeps his word "will never see death," v. 51, takes the dialogue to another level, convincing "the Jews" that he is "possessed" (v. 52). Since Abraham and the prophets all died, who does Jesus make himself to be?[156] Jesus affirms not only that Abraham saw Jesus' day and rejoiced, but also, before Abraham came into being, "I am" (ἐγώ εἰμι), equivalent to the divine name אֲנִי־הוּא. During the feast, the worshipers would have held their willow branches and prayed, אֲנִי וְהוּא "(I and He) come to our aid."[157] Here Jesus is the answer to that prayer; his fivefold repetition of the phrase ἐγώ εἰμι, within the context of the feast, giving his self-disclosure the character of a theophany.[158] "The Jews" reject this as blasphemy. At their attempt to stone him, Jesus hides himself and departs from the Temple. Davies believes that Jesus' leaving here is decisive, "'I am' has departed from the Temple, that 'holy space' is no longer the abode of the Divine Presence. The Shekinah is no longer *there*, but is now found wherever Christ is."[159] Since Jesus will again be found in the Temple precincts it is more likely that this is part of a gradual withdrawal. Ominously, in Ezek 10:1–22, a similar departure foreshadowed the destruction of Jerusalem in 587 B.C.

THE NE AS DELIVERANCE FROM SIN, DEATH, AND THE REALM OF SATAN

The importance of this dialogue is that it shows the true nature of the NE as deliverance from sin, death, and the dominion of the devil. Jesus stands before "the Jews," as an epiphany of God, offering to free them, not from Roman dominion, but from the root cause of their problem (universal to all mankind), their slavery to sin and death, under the curse of the law, restoring paradise. It also explains the judgement that would fall upon Jerusalem. Rejecting God's Son, the unbelieving "Jews" have chosen to remain slaves to sin, aligning themselves with the devil. The Father would judge them.

---

154. Walker, *Holy City*, 172. Cf. Johnston, *Spirit-Paraclete*, 69.
155. Cf. 1 Cor 3:9–16; Eph 2:19–22; 1 Pet 2:5.
156. See above on John 5:18, where Jesus is accused of "making himself" equal to God.
157. Cf. Dodd, *IFG*, 349–50; Coloe, *God Dwells*, 137; Bruce, *John*, 193.
158. See Coloe, *God Dwells*, 142. Cf. John 8:12, 18, 24, 28, 58.
159. Davies, *Gospel and the Land*, 295. Cf. Kerr, *Temple*, 248.

Pauline parallels

THE PAULINE ANTITHESIS BETWEEN THE SLAVE AND THE SON

We cannot leave this passage without noting the remarkable parallels with Pauline theology. Thus, in Gal 4:21–31, Paul makes a similar allusion to the casting out of Ishmael to that made (in John 8:35) by Jesus.[160] He argues that Hagar and Sarah, together with their sons, are types of two covenants, the law and the Gospel (Gal 4:24). Hagar and Ishmael, "the slave woman and her son," represent Mount Sinai and the law, and correspond "to the present Jerusalem . . . in slavery with her children" (Gal 4:25). Sarah and Isaac, the "free woman" and her son, represent the Gospel, God's gracious covenant announced to Abraham, and correspond to the heavenly Jerusalem, which is "above,"[161] (the NT people of God).

Moreover, as these two sons of Abraham were conceived in different ways and had different ends, even so it is with those under the respective covenants. Ishmael was conceived naturally, of the flesh, and was cast out as the son of a slave woman (Gen 21:10). So also, those who are under the law are seeking to please God according to the flesh (fallen human nature), by "the works of the law," and will thus be cast out as slaves.[162] Isaac, however, was born miraculously, according to God's promise, and became Abraham's freeborn son and heir. So also, those who are born by the power of the Holy Spirit, who believe the Gospel promise, are set free from the law (and sin and death)[163] by Christ[164] and become children and heirs of God. Importantly, these children of promise are those envisaged in Isa 54, the fruit of the Servant's vicarious suffering (Isa 52:13–53:12), who in the NE repopulate the "heavenly" Jerusalem.

THE JOHANNINE ANTITHESIS BETWEEN THE FLESH AND THE SPIRIT

In his Gospel, John presents the same antitheses between the Law and the Gospel (John 1:17; 9:28), and the flesh and the Spirit (John 3:6; 6:63). He shows us that it is not enough to be born of Jewish descent and to be under the law to enter the kingdom of Heaven. Rather, it is necessary to be born again (ἄνωθεν, from above) of the Holy Spirit (John 3:3, 5). This is because all people are in bondage as servants of sin, under the penalty of the law. The way of redemption is through the vicarious sacrifice of

---

160. See also Rom 9:7–9, where Isaac is the promised seed as opposed to Ishmael.

161. Cf. Heb 12:22.

162. The reader will note that I stand in the traditional Reformed position on Pauline interpretation of "the works of the law." Thus I reject the "new perspective(s)" on Paul and the "covenantal nomism" theory that the Jews (in general) viewed the law (circumcision, Jewish food laws, Sabbaths, and festivals) as a "badge of covenant membership," *rather than* as a means of obtaining righteousness. For a defence of the traitional Protestant doctrine of Justification by faith, expounded in the teaching of Galatians 2–3, see Silva, "Faith Versus Works of Law in Galatians," 217–48.

163. Cf. Rom 6:22; 7:5–6; 8:2, 6.

164. They are justified by faith. Cf. Gal 2:16; 3:24; Rom 7:5–6; 8:2, 6; Bruce, *Galatians*, 219.

PART II—DETAILED EXEGETICAL EXAMINATION OF JOHN 5–10

Jesus, the Paschal Lamb, and Suffering Servant. By faith in Jesus, Men are set free from sin and death and the curse of the law. To those who receive salvation through faith in Jesus, who are born not "of the will of the flesh nor of the will of man," the right is given to become children and heirs of God (John 1:12).

Conclusion

Chapters 7–8 show the nature of Jesus' NE fulfilment of Tabernacles. He did not come to bring eschatological consummation in terms of Last Day judgement of the nations and final manifestation of his glorious kingdom along Tabernacles lines. Rather, he came to inaugurate the NE by his paschal death, setting people free from slavery to sin. To believers, Jesus is the water of life, granting present enjoyment of eternal life; he is the light of the world, guiding them to the New Jerusalem and the heavenly Temple. In an already/not yet eschatology, Jesus' followers already enjoy these benefits, but will know the full experience of them when eschatological Tabernacles finally dawns on the Last Day.

Jesus has manifested himself to unbelieving "Jews," but they have failed to recognize him, siding with the satanic ruler of this world, seeking to destroy Jesus. Consequently, like those who died in the wilderness, they will be judged, suffering destruction along with their Jerusalem Temple some thirty-eight years hence.

11

Episode 4 Narrative
The Sabbath Healing of a Man-Born-Blind, John 9

IN THIS EPISODE JESUS heals a man who was blind from birth. The healing possibly took place on or shortly after the last day of the Feast of Tabernacles. It is connected thematically to Tabernacles by the twin themes of light and water.[1] Jesus is the light of the world, who imparts physical and spiritual sight to the man-born-blind. Moreover, the water of Siloam, used in the healing, is the same water used in the Tabernacles water pouring ceremony.[2] The Good Shepherd discourse, which also belongs to this episode, will be dealt with in chapter 12 below.

FORM AND STRUCTURE

John 9 commences the fourth Festival Cycle episode, John 9:1—10:21.[3] Consisting mainly of narrative it divides into three main sections: In vv. 1–12, Jesus performs a NE sign on a man-born-blind. In vv. 13–34, the man-born-blind is tried before the Pharisees. In vv. 35–41, he worships Jesus outside the synagogue. These main sections subdivide again, so that the entire chapter can be thought of as a dramatic presentation in seven scenes.[4] This does not mean that a miracle story has been expanded to reflect a church versus synagogue situation (contra Martyn), but rather it is a testimony to the artistry of John who recounts not only the miraculous sign that Jesus performed, but also the dramatic events that immediately followed.

THE RELATIONSHIP BETWEEN JOHN 9 AND JOHN 5

Before we explore this episode in greater detail, it is important to highlight the relationship between John 5 and John 9.

1. See the Tabernacles festal background, above.
2. See *m. Sukkah* 4:9–10.
3. See Dodd, *IFG*, 354, who treats 9:1—10:21 as a complete episode with 10:22–39 as an appendix.
4. Cf. Martyn, *History and Theology*, 37; Lincoln, *John*, 280.

PART II—DETAILED EXEGETICAL EXAMINATION OF JOHN 5-10

Their similarities and differences

John 9 directly parallels John 5. In both a man has been subject to an affliction for a great many years, lameness or blindness, causing him to be "exiled" from the Temple and its worship. Jesus sees and knows about each man and the question of sin in relation to his infirmity is alluded to. Jesus heals each man, on the Sabbath, by a creative act and NE sign, effectively calling him out of "exile." Each healing is related to water. After each healing, Jesus withdraws, but later seeks out the healed man. Each healing results in a trial scene in which the Pharisees make accusations against the man and Jesus. Each, however, has important differences from the other: In particular, the manner of healing, the response of the person healed towards Jesus, and the consequences of that response.

The purpose of these accounts

As previously argued, the accounts of the healings form two halves of a theodicy defending God's actions concerning the A.D. 70 judgement visited upon Jerusalem. Each man represents a different part of Israel confronted by the claims of Jesus in the "probationary" period before the destruction of the Temple. The lame man represents ordinary Jewish people who, having experienced the divine power of Jesus, and heard his call, have disobeyed his voice. Turning their back on Jesus they have sided with the "Jewish" authorities, in opposition to Jesus, and chosen the legalistic worshipping community of the Jerusalem Temple. As such they perished with the Temple. The blind man, however, represents those who, having been called out of "exile," obeyed Jesus and chose to worship him, the embodiment of God and God's new Temple, outside the Second Jerusalem Temple. As such they have escaped judgement and enjoy eternal life.

More than this however, the two narratives manifest the divine glory of Jesus, who has come down from heaven to save fallen men and women, to take upon himself our sins and infirmities, to make atonement for us before his Father, and to initiate a NE and new creation. Moreover, the two men are examples of the wrong and right ways to respond to Jesus. While the lame man responded in unbelief and sided with Jesus' enemies, bringing judgement upon himself, the blind man responded to Jesus in faith and worshipped him, receiving spiritual sight and the gift of eternal life.

NE INTERPRETATION OF JOHN 9

Jesus performs a NE sign on a man-born-blind, John 9:1–12

Jesus sees the man, vv. 1–5

"[And] as he passed by," connects this chapter to John 8:59, suggesting that it took place on or shortly after the last day of Tabernacles. Thus it takes place under the

The Sabbath Healing of a Man-Born-Blind, John 9

Tabernacles rubric, when Jesus is still in Jerusalem, but *after* the festivities have ceased and *outside* the Temple. Moreover, Jesus' passing by[5] may be a theophanic representation, continuing from his use of the absolute "I am," his "seeing" the blind man echoing that of the Lord, who saw Moses and the affliction of his people in Egypt.[6] This divine "seeing" is confirmed by his intimate knowledge of the man, blind from birth through no fault (sin) of his own or of his parents.

The reason for the man's suffering

The disciples' question, "Rabbi, who sinned?" reflects belief in a direct causal relationship between sickness or suffering and sin, either the sin of the parent or that of the individual.[7] Congenital blindness might be due to sin in the womb.[8] "Who sinned?" was also a question that Jews might ask when the Temple was destroyed.[9] The lame man's sin was mentioned in connection to his misfortune, but here Jesus absolves the man-born-blind. The Jewish believers he represents would also feel absolved, particularly post A.D. 70, for the judgements that came upon Jerusalem and the Temple. The reason for his suffering, that God's works might be manifest in him, would also give them hope and encouragement that, like the man, God had a purpose in their trials.

Jesus, the light to the world

Jesus' saying, "We must work the works of him who sent me while it is day," v. 4, may employ the plural of majesty. "Night is coming, when no one can work," refers to Jesus' departure by death. This is confirmed by Jesus' reference to "as long as I am in the world, I am the light of the world," v. 5, and the declaration that "it was night" when Judas went out to betray Jesus.[10] Those who came to take him kindled a fire and equipped themselves with burning torches, echoing the rebellious acts of those who have no light, Isa 50:11.[11] Here, though not an ἐγώ εἰμι saying, "I am the light of the world" echoes the John 8:12 declaration where Jesus fulfils Tabernacles imagery: light that guided Israel in the Exodus, and light synonymous with the eschatological consummation of redemption in the New Jerusalem. In the NE God would lead the blind, making darkness light before them (Isa 42:16, 18) and the Servant would be a light to the Gentiles that God's salvation should reach to the ends of the earth (Isa 49:6). Here Jesus gives physical and spiritual light to the man-born-blind, a sign of the

---

5. Cf. Exod 33:22; 34:6; 1 Kgs 19:11ff.; Mark 6:47; Lane, *Mark*, 236.
6. Exod 3:4, 7.
7. Cf. Carson, *John*, 361–62; Lincoln, *John*, 280.
8. Cf. Ps 58:3; Str-B 2.527–29; Brown, *John I-XII*, 371; Beasley-Murray, *John*, 155.
9. See Motyer, *Your Father*, 80–82.
10. John 13:30 cf. Exod 12:29–31, where the destroying angel passed over at midnight.
11. Cf. John 18:3, 18; Luke 22:53, "this is your hour, and the power of darkness."

PART II—DETAILED EXEGETICAL EXAMINATION OF JOHN 5-10

NE. Importantly, Jesus had performed no sign at the "Jewish" Tabernacles celebration, but now, outside the Temple, he performs a sign that directly relates to Tabernacles, indicating that the locus of God's revelation has now changed.

Jesus heals the man, vv. 6–7

Jesus' *modus operandi* here is distinctly different from that which he used in healing the lame man. His use of mud, made from spittle, to anoint the blind man's eyes, probably alludes to the creation of man from the earth. "That which the artificer—the Word—had omitted to form in the womb he supplied in public."[12] In later rabbinic texts, the saliva of a firstborn son was thought to have healing properties.[13] If this concept is at all in mind, it may signify a recreation of man by virtue of God's firstborn Son, the Second Adam. To Jewish ears ἐπέχρισεν (smear/anoint) might be a reminder of the Messiah.

Importantly, Jesus commands the man to "Go wash in the pool of Siloam." This recalls Elisha's command to Naaman, to wash in the Jordan, which required an active demonstration of Naaman's faith that resulted in him being cleansed of leprosy and coming to acknowledge Israel's one true God.[14] That the man-born-blind had faith in Jesus is demonstrated by his instant unquestioning obedience to Jesus' command, "So he went and washed and came back seeing," v. 7.

The significance of the water of Siloam

Siloam was "living water," fed from the Gihon spring, conducted to the pool by a canal. Its significance goes back to OT times where, supplying water to Jerusalem, it became identified with David[15] and Yahweh, Israel's true King, who graciously provided for his people.[16] Moreover, it "stood for Jerusalem as the city of faith."[17] Thus when Jerusalem trusted in Assyria to destroy their enemies, rather than in God, Isaiah compared their trust to preference for the Euphrates over Siloam.[18] The former represented the visible might of Assyria, the latter, "insignificant water," the "Lord of the whole world . . . [who

---

12. Irenaeus *Haer.* 5:15:2, cited by Beasley-Murray, *John*, 155. Cf. Brown, *John I–XII*, 372; Gen 2:7; Job 4:19.

13. *b. Baba Bathra* 126b. Cf. Jesus' use of saliva in Mark 8:23; 7:33.

14. Cf. 2 Kgs 5:10–15; Beasley-Murray, *John*, 155; Keener, *John*, 781.

15. Motyer, *Isaiah*, 91. Motyer points out that the Gihon spring, from which the Shiloah waters came, symbolized David, "For it was at Gihon that the monarchy passed from David to his sons." Moreover, the waters "Stood for Jerusalem as the city of faith."

16. See Zimmerli, *Ezekiel 2*, 511. "By this quite unrepresentative, small amount of water there is meant . . . Yahweh who is enthroned on the height of the temple mount above these waters of Gihon."

17. Motyer, *Isaiah*, 91 cf. Ps 46:4.

18. Isa 8:6. Cf. Oswalt, *Isaiah 1–39*, 226.

is also the] hidden, real king."[19] God would judge Judah's disbelief by bringing Assyria's armies, like a flood that would cover Judah, rising up to Jerusalem. This disbelief is echoed here by the "Jewish" leader's perceptions of Jesus. Moreover, it resonates with the κρυπτός/παρρησία motif in John 7, where Jesus is the hidden Messiah.

In later Jewish thought, free flowing water from Siloam indicated God's blessing, especially in the messianic era, and a dry fountain indicated his wrath. At the Babylonian exile, Jeremiah "said" to Israel, "had you been worthy you would be dwelling in Jerusalem and drinking the waters of Shiloah (Siloam) whose waters are pure and sweet; but now that you are unworthy, you are exiled to Babylon and drink the waters of the Euphrates whose waters are impure and evil-smelling."[20] According to the sign of Isaiah, God "sent" him water from Siloam,[21] from which the rabbis derived their etymology. Seeking to ingratiate himself with Rome, Josephus noted that the waters of Siloam flowed copiously in Jerusalem for Titus, whereas in times past God dried up the waters for disobedient Israel.[22]

Further significance is found in the Tabernacles water ceremony: Siloam was the source of the water poured out beside the altar with the wine from the sacrifice, thought to flow from the temple and down through the rock for the world's healing.[23] Moreover, in a cultic sense, Siloam's "living waters" were revered as suitable for ritual purification and cleansing.[24] Grigsby believes the (John 9:7) washing in Siloam symbolized the believer's salvific "bath" in the "fountain of cleansing waters at Calvary."[25]

From the above, the John 9 washing can be seen as a development of the "living water" motif first introduced in John 4.[26] Christ is the new Temple from which will flow living water in the new age.[27] This water, referred to in John 7:37–39, flows from Jesus' side, after his glorification and death, when blood and water flowed from Jesus' body.[28] As Moses provided water by striking the rock, so Christ will provide rivers of living water by being pierced. John 9 develops this living water motif in three ways:

1. Siloam waters symbolically impart eternal life.[29] The blind man received spiri-

---

19. Zimmerli, *Ezekiel 2*, 511. Cf. Oswalt, *Isaiah 1–39*, 225, "What is mightiest seems least so in appearance . . . Those who trust in God must look deeper than appearance."

20. *Lam. Rab.* 19, in Freedman, 7:24.

21. According to the pseudepigraphal *Lives of the Prophets*, Isaiah, v. 2, God gave Isaiah the "sign of siloam." When he prayed for water when close to death, God miraculously sent him water from the fountain of Siloam. On the *Lives of the Prophets* see Young, "Relation of Isaiah," 219, n. 18.

22. Josephus *War* 5:409–10.

23. Cf. Ezek 47; *m. Sukkah* 4:9–10; Str-B 2.490–93.

24. This "water of expiation" (מֵי הַמָּאָה) is only effective because it is "living water." See rabbinic commentary on Numbers 19:1–22, *m. Parah* 3:2–3, 5:2, 8:8.

25. Grigsby, "Washing," 227–35.

26. So Grigsby, "Washing," 227–35.

27. Cf. Ezek 47:1–2; Zech 14:8; Joel 3:18; Isa 35:5–7.

28. John 19:34.

29. Cf. John 3:5, where one must be "born of water and the Spirit" to "enter the kingdom of God."

tual sight, passing from darkness and death to light and life, simply by obeying Christ's command to "go, wash." In the NE, the Servant would be "a light for the nations," that . . . [God's] salvation may reach to the end of the earth," Isa 49:6.

2. The water of Siloam symbolically cleansed from sin. The John 19:34–37 allusion to Zechariah's pierced one relates the water from Jesus' side to the "fountain . . . to cleanse . . . from sin and uncleanness," Zech 13:1. This is anticipated in Jesus' humiliation of John 13:1–20, where he washed the disciples' feet, rendering them clean and enabling them to be part of Christ's kingdom-Temple.[30]

3. The waters of Siloam are Messianic, dispensed through Christ who was "sent." That John intended this messianic significance is indicated by the evangelist's hermeneutic, "which means Sent" (John 9:7).[31]

Comparison with John 5

In the light of these conclusions, the difference between the two healings is sharpened. The Bethesda pool, like the ritual water of the six stone water-pots (John 2:6) and the water of the well that Jacob himself had dug (John 4:12–14), is ineffectual. It cannot impart eternal life. Moreover, though adjacent to water, the lame man had made no attempt to avail himself of that water in order to wash in it and be healed. Jesus' question, "Do you want to be healed?" suggests that he had given up all hope of a cure. Furthermore, though both signs are creative acts on the part of Jesus, the lame man was passive, taking up his bed and walking *after* Jesus had healed him (John 5:9). The blind man, however, has an active faith in Jesus' word, immediately obeying his command, "go, wash," and having believed and obeyed, he returns seeing.

The reaction of the neighbors, vv. 8–12

Amazed by the transformation, those who knew the man previously interrogate him, and this presents an opportunity for witness. The discussion as to his identity, "Is this not the man who used to sit and beg?" is not directly addressed to the man as one capable of speaking for himself, but neighbors discuss him in his presence. "He kept saying, 'I am the man,'" indicates his insistence on testifying to his experience. "Then how were your eyes opened?" is a leading question. Mention of *opened eyes* is made seven times in the narrative.[32] In terms of the sign, the man is a faithful witness of what took place, reporting how he was healed and (unlike the man of John 5) by whom—Jesus. However, the question goes deeper than the mere mechanics of what transpired:

---

30. Cf. Boismard "Lavement des Pieds," 8–10; Dunn, "Washing of the Disciple's Feet," 247–52; Brown, *John XIII-XXI*, 568.

31. Cf. Brown, *John I-XII*, 372, 381; Carson, *John*, 365.

32. Cf. John 9:10, 14, 17, 21, 26, 30, 32.

The Sabbath Healing of a Man-Born-Blind, John 9

"Your eyes will be opened," was promised to Adam and Eve by the serpent, prior to man's fall.[33] Obedience to his lie, however, brought spiritual darkness, slavery to sin, and death.[34] This spiritual blindness led the nations to commit idolatry, by which even Israel was seduced.[35] Indeed, called as God's witness in his lawsuit against the nations, Israel herself was indicted as being spiritually blind.[36] Nevertheless, God promised that the eyes of the blind would be opened and that this would be a sign of his coming to redeem his people.[37] Moreover, this divine prerogative of opening blind eyes (Ps 146:8) would be conferred upon God's Servant so that he might lead the "blind" from captivity in a NE.[38]

The fact that Jesus opened the blind mans eyes, something never previously accomplished, was thus a sign that God had come to redeem his people from spiritual bondage, sin, and death. Moreover, it marked Jesus out as God's Servant and God's Son, who mediates God's presence, works his divine works, and leads a NE. (It is interesting that Jesus' opening of blind eyes was the first of the signs to be reported to JBap to confirm Jesus' messianic identity, Matt 11:5; Luke 7:22). In the case of the blind man, not only was his physical sight restored, but he also received spiritual illumination. Thus he became part of the true Israel and a witness to God's new redemptive work, that would eclipse the Exodus, that God beforehand had said that he would do.[39] Here this witness, and that of those he represents, is directed to "the Jews" in God's lawsuit against them.

The question, "Where is he?" (Jesus) and the man's reply, "I do not know," v. 12, indicate that, as in John 5:13, Jesus has withdrawn. It may also remind the reader of Jesus' ability to elude his foes, going and coming as he chose to do.

The man-born-blind is tried before the Pharisees, John 9:13–34

Interrogation of the man, vv. 13–17

The neighbors lead the man before the Pharisees' synagogue court as a test case, particularly because "it was a Sabbath day when Jesus made the mud and opened his eyes," v. 14. Jesus' actions contravened "Jewish" Sabbath laws in several ways:[40]

1. The man's life was not in danger, and Jesus could have waited to heal him on another day.

---

33. Gen 3:5, 7.
34. Gen 3:8–19 cf. Rom 5:12–19.
35. Cf. Isa 44:9–20; Ps 115:4–8; Ps 135:15–18; 2 Kgs 17:7–12; Rom 1:21–23.
36. Cf. Isa 42:19–25; 43:8–21; 59:10.
37. Cf. Isa 35:5; 42:16; Ps 146:8.
38. Cf. Isa 42:6–7, 16.
39. Isa 43:16–19.
40. Cf. Brown, *John I–XII*, 373; Carson, *John*, 367.

2. Jesus had kneaded clay, one of the thirty-nine works forbidden on the Sabbath.[41]
3. According to later tradition it was not permitted to anoint the eye on the Sabbath.[42]

As custodians of the "Jewish" worship, the Pharisees question the man to find out for themselves exactly what happened. Interestingly, while reporting the incident, he relates the bare facts, but omits such details as Jesus' name, making the clay, and the anointing of his eyes, that might incriminate Jesus. This contrasts with John 5 where the lame man, seeking to protect himself, effectively blamed Jesus for breaking the Sabbath.

As the world's light, Jesus always divides people.[43] The Pharisees are no exception. The verdict, "this man is not from God," is based upon the view that Jesus has broken the Sabbath. Thus, like the False Prophet, he teaches rebellion against God, who brought Israel out of Egypt, and must not be believed, even though he performs miracles (Deut 13:1–5). Jesus himself predicts that false messiahs would show great signs and lead many astray (Matt 24:24). At the Exodus Pharaoh's magicians were able to imitate Aaron's miracles. There were some signs, however, that the magicians (not being able to replicate) declared to be "the finger of God" (Exod 8:19). The alternative verdict, "how can a man who is a sinner do such signs?" is an acknowledging of the unprecedented nature of Jesus' sign. Moreover, it tends to confirm for John's readers not only Jesus' divine mission, but also his sinlessness.

Unable to decide for themselves, the Pharisees ask the opinion of the man Jesus healed. "He is a prophet," v. 17, expresses his accurate, but as yet insufficient, view of Jesus' person.

Interrogation of his parents, vv. 18–23

The parents are called to testify because, unable to reconcile their view of Jesus as a sinner with his performance of an undeniable work of God, the Pharisees doubt the reality of the miracle. The parents' testimony, however, confirms the facts: their son was born blind, but now he sees, v. 21. They deny further knowledge of what transpired, directing their interrogators back to their son, because they fear the "Jewish" leaders, v. 22. Readers familiar with the Synoptics would be aware of Jesus' warning that families would be divided because of him.[44] Johannine believers would be aware of this first hand.

---

41. *m. Shabbath* 7:2.

42. See *b. Abodah Zarah* 28b. *y. Shabbath* 14d, 17–18, says that one must not put fasting spittle on the eyes on the Sabbath.

43. Cf. John 3:19–21; 7:43.

44. Matt 10:34–36.

The Sabbath Healing of a Man-Born-Blind, John 9

The threat of exclusion from the synagogue

Many scholars consider that confession of Jesus as the Christ and the decision to exclude those that made it from the synagogue (ἀποσυνάγωγος) is anachronistic, and thus evidence of a "two level drama," *read back* into Jesus' ministry.[45] Certainly this incident would have a considerable bearing upon Johannine Christians, but there are important reasons for upholding its authenticity in the present setting. Since "messianic fever was in the air,"[46] it is hardly surprising that some people speculated that Jesus was the Christ. As we have seen, there was much speculation about Jesus' identity at Tabernacles.[47] Moreover, the authorities clearly feared losing control.[48] Thus it seems inconceivable that, along with their determined efforts to destroy Jesus, they would not have also decided upon measures, such as exclusion, to preserve their position of authority. Schürer argues that, from the days of Ezra,

> The strict infliction of this punishment [exclusion] was nothing less than vital to post-exilic Judaism . . . the Jewish communities could only preserve themselves by constantly and carefully eliminating alien elements . . . by way of community discipline.[49]

As to the exclusion itself, later rabbinic categories seem not exactly to fit what is described here; the most severe, *herem*, seems not to have excluded people from religious duties.[50] Nevertheless, we cannot be sure about first century synagogue legislation.[51] Moreover, it is not impossible that this was a desperate *ad hoc* measure, possibly local, brought in to avert a potential crisis. Certainly the authorities later employed such measures sporadically from the earliest history of the Church.[52]

The man-born-blind is recalled and cast out, vv. 24–34

Having been unable to disprove the sign, the Pharisees seek to make the man-born-blind a witness against himself and Jesus. "Give glory to God (Δὸς δόξαν τῷ θεῷ)" echoes Joshua 7:19, where Achan, having brought a curse upon Israel, was exhorted

---

45. Cf. Martyn, *History and Theology*, 24ff.; Barrett, *John*, 361–62; Lincoln, *John*, 284.
46. Carson, *John*, 372.
47. Cf. John 7:26–27; 31; 41–42.
48. Cf. John 11:47–48; 12:19.
49. Schürer, *History of the Jewish people*, 2:431. Cf. Ezra 10:8.
50. Cf. *m. Middoth* 2.2; Carson, *John*, 370; Brown, *John I–XII*, 374.
51. So Brown, *John I–XII*, 374. Cf. Carson, *John*, 371.
52. Cf. Robinson, *Priority*, 80–81, and the passages cited there; idem, *Redating*, 273. "The word describing the action in John 9:34f., ἐκβάλλειν to throw out, is so common as to be used in similar circumstances of Jesus himself (Luke 4:29), Stephen (Acts 7.58), Paul (Acts 13.50), and of Christians by other Christians (III John 10)." Cf. Hengel, *Question*, 114–15; idem, *Between Jesus and Paul*, 1–29, 133–56. Cf. John 16:2; Luke 6:22; 12:11; Matt 10:17ff.

to confess his sin.[53] The confident assertion, "we know that this man is a sinner," v. 24, made by the authorities, puts pressure on the man in an attempt to bully him into submission to their judgement. John's readers are aware, however, that these authorities have been perplexed and divided by Jesus' sign.

The man-born-blind does indeed "give glory to God," but by boldly standing his ground rather than making confession of guilt. Thus, rather than being intimidated into accepting their verdict, as an ideal witness he reports just what he knows, "though I was blind, now I see." They have no answer to his testimony, but can only proceed to probe further. He, however, perceives the true reason for their obduracy; he has already told them, but they "would not listen," v. 27. This echoes God's word through Isaiah: "keep on hearing, but do not understand; keep on seeing but do not perceive."[54] "Do you also want to become his disciples?" is ironic. The man knows that this is the furthest thing from their minds; it indicates, however, his own bold commitment to Jesus.

The lines are now drawn. "You are his disciple, but we are disciples of Moses," v. 28, goes to the heart of the conflict. Whereas the man is committed to Jesus, the Pharisees are committed to Moses and the Torah. "We know that God has spoken to Moses" refers to the OC given at Sinai. Ironically, as the reader will understand, they do not listen to Moses, who spoke of Jesus as the one to whom they must listen.[55] Moreover, failure to keep the OC led Israel into exile and bondage. As we have seen, these "Jews" are in bondage to sin.[56] "As for this . . . [fellow], we do not know where he comes from," v. 29, contradicts what they had previously said about knowing that Jesus is a sinner. Moreover, it reinforces Jesus' earlier teaching that they do not know either him or his Father (John 8:19).

The "Jewish" leaders have ridiculed the man-born-blind for his commitment to Jesus, but now, though humble, he puts these teachers of the law to shame by pointing out their wilful ignorance: it is amazing that they do not know where Jesus is from and yet he opened the man's eyes. He, however, knows that Jesus is from God, because God only hears those who do his will, not sinners.[57] Moreover, since the world began, no one has opened the eyes of the blind, v. 32. This reinforces the nature of Jesus' sign and mission, pointing to the Lord's return to Zion and his initiation of a NE from bondage. It also indicates that a humble believer in Jesus can attain a greater understanding of the truth than learned teachers of the law.

The "Jewish" authorities have no answer to the man, apart from accusing him of being completely born in sin (because of his congenital blindness), upbraiding him for lecturing them, and excluding him from the synagogue.

---

53. Cf. Brown, *John I–XII*, 374; Bruce, *John*, 216; Keener, *John*, 790.
54. Isa 6:9–10, cited in John 12:40.
55. Deut 18:15–19. See above on John 5:45–47.
56. See above on John 8:34.
57. John 9:30–31. Cf. Ps 66:18; Isa 1:15–17.

The Sabbath Healing of a Man-Born-Blind, John 9

An echo of Isa 66:5

"They cast him out," together with, "give glory to God," echoes,

> Hear the word of the LORD, you who tremble at his word: "Your brothers who hate you and *cast you out* for my name's sake have said, '*Let the LORD be glorified* . . .'; but it is they who shall be put to shame." Isaiah 66:5 (emphases mine).

The return from exile context, foreseen by Isaiah, is particularly appropriate: Those who fear God's word would be cast out of the worshipping community by their own leaders and religious authorities.[58] The outcasts, generally not the powerful, are those who seek to keep God's covenant from the heart, who treat the poor with equity, observe the Sabbath, and keep the divine ordinances as God has prescribed. Those who cast them out are the wealthy, priests, and nobles, whose major concern is their own aggrandizement. Though they want to appear to be religious, they are embarrassed by, and scornful of, their rustic brethren who exhibit true religious zeal.[59] Pinning their hopes upon cult practices, they do not understand that God does not require the ostentatious Temple they seek to build and that their sacrifices are detestable.[60] It is *they* who will be put to shame while the outcasts will enjoy the New Jerusalem (Isa 66:5–14). Oswalt cites Luke 6:22 and John 16:2, "they will put you out of the synagogues," as examples of the way this behavior would later be experienced by the apostles.[61]

He worships Jesus outside the synagogue, John 9:35–41

Exclusion meant that the man-born-blind was cut off from his brethren. However, Jesus, the "Good Shepherd," finds him, outside the synagogue. "Do you believe in the Son of Man?" is used to further instruct the man and to elicit his confession. In Johannine context, Son of Man has connotations of the Danielic Son of Man and Second Adam, who suffers and is lifted up for his people, inherits the Davidic kingdom, and judges on the last day.[62] Willing to believe, the man asks Jesus to whom he is referring. By his reply, "You have seen him, and it is he who is speaking to you," reminiscent of John 4:26, Jesus discloses his identity to the man. "You have seen him" implies spiritual as well as physical sight. The man acknowledges his faith in Jesus by his words, "Lord, I believe," and by his actions, worshipping Jesus. Unlike the lame man, who adhered to the Temple community under the "Jewish" authorities, the man-born-blind finds worship in Spirit and truth, outside the Temple.

---

58. Blenkinsopp, *Isaiah 56–66*, 299. Cf. Delitzsch, *Isaiah 28–66*, 498.
59. See Oswalt, *Isaiah 40–66*, 670.
60. Isaiah 66:1–2. Cf. Delitzsch, *Isaiah 28–66*, 496–97; Oswalt, *Isaiah 40–66*, 670.
61. Oswalt, *Isaiah 40–66*, 670.
62. See above on John 5.

Jesus sums up this incident with his words, "For judgement I came into this world, that those who do not see may see, and those who see may become blind." Alluding to Isa 6:10, and to such NE promises as Isa 42:16, his language indicates the division his mission brings: spiritual illumination of the blind coupled with judicial blinding of those who claim to see. To the Pharisees' question "Are we also blind?" Jesus responds by pointing out their culpability: If they truly were blind they would be innocent, but because they see their guilt remains, v. 41. Like the wicked tenants in the parable of the vineyard (Matt 21:33–41), they not only recognize the heir, but also seek to kill him.

Conclusion

In John 9, Jesus begins to fulfil the symbolism of Tabernacles outside the second Temple and the Synagogue. He is the light of the world, the one who imparts living water to the thirsty. He is leading his true people in a NE away from the earthly Jerusalem with its Temple to the heavenly Jerusalem and the Temple of his Father's house.

John 9 also forms the second part of a two-part theodicy, concerning the destruction of the Temple, where the man-born-blind represents those Israelites who, called out of "exile"[63] by Jesus, follow him to find true worship outside the Second Temple and synagogue in Jesus' new Temple and new worshipping community. Absolved from guilt, they receive spiritual sight and forgiveness of sins and become witnesses of the return of the Lord to his people and the dawn of the NE. As a consequence, they suffer exclusion by their unbelieving "Jewish" brethren who persist in spiritual blindness and cause division within families. Nevertheless, they escape the judgement brought upon Jerusalem and its Temple, the responsibility for which falls upon the shoulders of the "Jewish" authorities who wilfully resisted the claims of God's Son.

The loss of the earthly (Second) Temple is not the end, because, in Jesus, God had already begun to withdraw from it. Indeed, Jesus is the new Temple and the new locus of God's revelation, from whom flows living waters and forgiveness of sins that will heal the land. He calls people out of the old institutions, enslaved by the "Jews," to himself, the reality to which they point, to follow him in a NE. The obedient believing response to Jesus, demonstrated by the man-born-blind, is the example that we all must follow.

---

63. See my discussion above.

12

Episode 4 Discourse
The Good Shepherd, John 10:1–21

FOLLOWING ON FROM JESUS' words of John 9:41, John 10:1–21 concludes the fourth Festival Cycle episode.[1] As such, Jesus' discourse, contained therein, directly relates to the John 9 narrative where Jesus heals the man-born-blind. Moreover, like John 9, it falls under the Tabernacles rubric. John 10:22–42 is a separate episode that takes place some three months later, at the Feast of Dedication. John has juxtaposed it with the Tabernacles episode because of the parallels between Dedication and Tabernacles and because of the thematic parallels between Jesus' discourses on each of these occasions.[2]

Although the Tabernacles background to this episode has been investigated, it is necessary to revisit one particular aspect of the feast, emphasized here: Yahweh as the Shepherd-King of Israel, his universal enthronement, and his relationship to his sacral king and under-shepherd.

THE SACRAL KINGSHIP BACKGROUND

Sacral kingship in the Ancient Near East

From Sumerian times, the ANE nations thought of their rulers as shepherds. Thus the Sumerian King List speaks of monarchs as "shepherds."[3] In fact, the god was viewed as the king (shepherd), who ruled over the city-state, the temple was his manor house, and the king-priest his representative.[4] The Babylonians and Egyptians also perceived their kings to be shepherds of the people, chosen by the gods to bring salvation.[5] Again their gods were often given the title and function of shepherds. Thus the Babylonian god Marduk was said to "exercise shepherdship over mankind"[6] and the Egyptian god Osiris

---

1. See Dodd, *IFG*, 354–57, for whom John 9:1–10:21 is a complete episode.
2. Cf. the similar juxtaposition of, and thematic parallels between, John 3:1–21 and John 3:22–36.
3. Cf. *ANET*, 265; Jacobson, *Sumerian King List*, 72–73, 80–81; Block, *Ezekiel 25–48*, 280.
4. Bright, *History of Israel*, 34.
5. Block, *Ezekiel 25–48*, 280–81.
6. See *Enuma Elish* 6:107, cited in Beale, *Temple*, 91.

PART II—DETAILED EXEGETICAL EXAMINATION OF JOHN 5-10

was thought to protect his subjects "as a shepherd tends his flock."[7] The king, the "*living image of the god*,"[8] was usually responsible for building the god's temple and serving him as priest. As the god's representative his function included gathering the dispersed, ruling justly, and caring for the weak.[9] Indeed, Babylonian and Egyptian proverbs liken a people without a king to "sheep without a shepherd."[10]

Sacral kingship in the OT

Though uniquely monotheistic, some of these ANE concepts are present in the OT as "embedded in the living piety of Israel."[11] As Beale argues, this correspondence is probably due, in part, to the collective human memory of the way things were "from the beginning."[12] As time progressed, for those outside of the covenant, this memory became "dim," their understanding was "darkened," and they "exchanged the glory of the immortal God for images resembling mortal man and birds and animals and reptiles" (Rom 1:21–23). Israel preserved the knowledge of God, however, having access to his special revelation. Moreover, "Israel intentionally alluded to facets of the pagan religion surrounding them," for polemical purposes,[13] to show that the Lord is the one true God, and "all the gods of the peoples are worthless idols" (Ps 96:5).

For Israel, Yahweh is Israel's Shepherd, they are his sheep,[14] and he appoints under-shepherds to oversee them.[15] Some have postulated that prophets and priests in general were designated "shepherds,"[16] but it is likely that the term only applied to rulers.[17] Sacral kingship, depicted and rooted in creation, would be the ultimate development (Zech 6:11–13), with a priest-king reigning throughout a worldwide Temple (Zech 14:20–21 cf. Hab 2:14):

---

7. Jeremias, "ποιμήν," 486.

8. Beale, *Temple*, 89 (emphasis original).

9. Jeremias, "ποιμήν," 486.

10. Block, *Ezekiel 25–48*, 281, citing Lambert, *Babylonian Wisdom Literature*, 229, 232. These words are remarkably similar to Num 27:17 and 1 Kgs 22:17. Cf. Mark 6:34.

11. Jeremias, "ποιμήν," 487.

12. See Beale, *Temple*, 29–30.

13. Ibid., 29–30. Beale cites Ps 29 as an example of this.

14. Cf. Gen 49:24; Ps 23; 78:52 79:13; 80:1; 95:7; 100:3.

15. These include Moses and (possibly) Aaron (cf. Ps 77:20; Num 33:1; 1 Sam 12:6), Joshua (Num 27:17), David (1 Chr 11:2–3), and David's seed (cf. 2 Sam 7:12–13; Jer 3:15; Mic 5:4).

16. So Calvin, *Jeremiah and Lamentations*, 1:181.

17. Cf. Hengstenberg, *Christology*, 643; Block, *Ezekiel 25–48*, 281.

At Creation

Yahweh is universal King by virtue of his work of creation.[18] Adam, God's "son" (Luke 3:38), bore the image of God and (in covenant relationship with God) acted as God's sacral king and prophet. As a king, Adam ruled, under God, over all creation (Gen 1:28). As a prophet, he was custodian of God's word. Moreover, he named the animals for God, designating each according to its characteristic (Gen 2:19). As a priest, in communion with God, he was given the task of cultivating (עָבַד) and keeping (שָׁמַר) the (temple[19]) garden, words used elsewhere of priests and Levites who *serve* in the Tabernacle or the Temple and who *guard and keep* the Tabernacle or Temple gates from intruders and anyone unclean.[20] In Gen 3:24, שָׁמַר is used to describe the cherubs who guarded the way to the tree of life.[21]

Adam failed in his priestly covenant duty to guard the temple garden from the entrance of sin. Being tempted by the serpent, both Adam and Eve transgressed God's commandment and, as a result, came under his judgement. This involved death, the curse, and expulsion from the garden. Nevertheless, God promised redemption for mankind in terms of one who would subdue the Serpent, crushing its head. Genesis 3:15 anticipates a special line (running through Genesis) leading to an Abrahamic dynasty, which would defeat its enemies and bring God's blessing to all nations.[22]

Under Moses

At Sinai, the formal application of Yahweh's kingship over Israel followed the suzerainty king-vassal treaty pattern.[23] Thus, having delivered the nation from Egyptian slavery, God covenanted to be their God and Israel to be his people and royal priesthood. Moses had previously been appointed as God's under-shepherd on the holy ground of the mountain of God and charged with delivering the people that he might return there with them to serve (עָבַד) God. Effectively Sinai became a temple-mountain, the summit representing the holy of holies where Moses, as a priest and as God's under-shepherd, met with God.[24] It was upon Sinai that Moses received both the law of God and the heavenly pattern for the Tabernacle. The latter would be God's dwelling place which, like a war tent, would accompany his people as they advanced

---

18. Cf. Pss 93–100.

19. On the garden as a Temple see Beale, *Temple*, 81–86.

20. Gen 2:15. Cf. Num 3:7–8; 4:23–24, 26; 8:25–26; 18:5–6; 1:53; 3:7–8; 1 Chr 23:32; Ezek 44:14; Wenham, *Genesis 1–15*, 67; Beale, *Temple*, 67; *Tg. Neof.* Gen 2:15; *Tg. Ps.-J.* Gen 2:15.

21. See Hamilton, *Genesis 1–17*, 171.

22. Gen 22:17–18. Cf. Alexander, "Messianic Ideology," 31.

23. See Bright, *History of Israel*, 150ff.

24. On Sinai as a temple-mountain see Beale, *Temple*,105. He cites Philo *Mos.* 2:75. Cf. Exod 19:12, 22–23; 24:1–2.

towards the new Eden of the Promised Land, and the place that God would choose for his Temple-dwelling.[25]

It is noteworthy that Moses acted both as Israel's shepherd, ruling and guiding the people according to God's law, and its priest, responsible for the Tabernacle and its sacrifice,[26] enjoying unique access to God, and making intercession for the people. Nevertheless, the duties of under-shepherd and priest were divided between Moses and his successors (Num 27:16–17) and Aaron and his sons respectively (Exod 28:1). This arrangement would continue under an envisaged monarchy.[27]

Rise of the Monarchy

Israel's desire to make a king was rebellion, not in itself (Deut 17:15), but because of their motivation, replacing trust in God with reliance upon an earthly monarch,[28] and because of the king they desired, "like the nations."[29] Saul was a concession to the will of the people and David, a man "after his [God's] own heart," 1 Sam 13:14, was the king that God always intended to shepherd his people (Ps 78:70–72). Block notes that, despite the fact that "the scepter shall not depart from Judah," Gen 49:10, Saul was a Benjamite.[30] Moreover, "The entire narrative of Saul's rise and reign is composed in ironical and farcical terms to serve as a foil against which to present David as Yahweh's anointed."[31]

Under David

David was regarded (typically) as Yahweh's son and "firstborn."[32] In this sense he was the "living image" of God. Moreover, in Ps 110, he prophetically declared his messianic descendant to be "a priest forever after the order of Melchizedek."[33] It is thought that the *Sitz im Leben* of this messianic psalm may have been the celebration

---

25. Cf. Deut 12:11; 16:11.

26. Cf. Exod 24:8ff.; 25:8–9; 26:1.

27. Anticipated in Num 24:17 cf. Deut 17:14–20; 28:36. The Priest would enquire of God for the king (Num 27:21 cf. 1 Sam 28:6) and the king would shepherd the people according to the Torah (Deut 17:18ff.). Cf. 2 Chr 26:16–18; 1 Sam 13:8ff. But cf. Hays, "If he looks like a Prophet," 67. See Kraus, *Psalms 60–150*, 351.

28. Cf. 1 Sam 8:7–8; 12:6–15.

29. Cf. 1 Sam 8:5, 10–20; Deut 17:14. See John 6:15, 26–27, where the people were culpable, not because they desired to make Jesus king, but because of their wrong motives and wrong conception of his kingship.

30. Block, "My Servant David," 38, n. 78.

31. Ibid., 78–79.

32. Cf. Ps 2:7; Ps 89:27, "I will make him the firstborn, the highest of the kings of the earth"; Zech 12:10.

33. Ps 110:4 cf. Matt 22:42–45. See Heb 5:5–6, which connects priesthood and sonship. Cf. Attridge, *Hebrews*, 145.

of the capture of Jerusalem and David's succession to the Jebusite king.[34] Since Jerusalem was probably the Salem of Gen 14:18, some scholars think that David inherited Melchizedek's priesthood[35] by covenant grant.[36] David's royal priesthood seems to be confirmed by his priestly actions,[37] in particular in connection with his bringing the ark to Jerusalem[38] and his desire to build God's House. David's intercession and vicarious self-offering for the people (sheep), invoking God's wrath against himself and his house, in a similar manner to Moses,[39] followed by his building an altar on the site of the future Temple,[40] may have been his supreme act as priest. The royal priesthood passed to David's sons,[41] in particular to Solomon, who offered sacrifices and built the Temple. David, himself a priest-king, was promised a greater son and priest-king, whose worldwide dominion would last forever[42] and whose dynasty would be the charter for mankind.[43]

The Divided Kingdom

Under Jeroboam I, the ten tribes of the Northern Kingdom defected from Davidic rule and from Yahweh.[44] "Not My People," Hos 1:9, they were taken into captivity and scattered. The Davidic dynasty continued in Judah, until the Babylonian captivity of 587 B.C. Though God "put away" his people at the exile, expelling them from the land, as Adam had been expelled from the garden-temple,[45] he did not totally forsake them, but promised to make a new covenant with the house of Israel and the house of Judah.[46] Indeed, the "Old" covenant provided for the eventuality of restoration after rebellion. Moreover, God's promises to David (2 Sam 7:12–16) that of his seed he would raise up a prophet-priest-king Messiah who would shepherd his people Israel would be fulfilled.

---

34. Cf. Allen, *Psalms 101–150*, 84–85; Merrill, "Royal Priesthood," 60ff.

35. He was "priest of God Most High," Gen 14:18.

36. Cf. Weinfeld, "Covenant of Grant," 185; Mowinckel, *Psalms*, 1:64; Gen 14:18–20, 22.

37. Cf. Kraus, *Psalms 60–150*, 351; Mowinckel, *Psalms*, 1:61.

38. See Merrill, "Royal Priesthood," 60 ff.

39. See *Mek. Exod.* 12:1, where David's intercession in 2 Sam 24:7 is compared to Moses' request, "blot me out of your book," Exod 32:32.

40. 2 Sam 24:17ff.

41. 1 Chron 18:17. Cf. Armerding, "David's Sons," 85–86; McComiskey, *Covenants of Promise*, 11, 21–25.

42. 2 Sam 7:13. Cf. Ps 72:5, 8, 11; 89:4, 19–37; 110:1–7.

43. 2 Sam 7:19. Cf. Block, "My Servant David," 39, 40, n. 83; Kaiser, *Messiah in the Old Testament*, 78–83.

44. 1 Kgs 12:16ff.

45. Cf. Wright, *RSG*, 92; Beale, *Temple*, 78; *Gen. Rab.* 21:8.

46. Jer 31:31ff.

PART II—DETAILED EXEGETICAL EXAMINATION OF JOHN 5-10

The Shepherd and the New Exodus in the OT

Deuteronomy

Envisaging Israel's rebellion, the Deuteronomic covenant uses shepherd imagery to speak of a NE, which became the basis of later prophecies. Thus, if Israel served other gods, the Lord would *scatter* them among the nations, but, if she repented and obeyed the Lord's *voice*, he would *gather* her outcasts and restore them to their land where they would again enjoy Edenic blessing. Moreover, he would circumcise their hearts so that they might love the Lord their God and live (Deut 30:1-6).

Isaiah

Contrary to its fragmentation in much recent scholarship, the book of Isaiah is a literary and theological unity, the work of Isaiah the prophet of Jerusalem, stemming from the reigns of Uzziah, Jotham, Ahaz, and Hezekiah, kings of Judah.[47] Nevertheless, Isaiah can be generally divided into three parts, according to the various situations that the prophet addresses.

Isaiah 1-39

In Isa 1-39, the nation has turned from God and Isaiah warns of coming judgement. Judah would be delivered from Syrian-Ephraim aggression (Isa 7:1-2) and even from the might of the Assyrian invasion (Isa 36:1-2), but ultimately the Davidic dynasty would be cut off and, because of its apostasy, the nation would go into Babylonian captivity. Nevertheless, mercy is promised in terms of a faithful remnant that would return to the Land and by way of the "rod of Jesse" who will rebuild the Davidic kingdom (Isa 11).

Isaiah 11:1—12:6 is one of the most important NE passages in connection with the Shepherd and the NE. Its tradition is taken up in Jer 23:1-6, which became the basis of Ezek 34, which in turn was elaborated in Zech 11.[48] Moreover, its shepherd imagery echoes Deut 30:1-6. Thus, "the Lord will extend his hand yet a second time to recover the remnant that remains of his people . . . and will *assemble* the banished of Israel, and *gather* the *dispersed* of Judah from the four corners of the earth."[49] The context is the apostasy of the house of David where Ahaz has turned away from God

---

47. On the unity of Isaiah, cf. Allis, *Unity*; Oswalt, *Isaiah 1-39*, 23-29, 44-46; Motyer, *Isaiah*, 25-30. Motyer notes that the fragmentation of Isaiah stems from "nineteenth-century rationalism."

48. Cf. also the allusions in Zech 3:8-10; 6:12-15. See below. Motyer, *Isaiah*, 14-16, notes that the Servant of Isa 40-55 and the Conqueror of Isa 56-66 are modified portraits of the same Davidic Messiah. Note the parallels with the Servant: He is a shoot/root Isa 11:1 cf. Isa 53:2; the Spirit of the Lord is upon him Isa 11:1 cf. Isa 61:1; his weapon is the rod/sword of his mouth, Isa 11:4 cf. Isa 49:2; Rev 1:16. Cf. Beale, *Use of Daniel*, 157.

49. Isa 11:11-12 (emphasis mine).

The Good Shepherd, John 10:1-21

and Judah's leaders cause the people to be destroyed (Isa 9:16). Moreover, Ephraim is confederate with Syria against Judah. But the Lord is judging his people, bringing the Assyrians, who like Egypt will lift up their staff against them (Isa 10:24). The northern kingdom will be destroyed and only a remnant of Judah will survive.[50] Though David's house will be cut off, however, Assyria in turn will be punished, and the Lord will cause the messianic Davidic branch (promised in Isa 7:14 and 9:1–6[51]) to reign. He will usher in universal righteousness, protect the poor and needy, and smite the wicked with the rod of his mouth.[52] His reign will usher in paradisal conditions and, in connection with God's holy temple-mountain, "the earth will be full of the knowledge of the LORD as the waters cover the sea," Isa 11:9.

The exaltation of this messianic King will be the signal to the nations for the NE, which the Lord himself will effect, *gathering* his people from all the earth. As at the Exodus, God will subdue Israel's enemies, destroy the tongue of the Egyptian Sea, and wave his hand over the river, leading his people across dry-shod, casting up a highway for their return. Moreover, in Zion God's people will celebrate an eschatological feast of Tabernacles with great joy (Isa 12:3).

Isaiah 2:1–5 is important as the ultimate goal of the NE, the eschatological Jerusalem temple-mountain, "the mountain of the house of the LORD," Isa 2:2, which grows to fills the whole world with God's glory.[53] Rising to become the highest of all the mountains, the Lord's word will go forth from Zion, and all nations will flow to it. Thus it envisages Yahweh's universal reign of righteousness and peace. Although not explicitly connected to the Shepherd and the NE, it is connected thematically with Isa 11:1—12:6 in terms of universal peace and justice,[54] universal knowledge of the Lord, and God's dwelling in Zion among his people. Moreover, the parallel vision in Micah *does* make NE connections since "in that day" the Lord will *assemble* the lame and *gather* those he had driven away, making them a strong nation, and reigning over them in Zion (Mic 4:1–7).

A similar concept is found in Isa 4:3–6 where the whole of latter-day Jerusalem will be covered with God's glory, manifest as the pillar of cloud by day and of fire by night that overshadowed the Exodus Tabernacle (Exod 13:21).

---

50. Cf. Isa 8:5–8; 10:20–22.

51. Cf. Oswalt, *Isaiah 1–39*, 277. Many scholars interpret such passages in terms of an ideal king. Indeed, some think that Hezekiah, Ahaz's son, is "Isaiah's first Messiah," intended in Isa 7:14. However, the promised restoration of paradise goes beyond historical expectations. Cf. Schribler, "Messianism," 87–104. See Stenning, *Targum of Isaiah*, 38, where the passage is referred to "Messiah."

52. Isa 11:4 cf. Isa 49:2; Rev 1:16.

53. Isa 2:2–3. Cf. Beale, *Temple*, 147; Dan 2:35.

54. Cf. Isa 2:3–4; 11:2–4, 9; 12:6.

PART II—DETAILED EXEGETICAL EXAMINATION OF JOHN 5-10

Isaiah 40-55

Here the context has changed and Isaiah foresees and addresses the situation of Israel in Babylonian captivity. The unit begins with a message of comfort: War is over, sin has been paid for and pardoned, and a highway is to be cast up[55] for the return of the Lord to Zion. The Lord himself as Shepherd will bring his exiles home[56] and will do so by destroying Babylon through Cyrus.[57] However, the people cavil at God's choice of a Persian king, their persistent "blindness and deafness," a consequence of idolatry,[58] leading them to reject his announcement of deliverance. Disobedience and unbelief lead to the postponement of the NE glory.[59] Nevertheless, an obedient Suffering Servant Israel is introduced, who will bring about NE fulfilment.[60]

In Isa 42:1-7, the Servant is given as "a covenant for the people, a light for the nations," to open blind eyes, and to bring out prisoners from the dungeon and darkness.[61] In Isa 49:8-13, the Lord appoints the Servant as Shepherd. He proclaims release to the captives (those in darkness),[62] and guides them back to their restored land. They neither hunger nor thirst,[63] for he leads them by springs of water, pastures them on the barren heights,[64] and protects them from wind and sun. Moreover, they come, not just from Babylon, but from every corner of the earth. In Isa 52:13—53:12, Israel is compared to sheep that have strayed. But the Servant, "like a lamb that is led to the slaughter" (Isa 53:7), bears their iniquities (Isa 53:11), being made a paschal sin offering. The Servant is thus a shepherd (and firstborn) who lays down his life for the sheep. Moreover, "when his soul makes an offering for sin, he shall see his offspring; he shall prolong his days," Isa 53:10, suggests his resurrection.

The Servant's identity has been the subject of much debate,[65] but in view of his shepherd function and royal overtones it is suggested that this is the Davidic Messiah of Isaiah 11, recast as Suffering Servant.[66] Bruce notes that the king was the one person who could sacrifice his own life in order to bear the nation's sin.

---

55. Isa 40:10-11 cf. 11:16; 35:8.
56. Isa 41:1—44:22.
57. Isa 44:23—47:15.
58. Watts, "Consolation," 44-45.
59. Ibid., 31.
60. Ibid., 54-55.
61. Cf. Ringe, *Biblical Jubilee*, 30; Isa 42:6-7, 20.
62. Cf. John 8:12ff.
63. Cf. John 4:14; 6:35; 7:37-38.
64. See above on John 6.
65. Suggestions include Moses or David *redivivus*, Isaiah, and the nation of Israel. Cf. the literature cited by Hugenberger, "Servant of the Lord," 105-140, esp. 106, n. 2.
66. Cf. Motyer, *Isaiah*, 13-16.

In ancient societies with a sacral kingship this was especially true; the king was not only his people's representative before God and men but was a representative of God to his people—in Israel, Yahweh's anointed one.[67]

As well as being a priest-king, however, like David, the Servant is also a prophet, declaring God's law to the nations (Isa 42:4). He is thus a Second Adam, undoing the fall that came through Adam the First, summing up a new humanity in himself.

In Isaiah 54, as a direct result of the Servant's sacrifice, Israel is restored to her own land and received back into new covenant relationship with the Lord. Moreover, she is to enlarge the place of her tabernacle, stretch out her curtains, and lengthen her cords, because she will *spread out* in all directions and her *seed* will possess the nations.

Isaiah 56–66

In Isa 56–66, in denouncing idolatry and child sacrifice, Isaiah speaks to the situation of his own day.[68] Nevertheless, in this third part of the book (at least in part) the prophet also foresees and addresses the situation following the return from exile, in terms of the rebuilding of the ruins and the rebuilding of the second Temple. The message is that the remnant of God's true people must remain faithful to him, keep his Sabbaths, obey his law, and wait for his salvation and the revelation of his righteousness.

Isaiah 56:8–12 addresses the situation of returnees,[69] their disappointment, and continuing rebellion. It promises mercy to the outcasts,[70] but castigates Israel's leaders as blind watchmen, dumb dogs, and undiscerning shepherds.[71] They want to build an ostentatious Temple (Isa 66:1), but do not understand that the Lord fills heaven and earth. Thus he rejects them, showing respect to the contrite who fear his word. Ultimately, Zion's birth-pangs will give way to a new heaven and earth, where the nations flow to the Jerusalem mountain-Temple and God takes some of them to serve him as priests and Levites (Isa 66:9–24).

Micah

Micah 2:12–13 speaks of the survival of the remnant. The Lord says,

> I will surely assemble all of you, O Jacob; I will gather the remnant of Israel;
> I will set them together like sheep in a fold, like a flock in its pasture, a noisy

---

67. Bruce, *Old Testament Themes*, 89.
68. See e.g. Isa 57:3–13; 65:2–5. See Motyer, *Isaiah*, 26.
69. See Watts, "Consolation," 31–32.
70. "The Lord GOD, who *gathers* the outcasts [eunuchs and foreigners] . . . will *gather* yet *others*," cf. John 10:16.
71. See Oswalt, *Isaiah 40–66*, 469. The threefold imagery suggests prophets, priests, and kings. Cf. "Priests, shepherds and prophets," Jer 2:8. It is interesting that, in John 9:39–41, the Pharisees were "blind."

multitude of men. He who opens the breach goes up before them; they break through and pass the gate, going out by it. Their king passes on before them, the LORD at their head.

Though many scholars think that the oracle refers to Israel's salvation from the Babylonian captivity, both Allen and Waltke interpret it as a reference to Jerusalem's deliverance from Sennacherib's blockade.[72] The *gate* is the gate of Jerusalem, the city from which the remnant are delivered. The release occurs in three stages:

1. The Shepherd-king breaks open the blockaded gate.
2. The sheep (people) pass through it in triumph.
3. The king takes his rightful position at their head.[73]

In Micah 3:1–4, God addresses Israel's rulers as those who "tear the skin from off my people and their flesh from off their bones, who eat the flesh of my people, and flay their skin . . . and break their bones . . . and chop them up like meat in a pot." The imagery suggests sheep killed for food. In Mic 5:1–6, however, a coming messianic shepherd-King, of David's line, born in Bethlehem,[74] "whose origin is from of old, from ancient days," will shepherd his flock and rule to the ends of the earth. In Micah 7:14–18, as at the Exodus, the Lord will "show . . . marvelous things," pardoning, *passing over*, and removing the people's sin.[75] Micah 4:1–7 shares the identical NE goal of Isa 2:1–5.

Jeremiah

The Lord will *scatter* his rebellious people among the nations and send a sword after them. Because they have broken the covenant which the Lord made with them when he brought them out of Egypt, and they have not *heard his voice*, the covenant curses will come upon them.[76] Responsibility lies with their shepherds who "destroy and scatter the sheep of my pasture," driving them away and not visiting them.[77] Nevertheless, Yahweh declares,

> I will gather the remnant of my flock out of all the countries where I have driven them, and I will bring them back to their fold, and they shall be fruitful

---

72. Cf. Allen, "Micah," 242–43; Waltke, "Micah," 652; 2 Kgs 19:31.

73. See Waltke, "Micah," 654, who compares this deliverance to that of the Exodus.

74. Cf. Matt 2:1–6.

75. Mic 7:14, 18. Cf. the Lord's passing over his people in mercy at the Exodus, Exod 12:13, 23, and at the cross, Rom 3:25; 1 Cor 5:7.

76. Cf. Jer 9:16; 11:1ff.

77. Jer 23:1–8 cf. Jer 10:21; 12:10; 50:6. Thompson, *Jeremiah*, 733, thinks that Jer 50:6 refers to "leaders, kings, priests, and prophets." But in view of Jer 23:1–4, where "shepherds" refers to kings, the same group is probably intended here.

and multiply. I will set shepherds over them who will care for them . . . neither shall any be missing.[78]

The NE of which Jeremiah speaks will completely overshadow the Exodus from Egypt (Jer 23:7–8). The Lord will "be the God of all the clans of Israel," reunifying Israel and Judah, and they will be his people.[79] Moreover, he will "bring them from the north country, and *gather them* from the farthest parts of the earth, among them the *blind* and the *lame*." He "will make them walk by brooks of *water*, in a straight path in which they shall not stumble," because the Lord is a father to Israel and Ephraim is his firstborn.[80] "He who scattered Israel will gather him, and will keep him as a shepherd keeps his flock. For the LORD has ransomed Jacob . . . from hands too strong for him" (Jer 31:10–11).

In this context of future hope, the Lord announces his new covenant with Israel and Judah, whereby he will be their God, and they will be his people. Thus he will write his law upon their hearts and forgive their sins.[81] Moreover, Yahweh will "raise up for David a righteous Branch, and he shall reign as king," executing justice in the land.[82] David's seed will be as innumerable as the stars and the sands of the sea[83] and he shall never lack a man to reign over Israel.

Ezekiel

Ezekiel 34:1–31 is based on Jer 23:1–6, "The linkages in theme and structure, style, and diction are too numerous and too specific to be accidental."[84] In Ezek 34:1–10, the Lord pronounces judgement upon the shepherds of Israel. They have ruled with harshness, slaughtering the flock to feed and clothe themselves, but have not strengthened the weak, healed the sick, bound the injured, brought back strays, or sought the lost. As a result the sheep have been scattered and become a prey for wild beasts. The Lord will rescue his sheep *from the shepherds*. He will seek out his sheep and rescue them from all the countries where they have been scattered, gathering them to their own land. He himself will be their shepherd, pasturing them, seeking the lost, bringing back the strays, binding the injured, and strengthening the weak. But he will judge the fat sheep who have scattered the lean. He will also set over them "one shepherd," his servant David. The Lord will be their God, and his servant David will be their prince (Ezek 34:23–24). "I am the LORD, I have spoken," Ezek 34:24, echoes Exod

---

78. Jer 23:3–4 cf. Ezek 34:11ff.; John 10:28–29.
79. Jer 31:1 cf. Jer 3:18.
80. Jer 31:8–9 (emphasis mine) cf. the cripple of John 5 and blind man of John 9.
81. Jer 31:31–34. cf. Jer 32:36–41; 50:4–5, 20.
82. Jer 23:5; 33:14–26. This reflects the Branch concept of Isa 11:1. Cf. Isa 53:2; Ps 80:15; Zech 3:8; 6:12.
83. Jer 33:22, echoing Gen 13:16; 15:5; 22:17.
84. Block, *Ezekiel 25–48*, 275.

3:14.⁸⁵ Moreover, the Lord will make a covenant of peace (בְּרִית שָׁלוֹם) associated with the turning away of God's anger.⁸⁶

In Ezek 36, the Lord will act unilaterally to deliver his people for the sake of his own name. He emphatically tells them that *he will* take them from the nations, gather them from all the lands, bring them into their own land, and sprinkle clean water upon them to cleanse them from all their uncleanness and idolatry.⁸⁷ He will also put his Spirit within them, restore Edenic blessing, and increase their number "like the flock at Jerusalem during her appointed feasts . . . Then they will know that I am the Lord," Ezek 36:38.

In Ezek 37, this NE deliverance is illustrated by two sign-acts, the raising of the bodies of people slain in battle, long dead, but not buried and thus under the curse,⁸⁸ and the joining of two sticks representative of Judah and Israel. By way of explanation, the Lord says,

> I will take the people of Israel from the nations . . . And I will make them one nation in the land . . . And one king shall be king over them all, and they shall be no longer two nations, and no longer divided into two kingdoms . . . I will save them . . . and will cleanse them; and they shall be my people, and I will be their God. My servant David shall be king over them, and they shall all have one shepherd.⁸⁹

Moreover, the people will dwell in the land forever, David will reign forever, and Yahweh will establish an everlasting covenant of peace with them. He will set his sanctuary in their midst forevermore and his dwelling place (Tabernacle) shall be with them (Ezek 37:26–27).

Zechariah

A remnant has returned to Jerusalem, but the return has born no resemblance to the NE expectation. The few who have returned are in disgrace, and after twenty years the Temple has still not been rebuilt. Moreover, since the nations are "at rest," Zech 1:11, there is little prospect that things would change. The angel of Yahweh asks, "O LORD of hosts, how long will you have no mercy on Jerusalem and the cities of Judah, against which you have been angry these seventy years?"⁹⁰ It is this question that Zechariah answers.

---

85. Cf. also Exod 29:46, and Jesus' "I am," John 10:7, 9, 11.
86. Ezek 34:25. Cf. Block, *Ezekiel 25–48*, 302; Num 25:12; Isa 54:7–10; 53:10–12.
87. Ezek 36:24–25 cf. Isa 52:15; Zech 12:10–11; 13:1.
88. Ezek 37:1–14 cf. 2 Sam 21; Deut 28:25–26; Jer 34:17–20.
89. Ezek 37:21–24 (emphasis mine). Cf. "One flock, one shepherd," John 10:16.
90. Zech 1:12 cf. Jer 25:11; 29:10.

Zechariah 1–8

These chapters contain Zechariah's night visions, intended to comfort and reassure the remnant, concerning God's gracious purposes. Thus the Lord will again choose and prosper Jerusalem, build his house, and dwell in her midst.[91] So great will be her prosperity that the city will be inhabited as towns without walls, because of the multitude of people and livestock, and the Lord will be "a wall of fire all around," and "the glory in her midst," Zech 2:5. Such imagery suggests that the whole of Jerusalem will ultimately become a Temple. In the light of this the people of God, scattered to the four winds, are urged to "flee" from Babylon and to "escape to Zion" in NE manner.[92] These promises are bolstered by sign acts, in which the prophet participates:

First, Joshua is reinstated as High Priest. His filthy garments (the peoples' sins, connected with exile) are removed and he is arrayed in costly robes. On condition that he walks in God's ways and keeps his charge, he is granted to rule over God's house (Temple), take charge over his courts, and have access to God's presence and the heavenly council. Joshua and his associates are a sign of "my servant the Branch," and the removal of iniquity "in a single day."[93] This extraordinary move associates Joshua the High Priest with the messianic Davidic branch.

Second, an elaborate crown is made, set on the head of Joshua the High Priest, and the Lord's word is announced,

> Behold, the man whose name is the Branch: for he shall branch out from his place, and he shall build the temple of the LORD. It is he who shall build the temple of the LORD and shall bear royal honor, and shall sit and rule on his throne. And there shall be a priest on his throne, and the counsel of peace shall be between them both.[94]

Thus Joshua becomes a symbolic portrayal of Messiah, combining the offices and function of priest and king.[95] The laying-up of the crown in the temple, as a memorial, together with prediction that "those who are far off shall come and help to build the temple of the LORD," suggests the expectation of a NE, Temple, and Messiah yet to come.[96] The vision of the two anointed ones who stand by the Lord, who supply oil to

---

91. Zech 1:16–17; 2:5, 10 cf. Deut 12:4ff.; Ps 78:70.

92. Zech 2:6–7. In Zech 2:9, God says, "I will shake my hand over them [the nations], and they shall become plunder for those who served them."

93. Zech 3:1–10.

94. Zech 6:12–13.

95. Some commentators have postulated that the royal functions are addressed to Zerubbabel, David's descendant, but it is more natural to understand them here of Joshua. See messianic psalm, Ps 110:1–4.

96. Zech 6:15 cf. Hag 2:7–9.

PART II—DETAILED EXEGETICAL EXAMINATION OF JOHN 5–10

the golden lampstand, may also support the concept of the offices of high priest and king coalescing in Messiah.[97]

Zechariah 9–14

These chapters contain oracles or burdens that show how the messianic NE promises will yet be fulfilled.[98] Thus the Lord will send his Davidic King to his people, whose reign will be from sea to sea.[99] However, Israel will again be disobedient, fall prey to wicked rulers, and be scattered. Nevertheless, the Lord will sow (scatter) them among the heathen and multiply them as they were multiplied in Egypt, bringing them home in a NE.[100] The Lord's companion and shepherd-king will be pierced, resulting in cleansing and repentance for David's house. The Lord will shake the nations, gathering them against Jerusalem with devastating consequences. He will then fight for his people and bring global salvation, to be commemorated in the feast of Tabernacles:

1. In Zech 9:9–17, Zion's king comes to her, "humble and mounted on a donkey." The Lord will establish a worldwide dominion for him. He will also set his prisoners free from the waterless pit because of the "blood of my covenant," fighting for and saving them "as the flock of his people."

2. In Zech 10:1–4, the situation is the same as that described in Jer 23:1–2 and Ezek 34:1–6: The sheep are scattered for want of a *good* shepherd, the existing shepherds being the objects of God's wrath. God will punish them and himself act as shepherd, whistling for his sheep, bringing them home through the "sea of troubles" from Egypt and Assyria.[101] He will also provide them with a good shepherd and messianic King.[102] The request for rain may associate this oracle with the feast of Tabernacles and the need to enthrone the Lord as King.

3. In Zech 11:4–17, Zechariah performs sign acts, probably in the Temple environs,[103] to critique the shepherds. First he takes the part of a good "shepherd," set over a flock "doomed to slaughter," whose owners do not pity them.[104] He takes two staffs and tends the sheep for a short period, dismissing three other shepherds. When

---

97. Zech 4:1–14. The concept of Messiah supplying the Spirit [oil] to the people of God [lampstand] is embraced by the author of the Fourth Gospel, John 14:16–17; 15:26; 16:7; 20:22 cf. Rev 1:20; 11:4.

98. See Duguid, "Messianic Themes," 266.

99. Zech 9:9–10 cf. Ps 72:8; Isa 11:9.

100. Zech 10:8–12.

101. Zech 10:8–10 cf. Jer 23:3–6; Ezek 34:11–16, 23–24.

102. Zech 10:4 cf. Isa 28:16; Ps 118:22; Isa 22:20–23. Cf. Cathcart and Gordon, *Targum of the Minor Prophets*, 209. The Targum on Zech 10:4 reads, "From them will be *their king*, from them *their anointed one* . . ." (emphasis original). Cf. Duguid, "Messianic Themes," 271–72.

103. So McComiskey, "Zechariah," 1191.

104. Zech 11:4–14.

The Good Shepherd, John 10:1-21

the people detest their shepherd and he becomes impatient with them, he refuses to continue, breaking his staffs. The shepherd's wages, thirty pieces of silver, are cast to the house of the potter.[105] Zechariah then takes the equipment of a "foolish shepherd," to symbolize a wicked ruler who will "devour" the sheep.

Importantly, this appears to be "a complete reversal of Ezekiel's prophecy."[106] Instead of shepherding the flock and appointing David as their "good" shepherd (Ezek 34:24), here the Lord (and his Davidic shepherd) abandons the flock and appoints a wicked shepherd over them. Moreover, rather than joining two sticks symbolising the union of Judah and Ephraim under David (as in Ezek 37:15-24), here the two staffs are broken, symbolising the breaking of the brotherhood between Judah and Ephraim (Zech 11:14) and the breaking of the covenant with the nations (Zech 11:10). From this background, the "good" shepherd of Zechariah 11 seems to represent both the Lord and his earthly under-shepherd David. That the reversal of Ezekiel is not permanent may be indicated by the nadir of the wicked shepherd.[107]

4. Similar ideas are expressed in Zech 13:7-9.[108] The sword strikes the shepherd and the sheep are scattered.[109] Only one third of the population (God's true covenant people) will survive. They will be tested and refined. The stricken shepherd is "the man who stands next to me," the Lord's vicegerent,[110] and Israel's king,[111] possibly identified with the Suffering Servant.[112]

5. In Zech 12, though the nations gather against Jerusalem to destroy her, God will make her a "cup of staggering" and a "heavy stone" to all who come against her. He will save and strengthen his people, pouring out a spirit of grace on David's house, so that they will mourn, as for a firstborn, when they "look on me, on him whom they have pierced."[113] In connection with this a fountain will be opened to

---

105. Cf. Matt 26:15; 27:9,10.

106. Duguid, "Messianic Themes," 272. See Ezek 34. Cf. Hanson, *Dawn of Apocalyptic*, 344-45. Hanson believes that Zech 11:7-17 is a conscious polemic against those who were building their leadership claims on Ezekiel. I would argue, however, that this passage is an elaboration of the Ezek 34 NE, indicating that Israel would yet again rebel and be scattered in the days of Messiah, prior to the ultimate NE fulfilment.

107. Zech 11:17. Cf. Duguid, "Messianic Themes," 273-74.

108. McComiskey, "Zechariah," 1214-5, thinks it a "virtual certainty" that the figure of Zech 13:7 is the same as that of Zech 12:10 and Zech 11:4-14. Moreover, he points up the "striking consonance" between Zech 12:10 and Zech 3:8-10. He also notes similarities between the sufferings of Zech 12:10 and those of the Servant of Isa 53.

109. Cf. the citation of this passage, and its application to Jesus, in Matt 24:36.

110. Zech 13:7 cf. Ps 80:17.

111. Cf. 1 Kgs 22:17, where the sheep are scattered because they have no master (king).

112. See Bruce, *Old Testament Themes*, 102-3. See above on John 6, and the Servant. Cf. Lamarche, *Zacharie IX-XIV*, 137, who concludes that, "les rapprochments entre Zech 13, 7-9 et le Deutero Isaie sont donc possibles, mais loin d'etre certains."

113. Zech 12:10 cf. Isa 53:5; John 19:37.

cleanse from sin.[114] The paschal nature of this passage and the connection with the Suffering Servant has been previously noted.[115] Moreover, the piercing suggests identification with the shepherd of Zech 13:7–9, the Suffering Servant of Isa 53:5, and the Righteous Sufferer of Ps 22:16.

6. Zechariah closes with an apocalyptic description of the end of the present order, where the nations are gathered to fight against Jerusalem and the Lord intervenes to save his people, Zech 14:1–5.[116] This ushers in the paradisal reign of God, described in terms of light at evening time, living waters flowing from Jerusalem, and the enthronement of the Lord over all the earth, all reminiscent of Tabernacles. The wealth of the nations is plundered and a plague shall fall upon them, Zech 14:12, reminiscent of the Exodus. Survivors of the nations will be joined to the Lord and celebrate the feast of Tabernacles. In Zech 14:20–21, the book of Zechariah comes full circle with Jerusalem effectively becoming God's Temple, every pot in the city becoming as sacred as the Temple vessels, and "holy to the LORD," the inscription worn by the High priest, being inscribed on the bells of horses.[117]

Connections between Zechariah 1–8 and 9–14

Can a parallel be demonstrated between the priest-king in Zech 1–8, and the shepherd-king of Zech 9–14? Many scholars emphasize what they consider to be the different atmosphere and style between the two parts of Zechariah concluding that they have different authors. Others have nevertheless pointed up the structural and thematic unity between chapters 1–8 and 9–14. Childs speaks of a "surprising compatibility" between them.[118] McComiskey notes several common themes linking the two parts of the book, which give "a distinctly Zecharian cast" to Zech 9–14. Lamarche has observed a chiastic arrangement within Zech 9–14, whereby the arrival of the King, Zech 9:9–10, parallels the rejected shepherd, Zech 11:4–17.[119] Thus Zech 9–14 presents four aspects of a single messianic conception, the "Shepherd King.[120] Baldwin follows this approach.[121] Kline suggests that Zechariah is structured as a diptych around a central

---

114. Zech 13:1 cf. 3:9; Ezek 36:25–26.

115. See above on John 6. Cf. Lamarche, *Zacharie IX–XIV*, 136. Although the Babylonian Talmud identifies the pierced one as Messiah ben Joseph of later period than the apostles, the Palestinian Talmud identifies him as Messiah. See Bruce, *Old Testament Themes*, 112.

116. Cf. Ezek 38–39; Rev 20:7–10.

117. Cf. Kline, *Glory in Our Midst*, 76; Beale, *Temple*, 143.

118. Childs, *Introduction*, 482. He nevertheless believes that Zech 9–14 are from a different author than Zech 1–8.

119. Lamarche, *Zacharie IX–XIV*, passim. Cf. Baldwin, *Haggai, Zechariah and Malachi*, 78.

120. Cf. Zech 9:9–10; 11:4–17; 12:10–13:1; 13:7–9; Lamarche, *Zacharie IX–XIV*, 145–47; Bruce, *Old Testament Themes*, 101ff.; Lindars, *John*, 110ff.; France, *Jesus and the Old Testament*, 103ff. This was noted above in the exposition of John 6, in connection with the Servant.

121. Baldwin, *Haggai, Zechariah and Malachi*, 78.

The Good Shepherd, John 10:1-21

hinge, Zech 6:9-15. Moreover, each half is itself a diptych, hinged at Zech 3:1-10 and Zech 11:1-17 respectively. Furthermore, the three hinge sections parallel each other, each representing commissioning to messianic office.[122] Thus the unity of Zechariah is established and the "good Shepherd" of the second half of the book represents the priest-king of the first.

The Shepherd and the New Exodus in the OT Pseudepigrapha

1 Enoch 85-90

Although having no direct bearing upon GJohn, 1 Enoch 85-90, "the animal apocalypse," illustrates the use of shepherd and sheep imagery by a Jewish intertestamental author in a visionary portrayal of Israel's history.[123] It also highlights the central importance of the Tabernacle and Temple to that history:

In Egypt, the children of Israel are portrayed as sheep among wolves. The Lord of the sheep visits and delivers them. He provides them with pasture and leads them, together with a sheep that becomes a man (Moses). At Sinai the sheep become blind, stray, and are punished. The sheep-turned-man builds the Lord's house (the Tabernacle) and places the sheep within it (1 Enoch 89:36). They are led to a pleasant land, with the house in their midst, "by which their eyes become opened."[124]

In the land, they became "dim-sighted until another sheep [Samuel] arose and led them . . . and their eyes became opened."[125] Attacked by wild beasts (the surrounding hostile nations), the Lord raises up rams (Saul and David) to deliver them. The house is made "great and spacious,"[126] and a tower is built upon it (the Temple), but the sheep abandon the house and become blind. The Lord sends sheep (prophets) to testify against them, but ultimately, when they completely go astray, he abandons them to wild beasts. Seventy shepherds (angels) are appointed over the sheep, but these kill, destroy, and abandon the sheep (1 Enoch 89:65). Wild beasts devour a majority of the sheep and the house is destroyed (at the Babylonian exile). The deeds of the shepherds are written in a book.

Three sheep return and start to rebuild the house and tower, but polluted food is offered before the tower (1 Enoch 89:72-73). The sheep are "dim-sighted" and cannot see this. The sheep are delivered to the shepherds for destruction and are "dispersed

---

122. Kline, *Glory In Our Midst*, 219. Cf. idem, "Structure of Zechariah," 173-79.

123. 1 Enoch is "composite." 1 Enoch 89-90 comes from the "Dream Visions" section of the book (1 Enoch 83-90) which an early scholarly consensus has dated to ca. 165-61 B.C. Other parts of 1 Enoch are thought to be much later. The "Similitudes" (1 Enoch 37-71), for example, are thought to date to the first century A. D. Cf. Isaac, "1 Enoch," in Charlesworth, *Pseudepigrapha*, 1:6-7.

124. 1 Enoch 89:40, in Charlesworth, *Pseudepigrapha*, 1:66.

125. 1 Enoch 89:41-42, in Charlesworth, *Pseudepigrapha*, 1:67.

126. 1 Enoch 89:50, in Charlesworth, *Pseudepigrapha*, 1:67.

into the woods."¹²⁷ Eagles, dogs, kites, and ravens devour the sheep (the persecution of the Jews under Antiochus IV "Epiphanes"). Lambs (who can see) are born from snow white sheep, but the sheep cannot see and will not listen to them (1 Enoch 90:6–7). The lambs grow horns, but are attacked by ravens (Seleucids). One of the sheep sprouts a huge horn (Judas Maccabeus). He opens the eyes of the sheep. He also battles with the ravens, cries to God, and is helped by the writer of the book.

The wild birds and sheep unite against the horn of the ram, but the Lord of the sheep smites the earth with a rod and the sheep are given a sword to smite the wild beasts and birds (1 Enoch 90:18–19). The judgement throne is set and one (God or possibly the Son of Man/Messiah[128]) sits upon it "for the Lord of the sheep."[129] The stars, seventy shepherds, and blind sheep are thrown into the "fiery abyss." The "ancient house" is transformed, and the "snow white" sheep that had been destroyed are gathered into the house with joy.

Points of interest

1 Enoch 85–90 surveys the history of God's people (sheep) from the Creation to the Final Judgement, dividing that history into several periods. From the time of the Exodus until the final judgement and beyond, the house of God (the Tabernacle and then the Temple) is of central importance to Israel's story. It is their sheepfold, the place to which the sheep are gathered, and it is a determining factor of their well-being. The building and beautifying of the "house" coincides with periods of spiritual prosperity; its abandonment and defilement, in conjunction with blindness and deafness, symbolic of rebellion against God, leads to exile and ruin.

From the time of the exile, God hands Israel over to seventy shepherds. Unlike the OT use of shepherd imagery, these are not human rulers but angelic beings, whose purpose is to punish Israel in measure, but who afflict her excessively. The seventy periods in which they rule seems to correspond in some way to the seventy years of Jer 25:11–12 and to the seventy weeks of Daniel 9:24. It is thought that these angelic beings are introduced by way of a theodicy, taking the blame (instead of God) for the excessive suffering of Israel, from the exile to the Final Judgement.[130]

The return from exile and the Second Temple does not solve Israel's problems, because they allow it to become polluted and are scattered by Seleucid rulers. Only the intervention of the Lord makes a difference. God (or Messiah on his behalf) judges the world and the wicked angels and impenitent people are cast into the abyss. The ultimate state of the blessed is to be gathered into a transformed house of the Lord.

---

127. 1 Enoch 89:75, in Charlesworth, *Pseudepigrapha*, 1:69.
128. Cf. 1 Enoch 61:8. Belonging to the "Similitudes," this reference is much later.
129. 1 Enoch 90:20, in Charlesworth, *Pseudepigrapha*, 1:70.
130. Cf. Olson, *Animal Apocalypse*, 190.

The Good Shepherd, John 10:1-21

Shepherds, sheep, and house building in the OT and in GJohn

From this survey, several points have emerged.

1. The OT prophets share a similar vision for the NE where Israel's shepherds are responsible for the exile, but Yahweh and his under-shepherd, the messianic Davidic Servant, will restore the people to their land where they will serve him in his Temple which will envelop the whole world.

2. This vision has been elaborated and developed by inner-biblical exegesis, according to God's progressive revelation. A particular twist to the story occurs in Zechariah, where the Davidic shepherd is rejected by his sheep and casts his wages of thirty pieces of silver into the Temple, to the potter. He breaks the covenant between Judah and Israel and his covenant with the nations, and he abandons his sheep to a worthless shepherd who presides over their destruction, Zech 11:4-17. Moreover, the Davidic shepherd is pierced and stricken, and the sheep are (again) scattered (Zech 12:10; 13:7-9).[131] Ultimately, however, the end result is the same. God's scattered people, Judah and Joseph, whom he has sown among the nations, are restored to the land (Zech 10:6-12). Moreover, the Spirit of grace and supplication is poured out upon them so that when they look upon their pierced Messiah they will mourn because of him. A fountain is also open for their sin and uncleanness (Zech 12:10—13:1). Furthermore, the whole of Jerusalem becomes God's Temple and Messiah's worldwide kingdom of peace is established (Zech 9:10).

3. The building of a worldwide temple, based on Jerusalem, is central to the NE hope. This parallels the Psalm 68 understanding of the Exodus, seen as a journey from Egypt to the Temple, where God, the divine warrior, having delivered his people, ascends into his rest among them within the Temple.[132]

4. There will be a final showdown between the forces of evil and the people of God in which the Lord will intervene for his people and usher in the new heavens and earth.

In GJohn, from the outset, Jesus is the builder of God's house; the "Jewish" leaders being those who bring destruction upon the Temple and the people. Jesus will raise up the Temple of his body within three days (John 2:19). This is not the whole story for (in an already/not yet eschatology)[133] Jesus' people become part of his ever-growing

---

131. Zech 13:7 is fulfilled when Jesus is smitten and his disciples are scattered, Matt 26:31; Mark 14:27. The resulting devastation of Zech 13:8-9, however seems to have a fulfilment in the events of A.D. 70 and in all that followed.

132. Ps 68 cf. Ps 118; Ps 132:8; 1 Chr 6:41. Cf. Kidner, *Psalms 1-72*, 238; Davis, *1 Kings*, 60-61. As previously noted, the divine warrior motif follows a particular pattern: Warfare, victory, kingship, housebuilding, and celebration. See Longman and Reid, *God is a Warrior*, 83-88.

133. See below.

PART II—DETAILED EXEGETICAL EXAMINATION OF JOHN 5-10

Temple. Moreover, he sanctifies and sends them out into the world, to represent God's Temple on earth, and to add to it "living stones." The ultimate assembly of this temple is in heaven.

INTEGRITY, FORM, AND STRUCTURE OF JOHN 10:1-21

Integrity

Because of the similarity of John 10:19-21 to John 9:39-41, Bernard has proposed that the text has been dislocated and that John 10:19-29 should follow John 9:41.[134] This would have the effect of making the Feast of Dedication, v. 22, the setting for the whole of chapter 10. Though plausible, this relocation is without textual evidence, and the text makes good sense as it stands.[135]

The integrity of vv. 1-5 has also been questioned. Derrett believes that John reconstructed a parable, which he "decoded" from the OT.[136] Robinson proposed that two parables that have been fused together: vv. 1-3a centers on the porter who refuses entrance to the bandit, but opens to the shepherd, while vv. 3b-5 deals with the relationship between the shepherd and his sheep.[137] Others find this distinction "tenuous," the events of vv. 1-5 being held together in good succession.[138]

Form and structure

There is general consensus that this section divides into two main parts consisting of an extended figure of speech or parable(s), vv. 1-5, and an explanation, vv. 7-18 (often subdivided), with v. 6 and vv. 19-21 consisting of editorial comments and the reaction of "the Jews."[139] Scholars disagree, however, concerning the figure of speech Jesus employs. The Greek, παροιμίαν, v. 6, figure of speech, parable, proverb, translates מָשָׁל, that covers all figurative illustrations including parable, proverb, allegory, and metaphor. Barrett argues that the shepherd theme is neither a parable nor an allegory, but (related to both) a symbolic discourse, alternating between symbols and statements.[140] Brown, noting the similarities to the synoptic parables that have explanations, posits parables, vv. 1-5, followed by allegorical explanations.[141] In fact, the hearer's failure to

---

134. Bernard, *John*, xxiv-xxv, 341.
135. Cf. Barrett, *John*, 367; Beasly-Murray, *John*, 166; Carson, *John*, 379.
136. Cf. Derrett, "Good Shepherd," 25-50; Barrett, *John*, 368.
137. Robinson, "Parable," 233-40. Cf. Dodd, *HTFG*, 383.
138. See Beasley-Murray, *John*, 167.
139. Cf. Beasley-Murray, *John*, 167; Brown, *John I-XII*, 391-400; Carson, *John*, 380-90; Hoskyns, *Fourth Gospel*, 371-81; Köstenberger, *John*, 299-308; Morris, *John*, 500-514; Schnackenburg, *John*, 2:278-98.
140. Barrett, *John*, 367. Cf. Dodd, *IFG*, 134-35.
141. Cf. Mark 4:13-20; Matt 13:3-43.

The Good Shepherd, John 10:1-21

understand (v. 6) preceding the explanation (vv. 7ff.) strengthens the Synoptic parable with explanation parallel.[142] To be sure, this parable lacks the introductory "kingdom of heaven is like" formula of many of the Synoptic parables, but it is not too dissimilar to the "allegorical" Parable of the Two Sons, and the Parable of the Tenants.[143]

Comparison with OT parabolic forms is instructive. If παροιμίαν echoes "parable," in Ps 78:2,[144] which it might, given John's echoes of this psalm,[145] its content might cast light on Jesus' parable.[146] In fact, Ps 78 summarizes Israel's redemptive history, from the Exodus onward (where God led Israel like a flock), in order to teach its lessons. Ezekiel's Parable of the Eagles and the Vine, Ezek 17, with its symbolic representation and explanation (relating to Babylonian exile), shares a similar structure to John 10:1-21. Moreover, his shepherd discourse of Ezek 34 provides a model upon which it was partially based. Accepting the prophetic and allegorical nature of OT parables, it is not difficult to place the parable of the Good Shepherd within this wider parable *genre*. Objections have been made that such "allegorical" parables add the Church's interpretation to Jesus' simpler stories which were calculated to put across one main point (Jülicher).[147] Lately, however, scholars are increasingly inclined to acknowledge the allegorical nature of Jesus' parables.[148]

Another question concerns symbolic reference. Commentators on John 10 often discuss Near Eastern pastoral practice, shepherds naming their sheep and leading them out of a shared enclosure, without mention of OT echoes or inferences *within these symbolic details*. But this is not the correct way of understanding Jesus' parables. As Wright points out, they frequently follow well-known Jewish models: The vine, for example, represents Israel and "the sheep and shepherd speaks of Israel and her king." Thus they tell the story of Israel, but as "subversive stories" they challenge the prevailing worldview of their hearers.[149] Moreover, in addition to one main referent, their symbols frequently contain multiple allusions to and resonances with the OT story.[150]

The parable of the Good Shepherd functions in a similar manner: Jesus decodes the main symbols of John 1–5 in John 7–19, but the unstated points of resonance, transumed from the many texts that he echoes,[151] carry a hidden "subversive" message. That this message is real and not imagined is seen, not only from the sheer number of

---

142. Cf. Lightfoot, *John's Gospel*, 210.
143. Matt 21:28–32; Matt 33–41.
144. Cf. Ps 49:4.
145. Cf. "beginning" (ἀρχῇ) in John 1:1; LXX Ps 78:2. Cf. Ps 78:24, echoed in John 6:31.
146. Cf. Matt 13:35, which cites Ps 78:2 as prophetic of Jesus' teaching.
147. Cf. Wright, *NTPG*, 433.
148. See Wright, *JVG*, 178.
149. Ibid.,175.
150. Cf. ibid., 178.
151. Cf. Hays, *Echoes*, 20.

PART II—DETAILED EXEGETICAL EXAMINATION OF JOHN 5–10

echoes, but also, more importantly, from their resonance and thematic coherence[152] with the text and with each other. Thus, from careful examination of possible echoes, certain patterns emerge.

NE INTERPRETATION OF JOHN 10:1–21, JESUS THE GOOD SHEPHERD

Shepherd and Sheep: a Subversive Parable, vv. 1–6

On a superficial level this parable speaks about access to sheep in an enclosure. Thieves and robbers climb up into the sheepfold in contrast to the shepherd who enters legitimately through the door. The sheep recognize the shepherd and follow him as he leads them out, but they eschew a stranger's voice. OT echoes and allusions, however, show that it refers on a deeper level to the people of God, the Temple, religious-political usurpers, and Israel's king; the Lord and his messianic under-shepherd.

Echoes and allusions

"The Shepherd of the sheep (ποιμήν . . . τῶν προβάτων)," v. 2.

1. This alludes first and foremost to the Lord as King over Israel.[153] Moreover, there is a connection between God as shepherd and the Exodus where he "led out his people like sheep and guided them in the wilderness like a flock."[154] In the NE Yahweh declares, "I myself will search for my sheep and will seek them out. As a shepherd seeks out his flock . . . that have been scattered."[155] A connection also exists with the Tabernacle and the Temple. It was by the pillar of fire, resident over the Tabernacle, and the ark of God that dwelt within it, symbolic of God's presence, that Israel was led through the wilderness to the Promised Land.[156] From above the mercy seat, Moses "*heard the voice* [of the Lord]."[157] In Ps 80:1, the "Shepherd of Israel" is enthroned "upon the cherubim" in the Temple. Moreover, in Pss 95 and 100 he calls Israel to worship before him in the Temple on the basis that he is their creator-king and they are his sheep, the people of his pasture. Interestingly the ultimate goal of Yahweh's shepherding of David was that he might "dwell in the house of the LORD forever."[158] It is also of interest that in

---

152. See Ibid., 30. See above on intertextuality.
153. Cf. Pss 80:1; 100:3; 79:13; 95:7; 23:1; Isa 40:11; Jer 31:10; Ezek 34:12; Mic 7:14.
154. Cf. Ps 78:52; cf. Pss 77:20; 80; Isa 63:11.
155. Ezek 34:11–12.
156. Cf. Exod 13:21; 40:34–38; Num 9:15–22; 10:35; Pss 68; 48:14.
157. Num 7:89 (emphasis mine).
158. Cf. Pss 23:6; 27:4; 43:3–4.

The Good Shepherd, John 10:1–21

the Dream Visions of 1 Enoch the Temple is the dwelling place of the sheep.[159]

2. "Shepherd of the sheep" also alludes to God's under-shepherd. In Num 27:16–17, Moses asked God to "appoint a man over the congregation who shall go out before them and come in before them, who shall lead them out and bring them in, that the congregation of the LORD may not be as sheep that have no shepherd." Ps 78 speaks of David's appointment, "to shepherd Jacob his [Yahweh's] people,"[160] as the culmination of God's gracious dealings with his rebellious people from the Exodus onward. In the NE God would set one shepherd over Israel, his messianic "servant David."[161]

THE WORD αὐλή, TRANSLATED "[SHEEP]FOLD," V. 1

This is used in the LXX of the court(s) of the Tabernacle and Temple.[162] The Hebrew חָצֵר (court) has a wide semantic range, and can mean:

1. Enclosures (in Egypt), perhaps courtyards or cattle yards.
2. The court of a private house (containing a well) or palace.
3. The court of the Tabernacle or the courts of Solomon's or Ezekiel's Temple.[163]

In the NT αὐλή has a similar semantic range and is frequently translated "courtyard."[164] It is suggested that Jesus has in mind the courts of God's house, as the place to which his sheep (people) gather. Other uses confirm these priestly/Temple overtones.

In John 18:15 αὐλή refers to the courtyard of the High Priest, entered by a door (θύρᾳ), guarded by a doorkeeper (θυρωρῷ), all echoing John 10.[165] Echoes of John 10 are also found in John 18:1–11, where Jesus is arrested within a walled garden.[166] The garden is reminiscent of Eden. Judas enters like a wolf, but Jesus is the Good Shepherd protecting his sheep. It may be significant that, "in the place where he was crucified there was a garden," John 19:41. This could well relate Jesus' death to the Eden garden-temple. The tomb certainly recalls the entrance of death into the first garden. Here, in the garden, Jesus will rise from the dead, overcoming death.

---

159. See above.
160. Ps 78:70–72 cf. 2 Sam 7:8.
161. Cf. Ezek 34:23–24; 37:24–25; Mic 5:2–4.
162. Cf. Exod 27:9, 12–13; Num 4:26; 1 Chr 23:28; 2 Chr 23:5; 33:5; Neh 8:16; 13:7; Ps 65:4; 84:2, 10; Isa 1:2; 62:9; Ezek 9:7; 46:21; Zech 3:7.
163. See Brown et al., *Lexicon*, 346–47.
164. Cf. Matt 26:58, 69; Mark 14:54, 66; Luke 22:55; John 18:15; Rev 11:2.
165. See Stibbe, *John as Storyteller*, 103–4.
166. Cf. ibid., 103.

PART II—DETAILED EXEGETICAL EXAMINATION OF JOHN 5-10

"The door," vv. 1, 7

This is probably an echo of the gate of Ps 118:19–20 and Ps 24:7– 9. This echo has been noted by several commentators, but dealt with at length by Brunson.[167] He argues that because of the double connection of θύρα with "I am," and the soteriological implications of its function within the passage, we should view here the door of the Temple.[168] He also notes that "court" of the sheepfold points in this direction, representing the Temple.[169] In this connection the doorkeeper echoes the Temple servants of Pss 24 and 118, who admit only the righteous into God's sanctuary. There is probably also a conceptual echo of the priestly role of guarding the temple-garden, committed first to Adam and then to the cherubim. In Johannine context, it is possible that JBap can be understood as fulfilling this role, admitting Jesus among the sheep, although ultimately the doorkeeper is the Father.

Specific allusion to Zechariah

Hanson suggests that αὐλή (court/fold), John 10:1, alludes specifically to Zech 3:7,[170] where Joshua is purged of his offenses, promised a position over God's people, and charge over his *courts*—if he continues to walk in God's ways.

> If you will walk in my ways and keep my charge, then you shall rule my house and have charge of my courts, and I will give you the right of access among those who are standing here (Zech 3:7).

He also believes that Zech 3:5–10 lies behind John 10:1–6. He points out that the name of the high priest (Joshua) is equivalent to "Jesus" and that the name of his adversary, ὁ διάβολος, is used in GJohn of Satan. Moreover, the Zech 3:8 reference to "the Branch" would have been regarded as messianic.[171] I would add that, both John 10 and Zech 3:5–10 deal with the same issue of messianic investiture and authority over God's house and people; Joshua judging God's house as a royal high priest and Jesus as priestly shepherd-king who lays down his life for his sheep. Important in this respect is the symbolic removal of Zechariah's filthy garments, symbolic of the sins of the exile. This may have been particularly significant for John, foreshadowing Jesus the paschal lamb, who takes away the world's sin.

Confirmation that GJohn alludes to Zechariah is found in Pilate's acclamation "behold the man," John 19:5, which echoes Zech 6:12, a parallel investiture of Joshua to that of Zech 3:5–10, but this time as king:

---

167. Brunson, *Psalm 118*, 317ff. Cf. the scholars he cites, Ibid., 317, n. 1. See below.
168. Ibid., 325–26.
169. Ibid., 339.
170. Hanson, *Prophetic*, 136.
171. Hanson, *Prophetic*, 136.

> *Behold, the man* whose name is the Branch: for he shall branch out from his place, and he shall build the temple of the LORD. It is he who shall build the temple of the Lord and shall bear royal honor, and shall sit and rule on his throne. And there shall be a priest on his throne, and the counsel of peace shall be between them both.[172]

Significantly, both the Johannine and Zechariah acclamations emphasize royal dignity: Joshua, being a priest-king and wearing a crown of gold, and (ironically) Jesus having been arrayed in a purple robe and wearing a crown of thorns. Meeks sees John 19:1–22 as Jesus' installation as eschatological king.[173] He takes note of Jesus' mock investiture followed by Pilate's two presentations of him to his people as their king.[174] He argues that the first presentation, "Behold the Man," ascribes a title and throne name to Jesus. "The Man" alludes to the Son of Man and the scene parallels Zech 6:12.

In John 19:13–16, Meeks thinks that it is Jesus who is seated on the βῆμα (judgement seat) rather than Pilate,[175] and presented as king of the Jews. In rejecting him, the "Jewish" authorities judge themselves to be among the nations who "have no king but Caesar." The precise moment of Jesus' enthronement, the sixth hour of the eve of the Passover, is the time when observation of Passover regulations begin. Meeks thinks that the Passover Haggadah *Nishmat* is echoed:

> From everlasting to everlasting you are God;
> Beside you we have no king, redeemer, or Savior,
> No liberator, deliverer, provider
> None who takes pity in every time of distress and trouble,
> We have no king but you.[176]

This implies that "the Jews" were not only rejecting Jesus, but also God as their king. The final exaltation of Jesus comes with the placard attached to Jesus' cross, "Jesus of Nazareth, the King of the Jews."[177]

Further support for these allusions may be found in the general importance of Zechariah for GJohn, not least in the allusion to Zech 14:21, where in the (judgement) day of the Lord, "there shall no longer be a trader in the house of the LORD."[178] This allusion occurs in connection with Jesus' Temple cleansing, signalling the judgement about to be visited upon it.[179] Significantly Jesus will build the Temple, which the "Jew-

---

172. Zech 6:12 (emphasis mine). Cf. Meeks, *Prophet-King*, 70; Bernard, *John*, 616; Lindars, *John*, 566; Hanson, *Prophetic*, 203–4.

173. Meeks, *Prophet-King*, 72.

174. Cf. John 19:1–7; 13–16.

175. Meeks, *Prophet-King*, 77. He takes ἐκάθισεν, John 19:13, as transitive.

176. Cf. Ibid., 77; Lincoln, *John*, 471. Meeks thinks the Nishmat is early, but it is not possible to date it.

177. Cf. John 19:19.

178. See John 2:16. Cf. Dodd, *IFG*, 300; Barrett, *John*, 198.

179. Cf. Dodd, *IFG*, 300; Kerr, *Temple*, 76–77.

PART II—DETAILED EXEGETICAL EXAMINATION OF JOHN 5–10

ish" leaders destroy, by raising up his body on the third day.[180] In addition, in view of John's citation of Zech 9:9 and Zech 12:10, it seems likely that he combined aspects of the messianic Shepherd of Zech 9–14 with the visions of Zech 3 and Zech 6 in his portrayal of Jesus as priest-king.[181]

"He calls his own sheep by name," v. 3

This seems to echo Moses' words to the Lord, "you have said, 'I know you by name.'"[182] The context is Moses' request that God, who has charged him to "bring up this people," would go with him and guide him. This idea is echoed in a NE verse, "I have called you by name, you are mine," Isa 43:1. The context here is the Lord's assurance that he will be with his people as once again he brings them through fire and through the waters, gathering them from the four corners of the earth. Similar promises, "I will go before you," and "I . . . call you by your name," are made to Cyrus, although he does not know the Lord, who works for his servant Jacob's sake (Isa 45:2–4).

"Leads them out," v. 3

This is Exodus terminology referring to the night that "All the hosts of the LORD went out from the land of Egypt," which night was commemorated in the Passover.[183] In Ezek 34:13, God would again "bring them out," in a NE, this time gathering his flock from all the peoples and countries where they had been scattered. "When he has brought out all his own, he goes before them," continues this theme. Thus ἐκβάλῃ, "brought out," echoes the expulsion, ἐκβαλεῖν, from Egypt, LXX Exod 12:33. It also echoes the expulsion of the man-born-blind by the "Jewish" leaders, ἐξέβαλον αὐτὸν ἔξω, John 9:34.[184]

"He goes before them," v. 4

This echoes "The LORD *went before them* by day in a pillar of cloud to lead them along the way, and by night in a pillar of fire to give them light, that they might travel by day and by night."[185] Deuteronomy recalls, "The LORD . . . went before you in the way to seek you out a place to pitch your tents . . . to show you by what way you

---

180. John 2:19.
181. Cf. allusions to Zech 12:10 in John 19:37; to Zech 9:9 in John 12:15, and to the Zech 14 Tabernacles imagery employed in John 7.
182. Exod 33:12 cf. 33:17.
183. Cf. Exod 12:41; 3:8, 12; 6:26.
184. Cf. Lincoln, *Trial*, 278; Bruce, *John*, 228.
185. Exod 13:21 (emphasis mine) cf. Num 10:33.

The Good Shepherd, John 10:1–21

should go."[186] In the NE, the Lord will "go before you, and ... be your rearguard," Isa 52:12. "Goes before them" may also echo Micah 2:13, where the king (and the Lord) "goes ... before" his sheep as he leads them out of the besieged city of Jerusalem.[187] If the setting is Sennacherib's blockade of Jerusalem, Isa 36:2, then the remnant escape fearful judgement. This might indicate the judgement about to fall on Jerusalem, that Jesus' disciples escape, by being led out of it.[188]

"The sheep hear his voice," v. 3

This probably echoes the words of Ps 95:7, "if you hear his voice." The Psalm may have been composed for the feast of Tabernacles, to help worshipers relive the wilderness experience.[189] It reminds worshippers that "the LORD is a great God, and a great king." Moreover, "he is our God, and we are the people of his pasture, and the sheep of his hand." The warning is given, "If you hear his voice, do not harden your hearts, as at Meribah [dispute], as on the day of Massah [testing] in the wilderness, when your fathers put me to the test . . . though they had seen my work." In the Johannine context, the Pharisees had recently experienced the Tabernacles reminder of the wilderness and had seen evidence of the works of God (John 9:3–4) that Jesus had performed upon the blind man. Despite this they had repeatedly hardened their hearts and refused to hear the shepherd's voice. The inevitable consequence would be their failure to enter his rest. The man-born-blind, however, had heard Jesus' voice and followed him, out of the "Jewish" worshipping community, to worship God, in Jesus (John 9:38), in Spirit and truth (John 4:24).

Specific allusion to Hosea

John 10:1, 8 is a particularly interesting echo of Hosea 6:7—7:2.[190] The Lord calls the northern *priests*, who make the king glad by their evil deeds, "thieves" and "robbers," LXX Hosea 7:1, "κλέπτης," who enter in, and "λῃστής," the same words that Jesus uses of those who climb into the sheepfold. In context, Yahweh called the nation to heart-repentance, desiring mercy rather than sacrifice. Hosea 6:1–3 is either the word of the nation's feigned repentance, or the response Yahweh desires from them.[191] Either way, the idea is expressed that God "will come to us as the showers," and "after two days [the period of time after which decomposition of a corpse sets in] he will revive us;

---

186. Deut 1:32–33.
187. See above.
188. Cf. Jesus' warning that a new captivity will come for Jerusalem, Luke 19:41–44; 21:20–24.
189. Kidner, *Psalms 73–150*, 343.
190. Hanson, *Prophetic*, 140–41.
191. See Kidner, *Hosea*, 64–65.

on the third day he will raise us up." This "anticipates the clearer accounts of national resurrection after death in exile."[192] But it is also, according to France,

> The nearest [verbal] parallel the Old Testament offers to Jesus' predictions of his resurrection, and its influence on them is widely accepted.[193]

In fact, Yahweh longs to revive the nation and will yet unconditionally return "the captivity (LXX αἰχμαλωσίαν)" of his people.[194] But the murderous acts of the priests, *breaking in to steal* and *waylaying outside*, prevented Yahweh's restoration and would bring a harvest of judgement upon Israel.[195] In John 10 context, this echo suggests that the corrupt religious hierarchy were bringing judgement upon the nation, as in the days of Hosea. This parallels the John 2 purging of merchants from God's house. Jesus, however, who would lay down his life that he might take it again, John 10:17–18, would embody and fulfil the hopes of Israel's restoration and resurrection[196] for his true sheep.

Decoding the story

"Truly, truly," never begins a new Johannine discourse, and here Jesus' words continue his address to the Pharisees, "If you were blind, you would have no guilt; but now that you say, 'We see,' your guilt remains" (John 9:41). As leaders over God's people they have recognized the unmistakable sign of the messianic deliverer, opening the eyes of the blind, but have nevertheless treated him as a false prophet and sinner, casting out his disciple. Jesus accordingly condemns those responsible, but does not stop there. Rather, using a cryptic parable, he relates the usurpation of the rule over God's people by the "Jewish" hierarchy, based around the Second Temple, seen as God's House and God's courts; Israel being the people (sheep) of God's courts. He also presents himself as the legitimate ruler over God's true people, appointed by God, who has come to lead his own sheep out from their midst in a NE.

Jesus' description of the one who climbs up into God's courts refers to the religious leaders, represented by the High Priest, the effective ruler of the Jewish people, successor to the corrupt Hasmonean king-priests. (Herod may also be implicated as a usurper-king).[197] This High Priest has usurped the position of shepherd (priest-king), and with his "hirelings" has imposed a tyrannical rule over the Lord's flock. This is not something new, but follows a pattern going back to the temple-garden where the serpent gained illegitimate access, imposing his rule over Adam's descendants. It is

---

192. Hubbard, *Hosea*, 125. Cf. Ezek 37.
193. France, *Jesus and the Old Testament*, 54. Cf. John 2:19–22.
194. KJV Hos 6:11.
195. Cf. Hubbard, *Hosea*, 131–32; Andersen and Freedman, *Hosea*, 432ff.
196. Cf. France, *Jesus and the Old Testament*, 55; Dodd, *According*, 103.
197. Cf. Wright, *John 1–10*, 149.

The Good Shepherd, John 10:1-21

likely that Jesus has this satanic usurpation in mind, especially as in John 8:44 he refers back to the fall and to unbelieving "Jews" as children of the devil who do his works. Moreover, he speaks of the *casting out* of the ruler of this world, a reference to Satan, in relation to his death, John 12:31.

Nevertheless, Jesus the true Shepherd has now entered God's courts, being recognized by the gatekeeper. This could be an implicit reference to JBap's acknowledgement and acceptance of Jesus. More likely it refers to the Father's recognition of Jesus' legitimacy and his ordination and investiture of Jesus to the office of messianic priest-king, on David's throne, ruling over the people of God.[198] Possibly the divine confirmation of Jesus as God's Son and Servant, at his baptism by JBap, is intended.[199]

This priest-king is now calling God's sheep, his true people, to follow him.[200] Like the man-born-blind they hear, recognize, and obey Jesus' voice, and he leads them out in a NE from bondage (enforced by the "Jewish" legalistic hierarchy) and slavery to Satan and to sin, to the freedom of the sons of God.[201] Indeed, the "Jewish" authorities expel Jesus' followers from their second-Temple worshipping community, just as Israel was ejected from Egypt. Jesus is providing atonement for his people's sin by means of a new paschal sacrifice, perhaps implicit here in the allusion to Zechariah 3, but becoming explicit later. He is also going before them to lead them home, as the new worshipping community, to the Father's house, understood as the new heavenly Temple, John 14:2-3. Moreover, he will embody their national resurrection and build the true Temple by his resurrection on the third day. They, as true Israelites, have recognized his teaching and the legitimacy of his rule[202] and followed him. Like the man-born-blind they refuse to follow the usurper and his regime.

Explanation and elaboration, John 10:7-18

Some argue that John 10:7-18 is not an explanation of John 10:1-5, but rather a meditation upon and elaboration of some of the metaphors found in those verses.[203] Bruce goes so far as to suggest that we have a short parable in which Jesus is compared to the door, inserted into the longer parable in which he is compared to the shepherd.[204] This is because there is an apparent incongruity between Jesus' description of himself as both the door and the Shepherd who enters by the door. Moreover, the "explana-

---

198. Cf. Ps 118:20; Ps 24:3-5; Ps 15, and God's charge to Joshua, Zech 3:7. Cf. John 6:27.
199. Cf. Mark 1:11; Matt 3:17; Luke 3:22.
200. Cf. John 1 as an example of the way Jesus called individuals, Peter, Philip, and Nathanael, by name, to be his followers.
201. John 8:31-36.
202. Cf. John 1:47, where Nathanael is called "an Israelite indeed," and John 1:49, where he confesses to Jesus, "You are the king of Israel."
203. See e.g. Carson, *John*, 383.
204. Bruce, *John*, 225.

tion" introduces new details such as hired hands and the death of the Shepherd. Some of these observations are at least partially correct. Jesus does not explain vv. 1–5 as a story. To do so *publicly* would have been dangerous. What he does do, however, is to focus on two key elements of the *paroimia*, and explain and elaborate them in terms of himself and his relationship with his people in contrast to the authorities.[205] Because of the danger of being accused of seditious speech, these amplifications are also allegorical.

In vv. 7–10, Jesus explains legitimate access to the court of the sheep by the door, v. 1. Jesus is the door, those who climb up another way are thieves, and those who enter by him are his sheep. There is no need to introduce "Christian shepherds," or distinguish door *to* the sheep from door *for* the sheep—all besides Jesus are either thieves or sheep.[206] In vv. 11–18, Jesus explains the behavior of the true (Good) Shepherd as opposed to hired hands whose only interest is reward. There is no need to interpret hired hands as being different individuals from the thieves. In both cases Jesus is speaking of the same people, the authorities, embodied in the High Priest, but from different perspectives. Hasmonean rulers and their successors were both thieves, bribing their way into the high priesthood and thus climbing up some other way, and hirelings, not caring for the sheep, but serving their own interests and deserting the sheep to wolves, fierce occupying nations.

I am the door, vv. 7–10

Echoes and allusions

"I AM . . ." V. 7

The ἐγώ εἰμι with explicit predicate echoes the revelation of the Lord's divine covenant name in the context of the Exodus and NE.[207] Jesus embodies this covenant Lord before his people as one who is all-sufficient to provide for them on their NE journey. Here he provides them with access to God and to the new worshipping community.

"THE DOOR," V. 7

As previously indicated, several commentators find that "the door" echoes the "gates of righteousness" and "gate of the Lord," Ps 118:19, 20.[208] This psalm concludes the "Egyptian *Hallel*,"[209] sung at Passover and at the Tabernacles water drawing ceremony.

---

205. See Morris, *John*, 505.
206. Cf. Ridderbos, *John*, 356; Schnackenburg, *John*, 2:289; Carson, *John*, 384.
207. See above.
208. Cf. John 10:7, 9. See on John 10:1, 2 above. Bowman, *Fourth Gospel*, 201, thinks the door is that of the Tabernacle and the sheepfold is the Tabernacle. Cf. Enz, "Type," 213; Keener, *John*, 811.
209. Pss 113–18.

The Good Shepherd, John 10:1-21

These psalms recall the Exodus redemption from Egypt, and the subsequent journey, culminating in a final deliverance at Jerusalem.[210] In Ps 118:5ff., the thanksgiving of the festal procession approaching the Temple[211] gives way to the testimony of a sole individual. He recounts his deliverance, being surrounded by all nations,[212] but rescued from death, in words taken from the Song of Moses at the Red Sea.[213] He demands, "wholly on his merits and perfected through suffering,"[214] that the Temple "gates of righteousness" be opened to him. The gatekeepers reply: "This is the gate of the LORD; the righteous shall enter through it." Thus "the door," Ps 118:20, is the way of access to the Lord.[215] This presents the human dilemma, that only the righteous may enter God's presence. In Ps 118:25–26, the suffering King is admitted to shouts of "Save us . . . Blessed is he who comes in the name of the LORD."

Similar ideas are present in the "gate liturgies,"[216] Pss 15 and 24, where the entrant to the Temple is examined by the gatekeepers and is required to give a confession of his righteousness. Thus in Ps 24 the Psalmist asks who is able to ascend to the hill of the Lord and stand before God in the holy place. The reply is that only "he who has clean hands and a pure heart" will receive blessings and righteousness from God. In the second part of Ps 24, the King of Glory and divine warrior[217] demands that the gates be opened to him and he is admitted as the conquering Lord.

Several considerations make the Ps 118 echo feasible:

1. Psalm 118 is frequently interpreted messianically in the NT, especially in terms of the rejected Temple cornerstone and the coming messianic King. In particular, in the Synoptics, in the context of the parable of the wicked Vinedressers, "wicked men," who recognize and destroy the heir, Jesus identifies himself as the Temple cornerstone and the "Jewish" authorities as the builders who rejected him.[218] This is conceptually similar to John 2:19, where Jesus is the new Temple whom the authorities seek to destroy,[219] and to the present John 10 context where "the Jews" have usurped authority, but Jesus is the door to the true Temple.

2. All Four Gospels cite "Hosanna! Blessed is he who comes in the name of the

---

210. See Kidner, *Psalms 73–150*, 401, 412.
211. Cf. Jer 33:11.
212. Cf. Zech 14:2; Ps 2:2.
213. Vv. 14–16 cf. Exod 15:2, 6, 12; Isa 12:2; Kidner, *Psalms 73–150*, 414.
214. Kidner, *Psalms 73–150*, 414–15. Cf. Heb 2:10; 9:24.
215. Brunson, *Psalm 118*, 338–39.
216. Kraus, *Psalms 60–150*, 395.
217. See Longman and Reid, *God is a Warrior*, 122. They see Jesus' Triumphal Entry as fulfilling the divine warrior imagery of Ps 118:10–16, 19–20.
218. Ps 118:22 cf. Isa 28:16; Matt 21:42; Mark 12:10; Luke 20:17. This "cornerstone" imagery is also used of Jesus in Acts 4:11; 1 Pet 2:4–7; Eph 2:20; Rom 9:32–33.
219. See Kerr, *Temple*, 88.

Lord," in the context of Jesus' triumphal entry.[220] John specifically links this with Zech 9:9, "your king is coming..."[221]

3. In the John 9–10 context there are a number of other possible echoes of Ps 118: "I am the light of the world," echoes "The LORD is God, and he has made his light to shine upon us." "I have come," echoes "he who comes." "If anyone enters by me," echoes "the righteous shall enter." "He will be saved," echoes "you have become my salvation." "I lay down my life for the sheep," may echo the binding of the "festal sacrifice" to the altar.[222]

4. As Brunson has demonstrated, there are several other important allusions to Ps 118 elsewhere in GJohn, not least in the John 10:24 surrounding of Jesus by the authorities.[223]

Given this echo it is possible that Messiah's entering the sanctuary through the door into the presence of God, representatively for his people, gaining access on their behalf,[224] stands behind Jesus' "I am the door" saying. "I am the way... No one comes to the Father except through me," John 14:6, employs a similar metaphor. He is the one who represents and goes before his people, by way of the cross, to prepare a place for them, that through his atoning sacrifice they might be where he is.[225] This is not too dissimilar to John 1:51, where the heavens open and Jesus is the ladder connecting heaven and earth, echoing Jacob's ladder (Gen 28:12–17) which he declared to be "the house of God... the gate of heaven." It is also not far from the thought expressed in Zech 3:7 where, on condition of his obedience, Joshua is given *access* to the heavenly council and *charge* over God's house and courts. Moreover, this understanding of Jesus' door saying may help solve any apparent incongruity between the pictures of Jesus as the Shepherd who enters through the door, and Jesus as the door through which people enter.

"HE WILL BE SAVED," V. 9

As previously suggested, this echoes Ps 118:21, where the Righteous Sufferer, entering through the door, exclaims, "You... have become my salvation." As he enters the people cry, "Save us, we pray, O LORD," a cry that is echoed at Tabernacles. (He) "will be saved," is also applied to God's people in Jeremiah, where the Lord will gather his

---

220. Ps 118:25, 26 cf. Matt 21:9; 23:39; Mark 11:9; Luke 13:35; 19:38; John 12:13.
221. Cf. John 12:13–15; Brown, *John I–XII*, 460–61; Hanson, *Prophetic*, 164; Beasley-Murray, *John*, 210.
222. Cf. John 9:5 with Ps 118:27; John 10:10 with Ps 118:26; John 10:9 with Ps 118:20; John 10:9 with Ps 118:21; John 10:15, 17, 18 with Ps 118:27.
223. John 10:24 cf. Ps 118:10–12; Brunson, *Psalm 118*, 351–61. See below.
224. Cf. Kidner, *Psalms 73–150*, 415, citing Heb 2:10; 9:24; Mays, *Psalms*, 376.
225. John 14:2–6.

flock in a NE, which will eclipse the deliverance from Egypt, and appoint a Davidic branch as King over them.[226]

"GO IN AND OUT," V. 9

Commentators suggest that, to "go in and out," John 10:9, represents freedom and security in everyday life, rather than entrance into and exit from the sheepfold.[227] I would suggest, however, that it also has other connotations. Joshua's going out and coming in as shepherd before the people suggests his leadership in warfare,[228] and perhaps their journey from Egypt to the Promised Land. Moses' confession that he could no longer "go out and come in" was in the context of his handing over to Joshua as the military leader who would cross the Jordan and possess the land (Deut 31:2). During the conquest of the land, Caleb confessed, "I am still as strong today as I was in the day that Moses sent me; my strength now is as my strength was then, for war and for going [out] and coming [in]," Josh 14:11. Similarly, David "led out and brought in Israel [in battle]. And the Lord said to [him], 'You shall be shepherd of my people Israel.'"[229] A similar thought is present in the movement of the Tabernacle. Thus, when the Tabernacle went forward on the journey, Moses said, "*Arise*, O LORD, and let your enemies be scattered . . ." When it rested he said, "*Return*, O LORD, to the ten thousand thousands of Israel."[230] In Ps 121:8, "the LORD will keep your going out and your coming in," is set in the context of the Lord's protection of pilgrims to mount Zion.

It is possible that the order of the words is significant. Thus in the context of warfare, the usual order is going out, coming in. In John 10:9, as in Deut 28:6, a blessing for obedience, the order is coming in and going out. Moreover, the Deuteronomic blessing is grouped with a number of beatitudes that suggest domestic happiness. Yet even here the "going out" is immediately followed by promise of victory in warfare against enemies that "come out against you."[231] Moreover, this warfare concept harmonizes with Jesus' sending out his disciples, as a spiritual army, "as lambs among wolves"[232]

"FIND PASTURE," V. 9

This is also associated with the NE journeys of the sheep and their ultimate destination. In Ps 23, the Lord, as David's shepherd, guides him into green pasture beside still

---

226. Cf. Jer 23:6; 31:7.
227. Cf. Schnackenburg, *John*, 2:358, citing Deut 31:2; Ps 121:8; Thompson, *Deuteronomy*, 270; Craigie, *Deuteronomy*, 336; Morris, *John*, 509; Josh 6:1.
228. Num 27:17. Cf. Milgroom, *Numbers*, 234–36.
229. Cf. 2 Sam 5:2; 1 Chr 11:2; 1 Kgs 22:17; Ezek 34:5; 1 Kgs 3:7; Isa 37:28.
230. Num 10:35–36 (emphasis mine).
231. Deut 28:7. Cf. Merrill, *Deuteronomy*, 354.
232. NKJV Luke 10:3. Cf. Longman and Reid, *God is a Warrior*, 105.

PART II—DETAILED EXEGETICAL EXAMINATION OF JOHN 5–10

waters. The ultimate movement of the Psalm, however, is towards David's dwelling in the house of the Lord forever. In Isa 49:9–10, the Servant frees the captives, leading them towards Zion; "they shall feed along the ways; on all bare heights shall be their pasture." A similar thought is expressed in Ezekiel, where the Lord as shepherd will gather his people from the countries, bringing them into their own land where he will "feed them with good pasture . . . they shall lie down in good grazing land, and on rich pasture they shall feed."[233]

"All who came before me," v. 8

This does not refer to OT prophets sent by God, but to false rulers and messiahs viewed as "thieves and robbers." Two such "messiahs" who preceded Jesus have been identified in the DSS. Wise thinks that the Damascus Document is a literal presentation of the departure of Judah and his followers from Jerusalem to eke out a living as bandits in the harsh terrain south of Damascus. Their persecution, and the death of Judah prior to 63 B.C., led to a great messianic movement.[234] Knohl thinks that Menahem, a respected Jewish scholar and member of the court of Herod the Great, is the suffering and exalted figure described in one of the hymns from Qumran. His followers subsequently thought that, having been killed and publicly disgraced, Menahem rose after three days.[235] Jesus' "all" is wide enough to include such figures and may well do so, but the Johannine context suggests that his words were also aimed at the Jerusalem "Jewish" hierarchy.

"steal and kill and destroy," v. 10

It was pointed out (above) that John's "thieves and robbers," echoes the description of the priests of Hosea's day that thrived under an evil king. The actions of John's thieves (λῃσταί), "steal and kill and destroy," John 10:10, also echo those of Hosea's priests: "As robbers lie in wait for a man, so the priests band together; they murder on the way to Shechem; they commit villainy," Hosea 6:9. It is interesting that θύσῃ is not the usual word for "to kill," but means "to sacrifice," or "to kill for food."[236] Thus there could be an allusion to the "Jewish" priests.[237] Killing the sheep for food is an accusation made against the shepherds (kings), responsible for the exile, of Ezek 34:3: "You eat the fat, you clothe yourselves with the wool, you slaughter the fat ones, but you do not feed the sheep." These same rulers are castigated in Jer 23:1[238] for *destroying* the sheep (LXX

---

233. Ezek 34:13–14. Cf. "plantations of renown" in Ezek 34:29.
234. Wise, *First Messiah*, cited by Hess, "Messiahs Here and There," 105.
235. Knohl, *Messiah Before Jesus*, 106.
236. Morris, *John*, 508, n. 33.
237. See Brown, *John I–XII*, 386.
238. Cf. Ezek 34, which is based on this passage.

ἀπόλλυμι, the same verb used in John 10:10). That these passages are echoed is made probable by other clear allusions that John makes to them here.

"Killing for food," (θύσῃ) may also echo Mic 3:1–4, where Israel's leaders skinned and cooked God's people for food. It is also possible that θύσῃ echoes the "flock for slaughter," Zech 11:4–5.[239] These sheep (Israel) are to be sold for meat.[240] Given one last chance by the Lord, they reject the Good Shepherd, paying him thirty pieces of silver. A worthless shepherd replaces him, who neglects his duties and "devours the flesh of the fat ones."[241] In an elaboration upon Ezek 34, things will get worse before they get better. The implication is that a (then future) worthless king would yet bring another dispersion of Israel. I suggest that John might well have understood this scattering as the A.D. 70 devastation visited by Titus on Jerusalem.[242] In support of this interpretation is the rejection of Jesus as king in favor of Caesar.[243] McComiskey writes,

> When we look for a shepherd-leader whom the nation's rulers rejected for thirty pieces of silver at a time when the nation fell into foreign hands, the New Testament stands insistently before us, urging us to look at Christ, the Good Shepherd . . . Only forty years after this rejection by the civil and religious leaders of his time, the cruel events of A.D. 70 occurred.[244]

Although John may have understood Caesar as the "worthless shepherd" of Zech 11:15–17, since in the OT the nations were portrayed as wild beasts, it is more likely that he understood this foreign power to be the wolf that scattered the sheep.[245] Moreover, in view of the Temple and synagogue background of John 10, as well as Zechariah's priest-king shepherd motif, it is more likely that the authorities, embodied in the High Priest, were John's thief and "worthless shepherd" (understood as collaborating with Caesar).

"I HAVE COME," V. 10 (NKJV)

This refers in GJohn to Jesus' coming from (and returning to) God,[246] but it also has connotations of an eschatological deliverer, promised in the OT. There are several strands to this OT expectation, including the eschatological Prophet, referred to in

---

239. Cf. Jer 25:34–35.
240. Cf. Baldwin, *Haggai, Zechariah and Malachi*, 179; McComiskey, "Zechariah," 1191.
241. Zech 11:12–16 cf. Ezek 34:2–5. Cf. Baldwin, *Haggai, Zechariah and Malachi*, 179.
242. Cf. McComiskey, "Zechariah," 1205.
243. Cf. John 18:33–40; 19:1–6; esp. "We have no king but Caesar," 19:15–16, 19–21. See above on the John 19:5, "behold the man," echo of Zech 6:12; 3:8. Cf. also, "They will look on him whom they have pierced," John 19:37, citing Zech 12:10.
244. McComiskey, "Zechariah," 1201. Cf. Matt 26:14–15.
245. Cf. Dan 7; Ps 74:19. See below.
246. NKJV John 10:10 cf. John 1:9, 11, 14–15, 17, 27; 3:13, 17, 31; 5:23, 37, 43; 6:50, 57; 7:33; 8:14; 42; 9:39; 11:42; 13:3; 17:11; 20:17.

PART II—DETAILED EXEGETICAL EXAMINATION OF JOHN 5-10

John 6:14.[247] But the main lines, regarding a "coming one," concern the coming Davidic Messiah and the coming of God to his people in a NE.

THE COMING DAVIDIC MESSIAH

The roots of royal messianism are found in Gen 1–2 where Adam is pictured as a royal viceroy in the garden. As we have seen, the sacral dimension of his role is hinted at in the use of the verbs עָבַד and שָׁמַר (serve and keep/guard), used later of priestly service in the Tabernacle and Temple.[248] The seed of the woman and future deliverer, promised in Gen 3:15, came to be seen as a royal figure:[249] a prototype of the Son of Man[250] and the Davidic priest-king who will subdue his enemies under his feet.[251] Other important allusions to a *coming* king are found in the Pentateuch: Kings would *come* from Abraham;[252] the sceptre would not depart from Judah until Shiloh *comes*;[253] a star shall *come* out of Jacob and a sceptre shall rise out of Israel.[254]

In the former and latter prophets, the messianic hope centers in David who fulfils the prophecy of 1 Sam 2:10, "The Lord . . . will give strength to his king."[255] In this respect 2 Sam 7 is particularly important. Here, David, God's under-shepherd, desired to build a house for the Lord, having been given rest from his enemies. But this rest is only an anticipation of a greater rest to come when the Lord will "appoint a place" for his people Israel, "so that they may dwell in their own place and be disturbed no more," 2 Sam 7:10. Indeed the Lord, having brought Israel up from Egypt, had "moved about in a tent," but had not asked any of his under-shepherds to build him a house. Rather, the Lord would build David a house, establishing the kingdom of his seed.[256]

---

247. This reference appears to subsume the Mosaic Prophet under the Messiah, as does the attempt to make Jesus king, John 6:14–15.

248. See above. See Block, "My Servant David," 37, n. 71.

249. Thus the Jewish interpretations found in the LXX and Targums (*Ps.-J., Neof.*, and poss. *Onq.*) take the Serpent as Satan over whom victory will be gained in the days of King Messiah. The NT alludes to this passage in a "broadly messianic sense" Cf. Wehnam, *Genesis 1–15*, 80–81; Rom 16:20; Heb 2:14; Rev 12.

250. Cf. Ps 8:6; Dan 7:14. Wenham, *Genesis 1–15*, 80–81, thinks "Son of Man," as a title for Jesus, may echo Gen 3:15, as may Jesus' use of "woman" for his mother in John 2:4; 19:26. Cf. Alexander, "Messianic Ideology," 28, n. 22.

251. Cf. Ps 110:1; 2:8f.; 72:9; 89:23. Cf. Alexander, "Messianic Ideology," 31ff. For allusions to Gen 3:15 in the Royal Psalms see Wifall, "Gen 3:15," 363.

252. Cf. Gen 17:6, 16; 35:11.

253. Gen 49:10–11. The mention of a donkey's colt and garments washed in the blood of grapes may be echoed in Zech 9:9 and Isa 63:3.

254. Num 24:17, where the King would conquer Agag. David conquered Agag in 1 Sam 15:8; 2 Sam 1:1.

255. Cf. 2 Sam 5:1–3.

256. Cf. the promised seed of Gen 3:15.

The Good Shepherd, John 10:1–21

Coming from David, he would be God's son and would build God's house.²⁵⁷ David spoke of this "covenant" as the charter "for mankind."²⁵⁸

Though the Davidic tree would be chopped down, the latter prophets speak of a shoot or branch that would *come* forth from its stump that would judge the poor, smite the earth, and bring in paradisal conditions.²⁵⁹ Micah speaks of a king, "whose origin is from of old, from ancient days," who would *come* forth from Bethlehem, Micah 5:2. Zechariah speaks of the *coming* of this Davidic king to Jerusalem, predicting that "his rule shall be from sea to sea, and from the River to the ends of the earth," Zech 9:9–10.

Several psalms specifically speak of messiah's "coming."²⁶⁰ In Ps 72:6, The King's Son will *come down* (יֵרֵד) "like rain." Psalm 24:7, 9 summons the gates of Zion to allow the "King of glory" to *come in*. The approaching King is greeted with "blessed is he who comes in the name of the LORD."²⁶¹ In Ps 40, Messiah declares, "Behold, I have come; in the scroll of the book it is written of me."²⁶² The importance of this verse to the NT is seen in Heb 10:5–14 where the author applies it to Jesus' sacrificial death as providing atonement for sin and abrogating the ineffectual Levitical sacrifices. An echo in John 10:10–11, indicates that Jesus' laying down his life provides vicarious atonement for sin.

As well as announcing the fact of Messiah's coming, the Psalms delineate its nature. Psalm 2:7 (cf. Heb 1:5) announces the Lord's decree that the Davidic Messiah is his Son. In Ps 89:26–27, he is referred to as God's Son and firstborn, the highest of the kings of the earth. In both these psalms he subdues the earth. The latter speaks of the covenant whereby David's seed and throne endure forever. Psalm 45:6 (cf. Heb 1:8) speaks of the Son in terms of deity, "Your throne, O God, is forever." Psalm 110 has the messianic King sit at God's right hand and declares him "a priest forever after the order of Melchizedek."

Several Davidic Psalms are understood in the NT as important witnesses to Messiah's sufferings, fulfilled by Jesus' passion.²⁶³ Psalm 16:10 is cited of Jesus' resurrection.²⁶⁴ Psalm 22, an important testimonial to Jesus' crucifixion, also suggests his resurrection, speaking of victory, and a seed, following suffering.²⁶⁵ In the Synoptics,

---

257. See 2 Sam 7:7–16.

258. Cf. 2 Sam 7:19; 23:5; Block, "My Servant David," 39, 40, n. 83; Kaiser, *Messiah in the Old Testament*, 78–83.

259. Cf. Isa 11:1; 4:2; 60:21; Ps 80:15; Jer 23:3–6; 33:12–17; Zech 3:8; 6:12.

260. About 15 Psalms are cited in the NT as messianic, although possibly all Davidic and Royal psalms were similarly regarded. Cf. Kidner, *Psalms 1–72*, 18, 25.

261. Ps 118:26 cf. John 12:13.

262. Ps 40:7 cf. Heb 10:9. See Kidner, *Psalms 1–72*, 159–60.

263. Cf. Ps 22, 35, 40, 41, 109, 69, 118.

264. Cf. Acts 2:27, 31; 13:3. John would also have had OT testimonia to Jesus' resurrection in mind when he wrote, "As yet they did not understand the Scripture, that he must rise from the dead," John 20:9.

265. Ps 22:22–31. Cf. the victory and seed promised to the Suffering Servant, Isa 53:10–12.

PART II—DETAILED EXEGETICAL EXAMINATION OF JOHN 5-10

this psalm is echoed in Jesus' cry of dereliction.[266] In GJohn it is "fulfilled" by the dividing of Jesus' clothes, and by Jesus' thirst.[267] This Davidic messianic suffering is also an important bridge between the anointed King, the Suffering Servant, and Zechariah's pierced one.[268]

THE COMING OF GOD

In addition to the above, there are several OT references to the *coming of God* to his people, particularly in Isaiah, where "the LORD of hosts will come down to fight on Mount Zion"; "the LORD . . . will come like a rushing stream"; "the LORD will come in fire."[269] Two passages are particularly important to the John 10 context, both involving the Lord's coming to the wilderness, to lead his redeemed people from captivity on the road back to Zion. In Isa 35:4–5, "God will come with vengeance . . . He will come and save you. Then shall the eyes of the blind be opened." Jesus' opening blind eyes, a sign never seen "since the world began"[270] is thus evidence of God's NE coming in the person of Jesus. In Isa 40:10–11, in NE context,

> The Lord GOD comes with might, and his arm rules for him; behold, his reward is with him, and his recompense before him. He will tend his flock like a shepherd; he will gather the lambs in his arms; he will carry them in his bosom, and gently lead those that are with young.[271]

In John 10, Yahweh's NE shepherding of the sheep is fulfilled by Jesus who declares, "I have come that they may have life . . . *I am* the Good Shepherd."[272]

Zechariah 14:5, "the LORD my God will come," is another important reference, relevant here because of its eschatological Tabernacles context: Jerusalem is surrounded by the nations, and a new captivity ensues, but the Lord comes to deliver his people, leading them out of the city, inaugurating the eschatological judgement and consummation. Malachi 3:1, 5, is also relevant, predicting the Lord's sudden coming to his Temple to purify and judge his people.[273]

---

266. Ps 22:1 cf. Matt 27:46; Mark 15:34.

267. Cf. Ps 22:18 and John 19:24; Ps 22:15 and John 19:28. Cf. Aland et al., *Greek New Testament*, 4th revised edn., 398.

268. Cf. "they have pierced my hands and feet," Ps 22:16, with Isa 53:5 and Zech 12:10.

269. Cf. Isa 31:4; 59:19–20; 66:15.

270. John 9:32.

271. Cf. Num 11:12, where Moses complained, "Did I conceive all this people? Did I give them birth, that you should say to me, 'Carry them in your bosom, as a nurse carries a nursing child,' to the land that you swore to give their fathers?"

272. NKJV John 10:10–11.

273. See above on the John 7:14 echo of Mal 3:1.

"Life," v. 10

"Life" is more than existence, connoting eternal life as opposed to destruction. "Life" finds OT echoes in the tree of life. "Abundant" life, suggests life in all its fullness—life that only God can bestow. Such conditions echo several OT passages associated with shepherd imagery. Thus in Isa 11:6–9, ferocious animals cease to harm: "They shall not hurt or destroy in all my holy mountain." In Isa 40:10–11, the Lord himself will protect the young and vulnerable. In Mic 5:4, under the Davidic shepherd, the sheep shall dwell secure. In Jeremiah the scattered sheep will be brought back to the fold and "shall be fruitful and multiply . . . shall fear no more . . . neither shall any be missing."[274] In Ezek 34, the Lord will feed the sheep with good pasture and they shall lie down. He will strengthen the weak and banish wild beasts. He will send showers of blessing and cause the land to be fruitful.[275] Such conditions imply a return to paradise.

The Story elaborated and explained: The door

Jesus is the door to God's true Temple and thus the eschatological "door" of salvation. God's presence is barred to all but the righteous, but Jesus, God's righteous Son and the Davidic Messiah, enters in, on behalf of his people, providing access to God and NE salvation for them. Thus they enter in and find salvation through him.

In doing so, Jesus leads them out and away from the Jerusalem Temple, controlled by corrupt "Jewish" authorities, and, more importantly, he leads them out of the dominion of sin and Satan (who usurped authority over humanity in Eden) in a NE back to the true Zion. He will deliver them from their enemies, leading them "in and out," on their pilgrimage, to the heavenly Jerusalem, providing "pasture" for their needs, bestowing upon them present possession of eternal life.

Others, messianic pretenders and the "Jewish" leaders, came for the sheep before Jesus, but they are "thieves and robbers," having laid claim to the people of God illegitimately, bypassing the true King. Their only intention is personal gain at the expense of the people's destruction. It is because of their wicked deeds, rejecting the Messiah, that God will bring judgement upon the earthly Jerusalem and its Temple, and its people will be destroyed and scattered. Jesus' true followers have not listened to them, but all that do will share in the judgement about to be visited by God.

Jesus is the true messianic King and Son of God, promised throughout the OT, now come for his sheep. He has come to vicariously lay down his life in death to atone for their sins and to rise again. As the Davidic Messiah, he will initiate his everlasting kingdom and subdue the world to himself. As the Lord God, he has come to visit his people whom he will gather to himself from the ends of the world in a NE.

---

274. Jer 23:3–7 cf. 33:14ff.
275. Ezek 34 cf. 36:22ff.; 37:11–14; 22–28.

PART II—DETAILED EXEGETICAL EXAMINATION OF JOHN 5–10

I am the Good Shepherd, vv. 11–18

Echoes and allusions

GOOD SHEPHERD, V. 11

"Good" Shepherd has no strong *verbal* echo of an OT passage, since nowhere in the OT does the adjective "Good" modify "Shepherd." Nevertheless, there are strong echoes of OT concepts: Thus, *the* Good Shepherd implies a *particular* (ultimate) Good Shepherd, whose coming has been foretold. To the question, "Who is *the* Good Shepherd?" the OT has a twofold answer. In terms of Israel's God, the Lord is the "Good" Shepherd.[276] In terms of human leadership, David is his ultimate under-shepherd.[277] Jesus' statement, "I am the Good Shepherd," suggests that in the earthly life of Jesus an epiphany is taking place in which Yahweh, the Shepherd and covenant God of Israel, is now manifest among his people.[278] This reflects several OT passages where Yahweh himself will come to shepherd his people, gathering them from all the countries in which they have been scattered,[279] appointing a Davidic messiah over them. Since John understands Jesus to be both Son of God and Messiah (John 20:31), it is likely that Jesus here represents *both* the Lord *and* his under-shepherd—his "living image" and representative.[280]

A further point of comparison with the OT is the juxtaposition and contrast of the Good Shepherd with wicked shepherds.[281] In John 10, Jesus *the* Good Shepherd is contrasted with the "Jewish" hierarchy who, as thieves and hirelings, destroy and scatter the sheep. In the OT the Lord contrasts himself with Israel's wicked rulers, who have destroyed and scattered the people (Ezek 34). Moreover, the Lord comes to shepherd his sheep precisely because of the failure of Israel's shepherds, just as Jesus shepherds the man-born-blind, who has been failed by "Jewish" leaders. He comes to renew the covenant, and to unite his people under one shepherd in one fold.[282]

A striking difference with the OT is found in the fact that Yahweh does not explicitly suffer on behalf of his sheep (although see Isa 63:7–9), but in John 10 the Good Shepherd lays down his life for them. If we think of an OT Good Shepherd who suffers

---

276. Cf. Pss 23; 80:1; 100:3; Isa 40:11; Ezek 43.

277. Prior to David, Moses would have been considered the outstanding under-shepherd, leading Israel out of the slavery of Egypt, but in the NE tradition, David has taken over the Mosaic role. It is possible that David is seen in some sense as a second Moses. Cf. Allison, *New Moses*, 35ff.

278. See above on "I am."

279. Cf. Isa 40:9–11; Jer 23:3; Ezek 34:11ff.; Zech 10:3; Deut 30:3–6.

280. Cf. Brown, *John I–XII*, 398, who understands it as *either or*.

281. Bruce, *John*, 226, notes that in speaking of the shepherd as "good," Jesus is contrasted with the Zech 11:17 "worthless shepherd." Carson, *John*, 386, thinks this allusion possible.

282. Cf. Ezek 34:23; 37:22, 24; John 10:16.

we are reminded of the Servant,[283] the shepherd-king of Zech 9–14,[284] and possibly the Son of Man of Dan 7.[285] In Zech 11, however, the shepherd seems to represent both the Lord and his earthly under-shepherd,[286] portrayed in the context of a critique of Israel's shepherds.[287] Moreover, they shall "look on me, on him whom they have pierced," Zech 12:10, seems to combine the Lord with a pierced Davidic king and first-born. This enigmatic passage may suggest that the Lord himself is pierced through.[288] Furthermore, John identifies this "pierced one" as Jesus (John 19:37).

Does the Good Shepherd reflect Zech 11:4–14? On the face of it, the answer is negative. Not only is this passage a "complete reversal" of Ezek 34 optimism, but the differences between the Good Shepherd of John 10 and that of Zech 11 are "striking."[289] However, if we think of the doomed flock of Zech 11 in terms of Israel, represented by her leaders, their rejection of Jesus is patent, not least in John 9:1—10:21. In Galilee many of his disciples "no longer walked with him." In Jerusalem, when they sought to arrest and stone him, he mysteriously departed from the Temple, indicating his rejection of those that rejected him. Moreover, Jesus could truly have said of Israel's leaders, "my soul was weary of them, and their soul also loathed me."[290] The rejection of Jesus came to a head with Judas' agreement with the chief priests to hand him over to them for thirty pieces of silver. Jesus' departure from the city, and his crossing the Kidron brook, pursued by Judas with a cohort, echo David's departure across Kidron, pursued by Absalom.[291] The ultimate rejection, however, was when Jesus was presented to the people as their king and they called for his crucifixion.[292]

If Zech 11 stands behind this rejection, as I argue that it does, then several implications follow:

1. Having rejected him, Jesus abandons the unbelieving "Jews" to their fate.

2. The Lord would break the covenants between Israel and the nations, and Judah and Ephraim.

---

283. Isa 53. Cf. Brown, *John I-XII*, 398.

284. Cf. Brown, *John I-XII*, 398; Schnackenburg, *John*, 2:295.

285. See Bruce, *Old Testament Themes*, 90–91.

286. See above on the Shepherd and the NE.

287. Cf. Carson, *John*, 386; Bruce, *John*, 116.

288. The idea of God suffering may be present in Gen 15:17. Cf. Robertson, *Christ of the Covenants*, 130–31. That God is impassive ("without body, parts and passion") is central to Christian theology. But in that the Son became a man he became capable of death in his human nature. In this sense, Charles Wesley was correct in speaking of the immortal dying and being amazed that "Thou, my God, shouldst die for me."

289. So Duguid, "Messianic Themes," 278.

290. ASV Zech 11:8.

291. John 18:1ff. cf. 2 Sam 15:23. It is interesting that David later wished that he could have died for his son, Absalom, whereas Jesus did die for his friends.

292. John 19:14–15. See above.

3. The nation would be left to the tender mercies of the anti-shepherd king of their choice.[293]
4. The situation is not permanent.[294]
5. A remnant will be tried, purified and cleansed, becoming part of the new Israel with whom the covenant is renewed.[295]

It may be objected that the Shepherd of Zechariah 11 does not suffer. This is answered by pointing up the parallels between the shepherd-king cameos in Zechariah 11–14 where the Shepherd *does* suffer. Moreover, John understood the whole of Zechariah 9–14 as testimony to Jesus.[296]

"LAYS DOWN HIS LIFE FOR THE SHEEP," V. 11

τὴν ψυχὴν αὐτοῦ τίθησιν ὑπὲρ τῶν προβάτων, is clearly a reference to Jesus' death on the cross. Any thought that this refers merely to the shepherd "risking his life" is dispelled by verses 17–18. Moreover, ὑπέρ indicates the vicarious sacrificial nature of that death.[297] In John 6:51, Jesus gives his flesh for (ὑπέρ) the life of the world. In John 13:37, in the context of Jesus' departure by way of the cross, Peter ironically protests "I will lay down my life for you" (τὴν ψυχήν μου ὑπὲρ σοῦ θήσω). In John 15:13 Jesus refers to the extent of his love for the disciples (friends) in that he lays down his life for them (τὴν ψυχὴν αὐτοῦ θῇ ὑπὲρ τῶν φίλων αὐτοῦ). The question here is whether this echoes the OT shepherd imagery? Though there are few clear verbal echoes, there are strong conceptual parallels.

Absent from the Levitical cult, vicarious human sacrifice is foreshadowed in the concept of sacral kingship. As shepherd, the king had a responsibility for his people (sheep), something David understood from his days as a shepherd-boy.[298] As leader of the people,[299] royal priest, and the Lord's firstborn,[300] the king represented both the people and the Lord, "the King of Israel, and his Redeemer."[301] Thus he had a unique responsibility, analogous to that of the firstborn at the first Passover, to offer himself to God for the redemption of the people.

---

293. Cf. Zech 11:6, 16.
294. See above on the demise of the wicked shepherd.
295. Cf. Zech 12:10–13:1; 13:8–9.
296. See Dodd, "Old Testament in the New," 174–75. Cf. GJohn's citations of Zechariah above.
297. See Carson, *John*, 386.
298. 1 Sam 17:34–7.
299. Cf. Mowinckel, *Psalms*, 1:44.
300. Ps 89:27.
301. Isa 44:6. Cf. Holland, *Contours*, 264. He notes that this verse is echoed in Rev 1:4–8, where Jesus is "firstborn," "King," and "first and last."

The Good Shepherd, John 10:1-21

There are at least two occasions when Israel's leader or king offered himself as a vicarious sacrifice:

1. Moses interceded for Israel asking God to forgive their sins, but if not to blot his name out of the book the Lord had written. The idea is that Moses' life should atone for their sin.[302] But the request is flatly refused, suggesting that vicarious human suffering was not an option for Moses.[303] Durham writes, "No one save Yahweh himself can undertake to do what Moses here wants to do."[304] Nevertheless, that God's under-shepherd Moses made this offer is significant.[305]

2. David interceded for Israel, asking that the Lord's hand be against him and his father's house rather than "these [innocent] sheep."[306] This differs from Moses' act in that David confessed his guilt and the people's "innocence." Nevertheless, it showed the same willingness on the part of Israel's shepherd to offer himself for the sheep.[307] Moreover, by invoking God's wrath upon himself and his father's house, he seems to have invoked the punishment of Israel upon his offspring, including the Messiah. Significantly, the Lord made no immediate response to David. Rather, he sent the prophet Gad to tell David to raise an altar at a location intended to be the site of the Temple.[308] There the fire (wrath) of God fell upon the sacrifice and the plague was stayed.[309] It is significant that this was the same site, mount Moriah, "chosen by the Lord," where Abraham, father of kings, offered his "firstborn" son, and where Solomon's Temple was to be built.[310] Though substituted with a ram, Heb 11:17-19 views Abraham's "firstborn" as being figuratively offered and received back from the dead. Moreover, as previously noted, in some Jewish traditions, the *Aqeda* (binding of Isaac) is viewed as the basis of God's acceptance of Temple sacrifice.[311]

At face value, these examples seem to attest to the unacceptability of vicarious human sacrifice on the part of Israel. Whenever human sacrifice might be required, animals were substituted, as at the Passover, where the lamb was substituted for the firstborn. Moreover, every firstborn thereafter was to be redeemed with a lamb. Whenever human sacrifice *was actually made*, it was viewed with abhorrence.[312] The very

---

302. Exod 32:33. Cf. Childs, *Exodus*, 571; Durham, *Exodus*, 432.
303. Cf. Paul's desire to sacrifice himself for his kinsmen, Rom 9:3.
304. Durham, *Exodus*, 432.
305. It was viewed by early Christian interpreters as typical of Christ. Cf. Childs, *Exodus*, 576-77.
306. Cf. 2 Sam 24:17; 1 Chr 21:17.
307. Cf. Baldwin, *1 and 2 Samuel*, 297.
308. 1 Chr 21:18; 22:1.
309. 1 Chr 21:26-27.
310. Cf. Williamson, *1 and 2 Chronicles*, 203-5; Anderson, *2 Samuel*, 283-84.
311. See above on the Passover, "Developments within Judaism."
312. Cf. Lev 18:21; Deut 18:10; 2 Kgs 16:3; 21:6; 2 Chr 33:6; Jer 32:35; Ezek 16:21.

fact that the examples of Abraham, Moses, and David are mentioned with approval, however, indicates that it was not the principle *per se* that was at fault, but that other factors were intolerable. The practice was associated with vengeful pagan gods, violated the sanctity of human life, and resulted in the death of countless innocent children. Above all, it was not efficacious as a means of atonement.[313] From the NT perspective, animal sacrifices could not take away sins either, but were a temporary measure pointing towards an ultimate solution.[314] God "passed over" sins, leaving them unpunished, until atoned for by the ultimate, acceptable, once for all, sacrificial offering of the Son of God himself.[315]

For some scholars another example of the king offering himself for the people is evidenced in a liturgy implicit within the psalms. For Mowinckel, the king is the "corporate representative," through whom the people approach Yahweh.[316] Not only does he receive the promises and power of blessing that are to benefit the whole congregation, but he is also its "breath of life," and happiness. His righteousness is their righteousness; his sin is their sin.[317] Moreover,

> He appears as the vicarious bearer of all the misfortunes and sufferings which have hit the people, and subjects himself to rites of expiation which have to be performed, and prays for help and salvation.[318]

According to the Myth and Ritual school, in the cultic New Year ritual the king took the part of the dying and reviving deity: Psalm 22 (for example) speaks of the "dying king" and "reviving ruler."[319] As Van Gemeren points out, however, this theory, based on the Babylonian New Year Festival, "[sacrifices] the principle of diversity, assuming that Israel's religious experience was no different than that of her neighbors."[320] Unlike the Babylonian god (Tammuz) who is caught up in the unending cycle of nature (seasons), Yahweh is transcendent over them. Moreover, Wright is adamant that there are no "dying and rising gods and goddesses in the Jewish world."[321] Similarly Kidner, noting that the theory lacks direct evidential support, rightly affirms that it is better to understand such psalms as Ps 22, as the NT does, as prophetic of the sufferings of Christ.[322]

Indeed, from the outset, Scripture predicts the coming of a messianic King who will suffer vicariously for his people: Genesis 3:15 "anticipates the creation of a royal

---

313. The victims were offered against the will of the Lord and their own will and lacked the sanctity and representative character necessary to make vicarious atonement.

314. Heb 10:11–12.

315. Cf. Rom 3:25; Heb 10:12ff.

316. Mowinckel, *Psalms*, 1:60.

317. Ibid., 61.

318. Ibid., 61. He cites Ps 102 as an example.

319. Kraus, *Psalms 1–59*, 293. This psalm is "fulfilled" in John 19:24, 28; Matt 27:46; Mark 15:34.

320. Van Gemeren, "Psalms," 12–13.

321. Wright, *RSG*, 81.

322. Kidner, *Psalms 1–72*, 105, citing Acts 2:30–31.

The Good Shepherd, John 10:1–21

line" through which the fall of man will be reversed.[323] Moreover, it suggests that Messiah, the woman's "seed," would be a second-Adam figure who in destroying the serpent would himself suffer. This messianic expectation is developed throughout the OT, in ever increasing detail, in types and shadows and by explicit prophetic predictions.

Of all the OT messianic prophecies, however, by far the most likely referent for the Johannine "lays down his life for the sheep," is the Servant of Isa 53. Thus Jesus' saying, "I lay down (τίθημι) my life (ψυχὴν) for the sheep" is "quite close" to the Hebrew of Isa 53:10 (נַפְשׁוֹ . . . תָּשִׂים).[324] I have previously argued that the Servant is a royal messianic figure who vicariously offers his life as a paschal sacrifice that initiates the NE.[325] Here I would also point out how conceptually close this is to John 10:11, 15; so close that the two are directly related.[326] Thus, the Servant (Davidic King-Messiah) makes his soul (נַפְשׁוֹ) an offering for sin (אָשָׁם), Isa 53:10, having "poured out his soul to death," הֶעֱרָה לַמָּוֶת נַפְשׁוֹ, Isa 53:12. Foretelling Messiah's death, the verb הֶעֱרָה[327] suggests that he actively caused this to happen.[328] Moreover, he died *for* "us," Isa 53:5, his people, the *sheep* that had gone astray; his death being a sin offering (אָשָׁם) that takes away his people's sin and makes them righteous.[329] Because of this God highly exalts him, just as Jesus is exalted by the Father.[330] Moreover, as a result of his sacrifice, he will see his seed and lengthen his days, Isa 53:10–11. This compares with Jesus' laying down his life in order that he may take it up again, John 10:17.

Scholars have objected to this interpretation of the Servant's sufferings on several counts.

1. It has been suggested that the Servant does not actually die. Rather, although he "risks his life," references to his death are only "metaphorical." But this is hardly credible in view of the mention of the Servant's grave, Isa 53:9.[331]

2. Likewise the Servant did not experience resurrection. Rather, he received a reversal of fortune having been released from imprisonment,[332] or, having died, his work was carried on by his disciples.[333] Certainly resurrection is not explicitly mentioned in the text, but given that the Servant died, it is hard to deny a subsequent reversal

---

323. Alexander, "Messianic Ideology," 31.
324. Cf. Westcott, *John*, 2:57; Hanson, *Prophetic*, 141.
325. See above on John 6, the Servant.
326. See Westcott, *John*, 2:56. "The whole portraiture of 'the Good Shepherd' is a commentary on Isa 53." Cf. Block, "My Servant David," 55; Young, *Isaiah 40–66*, 348.
327. hiphil perfect 3rd person masculine singular from ערה.
328. See Oswalt, *Isaiah 40–66*, 406. Cf. John 10:18.
329. See Ibid., 406.
330. Cf. John 3:14; 17:1.
331. Cf. Childs, *Isaiah*, 416; Young, *Isaiah 40–66*, 352–53.
332. Cf. Oswalt, *Isaiah 40–66*, 405, who finds this suggestion "hard to believe."
333. Cf. Blenkinsopp, *Isaiah 40–55*, 355.

PART II—DETAILED EXEGETICAL EXAMINATION OF JOHN 5-10

that not only restored his life but also exalted him to the heavens.[334] Moreover, accounts of personal *bodily* resurrection are found in the OT.[335]

3. The Servant's sufferings were not vicarious: He suffered along with sinners, or as a result of his dangerous mission, rather than suffering in their place and on their behalf.[336] The main objection to the Servant's vicarious suffering, raised by scholars who hold this view, is theological: The only provision for the expiation of sins within the OT was within the Levitical cult, by means of animal sacrifices, and the introduction of vicarious *human* suffering is improbable or against the grain of the OT.[337] The answer to this is the same as that given to Myth and Ritual school: The Servant's vicarious sufferings, just like those described in the messianic psalms, are prophetic of Christ.[338] There was no historical figure, in Isaiah's time or at the time of the Babylonian Captivity, who vicariously atoned for sin. Rather the delineation of the Servant's work provides a prophetic portrait of the vicarious death and glorious resurrection of the Son of God.[339] Moreover, as Hebrews insists, the Levitical sacrifices themselves had no efficacy to take away sins, but were rather types and shadows that pointed to the once for all sacrifice of Jesus, which alone could atone for sin (Heb 10:11–12). Once this was made, the types and shadows were abrogated and eventually disappeared (Heb 8:13).

I conclude that the Servant's vicarious sufferings point forward to those of the Good Shepherd of John 10 who laid down his life for his sheep and rose again from the dead, victorious over death.

As indicated above, the Shepherd-King of Zech 9–14 is closely related to the Servant of Isa 53. Moreover, it too suggests the sacrifice of the messianic King on behalf of his people.[340] He also is struck with a sword or pierced.[341] The result is the bestowal of a spirit of grace and the opening of a fountain for sin and uncleanness for the house of David.[342] The implication is that the slaying of the Shepherd results in the benefit of his people. That this idea lies behind John's passion narrative is confirmed by the citation of Zech 12:10 in John 19:37.[343] Moreover, the blood and water that flowed from Jesus' side as a result of the piercing are a testimony, not only to Jesus' death,

---

334. Cf. Ps 22:22ff. John may also have had such OT testimonia to Jesus' resurrection in mind when he wrote, "As yet they knew not the scripture, that he must rise from the dead," John 20:9.

335. Cf. 1 Kgs 17:17–24; 2 Kgs 4:18–37; 13:21.

336. See discussion in Childs, *Isaiah*, 415, where Childs dissents from such views.

337. Cf. discussion in ibid., 415.

338. Cf. Acts 2: 25–31, where Ps 16:8 –11 speaks of the resurrection of Christ, not of David.

339. Cf. e.g. John 12:38; Matt 8:17; 12:18–21.

340. Provan, "Messiah in the Book of Kings," 83, writes, "The suggestion of vicarious suffering in Zechariah 13:1 reminds us . . . of Isaiah 52:13–53:12."

341. Cf. Zech 13:7; 12:10.

342. Cf. Zech 12:10 13:1; John 14:34–37.

343. Cf. also Rev 1:7.

but also to his messiahship (1 John 5:6–8). They are also the twin OT symbols of cleansing,[344] a cleansing also spoken of in NE shepherd context.[345] Other (Zech 9–14) indications of vicarious suffering may include allusions to David, the Servant, and the messianic King's designation as firstborn within the context of a paschal sacrifice.[346] The John 19:37 reference to piercing is immediately preceded by a reference to the Paschal lamb whose bones were not broken, John 19:36, which lamb was offered for Israel's redemption.

A further possible OT indication of vicarious messianic suffering, related to the Servant, is present in the Danielic Son of Man. As previously noted, Dan 9:26, "an anointed one shall be cut off," echoes Isa 53:8, "he was cut off out of the land of the living." Moreover, the verb "cut off" (כָּרַת) is used of cutting a covenant, involving the death of a sacrificial victim. "And he shall make a strong covenant with many," Dan 9:27, reflects the "*He* and the *many*" contrast of Isa 52:13–53:12. It has also been suggested that the Son of Man of Dan 7 is the Davidic messianic King who suffers and obtains a kingdom on behalf of his people.

THE HIRELING WHO "LEAVES THE SHEEP . . . AND THE WOLF . . . SCATTERS THEM," V. 12

This possibly alludes to Zechariah's words, "woe to my worthless shepherd, who deserts the flock! May the sword strike his arm and his right eye! Let his arm be wholly withered, his right eye utterly blinded!"[347] Interestingly, the curse invoked upon this shepherd involves blindness and physical withering; afflictions Jesus healed in John 5 and John 9. Similar woes are pronounced on the shepherds of Jer 23:1–2, who "destroy and scatter the sheep." Since they have "scattered my flock and have driven them away, and . . . have not attended to them," the Lord declares that he will "attend" to them for their evil deeds. Moreover, he will himself "gather the remnant" of his flock "out of all the countries" where he has driven them, and he will "bring them back to their fold." Perhaps the closest parallel is that of Ezek 34:5, where the sheep were "scattered, because there was no shepherd, and they became food for all the wild beasts." Once again a "woe" is pronounced upon the shepherds, and the Lord himself will seek his sheep from all the countries where they have been scattered and bring them back to their own land.[348]

Bowman thinks that John 10:12 may specifically refer to Johanan ben Zakkai and his disciples who deserted Jerusalem and its people prior to its fall to the Romans,

---

344. See Duguid, "Messianic Themes," 279. Cf. Menken, "Textual Form and Meaning," 494–511; Hanson, *Prophetic*, 225; Moo, *Old Testament*, 136.

345. Cf. Ezek 36:25, 33; 37:23; Jer 33:8. They are also connected with the wine and water poured from the silver bowls on the last day of Tabernacles.

346. Cf. Zech 12:10, set in a paschal context.

347. Zech 11:17. So Duguid, "Messianic Themes," 278.

348. Ezek 34:1–16.

PART II—DETAILED EXEGETICAL EXAMINATION OF JOHN 5–10

and made a deal with Vespasian to set up the Jamnia academy.[349] Although this is not impossible, it is more probable that Jesus' words refer to the "Jewish" hierarchy generally. Moreover, it is probable that "the wolf," that snatches and scatters the sheep, refers to the Romans and their impending A.D. 70 destruction of Jerusalem and subsequent scattering of the Jewish people. Thus Jer 5:6, predicting the Babylonian captivity, speaks of a nation coming against Jerusalem from afar, as a "desert wolf," that will destroy God's impenitent people. Wild beast imagery is also used in Isa 56:9, (closely paralleled by Ezek 34:5, 8) of fierce invading nations.[350]

"I KNOW MY OWN [SHEEP] . . ." V. 14

This possibly echoes the LXX wording of Num 16:5, "the Lord knows those that are his,"[351] spoken regarding the rebellion of Korah. In GJohn, Jesus has intimate knowledge of his disciples. In answer to Nathaniel's question, "How do you know me?" Jesus can reply, "Before Philip called you . . . I saw you." Moreover, the Samaritan woman could say, "Come, see a man who told me all that I ever did."[352] Jesus knew the man-born-blind even prior to his birth (John 9:3). Elsewhere Jesus refers to his disciples as "his own" (τοὺς ἰδίους). Specifically these people are "all that the Father gives [to Jesus]."[353] They come to him and, unlike the Pharisees, he will not cast them out.

"MY OWN KNOW ME," V. 14

This echoes the covenant recognition formula where, in the context of his tabernacling among his people, God says, "I will dwell among the people of Israel and will be their God . . . *They shall know that I am the LORD their God*, who brought them out of the Land of Egypt that I might dwell among them."[354] Similarly, in Ezek 34:30–31, "they shall know that I am the LORD their God with them, and that they, the house of Israel, are my people, declares the Lord." A similar echo comes from Jeremiah's NC context where God will write his law upon his people's hearts, forgive their sins, and it will no longer be necessary for them to teach their neighbors, "for they shall all know me," Jer 31:34.

In John 17 Jesus speaks of his manifesting his Father's name, and thus character, to the people whom God gave him out of the world. Moreover, they have known that everything God gave Jesus is from the Father, and they have known that Jesus came from the Father. Such knowledge is illustrated in Peter's confession that Jesus is "the

---

349. Bowman, *Fourth Gospel*, 201.
350. Cf. Isa 5:5, 26–30; Jer 12:9; John 10:12–13.
351. So Bruce, *John*, 227. He notes that this is cited verbatim in 2 Tim 2:19.
352. Cf. John 1:48; 4:29.
353. Cf. John 6:37; 13:1; 17:2.
354. Exod 29:45–46 (emphasis mine).

Holy One of God," John 6:69. Furthermore, the goal of eternal life is that they should know the Father and the Son. The world, however, would expel and kill believers, because they have not known the Father or Jesus.[355]

"I HAVE OTHER SHEEP THAT ARE NOT OF THIS FOLD, I MUST BRING THEM ALSO (κἀκεῖνα δεῖ με ἀγαγεῖν)," v. 16

This echoes Isa 56:6–8, "'And the foreigners who join themselves to the LORD . . . these I will bring (LXX εἰσάξω) to my holy mountain . . .' The Lord GOD, who gathers the outcasts of Israel, declares, 'I will gather yet others to him besides those already gathered (LXX συναγωγήν).'" In context, the Lord declares that he will gather foreigners (Gentiles), who attach themselves to the Lord to serve and love him, keep his Sabbath, and hold fast his covenant. He will bring them to his holy mountain and make them joyful in his house of prayer (Temple); "for my house shall be called a house of prayer for all peoples."[356] Jesus' calling Gentiles has previously been intimated in the gathered leftover fragments and in the ironic question, "Does he intend to go to the Dispersion among the Greeks and teach the Greeks?" (John 7:35). Further indications of this are given in the Greeks who wish to see Jesus (John 12:20) and in Caiaphas's prophetic words: "one man should die for the people . . . and not for the nation only, but also to gather into one the children of God who are scattered abroad," John 11:50–52.

There is probably also an echo of Ezek 34:11–13, where the Lord declares, "I myself will search for my sheep and will seek them out . . . I will bring them out from the peoples (LXX ἐξάξω αὐτοὺς ἐκ τῶν ἐθνῶν) and gather them from the countries, and will bring them into their own land." The context is Yahweh's gathering of his people from the nations where they were "scattered, because there was no (good) shepherd, and they became food for all the wild beasts," Ezek 34:5.

"ONE FLOCK, ONE SHEPHERD," v. 16

This echoes "I will rescue my flock . . . I will set up over them one shepherd, my servant David."[357] Block argues that reinstatement of the Davidic prince becomes part of the covenant promise, "I will be your God and you will be my people."[358] Thus God says, "I, Yahweh, will be their God, and my servant David will be ruler among them," reserving the second part of the covenant formula, "they shall be my people," until Ezek 34:30. Furthermore, David's dwelling among them is reminiscent of the auxiliary affirmation, often thought of as part of the covenant formula, "I will dwell in your

---

355. Cf. John 17:3, 6–8; 16:3.
356. Cf. Isa 56:7; Mark 11:17.
357. Ezek 34:22–23. Cf. Jer 3:8–10.
358. Block, *Ezekiel 25–48*, 301.

midst."[359] Thus David symbolizes Yahweh's presence among his people.[360] In GJohn, Jesus is the Word of God who became flesh and "dwelt [in a Tabernacle] among us," John 1:12, mediating God's covenant presence. The restoration of David as shepherd is also in accordance with God's promises to David. In 2 Sam 7:10, God says, "I will appoint a place (LXX τόπον) for my people Israel," establishing the kingdom of David's seed, who shall build God's house and reign forever. In Ps 89:33–37 these promises are confirmed by covenant oath. In GJohn Jesus builds God's house, John 2:19, and prepares a place (τόπον) for his people, John 14:2.

Block also notes that Yahweh restores his flock because of his covenant with them.[361] When God appoints the Davidic shepherd, he establishes a covenant of peace for Israel, associated with the turning away of his wrath. This same covenant of peace is confirmed following the sacrificial death of the Servant.[362] In GJohn, the Father gives his Son, so that whosoever believes in him might not perish. In 1 John 4:9–10 this gift makes propitiation for our sins, the turning away of God's wrath.

"One flock one shepherd" also echoes Ezek 37:22, where, by a prophetic sign act, the joining of two sticks or staffs, God indicates that he will make one nation of Israel and Judah, under one king.

> I will make them one nation in the land, on the mountains of Israel. And one king shall be king over them all, and they shall be no longer two nations, and no longer divided into two kingdoms . . . My servant David shall be king over them, and they shall all have one shepherd . . . David my servant shall be their prince for ever. I will make a covenant of peace with them . . . And I will . . . set my sanctuary in their midst forevermore. My dwelling place shall be with them, and I will be their God, and they shall be my people (Ezek 37:22–27).

Importantly, referred to as "Not my people," the Northern Kingdom of Israel had gone into captivity under Assyria. Nevertheless, God would restore them, and "in the place where it was said to them, 'You are not my people,' it shall be said to them, 'Children of the living God,'" Hosea 1:10. Paul notes the fulfilment of this prophecy, at least in part, in the calling of Gentiles to belong to the people of God.[363]

The Story elaborated and explained: The Good Shepherd

The "Jewish" leaders are "worthless" shepherds, responsible for the coming destruction that will be visited upon Jerusalem and a further dispersion that will be endured by the Jewish people. The "Jewish" authorities do not care for the people, but will

---

359. Cf. Gen 17:7, Exod 29:45–46; Lev 26:12–13.
360. Block, *Ezekiel 25–48*, 301.
361. Block, *Ezekiel 25–48*, 301. Cf. Deut 4:31.
362. Isa 54:7–10 cf. Ezek 37:26.
363. Rom 9:26 cf. 1 Peter 2:9.

desert them in the face of the cruel Roman onslaught that will soon eventuate in A.D. 70. Jesus, in contrast, is the Good Shepherd. He is the manifestation of Yahweh, come to deliver his sheep, searching for them, and seeking them out in all the places where they have been scattered. At the same time he is the Davidic King and Messiah, come to give his life for them and to reign over them. His people have been given to him by his Father and he knows each one of them personally and intimately. As God's Servant and paschal sacrifice he will effect their redemption, atoning for their sins, by voluntarily laying down his life unto death on their behalf and taking it up again. This inaugurates the NC and NE whereby he will lead his people out of "exile" to the true Temple, the Father's house, the place he prepares for them. In fact Jesus builds this Temple, commensurate with his raising his body from the dead. Ultimately, this will result in a worldwide Temple, comprising all the people that the Father has given to him as his seed, the reward of his suffering. They will spread abroad in a new heaven and earth that will be filled with God's glory.

Although Jesus has come to call out a people from among the Jewish nation, his salvation is not confined to them, but extends to the Gentiles of every nation. These Jesus will also lead to the heavenly Jerusalem, where they will be united with Jewish believers as one people under God. However, unbelieving "Jews," who reject Jesus, will be abandoned to the worthless shepherd they have chosen, who will leave them to be scattered and destroyed by the Romans. This situation is not irreversible, however, since all who turn to Jesus will be caught up in the restoration from "exile."

Aftermath, vv. 19–21

Jesus' words divide his "Jewish" hearers. Some maintain that he is demon possessed and mad, not to be listened to. Others, however, point out the two unmistakable evidences that Jesus is from God: his words are not those of one demon possessed and he has opened the eyes of the blind.

Conclusion

The parable of the Good Shepherd is a subversive story that turns the world of the Pharisees on its head. Instead of being Israel's true leaders, they are hirelings and villains who plunder God's people. Jesus, however, is Israel's true King and redeemer, and his followers, cast out by some, are the true people of God. Jesus' death is the paschal sacrifice that initiates their NE redemption, a deliverance that extends to the Gentiles. Jesus leads his people to the New Jerusalem and new Temple. Under the leadership of the "Jewish" hierarchy, however, earthly Jerusalem will be destroyed and its people scattered in a new exile. Thus the hope of reunification for the Jewish people will be reversed. Nevertheless, after this new scattering, Jews (together with Gentiles) will ultimately be united, being called by the uplifted cross to participate in a NE to the heavenly Jerusalem.

13

Episode 5

Jesus Sanctified and Sent by the Father, John 10:22–42

DODD CONSIDERS THIS PASSAGE to be an epilogue to the previous episode,[1] but in fact it comprises a short episode in its own right. John has juxtaposed it with the Good Shepherd discourse because of its similar setting and themes that complement the latter.

THE DEDICATION FESTAL BACKGROUND

This feast was instituted during intertestamental times following the recapture ("from an Antichrist"[2]) and reconsecration of the Temple on 25 Kislev, 164 B.C., after its desecration by Antiochus IV three years earlier. This Seleucid king had sought to tighten his control on Palestine, the unruly Jewish state, by Hellenizing the Jews with the help of collaborators within the Jewish priests and aristocracy (1 Macc 1:11–13). In response to a large bribe, Antiochus deposed the lawful "godly"[3] High Priest, Onias III, who was zealous for the law (2 Macc 4:2), and gave his office to his brother Joshua, who took the Greek name Jason and actively encouraged the process of Hellenization.[4] A "place of exercise" was built where Jewish boys, competing naked, hid their covenant mark of circumcision (1 Macc 1:14–15).

Jason was later deposed in favor of Menelaus, a non-Zadokite, who offered the king even more money and was an even more zealous Hellenizer. Menelaus was responsible for the murder of the lawful High Priest, Onias III.[5] While Antiochus was busy campaigning against Egypt, however, Jason staged a rebellion, seizing control of Jerusalem and ousting Menelaus (2 Macc 5:5). On his return from Egypt, Antiochus

---

1. Dodd, *IFG*, 354–57.
2. Beasley-Murray, *John*, 173.
3. See 2 Macc 3:1.
4. See Bruce, *New Testament History*, 3.
5. 2 Macc 4:34–35. See Schürer, *History of the Jewish people*, 1:149–50.

Jesus Sanctified and Sent by the Father, John 10:22-42

punished the rebellious city, committing dreadful atrocities and looting the Temple to help pay for his military campaign against Egypt.[6]

The crisis culminated when Antiochus' military ambitions were thwarted by the Romans and, returning home, he vented his ire against Jerusalem.[7] Apollonius, Antiochus's envoy, attacked Jerusalem on the Sabbath, setting up a military fortress (the "Akra") that was occupied by "wicked" Syrian troops.[8] Moreover, Antiochus sought to "change the times and the laws,"[9] forcibly compelling the Jews to offer pagan sacrifices, making circumcision and the possession of the Scriptures punishable by death (1 Macc 1:57), and declaring himself "Epiphanes," the manifest (god, i.e. Zeus).[10] His ultimate "madness"[11] was the "abomination of desolation": swine's flesh was offered upon the altar and a pagan altar to Zeus Olympios was erected in the Temple.[12]

When Mattathias and his sons rebelled, a protracted struggle followed, Judas Maccabeus becoming their leader and waging a campaign of gorilla warfare from the caves and hills.[13] When Antiochus was defeated, the Temple and altar were re-consecrated three years to the day after they had been defiled. The Temple was illuminated with great lights and a feast was celebrated for eight days. Because of this, and the lighting of lamps in Jewish homes, symbolic of the shining upon them of the right to worship, the feast would be called *Hanukkah*, the Feast of Lights.[14] In view of the re-dedication of the Temple, the feast was also referred to as the Feast of Dedication, and it was decreed that this feast should be held annually.[15]

Since the lights recalled Tabernacles, and the reconsecration recalled both the consecration of Solomon's Temple and the consecration of the altar by the returnees from captivity, both celebrated at Tabernacles, the feast was also referred to as "the feast of Tabernacles in the month Kislev" (2 Macc 1:9). Indeed, the rational for Dedication is similar to that of Tabernacles, to recall God's preservation of his people in the wilderness, after they had fled from the city and hid in caves and mountains.[16] Moreover, the books of Maccabees indicate that the celebrations for both feasts were similar: both lasted for eight days and both were characterized by joy and light, the

---

6. Cf. 2 Macc 5:11–16, 21; Schürer, *History of the Jewish people*, 1:148.

7. Cf. ibid., 1:151–52. See Dan 11:29–31, that predicted these events.

8. Cf. 1 Macc 1:29–35; 2 Macc 5:24–26; Yee, *Jewish Feasts*, 85; Schürer, *History of the Jewish people*, 1:152.

9. Dan 7:25 cf. 1 Macc 1:41–50, 56–58, 60–64.

10. See Bruce, *John*, 230, 237, n. 8.

11. The Jews referred to Antiochus as "epimannes," or madman.

12. 1 Macc 1:59 cf. Dan 11:31.

13. 1 Macc 2:1–4:35. Cf. Bruce, *New Testament History*, 4–5.

14. See Josephus *Ant.* 12:325.

15. Cf. 1 Macc 4:59; 2 Macc 1:9, 18; 10:1–8. Whether or not they took over an earlier festival celebration of the winter solstice is disputed. Cf. Bruce, *John*, 230.

16. 2 Macc 10:6. Cf. Yee, *Jewish Feasts*, 86.

waving of palms, and the singing of the *Hallel*.[17] Furthermore, both recalled the sacred fire that fell upon the altar in Solomon's Temple and both were viewed eschatologically in terms of the consummation, where "every man sat under his vine and his fig tree."[18]

The Maccabean victory was significant because it ensured the survival of Jewish identity.[19] *Hanukkah* was an annual reminder of the danger, not only of hostile powers, but also of the enemy within that might lead to apostasy and assimilation by the nations. As Yee notes, there was a "Genuine possibility that another Antiochus might set up another 'desolating sacrilege.'" Dedication called the Jews to remain faithful to the Torah, circumcision, and the Temple, and so proclaim, "Never again!"[20]

FORM AND STRUCTURE OF JOHN 10:22–42

This passage takes the form of a trial, where Jesus is set upon by the "Jewish" authorities in the Temple precincts and questioned regarding his messianic status. It divides into four parts: Verses 22–24 provide the background and circumstances to an encounter of Jesus by the authorities. Verses 25–31 report Jesus' initial defense culminating in an attempt to stone him. In vv. 32–39, Jesus gives a further defense and the "Jewish" authorities make a further attempt to apprehend him. Verses 40–42 are an epilogue relating Jesus' departure, concluding both the episode and the Festival Cycle.

JESUS' TRIAL AT DEDICATION, JOHN 10:22–42

Jesus encountered by the authorities in the Temple, John 10:22–24

Jesus did not leave Judea at the conclusion of Tabernacles and now, three months later, he is again in Jerusalem, walking in the Temple precincts at Dedication. "Solomon's Portico" is thought to be the only part of Solomon's Temple that had survived destruction,[21] and so its mention is a link to the first Temple. John may also have mentioned it as anticipating the place where believers would regularly meet after Jesus' ascension.[22] If this is correct he may have associated it with persecution of the primitive Church since, on both occasions when it is mentioned in Acts, the priests and Sadducees rise up against the believers.[23] Its covered colonnades would have offered Jesus

---

17. Cf. 1 Macc 4:52–59; 2 Macc 10:5–8; Yee, *Jewish Feasts*, 86–87; Schürer, *History of the Jewish people*, 1:163, n. 65.

18. 1 Macc 14:12. Cf. 1 Kgs 4:25; Mic 4:4. Cf. Wright, *RSG*, 26, 600–1.

19. Cf. Yee, *Jewish Feasts*, 88; Skarsaune, *Temple*, 25.

20. Yee, *Jewish Feasts*, 88.

21. Cf. Brown, *John I–XII*, 402; Brunson, *Psalm 118*, 356, citing Josephus *War* 5:185; *Ant.* 15:401; 20:221.

22. So Carson, *John*, 391.

23. Cf. Acts 3:11; 4:1; 5:12, 17.

Jesus Sanctified and Sent by the Father, John 10:22–42

some shelter from the cold winter winds, but there was no protection from the "winter" that now characterized the relationship of the "Jewish" leaders to Jesus.[24]

"The Jews gathered around (ἐκύκλωσαν) him" echoes Ps 118:10, "all nations surrounded (ἐκύκλωσάν) me."[25] As previously noted, the Ps 118 context is the culmination of the journey from the Exodus to the Temple; its theme recounts the struggles of a messianic individual, his deliverance from death, and his victorious entrance into the Temple. The "ring of foes" that surround him have been compared to the nations that surround Jerusalem in Zech 14:2.[26] Midrash on Ps 118 speaks of Gog and Magog encircling Jerusalem three times in the end times as Nebuchadnezzar ascended three times against Jerusalem.[27] Revelation 20:8–9 applies the same detail to the encompassing (ἐκύκλευσαν) of the camp of the saints and the beloved city.[28] The Ps 2:2 rejection of Messiah is even more appropriate, however, especially as the conspirators would include Israel itself, Acts 4:27. Tellingly, Kidner equates these foes to the builders (authorities) who reject the chosen Temple cornerstone.[29] In Luke 21:20, however, κυκλόω is used of Jerusalem surrounded by armies, indicating that its *desolation* is near. Only too familiar with Jesus' warning of these events, John may be inferring that the "Jewish" leaders had brought the A.D. 70 desolation upon themselves as retribution for their treatment of God's Son. Moreover, the Revelation allusion infers a further fulfilment in terms of a final showdown between the forces of evil and Jesus' Church.

Such echoes indicate that the "Jewish" leaders have no interest in believing, but only want to catch Jesus in his speech. Moreover, their question, "If you are the Christ, tell us plainly," and Jesus' reply, "I told you, and you do not believe," John 10:24, corresponding almost exactly to Luke 22:67, where Jesus was tried before the Sanhedrin, indicate that Jesus is effectively on trial. "Plainly" (παρρησίᾳ) picks up the secret/public motif of John 7. The "Jewish" authorities want Jesus to confess his messiahship publicly in order that they might accuse him before Pilate. "How long do you keep us in suspense" is probably a play on words: τὴν ψυχὴν ἡμῶν αἴρεις is literally "you take away our lives," echoing Jesus' words, τίθημι τὴν ψυχήν μου . . . οὐδεὶς αἴρει αὐτὴν ἀπ' ἐμοῦ, "I lay down my life . . . No one takes it from me," John 10:17–18. Thus, ironically, they consider Jesus to be destroying them, perhaps as the "desolating sacrilege."

---

24. Cf. Beasley-Murray, *John*, 173; Hoskyns, *Fourth Gospel*, 386. Moloney, *Signs and Shadows*, 150, notes that previously there was a glimmer of hope in Tabernacles where opinion was divided, but now in the middle of winter hope disappears.

25. Cf. Hanson, *Prophetic*, 142–43; Brunson, *Psalm 118*, 351–62.

26. Kidner, *Psalms 73–150*, 413–14.

27. Braude, *Midrash on Psalms*, 2:239–40.

28. See Hanson, *Prophetic*, 143.

29. Kidner, *Psalms 73–150*, 414–15.

PART II—DETAILED EXEGETICAL EXAMINATION OF JOHN 5-10

Jesus' initial defense, vv. 25–31

Jesus' defense is to turn the tables. Moreover, just as in Ps 118:10–12 the encircled Messiah repels his foes "in the name of the LORD" (LXX Ps 117:10–12 τῷ ὀνόματι κυρίου), so also Jesus answers the "Jewish" leaders in the name of his Father (ἐν τῷ ὀνόματι τοῦ πατρός μου).[30] He has not failed to tell them who he is, but they have not believed him. His works, done *in the name of his Father*, are self-authenticating signs, revealing his identity as the Son of God. In particular, Jesus' healing the lame and opening the eyes of the blind, have signalled the coming of God among them to lead a NE. Like their fathers in the wilderness, however, they have seen God's works, but disbelieved (Ps 78:32).

The reason they do not believe is because they are not Jesus' sheep (people). As in John 10:3–4, Jesus' sheep recognize the Shepherd's voice, he knows them and they follow him. Jesus' gift to them of eternal life is contrasted with perishing.[31] The denial that his people will ever perish is emphatic. That none can snatch them out of Jesus' "hand," v. 28, speaks of his power to keep and protect his people from the wolf who would try to snatch them away. In this respect he has the same power to deliver as his Father who is "greater than all." There is an allusion here, in John 10:29, to Isa 43:12–13, "I am God. Also henceforth I am he; there is none who can deliver from my hand."[32] Coming from "a favorite scriptural passage [of John],"[33] it proclaims Yahweh's future NE gathering of his people, calling upon Israel to bear witness before the gathered nations. Thus Jesus' people will not be destroyed by fierce invading powers.

"I and the Father are one," John 10:30, expresses not only Jesus' complete unity of mind and spirit with the Father, but also his equality in terms of his ability to bestow eternal life on his people and to guard them from being snatched.[34] To the "Jewish" leaders this is blasphemy, punishable by death. Moreover, they see him as another Antiochus, proclaiming himself to be "God manifest," bringing wrath upon them. Immediately they indicate their willingness to administer the appropriate penalty by picking up stones to destroy Jesus.

Jesus' further defense, vv. 32–39

Jesus halts the attempt to do away with him by reminding the "Jewish" authorities of the good works he has shown them from the Father. Since they had found great difficulty in finding fault with such signs as Jesus' opening blind eyes, the remembrance

---

30. John 10:25 cf. Ps 118:10–12. Cf. Brunson, *Psalm 118*, 352–53, who notes that both encounters take place in the context of the Temple.

31. As in John 3:15–16.

32. Cf. Hoskyns, *Fourth Gospel*, 388; Hanson, *Prophetic*, 143.

33. So Hanson, *Prophetic*, 119, 143. See above on the allusions to Isa 43 in John 6.

34. Cf. Bruce, *John*, 232–33; Carson, *John*, 394–95; Neyrey, "'I Said You are Gods,'" 651–52.

Jesus Sanctified and Sent by the Father, John 10:22-42

cannot but have pricked their consciences. Their retort is that it is not for his good works that they will stone him, but for blasphemy. Their charge that Jesus makes himself God (John 10:23) is reminiscent of Antiochus's claims. It is also equivalent to that of John 5:18, where Jesus' defense was that his Father has bestowed upon him divine honors. Here Jesus defends his eternal unity with the Father by using an *a minori ad maius* (from the lesser to the greater) argument[35] based on his citation of Ps 82:6, "I said, you are gods." If God called them gods, or sons of God, to whom God's word came, [much more] the one who the Father has sanctified and sent into the world is entitled to call himself the Son of God.

As Hanson points out, to understand this citation, we "must . . . read Psalm 82 as a whole."[36] Nevertheless, there are considerable difficulties in understanding how Jesus interprets and applies this psalm. In particular, who are those addressed as "gods"? Three main possibilities have been identified:

1. God may be addressing angels who have abused their powers and "will die like men."[37] This seems unlikely because they are exhorted to judge justly among people, giving justice to the poor and fatherless, Ps 82:3-4. Moreover, it is hard to see how such "gods" are referred to as those "to whom the word of God came."[38] Furthermore, Jesus would have failed to find a Scripture to prove that a man could be called god.[39] Menken's modified form of this theory, that the "gods" are human recipients of divine revelation, such as Jeremiah, admitted to the heavenly council,[40] also has problems since it is hard to believe that Jesus would have thought of Jeremiah as under God's judgement.

2. A second possibility is that God addresses Israel's judges—called "gods" by virtue of their judicial function, but falling under God's judgement because of their failure to uphold his law.[41] Kidner notes that support for this view relies on Exod 21:6; 22:8-9, where Israelites, who came for judgement, came before God (or possibly "the god") to be judged by God's word. He also notes that in Exod 22:28 it might be possible to understand God (or "the gods" KJV) as synonymous with a ruler of the people.[42]

    This view is attractive, because it suggests the judgement of Israel's shepherds, relevant to the John 10 context. Moreover, Midrash on Ps 82 relates the

---

35. According to the first of Hillel's rules, *Qal wahomer*. Cf. Manns, "*Exégese* rabbinic," 525-38. He believes that *Qal wahomer* reasoning is also present in 7:22-23.

36. Hanson, *Prophetic*, 144.

37. Cf. Ashton, *Understanding*, 147-50.

38. John 10:35. Cf. Daly-Denton, *David*, 164-176.

39. See Barrett, *John*, 385.

40. Menken, "Use of the Septuagint," 375ff.

41. So Calvin, *Psalms*, 3:334. Cf. Brown, *John I-XII*, 409ff.; Daly-Denton, *David*, 170ff.; Lindars, *John*, 374.

42. Kidner, *Psalms 73-150*, 296-97.

PART II—DETAILED EXEGETICAL EXAMINATION OF JOHN 5-10

psalm to Moses' charge to the judges of Israel.[43] Other possible "judges" include Moses,[44] David, and David's royal line.[45]

3. The most likely suggestion, however, is that the congregation which God addresses in Ps 82, among whom he stands, is Israel at Sinai.[46] There is plenty of support for this third view in the rabbinic writings. For example, Midrash on Exodus 32:7 says,

> It is written, *'I said: Ye are godlike beings,' and all of you sons of the most high* ([Ps.] LXXXII, 6). When Israel stood at Sinai and received the Torah, the Holy One, blessed be He, said to the Angel of Death: 'Thou hast power over all the heathen but not over this people, for they are My portion, and just as I live forever, so will My children be eternal' . . . 'Yet you refused . . . and corrupted your deeds and said to the calf: "*This is thy god, O Israel*" (Ex. XXXII, 4), and for this reason *Ye shall die like men* (Ps. LXXXII, 7).'[47]

The implication of this (and several other similar rabbinic writings) is that mere reception of the Torah was thought somehow to convey eternal life and godlike status. This godlike status and eternal life were considered lost, however, because of Israel's transgression with the golden calf, likened unto Adam's fall.[48] Although neither Jesus nor the OT or NT Scriptures endorse the teaching that mere reception or possession of the Torah (externalised on tablets of stone) can convey life,[49] or that the golden calf incident was a second "fall," it was pre-eminently to this people, on this occasion (at Sinai), that the word of God came. Moreover, it was God's word and covenant that graciously set them apart to be a royal priesthood and holy nation unto God (Exod 19:5-6), designating them "gods." Their collective "godlike" ability to administer God's judgement, being in possession of his law (as in suggestion 2 above), may also have been an important factor. Israel's mistake was to believe that mere possession of the Torah (and circumcision) bestowed life.[50] In fact, although the law is holy, transgression of the law

---

43. Cf. Braude, *Midrash on Psalms*, 2:59; Deut 1:17. See also, *b. Sahn.* 6b-7a, *b. Sota* 47b, *b. Ber.* 6a, *Midr. Teh.* 82.1.

44. The great judge who was made a "god" to Pharaoh (Exod. 7:1).

45. In view of their designation as sons of God or godlike. Cf. Ps 2:7; 2 Sam 7:14; Zech 12:8; Isa 9:6. The word of God came to David and to Solomon. Cf. 1 Chr 22:8; 1 Kgs 6:11; Daly-Denton, *David*, 172-73.

46. Cf. Neyrey, "I Said You are Gods," 655ff.; Carson, *John*, 398-99.

47. *Exod. Rab.* 32:7, in Freedman, 3:411.

48. Cf. Neyrey, "I Said You are Gods," 655-59, and the rabbinic writings he cites; Ackerman, "Rabbinic," 187; *Exod. Rab.* 32:1; *Lev. Rab.* 4:1.

49. Cf. e.g. John 5:39-40; Lev 18:5; Gal 3:21.

50. Cf. Rom 2:17-29.

brings death.[51] Israel fell under condemnation because, although she had the law she did not keep it.

Given this third view, Jesus' argument becomes, "if the Israelites were declared gods, or God's sons, when God's gracious word (and covenant) came to them at Sinai, how much more is he (God's incarnate Word) whom God has sanctified and sent into the world entitled to be called God's Son."

In addition to this comparison, however, other comparisons are implicit. In particular, the verb ἁγιάζω is used in Maccabees to describe the consecration of the Temple courts (αὐλὰς).[52] Thus in describing himself as the one "whom the Father consecrated (ὃν ὁ πατὴρ ἡγίασεν) and sent into the world," John 10:36, Jesus implies that he is God's new Temple, whom God himself has dedicated and sent into the world.[53] It is also important to note that ἁγιάζω and ἀποστέλλω are used of Jesus' sanctifying and sending his disciples into the world, in connection with his departure, in the same manner that the Father sanctified and sent him, John 17:17–19.[54] In John 20:21–22, Jesus not only sends his disciples into the world, but also bestows on them the Holy Spirit, making them temples of God.[55] Moreover, Jesus has given them God's word and bestowed upon them the title, sons of God.[56] This might imply that the Isaianic vision of the latter day going forth of the law from Zion to all the world[57] is accomplished by Jesus, God's new heavenly Temple, sending out his people, expanding his Temple throughout the world. Importantly for John's readers, although the earthly Temple has been destroyed, Jesus and his people, who mediate God's presence in the world, have replaced it. Returning to Jesus' argument, this means that he is contrasting himself (and his people), the fulfilment of all that the Temple represented, with Israel at Sinai—consecrated and made God's sons, a royal priesthood, and effectively part of God's Temple, but who transgressed the law and "died like men."

A further comparison exists between the Torah, received by Israel at Sinai, which could not bestow life, but rather, through indwelling sin produced death (Rom 7:9–13), and Jesus the living incarnate Word of God sent into the world to bestow life on all who receive him. Ackerman is probably correct to draw parallels between Sinai and the Prologue.[58] Thus although the rabbis thought that reception of the Torah conferred eternal life, Jesus, God's Word, does do so to all who receive him.[59] The implication is that the "Jewish" leaders are defending the Torah, in the (vain) hope of

51. Cf. Rom 6:23; 7:10–13.
52. Cf. 1 Macc 4:48; 3 Macc 2:9, 16; Coloe, *God Dwells*, 153.
53. Cf. Brown, *John I–XII*, 401–2; Kerr, *Temple*, 254; Moloney, *Signs and Shadows*, 149–50.
54. Cf. Coloe, *God Dwells*, 154; Walker, *Holy City*, 170–74.
55. Cf. 1 Cor 6:19; John 2:21.
56. Cf. John 17:14; 1:12.
57. Isa 2:2-4 cf. Heb 12:22–25.
58. Ackerman, "Rabbinic," 188ff.
59. Cf. John 1:12; 5:39.

life (because they cannot keep it), but before them is God's Son and Word who alone can give life. They seek to protect the Temple that harbors corruption, yet Jesus is the true Temple, locus of God's Word and presence, whom they seek to destroy.

Jesus' final appeal is to his works. If they do not believe his words, his works are irrefutable evidence of his identity. Moreover, they demonstrate the mutual indwelling of the Father and the Son. Once again this is Temple imagery. In Jesus, God dwells among his people.

> How serious, then, is the situation of 'the Jews' who stand accused of not accepting the visible presence of God in the works of Jesus. They celebrate their allegiance to the God of Israel present in the Temple, but they are not prepared to accept that God, visible in the works of Jesus.[60]

The fact that "they sought to arrest him, but he escaped from their hands," v. 39, points to their powerlessness to take Jesus until his time came. "Their hands," are in contrast to the hand of Jesus and of the Father. "The Jews" enjoyed a limited authority, but all power and authority belong to the Father and the Son, something which John's churches must remember in times of conflict and persecution.

Epilogue, vv. 40–42

Jesus has appeared in the Temple for the last time in GJohn and has been finally rejected by the "Jewish" authorities who have also sought to kill him. The glory has departed from the Jerusalem Temple and once again Jesus goes away, signalling his NE. Moreover, like Joshua before him, he crosses the Jordan, but this time in a direction away from the earthly Jerusalem and "the Jews." Rather he returns to the place where his ministry commenced with the baptism of JBap. Here, away from earthly Jerusalem, many believe on him and validate JBap's testimony: "everything that John said about this man was true," John 10:41. As Moloney comments, this return not only brings to a close Jesus' presence in Jerusalem for the "feasts of the Jews," but also looks back to the beginning, bringing Jesus' ministry full circle.[61]

Conclusion

Set against the backdrop of Dedication, Jesus is once again on trial before the "Jewish" authorities. They fear that he is bringing God's anger upon Jerusalem and its Temple by his messianic claims, of which they seek a confession. In his defense, Jesus points to his NE signs that authenticate his mission. That the "Jewish" leaders do not believe is evidence that they are not his true people, on whom he bestows eternal life and saving power. In this salvation he is equal to his Father. The "Jewish" authorities consider this

---

60. Moloney, *Signs and Shadows*, 150.
61. Ibid., 151.

claim as equivalent to the blasphemy of Antiochus. Consequently, they are seeking to destroy Jesus by stoning him. Jesus defends himself by appealing to Ps 82:6, where Israel, the people to whom God's word came at Sinai, are referred to as gods. How much more should the one who is the incarnate Word, the true Temple and dwelling place of God, be referred to as God's Son. Jesus avoids further attempts to apprehend him, leaving the Temple to its destruction.

The incident is particularly important for John's readers. Though they have suffered the loss of the earthly Temple, Jesus is the new locus of God's revelation. Though he has gone away to heaven, he has also sent forth his disciples into the world as the earthly representation of the heavenly Temple. Though the "Jews" do not believe, away from Jerusalem and throughout the world, many will believe, become part of the NE to the Father's house, and be joined to the ever expanding heavenly Temple, dedicated by God himself. Though the "Jews" seek to persecute them, none can snatch those who trust in Jesus from his hand or from the hand of his Father.

14

Summary and Conclusions

IN THIS STUDY I have sought to demonstrate that the Paschal NE paradigm is a major interpretative key to John's Gospel.

In Part I, I began by setting out my intertextual methodology: reading GJohn against the OT background, using Johannine echoes and allusions as pointers to their OT context in order to illuminate GJohn's meaning. I argued that giving precedence to OT echoes is legitimate, given that an appropriate historical context for GJohn could be established.

I established such a context by delineating a feasible historical model and *Sitz im Leben* in which the Apostle John authored his Gospel in the Roman province of Asia following the A.D. 70 destruction of the Jerusalem Temple. His purpose was to strengthen his churches, particularly Jewish believers, under pressure from the local synagogues, questioning the purpose of God in the disaster that had befallen Jerusalem and its Temple, and wavering in their faith in Jesus. By using the Paschal NE paradigm to portray Jesus' ministry, John was able to vindicate Jesus as the Christ and Son of God who had fulfilled OT NE expectations. Thus Jesus has inaugurated a NE from bondage to sin and death, by his paschal sacrifice, to the new Temple of the Father's house, from whence the Word of God is still going forth into all the world. This NE has already commenced and will culminate in Last Day resurrection, judgement, and Sabbath rest in a re-created universe. Moreover, John was able to vindicate Jewish believers who had been cast out by their brethren and perhaps blamed for the Temple's destruction because of their faith in Jesus.

The feasibility of my method was further established from an ideological, Christological, and literary perspective. Hellenistic and Gnostic thought, previously considered by some to provide the background for many Johannine concepts, was found to be alien to GJohn. Rather, the OT NE paradigm provided a more suitable context, one fully able to explain Johannine thought. Moreover, Johannine Christological tensions do not arise from a plurality of ideologically conflicting sources or editors, or from the development of doctrine within a Johannine school. Rather, GJohn is the product of a single great mind and its tensions arise from his dialogue with the diverse OT

Summary and Conclusions

Christological expectations and from Jesus' nature as an infinite person, both God and man. New literary criticism was also found to support a paschal NE reading of GJohn.

It should be noted that Part I offers my solution to the "Johannine puzzle," the reason why GJohn is so different from the Synoptics. Those Gospels follow the same basic pattern of the primitive apostolic message as it was first presented by Peter (e.g., in Acts 10:36–43): Jesus' Davidic descent, the baptism of JBap, Jesus' anointing with the Holy Spirit, his itinerant ministry from Galilee to Jerusalem, the powerful signs and healings he performed, his betrayal, death, resurrection, and appearances to eye-witnesses, the great commission, and his ascent to heaven. While John acknowledges and complements this pattern, his purpose is not to present a new version of the Synoptic Gospel kerygma. Rather, as the only remaining apostle, at the close of the apostolic era, he uses previously unpublished apostolic tradition to address the radically different post A.D. 70 situation in which he finds himself. In particular, following the destruction of the Temple and persecution by "Jews," members of his churches were beginning to despair of the fulfilment of the NE promises through Jesus and needed encouragement to continue to believe in Jesus the Christ and Son of God.

In Part II, I commenced by giving a "road map" of the Festival Cycle, John 5–10, which comprises five individual episodes of Jesus' ministry. Each episode is set against the background of a particular Jewish feast that illuminates the situation of crisis that Jesus encounters when he visits the Jewish people. The feasts form the background to Jesus' NE signs and discourses, against which he reveals himself to be Israel's Lord and Messiah, come to deliver his people in a NE. In this, the feasts point backward to the Exodus and forward to the eschatological NE that Jesus came to fulfil.

Although the Jewish people are no longer in Babylonian exile, they are under the dominion of foreigners and the great NE promises of salvation have not yet been fulfilled. More importantly, the people need to be delivered from the realm of sin and death and the devil, in a NE to the realm of life and salvation. Jesus initiates this NE by laying down his life as a paschal sacrifice. In this he is resisted (as Moses was resisted by Pharaoh at the Exodus) by "the Jews." Consisting largely of the chief priests and Pharisees, the latter are the powerful religious elite, who exercise authority over the Temple and over the people. By resisting God's Son, they will bring destruction upon their Temple.

Jesus visits the Temple in order to identify with it as the one who fulfils its feasts and symbolism. He leads his people from their "Jewish" Second Temple worship to the new worshipping community of his Father's house. Jesus, together with his people, comprise this new Temple. Though many of the people reject Jesus, a minority believe and follow him, becoming the New Israel. His departure from the Jerusalem Second Temple is a sign that its glory is departing and that it will soon be destroyed.

From this overview, I proceeded to investigate each of the Festival Cycle episodes using Johannine OT echoes and the NE paradigm as an interpretative key:

In John 5, the lame man at the pool represents Jewish people who suffered in "exile," despairing of help, and hoping for divine intervention. Jesus' Sabbath day healing of the lame man was a NE sign, signalling the breaking in of Sabbath rest through Jesus. Although the man is healed by Jesus, however, he turns his back upon him, fearing the "Jews." His unbelief and betrayal provides a model of the wrong response to Jesus. The healing also forms part of a two-part theodicy, vindicating God concerning the A.D. 70 destruction visited by the Romans upon Jerusalem. The man represents a particular section of the Jewish people. Called out of "exile" by Jesus' powerful signs, they had been tested by opposition from the "Jewish" authorities, hostile to Jesus. The man, and those he represented, turned back from Jesus to side with the "Jewish" authorities and their Second Temple worshipping community. Ironically, the Second Temple would finally be destroyed some thirty-eight years later.

Put on trial by "Jewish" leaders, Jesus is accused of breaking the Sabbath and *making himself* equal to God. His defense is that he is not a rebellious son, but the Father has bestowed upon him the twin powers of judging the world and raising the dead, in order that he might do the Father's work. As the Son of Man and last Adam, he is inaugurating a NE return from "exile," and Sabbath rest, by his paschal sacrifice. This takes place in two stages. Here and now the spiritually dead are called to new life by Jesus' word. In the last day, Jesus will raise the dead and judge the world. The Father witnesses to Jesus by the signs, directly by his voice, and through Scripture. The "Jewish" leaders have not received God's testimony, but prefer the honor that comes from one another. Though they think that the Scriptures bestow eternal life, the Scriptures testify to Jesus. Though they look to Moses, he spoke of Jesus and will become their chief prosecutor.

John 6:1–24 is a symbolic narrative in which, against the Passover background, Jesus signals his paschal NE. It commences with Jesus performing a prophetic sign-act: departing from Judea, crossing the sea, followed by multitudes, he ascends the mountain. Reflecting the Exodus, this becomes a paradigm for Jesus' paschal departure to his Father's house, by way of the cross, by which he initiates the NE.

This leads to a crisis (typical of the Exodus and NE): the need to provide the multitudes with bread—not merely physical bread, but a paschal messianic banquet, and God's NC mercies. Jesus is this bread of life, God's Son, Servant, and Word from heaven, who feeds the multitudes by virtue of his paschal sacrifice. His disciples must learn to trust this Word. The gathering of the fragments, that none may perish, represents the NE gathering of "exiles" from all the world and the reconstitution of twelve tribes in one NI, comprising believing Jews and Gentiles. The crowds, however, failing to understand or to perceive Jesus' true identity, seek to make him a political deliverer and source of perishable bread.

The disciples' deliverance from death upon the sea is a further NE sign. Jesus' absence, perhaps symbolic of his death, leads to imminent danger and death by which they are "baptized" into Jesus. He, however, manifests his divine glory, revealing himself to be the embodiment of the covenant God, the "I am," who delivers his people through the NE waters. This separates them from the left-behind crowd, who, in vain, search for Jesus in hope of physical bread.

When the crowds catch up with Jesus, he brings a lawsuit against them, whereby he warns them not to work for bread, under the curse, that causes (people) to perish, but for bread that he the Son of Man gives that leads to eternal life. They interpret Jesus' words as referring to works that they must perform to enable them to eat the sanctified bread, but Jesus directs them to faith in himself. In hope of physical bread, they ask him to repeat the sign of the manna, but Jesus corrects them: the Mosaic gift was just a shadow of the one who comes down from heaven to give eternal life to the world. Using God's covenant name, "I am," Jesus discloses himself to be the true bread and Word of God come down from heaven to lead a NE from hunger, thirst, and death, under the curse.

Though the crowds do not believe, the Father has given to Jesus a people. As such, he is the Last Adam and the one in whom the promises made to Abraham are fulfilled. Jesus' people will come to him and he will not cast them out or lose them. Rather, on the last day he will raise them up to eternal life in a new heaven and earth. For the crowds, however, like their fathers, the physical bread which they crave will only lead to their death. The unbelieving "Jews" show that they are truly the descendants of their wilderness fathers by murmuring and despising Jesus, the bread of God. In contrast to the unbelieving "Jews," Jesus' true people will be taught by the Father, who will draw them out of bondage and lead them to Jesus, lifted up as a signal of NE salvation. Jesus bestows eternal life on them, as God's Servant, by giving his flesh as a paschal sacrifice, vicariously bearing the wrath of God for them, initiating a NE from sin and death to righteousness and life. They partake of this sacrifice by faith, becoming part of God's new Temple.

For many of Jesus' disciples his words cause offense and they turn back. Greater offenses are ahead when Jesus will die on the cross. These disciples turn back because they do not have true faith in Jesus and lack spiritual illumination. The Twelve, however, the basis of the NI, have come to know and to believe that Jesus is God's holy one, the messianic King, and the locus of his divine presence. Even among them, however, there is a traitor.

Jesus' discourse explains why those who rejected their Messiah were left to "wander in the wilderness" for some thirty-eight years before the destruction of the Second Temple. It also explains defections from the Johannine community—they were offended by Jesus' cross and did not have true faith or spiritual illumination.

In John 7–8, Jesus does not fulfil the expectation of the worshippers at the Feast by ascending to the Father in Last Day fulfilment of Tabernacles. He did not (initially) come to bring eschatological consummation in terms of Last Day judgement of the nations and final manifestation of his glorious kingdom. Rather, he came to inaugurate the NE, initiating the Tabernacles journey by his paschal death. Thus he sets people free from slavery to sin, provides the Holy Spirit as the water of life, and grants spiritual illumination to his people as they travel to the New Jerusalem and the heavenly Temple. In an already/not yet eschatology, Jesus' people enjoy these benefits now, but will know the full experience of them in God's rest, when eschatological Tabernacles finally dawns on the Last Day. Jesus manifests himself to many of the "Jews" as their covenant Lord and "I am." They, however, reject him, siding with the satanic ruler of this world, seeking to destroy Jesus. Consequently, they themselves will not abide as God's children in his new heavenly Temple, but will suffer destruction along with *their* Temple.

In John 9, the man-born-blind (like the lame man of John 5) represents Jewish people in "exile," who are encountered by Jesus, the light of the world, the Lord who has come to deliver his people. Unlike the lame man, however, this man (and those whom he represents) demonstrates the correct way to respond to Jesus, by faith and in humble obedience to his word. The chapter also forms the second part of the two-part theodicy, where the man-born-blind and those whom he represents are called out of "exile," in a NE, and follow Jesus to find true worship outside the Jerusalem Temple and synagogue in Jesus' new worshipping community. Absolved from guilt and cleansed from sin, they receive spiritual sight and become God's witnesses of the return of the Lord (who alone can open blind eyes) to his people and the dawn of the NE. As a consequence, they suffer exclusion by the "Jewish" leaders who persist in their spiritual blindness and cause division within families. Nevertheless, they escape the judgement brought upon Jerusalem, the responsibility for which falls upon the shoulders of the "Jewish" authorities who wilfully resisted the claims of God's Son.

In John 10:1–21, the parable of the Good Shepherd is a subversive story that turns the world of the Pharisees on its head. Instead of being Israel's true leaders, they are in fact no better than thieves and hirelings who follow Satan in usurping God's rule over the Temple and over his people. Jesus, the legitimate ruler over the people of God has now entered the Jewish sheepfold to lead his own people out in a NE from bondage to sin, death, and Satan. His true people recognise him and he leads them in and out on a journey to the heavenly Jerusalem. He embodies their national resurrection and raises the new Temple by his resurrection from the dead on the third day.

Jesus is the door of God's new Temple, the only means of access to God. He alone is the Davidic Messiah, who has entered single-handedly, by virtue of his righteousness and atoning death, into the presence of God, obtaining access on behalf of his people. Others who came before for the people were thieves and robbers who cared nothing for the people, but sought to exploit them for their own advantage. Jesus has come to give them life to the full. He makes abundant provision for them as he leads them to their heavenly destination.

Jesus is Israel's Good Shepherd, its true King and Redeemer. He has come, both as the Lord from heaven, to seek out his sheep, and as the Davidic Servant who lays down his life for them. His followers, who are (like the man-born-blind) cast out by the "Jewish" authorities, are the true people of God. Jesus' vicarious death is the paschal sacrifice that atones for their sin and initiates their NE redemption, a deliverance

Summary and Conclusions

that extends to the Gentiles. In the New Jerusalem and new heavenly Temple, all true believers in him, both Jews and Gentiles, will be united under his reign. Under the leadership of the "Jewish" hierarchy, however, earthly Jerusalem will be destroyed and its people scattered in a new exile. This is because they have rejected the Good Shepherd in favor of a wicked ruler who will desert them to a savage onslaught by the Romans. Thus the hope of reunification for the Jewish people will be reversed. Nevertheless, in a new dispersion, the Jews scattered among the Gentiles will ultimately be united, being called by the uplifted cross, through faith in Christ, to participate in a NE to the heavenly Jerusalem.

In John 10:22–42, against the backdrop of Dedication, Jesus is once again on trial before the "Jewish" authorities. They fear that he is bringing God's anger upon Jerusalem and its Temple by his messianic claims. In his defense, Jesus points to his NE signs that authenticate his mission. That the authorities do not believe is evidence that they are not his true people. On these he bestows eternal life and saving power. In this salvation he is equal to his Father. The "Jewish" leaders consider this claim as equivalent to the blasphemy of Antiochus. Consequently they seek to destroy Jesus by stoning him. Jesus defends himself by appealing to Scripture: Since Israel who received God's word at Sinai are referred to as gods, how much more should the one who is the incarnate Word, the true Temple, and dwelling place of God be referred to as God's Son? This contrasts Jesus and his people as the new Temple with the "Jewish" leaders and their followers as the "Sinai Temple," under the law. Moreover, it contrasts his powerful Word with the law that is unable in itself to impart life. Jesus demonstrates that the "Jewish" leaders are powerless to apprehend him by leaving their Temple. This departure from the "Jewish" controlled Temple signals its impending destruction.

The incident is important for the Jewish believers of John's churches. Though they have suffered the loss of the earthly Temple, and been cast out of the synagogues, Jesus is the new locus of God's revelation. Though he has gone away to heaven he has sent forth his disciples into the world, as the earthly representation of the heavenly Temple, that they might call others to follow in the NE. Though they suffer persecution, they are safe in the almighty hand of the Son of God.

Examination of the Festival Cycle has demonstrated that the Paschal NE is a major interpretative key to this section. It has further pointed to the importance of the paradigm for the whole Gospel and indicated the necessity of further research. Further work is needed particularly to investigate the upper room discourse and Jesus' passion and resurrection narratives. It is hoped that the present work will be an inspiration to those who seek to undertake further exploration of the NE in GJohn and to all who read this marvellous Gospel.

Bibliography

SOURCES AND REFERENCE WORKS

Abbot, E. A. *Johannine Grammar*. London: A. & C. Black, 1905.

Aland, B., K. Aland, J. Karavidopoulos, C. M. Martini and B. M. Metzger (eds.). *The Greek New Testament*. 4th revised edn. Stuttgart: Deutsche Bibelgesellschaft, 2001.

Alexander, T. D., and B. S. Rosner, (eds.). *The New Dictionary of Biblical Theology*. Leicester: IVP, 2000.

Bauer, W., W. F. Arndt, F. W. Gingrich, and F. W. Danker. *A Greek-English Lexicon of the New Testament and Other Early Christian Literature*. 2nd edn. Chicago: University of Chicago Press, 1979.

Braude, W. G., (trans.). *Pesikta De-Rab Kahana*. Philadelphia: JPS, 2002.

———. (trans.). *The Midrash on Psalms*. Yale Judaica Series vol. XIII. 2nd edn. 2 vols. New Haven: YUP, 1987.

Bromiley, G. W. (ed.). *ISBE*. Rev. edn. 4 vols. Grand Rapids: Eerdmans, 1986.

Brown, F., S. R. Driver, C. A. Briggs. *The New Brown-Driver-Briggs-Gesenius Hebrew and English Lexicon*. Peabody: Hendrickson, 1979.

Cathcart, K. J. (trans.), and R. P. Gordon, (trans.). *The Targum of the Minor Prophets*. In K. J. Cathcart, M. Maher, and M. McNamara (eds.). *The Aramaic Bible*. Vol. 14. Edinburgh: T. & T. Clark, 1989.

Charlesworth, J. H., (ed.). *The Old Testament Pseudepigrapha*. 2 vols. New York: Doubleday, 1983–1985.

Danby, H. *The Mishnah: Translated from the Hebrew with Introduction and Brief Explanatory Notes*. London: OUP, 1933.

Epstein, I., (trans.). *The Babylonian Talmud*. London: Soncino Press, 1935.

Freedman, D. N., (ed.). *The Anchor Bible Dictionary*. 6 vols. New York: Doubleday, 1992.

Freedman, R. H., and M. Simon, (eds.). *Midrash Rabbah*. 3rd edn. 10 vols. New York: The Soncino Press, 1983.

Green, J. B., S. McKnight, and H. Marshall, (eds.). *Dictionary of Jesus and the Gospels: A Compendium of Contemporary Biblical Scholarship*. Leicester: IVP, 1992.

Hammer, R., (trans.). *The Classic Midrash: Tannaitic Commenteries on the Bible*. New York: Paulist Press, 1995.

Hübner, H. *Vetus Testamentum in Novo: Evangelium secundum Iohannum*. 2 vols. Göttingen: Vandenhoek & Ruprecht, 2003.

Kittel, G., and G. Freidrich, (eds.). *Theological Dictionary of the New Testament*. G. W. Bromiley, (trans.). 10 vols. Grand Rapids: Eerdmans, 1988.

Kittel, R., (ed.). *Biblia Hebraica Stuttgartensia*. Stuttgart: Deutsche Bibelgesellschaft, 1997.

Bibliography

Lauterbach, J. Z. *Mekhilta De-Rabbi Ishmael*. 2nd edn. 2 vols. Philadephia: Jewish Publication Society of America, 2004.

Lightfoot, J. B, (ed.). *The Apostolic Fathers Part One: Clement*. Vols. 1–2, Peabody: Hendrickson, 1989.

———. *The Apostolic Fathers Part Two: Ignatius and Polycarp*. Vols. 1–3. Peabody: Hendrickson. 1989.

McNamara, M., (trans.). *Targum Neofiti 1: Genesis*. In K. J. Cathcart, M. Maher, and M. McNamara (eds.). *The Aramaic Bible*. Vol. 1a. Edinburgh: T. & T. Clark, 1992.

———. *Targum Neofiti 1: Exodus*. In K. J. Cathcart, M. Maher, and M. McNamara (eds.). *The Aramaic Bible*. Vol. 2. Edinburgh: T. & T. Clark, 1992.

———. *Targum Neofiti 1: Deuteronomy*. In K. J. Cathcart, M. Maher, and M. McNamara (eds.). *The Aramaic Bible*. Vol. 5a. Edinburgh: T. & T. Clark, 1997.

Melito of Sardis. *Peri Pascha* ("On The Passover.") G. F. Hawthorne (trans.). *Kerux: The Journal of Northwest Theological Seminary* 4 (1989): 5–35.

Moulton, J. H., and G. Milligan. *The Vocabulary of the Greek New Testament: Illustrated from the Papyri and other Non-Literary Sources*. London: Hodder & Stoughton, 1948.

Neusner, J. *The Tosefta: Translated From the Hebrew with a New Introduction*. Peabody: Hendrickson, 2002.

———. *The Babylonian Talmud: A Translation and Commentary*. 37 vols. Peabody: Hendrickson, 2005.

Orr, J. *The International Standard Bible Encyclopaedia*. 4 vols. Peabody: Hendrickson, 1996.

Pritchard, J. B. (ed.). *Ancient Near Eastern Texts Relating to the Old Testament*. 3rd edn. Princeton, 1969.

Richardson, C. C. (ed.). *Early Christian Fathers*. New York: Touchstone, 1996.

Roberts, A., and J. Donaldson, (eds.). *The Ante-Nicene Fathers: Translation of the Writings of the Fathers down to A.D. 325*. Revised by A. C. Coxe. 14 vols. 1885. Reprinted, Grand Rapids: Eerdmans 1993.

Robinson, J. M, (ed.). *The Nag Hammadi Library: The Definitive Translation of the Gnostic Scriptures Complete in One Volume*. San Francisco: Harper Collins, 1990.

Ryken, L., J. C. Wilhoit, and T. Longman III. *Dictionary of Biblical Imagery: An Encyclopaedic Exploration of the Images, Symbols, Motifs, Metaphors, Figures of Speech and Literary Patterns of the Bible*. Leicester: IVP, 1998.

Schaff, P., and H. Wace, (eds.). *The Nicene and Post-Nicene Fathers*. Second series. 14 vols. 1890. Reprinted, Grand Rapids: Eerdmans, 1991.

Schürer, E. *The History of the Jewish People in the Age of Jesus Christ*. 4 vols. Rev. edn. Edinburgh: T. & T. Clark, 1973–1987.

Smith, G. A. *Historical Geography of the Holy Land*. 25th edn. London, 1931.

Stenning, J. F., (trans.). *The Targum of Isaiah*. Oxford: Clarendon Press, 1949.

Vermes, G., *The Complete Dead Sea Scrolls in English*. New York: Penguin, 1997.

Vanhoozer, K. J., (ed.). *Dictionary for Theological Interpretation of the Bible*. Grand Rapids: Baker, 2002.

Whiston, W., (trans.). *The Works of Josephus: Complete and Unabridged. New Updated Edition*. USA: Hendrickson, 1995.

Yonge, C. D., (trans.). *The Works of Philo: Complete and Unabridged*. USA: Hendrickson, 1995.

Bibliography

GENERAL

Ackerman, J. S. "The Rabbinic Interepretation of Psalm 82 and the Gospel of John: John 10:34." *Harvard Theoligical Review* 59 no. 2 (1966): 186–91.

Alexander, T. D. *From Paradise to the Promised Land: An Introduction to the Pentateuch.* 2nd edn. Grand Rapids: Baker, 2002.

———. "Messianic Ideology in Genesis." In P. E. Satterthwaite, R. S. Hess, and G. J. Wenham, (eds.). *The Lord's Anointed: Interpretation of Old Testament Messianic Texts.* Carlisle: Paternoster, 1995, 19–39.

Allen, L. C. *Ezekiel 1–19.* WBC vol. 28. Dallas: Word, 1994.

———. *Ezekiel 20–48.* WBC vol. 29. Waco: Word, 1990.

———. *The Books of Joel, Obadiah, Jonah and Micah.* NICOT. Grand Rapids: Eerdmans, 1976.

———. "Joel." In Idem. *The Books of Joel, Obadiah, Jonah and Micah.* NICOT. Grand Rapids: Eerdmans, 1976, 17–126.

———. "Micah." In In Idem. *The Books of Joel, Obadiah, Jonah and Micah.* NICOT. Grand Rapids: Eerdmans, 1976, 237–404.

———. *Psalms 101–150.* WBC vol. 21. Waco: Word, 1983.

Allis, O. T. *The Unity of Isaiah: A Study in Prophecy.* Phillipsburg: P. & R., 1980.

Allison, D. C. "The Living Water." *St Vladimir's Quarterly* (1973): 143–57.

———. *The New Moses: A Matthean Typology.* Edinburgh: T. & T. Clark, 1993.

Alter, R. *The Art of Biblical Narrative.* New York: Basic Books, 1981.

Andersen, F. I., and D. N. Freedman. *Hosea.* AB vol. 24. New York: Doubleday, 1980.

Anderson, A. A. *2 Samuel.* WBC vol. 11. Dallas: Word, 1989.

Anderson, P. N. *The Christology of the Fourth Gospel: Its Unity and Disunity in the Light of John 6.* Valley Forge: Trinty Press International, 1996.

———. "The Having-Sent-Me Father: Aspects of Agency, Encounter, and Irony in the Johannine Father-Son Relationship." *Semeia* 85 (1991): 33–57.

———. "The *Sitz im Leben* of the Johannine Bread of Life Discourse and its Evolving Context." In R. A. Culpepper, (ed.). *Critical Readings of John 6.* Leiden: Brill, 1997, 1–60.

Appold, M. L. *The Oneness Motif in the Fourth Gospel.* Tübingen: Mohr, 1976.

Armerding, C. E. "Were David's Sons Really Priests." In G. F. Hawthorne, (ed.). *Current Issues in Biblical and Patristic Interpretation.* Grand Rapids: Eerdmans, 1975, 85–86.

Ashton, J. *Studying John: Approaches to the Fourth Gospel.* Oxford: Clarendon Press, 1994.

———. *Understanding the Fourth Gospel.* Oxford: OUP, 1991.

———. (ed.). *The Interpretation of John.* 2nd edn. Edinburgh: T. & T. Clark, 1997.

Attridge, H. W. *Hebrews: A Commentary on the Epistle to the Hebrews.* Hermeneia. Philadelphia: Fortress, 1989.

Bacon, B. W. *The Gospel of the Hellenists.* New York: Henry Holt, 1933.

Baily, D. P. "The Intertextual Relationship of Daniel 12:2 and Isaiah 26:19." *TynBul* 51 (2000): 305–8.

Baker, D. W., T. D. Alexander, and B. K. Waltke. *Obadiah, Jonah and Micah.* TOTC. Leicester: IVP, 1992.

Baldwin, J. G. *Daniel.* TOTC. Leicester: IVP, 1978.

———. *Haggai, Zechariah and Malachi.* TOTC. Leicester: IVP, 1972.

———. *1 and 2 Samuel.* TOTC. Leicester: IVP, 1988.

Balentine, G. L. *The Concept of the New Exodus in the Gospels.* Th.D. Thesis. Louisville: Southern Baptist Theological Seminary, 1961.

Bibliography

Ball, D. M. *'I Am' in John's Gospel: Literary Function, Background and Theological Implications.* JSNTSup 124. Sheffield: Sheffield Academic Press, 1996.

Barclay, W. *The Gospel of John.* 2 vols. Louisville: Westminster John Knox, 2001.

Barnett, P. "The Jewish Sign Prophets A.D 40–70: Their Intentions and Origin." *NTS* 27 (1980–81): 679–97.

Barrett, C. K. *The Gospel According to St John.* 2nd edn. London: SPCK, 1978.

———. *The Gospel of John and Judaism: The Franz Delitzsch Lectures, University of Münster 1967.* D. M. Smith, (trans.). London: SPCK, 1975.

———. "The Dialetical Theology of St John." In *Idem. New Testament Essays.* London: SPCK, 1972, 49–69.

———. "The Background of Mark 10:45." In A. J. B. Higgins, (ed.). *New Testament Essays: Studies in Memory of T. W. Manson.* Manchester: 1959, 1–18.

———. "The Lamb of God." *NTS* 1 (1955): 210–18.

———. "The Old Testament in the Fourth Gospel." *JTS* 48 (1947): 155–69.

Bauckham, R. "For Whom were the Gospels Written?" In *Idem* (ed.). *The Gospels for all Christians: Rethinking the Gospel Audiences.* Grand Rapids: Eerdmans, 1998, 9–48.

———. *The Climax of Prophecy: Studies on the Book of Revelation.* Edinburgh: T. & T. Clark, 1993.

———. *Jesus and the Eyewitnesses: The Gospels as Eyewitness Testimony.* Grand Rapids: Eerdmans, 2006.

———. *The Testimony of the Beloved Disciple: Narrative, History, and Theology in the Gospel of John.* Grand Rapids: Baker, 2007.

———. "Papias and Polycrates on the Origin of the Gospel of John." In *Idem. The Testimony of the Beloved Disciple: Narrative, History, and Theology in the Gospel of John.* Grand Rapids: Baker, 2007, 33–72.

———. "Historiographical Characteristics of the Gospel of John." In *Idem. The Testimony of the Beloved Disciple: Narrative, History, and Theology in the Gospel of John.* Grand Rapids: Baker, 2007, 93–112.

———. "Jewish Messianism According to the Gospel of John." In *Idem. The Testimony of the Beloved Disciple: Narrative, History, and Theology in the Gospel of John.* Grand Rapids: Baker, 2007, 207–38.

———. "Monotheism and Christology in the Gospel of John." In *Idem. The Testimony of the Beloved Disciple: Narrative, History, and Theology in the Gospel of John.* Grand Rapids: Baker, 2007, 239–52.

———. "The 153 Fish and the Unity of the Fourth Gospel." In *Idem. The Testimony of the Beloved Disciple: Narrative, History, and Theology in the Gospel of John.* Grand Rapids: Baker, 2007, 271–84.

———. "John for Readers of Mark." In *Idem* (ed.). *The Gospel for All Christians: Rethinking the Gospel Audiences.* Grand Rapids: Eerdmans, 1998, 147–71.

———. (ed.). *The Gospels for All Christian: Rethinking the Gospel Audiences.* Grand Rapids: Eerdmans, 1998.

Bauckham, R., and C. Mosser, (eds.). *The Gospel of John and Christian Theology.* Grand Rapids: Eerdmans, 2008.

Bauer, W. *Rechtgläubigkeit und Ketzerei im ältesten Christentum.* Tübingen: 1934. ET *Orthodoxy and Heresy in Earliest Christianity.* Philadelphia, 1971.

Beale, G. K. *A New Testament Biblical Theology: The Unfolding of The Old Testament in The New.* Grand Rapids: Baker Academic, 2011.

Bibliography

———. *John's Use of the Old Testament in Revelation*. Sheffield: Sheffield Academic Press, 1998.

———. *The Use of Daniel in Jewish Apocalyptic Literature and in the Revelation of St. John*. New York: University Press of America, 1984.

———. *The Book of Revelation*. Grand Rapids: Eerdmans, 1999.

———. *The Temple and the Church's Mission: A Biblical Theology of the Dwelling Place of God*. Downers Grove: IVP, 2004.

———. "Revelation." In D. A. Carson and H. M. G. Williamson, (eds.). *It is written: Scripture Citing Scripture. Essays in Honour of Barnabas Lindars*. Cambridge: CUP, 1988, 318-32.

———. (ed.). *The Right Doctrine from the Wrong Texts: Essays on the Use of the Old Testament in the New*. Grand Rapids: Baker, 1994.

Beale, G. K., and D. A. Carson, (eds.). *Commentary on the New Testament Use of the Old Testament*. Grand Rapids: Baker, 2007.

Beasley-Murray, G. R. *John*. WBC vol. 36. Waco: Word, 1987.

———. *The Book of Revelation*. Grand Rapids: Eerdmans, 1981.

———. "The Interpretation of Daniel 7." *CBQ* 45 (1983): 44-58.

Beckwith, I. T. *The Apocalypse of John*. London: MacMillan, 1922.

Bentzen, A. *King and Messiah*. ET London: Lutterworth, 1955.

Bernard, J. H. *A Critical and Exegetical Commentary on the Gospel according to St. John*. 2 vols. ICC. Edinburgh: T. & T. Clark, 1928.

Berkhof, L. *Systematic Theology*. Edinburgh: The Banner of Truth Trust, 1958.

Beutler, J. *Martyria*. Frankfurt: J. Knecht, 1972.

Beutler, J. and R. T. Fortna, (eds.). *The Shepherd Discourse of John 10 and its Context: Studies by Members of the Johannine Writings Seminar*. Cambridge: CUP, 1991.

Bieringer, R., D. Pollefeyt, and F. Vandecasteele-Vanneuville, (eds.). *Anti Judaism and the Fourth Gospel*. London: Westminster John Knox, 2001.

Blank, J. *Krisis: Untersuchungen zur johanneischen Christologie und Eschatologie*. Freiburg im Breisgau: Lambertus-Verlag, 1964.

Blenkinsopp, J. *Isaiah 1-39. A New Translation with Introduction and Commentary*. AB vol. 19. New York: Doubleday, 2000.

———. *Isaiah 40-55. A New Translation with Introduction and Commentary*. AB vol. 19A. New York: Doubleday, 2002.

———. *Isaiah 56-66. A New Translation with Introduction and Commentary*. AB vol. 19B. New York: Doubleday, 2003.

Block, D. I. *The Book of Ezekiel Chapters 1-24*. NICOT. Grand Rapids: Eerdmans, 1997

———. *The Book of Ezekiel Chapters 25-48*. NICOT. Grand Rapids: Eerdmans, 1998.

———. "My Servant David." In R. S. Hess, and M. D. Carroll. *Israel's Messiah in the Bible and the Dead Sea Scrolls*. Grand Rapids: Baker, 2003, 17-56.

Blomberg, C. L. *The Historical Reliability of John's Gospel: Issues and Commentary*. Leicester: Apollos, 2001.

Bock, D. L. *Acts*. Baker Exegetical Commentary on the New Testament. Grand Rapids: Baker, 2007.

Boice, J. M. *Witness and Revelation in the Gospel of John*. Grand Rapids: Zondervan, 1970.

Boismard, M. E. "Le Lavement des Pieds (Jn xiii, 1-17)." *Revue Biblique* 71 (1964): 5-24.

———. *Moses or Jesus: An Essay in Johannine Christology*. B. T. Viviano (trans). ET Minneapolis: Fortress, 1993.

Borchert, G. L. *John 1-11*. NAC vol. 25A. Nashville: Broadman & Holman, 1996.

———. *John 12-21*. NAC vol. 25B. Nashville: Broadman & Holman, 2002.
Borgen, P. *Bread From Heaven: An Exegetical Study of the Concept of Manna in the Gospel of John and the Writings of Philo*. Leiden: Brill, 1965.
———. *Logos Was The True Light and Other Essays on the Gospel of John*. Trondheim: Tapir Publishers, 1983.
Bowman, J. *The Fourth Gospel and the Jews: A Study in R. Akiba, Esther and the Gospel of John*. Pittsburgh Theological Monograph Series 8. Oregon: Wipf and Stock, 1975.
Boyarin, D. "Semantic Differences; or 'Judaism'/'Christianity.'" In A. H. Becker and A. Y. Reed, (eds.). *The Ways that Never Parted: Jews and Christians in Late Antiquity and the Early Middle Ages*. Texts and Studies in Ancient Judaism 95. Tübingen: Mohr Siebeck, 2003, 65–85.
———. "The Ioudaioi in John and the Prehistory of 'Judaism.'" In J. C. Anderson, P. Sellew, and C. Setzer, (eds.). *Pauline Conversations in Context: Essays in Honour of Calvin J. Roetzel*. JSNTSup 221. London: Sheffield Academic Press, 2002, 216–39.
———. *Border Lines: The Partition of Judaeo-Christianity*. Philadelphia: University of Pennsylvania Press, 2004.
Braun, F. M. *Jean le Théologien et son Évangile dans l'Église ancienne*. Paris: Gabalda, 1959.
———. "L'Evangile de Saint Jean et les Grandes Traditions d'Israel, IV: Moise et l'Exode." *Revue Thomiste* 68 (1960): 165–84.
Bright, J. *A History of Israel*. 3rd edn. London: SCM, 1981.
Brodie, T. L. *The Gospel According to John: A Literary and Theological Commentary*. Oxford: OUP, 1993.
———. *The Quest for the Origin of John's Gospel: A Source-Oriented Approach*. Oxford: OUP, 1993.
Broer, I. "Knowledge of Palestine in the Fourth Gospel?" In R. T. Fortna and T. Thatcher. *Jesus in Johannine Tradition*. Louisville: Westminster John Knox, 2001, 83–99.
Brooke, G. J. "Christ and the Law in John 7–10." In B. Lindars, (ed.). *Law and Religion: Essays on the Place of the Law in Israel and Early Christianity*. Cambridge, 1988, 102–12.
———. *Exegesis at Qumran: 4Q Florilegium in Its Jewish Context*. JSOTSup 29. Sheffield: JSOT Press, 1985.
Brown, R. E. "Incidents that are Units in the Synoptic Gospels but Dispersed in St. John." *CBQ* 23 (1961): 143–60.
———. "Other Sheep Not Of This Fold. The Johannine Perspective on Christian Diversity in the Late First Century." *JBL* 97 1 (1978): 5–22.
———. "The Dead Sea Scrolls and the New Testament." In J. H. Charlesworth, (ed.). *John and the Dead Sea Scrolls*. New York: Crossroad, 1991, 1–8.
———. *An Introduction to the New Testament*. New York: Doubleday, 1997.
———. *The Community of the Beloved Disciple: The Life, Loves, and Hates of an Individual Church in New Testament Times*. New York: Paulist Press, 1979.
———. *The Epistles of John: A New Translation with Introduction and Commentary*. AB vol. 30. New York: Doubleday, 1982.
———. *The Gospel According to John 1–XII*. AB vol. 29. New York: Doubleday, 1966.
———. *The Gospel According to John XIII–XXI*. AB vol. 29a. New York: Doubleday, 1970.
———. *An Introduction to the Gospel of John*. F. J. Moloney (ed.). London: Doubleday, 2003.
Bruce, F. F. *The Acts of the Apostles: The Greek Text with Introduction and Commentary*. Grand Rapids: Eerdmans, 1951.

Bibliography

———.*The Book of the Acts: The English Text with Introduction, Exposition and Notes.* London: Marshall, Morgan & Scott, 1968.

———. *The Canon of Scripture.* Illinois: IVP, 1988.

———.*The Epistles of John.* Basingstoke: Pickering, 1970.

———. *The Epistle to the Hebrews.* NICNT. Rev. edn. Grand Rapids: Eerdmans, 1990.

———. *The Epistle to the Galatians.* NIGTC. Grand Rapids: Eerdmans, 1992.

———. *The Gospel of John.* Grand Rapids, Eerdmans, 1983.

———. *New Testament Development Of Old Testament Themes.* Grand Rapids: Eerdmans, 1969.

———. "Some Notes on the Fourth Evangelist." *EvQ* 16 (1944): 101–9.

———. *New Testament History.* London: Thomas Nelson, 1969.

Brunson, A. C. *Psalm 118 in the Gospel of John: An Intertextual Study of the New Exodus Pattern in the Gospel of John.* WUNT 2 158. Tübingen: Mohr Siebeck, 2003.

Bühner, J. A. *Der Gesandte und sein Weg im vierten Evangelium: Die kultur- und religionsgeschichliche Grundlagen der johanneischen Sendungschristologie sowie ihre traditionsgeschichliche Entwicklung.* Tübingen: 1977.

Bultmann, R. *Theology of the New Testament.* K. Grobel, (trans.). 2 vols. London: SCM, 1952–55.

———. *The Gospel of John: A Commentary*, G. R. Beasley-Murray, (trans.). Oxford: Basil Blackwell, 1971.

Burridge, R. A. *What Are the Gospels? A Comparison with Graeco-Roman Biography.* 2nd edn. Grand Rapids: Eerdmans, 2004.

Buchanan, G. *Introduction to Intertextuality.* New York: Edwin Mellen, 1994.

Burge, G. M. *John.* NIV Application Commentary. Grand Rapids: Zondervan, 2000.

———. *Interpreting the Gospel of John.* Grand Rapids: Baker, 1992.

———. *The Letters of John.* NIV Application Commentary. Grand Rapids: Zondervan, 1996.

Burney, C. F. *The Aramaic Origin of the Fourth Gospel.* Oxford: Clarendon Press, 1922.

Bush, G. *Commentary on Exodus.* New York, 1843. Repr. Grand Rapids: Kregel, 1989.

Byrskog, S. *Story as History—History as Story: The Gospel Tradition in the Context of Ancient Oral History.* WUNT 123. Tübingen: Mohr Siebeck, 2000.

Caird, G. B. *The Revelation of Saint John.* BNTC. London: A. & C. Black, 1966.

Calvin, J. *Commentary on the book of Psalms.* J. Anderson (trans.). 5 vols. Edinburgh: Calvin Translation Society, 1845–49.

———. *Commentary on the book of the Prophet Isaiah.* W. Pringle (trans.). 4 vols. Edinburgh: Calvin Translation Society, 1850.

———. *Commentaries on the book of the Prophet Jeremiah and the Lamentations.* J. Owen (trans.). 5 vols. Edinburgh: Calvin Translation Society, 1850.

———. *Commentaries on the Prophet Daniel.* T. Myers (trans.). 2 vols. Edinburgh: Calvin Translation Society, 1853.

———. *The Gospel According to St. John.* T. H. L. Parker (trans.). 2 vols. Edinburgh: Oliver and Boyd, 1959.

Carlson, R. A. *David the Chosen King: A Traditio-Historical Approach to the Second Book of Samuel.* Stockholm: Almqvist and Wiksell, 1964.

Carson, D. A. *Divine Sovereignty and Human Responsibility: Biblical Perspectives in Tension.* Eugene: Wipf and Stock, 2002.

———. *The Gospel According to John.* Leicester: IVP, 1991.

Carson, D. A., D. J. Moo, and L. Morris. *An Introduction to the New Testament*. Grand Rapids: Zondervan, 1992.

Carson, D. A., and H. G. M. Williamson, (eds.). *It is Written: Scripture Citing Scripture*. Cambridge: CUP, 1988.

Carson, D. A., P. T. O'Brien, and M. Seifrid. *Justification and Variegated Nomism*. 2 vols. Grand Rapids: Baker, 2001–4.

Casey, M. "Where Wright is Wrong: A Critical Review of N. T. Wright's *Jesus and the Victory of God*." *JSNT* 69 (1998): 95–103.

Charlesworth, J. H. *The Beloved Disciple: Whose Witness Validates the Gospel of John?* Valley Forge: Trinity Press International, 1995.

———. (ed.). *John and the Dead Sea Scrolls*. New York: Crossroad, 1991.

Childs, B. S. *Introduction to the Old Testament as Scripture*. London: SCM, 1996.

———. *Biblical Theology of the Old Testament*. London: SCM, 1992.

———. *Exodus*. OTL. London: SCM, 1974.

———. *Isaiah*. Louisville: Westminster John Knox, 2001.

Chilton, B. D. *Templum Amicitiae: Essays on the Second Temple Presented to Ernst Bammel*. JSNTSup 48. Sheffield: JSOT Press, 1991.

Clark, D. K. "Signs in Wisdom and John." *CBQ* (1993): 201–9.

Cole, A. *Exodus*. TOTC. Leicester: IVP, 1973.

Collins, J. J. *A Commentary on the Book of Daniel*. Hermeneia. Minneapolis: Fortress, 1993.

Coloe, M. L. *God Dwells with Us: Temple Symbolism in the Fourth Gospel*. Minnesota: Liturgical Press, 2001.

Colpe, C. "New Testament and Gnostic Christology." In J. Neusner, (ed.). *Studies in the History of Religions*. XIV. Leiden: Brill, 1968, 227–43.

Cooke, G. A. *Ezekiel*. ICC. Edinburgh: T. & T. Clark, 1936.

Cotterell, P. C., and M. Turner. *Linguistics and Biblical Interpretation*. Downers Grove: IVP, 1989.

Coxon, P. S. *The Paschal New Exodus in John's Gospel: An Interpretative Key, With Particular Reference to Chapters 5–10*. Ph.D. Thesis. Lampeter: University of Wales, 2010.

Craigie, P. C. *The Book of Deuteronomy*. NICOT. Grand Rapids: Eerdmans, 1976.

———. *Psalms 1–50*. WBC vol. 19. Waco: Word, 1983.

Cranfield, C. E. B. *A Critical and Exegetical Commentary on the Epistle to the Romans*. 2 vols. ICC. Edinburgh: T. & T. Clark, 1979.

Cross, F. L., (ed.), *The Jung Codex*. London: Mowbray, 1955.

Culler, J., *The Pursuit of Signs: Semiotics, Literature, Deconstruction*. New York: Cornell University Press, 2002.

Cullmann, O. *The Johannine Circle: Its Place in Judaism, Among the Disciples of Jesus and in Early Christianity: A Study in the Origin of the Gospel of John*. London: SCM, 1976.

———. *The Christology of the New Testament*. London: SCM. 1983.

———. "Sabbat und Sonntag nach dem Johannesevangelium." In W. Schmauch, (ed.). *In Memoriam Ernst Lohmeyer*. Stuttgart: Evangelisches Verlag, 1951, 127–31.

Culpepper, R. A. *Anatomy of the Fourth Gospel: A Study in Literary Design*. Philadelphia: Fortress, 1983.

———. *John the Son of Zebedee: The Life of a Legend*. Minneapolis: Fortress, 2000.

———. *The Gospel and Letters of John*. Nashville: Abingdon, 1998.

Culpepper, R. A., (ed.). *Critical readings of John 6*. Leiden: Brill 1997.

Culpepper, R. A., and C. C. Black, (eds.). *Exploring the Gospel of John: In Honor of D. Moody Smith*. Louisville: Westminster John Knox, 1996.

Cyril of Alexandria. *The Gospel According to John*. P. E. Pusey (trans.). London, 1885.

Dahms, J. V. "Isaiah 55:11 and the Gospel of John." *EvQ* 53 (1981): 78–88.

Dahood, M. *Psalms I 1–50: A New Translation with Introduction and Commentary*. AB vol. 16. New York: Doubleday, 1966.

———. *Psalms II 51–100: A New Translation with Introduction and Commentary*. AB vol. 17. New York: Doubleday, 1968.

———. *Psalms III 101–150: A New Translation with Introduction and Commentary*. AB vol. 17a. New York: Doubleday, 1970.

Daly-Denton, M. *David in the Fourth Gospel: The Johannine Reception of the Psalms*. Leiden: Brill, 2000.

Daniélou, J. *Sacramentum Futuri*. Paris: Beauchesne, 1950.

Daube, D. *The Exodus Pattern in the Bible*. London: Faber and Faber, 1963.

———. *The New Testament and Rabbinic Judaism*. London: Athlone Press, 1956.

Davids, P. H. *The First Epistle of Peter*. NICNT. Grand Rapids: Eerdmans, 1990.

Davies, M. *Rhetoric and Reference in the Fourth Gospel*. JSNTSup 69. Sheffield: Sheffield Academic Press, 1992.

Davies, W. D. "Paul and the New Exodus." In C. Evans, and S. Talmon, (eds.). *The Quest for Context and Meaning: Studies in Biblical Intertextuality in Honor of James A. Sanders*. Leiden: Brill, 1997, 443–63.

———. *Paul and Rabbinic Judasism*. London: SPCK, 1948.

———. *Torah in the Messianic Age and/or the Age to Come*. SBLMS 7. Philadelphia: SBL, 1952.

———. *The Gospel and the Land: Early Christianity and Jewish Territorial Doctrine*. Berkeley: University of California Press, 1974.

Davies, W. D., and D. C. Allison. *The Gospel According to Saint Matthew*. ICC. 3 vols. Edinburgh: T. & T. Clark, 1988.

Davis, D. R. *1 Kings: The Wisdom and the Folly*. Fearn: Christian Focus, 2002.

Day, J., (ed.). *King and Messiah in Israel and the Ancient Near East: Proceedings of the Oxford Old Testament Seminar*. Sheffield: Sheffield Academic Press, 1998.

De Boer, M. C., (ed.). *From Jesus to John: Essays on Jesus and New Testament Christology in Honour of Marinus de Jonge*. JSNTSup 84. Sheffield: Sheffield Academic, 1993.

Deeley, M. K. "Ezekiel's Shepherd and John's Jesus: A Case Study in the Appropriation of Biblical Texts." In C. A. Evans and J. A. Sanders (eds.). *Early Christian Interpretations of the Scriptures of Israel*. JSNTSup 148. Sheffield: Sheffield Academic Press, 1997, 252–63.

De Jonge, M. "Eschatology and Ethics in the Fourth Gospel." In Idem. *Jesus: Stranger from Heaven and Son of God*. J. E. Steely, (trans.). Missoula: Scholars Press, 1977.

Delitzsch., F. *Isaiah 28–66*. J. Martin, (trans.). Edinburgh: T. & T. Clark, 1877. Repr. in C. F. Keil, and F. Delitzsch. *Commentary on the Old Testament*. Peabody: Hendrickson, 1989.

Denis, A. M. "Jesus' Walking on the Waters: A Contribution to the History of the Pericope in Gospel Tradition." *Louvain Studies* 1 (1967): 284–97.

Derrett, J. D. M. "The Good Shepherd: St. John's use of Jewish Halakah and Haggadah," *Studia Theologica* 27 (1973): 25–50.

———. "The Parable of the Wicked Vinedressers." In Idem. *Law in the New Testament*. London: 1970, 286–312.

De Solages, B. *Jean et les synoptiques*. Leiden: Brill, 1979.

De Vries, S. J. *1 Kings.* WBC vol. 12. Waco: Word, 1985.

Dillard, R. B., "Joel." In T. E. McComiskey (ed.). *The Minor Prophets: An Exegetical and Expository Commentary.* 3 vols. Grand Rapids: Baker, 1992–2003, 239–313.

Dodd, C. H. *About the Gospels.* Cambridge: CUP, 1950.

———. *According to the Scriptures: The Sub-Structure of New Testament Theology.* London: Nisbet & Co., 1952.

———. *Historical Tradition in the Fourth Gospel.* Cambridge: CUP, 1963.

———. *The Apostolic Preaching and its Developments.* London: Hodder & Stoughton, 1963.

———. "A Hidden Parable in the Fourth Gospel." In *Idem. More New Testament Studies.* Manchester, 1968, 30–40.

———. *The Interpretation of the Fourth Gospel.* Cambridge: CUP, 1953.

———. "The Old Testament in the New." In G. K. Beale (ed.). *The Right Doctrine from the Wrong Texts.* Grand Rapids: Baker, 1994, 167–81.

Duguid, I. "Messianic Themes in Zechariah 9–14." In P. E. Satterthwaite, R. S. Hess, and G. J. Wenham, (eds.). *The Lord's Anointed: Interpretation of Old Testament Messianic Texts.* Carlisle: Paternoster, 1995, 255–80.

Duke, P. D. *Irony in the Fourth Gospel.* Atlanta: Westminster John Knox, 1985.

Dunn J. D. G. *Baptism in the Holy Spirit: A Re-Examination of the New Testament Teaching on the Gift of the Spirit in Relation to Pentecostalism Today.* Philadelphia: Westminster, 1970.

———. *Romans 9–16.* WBC vol. 38b. Dallas: Word, 1988.

———. *Christology in the Making: A New Testament Inquiry into the Origins of the Doctrine of the Incarnation.* 2nd edn. Grand Rapids: Eerdmans, 1989.

———. *The Epistle to Colossians and Philemon.* NIGTC. Grand Rapids: Eerdmans, 1996.

———. *Jews and Christians: The Parting of the Ways A.D. 70 To 135.* Grand Rapids: Eerdmans, 1999.

———. *The Partings of the Ways: Between Christianity and Judaism and their Significance for the Character of Christianity.* 2nd edn. London: SCM, 2006.

———. *Unity and Diversity in the New Testament: An Inquiry into the Character of Earliest Christianity.* 3rd edn. Suffolk: SCM, 2006.

———. "Let John Be John: A Gospel for Its Time." In P. Stuhlmacher, (ed.). *Das Evangelium und die Evangelien. Vorträge vom Tübinger Symposium 1982.* WUNT 28. Tübingen: Mohr, 1983.

———. "The Washing of the Disciple's Feet in John 13:1–20." *ZNW* 61 (1970): 247–52.

———. "The Embarrassment of History: Reflections on the Problem of 'Anti Judaism' in the Fourth Gospel." In R. Bieringer, D. Pollefeyt, and F. Vandecasteele-Vanneuville, (eds.), *Anti Judaism and the Fourth Gospel.* London: Westminster John Knox, 2001, 41–60.

Durham, J. I. *Exodus.* WBC vol. 3. Waco: Word, 1987.

Edersheim, A. *The Temple: Its Ministry and Services as They Were at the Time of Jesus Christ.* London, 1898. Repr. Grand Rapids: Eerdmans, 1992.

Edwards, R. B. *Discovering John.* London: SPCK, 2003.

Ellis, E. E. *Paul's Use of the Old Testament.* 1957. Repr. Grand Rapids: Baker, 1981.

Ellis, P. F. *The Genius of John: A Composition-Critical Commentary on the Fourth Gospel.* Minnesota: Liturgical Press, 1984.

Engnell, I. *Critical Essays on the Old Testament.* London: SPCK, 1970.

Enz, J. J. "The Book of Exodus as a Literary Type for the Gospel of John." *JBL* 76 no. 3 (1957): 208–15.

Bibliography

Evans, C. A. "Obduracy and the Lord's Servant: Some Observations on the Uses of the Old Testament in the Fourth Gospel." In C. A. Evans and W. F. Stinespring (eds.). *Early Jewish and Christian Exegesis Studies. In Memory of William Hugh.* Atlanta: Scholars Press (1987): 221–34.

———. "Root Causes of the Jewish-Christian Rift from Jesus to Justin." In S. E. Porter and B. W. R. Pearson, (eds.). *Christian-Jewish Relations through the Centuries.* JSNTSup 192. Sheffield: Sheffield Academic Press, 2000, 20–35.

———. "Jesus and the Continuing Exile of Israel." In C. C. Newman, (ed.). *Jesus and the Restoration of Israel: A Critical Assessment of N. T. Wright's Jesus and The Victory of God.* Downers Grove: IVP, 1999, 77–100.

Eveson, P. H. *The Great Exchange: Justification by Faith Alone in the Light of Recent Thought.* Bromley: Day One Publications, 1996.

Fairbairn, P. *Ezekiel.* Edinburgh, 1851. Repr. Grand Rapids: Kregel, 1989.

Ferreira, J. *Johannine Ecclesiology.* JSNTSup 160. Sheffield: Sheffield Academic Press, 1998.

Feuillet, A. *Johannine Studies.* New York: Alba House, 1965.

Finch, R. G. *The Synagogue Lectionary and the New Testament.* London: SPCK, 1939.

Finkelstein, L. "Pre-Maccabean Documents in the Passover Haggadah." *Harvard Theological Review* 35 (1942): 291–332.

Fishbane, M. *Biblical Interpretation in Ancient Israel.* Oxford: OUP, 1988.

———. *Text and Texture: Close Readings of Selected Biblical Texts.* New York: Schocken, 1979.

Fischer, J. "Das Problem des neuen Exodus in Js 40-55." *Theologische Quartalschrift* 110 (1929): 111–30.

Fioreaza, E. S. *The Book of Revelation: Justice and Judgment.* Philadelphia: Fortress, 1985.

Fortna, R. T. *The Fourth Gospel and its Predecessor: From Narrative Source to Present Gospel.* Edinburgh: T. & T. Clark, 1988.

———. *The Gospel of Signs: A Reconstruction of the Narrative Source Underlying the Fourth Gospel.* Cambridge: CUP, 1970.

Fortna, R. T., and B. R. Gaventa, (eds.). *The Conversation Continues: Studies in Paul and John. In Honor of J. Louis Martyn.* Nashville: Abingdon, 1990.

Fortna, R. T. and T. Thatcher, (ed.). *Jesus in Johannine Tradition.* London: Westminster John Knox, 2001.

France, R. T. *Jesus and The Old Testament.* London: Tyndale Press, 1971.

———. "The Servant of the Lord in the Teaching of Jesus." *TynBul* 19 (1968): 26–52.

———. *Matthew: Evangelist and Teacher.* Grand Rapids: Zondervan, 1989.

———. *The Gospel of Mark.* NIGTC. Grand Rapids: Eerdmans, 2002.

———. *The Gospel of Matthew.* NICOT. Grand Rapids: Eerdmans, 2007.

Fredrickson, D. E. "Eucharistic Symbolism in the Gospel of John." *Word and World* 17 (1997): 40–44.

Fredriksen, P. *Jesus of Nazareth, King of the Jews: A Jewish Life and the Emergence of Christianity.* New York: Knopf, 2000.

Garrett, S. R. "Exodus From Bondage: Luke 9:31 and Acts 12:1–24." *CBQ* 52 (1990): 656–80.

Gartner, B. *John 6 and The Jewish Passover.* Lund: Gleerup, 1959.

Gaster, M. *The Samaritan Oral Law and Ancient Traditions.* London: Search, 1932.

Gemser, B. "The Rib-or Controversy-Pattern in Hebrew Mentality." In M. Noth and D. Winton Thomas, (eds.). *Wisdom in Israel and the Ancient Near East.* Leiden: Brill, 1955, 120–37.

Bibliography

Gerhardson, B. *The Reliability of the Gospel Tradition*. Massachusetts: Hendrickson, 2001.

Gispen, W. H. *Exodus*. E. van der Maas (trans.). Grand Rapids: Zondervan, 1982.

Glasson, T. F. *Moses in The Fourth Gospel*. London: SCM, 1963.

———. "The 'Passover,' a Misnomer: The Meaning of the verb Pasach." *JTS* 10, (1959): 79-84.

Godet, F. L. *Commentary on John's Gospel*. 1900. Repr. Grand Rapids: Kregel, 1987.

Goldingay, J. E. *Daniel*. WBC vol. 30. Dallas: Word, 1989.

Goodman, M. *Rome and Jerusalem: The Clash of Ancient Civilizations*. London: Allen Lane, 2007.

———. "The Function of the Minim in Early Rabbinic Judaism." In H. Cancik, H. Lichtenberger, and P. Schäfer (eds.). *Geschichte-Tradition-Reflection: Festschrift für Martin Hengel zum 70. Geburtstag*. Tübingen: *Mohr, 1966, 501-10.*

Goppelt, L. *Typos: Die Typologische Deutung des Alten Testaments im Neuen*. Bertelsmann Verlag: 1939. ET *The Typological Interpretation of the Old Testament in the New*. D. H. Madvig, (trans.). Grand Rapids: Eerdmans, 1982.

Grant, R. M. *A Historical Introduction to the New Testament*. New York, 1963.

———. *Gnosticism, A Sourcebook of Heretical Writings from the Early Christian Period*. New York, 1961.

Green, J. B. *The Gospel of Luke*. NICOT. Grand Rapids: Eerdmans, 1997.

Greimas, A. J. *Sémantique structurale*. Paris: Larousse, 1966.

Grelot, P. "Soixante-dix semaines d'années." *Biblica* 50 (1969): 178-81.

Grigsby, B. "Washing in the Pool of Siloam: A Thematic Anticipation of the Johannine Cross." *NovT* 27 3 (1985): 227-35.

———. "The Reworking of the Lake-Walking Account in the Johannine Tradition," *Expository Times* 100 (1989): 295-97.

Grudem, W. *1 Peter*. TNTC. Leicester: IVP, 1988.

Guilding, A. *The Fourth Gospel and Jewish Worship: A study of the Relation of John's Gospel to the Ancient Jewish Lectionary System*. Oxford: Clarendon, 1960.

Guthrie, D. *Hebrews*. TNTC. Leicester: IVP, 1983.

———. *New Testament Introduction*. Rev. edn. Leicester: IVP, 1983.

———. *New Testament Theology*. Leicester: IVP, 1981.

Haenchen, E., *John 1: A Commentary on the Gospel of John, Chapters 1-6*. R. W. Funk (trans.). Hermeneia. Philadelphia: Fortress, 1984.

———. *John 2: A Commentary on the Gospel of John, Chapters 7-21*. R. W. Funk (trans.). Hermeneia. Philadelphia: Fortress, 1984.

———. "Der Vater, der mich gesandt hat" *NTS* 9 (1962-63): 208-16.

Hailey, H. *A Commentary on the Minor Prophets*. Grand Rapids: Baker, 1991.

Hamilton, V. P. *The Book of Genesis Chapters 1-17*. NICOT. Grand Rapids: Eerdmans, 1991.

Harner, P. B. *The "I Am" of the Fourth Gospel: A Study in Johannine Usage and Thought*. Philadelphia: Fortress, 1970.

Hanson, A. T. *The Living Utterances of God: The New Testament Exegesis of the Old*. London: Longman and Todd, 1983.

———. *The Prophetic Gospel: A Study of John and the Old Testament*. Edinburgh: T. & T. Clark, 1991.

———. *The Wrath of The Lamb*. London: SPCK, 1957.

———. "John's use of Scripture." In C. A. Evans, and W. R. Stegner, (eds.). *The Gospels and the Scripture of Israel*. JSNTSup 104. Sheffield, 1994: 365.

Bibliography

Hanson, P. D. *The Dawn of Apocalyptic.* Philadelphia: Fortress, 1975.
Harvey, A. E. *Jesus on Trial: A Study in the Fourth Gospel.* London: SPCK, 1976.
Harris, E. *Prologue and Gospel, The Theology of the fourth Evangelist.* JSNTSup 107. Sheffield: Sheffield Academic Press, 1994.
Harrison, R. K. *Leviticus.* TOTC. Leicester: IVP, 1980.
Hays, R. B. *Echoes of Scripture in the Letters of Paul.* New Haven: YUP, 1989.
———. *The Conversion of the Imagination: Paul as Interpreter of Israel's Scripture.* Grand Rapids: Eerdmans, 2005.
Hays, J. D. "If he looks like a Prophet . . . " In R. S. Hess, and M. D. Carroll, (eds.). *Israel's Messiah in the Bible and the Dead Sea Scrolls.* Grand Rapids: Baker, 2003, 57–69.
Heil, J. P. *Jesus Walking on the Sea: Meaning and Gospel Functions of Matthew 14:22-33, Mark 6:45-52 and John 6:15b-21.* Rome: Biblical Institute Press, 1981.
Hemer, C. J. *The Letters to the Seven Churches of Asia in their Local Setting.* Grand Rapids: Eerdmans, 1989.
Hendricksen, W. *More Than Conquerors: An Interpretation of the Book of Revelation.* Grand Rapids: Baker, 1967.
Hengel, M. M. *Judaism and Hellenism.* London: SCM, 1996.
———. *The Atonement: The Origins of the Doctrine in the New Testament.* Philadelphia: Fortress, 1981.
———. *Between Jesus and Paul.* London: SCM, 1983.
———. *Studies in Mark.* Philadelphia: Fortress, 1985.
———. "The Effective History of Isaiah 53 in the Pre-Christian Period." In B. Janowski and P. Stuhlmacher, (eds.). *The Suffering Servant: Isaiah 53 in Jewish and Christian Sources.* Grand Rapids: Eerdmans, 2004.
———. *The Four Gospels and the One Gospel of Jesus Christ: An Investigation of the Collection and Origin of the Canonical Gospels.* Harrisburg Pa: Trinity Press International, 2000.
———. *The Johannine Question.* London: SCM, 1990.
———. "The Old Testament in the Fourth Gospel." *HBT* 12 (1990): 31–32.
———. "Das Gleichnis von den Weingartnern Mc 12, 1–12 im Licht der Zenonpapyri und der rabbinischen Gleichnisse." *ZNW* 29 (1968): 28.
———. "Das Johannesevangelium als Quelle fur die Geschichte des antiken Judentums." In *Judaica, Hellenistica et Christiana: Kleine Schriften II.* Tübingen, 1999.
Hengstenberg, E. W. *Christology of the Old Testament: And a Commentary on the Messianic Predictions.* T. Meyer, (trans.). 2 vols. Edinburgh: T. & T. Clark, 1868. Abridged edn. Grand Rapids: Kregel: 1970.
———. *Commentary on the Gospel of St. John.* 2 vols. ET. Edinburgh: T. & T. Clark, 1868.
Hess, R. S. "Messiahs Here and There." In R. S. Hess, and M. D. Carroll (eds.). *Israel's Messiah in the Bible and the Dead Sea Scrolls.* Grand Rapids: Baker, 2003, 103–108.
Hess, R. S., and M. D.Carroll, (eds.). *Israel's Messiah in the Bible and the Dead Sea Scrolls.* Grand Rapids: Baker, 2003.
Hill, C. E. *The Johannine Corpus in the Early Church.* Oxford: OUP, 2004.
———. "Epistula Apostolorum," *JECS* 7 (1999): 1–53.
Hirsch, E. D. *Validity in Interpretation.* New Haven: YUP, 1967.
Hodge, C. *Romans.* Edinburgh: The Banner of Truth Trust, 1975.
———. *I&II Corinthians.* Edinburgh: The Banner of Truth Trust, 1974.
———. *Systematic Theology.* 3 vols. Grand Rapids: Eerdmans, 1993.

Holladay, W. L., *Jeremiah 1: A Commentary on the Book of the Prophet Jeremiah, Chapters 1–25*. Hermeneia. Minneapolis: Fortress, 1986.

———. *Jeremiah 2: A Commentary on the Book of the Prophet Jeremiah, Chapters 26–52*. Hermeneia. Minneapolis: Fortress, 1989.

Holland, T. *Contours of Pauline Theology: A Radical New Survey of the Influences on Paul's Biblical Writings*. Fearn: Christian Focus, 2004.

———. *Romans. The Divine Marriage: A Biblical Theological Commentary*. Eugene, Oregon: Pickwick Publications, 2011.

Hollander, J. *The Figure of Echo: A Mode of Allusion in Milton and After*. Berkeley: University of California Press, 1981.

Hooker, M. D. *Jesus and the Servant*. London: 1959.

Horbury, W. "Extirpation and Excommunication." *VT* 35 (1985): 13–38.

Horsley, R. A., "Popular Messianic Movements around the time of Jesus." *CBQ* 46 (1984): 471–95.

Horsley, R. A., and J. S. Hanson. *Bandits, Prophets and Messiahs: Popular Movements in the Time of Jesus*. Harrisburg: Trinity Press International, 1999.

Hort. J. A. *The Apocalypse of St. John I–III*. London: Macmillan, 1908.

Hoskyns, E. C., F. N. Davey, (ed.). *The Fourth Gospel*. London: Faber and Faber, 1947.

Houlden, J. L. *Commentary on Johannine Epistles*. London, 1973.

Howard, J. K. "Passover and Eucharist in the Fourth Gospel." *SJT* 20 (1967): 329–37.

———. "'Christ our Passover.' A Study of the Passover Exodus Theme in 1 Corinthians." *EvQ* 41 (1963): 97–108.

Howard, W. F. "The Common Authorship of the Johannine Gospel and Epistles." *JTS* 48 (1947): 12–25. Reprinted in W. F. Howard. *The Fourth Gospel in Recent Criticism and Interpretation*. London: 1955, 282–95.

Hubbard, D. A. *Hosea*. TOTC. Leicester: IVP, 1989.

Hugenberger, G. P., "The Servant of the Lord in the 'Servant Songs' of Isaiah: A Second Moses Figure." In P. E. Satterthwaite, R. S. Hess, and G. J. Wenham, (eds.). *The Lord's Anointed: Interpretation of Old Testament Messianic Texts*. Carlisle: Paternoster, 1995, 105–40.

Hughes, P. E. *A Commentary on the Epistle to the Hebrews*. Grand Rapids: Eerdmans, 1979.

Hunt, B. P. W. Stather, *Some Johannine Problems*. London, 1958.

Isaac, E., (trans.). "1 (Ethiopic Apocalypse of) Enoch." In J. H. Charlesworth, (ed.). *The Old Testament Pseudepigrapha*. New York: Doubleday, 1982, vol. 1, 1–6.

Jacobson, T. *The Sumerian King List*. Chicago: University of Chicago Press, 1939.

Janowski, B. and P. Stuhlmacher, (eds.). *The Suffering Servant: Isaiah 53 in Jewish and Christian Sources*. Grand Rapids: Eerdmans, 2004.

Jeremias, J. *The Eucharistic Words of Jesus*. Oxford: Basil Blackwell, 1955.

———. *The Rediscovery of Bethesda: John 5:2*. Louisville, Southern Baptist Theological Seminary, 1966.

———. "λίθος," *TDNT* 4:268–80.

———. "Μωυσῆς." *TDNT* 4:848–73.

———. "παῖς θεοῦ," *TDNT* 5:712–17.

———. "ποιμήν," *TDNT* 6:485–502.

———. "πολλοί," *TDNT* 6:536–45.

Johnston, G. *The Spirit-Paraclete in the Gospel of John*. SNTSMS 12. Cambridge: CUP, 1970.

Jones, L. P. *The Symbol of Water in the Gospel of John*. JSNTSup 145. Sheffield: Sheffield Academic Press, 1997.

Bibliography

Kaiser, O. *Isaiah 1–12*. OTL. London: SMC, 1996.

———. *Isaiah 13–39*. OTL. London: SMC, 1996.

Kaiser, W. C. Jr. *The Messiah in the Old Testament*. Grand Rapids: Zondervan,1995.

———. *The Uses of the Old Testament in the New*. Eugene: Wipf and Stock, 2001.

Käsemann, E. *The Testament of Jesus: A Study of the Gospel of John in the Light of Chapter 17*. London: SCM, 1968.

Keener, C. S. *The Gospel of John: A Commentary*. 2 vols. Massachusetts: Hendrickson, 2003.

Kellermann, U. "Das Danielbuch und die Märtyrertheologie der Auferstehung." In J. W. Van Henten (ed.). *Die Entstehung der Jüdischen Martyrologie*. Studia Post-Biblica vol. 38. Leiden: Brill, 1990. 50-75.

Kerr, A. R. *The Temple of Jesus' Body: The Temple Theme in the Gospel of John*. JSNTSup 220. Sheffield: Sheffield Academic Press, 2002.

Keil, C. F. *The Book of Daniel*. M. G. Easton, (trans.). Edinburgh: T. & T. Clark, 1872. Repr. in C. F. Keil, and F. Delitzsch. *Commentary on the Old Testament*. Peabody: Hendrickson, 1989.

———. *The Books of the Kings*. J. Martin (trans.). Edinburgh: T. & T. Clark, 1883. Repr. in C. F. Keil, and F. Delitzsch. *Commentary on the Old Testament*. Peabody: Hendrickson, 1989.

Keil, C. F., and F. Delitzsch. *Biblical Commentary on the Old Testament: The Pentateuch*. Vol. 3. *Numbers, Deuteronomy*. J. Martin (trans.). Edinburgh: T. & T. Clark, 1865. Repr. in C. F. Keil, and F. Delitzsch. *Commentary on the Old Testament*. Peabody: Hendrickson, 1989.

Keown, G. L., P. J. Scalise, and T. G. Smothers. *Jeremiah 26–52*. WBC vol. 27. Dallas: Word, 1996.

Kidner, K. *Psalms 1–72*. TOTC. Leicester: IVP, 1973.

———. *Psalms 73–150*. TOTC. Leicester: IVP, 1975.

———. *The Message of Hosea*. BST. Leicester: IVP, 1981.

Kitchen, K. A. *Ancient Orient and The Old Testament*. London: The Tyndale Press, 1966.

Klausner, J. *Messianic Idea in Israel*. London: Allen and Unwin, 1956.

Klijn, A. F. J. "The Study of Jewish Christianity." *NTS* 20 (1974): 119-31.

Kline, M. G. *Glory in Our Midst: A Biblical-Theological Reading of Zechariah's Night Visons*. Eugene: Wipf and Stock, 2001.

———. "The Structure of the Book of Zechariah." *JETS* 34 2 (1991): 173–79.

———. *Treaty of the Great King: The Covenant Structure of Deuteronomy: Studies and Commentary*. Grand Rapids: Eerdmans, 1963.

Knight, G. A. F. *Isaiah 40–55: Servant Theology*. ITC. Grand Rapids: Eerdmans,1984.

———. *Isaiah 56–66: The New Israel*. ITC. Grand Rapids: Eerdmans, 1985.

Knohl, I. *The Messiah Before Jesus: The Suffering Servant of the Dead Sea Scrolls*. Berkeley: University of California Press, 2000.

Koester, C. R. *The Word of Life: A Theology of John's Gospel*. Grand Rapids: Eerdmans, 2008.

———. *Symbolism in the Fourth Gospel: Meaning, Mystery, Community*. 2nd edn. Minneapolis: Fortress, 2003.

Koester, H. *Ancient Christian Gospels: Their History and Development*. Harrisburg: Trinity Press International, 1990.

———. *Introduction to the New Testament*. Vol. 2: *History and Literature of Early Christianity*. 2nd edn. New York: Walter De Gruyter, 2002.

Bibliography

Köstenberger, A. J. *John.* Baker Exegetical Commentary on the New Testament. Grand Rapids: Baker, 2004.

———. *Encountering John: The Gospel in Historical, Literary, and Theological Perspective.* Grand Rapids: Baker, 1999.

———. "The Destruction of the Second Temple and the Composition of the Fourth Gospel." In J. Lierman (ed.), *Challenging Perspectives on the Gospel of John.* Tübingen: Mohr, (2006). 69-108.

———. *The Missions of Jesus and the Disciples according to the Fourth Gospel: With Implications for the Fourth Gospel's Purpose and the Mission of the Contemporary Church.* Grand Rapids: Eerdmans, 1998.

Kooevar, H. J. *De Opbouw van het boek Jozua.* Heverlee: Centrum voor Bijbelse Vorming Belgie, v.z.w., 1990.

Koptak, P. E. "Intertextuality." In K. J. Vanhoozer, (ed.). *Dictionary for Theological Interpretation of the Bible.* Grand Rapids: Baker, 2002.

Kraus, H. J. *Worship in Israel.* G. Bushwell (trans.). Oxford: Blackwell, 1966.

———. *Psalms 1-59: A Continental Commentary.* H. C. Oswald (trans.). Minneapolis: Fortress, 1993.

———. *Psalms 60-150: A Continental Commentary.* H. C. Oswald (trans.). Minneapolis: Fortress, 1993.

Kruse, C. G. *The Letters of John.* Grand Rapids: Eerdmans, 2002.

———. *John.* TNTC. Grand Rapids: Eerdmans, 2003.

Kümmel, W. G. *Introduction to the New Testament.* London: SCM, 1975.

Kysar, R. "The Source Analysis of the Fourth Gospel, A Growing Consensus?" *NovT* 15 2 (1973): 134-52.

———. *John.* Minneapolis: Augsburg, 1986.

———. *John The Maverick Gospel.* Rev. edn. London: Westminster John Knox, 1993.

———. *The Fourth Evangelist and his Gospel: An Examination of Contemporary Scholarship.* Minneapolis: Augsburg 1975.

———. *Voyages with John: Charting the Fourth Gospel.* Waco: Baylor, 2006.

Laetsch, T. *The Minor Prophets.* Saint Louis: Concordia, 1965.

Lamarche, P. *Zacharie IX-XIV: Structure Littéraire et Messianisme.* Paris: Librairie Lecoffre, 1961.

Lambert, W. G. *Babylonian Wisdom Literature.* Oxford: OUP, 1960.

Lane, W. L. *The Gospel of Mark.* NICNT. Grand Rapids: Eerdmans, 1990.

———. *Hebrews 1-8.* WBC vol. 47A. Dallas: Word, 1991.

Lawlor, H. *Eusebiana: Essays on the Ecclesiastical History of Eusebius.* Oxford, 1912.

Leaney, A. R. C. "The Johannine Paraclete and Qumran." In J. H. Charlesworth (ed.). *John and the Dead Sea Scrolls.* New York: Crossroad, 1991, 38-61.

Lee, D. A. *The Symbolic Narratives of the Fourth Gospel: The Interplay of Form and Meaning.* JSNTSup 95. Sheffield: Sheffield Academic Press, 1994.

Lenski, R. C. H. *The Interpretation of St. Paul's Epistle to the Romans.* Minneapolis: Augsburg, 1961.

Letham, R. *The Holy Trinity: In Scripture, History, Theology, and Worship.* Phillipsburg: P. & R., 2004.

Leupold, H. C. *Exposition of Genesis.* 2 vols. Grand Rapids: Baker, 1949.

———. *Exposition of Daniel.* Grand Rapids: Baker, 1969.

Bibliography

Lierman, J., (ed.). *Challenging Perspectives on the Gospel of John*. Tübingen: Mohr Siebeck, 2006.

Lieu, J. *The Second and Third Epistles of John*. Edinburgh: 1986.

Lightfoot, R. H. *St. John's Gospel: A Commentary*. C. F. Evans (ed.). London: OUP, 1960.

Lincoln, A. T. *The Gospel According to St. John*. BNTC. London: Hendrickson, 2005.

———. *Truth on Trial: The Lawsuit Motif in the Fourth Gospel*. Peabody: Hendrickson, 2000.

———. "The Beloved Disciple as Eyewitness and the Fourth Gospel as Witness." *JSNT* 85 (2002): 3–26.

Lindars, B. *Behind the Fourth Gospel: Studies in Creative Criticism*. London: SPCK, 1971.

———. *Essays on John*. Leuven: Leuven University Press, 1992.

———. *John: New Testament Guides*. Sheffield: Sheffield Academic Press, 1990.

———. *New Testament Apologetic: The Doctrinal Significance of the Old Testament Quotations*. London: SCM, 1961.

———. *The Gospel of John*. New Century Bible Commentary. Grand Rapids: Eerdmans, 1995.

———. "The Place of the Old Testament in the Formation of the New Testament Theology." In G. K. Beale, (ed.). *The Right Doctrine from the Wrong Texts*. Grand Rapids: Baker, 1994, 137–45.

Lloyd-Jones, D. M. *Romans: An Exposition of Chapter 11: To God's Glory*. Edinburgh: The Banner of Truth Trust, 1998.

Loader, W. *The Christology of the Fourth Gospel*. Frankfurt: Verlag Peter Lang, 1989.

Lohse, E. "σάββατον." *TDNT* 7:1–35.

Loisy, A. *Le Quatrième évangile; Les épitres dites de Jean*. 2nd edn. Paris: Emile Nourry, 1921.

Longman, T. and D. G. Reid. *God is a Warrior*. Grand Rapids: Zondervan, 1995.

Lowe, M. "Who were the IOUDAIOI?" *NovT* 18 (1986): 101–30.

Maccini, R. *Her Testimony is True: Women as Witnesses according to John*. Sheffield: Sheffield Academic Press, 1996.

Mackay, J. L. *Exodus*. Mentor. Fearn: Christian Focus, 2001.

———. *Jeremiah: An Introduction and Commentary. Vol. 2: Chapters 21–52*. Fearn: Christian Focus, 2004.

MacRae, G. W. "The Meaning and Evolution of the Feast of Tabernacles." *CBQ* 22 (1960): 251–76.

Malina, B. J. *The New Testament World: Insights from Cultural Anthropology*. 3rd edn. Louisville: Westminster John Knox, 2001.

———. *The Palestinian Manna Tradition: The Manna Tradition in the Palestinian Targums and its Relationship to the New Testament Writings*. Leiden: Brill, 1968.

Malina, B. J. and R. L. Rohrbaugh. *Social-Science Commentary on the Gospel of John*. Minneapolis: Fortress, 1998.

Manek, J. "The New Exodus in the Book of Luke." *NovT* 2. (1957): 8–23

Manning, G. T. Jr. *Echoes of a Prophet: The Use of Ezekiel in the Gospel of John and in Literature of the Second Temple Period*. JSNTSup 270. London: T. & T. Clark, 2004.

Manns, F. "*Exégèse* rabbinic et *exégèse* johannique." *RB* 92 (1985): 525–38.

Marcus, J. *The Way of the Lord: Christological Exegesis of the Old Testament in the Gospel of Mark*. Westminster John Knox, 1992

Mare, W. H. *The Archaeology of the Jerusalem Area*. Grand Rapids: Baker, 1987.

Marshall, I. H. "An Assessment of Recent Developments." In D. A. Carson, and H. G. M. Williamson, (eds.). *It is Written: Scripture Citing Scripture*. Cambridge: CUP, 1988,

1-21. Reprinted in In G. K. Beale, (ed.). *The Right Doctrine from the Wrong Texts.* Grand Rapids: Baker, 1994, 195-216.

Martin, R. P. "Some Reflections on New Testament Hymns." In H. H. Rowden, (ed.). *Christ the Lord: Studies Presented to D. Guthrie.* Illinois: IVP, 1982, 37-49.

Martyn, J. L. *History and Theology in the Fourth Gospel.* 3rd edn. London: Westminster John Knox, 2003.

Mauser, U. *Christ in the Wilderness: The Wilderness Theme in the Second Gospel and its Basis in Biblical Tradition.* Studies in Biblical Theology 39. Naperville: Allenson, 1963.

Mays, J. L. *Psalms.* Interpretation. Louisville: John Knox, 1994.

McCasland, S. V. "Matthew Twists the Scriptures." In G. K. Beale, (ed.). *The Right Doctrine from the Wrong Texts.* Grand Rapids: Baker, 1994, 146-52.

———. "Signs and Wonders." *JBL* 76 (1957): 149-52.

McComiskey, T. E. (ed.). *The Minor Prophets: An Exegetical and Expository Commentary.* 3 vols. Grand Rapids: Baker, 1992-2003.

———. "Hosea" in Idem., *The Minor Prophets: An Exegetical and Expository Commentary.* 3 vols. Grand Rapids: Baker, 1992-2003, 1-237.

———. "Zechariah" in Idem., *The Minor Prophets: An Exegetical and Expository Commentary.* 3 vols. Grand Rapids: Baker, 1992-2003, 1003-1244.

———. *The Covenants of Promise: A Theology of the Old Testament Covenants.* Grand Rapids: Baker, 1985.

McConville, J. G. *Grace in the End: A Study in Deuteronomic Theology.* Grand Rapids:Zondervan, 1993.

———. *Judgment and Promise: An Interpretation of the Book of Jeremiah.* Leicester: Apollos, 1993.

———. *Deuteronomy.* Apollos. Leicester: IVP, 2002.

McGrath, J. F. *John's Apologetic Christology: Legitimation and Development in Johannine Christology.* SNTSMS 111. Cambridge: CUP, 2001.

———. "A Rebellious Son? Hugo Odeberg and the Interpretation of John 5.18." *NTS* 44 (1998): 470-73.

McHugh, J. "In Him was Life." In J. Dunn, (ed.). *Jews and Christians: The Partings of the Ways A. D. 70-135.* Grand Rapids: Eerdmans, 1999.

Mead, R. T. "A Dissenting Opinion about Respect for Context in Old Testament Quotations." In G. K. Beale, (ed.). *The Right Doctrine from the Wrong Texts.* Grand Rapids: Baker, 1994, 153-63.

Meeks, W. A. "'Am I a Jew?' Johannine Christianity and Judaism." In J. Neusner, (ed.). *Christianity, Judaism and Other Graeco-Roman Cults: Studies for Morton Smith at Sixty.* Studies in Judaism in Late Antiquity 12. Leiden: Brill, 1972. 163-86.

———. The Man from Heaven in Johannine Sectarianism." *JBL* 91 (1972): 44-72.

———. *The Prophet-King: Moses Traditions and the Johannine Christology.* NovT sup. 14 Leiden: Brill, 1967.

———. "Galilee and Judea in the Fourth Gospel." *JBL* 85.2 (1996): 159-69.

Meir, J. P. *A Marginal Jew: Rethinking the Historical Jesus.* 3 vols. New York: Doubleday, 1991-2001.

Menken, M. J. J. "The Textual Form and Meaning of the Quotation from Zech. 12:10 in John 19:37." *CBQ* 55 (1993): 494-511.

———. *Numerical Literary Techiques in John.* NovTSup 55. Leiden: Brill, 1985.

———. "The Origin of the Old Testament Quotation in John 7:38." *NovT* 38 (1996): 160-75.

Bibliography

———. *Old Testament Quotations in the Fourth Gospel: Studies in Textual Form*. Kampen: Pharos, 1996.

———. "The Use of the Septuagint in Three Quotations in John: John 10:34; 12:38; 19:24." In C. M. Tuckett (ed.). *The Scriptures in the Gospels*. Leuven: Leuven University Press, (1997): 367–93.

Merrill, E. H. "Royal Priesthood: An Old Testament Messianic Motif." *Bibliotheca Sacra* 150 (Jan-March, 1993): 50–61.

———. *Deuteronomy*. NAC vol. 4. Nashville: Broadman & Holman, 1994.

Meyer, R. "Μάννα." *TDNT* 4:462–66.

Michel, O. "σπένδομαι." *TDNT* 7:528–36.

Milgroom, J. *Numbers*. JPS Torah Commentary. Philadelphia: JPS, 1989.

Minear, P. *John: The Martyr's Gospel*. Oregon: Wipf and Stock, 2003.

Moloney, F. J. *The Gospel of John*. Sacra Pagina 4. Minnesota: The Liturgical Press, 1998.

———. *Signs and Shadows: Reading John 5–12*. Minneapolis: Fortress, 1996.

Montgomery, J. A. *A Critical and Exegetical Commentary on the Book of Daniel*. Edinburgh: T. & T. Clark, 1927.

Moo, D. *The Epistle of the Romans*. NICNT. Grand Rapids: Eerdmans, 1996.

———. *The Old Testament in the Gospel Passion Narratives*. Sheffield: The Almond Press, 1983.

Morgan, R. "Fulfilment in the Fourth Gospel." *Interpretation* 11 (1957): 155–65.

Morris, L. *The Apostolic Preaching of the Cross*. 3rd edn. Grand Rapids: Eerdmans, 1965.

———. *The Gospel According to John*. NICNT. Grand Rapids: Eerdmans, 1971.

———. *Studies in the Fourth Gospel*. Grand Rapids: Eerdmans, 1969.

———. *Luke*. TNTC. Rev. edn. Leicester: IVP, 1988.

Moule, C. F. D. "A Note on Didache IX. 4." *JTS* 6 (1955): 240–43.

———. *The Birth of the New Testament*. 3rd edn. London: A. & C. Black, 1981.

Motyer, A. *The Prophecy of Isaiah*. Leicester: IVP, 1993.

Motyer, S. *Your Father the Devil? A New Approach to John and 'the Jews'*. Carlisle: Paternoster, 1997.

———. "The Fourth Gospel and the Salvation of Israel: An Appeal for a New Start." In R. Bieringer, D. Pollefeyt, and F. Vandecasteele-Vanneuville, (eds.). *Anti Judaism and the Fourth Gospel*. London: Westminster John Knox, 2001, 83–100.

Mowinckel, S. *The Psalms in Israel's Worship*. D. R. Ap-Thomas, (trans.). 2 vols. Grand Rapids: Eerdmans, 2004.

Moyise, S. (ed.). *The Old Testament in the New Testament: Essays in Honour of J. L. North*, JSNTSup 189. Sheffield: Sheffield Academic Press, 2000.

———. "Intertextuality and the Study of the Old Testament in the New." In *Idem*. *The Old Testament in the New Testament*. 14–19.

———. *The Old Testament in the New: An Introduction*. London: Continuum, 2001.

Moyise, S. and M. J. J. Menken, (eds.). *Isaiah in the New Testament*. London: T. & T. Clark, 2005.

Mueller, J. R. "The Apocalypse of Abraham and the Destruction of the Second Jewish Temple." *SBL Seminar papers* 21 (1982): 341–49.

Murray, J. *The Epistle to the Romans*. 2 vols. NICOT. Grand Rapids: Eerdmans, 1965.

Nash, R. H. *The Gospel and the Greeks: Did the New Testament Borrow from Pagan Thought?* Richardson: Probe, 1992.

Bibliography

Neill, S. and N. T. Wright. *The Interpretation of the New Testament 1861–1986.* 2nd edn. Oxford: OUP, 1988.

Neugebauer, F. "Miszelle zu Joh 5:35," *ZNW* 52 (1961): 130.

Neusner, J. "Judaism after the Destruction of the Temple: An Overview." In *Idem., Formative Judaism: Religious, Historical and Literary Studies, Third Series: Torah, Pharisees and Rabbis.* BJS 46. Chicago: Scholars Press, 1983, 83–98.

Newman, C. C, (ed.). *Jesus and The Restoration of Israel: A Critical Assessment of N. T. Wright's Jesus and The Victory of God.* Illinois Downers Grove: IVP, 1999.

Neyrey, J. H. *An Ideology of Revolt: John's Christology in Social-Science Perspective.* Philadelphia: Fortress, 1988.

———. *The Gospel of John.* Cambridge: CUP, 2007.

———. "Despising the Shame of the Cross: Honour and Shame in the Johannine Passion Narrative." *Semeia* 69 (1996): 113–37.

———. "Jacob Traditions and the Interpretation of John 4:10–26," *CBQ,* 41 (1979): 419–37.

———. "'I Said You Are Gods': Psalm 82:6 and John 10." *JBL* 108 4 (1989): 647–63.

———. " The 'Noble Shepherd' in John 10: Cultural and Rhetorical Background." *JBL* 120 2 (2001): 267–91.

Nielson, K. "Shepherd, Lamb and Blood: Imagery in the Old Testament—Use and Re-Use." *Studia Theologica* 46 (1992): 121–32.

———. *Yahweh as Prosecutor and Judge.* Sheffield: JSOT Press, 1978.

Nixon, R. E. *The Exodus in the New Testament.* London: Tyndale Press, 1963.

Nolland, J. *The Gospel of Matthew.* NIGTC. Grand Rapids: Eerdmans, 2005.

North, C. R. *The Second Isaiah: Introduction, Translation and Commentary to Chapters 49-55.* Oxford: OUP, 1964.

———. *The Suffering Servant in Deutero-Isaiah: An Historical and Critical Study.* London; OUP, 1956.

O'Brien, P. T. *The Epistle to the Philippians: A Commentary on the Greek Text.* NIGTC. Grand Rapids: Eerdmans, 1991.

O'Day, G. R. and S. E. Hylen, *John.* Louisville: Westminster John Knox, 2006.

Odeberg, H. *The Fourth Gospel: Interpreted in its Relation to Contemporaneous Religious Currents in Palestine and the Hellenistic-Oriental World.* Uppsala: Almqvist and Wiksells, 1929. Repr. Amsterdam: B. R. Grüner, 1974.

Olson, D. C. *A New Reading of the Animal Apocalypse of 1 Enoch.* Studia in Veteris Testamenti Pseudepigrapha 24. Leiden: Brill, 2013.

Olyott, S. *Dare to Stand Alone.* Welwyn: Evangelical Press, 1982.

Orlinsky, H. M. *Studies on the Second Part of the Book of Isaiah: The So-Called "Servant of the Lord" and "Suffering Servant in Second Isaiah."* VTSup 14. Leiden: Brill, 1967.

Orton, D. E. *The Composition of John's Gospel: Selected Studies from Novum Testamentum.* vol. 2. Leiden: Brill, 1999.

Osborne, G. R. *The Hermeneutical Spiral: A Comprehensive Introduction to Biblical Interpretation.* Illinois: IVP, 1991.

———. *Revelation.* Baker Exegetical Commentary on the New Testament. Grand Rapids: Baker, 2002.

Oswalt, J. N. *The Book of Isaiah Chapters 1–39.* NICOT. Grand Rapids: Eerdmans, 1986.

———. *The Book of Isaiah Chapters 40–66.* NICOT. Grand Rapids: Eerdmans.1998.

Ozanne, C. G. "The Language of the Apocalypse." *TynBul* 16 (1965): 3–9.

Bibliography

Painter, J. *The Quest for the Messiah: The History, Literature and Theology of the Johannine Community.* 2nd edn. Nashville: Abingdon, 1993.

Pancaro, S. *The Law in the Fourth Gospel: The Torah and the Gospel, Moses and Jesus, Judaism and Christianity According to John.* Leiden: Brill, 1975.

Pao, D. W. *Acts and the Isaianic New Exodus.* Grand Rapids: Baker, 2000.

Pedersen, J. *Israel: Its Life and Culture.* 4 vols. Copenhagen: Provl Banner, 1974.

Peterson, D. L. *Zechariah 9–14 and Malachi.* OTL. London: SCM, 1995.

Pétrement, S. "Le Colloque de Messine et le *Problème* du Gnosticisme." *Revue de Métaphysique et de Morale* 72 (1967): 344–73.

Pfeiffer, C. F. *Between the Testaments.* Grand Rapids: Baker, 1959.

Piper, O. A. " Unchanging Promises. Exodus in the New Testament." *Interpretation* 11 (1957): 3–22.

Porter, S. E., and C. A. Evans, (eds.). *The Johannine Writings.* Biblical Seminar 32. Sheffield: Sheffield Academic Press, 1995.

Poythress, V. S. *The Returning King: A Guide to the Book of Revelation.* Phillipsburg: P. & R., 2000.

———. "The Use of the Intersentence Conjunctions De, Oun, Kai, and Asyndeton in the Gospel of John." *NovT* 26 (1984): 312–40.

Preiss, T. "Justification in Johannine Thought." In Idem. *Life in Christ.* London: SCM, 1957, 9–31.

Price, J. L. "Light from Qumran upon Some Aspects of Johannine Theology." In J. H. Charlesworth (ed.). *John and the Dead Sea Scrolls.* New York: Crossroad, 1991, 9–37.

Provan, I. W., "The Messiah in the Book of Kings." In P. E. Satterthwaite, R. S. Hess, and G. J. Wenham, (eds.). *The Lord's Anointed: Interpretation of Old Testament Messianic Texts.* Carlisle: Paternoster, 1995, 67–85.

Pryor, J. W. *John: Evangelist of the Covenant People: The Narrative and Themes of the Fourth Gospel.* London: Darton, Longman & Todd, 1992.

Ramsay, W. M. *The Letters to the Seven churches.* 4th edn. USA: Kessinger Reprints, 1912.

Rankin, O. S. *The Origins of the Festival of Hanukkah.* Edinburgh: T. & T. Clark, 1930.

Ravens, D. *Luke and the Restoration of Israel.* JSNTSup 119. Sheffield: Sheffield Academic Press 1995.

Reymond, R. L. *A New Systematic Theology of the Christian Faith.* Nashville: Thomas Nelson, 1998.

Reicke, B. *The New Testament Era: The World of the Bible from 500 B.C. to A.D. 100.* D. E. Green (trans.). Philadelphia: Fortress, 1968.

Reim, G. *Studien zum alttestamentlichen Hintergrund des Johannesevangeliums.* SNTSMS 22. London: CUP, 1974.

Reinhartz, A. *Befriending the Beloved Disciple: A Jewish Reading of the Gospel of John.* London: Continuum, 2001.

———. "The Johannine Community and its Jewish Neighbours: A Reappraisal." In F. F. Segovia, (ed.). *'What is John?' Vol. II: Literary and Social Readings of the Fourth Gospel.* Society of Biblical Literature Symposium Series 7. Atlanta: Scholars Press, 1998, 111–38.

———. "'Jews' and Jews in the Fourth Gospel." In R. Bieringer, D. Pollefeyt, and F. Vandecasteele-Vanneuville, (eds.). *Anti Judaism and the Fourth Gospel.* London: Westminster John Knox, 2001, 213–27.

———. "The Gospel of John: How the 'Jews' became part of the plot." In P. Fredriksen, and A. Reinhartz, *Jesus, Judaism and Christian Anti-Judaism: Reading the New Testament after the Holocaust*. Louisville: Westminster John Knox, 99–116.
Rengstorf, K. H. "ἀποστέλλω." *TDNT* 1:398–447.
Rensberger, D. *Johannine Faith and Liberating Community*. Philadelphia, The Westminster Press, 1988.
Richardson, A. *The Miracle Stories of the Gospels*. London: SCM, 1941.
Ridderbos, H. *The Gospel of John: A Theological Commentary*. Grand Rapids: Eerdmans, 1997.
Ridderbos, J. *Isaiah*. BSC. Grand Rapids: Zondervan, 1983.
———. *Deuteronomy*. BSC. Grand Rapids: Zondervan, 1984.
Ringe, S. H. *Jesus, Liberation, and the Biblical Jubilee: Images for Ethics and Christology*. Philadelphia: Fortress, 1985. Repr. Oregon: Wipf and Stock, 2004.
Robertson, O. P. *The Christ of the Covenants*. Grand Rapids: Baker, 1982.
———. *Understanding the Land of the Bible: A Biblical-Theological Guide*. Phillipsburg: P. & R., 1996.
———. *Prophet of the Coming Day of the Lord: The Message of Joel*. Darlington: Evangelical Press, 1995.
Robinson, J. A. "The Problem of the Didache." *JTS* 13 (1911–12), 339–56.
Robinson, J. A. T. *Redating the New Testament*. London: SCM, 1976.
———. "The Parable of John 10:1–5." *ZNW* 46 (1955): 233–40.
———. *Twelve New Testament Studies*. London: SCM, 1962.
———. *The Priority of John*. London: SCM, 1985.
———. "The New Look on the Fourth Gospel." *Studia Evangelica, Texte und Untersuchungen* 73 (1959): 338–50. Reprinted in J. A. T. Robinson. *Twelve New Testament Studies*. London: SCM, 1962, 94–106.
Röhl, W. G. *Die Rezeption des Johannesevangeliums in christlich-gnostichen Schriften aus Nag Hammadi*. Frankfurt am Main: Peter Lang, 1991.
Ross, A. P. *Creation and Blessing: A Guide to the Study and Exposition of Genesis*. Grand Rapids: Baker, 1988.
Rubenstein, J. L. *The History of Sukkot in the Second Temple and Rabbinic Periods*. Atlanta: Scholars Press, 1995.
Ruckstuhl, E. *Die literarische Einheit des Johannevangeliums*. Paulus, 1951.
Rudolph, W. *Haggai—Sacharja 1–8—Sacharja 9–14—Maleachi*, Kommentar zum Alten Testament XIII 4. Gütersloh: Gerd Mohn, 1976.
Sahlin, H. "The Exodus of Salvation according to St. Paul." In A. J. Fridrichsen, (ed.). *The Root of the Vine*. Westminster: Dacre, 1953, 81–95.
———. *Zur Typologie des Johannesevangeliums*. Acta Universiatis Upsaliensis, 1950.
Saldarini, A. J. *Jesus and Passover*. New York: Paulist Press, 1984.
Sanders, E. P. *Jesus and Judaism*. Philadelphia: Fortress, 1985.
———. *Paul and Palestinian Judaism*. London: SCM, 1977.
———. *Jewish Law from Jesus to the Mishnah: Five Studies*. London: SCM. 1990.
Sanders J. N. *The Fourth Gospel in the Early Church: Its Origin and Influences on Christian Theology up to Irenaeus*. Cambridge: 1943.
Sarna, N. M. *Exploring Exodus: The Origins of Biblical Israel*. New York: Schocken Books, 1996.

Bibliography

Satterthwaite, P. E., R. S. Hess, and G. J. Wenham, (eds.). *The Lord's Anointed: Interpretation of Old Testament Messianic Texts*. Carlisle: Paternoster, 1995.

Schnackenburg, R. *The Gospel According to St. John*. Vol. 1. K. Smith, (trans.). New York: Herder and Herder, 1968.

———. *The Gospel According to St. John*. Vol. 2. New York: Seabury, 1980.

———. *The Gospel According to St. John*. Vol. 3. New York: Crossroad, 1982.

———. *The Johannine Epistles: Introduction and Commentary*. R. Fuller, (trans.), and I. Fuller, (trans.). New York: Crossroad, 1992.

Schneck, R. *Isaiah in the Gospel of Mark*. Berkely: Bibal, 1994.

Scholem, G. *Jewish Gnosticism, Merkabah Mysticism and Talmudic Tradition*. New York: Jewish Theological Seminary of America, 1960.

Schneider, J. "ἔρχομαι." *TDNT* 2:666–84.

Schribler, D. "Messianism and Messianic Prophecy in Isaiah 1–12 and 28–33." In P. E. Satterthwaite, R. S. Hess, and G. J. Wenham, (eds.). *The Lord's Anointed: Interpretation of Old Testament Messianic Texts*. Carlisle: Paternoster, 1995, 87–104.

Schultz, R., "The King in the Book of Isaiah." In P. E. Satterthwaite, R. S. Hess, and G. J. Wenham, (eds.). *The Lord's Anointed: Interpretation of Old Testament Messianic Texts*. Carlisle: Paternoster, 1995, 141–165.

Schweitzer, A., *The Mysticism of Paul the Apostle*. W. Montgomery, (trans.). 2nd edn. Baltimore: John Hopkins University Press. 1953.

Schweizer, E., *Ego Eimi*. Vandenhoeck and Ruprecht, 1939.

Scott, E. F. *The Fourth Gospel: Its Purpose and Theology*. Edinburgh, 1908.

Segal, J. B. *The Hebrew Passover from the Earliest Times to A.D. 70*. London: OUP, 1963.

Segovia, F. F. (ed.). *'What is John?' Readers and Readings in the Fourth Gospel*. Society of Biblical Literature Symposium Series 3. Atlanta: Scholars Press, 1996.

———. *'What is John?' Vol. II: Literary and Social Readings of the Fourth Gospel*. Society of Biblical Literature Symposium Series 7. Atlanta: Scholars Press, 1998.

Selwyn, E. C. *The Christian Prophets and the Prophetic Apocalypse*. London: MacMillan, 1990.

———. *The First Epistle of Peter*. London: MacMillan, 1952.

Silva, M. *Exegetical Method*. Grand Rapids: Baker, 1996.

———. *Philippians*. Grand Rapids: Baker, 1992.

———. "Faith Versus Works of Law in Galatians." In Carson, D. A., P. T. O'Brien, and M. Seifrid. *Justification and Variegated Nomism*. Vol. 2. Grand Rapids: Baker, 2004, 217–48.

Skarsaune, O. *In the Shadow of the Temple: Jewish Influences on Early Christianity*. Downers Grove: IVP, 2002.

Sloyan, G. *John: A Bible Commentary for Teaching and Preaching*. Atlanta: Westminster John Knox, 1988.

Smalley, S. S. *John: Evangelist and Interpreter*. 2nd edn. Guernsey: Paternoster, 1998.

———. "The Johannine Son of Man Sayings." *NTS* 15 (1969), 278–301.

———. *1, 2, 3 John*. WBC vol. 51. Rev. edn. Milton Keynes: Word, 2007.

———. *The Revelation to John: A Commentary on the Greek Text of the Apocalypse*. Illinois: IVP, 2005.

———. *Thunder and Love: John's Revelation and John's Community*. Milton Keynes: Word, 1994.

Smick, E. B. "Ugaritic and the Theology of the Psalms." In J. B. Payne (ed.). *New Perspectives on the Old Testament*. Waco: Word, 1970, 104–16.

Smith, D. Moody. *Johannine Christianity*. Edinburgh: T. & T. Clark, 1987.

———. "The Sources of the Gospel of John: An Assessment of the Present State of the Problem," *NTS* 10 (1963–64), 336–51.

———. *John*. Abingdon New Testament Commentaries. Nashville: Abingdon, 1999.

———. *John Among the Gospels*. 2nd edn. Columbia: USC, 2001.

———. *The Composition and Order of the Fourth Gospel: Bultmann's Literary Theory*. New Haven: YUP, 1965.

———. "The Contribution of J. Louis Martyn." In R. T. Fortna and B. R. Gaventa, (eds.). *The Conversation Continues: Studies in Paul and John in Honor of J. Louis Martyn*. Nashville: Abingdon, 1990, 275–94.

———. *The Fourth Gospel in Four Dimensions: Judaism and Jesus, the Gospels and Scripture*. Columbia: USC, 2008.

———. *The Theology of the Gospel of John*. Cambridge: CUP, 1995.

Smith, R. H. "Exodus Typology in the Fourth Gospel." *JBL* 81 (1962): 329–42.

Spieckermann, H. "The Conception and Prehistory of the Idea of Vicarious Suffering in the Old Testament." In B. Janowski and P. Stuhlmacher, (eds.). *The Suffering Servant: Isaiah 53 in Jewish and Christian Sources*. Grand Rapids: Eerdmans, 1996, 1–15.

Staley, J. L. *The Print's First Kiss: A Rhetorical Investigation of the Implied Reader in the Fourth Gospel*. Society of Biblical Literature Dissertation Studies 82. Atlanta: Scholars Press, 1988.

Stanton, G. N. *Jesus of Nazareth in New Testament Preaching*. SNTSMS 27. Cambridge: CUP, 1974.

———. *Jesus and Gospel*. Cambridge: CUP, 2004.

———. *The Gospels and Jesus*. 2nd edn. Oxford Bible Series. Oxford: OUP, 2002.

Stanton, G. N., B. W. Longenecker, and S. C. Barton, (eds.). *The Holy Spirit and Christian Origins: Essays in Honour of James D. G. Dunn*. Grand Rapids: Eerdmans, 2004.

Stendahl, K. *The School of St. Matthew, and Its Use of the Old Testament*. Acta Seminarii Neotestamentici Uppsaliensis 20. Lund: Gleerup,1954. 2nd ed. 1968.

Stibbe, M. W. G. *John's Gospel*. New Testament Readings. London: Routledge, 1994.

———. *John as Storyteller: Narrative Criticism and the Fourth Gospel*. SNTSMS 73, Cambridge: CUP, 1994.

———. (ed.). *The Gospel of John as Literature: An Anthology of Twentieth Century Perspectives*. Leiden: Brill, 1993.

Stott, J. R. W. *The Epistles of John*. TNTC. Grand Rapids: Eerdmans, 1964.

———. *The Message of Romans*. BST. Leicester: IVP, 1994.

———. *The Cross of Christ*. Leicester: IVP, 1989.

Strathmann, H. *Evangelium nach Johannes*. Göttingen, 1963.

Stuhlmacher, P. "Spiritual Remembering: John 14:26." In G. N. Stanton, B. W. Longenecker,and S. C. Barton, (eds.). *The Holy Spirit and Christian Origins: Essays in Honor of James D. G. Dunn*. Grand Rapids: Eerdmans, 2004, 55–68.

———. "Isaiah 53 in the Gospel and Acts." In B. Janowski and P. Stuhlmacher, (eds.). *The Suffering Servant: Isaiah 53 in Jewish and Christian Sources*. Grand Rapids: Eerdmans, 2004.

Swartley, W. M. *Israel's Scripture Traditions and the Synoptic Gospels: Story Shaping Story*. Peabody: Hendrickson, 1994.

Swetnam, J. *Jesus and Isaac: A Study of the Epistle to the Hebrews in the Light of the Aqedah*. Analecta Biblica 94. Rome: Biblical Institute Press, 1981.

Tasker, R. V. G. *John*. TNTC, Leicester: IVP, 1994.

Bibliography

Tate, M. E. *Psalms 51–100*. WBC vol. 20. Dallas: Word, 1990.

Taylor, V. *Jesus and his Sacrifice*. London: Macmillan, 1937.

Teeple, H. M. *The Mosaic Eschatological Prophet*. SBLMS 10. Philadelphia: SBL, 1957.

Temple, W. *Readings in St. John's Gospel: First and Second Series*. London: Macmillan, 1939. Repr. 1952.

Terrien, S. *The Psalms: Strophic Structure and Theological Commentary*. Grand Rapids: Eerdmans, 2002.

Thiselton, A. C. *The Two Horizons. New Testament Hermeneutics and Philosophical Description with Special Reference to Heidegger, Bultmann, Gadamer, and Wittgenstein*. Grand Rapids: Eerdmans, 1993.

Thompson, J. A. *The Book of Jeremiah*. NICOT. Grand Rapids: Eerdmans, 1992.

———. *Deuteronomy*. TOTC. Leicester: IVP, 1974.

Thompson, M. M. *The God of the Gospel of John*. Grand Rapids: Eerdmans, 2001.

———. *The Incarnate Word: Perspectives on Jesus in the Fourth Gospel*. Peabody: Hendrickson, 1988.

———. "The Breath of Life: John 20:22–23 Once More." In G. N. Stanton, B. W. Longenecker, and S. C. Barton, (eds.). *The Holy Spirit and Christian Origins: Essays in Honor of James D. G. Dunn*. Grand Rapids: Eerdmans, 2004, 69–78.

Trites, A. A. *The New Testament Concept of Witness*. SNTSMS 31. Cambridge: CUP, 1977.

Van Bell, G., J. G. Van der Watt, and P. Maritz. *Theology and Christology in the Fourth Gospel*. Leuven: Leuven University Press, 2005.

Vanhoozer, K. J. *Is There a Meaning in This Text? The Bible, The Reader, and the Morality of Literary Knowledge*. Grand Rapids: Zondervan, 1998.

Van Gemeren, W. A. "Psalms." In F. E. Gaebelein (ed.). *The Expositors Bible Commentary*. Grand Rapids: Zondervan, 1991, vol. 5, 1–880.

Vermes, G. *Scripture and Tradition in Judaism: Haggadic Studies*. Studia Post-Biblica vol. 4. Leiden: Brill, 1961.

———. "Redemption and Genesis 22." In *Idem. Scripture and Tradition in Judaism: Haggadic Studies*. Studia Post-Biblica vol. 4. Leiden: Brill, 1961, 193–227.

Von Rad, G. *Old Testament Theology: The Theology of Israel's Prophetic Traditions*. Vol. 2. London: SCM, 1975.

———. "There Remains Still a Rest for the People of God: An Investigation of a Biblical Conception." In *Idem. The Problem of the Hexateuch: and other Essays*. London: SCM, 1984.

Von Wahlde, U. C. "The Johannine 'Jews': A Critical Survey." *NTS* 28 (1982): 33–60.

Vos, G. *Biblical Theology: Old and New Testaments*. Edinburgh: The Banner of Truth Trust, 1975.

———. "The Idea of Biblical Theology as a Science and as a Theological Discipline." In G. Vos, and R. B. Gaffin (ed.). *Redemptve History and Biblical Interpretation: The Shorter Writings of Geerhardus Vos*. Phillipsburg: P. & R., 1980, 3–24.

Walker, P. W. L. *Jesus and the Holy City: New Testament Perspectives on Jerusalem*. Grand Rapids: Eerdmans, 1996.

Wallace, R.S. *The Message of Daniel*. BST. Leicester: IVP, 1973.

Waltke, B. K. "Micah." In D. W. Baker, T. D. Alexander, and B. K. Waltke. *Obadiah, Jonah and Micah*. TOTC. Leicester: IVP, 1988, 133–207.

Walton, J. H. *Genesis*. NIV Application Commentary. Grand Rapids: Zondervan, 2001.

———. "The Imagery of the Substitute King Ritual in Isaiah's Fourth Servant Song." *JBL* 122 (November, 2003): 734–43.
Watts, J. D. *Isaiah 34–66*. WBC vol. 25. Waco: Word, 1987.
Watts, R. E. *Isaiah's New Exodus in Mark*. Grand Rapids: Baker, 1997.
———. "Consolation or Confrontation? Isaiah 40–55 and the Delay of the New Exodus." *TynBul* 41 (1990): 31–59.
Webster, J. S. *Ingesting Jesus: Eating and Drinking in the Gospel of John*. SBL Academia Biblica 6. Atlanta, 2003.
Weinfeld, M. *Deuteronomy 1–11*. AB vol. 5. New York: Doubleday, 1991.
———. "The Covenant of Grant in the Old Testament and in the Ancient Near East." *Journal of American Oriental Society* 90 (1970): 184–203.
Weiser, A. *The Psalms*. H. Hartwell, (trans.). OTL. Philadelphia: Westminster, 1962.
Wellhausen. J. *Prolegomena to the History of Ancient Israel*. Edinburgh: A. & C. Black, 1885.
Wenham, G. J. *The Book of Leviticus*. NICOT. Grand Rapids: Eerdmans, 1979.
———. *Genesis 1–15*. WBC vol. 1. Dallas: Word, 1987.
Westcott, B. F. *The Epistles of St. John*. London: Macmillan, 1909.
———. *The Gospel According to St. John: The Greek Text with Introduction and Notes*. 2 vols. 1908. Repr. Grand Rapids: Baker, 1980.
Westermann, C. *Isaiah 40–66*. OTL. Wiltshire: SCM, 1985.
Whybray, R. N. *Thanksgiving for a Liberated Prophet: An Interpretation of Isaiah Chapter 53*. JSOTSup 4. Sheffield: JSOT Press, 1978.
Wifall, W. "Gen. 3:15—A Protevangelium?" *CBQ* 36 (1974): 361–65.
Williams, G. H. *Wilderness and Paradise in Christian thought*. New York: Harper, 1962.
Williamson, G. I. *The Shorter Catechism: For Study Classes*. 2 vols. Phillipsburg: P. & R., 1970.
Williamson, H. G. M. *1 and 2 Chronicles*. New Century Bible Commentary. Grand Rapids: Eerdmans, 1982.
Wilson, M. R. "Passover." In G. W. Bromiley (ed.). *ISBE*. Rev. edn. Grand Rapids: Eerdmans, 1986, vol. 3, 675–79.
Windisch, H. "John's Narrative Style." In M. W. G. Stibbe (ed.). *The Gospel of John as Literature: An Anthology of Twentieth Century Perspectives*. Leiden: Brill, 1993, 25–64.
Wise, M. O. *The First Messiah: Investigating the Saviour Before Jesus*. New York: Harper Collins, 1999.
Wiseman, D. J. *1 and 2 Kings*. TOTC, Leicester: IVP, 1993.
Witherington, B. *John's Wisdom: A Commentary on the Fourth Gospel*. Cambridge: The Lutterworth Press, 1995.
———. *The Acts of the Apostles: A Socio-Rhetorical Commentary*. Grand Rapids: Eerdmans, 1998.
Wolff, H. W. *Hosea: A Commentary on the Book of the Prophet Hosea*. G. Stansell (trans.). Hermeneia. Philadelphia: Fortress, 1974.
———. *Joel and Amos: A Commentary on the Books of the Prophets Joel and Amos*. W. Janzen, S. D. McBride and C. A. Muenchow (trans.). Hermeneia. Philadelphia: Fortress, 1977.
Woudstra, M. H. *The Book of Joshua*. NICOT. Grand Rapids: Eerdmans, 1991.
———. "The Tabernacle in Biblical-Theological Perspective." In J. B. Payne, (ed.). *New Perspectives on the Old Testament*. Waco: Word, 1970, 88–103.
Wright, N. T. *John for Everyone: Part 1 Chapters 1–10*. London: SPCK, 2002.
———. *John for Everyone: Part 2 Chapters 11–21*. London: SPCK, 2002.
———. *The New Testament and the People of God*. London: SPCK, 1992.

———. *Jesus and the Victory of God*. London: SPCK, 1996.

———. *The Resurrection of the Son of God*. London: SPCK, 2003.

———. *Paul and the Faithfulness of God*. 2 vols. Minneapolis: Fortress, 2013.

———. "In Grateful Dialogue." In C. C. Newman, (ed.). *Jesus and the Restoration of Israel: A Critical Assessment of N. T. Wright's Jesus and The Victory of God*. Downers Grove: IVP, 1999: 244–77.

———. "Poetry and Theology in Colossians 1:15-20." *NTS* 36 (1990): 444–60.

———. *Colossians and Philemon*. TNTC. Leicester: IVP, 1991.

———. *The Climax of the Covenant*. Edinburgh: T. & T. Clark, 1991.

———. *What Saint Paul Really Said*. Oxford: Lion, 1997.

———. *Paul in Fresh Perspective*. Minneapolis: Fortress, 2006.

———. *Pauline Perspectives: Essays on Paul, 1978-2013*. London: SPCK, 2013.

Yahuda, A. S. *The Accuracy of the Bible*. London: Heinemann, 1934.

Yamauchi, E. M. *Pre-Christian Gnosticism: A Survey of the Proposed Evidences*. Eugene: Wipf and Stock, 1983.

Yee, G. A. *Jewish Feasts and the Gospel of John*. Wilmington: Michael Glazier, 1989.

Young, E. J. *A Commentary on Daniel*. Grand Rapids: Eerdmans, 1949.

———. *The Book of Isaiah Chapters 1-18*. Vol. 1. Grand Rapids: Eerdmans, 1992.

———. *The Book of Isaiah Chapters 19-39*. Vol. 2. Grand Rapids: Eerdmans, 1992.

———. *The Book of Isaiah Chapters 40-46*. Vol. 3. Grand Rapids: Eerdmans, 1992.

———. "The Interpretation of *yzh* in Isaiah 52:15." *WTJ* 3 (1941): 125–32.

———. *Thy Word is Truth: Some Thoughts on the Biblical Doctrine of Inspiration*. Edinburgh: The Banner of Truth Trust, 1980.

Young, F. W. "A Study of the Relation of Isaiah to the Fourth Gospel." *ZNW* 46. (1955): 223–24.

Zimmerli, W. *Ezekiel 1: A Commentary on the Book of the Prophet Ezekiel, Chapters 1-24*. R. E. Clements (trans.). Hermeneia. Philadelphia: Fortress, 1979.

———. *Ezekiel 2: A Commentary on the Book of the Prophet Ezekiel, Chapters 25-48*. J. D. Martin (trans.). Hermeneia. Philadelphia: Fortress, 1983.

Zimmerli, W., and J. Jeremias. *The Servant of God: Studies in Biblical Theology*. London: SCM, 1957.

www.ingramcontent.com/pod-product-compliance
Lightning Source LLC
Chambersburg PA
CBHW080406300426
44113CB00015B/2412